Giuseppe Chirichiello

DSGE Models for Real Business Cycle and New Keynesian Macroeconomics

Theoretical Methods and Numerical Solutions with DYNARE

Springer

Giuseppe Chirichiello
Department of Legal and Economic Studies
Sapienza University of Rome
Roma, Italy

ISSN 2192-4333 ISSN 2192-4341 (electronic)
Springer Texts in Business and Economics
ISBN 978-3-031-56033-0 ISBN 978-3-031-56034-7 (eBook)
https://doi.org/10.1007/978-3-031-56034-7

This Springer imprint is published by the registered company Springer Nature Switzerland AG
The registered company address is: Gewerbestrasse 11, 6330 Cham, Switzerland

To my complex, but vital family

Preface

This book realizes a project that can be dated at least 23 years ago, since 2000, the year of the publication of my text entitled *Intertemporal Macroeconomic Models, Money and Rational Choices*, by McMillan. At the time, with the release of the aforementioned text, the work agenda also included a project for subsequent work, with the then provisional title *Intertemporal Stochastic Macroeconomic Models*. Academic and life vicissitudes delayed in various ways the realization of that project, but I didn't stop elaborating and keeping notes, with, among other things, a continuous chasing of literature, which, in 20 years, has grown and expanded to multiple themes impressively. I decided, after a few years of retirement from active teaching, to resume that project and reworking notes collected in the previous 20 years.

The text that I am presenting to readers and scholars, today has been born. Some brief notes on the reasons that led the author, despite the current state of retirement, to resume studies on the subject. As I hope readers will appreciate from the work setting, the first reason is that it would have been a pity to leave my notes sleeping. In this regard, I had a long 2-year period of "feelings of guilt" towards students (especially Italians) who would decide to continue their studies towards a PhD, especially at American Universities. In almost all universities, and above all in those most quoted among the top ten, DSGE models are an integral part of PhD courses. The initial impact of these courses creates many difficulties for students, except, perhaps, for a lucky few, who venture to study at internationally quoted universities.

The second reason, most intimate and scientifically irrelevant, is that I enjoyed in writing this book. Among other things, the revitalization of my notes has, in confidence, fueled the hope of still being able to continue my studies, albeit in an uncertain future.

In conclusion, I wish to thank my friends and colleagues Giorgio Di Giorgio and Enrico Cervellati, who kindly read and commented on chapters of the book.

Moreover, I wish to thank Niko Chtouris for his professional and very friendly editorial support, and last, but not least, I also wish to thank the publisher who, with the acceptance of the manuscript, took on the entrepreneurial risk associated with the publication of a text by an author who is now retired from active teaching.

Rome, Italy
July 2023

Giuseppe Chirichiello

Contents

1 Introduction 1
References 3

2 Finite-Difference Equations and Systems of Difference Equations in Rational Expectations 5
2.1 Review of Solutions of Linear First-Order Difference Equations 5
2.2 Solution by Factorization Method 10
2.3 First-Order Difference Equation in Rational Expectations 14
2.4 Forward Solution for the Case $|a| < 1$ 15
2.4.1 Method of Iterated Forward Substitution of Expectations 16
2.4.2 Factorization Method 19
2.4.3 Method of Indeterminate Coefficients 20
2.4.4 A Simple Example of a Forward Solution with the Method of Indeterminate Coefficients 21
2.5 Case $|a| > 1$ and Solution with the Backward Iteration Method 22
2.6 Bubbles 26
2.7 Second-Order Finite-Difference Equations and Related Equations with Expectations 28
2.8 Properties of Characteristic Equation Associated with a Second-Order Difference Equation 30
2.9 Stability Conditions for Second-Order Finite-Difference Equation 34
2.10 Solution Method by Factorization 35
2.11 Sargent's Approach to Solution Method by Factorization 38
2.12 Method for Reduction of a Rational Polynomial to Partial Fractions 42

2.13 Partial Fractions and Discussion of Solutions of Finite-Difference Equation of Second Order 44
2.14 Second-Order Difference Equations with Expectations 48
2.14.1 Method of Solution of Indeterminate Coefficients 49
2.14.2 Solution Method by Factorization 52
2.15 Solution to Second-Order Finite-Difference Equation with the Matrix Approach 54
2.16 Systems of Finite-Difference Equations 59
2.17 Systems of Finite-Difference Equations with Rational Expectations 63
2.18 Analytical Solution of Systems of Rational Expectations 65
2.19 Saddle Point Path 66
2.20 Solving System with the Blanchard-Kahn Procedure 67
2.21 The Case of Indeterminacy 70
2.22 The Case of Singular Problems: Outlines 73
2.23 An Elaborate Example of Economic Theory 74
2.23.1 Solution with the Method of Factorization 77
2.23.2 Solution with the Method of Indeterminate Coefficients 80
2.23.3 Solution with the Matrix Method and Application of the Blanchard-Kahn Procedure 84
Appendix 93
A.1 Introduction 93
References 105

3 Models of Representative Agents and Real Business Cycle Models 107
3.1 Use of the Lagrangian in Intertemporal Maximization 107
3.2 A Discussion of the Transversality Condition 109
3.3 An Application of the Intertemporal Maximization: The Case of Adjustment Costs of Capital and the Relationship with "Tobin's q" Theory 110
3.4 From Micro to Macro: A Simple Dynamic General Equilibrium Model (DGE) of Representative Agents (Ramsey) for a Decentralized Economy 114
3.5 Discussion of Solution of Simple DGE Macroeconomic Model 117
3.6 Log-Linear Approximation of DGE Macroeconomic Model 118
3.7 Methods of Solution of a Log-Linearized System: Indeterminate Coefficients 121
3.8 A Model of a Decentralized Economy, with Inelastic Labor Supply, as a Basic Model of Real Business Cycle 124

3.9 The Blanchard-Kahn Method for Solving Systems with Rational Expectations 126
3.10 Solution of the Basic Real Business Cycle Model with Blanchard-Kahn Method 129
3.11 Jordan Transformation Applied to System in Expectations in the Basic Real Business Cycle Model 130
3.12 Basic RBC Model of Centralized Economy with (a) Flexible Labor Supply and (b) Stochastic Shocks to Technology and Aggregate Demand 134
3.12.1 Steady-State Variables as Functions of Parameters 135
3.13 An Application of the Blanchard-Kahn Method to Hansen's DSGE Model 137
3.14 The Model of a Decentralized Economy, with Flexible Labor Supply and Exogenous Public Spending 148
3.15 A Complete Analysis of the RBC Model of the Centralized Economy, with Log-CRRA Utility Function in Consumption and Labor 151
3.15.1 Steady-State Solution 154
3.15.2 Log-Linearization of the Model 155
3.15.3 The State-Space Representation of the Log-Linear System 157
3.15.4 Transformation of the Real Cycle Model into a System of Rational Expectations 161
3.15.5 The Blanchard-Kahn Transformation of the RBC Model of the Centralized Economy 169
Appendix 172
A.1 Bellman and Dynamic Programming 172
A.2 An Economic Example of the Application of Bellman's Principle: Aggregate Savings in an Intertemporal Context Under Conditions of Uncertainty 180
References 184

4 A Simplified Illustration of Numerical Solution Methods of DSGE Models with DYNARE Software 187
4.1 DYNARE Coding as a Method for Numerical Solving DSGE Models 187
4.2 Three Different Ways of Writing Model Block Equations 189
4.3 The Code of the Centralized Economy Model, with Flexible Labor Supply, in the Form of Levels 189
4.4 A Comment on DYNARE's Numerical Simulation of the Model of the Centralized Economy in Level Form, with a Flexible Labor Supply 191
4.5 The Code of Model of the Centralized Economy with Flexible Labor Supply, in Exp-Log Form 195

4.6 The Code of the Model of the Centralized Economy in (Log) Linear Form, i.e., in the Form of Percentage Deviations from the Steady State . . . 197
4.7 An Alternative Way of Encoding Model Block . . . 198
4.8 Code of the Basic RBC Model with a CRRA Utility Function and Government Spending as a Shock . . . 202
4.8.1 Steady-State Variables as Functions of Parameters of the Model . . . 203
4.9 The Complete DYNARE Code of the Log-Linearized Model with Public Expenditure . . . 205
4.10 A Note on CALIBRATION, i.e., Assigning Numerical Values to Parameters . . . 207
4.11 Different Ways for Calculating the Steady State in DYNARE . . . 208
4.11.1 Method 1: *steady_state_model* Block . . . 208
4.11.2 Method 2: steady_state with the *steady state_helper* Function . . . 212
4.11.3 Method 3: Assigning Initial Values in the *initval* Block . . . 214
4.11.4 A Focus on External Steady-State File . . . 216
4.12 Another DYNARE Focus: Model with Different Parameter Values . . . 219
References . . . 220

5 A Basic Version of the Micro-founded Neo-Keynesian Model . . . 221
5.1 A Decentralized Economy: Choices of Representative Household . . . 221
5.2 Firms' Choices in the Case of Linear Production Technology and Flexible Prices . . . 227
5.3 Firm Choices in the Case of Cobb-Douglas Production Technology . . . 230
5.4 Firm Choices in the Case of Production Technology CES for Final Goods, Cobb-Douglas Technology for Intermediate Goods, and Full Flexible Prices . . . 233
5.4.1 Choices of Firm Producing Final Good . . . 233
5.4.2 Choices of Firm Producing Intermediate Goods . . . 235
5.5 Firms' Pricing in the Presence of Price Stickiness: (a) The Case of Costs of Price Adjustment . . . 237
5.6 Firm's Pricing in the Presence of Price Stickiness: (b) Price Stickiness a-la-Calvo in a Model of Linear Production Technology . . . 239
5.7 Firm's Pricing in the Presence of Price Stickiness: (c) Price Stickiness a-la-Calvo and Nonlinear Production Technology . . . 243
5.8 Differences Between Rotemberg and Calvo Price Stickiness . . . 244

5.9 Implications for the Inflation Rate of Firm's Way of Setting Prices 244
5.10 The Aggregate Economic System with Price Stickiness a-la-Calvo and Linear Production Technology: The Demand Side 245
5.11 The Aggregate Economic System with Price Stickiness a-la-Calvo and Linear Production Technology: The Supply Side 248
5.12 General Equilibrium of NKE Model with Linear Technology 249
5.12.1 The Log-Linear Version of Model 250
5.13 Dynamics of the Equilibrium Inflation 252
5.14 The Notion of GDP Gap and the New Keynesian Phillips' Curve 257
5.15 The Definitive Basic Model of the New Keynesian Economics (NKE) 259
5.16 Blanchard-Kahn Conditions for Stability and Uniqueness of Solutions of the Basic NKE Model 260
5.17 Numerical Solution of the Basic NKE Model and the DYNARE Code 266
References 267

6 More Complex NKE Models: Stickiness in Money Wages, Real Stickiness, and Extensions to a Medium-Size Model 269
6.1 Complex Model of the NKE with (a) Nonlinear Production Technology and Capital Accumulation; (b) Money Wages Setting by Households Acting as Monopolists in Specific Labor Market Services 270
6.1.1 The Representative Firm Producing Final Good 270
6.1.2 Firms Producing Intermediate Goods 272
6.1.3 Households 275
6.1.4 General Wage Index 278
6.2 Nominal Wage's Setting for Labor Service by the Representative Household 281
6.3 The Aggregate Labor Supply and Representative Trade Union 283
6.4 The Public Administration and the Central Bank 285
6.5 Equilibrium of Model with Rotemberg Price Stickiness and Flexible Wages 286
6.6 The Phillips Curve with Rotemberg Price Adjustment Costs . . . 290
6.7 Steady State and Details of Log-Linearization Algebra 292
6.8 The Complete Log-Linearized NKE Model, with Physical Capital and Price Adjustment Costs 298
6.9 DYNARE's Code for the Numerical Solution of the NKE Model with Physical Capital and Price Adjustment Costs 298

6.10 Some Specific Extensions of the NKE Model 300
6.10.1 Calvo Stickiness in Wage Modifications 300
6.10.2 Habit Persistence and Adjustment Costs of Capital and Labor 302
6.10.3 "Rules of Thumb" and Non-Ricardian Households 305
6.11 The Medium-Sized Micro-founded Keynesian Model (E. Sims 2016) 307
6.12 Labor's Supply Aggregation and Representative Trade Union Choices 309
6.12.1 Households 312
6.12.2 Firm Producer of the Final Good 323
6.12.3 Firm Producer of Intermediate Goods 324
6.12.4 Public Administration and Central Bank 331
6.13 Equilibrium and Aggregation 332
6.13.1 Exogenous Stochastic Processes 336
6.14 The Complete Set of Equilibrium Equations 337
6.14.1 Calculation of the Steady-State Solution 339
6.14.2 The Complete Set of Steady-State Equations 345
6.15 DYNARE Code for the Numerical Solution of the Medium-Sized NK Model 347
6.16 The Results of the DYNARE code for the Medium-Sized NK Model 350
References 358

Index 359

List of Figures

Fig. 2.1 Dynamics of expectations, case $|a| < 1$ 15
Fig. 2.2 Dynamics of expectations, case $|a| > 1$ 23
Fig. 2.3 A graphical representation of Eigenvectors 57
Fig. 2.4 Case of a source 57
Fig. 2.5 Case of a vortex 58
Fig. 2.6 Case of saddle-point 58
Fig. 2.7 Representation of points in the complex plane 103
Fig. 4.1 Transition functions 195
Fig. 6.1 Orthogonalized shock to e_G 356
Fig. 6.2 Orthogonalized shock to e_G 356
Fig. 6.3 Orthogonalized shock to e_A 357
Fig. 6.4 Orthogonalized shock to e_A 357

List of Tables

Table 4.1 Policy and transition functions 192
Table 4.2 Approximated theoretical moments 193
Table 4.3 Approximated matrix of correlations 193
Table 4.4 Approximated coefficients of autocorrelation 194
Table 6.1 Eigenvalues 352
Table 6.2 Matrix of covariance of exogenous shocks 352
Table 6.3 Policy and transition functions 353
Table 6.4 Theoretical moments 354
Table 6.5 Variance decomposition (in percent) 354
Table 6.6 Matrix of correlations 355

Chapter 1
Introduction

The book, submitted here to the reader, consists of five chapters in addition to Introduction and follows a definitely red thread of methodological nature.

Indeed, the aim is to guide the reader through the labyrinth of methods and theories that have characterized and contributed to the development of modern macroeconomics around the Stochastic Dynamic Models of Real Business Cycle.

The models of the New Keynesian Macroeconomics then followed and detached themselves from RBC models, by maintaining the same methods.

Both strands of research are characterized by the use of DSGE models, an acronym that indicates Dynamic Stochastic General Equilibrium.

At odds, Dynamic General Equilibrium models (DGE), of which Frank Ramsey (1927, 1928) was the initiator, with unforgettable contributions, reproduce the canonical results of the neoclassical theory (equilibrium Pareto optimality and full employment) in a dynamic context and an approach of "representative agents." Both properties, Pareto optimality and full employment, were considered sufficient to exclude the occurrence of economic cycles.

The introduction of stochastic elements in deterministic DGE models (particularly pioneered by Edward Prescott, (Kydland and Prescott 1982; Prescott 1986) by transforming those models from DGE into DSGE models) can be compared, in terms of effects and theoretical consequences, to the introduction of quanta in classical Newtonian mechanics, especially in modern quantum mechanics. Specifically, by assuming that global productivity follows a stochastic AR(1) induce in the DGE model, a Business Cycle, the cause of which is real, rather than a monetary or demand-related cause.

I have attempted to clarify this important aspect to the reader in Chap. 3 entitled "Dynamic Models of General Equilibrium as Real Business Cycle Models." In that chapter, Sect. 3.4 reconstructs an optimal macroeconomic model in a purely deterministic context, anticipating the same solution methods employed in the Real Business Cycle model discussed in the subsequent Sect. 3.8.

G. Chirichiello, *DSGE Models for Real Business Cycle and New Keynesian Macroeconomics*, Springer Texts in Business and Economics,
https://doi.org/10.1007/978-3-031-56034-7_1

The remainder of Chap. 3 primarily focuses on the methodology developed by Blanchard and Kahn (1980) for the "theoretical" resolution of dynamic models with rational expectations.

The systematic consideration of Blanchard-Kahn's methodology, in successive models, only slightly more complex than the basic model of the Real Business Cycle, makes it evident that the Blanchard-Kahn method, elegant and impeccable from a theoretical point of view, becomes essentially impractical due to the extensive number of algebraic calculations it necessitates. Consequently, it becomes evident that macroeconomic models aiming to describe more realistic economic systems, and oriented toward studying economic policy interventions, must rely on numerical solution methods. Such solutions in turn require elaborate software systems (notably Matlab and Dynare, but other types are also prevalent in the literature). This discussion sheds light on why the text commences with Chap. 2, entitled "Finite Difference Equations and Systems of Equations in Rational Expectations." It is essential for an average reader, especially those studying dynamic models for the first time (I am primarily thinking of Italian graduates, but also many PhD. students), to be equipped with the mathematical methods required to comprehend such models. This approach also explains why, contrary to the customary placement of mathematical references in appendices, I have chosen to begin the text with an examination of the mathematical methods extensively used throughout the work.

The significance of methodological aspects is further emphasized at the beginning of Chap. 3, where, sequentially, there are three paragraphs titled: "The Use of the Lagrangian in Intertemporal Maximization," "A Discussion on the Condition of Transversality," and "An Application of Intertemporal Maximization: The Case of Adjustment Costs of Capital and the Relation with Tobin's q."

The common thread highlighting the methodological reasons remains evident in the discussion of Chap. 4.

Here, in contrast to the complexity of the theoretical solutions, the item is to search for numerical solutions using the DYNARE software.

In presenting the properties of this software, I have chosen to provide a description of the minimal elements necessary for correctly coding the various RBC models to be simulated. Additionally, I have directly provided the codes for each of the RBC models considered. This should enable the reader to independently reproduce the same results outlined and discussed in this work.

Chapter 5, entitled "A Basic Version of Micro-founded Neo-Keynesian Model" introduces the reader to the study of New Keynesian Economics (NKE).

It does so by considering and analytically comparing various production technology formats (linear, Cobb-Douglas, and CES) and elaborating on the aspects of monopolistic competition, a fundamental contribution by Dixit and Stiglitz (1977) (see Bibliography). The chapter also presents different approaches to price stickiness in the basic model and, in subsequent models, wage stickiness according to the Calvo-Rotemberg dichotomy, along with their respective results and distinctions. Chapter 4 concludes with both the application of the Blanchard-Kahn methodology to the basic NKE model and numerical analysis, including the presentation of the corresponding DYNARE code.

The elaboration of various codes makes use of free software GNU Octave, version 6.2.0. There are more up-to-date versions of this software, but the version indicated was preferred because it is the one more compatible with DYNARE, a version of which in turn was more compatible with that just indicated of Octave. Such a version turned out to be the DYNARE 4.6.4, although updated DYNARE's versions up to 5.3 were even available.

The text concludes with Chap. 6, entitled "Complex Models of NKE: Stickiness in Money Wages, Real Stickiness, and Extension to a Medium-Sized Model." Two primary reasons for this growing complexity can be identified, one of a theoretical nature and the other of a practical-applicative nature.

Theoretical complexity arises from the ongoing debate, previously referred to as "Classics vs. Keynes," which has now resurfaced as the "RBC vs. NKE."

The introduction of real rigidities, such as costs related to capital and labor usage, investment costs, and variable capital utilization, in addition to the traditional stickiness of nominal prices and wages, aims to consider significant aspects of the "flesh-and-blood" economy while also countering efforts to "resuscitating" the RBC models (King and Rebelo 1999). Actually, NKE models have gained prominence, particularly as reference models for numerous research centers in central banks of major economies, both Western and non-Western. This diffusion constitutes the second reason for the growing complexity of NKE models. Explaining empirically relevant phenomena and designing economic policy interventions necessitates the inclusion of previously unconsidered phenomena and precise definitions of economic policy objectives.

For this second strand of DSGE's NKE models, the text provides only a representation of some theoretical aspects in Chap. 6. Section 6.11 presents a model titled "The Medium-Sized Micro-Founded Keynesian Model," developed by E. Sims (2016) in his Graduate lessons. This model consists of 26 equations in 26 unknowns, and a DYNARE code is also included.

Two elements are noticeably absent from the text. The first pertains to the estimation methods of various DSGE models. The second is the study of economic policy models, notably the topic of optimal monetary policy (and, aside from a few hints, fiscal policy as well), which is conspicuously missing.

This absence is particularly striking given the writer's past scientific interests. However, both themes, in terms of methodological aspects and theoretical debates, would warrant a separate text.

At this point, I can only wish a fruitful study to those who, out of their personal interest, choose to dedicate part of their time to exploring the following pages.

References

Blanchard, O. and Kahn, C. (1980) 'The Solution of Linear Difference Models under Rational Expectations', *Econometrica*, 48(5), pp. 1305-1311.

Dixit, A. and Stiglitz, J. (1977) 'Monopolistic Competition and Optimum Product Diversity', *American Economic Review*, 67(3), pp. 297-308.

King, R. and S. Rebelo (1999) 'Resuscitating real business cycles', in J. Taylor, M. Woodford(eds) *Handbook of Macroeconomics*, Vol.IB, Amstram, Elsevier Science North-Holland, pp. 927-1007.

Kydland, F. E., Prescott, E. C., (1982), Time to Build and Aggregate Fluctuations, Econometrica, 50(6).

Ramsey, F. (1927) 'A contribution to the theory of taxation', Economic Journal, 37(145), pp. 47-61.

Ramsey, F. (1928) 'A mathematical theory of saving', Economic Journal, 38(152), pp. 543-559.

Chapter 2
Finite-Difference Equations and Systems of Difference Equations in Rational Expectations

In the following, we discuss the solutions of difference equations of the first and second order, and the same difference equations in rational expectations. After considering the extension to systems of difference equations, the chapter extensively reviews the various methods of solution and the Blanchard-Khan procedure for solving systems of rational expectations. In closing, the chapter considers a case study of economic theory with the systematic application of the various solution methods previously considered, to this case. The chapter includes a mathematical appendix that review elementary quadratic equations and some useful notions on complex numbers and trigonometric identities.

2.1 Review of Solutions of Linear First-Order Difference Equations

Consider a function $y_t = f(y_{t-1})$ and assume that it is linear homogeneous. It corresponds to a first-order finite linear difference equation

$$y_t = a\, y_{t-1} \tag{2.1}$$

where the known term is absent and $a \neq 0$ is a given real number.

A dynamical system governed by Eq. (2.1) admits a single steady state $\overline{y} = 0$ and its stability depends on the value of the coefficient a. Steady state $\overline{y}$ is asymptotically stable if $\lim_{t \to \infty} y_t = \overline{y}$, at least starting from a neighborhood $|y - \overline{y}| < \varepsilon$ for $\varepsilon > 0$ arbitrarily small.

Stability of $\overline{y} = f(\overline{y})$ requires $|f'(\overline{y})| < 1$. Since $f'(\overline{y}) = a$, stationary solution $\overline{y} = 0$ is asymptotically stable if $|a| < 1$.

G. Chirichiello, *DSGE Models for Real Business Cycle and New Keynesian Macroeconomics*, Springer Texts in Business and Economics,
https://doi.org/10.1007/978-3-031-56034-7_2

The path toward a steady state is further characterized by the sign of a. It determines the regular path toward a steady state, in an increasing or decreasing mode, if a > 0, or oscillatory mode if a < 0.

The exact solution of the path toward the steady state is obtained by induction and by substitution.

Given an initial value y_0, it must be

$$y_1 = a\, y_0$$

$$y_2 = a\, y_1 = a(a\, y_0) = a^2 y_0$$

$$\ldots\ldots\ldots\ldots\ldots\ldots\ldots\ldots$$

$$y_t = a\, y_{t-1} = \ldots = a^t y_0$$

Therefore, the general solution of linear homogeneous first difference equation is

$$y_t = a^t y_0 \tag{2.2}$$

Here, the word *general* means that the expression (2.2) encompasses the entire family of solutions, each of which differs from the others by the initial condition y_0.

Let us now consider the nonhomogeneous linear equation

$$y_t = a\, y_{t-1} + b_t \tag{2.3}$$

It differs from the homogeneous equation (2.1) by the addition in each period t of an exogenous quantity b_t.

The solution of Eq. (2.3) must surely contain the entire family of solutions of the homogeneous equation since it is valid

$$y_t - b_t = a\, y_{t-1} \tag{2.4}$$

And so

$$y_t - b_t = a^t y_0$$

Since y_0 is an arbitrary constant, it can be set

$$y_t - b_t = ca^t$$

However, the family of solutions of homogeneous equation (2.4) does not exhaust all solutions of (2.3). Indeed, the general solution of (2.3) takes the form

$$y_t^g = ca^t + y_t^p \tag{2.5}$$

where y_t^p is any solution of the nonhomogeneous equation.[1]

To find a particular solution y_t^p one can proceed by backward iteration of the initial equation (2.3). In fact, moving the period t back to time t−1, Eq. (2.3) becomes

$$y_{t-1} = a\, y_{t-2} + b_{t-1}$$

This value appears in the initial equation (2.3), so by substituting for it, it follows

$$\begin{aligned} y_t &= a\, y_{t-1} + b_t = a\,(a\, y_{t-2} + b_{t-1}) + b_t \\ &= a^2 y_{t-2} + a\, b_{t-1} + b_t \end{aligned}$$

Now in this expression appears the term y_{t-2}. It is

$$y_{t-2} = a\, y_{t-3} + b_{t-2} \tag{2.6}$$

and by substituting into the previous, one gets

$$\begin{aligned} y_t &= a\left(a^2 y_{t-2} + ab_{t-2}\right) + a\, b_{t-1} + b_t \\ &= a^3 y_{t-3} + a^2\, b_{t-2} + a\, b_{t-1} + b_t \end{aligned}$$

By observing that $b_t = a^0\, b_t$, and using the summation symbol it can be written

$$y_t = a^3 y_{t-3} + \sum_{j=0}^{2} a^j\, b_{t-j}$$

After T iterations, you will obtain

---

[1] That the expression (2.5) is a solution of inhomogeneous equation is verified by observing that if y_t^g is a solution of (2.3), it must be

$$a\, y_{t-1} + b_t = a\left(ca^{t-1} + y_{t-1}^p\right) + b_t = ca^t + ay_{t-1}^p + b_t$$

But the first term ca^t is a solution of homogeneous equation (2.2), while for the residual term, one has

$$ay_{t-1}^p + b_t = y_t^p$$

So that
$y_t = a\, y_{t-1} + b_t = ca^t + y_t^p$.

$$y_t = a^T y_{t-T} + \sum_{j=0}^{T} a^j b_{t-j} \tag{2.7}$$

If the system has a natural starting point y_0, then t−T = 0 and, therefore, T = t, and the solution becomes

$$y_t = a^t y_0 + \sum_{j=0}^{t} a^j b_{t-j} \tag{2.8}$$

The system's position at each instant, therefore, is determined by its initial value, by time elapsed up to t, and by the sum of disturbances b_t, weighted by a^j,that hit the system from the initial instant up to the moment t.

However, the system does not always admit an initial position y_0. In this case for T→ ∞, the solution becomes

$$y_t = \lim_{t \to \infty} a^T y_{t-T} + \sum_{j=0}^{\infty} a^j b_{t-j}$$

This solution becomes indefinite if the limit of the first term, and/or the summation assumes infinite value. However, if disturbances b_t are bounded and $|a| < 1$, one has

$$y_t = \sum_{j=0}^{\infty} a^j b_{t-j} \tag{2.9}$$

If instead $|a| > 1$, then this solution explodes to infinity. Even in the case $|a| > 1$, however, it is still possible to find a bounded solution in the family of solutions for y_t.

Given Eq. (2.3), the differences' order does not change if one changes the current instant considered. In fact, at the instant t the difference between the indices equals t−(t−1) = 1, and analogously at the instant t+1 this difference equals t+1−t = 1, so that the equation remains of first order if we update the index at time t+2.

In that case the following is valid

$$y_{t+1} = a\, y_t + b_{t+1} \tag{2.10}$$

From this, it follows

$$y_t = \frac{1}{a}\, y_{t+1} - \frac{1}{a}\, b_{t+1} \tag{2.11}$$

Equation (2.11) contains y_{t+1}. Moving the time index forward by one, one has

$$y_{t+1} = \frac{1}{a}\, y_{t+2} - \frac{1}{a}\, b_{t+2}$$

and by substituting y_{t+1} into (2.11) one gets

$$y_t = \frac{1}{a^2}\, y_{t+2} - \frac{1}{a^2}\, b_{t+2} - \frac{1}{a}\, b_{t+1} \tag{2.12}$$

Equation (2.11) contains y_{t+2}.
Moving the time index forward by one, it gives

$$y_{t+2} = \frac{1}{a}\, y_{t+3} - \frac{1}{a}\, b_{t+3}$$

and by substituting y_{t+2} into (2.12)

$$y_t = \frac{1}{a^3}\, y_{t+3} - \frac{1}{a^3}\, b_{t+3} - \frac{1}{a^2}\, b_{t+2} - \frac{1}{a}\, b_{t+1}$$

That is

$$y_t = \frac{1}{a^3}\, y_{t+3} - \sum_{j=1}^{3} \frac{1}{a^j}\, b_{t+j} \tag{2.13}$$

After T periods and substitutions,[2] one gets

$$y_t = \frac{1}{a^T}\, y_{t+T} - \sum_{j=1}^{T} \frac{1}{a^j}\, b_{t+j} \tag{2.14}$$

For $T \to \infty$, since $|a| > 1$, it follows $\frac{1}{a^T}\, y_{t+T} \to 0$, and therefore,

$$y_t = - \sum_{j=1}^{\infty} \frac{1}{a^j} b_{t+j} \tag{2.15}$$

Equation (2.11), again because $|a| > 1$, is finite.

[2]The same result is achieved if initial equation $y_t = a\, y_{t-1} + b_t$ directly is solved for y_{t-1}, yielding $y_{t-1} = \frac{1}{a}\, y_t - \frac{b_t}{a}$. Advancing one time step, this becomes $y_t = \frac{1}{a}\, y_{t+1} - \frac{b_{t+1}}{a}$. Continuing this process, we find that $y_{t+1} = \frac{1}{a}\, y_{t+2} - \frac{b_{t+2}}{a}$. By substituting and advancing one time step up to time T, we obtain the expression $y_t = \frac{1}{a^T}\, y_{t+T} - \sum_{j=1}^{T} \frac{1}{a^j}\, b_{t+j}$.

2.2 Solution by Factorization Method

The method of solution by factorization makes use of lag operator L or its inverse forward operator F.

Lag operator L applied to a sequence y_t maps that sequence onto itself by transforming the index t into the index t−1, i.e.,

$$\mathrm{L}y_t = y_{t-1} \tag{2.16}$$

Repeated application of the L operator yields

$$\mathrm{L}(\mathrm{L}y_t) = L^2 y_t = y_{t-2};\ \ldots;\mathrm{L}\left(L^{n-1}y_t\right) = L^n y_t = y_{t-n} \tag{2.17}$$

The lag operator has an inverse L^{-1} which by definition is

$$L^{-1}(Ly_t) = \left(L^{-1}L\right)y_t = y_t \tag{2.18}$$

Applied to y_t, it functions as follows:

$$L^{-1}y_t = y_{t+1} \tag{2.19}$$

Sometimes operator L^{-1} is called the forward operator and is also denoted by F, so that it is equivalently set

$$\left(L^{-1}L\right)y_t = (FL)y_t = F(L\,y_t) = \mathrm{F}y_{t-1} = y_t \tag{2.20}$$

We define a polynomial in the lag operator formed with powers of L and denote it as A(L), i.e.,

$$A(L) = a_0L^0 + a_1L^1 + a_2L^2 + \ldots + a_nL^n + \ldots \sum_{i=0}^{\infty} a_iL^i$$

When applied to a sequence y_t, the polynomial in the L operator works as follows:

$$\mathrm{A(L)}y_t = \sum_{i=0}^{\infty} a_iL^iy_t = \sum_{i=0}^{\infty} a_iy_{t-i} \tag{2.21}$$

It is often convenient to work with a rational polynomial $A(L) = \frac{B(L)}{C(L)}$ and of particular interest is the polynomial obtained by setting $B(L) = 1$; $C(L) = 1 - \lambda L$. In that case polynomial in L is

$$A(L) = \frac{1}{1 - \lambda L} \tag{2.22}$$

Since λ is a constant and Lλ = λ, it is legitimate to interpret the denominator as a parameter. If |λ| < 1 the polynomial A(L) can formally be regarded as the limit of a geometric series, and therefore, it is possible to write

$$A(L) = \frac{1}{1 - \lambda L} = 1 + \lambda L + (\lambda L)^2 + (\lambda L)^3 + \ldots = \sum_{i=0}^{\infty} \lambda^i L^i$$

Applied to a series y_t the polynomial $\frac{1}{1-\lambda L}$ works by transforming the series into an infinite sum as follows:

$$\frac{1}{1 - \lambda L} y_t = \left[1 + \lambda L + (\lambda L)^2 + (\lambda L)^3 + \ldots\right] y_t = \sum_{i=0}^{\infty} \lambda^i \left(L^i y_t\right)$$

$$= \sum_{i=0}^{\infty} \lambda^i y_{t-i} \tag{2.23}$$

The sequence (2.23) with |λ| < 1 is bounded. Indeed, suppose that for every i ≥ 0, there exists finite M $\geq y_{t-i}$, ∀ i. It turns out

$$\sum_{i=0}^{\infty} \lambda^i y_{t-i} \leq \sum_{i=0}^{\infty} \lambda^i M = M \sum_{i=0}^{\infty} \lambda^i$$

But $\sum_{i=0}^{\infty} \lambda^i = \frac{1}{1-\lambda}$ and this is a finite number. Therefore, the summation to the left of the equality sign is also a finite number.

The sequence obtained by applying the polynomial $\frac{1}{1-\lambda L}$ is called a backward expansion, as all terms y_{t-i} contained in it refer to the past.

When |λ| > 1, the sequence obtained with the backward expansion is not bounded but divergent. However, even in the case |λ| > 1, it is possible to obtain a bounded sequence, by transforming the polynomial L in the following way.

By multiplying the numerator and denominator of $\frac{1}{1-\lambda L}$ by −1/λL, it follows

$$\frac{1}{1 - \lambda L} = \frac{-\frac{1}{\lambda L}}{(1 - \lambda L)\left(-\frac{1}{\lambda L}\right)} = \frac{-\frac{1}{\lambda L}}{\left(-\frac{1}{\lambda L} + 1\right)} = -\left(\frac{1}{\lambda L}\right) \frac{1}{1 - \frac{1}{\lambda L}} \tag{2.24}$$

The last term to the right of the sign of equality in (2.24) contains a polynomial $\frac{1}{1-\frac{1}{\lambda L}}$ which multiplies $-\left(\frac{1}{\lambda L}\right)$, and therefore, it admits the following expansion in L:

$$-\left(\frac{1}{\lambda L}\right)\left[1+\frac{1}{\lambda L}+\frac{1}{\lambda^2 L^2}+\ldots+\frac{1}{\lambda^n L^n}+\ldots\right]$$

$$=-\frac{1}{\lambda L}-\frac{1}{\lambda^2 L^2}-\frac{1}{\lambda^3 L^3}-\ldots-\frac{1}{\lambda^{n+1} L^{n+1}}= \; -\sum_{i=1}^{\infty}\frac{1}{\lambda^i L^i}$$

$$=-\sum_{i=1}^{\infty}\lambda^{-i}L^{-i} \tag{2.25}$$

By applying the transformation (2.25) to the sequence y_t results

$$y_t=-\sum_{i=1}^{\infty}\lambda^{-i}L^{-i}y_t=-\sum_{i=1}^{\infty}\lambda^{-i}y_{t+i} \tag{2.26}$$

The series (2.26), being $|\lambda| > 1$, is bounded. Furthermore, it is a weighted average of the terms iterated into the future, and for this reason, the expansion is called forward expansion or even forward factorization.

Factorizations just shown can be used to solve linear finite-difference equations of the first order, thus obtaining bounded solutions.

Consider again (2.3) and suppose that $|a| < 1$. Given that $y_{t-1} = Ly_t$, by substituting in (2.3), you get

$$y_t=a\,Ly_t+b_t \tag{2.27}$$

That is to say

$$(1-aL)y_t=b_t \tag{2.28}$$

From which

$$y_t=\frac{1}{1-aL}b_t=\sum_{i=1}^{\infty}a^iL^ib_t=\sum_{i=1}^{\infty}a^ib_{t-i} \tag{2.29}$$

If shocks b_t are bounded and $|a| < 1$, the sequence (2.29) coincides with the backward one, under the assumption that $\lim_{t\to\infty}a^Ty_{t-T}=0$. This is a particular solution, and for convenience, it can be indicated as

$$y_t^p=\sum_{i=1}^{\infty}a^ib_{t-i} \tag{2.30}$$

Since the solution of a nonhomogeneous equation is the sum of homogeneous and a particular solution, by adding y_t^p to the homogeneous solution, the general solution to the first-order finite-difference equation becomes (2.5). In (2.5), the constant c is arbitrary, so the number of obtainable solutions is infinite. However, as soon as a value is assigned to the constant c, the solution becomes determined.

Suppose now that $|a| > 1$. If we take the general solution y_t^g previously obtained with the backward factorization, the y_t^gdiverges, i.e., as is often stated, the backward solution, for $|a| > 1$ becomes explosive.

To search for a bounded solution even for the case $|a| > 1$, consider the transformation obtained by shifting forward by one step the time index, in the starting equation (2.3). It becomes

$$y_{t+1} = a\, y_t + b_{t+1} \tag{2.31}$$

By imposing the transversality condition $\lim_{t \to \infty} \frac{1}{a^T} y_T = 0$, it results

$$y_t = \lim_{t \to \infty} \frac{1}{a^T} y_T - \sum_{i=0}^{\infty} \frac{1}{a^i}\, b_{t+i} = -\sum_{i=0}^{\infty} \frac{1}{a^i}\, b_{t+i} \tag{2.32}$$

The same solution (2.31) is obtained by the factorization method. Indeed, it is

$$y_t = \frac{1}{a} L^{-1} y_t - \frac{1}{a} L^{-1} b_t = (aL)^{-1} y_t - (aL)^{-1}\, b_t \tag{2.33}$$

And so

$$\left[1 - (aL)^{-1}\right] y_t = -(aL)^{-1}\, b_t \tag{2.34}$$

That is to say

$$\begin{aligned} y_t &= \frac{-(aL)^{-1}}{1-(aL)^{-1}}\, b_t = \\ &-(aL)^{-1}\left[1 + (aL)^{-1} + (aL)^{-2} + \ldots\right] b_t = \\ &\left[-(aL)^{-1} - (aL)^{-2} - (aL)^{-3} - \ldots\right] b_t = \\ &-\sum_{i=1}^{\infty} a^{-i} L^{-i} b_t = -\sum_{i=1}^{\infty} a^{-i} b_{t+i} \end{aligned} \tag{2.35}$$

Since $|a| > 1$, solution (2.35) is bounded.

The associated homogeneous equation is $y_{t+1} = a\, y_t$, that is $y_t = a\, y_{t-1}$ and the complete general solution of the linear first difference equation becomes

$$y_t = ca^t - \sum_{i=1}^{\infty} a^{-i} b_{t+i} \tag{2.36}$$

Since $|a| > 1$, the first term diverges, so that to guarantee the boundedness of the general solution in this case, the only admissible value of the constant c is $c = 0$.

2.3 First-Order Difference Equation in Rational Expectations

A first-order difference equation in expectations, in the canonical form is as follows:

$$y_t = aE_t y_{t+1} + bx_t \tag{2.37}$$

where E_t is the expectation operator, i.e., the mean of the stochastic variable y_{t+1}, conditioned on the information available at time t.

Note that $E_t\, y_t = y_t$ so that if it is written $E_t\, y_t = aE_t y_{t+1} + bx_t$, it becomes evident that (2.37) also formally can be regarded as a finite-difference equation, in the sequence of expectations $\{E_t\, y_{t+i}\}$.

Solving Eq. (2.37) means searching for sequence $\{y_t\}$ for which the sequence of expectations $\{E_t\, y_{t+i}\}$ satisfies (2.37).

Among all feasible solutions, we are interested in finding the set for which terms $E_t\, y_{t+i}$ are bounded, i.e., for which $E_t\, y_{t+i}$ assume finite values.

Solving a difference in expectations equation with bounded terms is equivalent to finding a solution that admits nonexplosive expectations.

Such a solution can be obtained by induction, by iterating equation (2.37)) for T forward or backward, depending on whether $|a| < 1$ or $|a| > 1$.

It should be noted that, in the case of equations with differences in expectations, terms backward and forward used in mathematical literature undergo a sort of inversion with respect to the use in the case of ordinary difference equations.

Indeed, the term backward in the case of expectations refers to the case in which $|a| > 1$.

The same inversion holds for forward expansion in the case that $|a| < 1$. The reason for this inversion will soon be clear and is connected to the presence of expectations.

When $|a| < 1$, the forward solution is the one obtained by iteration of index t of equation forward from t+1 onward.

When $|a| > 1$, the solution is found by iterating the index t of equation backward from t−1 onward, precisely with the backward procedure.

Actually, the terms forward and backward in the language of rational expectations are synonyms, in the forward case, of "solution containing only terms referring to the future," and therefore, in conditions of uncertainty, "expected" terms or, in the backward case, as "solutions containing terms known with certainty", and in a certain sense referring to events or values that have already occurred or realized in the past.

2.4 Forward Solution for the Case |*a*| < 1

To start studying forward solution (containing future terms in solution), it is useful first to consider graphically, the dynamics of expectations described by the following equation:

$$E_t y_{t+1} = \frac{1}{a} y_t - \frac{b}{a} x_t \tag{2.38}$$

Let us consider the phase diagram (y_t, $E_t\, y_{t+1}$) represented in Fig. 2.1 for $x_t = x^* =$ constant.

Let y^* be the point where $E_t\, y_{t+1} = 0$, which verifies $y^* = b\, x^*$. Starting from this point, for increasing values of y_t in the interval $y_t < \bar{y}$, the expected value $E_t\, y_{t+1}$ moves toward the value $\bar{y}$, while it moves away from $\bar{y}$ for increasing values of y_t in the interval $y_t > \bar{y}$. Therefore, for an initial value $y_0 > \bar{y}$, the system highlights a speculative bubble, in which increasing current values of y_t feed ever-increasing values of expectations $E_t\, y_{t+2.}$

Figure 2.1 represents this dynamic.

Figure 2.1 shows that at point $y_0 > \bar{y}$, at $t = 1$, the expected value Ey_0 implies that at $t = 2$ the value y_1 will actually be greater than y_0. At y_1, the matured expectation $E_t\, y_1$ is such that $E_t\, y_1 > y_1$, and the expectation $E_t\, y_1$ requires, indeed, that $y_2 > y_{1.}$

The occurrence of y_2 confirms the expectation of increasing y value. We are faced, therefore, with *self-fulfilling* increasing expectations, and therefore, we are faced with a speculative bubble.

More interesting is the case already considered when the variable y_t does not have an initial position but is bound by a terminal condition.

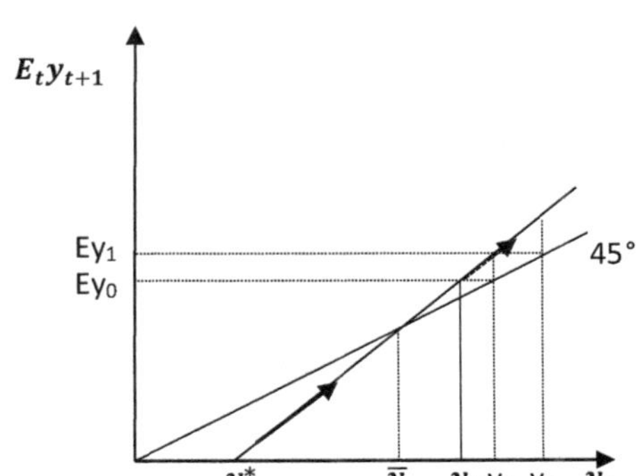

Fig. 2.1 Dynamics of expectations, case |a| < 1

We have already seen this condition, which takes the form of a limit $\lim_{t\to\infty} |y|_t < \infty$, imposes boundedness on the sequence $\{y_t\}$.

The methods of solution of (2.37) are the three already seen, namely:

1. Iterated substitution of expectations
2. Factorization
3. Method of indeterminate coefficients

We will go over these methods in the next sections by applying them to the search for the solutions of (2.37).

2.4.1 *Method of Iterated Forward Substitution of Expectations*

In the forward solution, the initial equation considered is (2.37), the canonical form. To solve (2.37), first iterate index t one step forward

$$y_{t+1} = aE_{t+1}y_{t+2} + bx_{t+1} \tag{2.39}$$

By applying the expectation operator, at time t, to y_{t+1}, it follows:

$$E_t y_{t+1} = a\ E_t E_{t+1} y_{t+2} + bx_{t+1} \tag{2.40}$$

The law of iterated expectations, which states that $(E_t\ (E_{t+1}\ y_{t+2}) = E_t\ y_{t+2}$, is valid, and therefore,

$$E_t y_{t+1} = a\ E_t y_{t+2} + bx_{t+1} \tag{2.41}$$

The term $E_t\ y_{t+1}$ in (2.41) appears in (2.37), and substituting one obtains

$$\begin{aligned} y_t &= a\left(aE_t y_{t+2} + bE_t x_{t+1}\right) + bx_t = a^2 E_t y_{t+2} + abE_t x_{t+1} + bx_t \\ &= a^2 E_t y_{t+2} + b\ (aE_t x_{t+1} + x_t) \end{aligned} \tag{2.42}$$

By iterating expectation at t+1 (2.41) one period ahead to time t+2 and by applying the law of iterated expectations, you get

$$E_t y_{t+2} = a\ E_t y_{t+3} + bE_t x_{t+2} \tag{2.43}$$

Substituting (2.43) in (2.42), it follows:

$$y_t = a^3 E_t y_{t+3} + \left(a^2 b\right) E_t x_{t+2}) + (ab) E_t x_{t+1} + b x_t$$
$$= a^3 E_t y_{t+3} + b\left(a^2 E_t x_{t+2} + a E_t x_{t+1} + x_t\right) \tag{2.44}$$

In general, by iterating the expectation operator forward, after successive substitutions, you will get

$$y_t = a^i E_t y_{t+i} + b(a^i E_t x_{t+i-1} + a^{i-1} E_t x_{t+i-1} + \cdots + a^2 E_t x_{t+2} + a E_t x_{t+1} + x_t) \tag{2.45}$$

By observing that $x_t = a^\circ E_t\, x_t$, using the summation symbol (2.45) can be rewritten

$$y_t = a^i E_t\, y_{t+i} + b \sum_{j=0}^{i} a^j\, E_t\, x_{t+j} \tag{2.46}$$

By iterating the time index for an infinite sequence of periods

$$y_t = \lim_{i \to \infty} a^{i+1} E_t y_{t+i+1} + b \lim_{i \to \infty} \sum_{j=0}^{i} a^j E_t\, x_{t+j} \tag{2.47}$$

The series (2.47) will converge if the two terms that compose it each converge to a finite value.

For the first term, the imposition of (the already known transversality condition) $\lim_{t \to \infty} |y_t| < \infty$ implies that the component $E_t y_{t+i}$ remains finite, while the $|a| < 1$ implies that series a^i tends to zero, so that $\lim_{i \to \infty} a^{i+1} E_t y_{t+i+1} = 0$ is verified. The solution of (2.37) then becomes

$$y_t = b \sum_{j=0}^{\infty} a^j E_t x_{t+j} \tag{2.48}$$

Series (2.48) is a multiple b of a linear combination of expectations of all shocks foreseen for the future (and this justifies the name solution forward-looking, i.e., it "looks to the future through expectations") for the exogenous stochastic variable x_t. Assuming an explicit stochastic process for x_t, it is also possible to further specify $E_t x_{t+j}$.

Let us assume that the stochastic process for $E_t x_{t+j}$ takes the AR(1) form

$$x_t = \rho x_{t-1} + (1 - \rho)\overline{x} + \varepsilon_t \tag{2.49}$$

where $|\rho| < 1$ is the persistence factor and ε_t is the innovation of process.

By iterating one period forward (2.49), and applying repeatedly the expectation operator, it is obtained

$$E_t x_{t+1} = \rho x_t + (1-\rho)\overline{x}$$

$$E_t x_{t+2} = \rho E_t x_{t+1} + (1-\rho)\overline{x} = \rho^2 x_t + \rho(1-\rho)\overline{x}$$
$$+(1-\rho)\overline{x} = \rho^2 x_t + (\rho+1)(1-\rho)\overline{x}$$

$$E_t x_{t+3} = \rho E_t x_{t+2} + (1-\rho)\overline{x} = \rho^3 x_t + \rho^2(1-\rho)\overline{x}$$
$$+(1+\rho)(1-\rho)\overline{x} = \rho^3 x_t + \left(\rho^2+\rho+1\right)(1-\rho)\overline{x}$$

$$\cdots\cdots\cdots\cdots\cdots\cdots\cdots\cdots\cdots\cdots\cdots\cdots$$

$$E_t x_{t+i} = \rho^i x_t + (1-\rho)\overline{x}\left(\rho^{i-1}\ldots+\rho^2+\rho+1\right)$$
$$= \rho^i x_t + (1-\rho)\overline{x}\sum_{j=0}^{i}\rho^j \tag{2.50}$$

The sum $\sum_{j=0}^{i}\rho^j$, since the number of terms is finite, equals $(1-\rho^i)/1-\rho$, so that

$$E_t x_{t+i} = \rho^i x_t + \left(1-\rho^i\right)\overline{x} = \rho^i(x_t-\overline{x}) + \overline{x} \tag{2.51}$$

The solution of (2.39) then will take the form

$$y_t = b\sum_{i=0}^{\infty} a^i E_t x_{t+i} = b\sum_{i=0}^{\infty} a^i\left[\rho^i(x_t-\overline{x}) + \overline{x}\right]$$
$$= b\sum_{i=0}^{\infty}\left[a^i\rho^i(x_t-\overline{x}) + a^i\overline{x}\right]$$
$$= b(x_t-\overline{x})\sum_{i=0}^{\infty} a^i\rho^i + b\overline{x}\sum_{i=0}^{\infty} a^i \tag{2.52}$$

from which

$$y_t = b\frac{(x_t-\overline{x})}{1-a\rho} + \frac{b\overline{x}}{1-a} = \frac{b}{1-a\rho}x_t - b\left(\frac{\overline{x}}{1-a\rho} + \frac{\overline{x}}{1-a}\right)$$

$$= \frac{b}{1-a\rho} x_t + \left[\frac{b(1-a\rho) - b(1-a)}{(1-a)(1-a\rho)} \right] \overline{x} = \frac{b}{1-a\rho} x_t + \frac{ba(1-\rho)}{(1-a)(1-a\rho)} \overline{x} \quad (2.53)$$

Compared to the deterministic solution, the stochastic solution (2.53) shows that the phenomenon exhibits fluctuations around the mean, i.e., it shows a cyclical path around the mean, and this is very important for purposes of studying economic phenomena.

2.4.2 Factorization Method

The factorization method for solving difference equations with expectations consists of the use of the forward operator F (or the equivalent operator $L^{-1} = F$) whose properties are

$$Fx_t = x_{t+1}, \ldots F^n x_t = x_{t+n}.$$

When the operator F is applied to expectations, it must be

$$F^i\,(E_t\, x_t) = E_t\,(F^i x_t) = E_t\, x_{t+i}.$$

By applying the operator F to (2.37) one obtains

$$y_t - aE_t F y_t = b x_t \quad (2.54)$$

Taking the expectation of (2.54), it is rewritten as

$$E_t y_t - aF E_t y_t = b E_t x_t \quad (2.55)$$

and so

$$(1 - aF) E_t y_t = b E_t x_t \quad (2.56)$$

By treating operator F as a parameter, the solution of (2.56) for $E_t y_t$ is

$$E_t y_t = b \frac{1}{1 - aF} E_t x_t \quad (2.57)$$

With |a| < 1, the term (1/1−aF) in (2.57) can be regarded as the limit of a geometric series with ratio aF, and therefore,

$$\frac{1}{1-aF}=\sum_{i=0}^{\infty}a^iF^i \tag{2.58}$$

And substituting (2.58) in (2.57), one has

$$E_ty_t=y_t=b\sum_{i=0}^{\infty}a^iF^iE_tx_t=b\sum_{i=0}^{\infty}a^i\ E_tx_{t+i} \tag{2.59}$$

The solution of Eq. (2.37) becomes

$$y_t=b\sum\nolimits_{i=0}^{\infty}a^{i+1}E_tx_{t+i} \tag{2.60}$$

The factorization method, however, allows one to obtain only fundamental solutions.

Moreover, it does not make explicit the use of the transversality condition, which, however, remains necessary for obtaining a finite solution.

2.4.3 *Method of Indeterminate Coefficients*

The method of indeterminate coefficient for solving finite-difference equations with expectations starts from an initial conjecture about the form of the solution.

A simplified but adequate conjecture is to assume that the solution for the problem at hand is a linear form in the expectations, i.e.,

$$y_t=\sum\nolimits_{i=0}^{\infty}\alpha_iE_tx_{t+i} \tag{2.61}$$

where α_i are coefficients to be determined.

Moving forward by one period the conjectured (2.61) and by taking its expectation, we obtain

$$E_ty_{t+1}=\sum\nolimits_{i=0}^{\infty}\alpha_iE_tx_{t+1+i} \tag{2.62}$$

Substituting in (2.37), we have

$$\sum\nolimits_{i=0}^{\infty}\alpha_iE_tx_{t+i}=a\left(\sum_{i=0}^{\infty}\alpha_iE_tx_{t+1+i}\right)+b\ x_t \tag{2.63}$$

Expanding the terms of (2.63), to the left and to the right of the sign's equality, gives

$$\alpha_0 x_t + \alpha_1 E_t x_{t+1} + \ldots + \alpha_i E_t x_{t+i} + \ldots$$
$$= bx_t + a\alpha_0 E_t x_{t+1} a\alpha_1 E_t x_{t+2} + \ldots + a\alpha_{i-1} E_t x_{t+i} + \ldots. \tag{2.64}$$

And by identifying the similar terms in (2.64) for i = 0, 1, .., ∞, we have

$$\alpha_0 = b$$
$$\alpha_1 = a\ \alpha_0 = ab$$
$$\alpha_2 = a\ \alpha_1 = \left(a^2\right)b$$
$$\cdots\cdots\cdots\cdots\cdots\cdots$$
$$\alpha_i = a\ \alpha_{i-1} = \left(a^i\right)b$$
$$\cdots\cdots\cdots\cdots\cdots\cdots$$

Therefore, by replacing the values of α_i in the hypothesized solution (2.61), it follows[3]

$$y_t = b\sum\nolimits_{i=0}^{\infty} a^i E_t x_{t+i} \tag{2.65}$$

2.4.4 A Simple Example of a Forward Solution with the Method of Indeterminate Coefficients

Let us assume that the variable x_t follows the same process AR(1), as before. In this case, we are faced with a dynamical system consisting of the following equations:

$$y_t = aE_t y_{t+1} + bx_t \tag{2.66}$$
$$x_t = \rho x_{t-1} + (1-\rho)\overline{x} + \varepsilon_t \tag{2.67}$$

Since y_t is linear in x_t, one can prove a linear solution in x_t with constant term, i.e., of the kind

$$y_t = \alpha_0 + \alpha_1 x_t \tag{2.68}$$

where α_0, α_1 are unknown coefficients.

Substituting (2.68) in (2.66), the following is obtained:

[3] A limit of this approach is that it requires a right guess about the solution, usually in economics based on knowledge of the model.

$$\alpha_0 + \alpha_1 x_t = aE_t(\alpha_0 + \alpha_1 x_{t+1}) + bx_t \tag{2.69}$$

and by computing expectations of (2.69)

$$\begin{aligned} \alpha_0 + \alpha_1 x_t &= a\alpha_0 + a\alpha_1 E_t x_{t+1} + bx_t \\ &= a\alpha_0 + a\alpha_1 \rho x_t + a\alpha_1 (1 - \rho)\overline{x} + bx_t \end{aligned} \tag{2.70}$$

By identifying the coefficients of similar terms, it follows

$$\alpha_0 = a\alpha_0 + a\alpha_1 (1 - \rho)\,\overline{x}$$

$$\alpha_1 = \alpha_1\ a\rho + b$$

That is

$$\alpha_0 = \alpha_1 \frac{a\,(1 - \rho)\overline{x}}{(1 - a)} \tag{2.71}$$

$$\alpha_1 = \frac{b}{1 - a\rho} \tag{2.72}$$

Substituting (2.72) in (2.71), it follows

$$\alpha_0 = \frac{ab(1 - \rho)}{(1 - a)(1 - a\rho)}\,\overline{x}$$

Solution is

$$y_t = \frac{ab(1 - \rho)}{(1 - a)(1 - a\rho)}\,\overline{x} + \frac{b}{1 - a\rho}\,x_t \tag{2.73}$$

which is the same as (2.53).

2.5 Case |a| > 1 and Solution with the Backward Iteration Method

In the case |a| > 1, the nature of the solution changes fundamentally.

Studying the dynamics of expectations described by (2.39), we now verify that, by setting $x_t = x^*$, with x^* constant, the series in expectations is convergent.

The graphic representation in the phase plane (y_t, $E_t y_{t+1}$) in Fig. 2.2 illustrates this property.

The system is stable, whatever the initial position y_0. There is an infinity of initial values y_0 for which the system returns to the stationary solution.

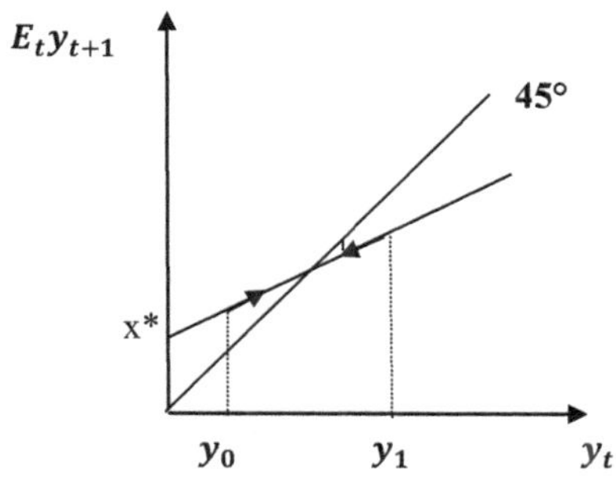

Fig. 2.2 Dynamics of expectations, case |a| > 1

For this reason, the system is said to be indeterminate, as trajectories leading to the stationary equilibrium are infinite. Often it is also said that a steady-state equilibrium is indeterminate. The language follows that of ordinary systems of linear equations, in which a system is indeterminate when the number of unknowns is greater than the number of equations. Now, refer to Cauchy's problem in the solution of finite-difference equations. Accordingly, when an initial condition is given, there is a single function that solves the considered difference equation. When initial conditions are infinite, there will be infinite solutions (just like when the number of unknowns is greater than the number of equations).

From the mathematical point of view, when |a| > 1 solution obtained with the forward method is divergent in expectations. Therefore, wanting a convergent solution, such a solution must be obtained differently, resorting to the backward iteration.

It is implemented as follows:

Concerning the initial canonical equation in the expectations (2.39), let us refer to (2.40) obtained by solving (2.39) for $E_t y_{t+1}$. Since we are looking for a solution for y_t, if we move (2.39) backward by one period, being $E_t y_t = y_t$, we get

$$y_t = \frac{1}{a} y_{t-1} - \frac{b}{a} x_t \tag{2.74}$$

the term y_{t-1} appears in (2.74). By shifting (2.74) one period back, it is

$$y_{t-1} = \frac{1}{a} y_{t-2} - \frac{b}{a} x_{t-1} \tag{2.75}$$

Substituting (2.73) in (2.72), we obtain

$$y_t = \frac{1}{a^2} y_{t-2} - \frac{b}{a^2} x_{t-2} - \frac{b}{a} x_{t-1} \tag{2.76}$$

After T iterations, we get

$$y_t = \frac{1}{a^T} y_{t-T} - \frac{b}{a^T} x_{t-T} - \ldots \frac{b}{a} x_{t-1} \tag{2.77}$$

That is

$$y_t = \frac{1}{a^T} y_{t-T} - b \sum_{i=1}^{T} \left(\frac{1}{a}\right)^i x_{t-i} \tag{2.78}$$

The series (2.78), since $|\boldsymbol{a}| > \mathbf{1}$, is bounded.

An equivalent way to search for the bounded solution is to "eliminate" the expectations from the starting equation (2.37), by referring to the definition

$$E_t y_{t+1} = y_{t+1} - \xi_{t+1} \tag{2.79}$$

where is $\xi_{t+1}$is the error such that $E_t\xi_{t+1} = 0$ and not correlated to the set of information (and therefore not correlated to y_t whose past and current values are part of the set of information).

Substituting in the initial (2.39) the expression of expectations (2.79), it becomes

$$y_{t+1} - \xi_{t+1} = \frac{1}{a} y_t - \frac{b}{a} x_t \tag{2.80}$$

From which

$$y_{t+1} = \frac{1}{a} y_t - \frac{b}{a} x_t + \xi_{t+1} \tag{2.81}$$

Shifting back (2.81) by one period, we get

$$y_t = \frac{1}{a} y_{t-1} - \frac{b}{a} x_{t-1} + \xi_t \tag{2.82}$$

Moving (2.82) further back, it is

$$y_{t-1} = \frac{1}{a} y_{t-2} - \frac{b}{a} x_{t-2} + \xi_{t-1} \tag{2.83}$$

and substituting (2.83) in (2.82), it follows

$$y_t = \frac{1}{a^2} y_{t-2} - \frac{b}{a^2} x_{t-2} - \frac{b}{a} x_{t-1} + \frac{1}{a} \xi_{t-1} + \xi_t \tag{2.84}$$

The term y_{t-2} appearing in (2.84) can be obtained by shifting (2.83) one period backward, i.e., by setting

$$y_{t-2} = \frac{1}{a} y_{t-3} - \frac{b}{a} x_{t-3} + \xi_{t-2} \tag{2.85}$$

and substituting (2.85) in (2.84) is obtained

$$y_t = \frac{1}{a^3} y_{t-3} - \frac{b}{a^3} x_{t-3} - \frac{b}{a^2} x_{t-2} - \frac{b}{a} x_{t-1} + \xi_t + \frac{1}{a} \xi_{t-1} + \frac{1}{a^2} \xi_{t-2} \tag{2.86}$$

After T iterations, we will have

$$y_t = \left(\frac{1}{a}\right)^T y_{t-T} - b \sum_{j=1}^{T} \frac{1}{a^j} x_{t-j} + \sum_{i=0}^{T-1} \frac{1}{a^i} \zeta_{t-j} \tag{2.87}$$

Equation (2.87) is the general solution of Eq. (2.74), the sum of the solution of the homogeneous equation, and two particular solutions. Indeed,

The term

$$\left(\frac{1}{a}\right)^T y_{t-T}$$

is the solution obtained by the back iteration of the homogeneous equation, resulting by setting $Ey_{t+1} = \left(\frac{1}{a}\right) y_t$.

The term

$$b \sum_{j=1}^{T} \frac{1}{a^j} x_{t-j}$$

is the weighted average, with declining weights, of deviations x_t from the mean, for an indefinite past, obtained by setting $\zeta_t = 0$ in (2.82).

Conversely, for $x_t = 0$ (2.82) becomes

$$y_t = \frac{1}{a} y_{t-1} + \zeta_t$$

By iterating for T periods, the latter admits the solution

$$y_t = \left(\frac{1}{a}\right)^T y_{t-T} + \sum_{i=0}^{T-1} \frac{1}{a^i} \zeta_{t-j} \tag{2.88}$$

and for T→∞ (2.88) becomes

$$y_t = \sum_{i=0}^{\infty} \frac{1}{a^i} \zeta_{t-j} \tag{2.89}$$

Since |a| > 1, (2.88) is bounded and it is a sunspot, i.e., it is the weighted average of stochastic shocks, occurred from a distant past up to now uncorrelated with themselves and with none of the fundamental variables of the economy.

This demonstrates that an equation with rational expectations also admits as a solution an equilibrium path guided over time exclusively by beliefs, or speculative factors. On this point, it is useful to carry out some further reflections in the next section.

2.6 Bubbles

The solution methods discussed above provide only limited solutions. If the constraint of searching only limited solutions is abandoned, the solution to the equation with rational expectations (2.36) appears in general as the sum of two types of solutions, a fundamental one y_t^f and one made up of bubbles y_t^b, i.e.,

$$\widetilde{y}_t = y_t^f + y_t^b \tag{2.90}$$

As we have seen, in case |a| < 1, a fundamental solution is the forward solution defined by

$$y_t^f = b \sum\nolimits_{j=0}^{\infty} a^j E_t x_{t+j} \tag{2.91}$$

What features does instead the bubble solution y_t^b have? We observe that if it is $\widetilde{y}_t = y_t^f + y_t^b$, by definition it must also be

$$E_t \widetilde{y}_{t+1} = E_t y_{t+1}^f + E_t y_{t+1}^b \tag{2.92}$$

And since it is $\widetilde{y}_t = a\, E_t \widetilde{y}_{t+1} + b\, x_t$, it must also be

$$y_t^f + y_t^b = aE_t y_{t+1}^f + aE_t y_{t+1}^b + bx_t \tag{2.93}$$

Since for fundamental solution is

$$y_t^f = aE_t y_{t+1}^f + bx_t \tag{2.94}$$

It follows

$$y_t^b = aE_t y_{t+1}^b \tag{2.95}$$

From which

$$E_t y_{t+1}^b = a^{-1} y_t^b \tag{2.96}$$

Any y_t^b satisfying (2.96) is such that $\widetilde{y}_t$ is a solution of (2.39). Since $|a| < 1$, explosive expectations are determined by y_t^b. For this reason, it is called a speculative bubble.

Thus, we found that a limited solution to the equation in expectations is obtained only because a priori bubbles are excluded from the general solution.

Let us now consider the case when $|a| > 1$.

As we have seen, shifting (2.80) back one period gives

$$y_t = a^{-1} y_{t-1} - a^{-1} bx_{t-1} + \xi_t \tag{2.97}$$

Equation (2.97) is a stochastic linear equation. It shows that the variable y_t is stochastic, subject to unpredictable shocks ξ_t. The shocks follow a given probability distribution, which can be characterized by a mean and a variance.

The solution to (2.97) is

$$y_t = \left(\frac{1}{a}\right)^T y_{t-T} - b \sum_{j=0}^{T} \frac{1}{a^j} x_{t-j} + \sum_{i=0}^{T} \frac{1}{a^i} \zeta_{t-j} \tag{2.98}$$

Which, being $|a| > 1$, is stable for $T \rightarrow \infty$.

The system is backward-looking, i.e., it is not guided by expectations but by events that have occurred in the past, including the history of the realization of past shocks that cannot be foreseen a priori. Being (2.97) the summation of stochastic variables, it remains a stochastic variable. Each term ξ_{t-i} is assumed to be serially uncorrelated to y_t, nor it is necessarily correlated with the innovation term x_t.

A shock with these characteristics, as we have seen, being not necessarily a fundamental shock, behaves like a sunspot. A sunspot captures a form of uncertainty that is purely extrinsic to the economy, i.e., generated by noneconomic factors such as beliefs in sunspots, and depending on the different volatility of the extrinsic uncertainty, the economy exhibits different pathways and, therefore, different solutions.

To point out this aspect, it is possible to characterize (2.97) by statistics. Sufficient statistics of a normal stochastic variable are mean and variance.

The mean can be expressed with the following difference equation:

$$E_t y_{t+1} = a^{-1} E_t y_t - a^{-1} b E_t x_{t+1} \tag{2.99}$$

That is, by using the unconditional mean symbol μ_t

$$\mu_{t+1} = a^{-1}\mu_t - \left(a^{-1}b\right)\mu_{x,t+1} \tag{2.100}$$

Equation (2.100) can be considered an ordinary finite-difference equation in μ_t. The solution obtained by recurrence is

$$\mu_t = a^{-T}\,\mu_0 + \sum_{i=0}^{T} \left(a^{-1}b\right)^i \mu_{x,t+i} \tag{2.101}$$

Also, for the variance σ^2_{t+1} of y_t, a similar difference equation is obtained starting from the definition

$$\sigma^2_{t+1} = \sigma^2_{t+1,\left[\,a^{-1}\;y_t\,-\,a^1 b\;x_t + \zeta_{t+1}\right]}$$

Computing variance of the term in square brackets (to right-hand of equality sign), by taking on account that each ξ_{t-i} is not serially correlated nor even correlated with the innovation term x_t, it results in a finite-difference equation of the variance, that is

$$\sigma^2_{t+1} = a^{-2}\,\sigma^2_t + \sigma^2_\zeta \tag{2.102}$$

with the initial position $\sigma^2_0 = 0$.

By treating these equations as usual finite-difference equations, it is possible to find a stationary solution for the mean and the variance, i.e.,

$$\mu = \frac{a^{-1}b\mu_x}{1 - a^{-1}}$$

$$\sigma^2 = \frac{\sigma^2_\zeta}{1 - a^{-2}}$$

2.7 Second-Order Finite-Difference Equations and Related Equations with Expectations

We will now proceed to the study of the finite-difference equation of the second order. The equation is given as

$$y_t = ay_{t-1} + by_{t-2} + cx_t \tag{2.103}$$

The order of differences of Eq. (2.103) is given by the difference between greater and lesser time index, i.e., t−(t−2) = 2.

The associated homogeneous equation is

$$y_t = ay_{t-1} + by_{t-2} \tag{2.104}$$

If, moving (2.104) forward by two indexes, we consider the equation

$$y_{t+2} = ay_{t+1} + by_t \tag{2.105}$$

that remains of the same order of (2.103), being t+2−t = 2.

The solution of (2.104) is obtained by a particular application of the method of indeterminate coefficients, which consists in hypothesizing a solution of the kind

$$y_t = \lambda^t \tag{2.106}$$

with λ a constant to be determined.

For (2.106) to be a solution of the homogeneous equation of the second order, it has to be

$$\lambda^{t+2} = a\lambda^{t+1} + b\lambda^t \tag{2.107}$$

That is to say

$$\lambda^t(\lambda^2 - a\lambda - b\lambda) = 0 \tag{2.108}$$

The latter (2.108), whatever λ^t, is true if the expression in parenthesis is null, i.e., if the equation of second degree in the unknown λ is verified

$$\lambda^2 - a\lambda - b = 0 \tag{2.109}$$

This is the *characteristic equation* associated with the second-order difference equation.

The roots of the characteristic equation (2.109) are calculated using the quadratic formula:

$$\lambda_1, \lambda_2 = \frac{a \pm \sqrt{(a^2 + 4b)}}{2} \tag{2.110}$$

The nature of roots depends on the sign of discriminant of the equation

$$\Delta = a^2 + 4b \tag{2.111}$$

In particular, if $\Delta > 0$, the roots are both real; if $\Delta < 0$ the roots are complex conjugate, if $\Delta = 0$ the roots are real and coincident, and therefore, the characteristic equation admits only one solution, counted twice.[4]

We will consider the three cases separately, but for the moment, we want to show that characteristic equations can also be deduced with the factorization method.

By applying operator L^{-1}, (2.105) can be rewritten

$$L^{-2}y_t - aL^{-1}y_t - by_t = 0 \tag{2.112}$$

From which

$$\left(L^{-2} - aL^{-1} - b\right) y_t = 0 \tag{2.113}$$

Expression in parentheses of (2.113) can be considered as the characteristic equation associated with finite-difference equation of second order if the symbol L^{-1} is interpreted as a parameter, i.e., if one set $\lambda = L^{-1}$. In fact, by substituting λ for $\lambda = L^{-1}$, we obtain

$$\lambda^2 - a\lambda - b = 0 \tag{2.114}$$

which is trivially (2.109).

Given the importance of characteristic equations for studying second-order difference equations, for the convenience of the reader in the Appendix, we review some properties of quadratic equations.

2.8 Properties of Characteristic Equation Associated with a Second-Order Difference Equation

In this section, we study the properties of the characteristic equation of a second-order finite-difference equation.

Three cases for the discriminant Δ are discussed: $\Delta > 0$, $\Delta < 0$, and $\Delta = 0$.

a) $\Delta > 0$. The roots of the characteristic equation, λ_1 and λ_2, are real and distinct. The solution to the homogeneous finite-difference equation (2.87) looks like:

---

[4]Descartes' rule also allows us to determine the sign of the roots. According to this rule, the number of positive roots is equal to the number of variations of the coefficients' sign, whereas the number of negative roots is equal to permanence's number in the coefficients' signs. On this point, see the review in Appendix.

$$y_t = A\,\lambda_1^t + B\lambda_2^t \tag{2.115}$$

with A and B constants to be determined.

Moving for two steps forward index t follows

$$A\,\lambda_1^{t+2} + B\,\lambda_2^{t+2} = a\left(A\,\lambda_1^{t+1} + B\,\lambda_2^{t+1}\right) + b\left(A\,\lambda_1^t + B\,\lambda_2^t\right) \tag{2.116}$$

That is to say

$$\mathrm{A}\lambda_1^t\left(\lambda_1^2 - a\lambda_1 - b\right) + \mathrm{B}\lambda_2^t\left(\lambda_2^2 - a\lambda_2 - b\right) = 0 \tag{2.117}$$

But λ_1 and λ_2 are roots of characteristic equation, and therefore, the terms in brackets are null. For each value λ_1^t and λ_2^t, the Eq. (2.117) is then verified.

Let us now refer to solution (2.115).

If $|\lambda_1|$ and $|\lambda_2|$ are both less than unity, this solution converges to zero; otherwise, it diverges.

Furthermore, the movement is monotonous if both roots are positive, while there will be oscillating values, negative or positive, if the roots are negative, as the power will be positive if the exponent is even, negative if the exponent is odd.

If one is positive and the other negative, movement will be impressed by the greater root in absolute value (called the *dominant root*), so that if the dominant root is the positive one, the dominant movement is monotone, while if the dominant root is negative, prevailing movement is oscillatory.

b) $\Delta = 0$

In this case, one solution of the characteristic equation for $\Delta = 0$ is $\lambda_1 = \lambda_2 = \frac{a}{2}$. Being $\lambda_*^t = \left(\frac{a}{2}\right)^t$ the common root, it follows that, together with the common root, the equation admits another solution represented by $t\lambda_*^t$.

Indeed, since it is also true that $y_{t+2} = ay_{t+1} + by_t$, by substituting for t λ_*^t one has

$$(\mathrm{t}+2)\,\lambda_*^{t+2} = \mathrm{a}\,(\mathrm{t}+1)\lambda_*^{t+1} + bt\lambda_*^t \tag{2.118}$$

That is to say

$$\lambda_*^t\,\left[(t+2)\lambda_*^2 - a(\mathrm{t}+1)\lambda_* - \mathrm{bt}\right] = 0 \tag{2.119}$$

But $\lambda_* = \frac{a}{2}$, and substituting it into (2.119), it follows

$$\left(\frac{a}{2}\right)^t\left[(t+2)\left(\frac{a}{2}\right)^2 - a(\mathrm{t}+1)\left(\frac{a}{2}\right) - \mathrm{bt}\right] = 0 \tag{2.120}$$

That is to say

$$\left(\frac{a}{2}\right)^t\left[\left(t\left(\frac{a}{2}\right)^2+2\left(\frac{a}{2}\right)^2\right)-\left(\frac{a^2}{2}\right)\mathrm{t}-\left(\frac{a^2}{2}\right)-\mathrm{bt}\right]=0$$

$$\left(\frac{a}{2}\right)^t\left[\left(t\frac{a^2}{4}+\frac{a^2}{2}\right)-\left(\frac{a^2}{2}\right)\mathrm{t}-\left(\frac{a^2}{2}\right)-\mathrm{bt}\right]=0$$

$$\left(\frac{a}{2}\right)^t\left[\left(\frac{a^2}{4}t-\frac{a^2}{2}\mathrm{t}-\mathrm{bt}\right)\right]=0$$

And putting in evidence in the round brackets, it will be

$$\left(\frac{a}{2}\right)^t\left[\left(\frac{a^2}{4}-\frac{a^2}{2}-\mathrm{b}\right)t\right]=0 \tag{2.121}$$

But $\Delta=0$ implies $a^2=-4\mathrm{b}$ and therefore $\frac{a^2}{4}=-b$ which substituted into (2.121) gives

$$\left(\frac{a}{2}\right)^t\left[\left(\frac{a^2}{4}-\frac{a^2}{2}+\frac{a^2}{4}\right)t\right]=\left(\frac{a}{2}\right)^t\left[\left(2\frac{a^2}{4}-\frac{a^2}{2}\right)=0\right. \tag{2.122}$$

Since the expression in parentheses of (2.122) vanishes, $t\lambda_*^t$ is effectively another solution of the second-order difference equation.

We therefore have found two distinct solutions λ_*^t, $\mathrm{t}\lambda_*^t$. Combined linearly with two arbitrary constants A and B, they give the general solution ([5]) of the second-order homogeneous equation, which is of kind

---

[5]That (2.123) is the general solution in the case $\Delta=0$ can also be verified directly by substitution in $y_{t+2}=ay_{t+1}+by_t$. Indeed

$$\left(\frac{a}{2}\right)^{t+2}(A+B\,(t+2))=a\left(\frac{a}{2}\right)^{t+1}(A+B(t+1))+\left(\frac{a}{2}\right)^t b(A+Bt)$$

That is to say $\left(\frac{a}{2}\right)^t\left[\frac{a^2}{4}(A+B\,(t+2))-\frac{a^2}{2}(A+B(t+1))-b(A+Bt)\right]=0$

$$\left(\frac{a}{2}\right)^t\left[\frac{a^2}{4}(A+B\,t)+\frac{a^2}{4}2-\frac{a^2}{2}(A+Bt)-\frac{a^2}{2}-b(A+Bt)\right]=0$$

$$\left(\frac{a}{2}\right)^t(A+B\,t)\left(\frac{a^2}{4}-\frac{2a^2}{4}-b\right)=-\left(\frac{a}{2}\right)^t\frac{(A+B\,t)}{4}(a^2+4b)=0$$

But $(a^2+4b)=0$, and therefore (2.123) verifies the second-order difference equation.

$$y_t = A\,\lambda_*^t + B\,t\lambda_*^t = \left(\frac{a}{2}\right)^t A + Bt\left(\frac{a}{2}\right)^t = \left(\frac{a}{2}\right)^t (A + Bt) \qquad (2.123)$$

The variable y_t, therefore, when $\Delta = 0$, follows a path resulting from the algebraic product of a linear trend (A+Bt) and an exponential trend $\left(\frac{a}{2}\right)^t$. The time path is dominated by the exponential component, and therefore, convergence depends on whether |a/2| > 1 or |a/2| < 1, while only if |a/2| = 1 does linear trend prevail.

c) Case $\Delta < 0$

In this case, the roots of the characteristic equation are complex conjugate. We write λ_1 and λ_2 in the exponential form

$$\lambda_1 = re^{i\theta} \qquad \lambda_2 = re^{-i\theta}$$

By substituting, the solution of the difference equation becomes

$$y_t = A\lambda_1^t + B\lambda_2^t = Ar^te^{i\theta t} + Br^te^{-i\theta t} = r^t\left(Ae^{i\theta t} + Be^{-i\theta t}\right) \qquad (2.124)$$

where A and B are constants to be determined.

Since y_t is a real number, A and B must be conjugate complex numbers. For example,

$$y_1 = Are^{i\theta} + Bre^{-i\theta} = r(A+B)cos\theta + ir(A-B)sen\theta \qquad (2.125)$$

and therefore, A+B must be real, and A-B a pure complex number such that if A = a +bi it must be B= a−bi. Therefore, A+B = a+bi+a−bi = 2a is real, while A−B = a +bi-a+bi = 2bi is a pure complex number.

Also, since A and B are complex numbers, can be written in exponential form

$$A = ae^{i\varphi} \text{ and } B = ae^{-i\varphi}$$

We can write

$$\begin{aligned} y_t &= Ar^te^{i\theta t} + Br^te^{-i\theta t} = ar^t\left[e^{i(\varphi+\theta t)} + e^{-i(\varphi+\theta t)}\right] \\ &= ar^t\ cos\,(\varphi+\theta t) + i\ sen(\varphi+\theta t) + cos\,(\varphi+\theta t) \\ &\quad - i\ sen(\varphi+\theta t)]\ 2ar^t\ cos\,(\varphi+\theta t) \end{aligned} \qquad (2.126)$$

We see from (2.126) that y_t is subject to cycles. In particular, if |r| > 1, the amplitude of oscillations diverges exponentially, while if |r| < 1, the amplitude of oscillations is damping down to zero. If |r| = 1, we will have a cycle of uniform amplitude, which always reappears in each period equal to itself.

Let's reconsider the solution formula of the characteristic equation when $\Delta < 0$. We have

$$\lambda_1 = \frac{a}{2} + i\,\frac{\sqrt{(a^2+4b)}}{2}; \qquad \lambda_2 = \frac{a}{2} - i\,\frac{\sqrt{(a^2+4b)}}{2}$$

By making use of properties

$$-\frac{a}{2} = r\ \cos\ \theta; \quad \frac{\sqrt{(a^2+4b)}}{2} = r\ sen\theta \ \text{ and } r = \sqrt{a^2+b^2}$$

Equation (2.125) can be rewritten

$$y_t = r^t[(A+B)cos\theta t + (A-B)i\ sen\theta t] \tag{2.127}$$

Also noting that $(A-B)i = i\frac{\sqrt{(a^2+4b)}}{2}\ i = i^2\frac{\sqrt{(a^2+4b)}}{2}$ $= -\frac{\sqrt{(a^2+4b)}}{2} = A_2$, (2.127) becomes

$$y_t = r^t[(A+B)cos\theta t + A_2\ sen\theta t] \tag{2.128}$$

and by symmetry, renaming $A + B = A_1$, we can write

$$y_t = r^t[A_1 cos\theta t + A_2\ sen\theta t] \tag{2.129}$$

Rewriting (2.129) becomes immediate to grasp considerations already made about the nature of temporal path of y_t.

The solution of finite-difference equation follows a cyclical trend, with cycles explosive or fading, depending on whether |r| > 1 or |r| < 1.

The constant r in terms of parameters of the characteristic equation now is $r = \sqrt{b}$.

Since $\sqrt{b} \geq\ < 1$ if $b \geq\ < 1$, the oscillatory movement will be increasing in amplitude if b > 1, will be constant if b = 1, and will be decreasing if b < 1.

2.9 Stability Conditions for Second-Order Finite-Difference Equation

The stability conditions of the second-order finite-difference equation have been expressed through the roots of the characteristic equation, while in the case of complex roots, they have been expressed, through the |r| value, in terms of parameters of the characteristic equation.

It is possible, however, to find symmetric conditions on coefficients of characteristic equations useful to verify the stability of solutions of finite-difference equations of second order.

Indeed, the conditions that will now be considered are valid in general and not only for the case of real roots and, therefore, also include those of complex roots. These conditions consist of the following inequalities on coefficients of the characteristic equation:

$$\begin{aligned} 1-a-b &> 0 \\ 1-b &> 0 \\ 1+a-b &> 0 \end{aligned} \tag{2.130}$$

Conditions (2.130) are necessary and sufficient for the roots of the characteristic equation to be less than unity in absolute value.

Note that the first inequality is equivalent to b < 1, being a+b < 1.

Considered the trinomial $f(\lambda) = \lambda^2 - a\lambda - b$. It is true that f(1) = 1−a−b. So, the first condition of (2.130) is equivalent to requiring that f(λ) is positive in correspondence of $\lambda = 1$; that is $f(1) > 0$.

Furthermore, f(−1) = 1+a−b, and the third condition of (2.130) states that in correspondence of λ = −1, the trinomial f(−1) must also be positive.

Finally, the second condition of (2.130) requires that the product b between the roots is positive, and together with the other two conditions, this implies that both roots are positive (therefore, greater than −1) and less than 1.

Lastly, for the second-order finite-difference equation even, the rule that the general solution is the sum of a homogeneous equation solution and a particular solution is true, i.e.,

$$y_t^g = A\lambda_1^t + B\lambda_2^t + y_t^p \tag{2.131}$$

2.10 Solution Method by Factorization

In Sect. 2.7, we applied the lag operator L to obtain characteristic equations by heuristically identifying L as a parameter.

Let us restart the reasoning, by considering the same L as operator Lag applied to the second-order canonical equation (2.102).

We'll have

$$\left(1 - aL - bL^2\right)y_t = cx_t \tag{2.132}$$

That is

$$\left(bL^2 + aL - 1\right)y_t = -cx_t$$

And dividing both sides by b, it is

$$\left(L^2 + \frac{a}{b}L - \frac{1}{b}\right)y_t = -\frac{c}{b}x_t \tag{2.133}$$

If the conditions $\lambda_1 + \lambda_2 = -\frac{a}{b}$ and $\lambda_1\lambda_2 = -\frac{1}{b}$ are imposed, the numbers λ_1 and λ_2 can be regarded as roots of the characteristic equation

$$\lambda^2 + \frac{a}{b}\lambda - \frac{1}{b} = 0 \tag{2.134}$$

So that we have

$$\begin{aligned} L^2 - (\lambda_1 + \lambda_2)L + \lambda_1\lambda_2 &= L^2 - \lambda_1 L - \lambda_2 L + \lambda_1\lambda_2 \\ &= L(L - \lambda_1) - \lambda_2(L - \lambda_1) \end{aligned} \tag{2.135}$$

and bringing out of the expression to the right of equality sign the term L-λ_1, we obtain

$$L^2 + \frac{a}{b}L - \frac{1}{b} = (\mathrm{L} - \lambda_2)(L - \lambda_1) \tag{2.136}$$

By substituting in (2.133), the difference equation now becomes

$$(\mathrm{L} - \lambda_2)(L - \lambda_1)y_t = -\frac{c}{b}x_t \tag{2.137}$$

From which

$$(L - \lambda_1)y_t = -\frac{c}{b}\frac{1}{\mathrm{L} - \lambda_2}x_t \tag{2.138}$$

By putting in (2.138) in evidence λ_1 on the left and $\frac{1}{\lambda_2}$ on the right, it is

$$\lambda_1\left(\frac{1}{\lambda_1}L - 1\right)y_t = -\frac{c}{b}\frac{1}{\lambda_2}\left(\frac{1}{\frac{1}{\lambda_2}L - 1}\right)x_t \tag{2.139}$$

Or

$$\lambda_1\lambda_2\left(\frac{1}{\lambda_1}L - 1\right)y_t = = -\frac{c}{b}\left(\frac{1}{\frac{1}{\lambda_2}L - 1}\right)x_t \tag{2.140}$$

But $\lambda_1\lambda_2 = -\frac{1}{b}$ so that

$$\left(\frac{1}{\lambda_1}L-1\right)y_t=c\left(\frac{1}{\frac{1}{\lambda_2}L-1}\right)x_t \tag{2.141}$$

Expanding the term to the right

$$-\frac{1}{1-\frac{1}{\lambda_2}L}cx_t=-\left(1+\frac{1}{\lambda_2}L+\ldots+\left(\frac{1}{\lambda_2}\right)^n L^n+\ldots\right)cx_t$$

$$=-c\sum_{i=0}^{\infty}\left(\frac{1}{\lambda_2}\right)^i x_{t-i} \tag{2.142}$$

From

$$\left(\frac{1}{\lambda_1}L-1\right)y_t==-c\sum_{i=0}^{\infty}\left(\frac{1}{\lambda_2}\right)^i x_{t-i},$$

the following particular solution is obtained:

$$y_t=\frac{1}{\lambda_1}y_{t-1}+c\sum_{0}^{\infty}\left(\frac{1}{\lambda_2}\right)^i x_{t-i} \tag{2.143}$$

The series (2.143) converges if $|\lambda_2| > 1$.

A general solution, by adding to the particular solution (2.143) just obtained, two solutions of the homogeneous equation $A\lambda_1^t$ and $B\lambda_2^t$, is

$$y_t=A\lambda_1^t+B\lambda_2^t+\frac{1}{\lambda_1}y_{t-1}+c\sum_{0}^{\infty}\left(\frac{1}{\lambda_2}\right)^i x_{t-i} \tag{2.144}$$

where A and B are constants to be determined.

The solution converges to a steady state if $|\lambda_1^t| < 1$ and $|\lambda_2^t| < 1$. But is $|\lambda_2^t| > 1$, so that the term $B\lambda_2^t$ diverges, unless $B = 0$. In this case, the convergent solution becomes

$$y_t=\frac{1}{\lambda_1}y_{t-1}+A\lambda_1^t+c\sum_{0}^{\infty}\left(\frac{1}{\lambda_2}\right)^i x_{t-i} \tag{2.145}$$

2.11 Sargent's Approach to Solution Method by Factorization

T. Sargent[6] provides an approach to the solution of a second-order finite-difference equation similar to the one proposed here, but different.

We earlier considered the factorization (2.136). Sargent considers the following factorization:

$$\left(1 - aL - bL^2\right) = (1 - \alpha_1 L)(1 - \alpha_2 L) \tag{2.146}$$

This factorization follows from the imposition of the following conditions on the coefficients of the trinomial of lags:

$$\alpha_1 + \alpha_2 = a \tag{2.147}$$

$$\alpha_1 \alpha_2 = -b \tag{2.148}$$

We will now study the relationship between the direct decomposition (2.146) proposed by Sargent and the usual one (2.136) relating to the canonical characteristic equation.

First, let's verify that Sargent's decomposition is true. From the condition

$$\left(1 - aL - bL^2\right) = 1 - (\alpha_1 + \alpha_2)L + \alpha_1 \alpha_2 L^2 \tag{2.149}$$

It follows

$$1 - \alpha_1 L - \alpha_2 L + \alpha_1 \alpha_2 L^2 = 1 - \alpha_1 L - \alpha_2 L(1 - \alpha_1 L) \tag{2.150}$$

Bringing out of the expression the term $(1 - \alpha_1 L)$, to the right hand of (2.150), it follows

$$1 - aL - bL^2 = (1 - \alpha_1 L)(1 - \alpha_2 L) \tag{2.151}$$

which is precisely the decomposition (2.146) proposed by Sargent.

The associated characteristic equation is now

$$1 - a\lambda - b\lambda^2 = 0 \tag{2.152}$$

The relationship between roots of Eq. (2.152) and terms of decomposition of trinomial lags (2.151) is

[6] Sargent, T. (1987).

$$(1-\alpha_1\lambda)(1-\alpha_2\lambda)=\alpha_1\left(\frac{1}{\alpha_1}-\lambda\right)\alpha_2\left(\frac{1}{\alpha_2}-\lambda\right) \tag{2.153}$$

Therefore, the characteristic equation is

$$(1-\alpha_1\lambda)(1-\alpha_2\lambda)=\alpha_1\left(\frac{1}{\alpha_1}-\lambda\right)\alpha_2\left(\frac{1}{\alpha_2}-\lambda\right)=0 \tag{2.154}$$

which admits roots

$$\lambda_1=\frac{1}{\alpha_1} \quad \text{and} \quad \lambda_2=\frac{1}{\alpha_2} \tag{2.155}$$

Concerning the canonical characteristic equation (2.136), therefore, the roots of Sargent's decomposition of trinomial in lags are the inverse of the roots of the associated characteristic equation.

Sargent's decomposition allows us to write the second-order finite-difference equation as

$$(1-\alpha_1 L)(1-\alpha_2 L)y_t=cx_t \tag{2.156}$$

And given the particular solution

$$y_t=\frac{c}{(1-\alpha_1 L)(1-\alpha_2 L)}x_t \tag{2.157}$$

the general solution becomes[7]

$$y_t=\frac{c}{(1-\alpha_1 L)(1-\alpha_2 L)}x_t+A\,\alpha_1^t+B\,\alpha_2^t \tag{2.158}$$

It is possible to obtain a particular solution by assigning two conditions that y_t must satisfy.

In particular, assigning two initial conditions $y_{t\,=\,0}=y_0$ and $y_{t\,=\,1}=y_1$, it is sufficient to determine constants A and B. To be able to determine them here, it is necessary to consider the method of reduction to partial fractions of a rational polynomial.

[7] That expression (2.158) is the general solution of (2.156) can be verified from $(1-\alpha_1 L)(1-\alpha_2 L)y_t=cx_t+A\alpha_1^t(1-\alpha_1 L)(1-\alpha_2 L)$

$$+B\alpha_2^t(1-\alpha_1 L)(1-\alpha_2 L)$$

Since $A(1-\alpha_1 L)(1-\alpha_2 L)\alpha_1^t=B(1-\alpha_1 L)(1-\alpha_2 L)\alpha_2^t=0$ as $\alpha_1 L=\frac{1}{\lambda_1}$ and $\alpha_2 L=\frac{1}{\lambda_2}$ and then $\alpha_1\left(\frac{1}{\alpha_1}-\lambda\right)\alpha_2\left(\frac{1}{\alpha_2}-\lambda\right)=0$.

For the moment, let us focus on an equivalent way to obtain the same solution for the second-order finite-difference equation.

We consider that equation in the following form:

$$y_t = \beta_1 y_{t-1} + \beta_2 y_{t-2} + bx_t + a \tag{2.159}$$

We rewrite (2.159) as

$$y_t - \beta_1 y_{t-1} - \beta_2 y_{t-2} = a + bx_t \tag{2.160}$$

By applying lag operators, (2.160) becomes

$$y_t - \beta_1 L y_t - \beta_2 L^2 y_t = a + bx_t$$

that is

$$\left(1 - \beta_1 L - \beta_2 L^2\right) y_t = a + bx_t \tag{2.161}$$

By replacing the symbol L with the auxiliary variable z, we get

$$1 - \beta_1 z - \beta_2 z^2 = 0 \tag{2.162}$$

This is the following characteristic equation:

$$\beta_2 z^2 + \beta_1 z - 1 = 0 \tag{2.163}$$

Being z_1 and z_2 roots of the characteristic equation (2.163), we can decompose it into the following linear factors:

$$\beta_2 z^2 + \beta_1 z - 1 = \beta_2\,(z - z_1)(z - z_2) \tag{2.164}$$

Bringing out of expression z_1 from the first term of (2.164), to the right hand of equality sign, it follows

$$\beta_2\, z_1 \left(\frac{z}{z_1} - 1\right)(z - z_2) \tag{2.165}$$

Bringing out of expression also z_2, from the second term of (2.165) to the right of equality, it follows

$$\beta_2\, z_1 z_2 \left(\frac{z}{z_1} - 1\right)\left(\frac{z}{z_2} - 1\right) \tag{2.166}$$

By recalling that from the relationship between the roots of a quadratic equation and its coefficients $z_1 z_2 = -\frac{1}{\beta_2}$, decomposition (2.164) becomes

$$\begin{aligned}\beta_2 z^2 + \beta_1 z - 1 &= -\left(\frac{z}{z_1} - 1\right)\left(\frac{z}{z_2} - 1\right) \\ &= \left(1 - \frac{z}{z_1}\right)\left(1 - \frac{z}{z_2}\right)\end{aligned} \tag{2.167}$$

It follows

$$\lambda_1 = (1/z_1) \text{ and } \lambda_2 = (1/z_2) \tag{2.168}$$

Characteristic equation (2.159) can be decomposed into the following product of monomials:

$$(1 - \lambda_1 z)(1 - \lambda_2 z) \tag{2.169}$$

By analogy, the second-degree polynomial in L can also be decomposed into a similar expression

$$\left(1 - \beta_1 L - \beta_2 L^2\right) = (1 - \lambda_1 L)(1 - \lambda_2 L) \tag{2.170}$$

With the decomposition (2.170), the second-order difference equation (2.159) now becomes

$$(1 - \lambda_1 L\ )(1 - \lambda_2 L) y_t = b x_t + a \tag{2.171}$$

Solving (2.171) for y_t, we obtain the following particular solution:

$$y_t = \frac{a}{(1 - \lambda_1 L)(1 - \lambda_2 L)} + \frac{b}{(1 - \lambda_1 L)(1 - \lambda_2 L)} x_t \tag{2.172}$$

The general solution (sum of a particular solution and solution of the homogeneous equation) appears as

$$y_t = \frac{a}{(1 - \lambda_1 L)(1 - \lambda_2 L)} + \frac{b}{(1 - \lambda_1 L)(1 - \lambda_2 L)} x_t + c_1 \lambda_1^t + c_2 \lambda_2^t \tag{2.173}$$

2.12 Method for Reduction of a Rational Polynomial to Partial Fractions

Consider a rational polynomial of the following form:

$$A(L) = \frac{F(L)}{G(L)} = \frac{F(L)}{(1-\lambda_1 L)(1-\lambda_2 L)\dots(1-\lambda_n L)} \tag{2.174}$$

where the degree of F(L) is assumed to be less than the degree of G(L).

The roots of the denominator G(λ) are

$$\lambda_1 = \frac{1}{\alpha_1}; \lambda_2 = \frac{1}{\alpha_2}, \dots . \lambda_n = \frac{1}{\alpha_n} \tag{2.175}$$

as each of these values satisfies the equation

$$(1-\alpha_1\lambda)\ (1-\alpha_2\lambda)\dots .(1-\alpha_n\lambda) = 0 \tag{2.176}$$

Suppose the n roots are distinct.

The method of partial fractions allows to decomposition of the single fraction of polynomials of kind (2.174) into the sum of n partial fractions

$$\frac{F(L)}{(1-\lambda_1 L)(1-\lambda_2 L)\dots(1-\lambda_n L)} = \frac{A_1}{(1-\lambda_1 L)} + \frac{A_2}{(1-\lambda_2 L)} + \dots \frac{A_n}{(1-\lambda_n L)} \tag{2.177}$$

where A_1, A_2, . . ., A_n are constants to be determined.

To determine the constants A_1, A_2, . . ., A_n, multiplying both sides of (2.177) by $(1-\lambda_1 L)(1-\lambda_2 L)\dots(1-\lambda_n L)$, one obtains

$$F(L) = \frac{A_1(1-\lambda_1 L)(1-\lambda_2 L)\dots(1-\lambda_n L)}{(1-\lambda_1 L)} + \frac{A_2(1-\lambda_1 L)(1-\lambda_2 L)\dots(1-\lambda_n L)}{(1-\lambda_2 L)}$$

$$+ \dots\dots$$

$$\dots + \frac{A_n(1-\lambda_1 L)(1-\lambda_2 L)\dots(1-\lambda_n L)}{(1-\lambda_n L)} \tag{2.178}$$

That is

$$F(L) = A_1(1-\lambda_2 L)\dots(1-\lambda_n L) + A_2(1-\lambda_1 L)\dots(1-\lambda_n L) + ..\\ + A_n(1-\lambda_1 L)(1-\lambda_2 L)\dots\dots(1-\lambda_{n-1} L) \quad (2.179)$$

With L$=\frac{1}{\lambda_1}$ (2.179) becomes

$$F\left(\frac{1}{\lambda_1}\right) = A_1\left(1-\frac{\lambda_2}{\lambda_1}\right)\dots\left(1-\frac{\lambda_n}{\lambda_1}\right) + A_2\left(1-\frac{\lambda_1}{\lambda_1}\right)\dots\\ \left(1-\frac{\lambda_n}{\lambda_1}\right) + \dots A_n\left(1-\frac{\lambda_1}{\lambda_1}\right)\left(1-\frac{\lambda_2}{\lambda_1}\right)\dots\left(1-\frac{\lambda_{n-1}}{\lambda_1}\right) \quad (2.180)$$

And

$$A_2\left(1-\frac{\lambda_1}{\lambda_1}\right)\dots\left(1-\frac{\lambda_n}{\lambda_1}\right) = 0\dots = A_n\left(1-\frac{\lambda_1}{\lambda_1}\right)\\ \times\left(1-\frac{\lambda_2}{\lambda_1}\right)\dots\dots\left(1-\frac{\lambda_{n-1}}{\lambda_1}\right) = 0 \quad (2.181)$$

So that

$$A_1 = \frac{F\left(\frac{1}{\lambda_1}\right)}{\left(1-\frac{\lambda_2}{\lambda_1}\right)\dots\left(1-\frac{\lambda_n}{\lambda_1}\right)} \quad (2.182)$$

And more generally

$$A_i = \frac{F\left(\frac{1}{\lambda_i}\right)}{\left(1-\frac{\lambda_1}{\lambda_i}\right)\dots\left(1-\frac{\lambda_{i-1}}{\lambda_i}\right)\left(1-\frac{\lambda_{i+1}}{\lambda_i}\right)\dots\left(1-\frac{\lambda_n}{\lambda_i}\right)} \quad (\text{i}=2,\dots,\text{n}) \quad (2.183)$$

As an example, we apply this transformation to the case in which the denominator is the second-order polynomial $(1-\lambda_1 L)(1-\lambda_2 L)$, i.e.,

$$A(L) = \frac{1}{(1-\lambda_1 L)(1-\lambda_2 L)} = \frac{A_1}{(1-\lambda_1 L)} + \frac{A_2}{(1-\lambda_2 L)} \quad (2.184)$$

It turns out

$$A_1 = \frac{1}{1-\frac{\lambda_2}{\lambda_1}} = \frac{\lambda_1}{\lambda_1-\lambda_2}; \qquad A_2 = \frac{1}{1-\frac{\lambda_1}{\lambda_2}} = \frac{\lambda_2}{\lambda_2-\lambda_1} \quad (2.185)$$

And so

$$\frac{1}{(1-\lambda_1 L)(1-\lambda_2 L)} = \frac{1}{\lambda_1-\lambda_2}\frac{\lambda_1}{(1-\lambda_1 L)} + \frac{1}{\lambda_2-\lambda_1}\frac{\lambda_2}{(1-\lambda_2 L)}$$
$$= \frac{1}{\lambda_1-\lambda_2}\left(\frac{\lambda_1}{(1-\lambda_1 L)} - \frac{\lambda_2}{(1-\lambda_2 L)}\right) \tag{2.186}$$

To complete the topic, consider the nth-order difference equation

$$(1-\lambda_1 L)(1-\lambda_2 L)\ldots(1-\lambda_n L)y_t = bx_t \tag{2.187}$$

The general solution is

$$y_t = \frac{b}{(1-\lambda_1 L)(1-\lambda_2 L)\ldots(1-\lambda_n L)}x_t + A_1\lambda_1^t + A_2\lambda_2^t + \ldots A_n\lambda_n^t \tag{2.188}$$

with A_i, i=2...n, constants to be determined.

In this case, n conditions on the path y_t are needed to determine the n constants A_1, A_2, . . A_n.

2.13 Partial Fractions and Discussion of Solutions of Finite-Difference Equation of Second Order

In this section, we study the second-order equation with the method of partial fractions.

We rewrite the rational polynomial as

$$\frac{1}{(1-\lambda_1 L)(1-\lambda_2 L)} = \frac{1}{\lambda_1-\lambda_2}\frac{\lambda_1}{(1-\lambda_1 L)} + \frac{1}{\lambda_2-\lambda_1}\frac{\lambda_2}{(1-\lambda_2 L)}$$
$$= \frac{1}{\lambda_1-\lambda_2}\left(\frac{\lambda_1}{(1-\lambda_1 L)} - \frac{\lambda_2}{(1-\lambda_2 L)}\right. \tag{2.189}$$

The general solution (of the second-order difference equation) can therefore be written as

$$y_t = \frac{bx_t}{\lambda_1-\lambda_2}\left(\frac{\lambda_1}{(1-\lambda_1 L)} - \frac{\lambda_2}{(1-\lambda_2 L)}\right) + A_1\lambda_1^t + A_2\lambda_2^t$$
$$= \frac{\lambda_1 b}{\lambda_1-\lambda_2}\frac{1}{(1-\lambda_1 L)}x_t - \frac{\lambda_2 b}{\lambda_1-\lambda_2}\frac{1}{(1-\lambda_2 L)}x_t + A\lambda_1^t + B\lambda_2^t \tag{2.190}$$

and by recalling that

$$\frac{1}{(1-\lambda_1 L)} = \sum_{i=0}^{\infty} \lambda_1^i L^i,$$

$$\frac{1}{(1-\lambda_2 L)} = \sum_{i=0}^{\infty} \lambda_2^i L^i, \tag{2.191}$$

And that $L^i x_t = x_{t-i}$, it follows

$$y_t = \frac{\lambda_1 b}{\lambda_1 - \lambda_2} \sum_{i=0}^{\infty} \lambda_1^i x_{t-i} - \frac{\lambda_2 b}{\lambda_1 - \lambda_2} \sum_{i=0}^{\infty} \lambda_2^i x_{t-i} + A\lambda_1^t + B\lambda_2^t \tag{2.192}$$

Equation (2.192) can be rewritten to discuss the solutions of homogeneous equations of the second-order finite differences.

Resorting to the artifice of rewriting the sums as "sum of sums," it is true that

$$\sum_{i=0}^{\infty} \lambda_1^i x_{t-i} = \sum_{i=0}^{t-1} \lambda_1^i x_{t-i} + \sum_{i=t}^{\infty} \lambda_1^i x_{t-i} \tag{2.193}$$

and likewise

$$\sum_{i=0}^{\infty} \lambda_2^i x_{t-i} = \sum_{i=0}^{t-1} \lambda_2^i x_{t-i} + \sum_{i=t}^{\infty} \lambda_2^i x_{t-i} \tag{2.194}$$

We have

$$y_t = \frac{\lambda_1 b}{\lambda_1 - \lambda_2} \sum_{i=0}^{t-1} \lambda_1^i x_{t-i} - \frac{\lambda_2 b}{\lambda_1 - \lambda_2} \sum_{i=0}^{t-1} \lambda_2^i x_{t-i} + \frac{\lambda_1 b}{\lambda_1 - \lambda_2} \sum_{i=t}^{\infty} \lambda_1^i x_{t-i}$$
$$- \frac{\lambda_2 b}{\lambda_1 - \lambda_2} \sum_{i=t}^{\infty} \lambda_2^i x_{t-i} + A\lambda_1^t + B\lambda_2^t \tag{2.195}$$

Since it is

$$\frac{\lambda_1 b}{\lambda_1 - \lambda_2} \sum_{i=t}^{\infty} \lambda_1^i x_{t-i} = \frac{\lambda_1 b}{\lambda_1 - \lambda_2} \lambda_1^t \sum_{i=0}^{\infty} \lambda_1^i x_{0-i} \tag{2.196}$$

$$\frac{\lambda_2 b}{\lambda_1 - \lambda_2} \sum_{i=t}^{\infty} \lambda_2^i x_{t-i} = \frac{\lambda_2 b}{\lambda_1 - \lambda_2} \lambda_2^t \sum_{i=0}^{\infty} \lambda_1^i x_{0-i} \tag{2.197}$$

We can put

$$\theta_0 = A + \frac{\lambda_1 b}{\lambda_1 - \lambda_2} \sum_{i=0}^{\infty} \lambda_1^i x_{0-i}$$

$$\eta_0 = B + \frac{\lambda_2 b}{\lambda_1 - \lambda_2} \sum_{i=0}^{\infty} \lambda_1^i x_{0-i}$$

and therefore,

$$y_t = \frac{\lambda_1 b}{\lambda_1 - \lambda_2} \sum_{i=0}^{t-1} \lambda_1^i x_{t-i} - \frac{\lambda_2 b}{\lambda_1 - \lambda_2} \sum_{i=0}^{t-1} \lambda_2^i x_{t-i} + \theta_0 \lambda_1^t + \eta_0 \lambda_2^t \tag{2.198}$$

For $x_{t-i} = 0$, for $i \leq t-1$, the solution coincides with the usual solution of homogeneous finite-difference equation of the second-order

$$y_t = \theta_0 \lambda_1^t + \eta_0 \lambda_2^t \tag{2.199}$$

Equation (2.199) shows that if λ_1 and λ_2 are both real, the solution converges to stationary solution, i.e., $\lim_{t \to \infty} y_t = 0$, if and only if roots of the characteristic equation are both lesser than the unit in absolute value, i.e., if and only if $|\lambda_1| < 1$ and $|\lambda_2| < 1$.

If $|\lambda_1| > 1$, $|\lambda_2| < |\lambda_1|$ and $\theta_0 > 0$, then $\lim_{t \to \infty} y_t = +\infty$, while for $|\lambda_1| > 1$ and $|\lambda_2| < |\lambda_1|$ with $\theta_0 < 0$, you have $\lim_{t \to \infty} y_t = -\infty$.

Now assume that roots are complex. In this case, they are complex conjugates and the previous considerations hold, showing that the solution of the homogeneous equation is of the type

$$y_t = 2ar^t \cos(\varphi + \theta t) \tag{2.200}$$

By recalling that

$$y_t = \frac{\lambda_1 b}{\lambda_1 - \lambda_2} \sum_{j=0}^{\infty} \lambda_1^j x_{t-j} - \frac{\lambda_2 b}{\lambda_1 - \lambda_2} \sum_{j=0}^{\infty} \lambda_2^j x_{t-j} \tag{2.201}$$

That is to say

$$\begin{aligned} y_t &= \frac{b}{\lambda_1 - \lambda_2} \sum_{j=0}^{\infty} \lambda_1^{j+1} x_{t-j} - \frac{b}{\lambda_1 - \lambda_2} \sum_{j=0}^{\infty} \lambda_2^{j+1} x_{t-j} \\ &= \frac{b}{\lambda_1 - \lambda_2} \sum_{j=0}^{\infty} \left(\lambda_1^{j+1} - \lambda_2^{j+1}\right) x_{t-j} \end{aligned} \tag{2.202}$$

By replacing in (2.193) the exponential expression of the roots $\lambda_1 = re^{i\theta}$, and $\lambda_2 = re^{-i\theta}$, it follows

$$y_t = \frac{b}{re^{i\theta} - re^{-i\theta}} \sum_{j=0}^{\infty} \left[\left(re^{i\theta}\right)^{j+1} - \left(re^{-i\theta}\right)^{j+1} \right] x_{t-j}$$

$$= \frac{b}{2risen\theta} \sum_{j=0}^{\infty} 2r^{j+1} i[sen\theta(j)] x_{t-j} \tag{2.203}$$

So that

$$y_t = b \sum_{j=0}^{\infty} r^j i \left[\frac{sen\theta(j+1)}{sen\theta} \right] x_{t-j} \tag{2.204}$$

The oscillations caused by the trigonometric component are weighted by r^i so that the amplitude of lag weight decreases as j increases if $r < 1$.

The case of equal roots for $\Delta = 0$ is obtained as follows:

The polynomial $\frac{1}{(1-\lambda L)(1-\lambda L)}$ equals

$$\frac{1}{(1-\lambda L)(1-\lambda L)} = \frac{1}{(1-\lambda L)} (1 + \lambda L + \ldots + \lambda^n L^n + \ldots)$$

$$= (1 + \lambda L + \ldots + \lambda^n L^n + \ldots) + \lambda L (1 + \lambda L + \ldots + \lambda^n L^n + \ldots)$$

$$+ \lambda^2 L^2 (1 + \lambda L + \ldots + \lambda^n L^n + \ldots) = 1 + 2\lambda L + 3\lambda^2 L^2 + \ldots$$

$$= \sum_{i=0}^{\infty} (i+1) \lambda^i L^i \tag{2.205}$$

The second-order finite-difference equation becomes[8]

$$(1 - \lambda L)^2 y_t = cx_t$$

The general solution is

---

[8]The component $(1 - \lambda L)^2$ is the result of the convolution of two sequences $\sum_{i=0}^{\infty} \lambda^i L^i$ and $\sum_{i=0}^{\infty} \lambda^i L^i$, and results from

$$\sum_{i=0}^{\infty} h_i = \sum_{i=0}^{\infty} \lambda^i L^i \lambda^i L^i = \sum_{i=0}^{\infty} \left(\lambda^i L^i\right)^2 = \frac{1}{(1-\lambda L)^2}$$

$$y_t = \frac{c}{(1-\lambda L)^2}\, x_t = c\sum_{i=0}^{\infty}(i+1)\lambda^i x_{t-i} + A\lambda^t + t\,B\lambda^t \tag{2.206}$$

with A and B real constants.

Rewriting summation in (2.197) as

$$\sum_{i=0}^{\infty}(i+1)\lambda^i x_{t-i} = \sum_{i=0}^{t-1}(i+1)\lambda^i x_{t-i} + \sum_{i=t}^{\infty}(i+1)\lambda^i x_{t-i} \tag{2.207}$$

and noting that

$$\sum_{i=t}^{\infty}(i+1)\lambda^i x_{t-i} = \sum_{j=0}^{\infty}(\,j+1+t)\lambda^{t+j}x_{0-J}$$

$$= \lambda^t\sum_{j=0}^{\infty}(\,j+1)\lambda^j x_{0-j} + t\lambda^t\sum_{j=0}^{\infty}\lambda^j x_{0-j} \tag{2.208}$$

The general solution becomes

$$y_t = c\sum_{i=0}^{t-1}(i+1)\lambda^i x_{t-i} + \theta_0\lambda^t + \eta_0\, t\lambda^t \tag{2.209}$$

where

$$\theta_0 = A + c\sum_{j=0}^{\infty}(\,j+1)\lambda^j x_{0-j}$$

and

$$\eta_0 = B + \sum_{j=0}^{\infty}\lambda^j x_{0-j}$$

with A and B obtained from two initial conditions $y_0 = 0$ and $y_1 = 0$.

For t $\geq$1 and $x_t = 0$, if $|\lambda| < 1$, the sequence (2.209) converges to the stationary value $y_t = 0$. If $|\lambda| > 1$, the convergence of (2.209) requires $\theta_0 = \eta_0 = 0$.

2.14 Second-Order Difference Equations with Expectations

A second-order difference equation with expectations is of the form:

$$y_t = a\, E_t y_{t+1} + b y_{t-1} + c x_t \tag{2.210}$$

It differs from an ordinary second-order difference equation in that it contains the term $E_t\, y_{t+1}$.

The solution of (2.210) can be found with the various methods already seen, i.e., by forward and backward induction, method of indeterminate coefficients, and method of factorization.

Here, we will first consider the method of indeterminate coefficients.

2.14.1 Method of Solution of Indeterminate Coefficients

With the method of indeterminate coefficients, as a tentative solution, we will assume the following sequence:

$$y_t = \mu y_{t-1} + \sum_{i=0}^{\infty} \alpha_i E_i x_{t+i} \tag{2.211}$$

with μ and α_i unknown coefficients to be determined.

If this is a solution, since moving the index t forward by one period and taking the expectation, it must be

$$E_t y_{t+1} = \mu y_t + \sum_{i=0}^{\infty} \alpha_i E_i x_{t+1+i} \tag{2.212}$$

Substituting both (2.211) and (2.212) in canonical equation (2.210), we will have

$$\mu y_{t-1} + \sum_{i=0}^{\infty} \alpha_i E_i x_{t+i} = a \left(\mu y_t + \sum_{i=0}^{\infty} \alpha_i E_i x_{t+1+i} \right) + b y_{t-1} + c x_t \tag{2.213}$$

Taking into account again the expression of y_t, it is

$$\mu y_{t-1} + \sum_{i=0}^{\infty} \alpha_i E_i x_{t+i}$$

$$= a \left[\mu \left(\mu y_{t-1} + \sum_{i=0}^{\infty} \alpha_i E_i x_{t+i} \right) + \sum_{i=0}^{\infty} \alpha_i E_i x_{t+1+i} \right] + b y_{t-1} + c x_t$$

$$= a\,\mu^2 y_{t-1} + a\mu \sum_{i=0}^{\infty} \alpha_i E_i x_{t+i} + a \sum_{i=0}^{\infty} \alpha_i E_i x_{t+1+i} + b y_{t-1} + c x_t$$

$$= \left(a\,\mu^2 + b\right) y_{t-1} + a\mu \sum_{i=0}^{\infty} \alpha_i E_i x_{t+i} + a \sum_{i=0}^{\infty} \alpha_i E_i x_{t+1+i} + c x_t \qquad (2.214)$$

To identify coefficients of similar terms, compare the terms containing $y_{t-1}$and those containing x_t and x_{t+i}.

It must be

$$\mu y_{t-1} = \left(a\,\mu^2 + b\right) y_{t-1} \qquad (2.215)$$

$$\alpha_0 x_t + \sum_{i=1}^{\infty} \alpha_i E_i x_{t+i} = (a\mu\alpha_0 + c)x_t + \sum_{i=1}^{\infty} a\mu\alpha_i E_i x_{t+i} + \sum_{i=1}^{\infty} a\alpha_{i-1} E_i x_{t+i}) \qquad (2.216)$$

And by identifying terms by terms, one has

$$\mu = a\,\mu^2 + b \qquad \text{(for terms containing } y_{t-1})$$

$$\alpha_0 = a\mu\alpha_0 + c \qquad \text{(for terms containing } x_t)$$

$$\alpha_i = a\mu\alpha_i + a\alpha_{i-1}\ (\mathrm{i} = 1, ., .\infty)(\text{for terms containing } E_i x_{t+i})$$

The first condition is equivalent to the following quadratic equation:

$$\mu^2 - \frac{1}{a}\mu + \frac{b}{a} = 0 \qquad (2.217)$$

Whose roots satisfy conditions

$$\mu_1 + \mu_2 = -\frac{1}{a}$$

$$\mu_1 \mu_2 = \frac{b}{a}$$

The three possible configurations that can emerge from the previous equation are as follows:

a) Both solutions are outside the circle of unit radius, and only one particular point, the steady state, is a solution of the equation.
b) One solution falls outside the unit circle, and the other is inside the circle: the model exhibits the saddle point property (among all the paths followed by solution, only one converges toward a steady state).

c) The two solutions are both in the unit circle: the model exhibits the property of indeterminacy (all infinite paths of solution converge toward a steady state). In models of rational expectations, we consider the property b) of saddle point, which corresponds to solution $|\mu_1| < 1$ and $|\mu_2| > 1$.

Taking the value of μ_1, solving for α_0, it follows

$$\alpha_0(1 - a\mu_1) = c \tag{2.218}$$

from which

$$\alpha_0 = \frac{c}{(1 - a\mu_1)} \tag{2.219}$$

Furthermore,

$$\alpha_i = a\mu_1\alpha_i + a\alpha_{i-1} \tag{2.220}$$

So that

$$\alpha_i = \frac{a}{1 - a\mu_1}\alpha_{i-1} = \frac{1}{\frac{1}{a} - \mu_1}\alpha_{i-1} = \frac{1}{\mu_1 + \mu_2 - \mu_1}\alpha_{i-1} = \left(\frac{1}{\mu_2}\right)\alpha_{i-1} \tag{2.221}$$

Equation (2.221) has solution $\alpha_i = \left(\frac{1}{\mu_2}\right)^i \alpha_0$, which, being $|\mu_2| > 1$, converges to zero.

Substituting the values of α_0, α_i, and μ_1 into the tentative solution, (2.211) follows

$$y_t = \mu_1 y_{t-1} + \frac{c}{(1 - a\mu_1)} \sum_{i=0}^{\infty} \left(\frac{1}{\mu_2}\right)^i E_i x_{t+i} \tag{2.222}$$

Even in this context, an interesting case for economists is the one in which the exogenous term follows a stochastic process of kind AR(1):

$$x_t = \rho\, x_{t-1} + \varepsilon_t \tag{2.223}$$

with $\varepsilon_t \sim N(0, \sigma)$.

In this case, a tentative solution for (2.210) is

$$y_t = \mu y_{t-1} + \alpha\, x_t \tag{2.224}$$

Moving one step forward time index and taking the expectation, it is

$$E_t y_{t+1} = \mu y_t + \alpha\, E_t x_{t+1} = \mu y_t + \rho\alpha\, x_t$$
$$= \mu^2 y_{t-1} + \mu\alpha\, x_t + +\rho\alpha\, x_t \tag{2.225}$$

Substituting and identifying

$$\mu y_{t-1} + \alpha\, x_t = a(\,\mu y_t + \rho\alpha\, x_t) + b y_{t-1} + \alpha\, x_t$$
$$= a\mu^2 y_{t-1} + a\mu\,\alpha\, x_t + a\rho\alpha\, x_t + b y_{t-1} + c\, x_t$$
$$= \left(a\mu^2 + b\right) y_{t-1} + [a\alpha\,(\mu + \rho) + c] x_t$$

and identifying terms by terms

$$\mu = a\mu^2 + b \tag{2.226}$$

$$\alpha = a\alpha\,(\mu + \rho) + c \tag{2.227}$$

As before, and as happens in the solution of the equations in rational expectations, we select stable root μ, the one for which $|\mu_1| < 1$ and such that

$$\alpha = \frac{c}{1 - a(\mu_1 + \rho)} \tag{2.228}$$

In contrast to the simple case, the solution inherits not only the persistence of the shock but also its self-persistence via μ_1 from first-order autocorrelation, as can be verified by considering first-order autocorrelation[9]

$$\rho(1) = \frac{\mu_1 + \rho}{1 + \mu_1 \rho}$$

2.14.2 Solution Method by Factorization

Let us now examine the method of solution by factorization. Moving in (2.210) the index t one period forward, and applying the expectation operator E_t, we have

$$E_t y_{t+1} = a\, E_t y_{t+2} + b E_t y_t + c\, E_t\, x_{t+1} \tag{2.229}$$

That is, by applying the forward operator L^{-1} to y_t

[9]The autocorrelation coefficient is defined by $\rho(1) = \frac{\text{cov}(y_t,\ y_{t-1})}{\sigma_t^2 \sigma_{t-1}^2}$.

$$E_tL^{-1}y_t = a\,E_tL^{-2}y_t + b\,y_t + c\,E_t\,x_{t+1} \tag{2.230}$$

Since in general $L^{-1}E_t\,y_t = E_t\,L^{-1}y_t$, we have

$$L^{-1}E_ty_t = a\;L^{-2}E_ty_t + b\,E_ty_t + c\,E_tx_{t+1} \tag{2.231}$$

which can be written

$$-c\,E_tx_{t+1} = a\;L^{-2}E_ty_t - L^{-1}E_ty_t + b\,E_ty_t \tag{2.232}$$

That is

$$-\frac{c}{a}\,E_tx_{t+1} = \left(L^{-2} - \frac{1}{a}L^{-1} + \frac{b}{a}\right)E_ty_t \tag{2.233}$$

Rewritten the expression in brackets of (2.233) in simple linear factors, (2.233) becomes

$$-\frac{c}{a}\,E_tx_{t+1} = (L^{-1} - \mu_1)(L^{-1} - \mu_2)E_ty_t \tag{2.234}$$

where μ_1 and μ_2 are roots of the characteristic equation $\mu^2 - \frac{1}{a}\,\mu + \frac{b}{a} = 0$ and therefore satisfy the conditions $\mu_1 + \mu_2 = \frac{1}{a}$ and $\mu_1\mu_2 = \frac{b}{a}$.

From (2.234) solving for $(L^{-1} - \mu_1)E_ty_t$, it is obtained

$$(L^{-1} - \mu_1)E_ty_t = -\frac{c}{a}\,\frac{1}{(L^{-1} - \mu_2)}E_tx_{t+1} \tag{2.235}$$

That is,

$$(L^{-1} - \mu_1)E_ty_t = -\frac{c}{a\mu_2}\,\frac{1}{(L^{-1}\mu_2^{-1} - 1)}E_tx_{t+1} \tag{2.236}$$

Taking the solution with $|\mu_1| < 1$ and $|\mu_2| > 1$ (saddle point), it is

$$\frac{1}{(1 - L^{-1}\mu_2^{-1})} = \sum_{i=0}^{\infty}\mu_2^{-i}L^{-i} \tag{2.237}$$

Therefore, moving the time index a step back

$$\left(L^{-1}-\mu_1\right)E_t y_{t-1}=\frac{c}{a\mu_2}\sum_{i=0}^{\infty}\mu_2^{-i}L^{-i}E_t x_t=\frac{c}{a\mu_2}\sum_{i=0}^{\infty}\mu_2^{-i}E_t x_{t+i} \tag{2.238}$$

By applying the operator L^{-1} to the left hand of (2.238) and remembering that $E_t y_{t-1}=y_{t-1}$, one has

$$y_t=\mu_1 y_{t-1}+\frac{c}{a\mu_2}\sum_{i=0}^{\infty}\mu_2^{-i}E_t x_{t+i} \tag{2.239}$$

Since $|\mu_2|>1$, (2.230) is convergent. Taking into account that $\mu_2=\frac{1}{a}-\mu_1$, it follows $\frac{c}{a\mu_2}=\frac{c}{1-\mu_1 a}$, and the solution by factorization coincides with (2.222) obtained with the method of indeterminate coefficients.

The general solution of the second-order difference equation is

$$y_t=\mu_1 y_{t-1}+\frac{c}{a\mu_2}\sum_{i=0}^{\infty}\mu_2^{-i}E_t x_{t+i}+\mathrm{A}\,\mu_1^t+\mathrm{B}\,\mu_2^t \tag{2.240}$$

The saddle point solution requires $\mathrm{A}=0$ and converges to the steady state $y_t=y_{t-1}=0$.

2.15 Solution to Second-Order Finite-Difference Equation with the Matrix Approach

In this section, we will consider the solution of the second-order ordinary finite-difference equation with the matrix approach. This exercise is also useful as an introduction to the more general approach to the solution of systems of finite-difference equations of the first order.

Indeed, by adding the auxiliary variable

$$z_t=y_{t-1} \tag{2.241}$$

Jointly with the original equation

$$y_t=ay_{t-1}+by_{t-2}+cx_t \tag{2.242}$$

One obtains the system

$$\begin{aligned} y_t &= ay_{t-1} + bz_{t-1} + cx_t \\ z_t &= y_{t-1} + 0\, z_{t-1} + 0\, x_t \end{aligned} \tag{2.243}$$

which in matrix form is

$$\begin{pmatrix} y_t \\ z_t \end{pmatrix} = \begin{pmatrix} a & b \\ 1 & 0 \end{pmatrix} \begin{pmatrix} y_{t-1} \\ z_{t-1} \end{pmatrix} + \begin{pmatrix} c \\ 0 \end{pmatrix} x_t \tag{2.244}$$

That is, in vector notation

$$v_t = A\, v_{t-1} + v^0 x_t \tag{2.245}$$

A system of finite differences of any form, with the appropriate change of variables, can be always traced back to a system of first-order differences.

The study of the system (2.245), and of dynamic tendencies nested into it, begins from the homogeneous system

$$v_t = A\, v_{t-1} \tag{2.246}$$

Associated with (2.246), there is a system of characteristic equations obtained from the following eigenvalue-eigenvector relationship:

$$\lambda x = A\, x \tag{2.247}$$

That is to say

$$0 = (A - \lambda I)\, x \tag{2.248}$$

System (2.247) can be thought of as resulting by applying the method of indeterminate coefficients to the homogeneous system (2.246), in which $v_t = x\, \lambda^t$, where $x = \begin{pmatrix} x_1 \\ x_2 \end{pmatrix}$ is a vector of constants to be determined, and the solutions have the form

$$x\, \lambda^t = \begin{pmatrix} x_1 \lambda^t \\ x_2 \lambda^t \end{pmatrix}.$$

If $x\, \lambda^t$ is a vector solution of the homogeneous system, it must be verified

$$x\, \lambda^t = A\, x \lambda^{t-1} \tag{2.249}$$

i.e.:

$$\lambda x = A\,x \tag{2.250}$$

System

$$(A - \lambda I)x = 0 \tag{2.251}$$

admits solutions x $\neq$ 0 only if $det|(A - \lambda I)| = 0$.

The condition for determinant vanishing corresponds to the characteristic equation associated with the initial dynamical system.

Matrix A can be diagonalized and written as

$$A = PDP^{-1} \tag{2.252}$$

where D is the diagonal matrix containing the eigenvalues and P is the matrix of eigenvectors.

With diagonalization, the system (2.246) can be rewritten in terms of eigenvectors and eigenvalues

$$v_t = PDP^{-1}\,v_{t-1} \tag{2.253}$$

That is, by defining the vector $y_t = P^{-1}v_t$, it follows

$$y_t = D\,y_{t-1} \tag{2.254}$$

Regarding the system (2.254), diagonalization allows to gathering in diagonal matrix D the roots or eigenvalues associated with initial matrix A, and in matrix P the corresponding eigenvectors.

One way to think about eigenvectors and eigenvalues is to refer to Fig. 2.3 below:

In Fig. 2.3, consider two eigenvectors, P_1 and P_2, which are associated to the eigenvalues $\mu_1$and μ_2. We can represent these eigenvectors as the direction along respective lines P_1 and P_2.

In the representation of Fig. 2.3, the root $\mu_1$is stable and the root μ_2 is unstable. Along P_1, a displacement occurs in the direction of the stationary point (y*, z*) whether displacement occurs from x_1 toward x_2 or from x_3 toward x_4, where along P_2 a displacement moves points away in the opposite direction to (y*, z*) as in x'_1 toward x'_2 and in x'_3 toward x'_4. Indeed, eigenvectors determine the direction along which the system evolves and eigenvalues determine the speed (step length) at which the movement takes place. For the case we are studying, given matrix A and eigenvector system λx=Ax, the equation corresponding to det|(A-λI)| = 0 is obtained by expanding the determinant

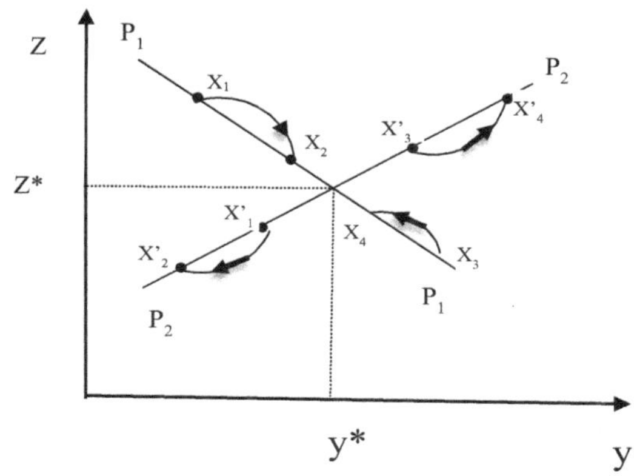

Fig. 2.3 A graphical representation of Eigenvectors

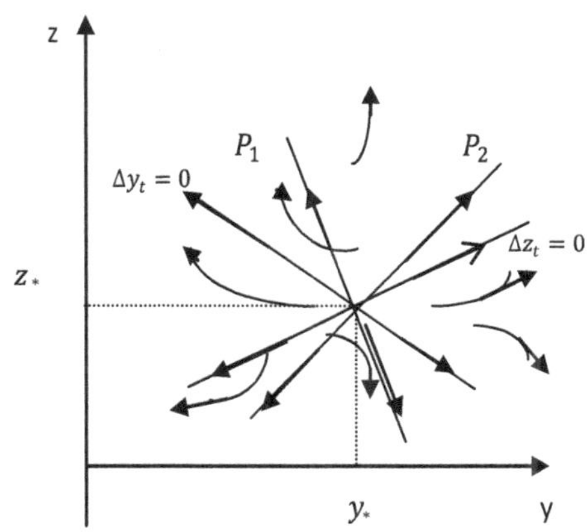

Fig. 2.4 Case of a source

$$\begin{vmatrix} a-\mu & b \\ 1 & 0-\mu \end{vmatrix} = \mu^2 - a\mu - b = 0 \tag{2.255}$$

We can use a phase diagram similar to Fig. 2.3 to examine the possible dynamics for the second-order finite-difference equation.

The first case considered in Fig. 2.4 is that of a *source*. In Fig. 2.5, the source is characterized by the fact that it admits only the stationary point as equilibrium. For any other starting point, other than the steady state, the system explodes, with each trajectory diverging toward infinity.

A second case of possible dynamics is that of a *vortex*, which is shown in Fig. 2.5.

The characteristic of the vortex is that whatever the starting point, the direction of a path starting from that point is oriented toward the stationary point. The system, therefore, is indeterminate because, whatever the initial point chosen by an observer, the system will be directed toward stationary point. A priori initial points are infinity, and this is the characteristic that causes indeterminacy.

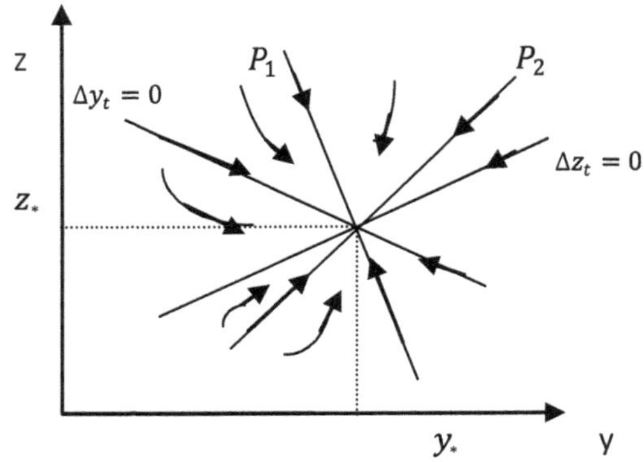

Fig. 2.5 Case of a vortex

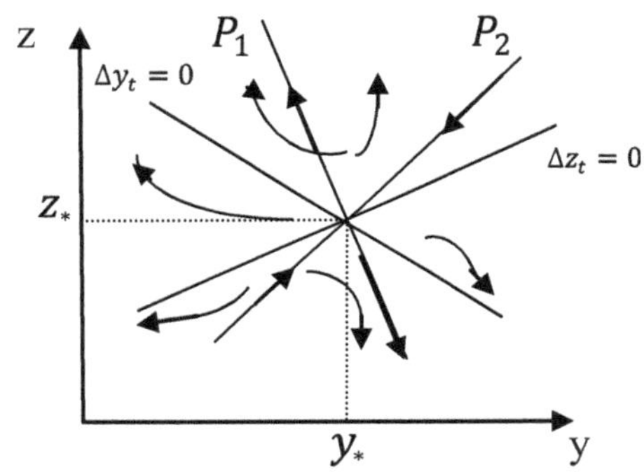

Fig. 2.6 Case of saddle-point

The third case, of particular interest in economic applications, is that of *saddle point* represented in Fig. 2.6.

In the saddle point case, only trajectories starting from points on the straight line P_2oriented toward the stationary state are convergent. Any other initial point leads the system toward the divergent trajectories. The saddle point situation is one most often represented in economic theory with rational expectations. At time t+1, the value z_{t+1} is perfectly expected. At time t, there is a single initial value $y_t$which allows the system to reach a steady state in the long run.

Let us now return to the vectorial system of homogeneous first difference equations (2.246).

Given an initial vector v_0, at t = 1, it follows

$$v_1 = A\, v_0 \tag{2.256}$$

At t = 2, it follows

$$v_2 = A\ v_1 = A \times A\ \ v_0 = A^2\ v_0 \tag{2.257}$$

At generic t, one has

$$\begin{aligned} v_t = A\ v_{t-1} = (A \times A) \times Av_{t-2} \ldots . = (A \times A) \ldots \times A\ v_{t-t-1} \\ = (A \times A) \ldots \times A\ A\ v_0 = A^t v_0 \end{aligned} \tag{2.258}$$

If A is diagonalizable, it can be written as $A = PDP^{-1}$, and the solution looks as

$$v_t = A^t v_0 = \left(PDP^{-1}\right)^t v_0 \tag{2.259}$$

That is, by putting $y_t = P^t v_t$

$$y_t = D^t y_0 \tag{2.260}$$

Solution (2.260) converges to the steady state $y_t = 0$ if and only if all eigenvalues contained in the diagonal matrix D are in absolute value less than unity.

In particular, in the case of the second-order difference equation, this is equivalent to requiring that both roots of characteristic equation μ_1 and μ_2 (that coincide with the eigenvalues of matrix D of order 2×2) are in absolute value less than unity.

2.16 Systems of Finite-Difference Equations

In general, a system of finite-difference equations can be thought of as directly resulting from a set of difference equations, e.g., for the 2×2 case, from two linear equations in two functions of the type

$$\begin{aligned} x_t = a\ x_{t-1} + b\ y_{t-1} + c \\ y_t = dx_{t-1} + f\ y_{t-1} + g \end{aligned} \tag{2.261}$$

By defining matrix, A$=\begin{pmatrix} a & b \\ d & f \end{pmatrix}$, and vectors $v_t = \begin{pmatrix} x_t \\ y_t \end{pmatrix}$, $\alpha = \begin{pmatrix} c \\ g \end{pmatrix}$, the system appears in the form

$$v_t = Av_{t-1} + \alpha \tag{2.262}$$

Consider now the stationary solution

$$v = Av + \alpha \tag{2.263}$$

It equals to

$$(I - A)v = \alpha \tag{2.264}$$

That is, if the inverse exists $(I - A)^{-1}$

$$v = (I - A)^{-1}\alpha \tag{2.265}$$

Therefore, a stationary solution depends on the existence of the inverse$(I - A)^{-1}$.

The nonhomogeneous system can be reduced to a homogeneous system by defining the deviation from stationary solution $z_t = v_t - v$. That is,

$$z_t = v_t - v = Av_{t-1} - Av + \alpha - \alpha = A(v_{t-1} - v) \tag{2.266}$$

which becomes

$$z_t = A\, z_{t-1} \tag{2.267}$$

For system (2.267), it is now possible to work out a solution with the method of indeterminate coefficients by proving a solution of the type

$$z_t = v\lambda^t \tag{2.268}$$

v being a vector of arbitrary constants and λ a number to be determined. Substituting (2.268) in (2.267) follows

$$v\lambda^t = Av\lambda^{t-1} \tag{2.269}$$

That is to say

$$v\lambda = Av \tag{2.270}$$

which is an eigenvalue-eigenvector problem of type

$$(\lambda I - A)v = 0 \tag{2.271}$$

We can now go on as seen previously. It is also worth considering the solution by backward recurrence, i.e., by iterating the time index backward. Noting that

$$z_{t-1} = A\, z_{t-2} \tag{2.272}$$

If we substitute in (2.267), we get

$$z_t = A\,(Az_{t-2}) = A^2 z_{t-2} \tag{2.273}$$

But

$$z_{t-2} = A\, z_{t-3} \tag{2.274}$$

By substituting (2.274) into (2.273)

$$z_t = A^2(Az_{t-3}) = A^3 z_{t-3} \tag{2.275}$$

After T iterations back of index t

$$z_t = A^{T-1}(Az_{t-T}) = A^T z_{t-T} \tag{2.276}$$

If we know the initial value for t−T = 0, i.e., T = t, we have

$$z_t = A^t z_0 \tag{2.277}$$

two observations. First, for the nonhomogeneous system

$$v_t = Av_{t-1} + \alpha \tag{2.278}$$

solution can be found in the following way. Shifting index t in (2.278) one period back, we get

$$v_{t-1} = Av_{t-2} + \alpha \tag{2.279}$$

And substituting (2.279) into (2.278), it follows

$$\begin{aligned} v_t &= A(Av_{t-2} + \alpha) + \alpha = A^2 v_{t-2} + A\,\alpha + \alpha \\ &= A^2 v_{t-2} + (A + I)\,\alpha \end{aligned} \tag{2.280}$$

Moving (2.279) one index back, we have

$$v_{t-2} = Av_{t-3} + \alpha \tag{2.281}$$

And substituting in (2.280), we get

$$\begin{aligned} v_t &= A\left[A^2 v_{t-3} + (A + I)\,\alpha\right] + \alpha = A^3 v_{t-3} + A^2\alpha + A\alpha + \alpha \\ &= A^3 v_{t-3} + \left(A^2 + A + I\right)\alpha \end{aligned} \tag{2.282}$$

And after T iterations, it will be

$$v_t = A^T v_{t-T} + \left(A^{T-1} + A^{T-2} + \ldots + A + I\right)\alpha \tag{2.283}$$

If the initial vector $v_{t\,-\,T\,=\,0} = v_0$ is known, the solution becomes

$$v_t = A^t v_0 + \left(A^{t-1} + A^{t-2} + \ldots + A + I\right)\alpha$$
$$= A^t v_0 + \sum_{j=0}^{t-1}\left(A^j \alpha\right) \tag{2.284}$$

Second, consider a particular case of the homogeneous system of (2.261), with b = d = 0. The system becomes

$$\begin{aligned} x_t &= a\, x_{t-1} \\ y_t &= f\, y_{t-1} \end{aligned} \tag{2.285}$$

Each of the equations of (2.285) is independent from the other and can be solved separately, giving the solution

$$\begin{aligned} x_t &= a^t\, x_0 \\ y_t &= f^t\, y_0 \end{aligned} \tag{2.286}$$

System (2.286) is a diagonal system, whose matrix has nonzero elements only on the main diagonal, i.e.,

$$A = \begin{pmatrix} a & 0 \\ 0 & f \end{pmatrix} \tag{2.287}$$

The study of the stability of this system is greatly simplified since it is reduced to the study of the convergence of two exponential functions (2.286). Convergence to a stationary solution requires simultaneously

$$\begin{aligned} \lim_{t\to\infty} x_t &= \lim_{t\to\infty} a^t\, x_0 = 0 \\ \lim_{t\to\infty} y_t &= \lim_{t\to\infty} f^t\, y_0 = 0 \end{aligned} \tag{2.288}$$

which requires $|a| < 1$; $|f| < 1$.

In general, however, the matrix that defines the path of a system is not diagonal. However, there is a transformation, called *Jordan transformation*, which allows us to rewrite many systems (those whose eigenvalues are all different)[10] in diagonal form, and after solving the transformed system, inverting transformation, we find the solution of the original system. This transformation in dynamic economic models is the object of the Blanchard-Kahn procedure.[11]

[10] See Hadley, G. (1961).

[11] Blanchard, O. and Kahn, C. (1980), work cited.

2.17 Systems of Finite-Difference Equations with Rational Expectations

To study systems with rational expectations, the initial step is to note that a system of finite-difference equations with expectations can be reduced to the following canonical representation in vectorial form:

$$E_t s_{t+1} = W_s s_t + W_E \, \varepsilon_{t+1} \tag{2.289}$$

In economic theory, (2.289) is often interpreted as a recurrent system that connects the expectations of vector of state variables $E_t \, s_{t+1}$ to the vector of current values of same state variables s_t.

This system, however, in general, does not directly arise from the equilibrium conditions of the model, but through a series of transformations, the initial system in rational expectations is brought back to the canonical form (2.289).

In economic models, the conditions of equilibrium are traced to two kinds of subsystems:

- A subsystem linking the vector of observable variables y_t to the vector of state variables s_t, i.e.,

$$M_{cc} y_t = M_{cs} s_t \tag{2.290}$$

And

- A subsystem of equations that relates the vector of expected variables (of both state variables and observable variables) $E_t \, s_{t+1}$and $E_t \, y_{t+1}$ to the vectors of observable variables, state variables, and stochastic variables.

This system is of the form

$$M_{ss_0} E_t s_{t+1} - M_{sc_0} E_t y_{t+1} = M_{sc_1} y_t - M_{ss_1} s_t + M_{sc} \varepsilon_{t+1} \tag{2.291}$$

For numerical solutions, one writes directly, e.g., in DYNARE (we will see it later), a program regarding the two subsystems (2.290) and (2.291).

For searching for analytic solutions, we proceed, as already said, at a preliminary step, by bringing back these two subsystems to the canonical system of expectations (2.289). For this reduction, the first step is to eliminate observable variables, for restricting our attention to the state variables only.

Admitted M_{cc} invertible, from (2.290) multiplying both sides by M_{cc}^{-1}, it follows

$$y_t = M_{cc}^{-1} M_{cs} s_t \tag{2.292}$$

and substituting (2.292) into subsystem (2.291), we obtain

$$M_{ss_0}E_t s_{t+1} - M_{sc_0}M_{cc}^{-1}M_{cs}E_t s_{t+1} = M_{sc_1}M_{cc}^{-1}M_{cs}s_t - M_{ss_1}s_t + M_{sc}\varepsilon_{t+1}$$

That is,

$$\begin{aligned}&\left(M_{ss_0} - M_{sc_0}M_{cc}^{-1}M_{cs}\right)E_t s_{t+1}\\&= \left(M_{sc_1}M_{cc}^{-1}M_{cs} - M_{ss_1}\right)s_t + M_{sc}\varepsilon_{t+1}\end{aligned} \tag{2.293}$$

Admitted $\left(M_{ss_0} - M_{sc_0}M_{cc}^{-1}M_{cs}\right)$ invertible, by solving (2.293) for $E_t\, s_{t+1}$, it follows

$$\begin{aligned}E_t s_{t+1} &= \left(M_{ss_0} - M_{sc_0}M_{cc}^{-1}M_{cs}\right)^{-1}\left(M_{sc_1}M_{cc}^{-1}M_{cs} - M_{ss_1}\right)s_t\\&+ \left(M_{ss_0} - M_{sc_0}M_{cc}^{-1}M_{cs}\right)^{-1}M_{sc}\,\varepsilon_{t+1}\end{aligned}$$

By letting

$$W_s = \left(M_{ss_0} - M_{sc_0}M_{cc}^{-1}M_{cs}\right)^{-1}\left(M_{sc_1}M_{cc}^{-1}M_{cs} - M_{ss_1}\right)$$

and

$$W_E = \left(M_{ss_0} - M_{sc_0}M_{cc}^{-1}M_{cs}\right)^{-1}M_{sc}$$

The resulting system is rewritten in the canonical form stated in (2.289).

It is also possible to carry out a further transformation. Following Farmer,[12] replace expectations with the equivalent expression

$$E_t s_{t+1} = s_{t+1} - z_{t+1} \tag{2.294}$$

where the expected error for z_{t+1} has the property $E_t\, z_{t+1} = 0$.

Going on with the substitution, and remembering that expectations of state variables coincide with the future values of these variables, it can be written

$$s_{t+1} = W_s s_t + W_E\,\varepsilon_{t+1} + z_{t+1} \tag{2.295}$$

This system (2.295) is typically solved numerically, e.g., with MATLAB software.

[12] R. Farmer (1993).

2.18 Analytical Solution of Systems of Rational Expectations

In traditional static economic models, depending on whether the variables involved, at the instant considered, are known or to be determined, a distinction is made between exogenous variables (known) and endogenous variables (to be determined by the model).

In dynamic models, in addition to the previous distinction, it is also necessary to specify whether the variables considered refer to the same period or to different periods.

Both the exogenous variables and the endogenous variables can be lagged variables or refer to the future. Endogenous variables, therefore, in addition to depending on exogenous variables (delayed or not) can depend on endogenous, but delayed, variables.

The exogenous, lagged exogenous, and lagged endogenous variables are *predetermined* variables.

In a system of differences with expectations, for variables subject to expectations, predetermined variables are distinguished from non-predetermined ones, the latter also called *jump variables* (the name *jump variables* for the latter derives from the characteristic that they assume precisely those values which guarantee uniqueness of solution).

By considering the value of expectation at time t+1, if expectation at time t+1 exactly coincides with the value assumed by the variable at time t+1, then that variable is predetermined (in expectations). If instead, the expectation is the expected value at time t+1 (value defined as expectation conditional to the set of information available at time t+1), then the variable is not predetermined.

Blanchard and Kahn proved that the existence and uniqueness of a solution depend on the position concerning the unit circle of the eigenvalues of the matrix of the canonical system W_s.

By calling N_p and N_{np}, the number of predetermined and non-predetermined variables, if we indicate with N_I and N_O the number of eigenvalues inside and outside the unit circle, the following rule (*Blanchard-Kahn conditions*) holds:

i) If the number of eigenvalues inside unit circle N_I is equal to the number N_p of predetermined variables, i.e., if $N_I = N_p$, the system of rational expectations satisfies the *saddle point property*. In that case, there is only one path that converges to a steady state.

ii) If the number of eigenvalues inside the unit circle is greater than the number of predetermined variables, i.e., $N_I > N_p$, the system of rational expectations satisfies the *vortex property*. In this case, every path is convergent at steady state, and the system is indeterminate.

iii) If the number of eigenvalues inside the unit circle is smaller than the number of predetermined variables $N_I < N_p$, the system is a *source* and there are no stable solutions. In that case, the system of rational expectations only admits explosive solutions (each different from the steady state).

The situations studied in economics generally are i) and ii).

We have already seen the operation of diagonalization. It is

$$W_s = PDP^{-1} \tag{2.296}$$

where D is the matrix of eigenvalues along the principal diagonal. Eigenvalues in the diagonal matrix are supposed ordered by absolute value in ascending order. That is, the eigenvalue in first place has less absolute value eigenvalue in the second place, less than the eigenvalue in the third place, and the eigenvalue in the n−1 place is less than the eigenvalue in the nth place.

The eigenvectors of matrix P are also ordered such that the eigenvector in the first position is associated with the eigenvalue in the first position, and the eigenvector in the last position is associated with the eigenvalue in the last position.

We will consider the two cases:[13]

1. The model satisfies the saddle point property $N_I = N_p$ (and $N_o = N_{np}$.
2. The model exhibits vortex property $N_I > N_p$ (and $N_o < N_{np}$) and therefore the model is indeterminate.

2.19 Saddle Point Path

As we have seen, in the case of the saddle point, the number N_I of eigenvalues in absolute value smaller than unit is exactly equal to the number N_p of predetermined variables, i.e., $N_I = N_p$.

Let us consider the system (2.295) which we report here for the reader's convenience

$$s_{t+1} = W_s s_t + W_E\, \varepsilon_{t+1} + z_{t+1} \tag{2.297}$$

Premultiplying (2.297) by P^{-1}

$$P^{-1} s_{t+1} = P^{-1} W_s s_t + P^{-1} W_E\, \varepsilon_{t+1} + P^{-1} z_{t+1} \tag{2.298}$$

Noting that $W_s s_t = W_s I s_t = W_s P P^{-1} s_t$, where I is the identity matrix, the system (2.298) is equivalent to

[13] The discussion in this and subsequent sections follows F. Collard (2005), *Quantitative Macroeconomics*, web edition (update in October 2015 at http://fabcol.free.fr/notes.htm), Retrieved *2 July 2023*.

$$P^{-1}s_{t+1} = P^{-1}W_s\, PP^{-1}s_t + P^{-1}W_E\, \varepsilon_{t+1} + P^{-1}z_{t+1} \tag{2.299}$$

Naming $\overline{s}_t$ the vector $P^{-1}s_t$, the system (2.299) can be rewritten as

$$\overline{s}_{t+1} = P^{-1}W_s\, P\, \overline{s}_t + P^{-1}W_E\, \varepsilon_{t+1} + P^{-1}z_{t+1} \tag{2.300}$$

Considering the Jordan transformation $W_s = PD\,P^{-1}$, it follows that $P^{-1}W_s\,P = D$, so that system (2.300) appears in the diagonal form

$$\overline{s}_{t+1} = D\overline{s}_t + R\varepsilon_{t+1} + P^{-1}z_{t+1} \tag{2.301}$$

where $R = P^{-1}W_E$

2.20 Solving System with the Blanchard-Kahn Procedure

The diagonal system (2.301) is the starting point for the next step of Blanchard-Kahn procedure.

We observe that matrices D, P, and P^{-1}, of Jordan transformation, can conveniently be partitioned in a way conforming to the positions of eigenvalues with respect to the unit circle, i.e.,

$$D = \begin{pmatrix} D_p & 0 \\ 0 & D_{np} \end{pmatrix}; \quad P = \begin{pmatrix} P_{p,p} & P_{p,np} \\ P_{np,p} & P_{np,np} \end{pmatrix};$$

$$P^{-1} = \begin{pmatrix} P^*_{pp} & P^*_{p,np} \\ P^*_{np,p} & P^*_{np,np} \end{pmatrix}$$

Also, matrix R and vector $\overline{s}_t$ can similarly be partitioned into

$$R = \begin{pmatrix} R_p \\ R_{np} \end{pmatrix} \quad \text{and} \quad \overline{s}_t = \begin{pmatrix} \overline{s}_{p,t} \\ \overline{s}_{np,t} \end{pmatrix}$$

Under these partitions, system (2.301) is rewritten as

$$\begin{pmatrix} \overline{s}_{p,t+1} \\ \overline{s}_{np,t+1} \end{pmatrix} = \begin{pmatrix} D_p & 0 \\ 0 & D_{np} \end{pmatrix} \begin{pmatrix} \overline{s}_{p,t} \\ \overline{s}_{np,t} \end{pmatrix} + \begin{pmatrix} R_p \\ R_{np} \end{pmatrix} \varepsilon_{t+1} + \begin{pmatrix} P^*_p \\ P^*_{np} \end{pmatrix} z_{t+1} \tag{2.302}$$

In (2.302), the system is partitioned into two subsystems, respectively, one referred to predetermined variables and the other to non-predetermined variables.

For the moment, we can ignore the subsystem of the predetermined variables $\overline{s}_{p,t+1}$ and look only for a solution for non-predetermined variables.

The respective subsystem is

$$\bar{s}_{np,t+1} = D_{np}\bar{s}_{np,t} + R_{np}\varepsilon_{t+1} + P^*_{np}z_{t+1} \tag{2.303}$$

Taking expectations of (2.303), since it is $E_t\, \varepsilon_{t+1} = E_t\, z_{t+1} = 0$, it follows

$$E_t\bar{s}_{np,t+1} = D_{np}\bar{s}_{np,t} \tag{2.304}$$

And by solving (2.304) for $\bar{s}_{np,t}$, it results

$$\bar{s}_{np,t} = D_{np}^{-1}E_t\bar{s}_{np,t+1} \tag{2.305}$$

With (2.305), we have a system of differences in expectations, which can be solved by iterating forward. For j periods it gives

$$\bar{s}_{np,t} = D_{np}^{-j}E_t\bar{s}_{np,t+j} \tag{2.306}$$

Considering the limit for j→∞ of (2.306), to the right of the equality sign, it results

$$\lim_{j\to\infty} D_{np}^{-j}E_t\bar{s}_{np,t+j} = 0 \tag{2.307}$$

and so, it follows

$$\bar{s}_{np,t} = 0 \tag{2.308}$$

Since by definition $\bar{s}_t = P^{-1}s_t$ and therefore from

$$\begin{pmatrix} \bar{s}_{p,t} \\ \bar{s}_{np,t} \end{pmatrix} = \begin{pmatrix} P^*_{pp} & P^*_{p,np} \\ P^*_{np,p} & P^*_{np,np} \end{pmatrix} \begin{pmatrix} s_{p,t} \\ s_{np,t} \end{pmatrix}$$

it results that for the component $\bar{s}_{np,t}$, the condition (2.307) is equivalent to

$$\bar{s}_{np,t} = P^*_{np,p}s_{p,t} + P^*_{np,np}s_{np,t} = 0 \tag{2.309}$$

System (2.309) can now be solved for $s_{np,\,t}$

$$s_{np,t} = -P^{*-1}_{np,np}P^*_{np,p}s_{p,t} \tag{2.310}$$

That is, writing $\Gamma = -P^{*-1}_{np,np}P^*_{np,p}$, it follows

$$s_{np,t} = \Gamma s_{p,t} \tag{2.311}$$

System (2.311) provides the initial conditions that non-predetermined variables (jump variables) must assume so that the economic system places itself all the time on the path that leads to the steady state.

We now note that as a consequence of the adopted partition of the matrices, the law of motion (2.297) can be conveniently rewritten as

$$\begin{pmatrix} s_{p,t+1} \\ s_{np,t+1} \end{pmatrix} = \begin{pmatrix} W_{pp} & W_{p,np} \\ W_{np,p} & W_{np,np} \end{pmatrix} \begin{pmatrix} s_{pt} \\ s_{np,t} \end{pmatrix} + \begin{pmatrix} W_{Ep} \\ W_{E,np} \end{pmatrix} \varepsilon_{t+1} + \begin{pmatrix} I_p \\ I_{np} \end{pmatrix} z_{t+1}$$

By rearranging the subsystem relative to $s_{p,\,t\,+\,1}$, it is

$$s_{p,t+1} = W_{pp} s_{pt} + W_{p,np}\, s_{np,t} + W_{Ep} \varepsilon_{t+1} + I_p z_{t+1} \tag{2.312}$$

In (2.312), it is $z_{t\,+\,1} = 0$, because, by definition, no forecasting error is made for the predetermined variables. Therefore, for (2.312), it must be

$$s_{p,t+1} = W_{pp} s_{pt} + W_{p,np} s_{np,t} + W_{Ep} \varepsilon_{t+1} \tag{2.313}$$

That is, by substituting $s_{np,\,t}$ obtained from (2.313), it follows

$$s_{p,t+1} = \left(W_{pp} + W_{p,np}\Gamma\right)\, s_{p,t} + W_{Ep} \varepsilon_{t+1} \tag{2.314}$$

System (2.314), by setting $M_{ss} = (W_{pp} + W_{p,\,np}\Gamma)$ and $M_{sE} = W_{Ep}$, rewrites:

$$s_{p,t+1} = M_{ss} s_{p,t} + M_{sE} \varepsilon_{t+1} \tag{2.315}$$

This is the solution of the predetermined variables in recursive form, i.e., as a function at time t+1 of the same predetermined variables at time t, and of stochastic shocks at time t+2.

It remains to obtain the expression of the vector of observable variables y_t according to the considered partition of matrices.

System (2.292), by setting $\phi = M_{cc}^{-1} M_{cs}$, becomes

$$y_t = \phi s_t \tag{2.316}$$

Partitioning matrix ϕ according to a criterion analogous to the one of previous partitions, we will set

$$\phi = \begin{pmatrix} \phi_p & 0 \\ 0 & \phi_{np} \end{pmatrix} \tag{2.317}$$

and (2.316) becomes

$$y_t = \begin{pmatrix} \phi_p & 0 \\ 0 & \phi_{np} \end{pmatrix} \begin{pmatrix} s_{pt} \\ s_{np,t} \end{pmatrix}$$
$$= \phi_p s_{pt} + \phi_{np} s_{np,t} = \left(\phi_p + \phi_{np}\Gamma\right) s_{pt} \tag{2.318}$$

And writing $\left(\phi_p + \phi_{np}\Gamma\right) = \Pi$, system (2.318) becomes

$$y_t = \Pi s_{pt} \tag{2.319}$$

Ultimately, then, the solution of the system in predetermined variables at time t +1, in the observable variables at time t, and the non-predetermined variables at time t becomes

$$\begin{aligned} s_{p,t+1} &= M_{ss} s_{p,t} + M_{sE} \varepsilon_{t+1} \\ y_t &= \Pi s_{pt} \\ s_{np,t} &= \Gamma s_{p,t} \end{aligned} \tag{2.320}$$

Finally, (2.320) is the *state-space* representation, according to which all the variables of the system (predetermined, observable, and non-predetermined variables) have a solution that at time t describes their path over time as a function of predetermined state variables.

2.21 The Case of Indeterminacy

For the sake of completeness, in this section, the case of indeterminacy will be considered.

Let us take up the transformed system (2.302) and admit that $N_I > N_p$, i.e., the number of roots inside the unit circle is greater than the number of predetermined variables.

This eventuality leads to the introduction of sunspot variables.

The sunspots are equal in number to the difference between the number of roots inside the unit circle and the number of predetermined variables, that is $N_I - N_B$, where for convenience the number of predetermined variables is now indicated with N_B.

In this case, the vector of state variables can be divided into three subsets

$$s_t = \left\{s_{B,t}, s_{s,t}, s_{np,t}\right\} \tag{2.321}$$

Jump variables, now include even sunspots so that this set is defined as $s_{s,\,t} \cup s_{np,\,t}$ with $s_{s,\,t}$ characterizing extrinsic uncertainty.

System (2.302) with the inclusion of the equations of the sunspot variables becomes

$$\begin{pmatrix} s_{B,t+1} \\ \\ s_{S,t+1} \\ s_{np,t+1} \end{pmatrix} = \begin{pmatrix} W_{BB} & W_{BS} & W_{B,np} \\ W_{SB} & W_{SS} & W_{S,np} \\ W_{np,B} & W_{np,S} & W_{np,np} \end{pmatrix} \begin{pmatrix} s_{Bt} \\ s_{s,t} \\ s_{np,t} \end{pmatrix} + \begin{pmatrix} W_{EB} \\ W_{SS} \\ W_{E,np} \end{pmatrix} \varepsilon_{t+1} + \begin{pmatrix} I_B \\ I_S \\ I_{np} \end{pmatrix} z_{t+1} \tag{2.322}$$

Diagonalization of W_s with $W_s = PDP^{-1}$ leads to the following representation:

$$\begin{pmatrix} \widetilde{s}_{B,t+1} \\ \\ \widetilde{s}_{S,t+1} \\ \widetilde{s}_{np,t+1} \end{pmatrix} = \begin{pmatrix} D_B & 0 & 0 \\ 0 & D_S & 0 \\ 0 & 0 & D_{np} \end{pmatrix} \begin{pmatrix} \widetilde{s}_{Bt} \\ \widetilde{s}_{s,t} \\ \widetilde{s}_{np,t} \end{pmatrix} + \begin{pmatrix} R_B \\ R_S \\ R_{np} \end{pmatrix} \varepsilon_{t+1}$$
$$+ \begin{pmatrix} P^*_{BB} & P^*_{BS} & P^*_{B,np} \\ P^*_{SB} & P^*_{SS} & P^*_{S,np} \\ P^*_{np,B} & P^*_{np,S} & P^*_{np,np} \end{pmatrix} \begin{pmatrix} z_{B,t+1} \\ z_{S,t+1} \\ z_{np,,t+1} \end{pmatrix} \tag{2.323}$$

Or in terms of components

$$\begin{aligned} \widetilde{s}_{B,t+1} &= D_B \widetilde{s}_{Bt} + R_B \varepsilon_{t+1} + P^*_{BB} z_{B,t+1} + P^*_{BS} z_{S,t+1} + P^*_{B,np} z_{np,t+1} \\ \widetilde{s}_{S,t+1} &= D_S \widetilde{s}_{s,t} + R_S \varepsilon_{t+1} + P^*_{SB} z_{B,t+1} + P^*_{SS} z_{S,t+1} + P^*_{S,np} z_{np,t+1} \end{aligned} \tag{2.324}$$

$$\widetilde{s}_{np,t+1} = D_{np,} \widetilde{s}_{np,t} + R_{np} \varepsilon_{t+1} + P^*_{np,B} z_{B,t+1} + P^*_{np,S} z_{S,t+1} + P^*_{np,np} z_{np,t+1}$$

It is admitted that $|D_{np}| > 1$ and $|D_B|$, $|D_S| < 1$. By eliminating the bubbles on non-predetermined variables, i.e., posing $\widetilde{s}_{np,t+1} = 0$, we will have by construction

$$\begin{aligned} & D_{np,} \widetilde{s}_{np,t} + R_{np} \varepsilon_{t+1} + P^*_{np,B} z_{B,t+1} \\ & + P^*_{np,S} z_{S,t+1} + P^*_{np,np} z_{np,t+1} = 0 \end{aligned} \tag{2.325}$$

Condition (2.325) imposes $D_{np,} \widetilde{s}_{np,t} = 0$, i.e., $\widetilde{s}_{np,t} = 0$ and by construction

$$\begin{pmatrix} P^*_{np,B} & P^*_{np,S} & P^*_{np,np} \end{pmatrix} \begin{pmatrix} s_{Bt} \\ s_{S,t} \\ s_{np,t} \end{pmatrix} = 0 \tag{2.326}$$

That is to say

$$P^*_{np,B} s_{Bt} + P^*_{np,S} s_{S,t} + P^*_{np,np}\, s_{np,t} = 0 \tag{2.327}$$

Solving (2.327) for $s_{np,\ t}$, we have

$$s_{np,t} = -\left(P^*_{np,np}\right)^{-1} P^*_{np,B} s_{Bt} - \left(P^*_{np,np}\right)^{-1} P^*_{np,S} s_{S,t} = \Gamma s_{Bt} + \Gamma s_{S,t} \tag{2.328}$$

Furthermore, the elimination of bubbles also imposes

$$R_{np}\varepsilon_{t+1} + P^*_{np,B} z_{B,t+1} + P^*_{np,S} z_{S,t+1} + P^*_{np,np} z_{np,t+1} = 0 \tag{2.329}$$

By solving (2.329) for $z_{np,\ t\ +\ 1}$

$$\begin{aligned} z_{np,t+1} = &-\left(P^*_{np,np}\right)^{-1} R_{np}\varepsilon_{t+1} - \left(P^*_{np,np}\right)^{-1} P^*_{np,B} z_{B,t+1} \\ &-\left(P^*_{np,np}\right)^{-1} P^*_{np,S} z_{S,t+1} \end{aligned} \tag{2.330}$$

Since predetermined variables are predicted with certainty, we will necessarily have $z_{B,\ t\ +\ 1} = 0$, and therefore,

$$z_{np,t+1} = -\left(P^*_{np,np}\right)^{-1} R_{np}\varepsilon_{t+1} - \left(P^*_{np,np}\right)^{-1} P^*_{np,S} z_{S,t+1} \tag{2.331}$$

By substituting these into the first two equations of the system (2.331), we will have

$$\begin{aligned} s_{B,t+1} &= \left(W_{BB} s_{Bt} + W_{B,np}\Gamma_{\mathrm{B}}\right) s_{Bt} + \left(W_{Bs} + W_{B,np}\,\Gamma_{\mathrm{s}}\right) s_{st} + W_{E,B}\,\varepsilon_{t+1} \\ s_{S,t+1} &= \left(W_{SB} s_{Bt} + W_{S,np}\Gamma_{\mathrm{B}}\right) s_{Bt} + \left(W_{ss} + W_{s,np}\,\Gamma_{\mathrm{s}}\right) s_{st} + W_{E,s}\,\varepsilon_{t+1} + z_{S,t+1} \end{aligned} \tag{2.332}$$

By defining

$$M_{ss} = \begin{pmatrix} W_{BB} s_{Bt} + W_{B,np}\Gamma_{\mathrm{B}} & W_{Bs} + W_{B,np}\,\Gamma_{\mathrm{s}} \\ W_{SB} s_{Bt} + W_{S,np}\Gamma_{\mathrm{B}} & W_{ss} + W_{s,np}\,\Gamma_{\mathrm{s}} \end{pmatrix}; M_{sE} = W_{E,B}; M_{sZ} = \begin{pmatrix} 0_{Bs} \\ I_{SS} \end{pmatrix}$$

System (2.332) can be rewritten

$$\begin{pmatrix} s_{B,t+1} \\ s_{S,t+1} \end{pmatrix} = M_{ss} \begin{pmatrix} s_{Bt} \\ s_{st} \end{pmatrix} + M_{sE}\varepsilon_{t+1} + M_{sZ}z_{S,t+1} \tag{2.333}$$

That is to say

$$\begin{aligned} s_{B,t+1} &= M_{ss}\ s_{Bt} + M_{sE}\varepsilon_{t+1} + M_{sZ}z_{S,t+1} \\ s_{S,t+1} &= M_{ss}\ s_{st} + M_{sE}\varepsilon_{t+1} + M_{sZ}z_{S,t+1} \end{aligned} \tag{2.334}$$

Finally, System (2.334) is in the usual backward-looking form and can be used to simulate the data.

2.22 The Case of Singular Problems: Outlines

For completeness, the case of singular problems will be also mentioned in this section. By tracking system to the canonical form (2.289), which connects the expected state variables to actual state variables, we assumed that the matrix $\left(M_{ss_0} - M_{sc_0}M_{cc}^{-1}M_{cs}\right)$ is invertible. In some circumstances, however, this is not possible because the matrix $\left(M_{ss_0} - M_{sc_0}M_{cc}^{-1}M_{cs}\right)$ is singular and therefore has no inverse. In this case, the model can be rewritten using the so-called *Schur decomposition*.

Even in the context of singularity of the above matrix, the first step consists in obtaining the solution y_t in the system (2.290) which requires that the matrix M_{cc} is invertible. If this were not the case, some variables would be redundant and could be ignored. Therefore, admitting invertible M_{cc} and writing solution (2.290) as

$$y_t = M_{cc}^{-1}M_{cs}s_t = \Psi s_t \tag{2.335}$$

System (2.291) becomes

$$M_{ss_0}E_t s_{t+1} - M_{sc_0}\Psi E_t s_{t+1} = M_{sc_1}\Psi s_t - M_{ss_1}s_t + M_{sc} \tag{2.336}$$

That is, by defining $A_0 = M_{ss_0} - M_{sc_0}$; $A_1 = M_{sc_1}\Psi - M_{ss_1}$; $A_2 = M_{sc}$, system (2.336) becomes

$$A_0 E_t s_{t+1} = A_1 s_t + A_2 \varepsilon_{t+1} \tag{2.337}$$

And again

$$A_0 s_{t+1} = A_1 s_t + A_2 \varepsilon_{t+1} + A_0 z_{t+1} \tag{2.338}$$

The system (2.338) is the model to be solved. For this type of model, the distinction between predetermined and non-predetermined variables is no longer sufficient, since static variables must also be considered.

Furthermore, non-predetermined variables are distinct into sunspot and non-sunspot variables. However, we will not go further into the topic, referring the reader to the original work of Klein (2000).

2.23 An Elaborate Example of Economic Theory

In the remainder of this chapter, an example is considered, taken from Sargent.[14] It concerns a firm's decision relative to demand for labor in an inter-temporal context, in the presence of costs for using labor.

The hypothesis is that for each unit of labor employed in production, in addition to the wage, the firm must bear a real unit cost for changing the level of labor employed for production. This cost is represented by a quadratic function whose argument is the current variation of labor employed, of the kind

$$\mathrm{CL} = \frac{\varphi}{2}\,(n_t - n_{t-1})^2 \tag{2.339}$$

It is also assumed that the firm has access to a production technology represented by a linear quadratic production function, depending on labor employed, i.e.,

$$Y_t = f_0 n_t - \frac{f_1}{2}\,n_t^2 \qquad \text{con } f_0 > 0, f_1 > 0 \tag{2.340}$$

Linear quadratic function exhibits the following properties:

a) Negative sign of squared term denotes diminishing marginal returns. Indeed, it is

$$\frac{dy_t}{dn_t} = f_0 - f_1 n_t \tag{2.341}$$

Therefore, the marginal product of labor is a decreasing linear function of labor employed by a firm;

b) Production function (2.340), while admitting decreasing marginal product, excludes that marginal product can be first increasing and then decreasing due to linearity of marginal product function.

[14] See Sargent (1987), op. cit.

c) The elasticity of production is not constant at all points along the curve, as in a power function, but decreases with the magnitude of the input. In fact, by considering the elasticity of production, we will have

$$\varepsilon_Y = \frac{\frac{dY_t}{Y_t}}{\frac{dn_t}{n_t}} = \frac{dY_t}{Y_t}\frac{n_t}{dn_t} = \frac{dY_t}{dn_t}\frac{n_t}{Y_t} = \frac{Pm_t}{PM_t} = 2\ \frac{f_0 - f_1 n_t}{2f_0 - f_1 n_t} \tag{2.342}$$

It turns out

$$\begin{aligned}\frac{d\varepsilon_Y}{dn_t} &= \frac{-2f_1(2f_0 - f_1 n_t) + 2f_1(f_0 - f_1 n_t)}{(2f_0 - f_1 n_t)^2} \\ &= \frac{-4f_1 f_0 + 2f_1^2 n_t + 2f_1 f_0 - 2f_1^2 n_t}{(2f_0 - f_1 n_t)^2} \\ &= -\frac{2f_1 f_0}{(2f_0 - f_1 n_t)^2}\end{aligned} \tag{2.343}$$

And it certainly is $\frac{d\varepsilon_Y}{dn_t} < 0$.

d) The Eq. (2.340) never allows for increasing marginal product. In fact, the equation of marginal product of labor is a decreasing straight line. It will have an angular coefficient that is always constant and negative.

Having stated the hypotheses admitted, the instantaneous firm's profit function is

$$\pi_t = f_0 n_t - \frac{f_1}{2}\ n_t^2 - w_t n_t - \frac{\varphi}{2}\ (n_t - n_{t-1})^2 \tag{2.344}$$

Over an infinite horizon, expected inter-temporal profit at constant interest rate r is

$$\begin{aligned} E_t \sum_{s=0}^{\infty}\left(\frac{1}{1+r}\right)^s &\left[f_0 n_{t+s} - \frac{f_1}{2}\ n_{t+s}^2 - w_{t+s} n_{t+s} - \frac{\varphi}{2}\ (n_{t+s} - n_{t+s-1})^2\right] \\ &- \left(\frac{1}{1+r}\right)^{s+1}\left[(n_{t+s+1} - n_{t+s})^2\right]\end{aligned} \tag{2.345}$$

and therefore, the firm's problem is

$$\max_{\{n_r\}_{r=0}^{\infty}} E_t \sum_{s=0}^{\infty}\left(\frac{1}{1+r}\right)^s \left\{\ \left[f_0 n_{t+s} - \frac{f_1}{2}\ n_{t+s}^2 - w_{t+s} n_{t+s} - \frac{\varphi}{2}\ (n_{t+s} - n_{t+s-1})^2\right]\right.$$

$$-\left(\frac{1}{1+r}\right)\left[\left(\mathrm{n}_{t+s+1}-\mathrm{n}_{t+s}\right)^2\right]\Big\} \tag{2.346}$$

Differentiating for n_{t+s}, first-order condition is[15]

$$E_t\left(\frac{1}{1+r}\right)^s\left[f_0-f_1n_{t+s}-w_{t+s}-\varphi(n_{t+s}-n_{t+s-1})+\left(\frac{1}{1+r}\right)\varphi(n_{t+s+1}-n_{t+s})\right]=0 \tag{2.347}$$

which requires

$$E_t\left[f_0-f_1n_{t+s}-w_{t+s}-\varphi(n_{t+s}-n_{t+s-1})+\left(\frac{1}{1+r}\right)\varphi(n_{t+s+1}-n_{t+s})\right]=0 \tag{2.348}$$

Expectation for s = 0 are

$$f_0-f_1n_t-w_t-\varphi(n_t-n_{t-1})+\left(\frac{\varphi}{1+r}\right)(E_tn_{t+1}-n_t)=0 \tag{2.349}$$

That is

$$\frac{\varphi}{1+r}E_tn_{t+1}=\varphi(n_t-n_{t-1})+\frac{\varphi}{1+r}n_t+f_1n_t-f_0+w_t \tag{2.350}$$

And this determines the following equation to differences in expectations:

$$E_tn_{t+1}=n_t-f_0\frac{(1+r)}{\varphi}+f_1\frac{(1+r)}{\varphi}n_t+\frac{(1+r)}{\varphi}w_t+(1+r)n_t$$
$$-(1+r)\,n_{t-1} \tag{2.351}$$

i.e.,

$$E_tn_{t+1}=n_t+(1+r)n_t+f_1\frac{(1+r)}{\varphi}n_t-(1+r)\,n_{t-1}+\frac{(1+r)}{\varphi}w_t$$
$$-f_0\frac{(1+r)}{\varphi} \tag{2.352}$$

And finally,

[15]The problem is solved by considering first derivative of the components of the objective function containing n_{t+s}.

$$E_t n_{t+1} - \left(1 + 1 + r + f_1 \frac{(1+r)}{\varphi}\right) n_t + (1+r) n_{t-1} + \frac{(1+r)}{\varphi} (f_0 - w_t) \ = 0 \tag{2.353}$$

Equation (2.353) is a second-order finite-difference equation with expectations, and in the next sections, it will be solved with each of three methods previously seen in Sects. 2.15–2.18.

2.23.1 *Solution with the Method of Factorization*

By applying the operator L^{-1} to n_t, it is possible to write[16]

$$E_t L^{-1} n_t = (2 + r + f_1 \frac{(1+r)}{\varphi}) n_t - (1+r) n_t + \frac{(1+r)}{\varphi} (w_t - f_0) \tag{2.354}$$

Applying again L^{-1} operator to both sides of (2.354), we have

$$E_t L^{-1} L^{-1} n_t = \left(2 + r + f_1 \frac{(1+r)}{\varphi}\right) L^{-1} n_t - (1+r) L^{-1} L n_t + \frac{(1+r)}{\varphi} \left(L^{-1} w_t - f_0\right) \tag{2.355}$$

And so

$$\left[L^{-2} - \left(2 + r + f_1 \frac{(1+r)}{\varphi}\right) L^{-1} + (1+r)\right] n_t = \frac{(1+r)}{\varphi} (w_{t+1} - f_0) \tag{2.356}$$

The trinomial $P(L^{-1}) = L^{-2} - \left(2 + r + f_1 \frac{(1+r)}{\varphi}\right) L^{-1} + (1+r)$, in the square brackets of (2.356), corresponds to the homogeneous equation of the associated finite-difference equation and can be factored as

$$\left(L^{-1} - \mu_1)\right)\left(L^{-1} - \mu_2\right) \tag{2.357}$$

The discriminant of trinomial is

[16] The developments in this section and the next two follow Collard, F. (2005), work cited.

$$\Delta=\left(2+r+f_1\ \frac{1+r}{\varphi}\right)^2-4(1+r)=(2+r)^2+\left(\ f_1\ \frac{1+r}{\varphi}\right)^2$$
$$+2\ (2+r)f_1\frac{1+r}{\varphi}-4(1+r) \tag{2.358}$$

The term $(2 + r)^2$ equals $4 + r^2 + 4r$, and therefore,

$$4(1+r)+r^2+\left(\ f_1\ \frac{1+r}{\varphi}\right)^2+2\ (2+r)f_1\frac{1+r}{\varphi}-4(1+r) \tag{2.359}$$

From which

$$\Delta=r^2+f_1\frac{1+r}{\varphi}\left(\ f_1\ \frac{1+r}{\varphi}+(4+2r)\right) \tag{2.360}$$

Being the sum of all positive terms, it is $\Delta > 0$, and the roots are both real. Furthermore,

$$P(1)=-f_1\ \frac{1+r}{\varphi}<0$$
$$P(-1)=2+2(1+r)+f_1\frac{(1+r)}{\varphi}=2(1+1+r)+f_1\frac{(1+r)}{\varphi}$$
$$=2(2+r)+f_1\frac{(1+r)}{\varphi}>0 \tag{2.361}$$

Of the two roots, one is discordant with the coefficient of L^{-2} and the other agrees, so that one root falls in the interval $(-1,1)$ and the other will be outside $(-1, 1)$. The root falling in the interval $(-1,1)$ can be further restricted since it is $P(0)=1+r > 0$. We will assume $\mu_1 < \mu_2$, and therefore, we will have $\mu_1 < 1$ and $\mu_2 > 1$. The discordant root satisfying $\mu_1 < 1$ falls in the interval (0, 1) and is therefore positive. The characteristic equation therefore has one positive root less than unity and the other greater than unity and therefore satisfies the saddle point property.

Rewritten the equation into linear factors, we get

$$\left[\left(L^{-1}-\mu_1\right)\left(L^{-1}-\mu_2\right)\right]n_t=\frac{(1+r)}{\varphi}(w_{t+1}-f_0) \tag{2.362}$$

That is

$$\left(L^{-1}-\mu_1\right)\ n_t=\frac{(1+r)(w_{t+1}-f_0)}{\varphi\left(L^{-1}-\mu_2\right)}=\frac{(1+r)(\ f_0-w_{t+1})}{\varphi\left(\mu_2-L^{-1}\right)} \tag{2.363}$$

Bringing $1/\mu_2$ outside of the expression in (2.363) to the right of the equality sign and taking into account that

$$\mu_1\mu_2 = (1 + \mathrm{r}) \quad \text{and} \quad \mu_1 = \frac{(1+r)}{\mu_2}$$

It follows

$$\left(L^{-1} - \mu_1\right)n_t = \frac{1}{\mu_2}\frac{(1+r)(f_0 - w_{t+1})}{\varphi\left(1 - \mu_2^{-1}L^{-1}\right)} = \frac{\mu_1}{\varphi}\frac{1}{\left(1 - \mu_2^{-1}L^{-1}\right)}(f_0 - w_{t+1}) \tag{2.364}$$

By shifting the t-index one period back,

$$\begin{aligned}\left(L^{-1} - \mu_1\right)n_{t-1} &= \frac{\mu_1}{\varphi}\frac{1}{\left(1 - \mu_2^{-1}L^{-1}\right)}(f_0 - w_t)\\ &= \frac{\mu_1}{\varphi}\sum_{i=0}^{\infty}\mu_2^{-i}L^{-i}(f_0 - w_t)\end{aligned} \tag{2.365}$$

Developing the series $\frac{\mu_1}{\varphi}\left[\sum_{i=0}^{\infty}\mu_2^{-i}f_0 - \sum_{i=0}^{\infty}\mu_2^{-i}L^{-i}w_t\right]$, you obtain

$$n_t = \mu_1 n_{t-1} + \frac{\mu_1}{\varphi}\frac{\mu_2 f_0}{\mu_2 - 1} - \frac{\mu_1}{\varphi}\sum_{i=}^{\infty}\mu_2^{-i}E_t w_{t+i} \tag{2.366}$$

That is,

$$n_t = \frac{f_0(1+r)}{\varphi(\mu_2 - 1)} + \mu_1 n_{t-1} - \frac{\mu_1}{\varphi}\sum_{i=}^{\infty}\mu_2^{-i}E_t w_{t+i} \tag{2.367}$$

Assuming for w_t a stochastic process AR(1)

$$w_t = \rho\, w_{t-1} + (1-\rho)\overline{w} + \varepsilon_t$$

it results

$$E_t w_{t+i} = \rho^i\, w_t + \left(1 - \rho^i\right)\overline{w} \tag{2.368}$$

And n_t becomes

$$n_t = \frac{f_0(1+r)}{\varphi(\mu_2 - 1)} + \mu_1 n_{t-1} - \frac{\mu_1}{\varphi} \sum_{i=}^{\infty} \mu_2^{-i} [(\rho^i\, w_t + (1-\rho^i)\overline{w})]$$

$$= \frac{f_0(1+r)}{\varphi(\mu_2 - 1)} + \mu_1 n_{t-1} - \frac{\mu_1}{\varphi} \sum_{i=0}^{\infty} [(\mu_2^{-i}\rho^i\, w_t + (\mu_2^{-i} - \mu_2^{-i}\rho^i)\overline{w})]$$

$$= \frac{f_0(1+r)}{\varphi(\mu_2 - 1)} + \mu_1 n_{t-1} - \frac{\mu_1}{\varphi}$$

$$\times \left\{ \sum_{i=0}^{\infty} \left[(\mu_2^{-i}\rho^i\, w_t] + \overline{w} \sum_{0}^{\infty} \mu_2^{-i} - \overline{w} \sum_{i=0}^{\infty} \mu_2^{-i}\rho^i \right] \right\} \tag{2.369}$$

That is,

$$n_t = \frac{f_0(1+r)}{\varphi(\mu_2 - 1)} + \mu_1 n_{t-1} - \frac{\mu_1}{\varphi}$$

$$\times \left(\frac{\mu_2}{\mu_2 - \rho} w_t + \frac{\overline{w}\mu_2}{\mu_2 - 1} - \frac{\overline{w}\mu_2}{\mu_2 - \rho} = \frac{f_0(1+r)}{\varphi(\mu_2 - 1)} + \mu_1 n_{t-1} - \frac{1}{\varphi} \left(\frac{\mu_1\mu_2}{\mu_2 - \rho} w_t + \frac{\overline{w}\mu_1\mu_2}{\mu_2 - 1} - \frac{\overline{w}\mu_1\mu_2}{\mu_2 - \rho} \right) \right. \tag{2.370}$$

The term $\frac{\overline{w}\mu_1\mu_2}{\mu_2 - 1} - \frac{\overline{w}\mu_1\mu_2}{\mu_2 - \rho}$ is equal to

$$\frac{\overline{w}(1+r)(\mu_2 - \rho) - (\mu_2 - 1)\overline{w}(1+r)}{(\mu_2 - 1)(\mu_2 - \rho)} = \frac{\overline{w}(1+r)(\mu_2 - \rho - \mu_2 + 1)}{(\mu_2 - 1)(\mu_2 - \rho)}$$

$$= \frac{\overline{w}(1+r)(1-\rho)}{(\mu_2 - 1)(\mu_2 - \rho)} \tag{2.371}$$

and therefore, $n_t$will be

$$n_t = \frac{f_0(1+r)}{\varphi(\mu_2 - 1)} + \mu_1 n_{t-1} - \frac{1+r}{\varphi(\mu_2 - \rho)} w_t - \frac{\overline{w}(1+r)(1-\rho)}{(\mu_2 - 1)(\mu_2 - \rho)} \tag{2.372}$$

Equation (2.372) is the solution of the finite-difference equation (2.353) with w_t following a stochastic process AR(1).

2.23.2 Solution with the Method of Indeterminate Coefficients

To apply the method of indeterminate coefficients, we try the solution

$$n_t = \alpha_0 + \alpha_1 n_{t-1} + \sum_{i=0}^{\infty} \gamma_i E_t w_{t+i} \tag{2.373}$$

with α_0, α_1, γ_i parameters to be determined.

Substituting (2.373) in the Eq. (2.353) to be solved, we obtain

$$\begin{aligned} & E_t\left(\alpha_0 + \alpha_1 n_t + \sum_{i=0}^{\infty} \gamma_i E_t w_{t+1+i}\right) \\ & - \left(2 + r + f_1 \frac{(1+r)}{\varphi}\right)\left(\alpha_0 + \alpha_1 n_{t-1} + \sum_{i=0}^{\infty} \gamma_i E_t w_{t+i}\right) \\ & + (1+r) n_{t-1} + \frac{(1+r)}{\varphi}(f_0 - w_t) = 0 \end{aligned} \tag{2.374}$$

Substituting again (2.373) into (2.374) follows

$$\begin{aligned} & \alpha_0 + \alpha_1\left(\alpha_0 + \alpha_1 n_{t-1} + \sum_{i=0}^{\infty} \gamma_i E_t w_{t+i}\right) + \sum_{i=0}^{\infty} \gamma_i E_t w_{t+1+i} \\ & - \left(2 + r + f_1 \frac{(1+r)}{\varphi}\right)\left(\alpha_0 + \alpha_1 n_{t-1} + \sum_{i=0}^{\infty} \gamma_i E_t w_{t+i}\right) \\ & + (1+r) n_{t-1} + \frac{(1+r)}{\varphi}(f_0 - w_t) = 0 \end{aligned} \tag{2.375}$$

That is

$$\begin{aligned} & \alpha_0(1 + \alpha_1) + \alpha_1^2 n_{t-1} + \alpha_1 \sum_{i=0}^{\infty} \gamma_i E_t w_{t+i}) + \sum_{i=0}^{\infty} \gamma_i E_t w_{t+1+i} \\ & - \left(2 + r + f_1 \frac{(1+r)}{\varphi}\right)\left(\alpha_0 + \alpha_1 n_{t-1} + \sum_{i=0}^{\infty} \gamma_i E_t w_{t+i}\right) \\ & + (1+r) n_{t-1} + \frac{(1+r)}{\varphi}(f_0 - w_t) = 0 \end{aligned} \tag{2.376}$$

By rearranging

$$(1 + \alpha_1)\alpha_0 - \left(2 + r + f_1 \frac{(1+r)}{\varphi}\right)\alpha_0 + \frac{(1+r)}{\varphi} f_0$$

$$+\alpha_1^2 n_{t-1} - \left(2 + r + f_1 \frac{(1+r)}{\varphi}\right)\alpha_1 n_{t-1} + (1+r)n_{t-1}$$

$$+\left\{\gamma_0\left[\alpha_1 - \left(2 + r + f_1 \frac{(1+r)}{\varphi}\right)\right] - \frac{(1+r)}{\varphi}\right\} w_t$$

$$+\left[\alpha_1 - \left(2 + r + f_1 \frac{(1+r)}{\varphi}\right)\right]\sum_{i=0}^{\infty} \gamma_{i+1} E_t w_{t+1+i} + \sum_{i=0}^{\infty} \gamma_i E_t w_{t+1+i} = 0 \quad (2.377)$$

Changing the index in the summations of (2.377) by setting j = i+1 and identifying term by term, you get the system

$$\alpha_0(1+\alpha_1) - \alpha_0\left(2 + r + f_1 \frac{(1+r)}{\varphi}\right) + \frac{(1+r)}{\varphi} f_0 = 0 \quad (2.378)$$

(coefficient of the null power term)

$$\alpha_1^2 - \left(2 + r + f_1 \frac{(1+r)}{\varphi}\right)\alpha_1 + (1+r) = 0 \quad (2.379)$$

(coefficient of the term n_{t-1})

$$\alpha_1\gamma_0 - \left(2 + r + f_1 \frac{(1+r)}{\varphi}\right)\gamma_0 - \frac{(1+r)}{\varphi} = 0 \quad (2.380)$$

(coefficient of the term w_t, which coincides with expectations for t=0)

$$\left[\alpha_1 - \left(2 + r + f_1 \frac{(1+r)}{\varphi}\right)\right]\gamma_j + \gamma_{j-1} = 0 \quad (2.381)$$

(coefficient of the term $E_t w_{t+j}$).

The Eq. (2.381) has exactly the coefficients of the characteristic equation corresponding to (2.356) solved previously, and therefore, the two equations coincide, and the system has a saddle point property with $\mu_1 \epsilon\ (0, 1)$ and $\mu_2 \epsilon\ (1, \infty)$.

Furthermore, remembering that

$$\mu_1 + \mu_2 = 2 + r + f_1 \frac{(1+r)}{\varphi}$$

we can rewrite the equations of coefficients as

$$\alpha_0(1+\alpha_1)-\alpha_0(\mu_1+\mu_2)+\frac{(1+r)}{\varphi}f_0=0$$
$$\gamma_0(\alpha_1-\mu_1)-\gamma_0\mu_2-\frac{(1+r)}{\varphi}=0 \tag{2.382}$$
$$\gamma_j(\alpha_1-\mu_1)-\gamma_j\mu_2+\gamma_{j-1}=0$$

But the last two equations of (2.382), being $\alpha_1=\mu_1$ the root of the quadratic equation, are equivalent to

$$-\gamma_0\mu_2-\frac{(1+r)}{\varphi}=0$$
$$\gamma_j=\frac{1}{\mu_2}\gamma_{j-1} \tag{2.383}$$

So, we have

$$\gamma_0=-\frac{(1+r)}{\varphi\mu_2}=-\frac{\mu_1\mu_2}{\varphi\mu_2}=-\frac{\mu_1}{\varphi}$$
$$\gamma_j=\frac{1}{\mu_2}\gamma_{j-1}=\left(\frac{1}{\mu_2}\right)^j\gamma_0=-\frac{\mu_1}{\varphi}\left(\frac{1}{\mu_2}\right)^j \tag{2.384}$$

Finally, the first equation of (2.382) becomes

$$\alpha_0(1+\alpha_1)-\alpha_0(\mu_1+\mu_2)+\frac{(1+r)}{\varphi}f_0$$
$$=\alpha_0(1+\alpha_1-\mu_1-\mu_2)+\frac{(1+r)}{\varphi}f_0=0 \tag{2.385}$$

But $\alpha_1-\mu_1=0$ and therefore

$$\alpha_0=-\frac{f_0(1+r)}{\varphi(1-\mu_2)}=\frac{f_0(1+r)}{\varphi(\mu_2-1)} \tag{2.386}$$

The solution for (2.363) is therefore

$$n_t=\frac{f_0(1+r)}{\varphi(\mu_2-1)}+\mu_1 n_{t-1}-\frac{\mu_1}{\varphi}\sum_{i=0}^{\infty}\left(\frac{1}{\mu_2}\right)^i E_t w_{t+i} \tag{2.387}$$

This coincides exactly with (2.367) obtained by the factorization method.

2.23.3 Solution with the Matrix Method and Application of the Blanchard-Kahn Procedure

With the matrix method, a numerical solution is wanted. Therefore, it is necessary to assign also a numerical value to the real wage. We assume, as previously, that real wage is determined by a stochastic process of type AR(1). Furthermore, in this approach, it is not necessary to deal with levels of labor demand, so we will express the model in terms of deviations from the steady state.

This model is obtained explicitly as follows:

A stationary solution n^* for (2.353) is

$$n^* - \left[2 + r + \frac{f_1(1+r)}{\varphi}\right]n^* + (1+r)n^* + \frac{(1+r)}{\varphi}(f_0 - \overline{w}) = 0 \tag{2.388}$$

Subtracting (2.388) from (2.353), we obtain

$$\begin{aligned} &E_t(n_{t+1} - n^*) - \left[2 + r + \frac{f_1(1+r)}{\varphi}\right](n_t - n^*) \\ &+(1+r)(n_{t-1} - n^*) - \frac{(1+r)}{\varphi}(w_t - \overline{w}) = 0 \end{aligned} \tag{2.389}$$

By defining $\widehat{n}_t = (n_t - n^*)$ and $\widehat{w}_t = (w_t - \overline{w})$, since $E_t(n_{t+1} - n^*) = E_t\widehat{n}_{t+1}$, it follows

$$E_t\widehat{n}_{t+1} - \left[2 + r + \frac{f_1(1+r)}{\varphi}\right]\widehat{n}_t + (1+r)\widehat{n}_{t-1} - \frac{(1+r)}{\varphi}\widehat{w}_t = 0 \tag{2.390}$$

This in a second-order difference equation with expectations in respect to $\widehat{n}_t$.

Given the equation that defines the AR(1) process for real wages $\widehat{w}_{t+1} = \rho\widehat{w}_t + \varepsilon_{t+1}$, by adding an auxiliary variable $\widehat{z}_t = \widehat{n}_{t-1}$, we transform the original equations in the following system of first-order difference equations in expectations:

$$E_t\widehat{z}_{t+1} - \widehat{n}_t = 0 \tag{2.391}$$

$$E_t\widehat{w}_{t+1} - \rho\widehat{w}_t - \varepsilon_{t+1} = 0 \tag{2.392}$$

$$E_t\widehat{n}_{t+1} + (1+r)\widehat{z}_t - \frac{(1+r)}{\varphi}\widehat{w}_t - \left[2 + r + \frac{f_1(1+r)}{\varphi}\right]\widehat{n}_t = 0 \tag{2.393}$$

The system (2.391)–(2.393) in matrix terms becomes

$$E_t\begin{pmatrix}\widehat{z}_{t+1}\\ \widehat{w}_{t+1}\\ \widehat{n}_{t+1}\end{pmatrix}+\begin{pmatrix}0 & 0 & -1\\ 0 & -\rho & 0\\ 1+r & -\dfrac{(1+r)}{\varphi} & -\left[2+r+\dfrac{f_1(1+r)}{\varphi}\right]\end{pmatrix}\begin{pmatrix}\widehat{z}_t\\ \widehat{w}_t\\ \widehat{n}_t\end{pmatrix}-\begin{pmatrix}0\\ 1\\ 0\end{pmatrix}\varepsilon_{t+1}=0 \tag{2.394}$$

That is to say

$$\begin{pmatrix}\widehat{z}_{t+1}\\ \widehat{w}_{t+1}\\ \widehat{n}_{t+1}\end{pmatrix}=-\begin{pmatrix}0 & 0 & -1\\ 0 & -\rho & 0\\ 1+r & -\dfrac{(1+r)}{\varphi} & -\left[2+r+\dfrac{f_1(1+r)}{\varphi}\right]\end{pmatrix}$$
$$\times\begin{pmatrix}\widehat{z}_t\\ \widehat{w}_t\\ \widehat{n}_t\end{pmatrix}+\begin{pmatrix}0\\ 1\\ 0\end{pmatrix}\varepsilon_{t+1}+\begin{pmatrix}\zeta_{z,t+1}\\ \zeta_{w,t+1}\\ \zeta_{n,t+1}\end{pmatrix} \tag{2.395}$$

In vector terms setting $x=\begin{pmatrix}0\\ 1\\ 0\end{pmatrix}$, the system (2.395) is

$$\widehat{v}_{t+1}=-A\widehat{v}_t+x\,\varepsilon_{t+1}+\zeta_{t+1} \tag{2.396}$$

Matrix (-A) is square. It admits a characteristic polynomial equation

$$P_A(\mu)=det(A-\mu I) \tag{2.397}$$

$P_A(\mu)$ is the determinant of matrix A−μI, obtained by adding A and −μI, being I matrix identity, with the same dimension of A, which has the unit value 1 for each element on the main diagonal. Therefore,

$$-A-\mu I=-(A+\mu I)=-\left[\begin{pmatrix}0 & 0 & -1\\ 0 & -\rho & 0\\ 1+r & -\dfrac{(1+r)}{\varphi} & -\left[2+r+\dfrac{f_1(1+r)}{\varphi}\right]\end{pmatrix}\right]$$
$$+\begin{pmatrix}\mu & 0 & 0\\ 0 & \mu & 0\\ 0 & 0 & \mu\end{pmatrix} \tag{2.398}$$

The determinant is

$$= -\det\begin{pmatrix} \mu & 0 & -1 \\ 0 & \mu-\rho & 0 \\ 1+r & -\dfrac{(1+r)}{\varphi} & \mu-\left[\left(2+r+\dfrac{f_1(1+r)}{\varphi}\right]\right) \end{pmatrix} =$$

$$(-1)\mu(\mu-\rho)\left(\mu-\left[2+r+\frac{f_1(1+r)}{\varphi}\right]+(1+\mathrm{r})(\mu-\rho)\right.$$

$$=(\rho-\mu)\left[\left(\mu^2-\left(2+r+\frac{f_1(1+r)}{\varphi}\right)\mu+(1+\mathrm{r})\right]=0 \quad (2.399)$$

The characteristic polynomial has three roots. The roots

$$\mu_1,\mu_2=\frac{\left(2+r+\frac{f_1(1+r)}{\varphi}\right)\pm\sqrt{\left(2+r+\frac{f_1(1+r)}{\varphi}\right)^2-4(1+\mathrm{r})}}{2} \quad (2.400)$$

are the same as in the previous characteristic equation, which now are in the square brackets of (2.399). A third root follows from

$$\mu_3=\rho \quad (2.401)$$

In computing eigenvectors associated with μ_1, μ_2 and μ_3, we start from μ_3, for convenience.

We have

$$\begin{pmatrix} \rho & 0 & -1 \\ 0 & 0 & 0 \\ 1+r & -\dfrac{(1+r)}{\varphi} & \rho+\left[2+r+\dfrac{f_1(1+r)}{\varphi}\right] \end{pmatrix}\begin{pmatrix} x \\ y \\ z \end{pmatrix}=0 \quad (2.402)$$

System (2.402) corresponds to the following equations:

$$\rho x-z=0 \quad (2.403)$$

$$(1+r)x-\frac{(1+r)}{\varphi}y+\left(\rho+\left[2+r+\frac{f_1(1+r)}{\varphi}\right]\right)z=0$$

System (2.403) has two equations but three unknowns, so one unknown must be arbitrarily chosen. We set $\mathrm{x}=1$. From the first of (2.403), it follows $\mathrm{z}=\rho$, and the second of (2.403) becomes

$$(1+r)-\frac{(1+r)}{\varphi}y+\rho\left(\rho+2+r+\frac{f_1(1+r)}{\varphi}\right)=0 \tag{2.404}$$

It follows

$$\frac{(1+r)}{\varphi}y=(1+r)+\rho\left(\rho+2+r+\frac{f_1(1+r)}{\varphi}\right) \tag{2.405}$$

And setting $\chi=\varphi+\frac{\rho\varphi}{(1+r)}\left(\rho+2+r+\frac{f_1(1+r)}{\varphi}\right)$, we obtain

$$y=\chi \tag{2.406}$$

Therefore, the eigenvector, associated with eigenvalue μ_3 is $\begin{pmatrix}1\\ \chi\\ \rho\end{pmatrix}$.

Let us now compute the eigenvector associated with μ_1. The corresponding system is

$$\begin{pmatrix}\mu_1 & 0 & -1\\ 0 & \mu_1-\rho & 0\\ 1+r & -\frac{(1+r)}{\varphi} & \mu_1+2+r+\frac{f_1(1+r)}{\varphi}\end{pmatrix}\begin{pmatrix}x\\ y\\ z\end{pmatrix}=0 \tag{2.407}$$

Namely, it is

$$\begin{aligned}\mu_1 x-z&=0\\ (\mu_1-\rho)y&=0\\ (1+r)x-\frac{(1+r)}{\varphi}y+\left(\mu_1+2+r+\frac{f_1(1+r)}{\varphi}\right)z&=0\end{aligned} \tag{2.408}$$

From the second of (2.408), it is y = 0, and therefore, (2.408) becomes

$$\begin{aligned}\mu_1 x-z&=0\\ (1+r)x+\left(\mu_1+2+r+\frac{f_1(1+r)}{\varphi}\right)z&=0\end{aligned} \tag{2.409}$$

From the first of (2.419), we obtain z = μ_1x, and so

$$\left[(1+r)+\left(\mu_1+2+r+\frac{f_1(1+r)}{\varphi}\right)\mu_1\right]x=0 \tag{2.410}$$

Equation (2.410) gives x = 0, and therefore, also z = 0. So, we have a trivial eigenvector. However, since we are looking for nontrivial solutions, this eigenvector must be excluded from the computation. To this end, it is necessary to exclude one equation, from the initial system of eigenvector (2.408). We exclude the last one, and the system becomes

$$\begin{aligned} \mu_1 x - z &= 0 \\ (\mu_1 - \rho) y &= 0 \end{aligned} \tag{2.411}$$

Therefore, from the second of (2.411), it is y = 0 and from the first it is $\mu_1 x = z$. Setting arbitrarily x = 1, we have z = μ_1. Hence, the eigenvector associated with the eigenvalue $\mu_1$is $\begin{pmatrix} 1 \\ 0 \\ \mu_1 \end{pmatrix}$.

Finally, we compute the eigenvector associated with μ_2, by referring to the system

$$\begin{pmatrix} \mu_2 & 0 & -1 \\ 0 & \mu_2 - \rho & 0 \\ 1 + r & -\dfrac{(1+r)}{\varphi} & \mu_2 + 2 + r + \dfrac{f_1(1+r)}{\varphi} \end{pmatrix} \begin{pmatrix} x \\ y \\ z \end{pmatrix} = 0 \tag{2.412}$$

System (2.412), apart from the reference to μ_2, is identical to the previous referred to the eigenvalue μ_1, whereby, the eigenvector associated with the eigenvalue μ_2 is $\begin{pmatrix} 1 \\ 0 \\ \mu_2 \end{pmatrix}$.

The matrix of eigenvectors is therefore

$$\mathrm{P} = \begin{pmatrix} 1 & 1 & 1 \\ 0 & \chi & 0 \\ \mu_1 & \rho & \mu_2 \end{pmatrix} \tag{2.413}$$

To compute the inverse matrix, we derive the determinant with Laplace expansion.[17]

Adjunct matrix is

[17]It is

$\text{Det P} = \begin{vmatrix} \chi & 0 \\ \rho & \mu_2 \end{vmatrix} - \begin{vmatrix} 0 & 0 \\ \mu_1 & \mu_2 \end{vmatrix} + \begin{vmatrix} 0 & \chi \\ \mu_1 & \rho \end{vmatrix} = \chi\mu_2 - \chi\mu_1 = \chi(\mu_2 - \mu_1).$

Conversely, the minors of matrix P are

$m_{11} = \begin{vmatrix} \chi & 0 \\ \rho & \mu_2 \end{vmatrix}; m_{12} = -\begin{vmatrix} 0 & 0 \\ \mu_1 & \mu_2 \end{vmatrix}; m_{13} = \begin{vmatrix} 0 & \chi \\ \mu_1 & \rho \end{vmatrix}$

$$\text{adjP} = \begin{pmatrix} m_{11} & m_{21} & m_{31} \\ m_{12} & m_{22} & m_{32} \\ m_{13} & m_{23} & m_{32} \end{pmatrix} = \begin{pmatrix} \mu_2\chi & \rho-\mu_2 & -\chi \\ 0 & \mu_2-\mu_1 & 0 \\ -\mu_1\chi & \mu_1-\rho & \chi \end{pmatrix} \tag{2.414}$$

and so, the inverse matrix is

$$P^{-1} = \frac{1}{\chi(\mu_2-\mu_1)} \begin{pmatrix} \mu_2\chi & \rho-\mu_2 & -\chi \\ 0 & \mu_2-\mu_1 & 0 \\ -\mu_1\chi & \mu_1-\rho & \chi \end{pmatrix} \tag{2.415}$$

Finally, the diagonal matrix is

$$D = \begin{pmatrix} \mu_1 & 0 & 0 \\ 0 & \rho & 0 \\ 0 & 0 & \mu_2 \end{pmatrix} \tag{2.416}$$

The system with matrix A incorporating change of sign is

$$E_t \begin{pmatrix} \widehat{z}_{t+1} \\ \widehat{w}_{t+1} \\ \widehat{n}_{t+1} \end{pmatrix} = \begin{pmatrix} 0 & 0 & 1 \\ 0 & \rho & 0 \\ -(1+r) & \dfrac{(1+r)}{\varphi} & \left[2+r+\dfrac{f_1(1+r)}{\varphi}\right] \end{pmatrix} \begin{pmatrix} \widehat{z}_t \\ \widehat{w}_t \\ \widehat{n}_t \end{pmatrix} + \begin{pmatrix} 0 \\ 1 \\ 0 \end{pmatrix} \varepsilon_{t+1} \tag{2.417}$$

The Jordan transformation applied to the matrix of system (2.417) is

$$\begin{pmatrix} 0 & 0 & 1 \\ 0 & \rho & 0 \\ -(1+r) & \dfrac{(1+r)}{\varphi} & \left[2+r+\dfrac{f_1(1+r)}{\varphi}\right] \end{pmatrix} \tag{2.418}$$

$m_{21} = -\begin{vmatrix} 1 & 1 \\ \rho & \mu_2 \end{vmatrix}$; $m_{22} = \begin{vmatrix} 1 & 1 \\ \mu_1 & \mu_2 \end{vmatrix}$; $m_{23} = -\begin{vmatrix} 1 & 1 \\ \mu_1 & \rho \end{vmatrix}$;
$m_{31} = \begin{vmatrix} 1 & 1 \\ \chi & 0 \end{vmatrix}$; $m_{32} = -\begin{vmatrix} 1 & 1 \\ 0 & 0 \end{vmatrix}$; $m_{33} = \begin{vmatrix} 1 & 1 \\ 0 & \chi \end{vmatrix}$

$$= \begin{pmatrix} 1 & 1 & 1 \\ 0 & \chi & 0 \\ \mu_1 & \rho & \mu_2 \end{pmatrix} \begin{pmatrix} \mu_1 & 0 & 0 \\ 0 & \rho & 0 \\ 0 & 0 & \mu_2 \end{pmatrix} \frac{1}{\chi(\mu_2 - \mu_1)} \begin{pmatrix} \mu_2\chi & \rho - \mu_2 & -\chi \\ 0 & \mu_2 - \mu_1 & 0 \\ -\mu_1\chi & \mu_1 - \rho & \chi \end{pmatrix}$$

Roots are two in number, $\mu_1$and ρ, and are less than unity, while μ_2, obviously one in number, is greater than unity.

Therefore, on the diagonal matrix, the following partition must be made

$$\begin{pmatrix} \mu_1 & 0 & 0 \\ 0 & \rho & 0 \\ 0 & 0 & \mu_2 \end{pmatrix} = \begin{pmatrix} \begin{pmatrix} \mu_1 & 0 \\ 0 & \rho \end{pmatrix} & (0) \\ (0 \quad 0) & \mu_2 \end{pmatrix} \tag{2.419}$$

Multiply (2.417) by the matrix P^{-1}, it follows

$$P^{-1}E_t \begin{pmatrix} \widehat{z}_{t+1} \\ \widehat{w}_{t+1} \\ \widehat{n}_{t+1} \end{pmatrix} = P^{-1} \begin{pmatrix} 0 & 0 & 1 \\ 0 & \rho & 0 \\ -(1+r) & \dfrac{(1+r)}{\varphi} & \left[2 + r + \dfrac{f_1(1+r)}{\varphi}\right] \end{pmatrix} PP^{-1} \begin{pmatrix} \widehat{z}_t \\ \widehat{w}_t \\ \widehat{n}_t \end{pmatrix}$$

$$+P^{-1} \begin{pmatrix} 0 \\ 1 \\ 0 \end{pmatrix} \varepsilon_{t+1} \tag{2.420}$$

By defining a vector $\widetilde{s}_{t+1} = P^{-1}s_t$, the system (2.420) becomes

$$\widetilde{s}_{t+1} = P^{-1} \begin{pmatrix} 0 & 0 & 1 \\ 0 & \rho & 0 \\ -(1+r) & \dfrac{(1+r)}{\varphi} & \left[2 + r + \dfrac{f_1(1+r)}{\varphi}\right] \end{pmatrix} P\widetilde{s}_t + P^{-1} \begin{pmatrix} 0 \\ 1 \\ 0 \end{pmatrix} \varepsilon_{t+1} \tag{2.421}$$

Since the product $P^{-1}AP=$ D, whence, by the Jordan transformation, is $A = P\,D\,P^{-1}$, the system (2.421) becomes

$$\widetilde{s}_{t+1} = D\widetilde{s}_t + R\varepsilon_{t+1} \tag{2.422}$$

That is

$$\frac{1}{\chi(\mu_2-\mu_1)}\begin{pmatrix}\mu_2\chi & \rho-\mu_2 & -\chi\\ 0 & \mu_2-\mu_1 & 0\\ -\mu_1\chi & \mu_1-\rho & \chi\end{pmatrix}E_t\begin{pmatrix}\widehat{z}_{t+1}\\ \widehat{w}_{t+1}\\ \widehat{n}_{t+1}\end{pmatrix}=\frac{1}{\chi(\mu_2-\mu_1)}\begin{pmatrix}\mu_1 & 0 & 0\\ 0 & \rho & 0\\ 0 & 0 & \mu_2\end{pmatrix}$$
$$\times\begin{pmatrix}\mu_2\chi & \rho-\mu_2 & -\chi\\ 0 & \mu_2-\mu_1 & 0\\ -\mu_1\chi & \mu_1-\rho & \chi\end{pmatrix}\begin{pmatrix}\widehat{z}_t\\ \widehat{w}_t\\ \widehat{n}_t\end{pmatrix}$$
$$+\frac{1}{\chi(\mu_2-\mu_1)}\begin{pmatrix}\mu_2\chi & \rho-\mu_2 & -\chi\\ 0 & \mu_2-\mu_1 & 0\\ -\mu_1\chi & \mu_1-\rho & \chi\end{pmatrix}\begin{pmatrix}0\\ 1\\ 0\end{pmatrix}\varepsilon_{t+1} \tag{2.423}$$

Expanding the vector products to the right of the system (2.423), it follows

$$\begin{pmatrix}\mu_2\chi\, E_t\, z_{t+1}+(\rho-\mu)E_t\, w_{t+1}-\chi E_t\, n_{t+1}\\ (\mu_2-\mu_1)E_t w_{t+1}\\ -\mu_1\chi\, E_t\, z_{t+1}+(\mu_1-\rho)E_t\, w_{t+1}+\chi E_t\, n_{t+1}\end{pmatrix}$$
$$=\begin{pmatrix}\mu_1 & 0 & 0\\ 0 & \rho & 0\\ 0 & 0 & \mu_2\end{pmatrix}\begin{pmatrix}\mu_2\chi\, z_t+(\rho-\mu_2)w_t-\chi n_t\\ (\mu_2-\mu_1)w_t\\ -\mu_1\chi z_t+(\mu_1-\rho)w_t+\chi n_t\end{pmatrix}+\begin{pmatrix}\rho-\mu_2\\ \mu_2-\mu_1\\ \mu_1-\rho\end{pmatrix}\varepsilon_{t+1} \tag{2.424}$$

The system (2.423) becomes

$$\begin{pmatrix}\mu_2\chi & \rho-\mu_2 & -\chi\\ 0 & \mu_2-\mu_1 & 0\\ -\mu_1\chi & \mu_1-\rho & \chi\end{pmatrix}\begin{pmatrix}z_t\\ w_t\\ n_t\end{pmatrix}=\begin{pmatrix}\mu_2\chi\, z_t+(\rho-\mu_2)w_t-\chi n_t\\ (\mu_2-\mu_1)w_t\\ -\mu_1\chi z_t+(\mu_1-\rho)w_t+\chi n_t\end{pmatrix}$$

and

$$\begin{pmatrix}\mu_2\chi & \rho-\mu_2 & -\chi\\ 0 & \mu_2-\mu_1 & 0\\ -\mu_1\chi & \mu_1-\rho & \chi\end{pmatrix}\begin{pmatrix}0\\ 1\\ 0\end{pmatrix}\varepsilon_{t+1}=\begin{pmatrix}\rho-\mu_2\\ \mu_2-\mu_1\\ \mu_1-\rho\end{pmatrix}\varepsilon_{t+1} \tag{2.425}$$

Carrying out the partition indicated in (2.419), we will have

$$\begin{pmatrix}s_{B,t+1}\\ -\mu_1\chi\, E_t\widehat{z}_{t+1}+(\mu_1-\rho)E_t\,\widehat{w}_{t+1}+\chi\, E_t\,\widehat{n}_{t+1}\end{pmatrix}$$

$$= \begin{pmatrix} D_B & 0 \\ 0 & \mu_2 \end{pmatrix} \begin{pmatrix} \bar{s}_{B,t} \\ -\mu_1\chi\widehat{z}_t + (\mu_1 - \rho)\widehat{w}_t + \chi\widehat{n}_t \end{pmatrix} + \begin{pmatrix} R_B \\ \mu_1 - \rho \end{pmatrix} \varepsilon_{t+1} \tag{2.426}$$

That is

$$\begin{pmatrix} \widetilde{s}_{B,t+1} \\ -\mu_1\chi\widehat{z}_{t+1} + (\mu_1 - \rho)\,\widehat{w}_{t+1} + \chi\widehat{n}_{t+1} \end{pmatrix}$$
$$= \begin{pmatrix} D_B\bar{s}_{B,t} \\ \mu_2[-\mu_1\chi\widehat{z}_t + (\mu_1 - \rho)\widehat{w}_t + \chi\widehat{n}_t] \end{pmatrix} + \begin{pmatrix} R_B\varepsilon_{t+1} \\ (\mu_1 - \rho)\varepsilon_{t+1} \end{pmatrix} \tag{2.427}$$

We take the expectations on both sides in the subsystem constituted by the last equation. Note that for the term to the right hand, $E_t\, \varepsilon_{t+1} = 0$ must be valid. By solving, and iterating to infinity, taking into account that $\|\mu_2| > 1$, and that, for the stability of the solution, it is required

$$-\mu_1\chi\widehat{z}_t + (\mu_1 - \rho)\widehat{w}_t + \chi\widehat{n}_t = 0 \tag{2.428}$$

it follows

$$\chi\widehat{n}_t = \mu_1\chi\widehat{z}_t + (\rho - \mu_1)\widehat{w}_t \tag{2.429}$$

so that

$$\widehat{n}_t = \mu_1\,\widehat{z}_t + \frac{(\rho - \mu_1)}{\chi}\widehat{w}_t \tag{2.430}$$

Equation (2.429) can be traced back to the solutions obtained with the previous methods. Since $\mu_1\widehat{z}_t = \mu_1 n_{t-1} - \mu_1 n^*$, it is

$$\widehat{n}_t = \mu_1\, n_{t-1} - \mu_1 n^* + \frac{(\rho - \mu_1)}{\chi}\widehat{w}_t \tag{2.431}$$

and taking into account that

$$\mathrm{n}* = \frac{f_0 - w}{f_1}$$

it follows

$$n_t = \mu_1\, n_{t-1} + (1 - \mu_1)n^* + \frac{(\rho - \mu_1)}{\chi}\widehat{w}_t \tag{2.432}$$

From which

$$n_t = \mu_1\, n_{t-1} + (1-\mu_1)\frac{f_0 - w}{f_1} + \frac{(\rho-\mu_1)}{\chi}\widehat{w}_t \tag{2.433}$$

The magnitude χ is

$$\chi = \varphi + \frac{\rho\varphi}{(1+r)}\left(\rho + 2 + r + \frac{f_1(1+r)}{\varphi}\right) \tag{2.434}$$

and $\widehat{w}_t$ is equal to

$$w_t = \rho w_{t-1} + \varepsilon_t$$

By computing expression $\frac{(\rho-\mu_1)}{\chi}\widehat{w}_t$, taking forward solution of w_t and operating the consequent simplifications, it allows to bring (2.433) back to the one previously obtained in (2.367) or (2.387).

The solution exercise with the Blanchard-Kahn procedure in the present section was carried out in full, to show its analytical complexity, even in the presence of a model ultimately very simple.

We will re-examine again Blanchard-Kahn procedure in the study of DSGE models, also to show its potential practical overcoming, thanks to the numerical calculus solutions considered in the literature.

Appendix

A.1 Introduction

This appendix contains some reviews of elementary mathematics, such as quadratic equations, and can be disregarded by readers already equipped with the notions covered here.

A.1.1 Review of Quadratic Equations

It will be known that a quadratic equation in the canonical form is of the kind

$$ax^2 + bx + c = 0 \tag{2.435}$$

Coefficient a of the second-degree term in (2.435) must always be considered $\neq 0$.

The solutions of (2.435) are called *roots of quadratic equations*. The study of roots of (2.435) can begin by considering the case c = 0 so that the quadratic equation becomes homogeneous

$$ax^2 + bx = 0 \tag{2.436}$$

Bringing x out of the expression (2.436), we have

$$x(ax + b) = 0 \tag{2.437}$$

From which it follows

$$x = 0 \quad and\ x = -\frac{b}{a} \tag{2.438}$$

Therefore, by (2.438), the equation admits two real roots, one of which is zero. Assuming now $b = 0$, $c \neq 0$ so that the equation in this hypothesis is in the form

$$ax^2 + c = 0 \tag{2.439}$$

It follows

$$x^2 = -\frac{c}{a} \tag{2.440}$$

$$x = \pm\sqrt{-\frac{c}{a}} \tag{2.441}$$

Also, in this case, the equation admits two roots whose nature depends on the signs of c and a. If the signs of both c and a coincide, so that $(c/a) > 0$, the negative sign under the radical indicates that the solution is a complex number.

Setting $\sqrt{(-1)} = i$, being i the symbol of the imaginary number, it follows

$$x = \pm\sqrt{(-1)}\sqrt{\frac{c}{a}} = \pm i\sqrt{\frac{c}{a}} \tag{2.442}$$

In this hypothesis, therefore, the roots are pure complex numbers (they lack real part), and since it is

$$x_1 = i\sqrt{\frac{c}{a}} \tag{2.443}$$

and

$$x_2 = -i\sqrt{\frac{c}{a}} \tag{2.444}$$

the two complex numbers (2.443) and (2.444) are conjugate to each other. Conversely, when the signs coefficients are discordant, it follows $-\frac{c}{a} > 0$, and therefore,

$$x = \pm\sqrt{\left(-\frac{c}{a}\right)}$$

The two roots are real and opposite

$$x_1 = \sqrt{\left(-\frac{c}{a}\right)} \tag{2.445}$$

$$x_2 = -\sqrt{\left(-\frac{c}{a}\right)}.$$

The last case to consider is when b=0=c, and the second degree equation becomes

$$ax^2 = 0 \tag{2.446}$$

In this case, the equation (2.446) admits a unique solution x = 0, but it is said that the equation admits double roots since x = 0 is counted twice.

Consider now the complete equation (2.435). It is solved by making the following transformations.

Multiplying (2.435) by 4a, it follows

$$4a^2x^2 + 4abx + 4ac = 0 \tag{2.447}$$

Adding b^2squared in (2.447) to both sides results

$$\left(4a^2x^2 + b^2 + 4abx\right) + 4ac = b^2 \tag{2.448}$$

That is,

$$(2\mathrm{ax} + \mathrm{b})^2 + 4ac = b^2 \tag{2.449}$$

and therefore,

$$(2\mathrm{ax} + \mathrm{b}) = \pm\sqrt{b^2 - 4ac} \tag{2.450}$$

From this, it follows

$$2\mathrm{ax} = -\mathrm{b} \pm \sqrt{b^2 - 4ac} \tag{2.451}$$

and then,

$$\mathrm{x} = \frac{-\mathrm{b} \pm \sqrt{b^2 - 4ac}}{2\mathrm{a}} \tag{2.452}$$

The general quadratic equation (2.435) admits two roots

$$\mathrm{x}_1 = \frac{-\mathrm{b} + \sqrt{b^2 - 4ac}}{2\mathrm{a}}; \quad \mathrm{x}_2 = \frac{-\mathrm{b} - \sqrt{b^2 - 4ac}}{2\mathrm{a}} \tag{2.453}$$

The nature of the solutions (2.453) depends on the magnitude

$$b^2 - 4ac = \Delta \tag{2.454}$$

which is *the discriminant* Δ of the quadratic equation.

If $\Delta > 0$, the roots are real and distinct; if $\Delta = 0$, the roots are real coincident; if $\Delta < 0$, we will have

$$\begin{aligned}\mathrm{x} = \frac{-\mathrm{b} \pm \sqrt{-(b^2 - 4ac)}}{2\mathrm{a}} &= -\frac{b}{2a} \pm \frac{1}{2a}\sqrt{-(1)(b^2 - 4ac)} \\ &= -\frac{b}{2a} \pm \frac{1}{2a}\, i\sqrt{(b^2 - 4ac)}\end{aligned} \tag{2.455}$$

and roots are complex numbers, with

$$-\text{real part} = -\frac{b}{2a} \tag{2.456}$$

and

$$-\text{imaginary part} = \pm\frac{1}{2a}\, i\sqrt{(b^2 - 4ac)} \tag{2.457}$$

Being the real part of the two solutions equal and the imaginary part also equal but with opposite signs, the roots are *complex conjugate.*

A.1.2 Relations Between Roots and Coefficients of Quadratic Equation

Given the complete canonical quadratic equation (2.435) between the coefficients (a, b, c) and the roots $x_1$and x_2, the following properties hold

$$x_1 + x_2 = -\frac{b}{a} \qquad (2.458)$$

$$x_1 x_2 = \frac{c}{a}$$

The proof is done by direct verification, i.e.,[18]

$$x_1 + x_2 = \frac{-\mathrm{b} + \sqrt{(b^2 - 4ac)}}{2\mathrm{a}} + \frac{-\mathrm{b} - \sqrt{(b^2 - 4ac)}}{2\mathrm{a}}$$

$$= \frac{-\mathrm{b} + \sqrt{(b^2 - 4ac)} - \mathrm{b} - \sqrt{(b^2 - 4ac)}}{2\mathrm{a}} = -\frac{2b}{2a} = -\frac{b}{a} \qquad (2.459)$$

$$x_1 x_2 = \frac{-\mathrm{b} + \sqrt{(b^2 - 4ac)}}{2\mathrm{a}} \frac{-\mathrm{b} - \sqrt{(b^2 - 4ac)}}{2\mathrm{a}} = \frac{\mathrm{b}^2 - b^2 + 4ac}{4\mathrm{a}^2}$$

$$= \frac{\mathrm{c}}{\mathrm{a}} \qquad (2.460)$$

Consider now the expression

$$f(x) = ax^2 + bx + c \qquad (2.461)$$

It is called a *second-degree trinomial.*

The roots of the second-degree equation are values for which

$$f(x_1) = 0 \qquad (2.462)$$

$$f(x_2) = 0$$

It follows that for $x \neq x_1$, $x \neq x_2$, it will be f(x) $\neq 0$ and it will be possible to establish the sign of the trinomial f(x).

For this purpose, we proceed as follows.

Bringing out of parentheses in (2.461) the coefficient a of the square term follows

[18] Descartes' rule, already referred to in footnote 4, states that in any equation with a positive or zero discriminant, each variation of signs of coefficients corresponds to a positive solution, and each permanence of signs of coefficients, to a negative solution. If the equation has discordant roots, the root that has the greatest absolute value is positive if sign variation precedes sign permanence, and instead, it is negative if permanence precedes the variation.

$$f(x)=a\left(x^2+\frac{b}{a}x+\frac{c}{a}\right) \tag{2.463}$$

But $\frac{b}{a}=-(x_1+x_2)$ and $\frac{c}{a}=x_1x_2$ so that

$$\begin{aligned} f(x)&=a\left(x^2-(x_1+x_2)x+x_1x_2\right)=a\left(x^2-xx_1-xx_2+x_1x_2\right)\\ &=a(x(x-x_1)-x_2(x-x_1)) \end{aligned} \tag{2.464}$$

Bringing out of expression in (2.144) the term $(x-x_1)$, we have

$$f(x)=a\ (x-x_1)(x-x_2) \tag{2.465}$$

Equation (2.465) shows that the trinomial f(x) can be decomposed into a product between the coefficient of quadratic term a, and two terms which, being linear in x, take the name of *linear factors*.

When the roots are complex conjugate, also the two linear factors $(x-x_1)$ and $(x-x_2)$ are complex conjugate, and therefore, in this case, the trinomial $f(x)$ cannot be broken down into real factors.

Let $\Delta>0$. Assume that $x_2>x_1$ and consider the values of x outside the interval of the roots $[x_1,x_2]$.

If $x>x_2$, it follows that $(x-x_1)$ and $(x-x_2)$ are both positive. Conversely, for $x<x_1$, both linear factors are negative. In both cases, the product $a\ (x-x_1)(x-x_2)$ will have the same sign of the coefficient a.

Therefore, f(x) has a sign agreeing with a for all x values *outside* the interval of the roots $[x_1, x_2]$, i.e.,

if $f(x)a>0$, then $x\notin[x_1,x_2]$, and verifies $x>x_2$ and $x<x_1$.

For values of x within the interval of roots, i.e., such that $x_2>x>x_1$, the two linear factors $(x-x_1)$ and $(x-x_2)$ disagree in sign, and the product $a\ (x-x_1)(x-x_2)$ has positive values if a is negative, and vice versa. Therefore, f(x) has the opposite sign to that of the first coefficient a, that is: $f(x)a<0$ for $x\in[x_1,x_2]$ or x verifying $x_2>x>x_1$.

Let $\Delta=0$. We will have $x_1=x_2$, and therefore,

$$f(x)=a(x-x_1)^2 \tag{2.466}$$

It follows that for $x\neq x_1$, the trinomial f(x) will have the same sign as a.

Let $\Delta<0$. The roots are complex conjugate and, in this case, we proceed as follows. Bringing in the general equation a outside of the expression, we will have

$$a\left(x^2+\frac{b}{a}x+\frac{c}{a}\right) \tag{2.467}$$

Adding and subtracting $\frac{b^2}{4a^2}$ to (2.147), it follows that

$$a\left[\left(x^2+\frac{b}{a}x+\frac{b^2}{4a^2}\right)+\frac{c}{a}-\frac{b^2}{4a^2}\right]=a\left[\left(x+\frac{b}{2a}\right)^2+\frac{4ac-b^2}{4a^2}\right]$$
$$=a\left[\left(x+\frac{b}{2a}\right)^2-\frac{\Delta}{4a^2}\right] \tag{2.468}$$

With $\Delta < 0$, both terms in square brackets are positive, and therefore, f(x) has the same sign as a and never vanishes so that $x \neq x_1 \neq x_2$) i.e., x does not assume values in the real field.

A.1.3 Comparison Between Roots of Quadratic Equation and Two Given Real Numbers

Let α and β be two parameters, and let us consider the values of the trinomial corresponding to the given parameters $f(\alpha)$ and $f(\beta)$.

Assume that α and β are such that $\alpha < \beta$. We now want to compare the roots, for which $f(x) = 0$, with the two given real numbers α and β to verify if the x roots of the equation are included between the two assigned numbers, i.e., if they satisfy the condition $\alpha < x < \beta$.

Let $\Delta > 0$ (therefore the two roots are real and distinct). We have the following cases:

First case

$f(\alpha)$ and $f(\beta)$ both have sign different from sign of a.

In this case, both α and β fall within the interval of the two roots. Therefore, $x_1 < \alpha < \beta < x_2$. Therefore, neither of the two roots is between α and β.

Second case

$f(\alpha)$ disagrees in sign with a, while $f(\beta)$ agrees in sign with a.

Since $f(\alpha)$ disagrees in sign with a, then α falls within the interval of the two roots.

Since $f(\beta)$ agrees in sign with a, then β falls outside the interval of the two roots.

Since by assumption it is $\beta > \alpha$, the number β falls outside to the right.

So, we have $x_1 < \alpha < x_2 < \beta$. We see now that the major x_2 root falls in the interval (α, β), while the minor root x_1 is external to the left of the interval (α, β).

Third case

$f(\alpha)$ agrees in sign with that of a, and $f(\beta)$ disagrees in sign with that of a, i.e., $a(f(\alpha) > 0$ and $af(\beta) < 0$. Since $f(\beta)$ and a disagree in signs, β falls within the interval of the two roots, while f(α), since agrees in sign with a, α falls outside the interval of the two roots. Furthermore, being $\alpha < \beta$, it must be $\alpha < x_1 < \beta < x_2$. Therefore, the minor root x_1 is inside the interval (α, β), and the greater root i outside the interval (α, β).

Fourth case

f(α) agrees in sign with a and f (β) agrees in sign with a.

Since f(α) and f (β) agree both in sign with the signs of a, α, and β, both fall outside the root interval.

In particular letting $\beta = 1, \alpha = -1$, if f (1)a > 0 and f(−1)a > 0, we have $-1 < x_1$, $x_2 < 1$. Both roots are in absolute value less than the unit so we can say the roots are internal to the circle of unitary radius.

To determine whether both parameters α and β both fall to the left, both to the right, or one outside left and one external to the right of roots interval, we consider the semi-sum of the roots, i.e.,

$$\Sigma = \frac{x_1 + x_2}{2} = \frac{1}{2}\left(\frac{-b + \sqrt{b^2 - 4ac}}{2a} + \frac{-b - \sqrt{b^2 - 4ac}}{2a}\right) = \frac{1}{2}\,\frac{-2b}{2a} = -\frac{b}{2a}$$

And since the half-sum certainly verifies $x_1 < \Sigma < x_2$ or $x_2 < \Sigma < x_1$, it is always included between the two added roots.

Therefore, we will study only the conditions $x_1 < \Sigma < x_2$, $\alpha < \sum$ and $\sum < \beta$.

We have the following subcases:

First sub case

The conditions $\alpha < \sum$ and $\sum < \beta$ are both satisfied.

In this case, α falls outside to the left and β to the right of the roots interval, i.e., $\alpha < x_1 < \sum < x_2 < \beta$. Therefore, both roots fall in the interval (α, β).

Second sub case

$\alpha < \sum$ (verified) and $\sum < \beta$ (not true). If $\sum < \beta$ is not true, then it will be $\beta < \sum$, therefore, β must fall to the left of the interval and a fortiori also α, since it is $\alpha < \beta$.

Therefore, it will have to be $\alpha < \beta < x_1 < \sum < x_2$, and both roots are outside to the right of the interval (α, β).

Third sub case

$\alpha < \sum$ (not true) and $\sum < \beta$ (verified). Since $\alpha < \sum$ is not true, it results $\sum < \alpha$; therefore, α will fall outside to the right of the root interval and a fortiori also β.

We have $x_1 < \sum < x_2 < \alpha < \beta$. Therefore, both roots are outside to the left of the interval (α, β).

The previous considerations apply to the study of second degree inequalities of the type f(x) < 0 and f(x) > 0.

In this circumstance, given the value of the discriminant $\Delta \geq 0$, it is necessary to verify the sign of the first coefficient and on these bases decide whether f(x) < 0 or f (x) > 0.

A.1.4 Some Review on Complex Numbers and Trigonometric Identities

As we have seen, in studying complex solutions of second-order homogeneous finite-difference equations in Sect. 2.8 of the present chapter, when converting complex numbers to the exponential form, it is necessary to take into account:

a) The trigonometric representation of complex numbers
b) Some trigonometric identities, which will be soon specified

From now on, we indicate the roots of quadratic equations with the same symbol λ used in the text. We know that given the discriminant Δ of the quadratic equation, in general, a complex root is of the type

$$\lambda_1 = (\mathrm{a}/2) + \mathrm{i}\sqrt{\Delta}/2$$

(and his conjugate is λ_2=(a/2) $-$ i $\sqrt{\Delta}/2$).

In the complex Cartesian plane, having the imaginary number as unit measure on the ordinate axis, the complex root has a graphical representation as in Fig. 2.7.

In Fig. 2.7, a segment originating from the origin can be thought of as the radius of a circle whose extreme point intersects the corresponding circle.

For any given r, the corresponding circle with unit radius admits the following cosine and sine:

$$\cos\theta = \frac{a_1/2}{r}; \qquad \sin\theta = \frac{\sqrt{\Delta}/2}{r} \tag{2.469}$$

It follows from this that trigonometric coordinates of point (a/2, $\sqrt{}\Delta$/2) are, respectively,

$$a_1/2 = r\ \cos\theta; \qquad \sqrt{\Delta}/2 = r\ \sin\theta; \tag{2.470}$$

For a given circle with radius r, the complex root of a quadratic equation can be written

$$\lambda_1 = (\mathrm{a}_1/2) + \mathrm{i}\sqrt{\Delta}/2 \ = \mathrm{r}\,(\cos\theta + i\ \sin\theta) \tag{2.471}$$

and complex conjugate root becomes

$$\lambda_2 = (a_1/2) - i\sqrt{\Delta}/2 \ = r\,(\cos\theta - i\,\sin\theta\,)) \tag{2.472}$$

Some useful trigonometric identities used for studying solutions of difference equations are

$$\begin{aligned}\cos(\theta_1 + \theta_2) &= \cos(\theta_1)\cos(\theta_2) - \sin(\theta_1)\sin(\theta_2)\\ \sin(\theta_1 + \theta_2) &= \sin(\theta_1)\cos(\theta_2) + \cos(\theta_1)\sin(\theta_2)\end{aligned} \tag{2.473}$$

When $\theta_1 = \theta_2$, we can ignore the index and set

$$\begin{aligned}\cos(2\theta) &= \cos^2\theta - \sin^2\theta\\ \sin(2\theta) &= 2\sin(\theta)\cos(\theta)\end{aligned} \tag{2.474}$$

These results are useful for studying the solutions of second-order finite-difference equation.

We know that the solution to a homogeneous second-order finite-difference equation is

$$y_t = A_1\lambda_1^t + A_2\lambda_2^t.$$

Consider the characteristic equation associated with complex conjugate roots. Squaring the roots, it follows

$$\begin{aligned}\lambda_1^2 = r^2(\cos\theta + i\,\sin\theta\,)^2 &= r^2\left(\cos^2\theta - \sin^2\theta + i\,2\sin\theta\cos\theta\right)\\ &= r^2(\cos(2\theta) + i\,\sin(2\theta))\end{aligned} \tag{2.475}$$

And

$$\lambda_2^2 = r^2(\cos(2\theta) - i\,\sin(2\theta)) \tag{2.476}$$

For any power t, it is

$$\begin{aligned}\lambda_1^t &= r^t(\cos(t\theta) + (i\,\sin(t\theta))\\ \lambda_2^t &= r^t(\cos(t\theta) - i\,\sin(t\theta))\end{aligned} \tag{2.477}$$

Furthermore, since y_t is real number, constants A_1 and A_2 in the solution to a homogeneous second-order finite-difference equation are also complex conjugate numbers, so that they can be written in the trigonometric form

$$A_1 = B_1(\cos B_2 + i\,\sin B_2)$$

Fig. 2.7 Representation of points in the complex plane

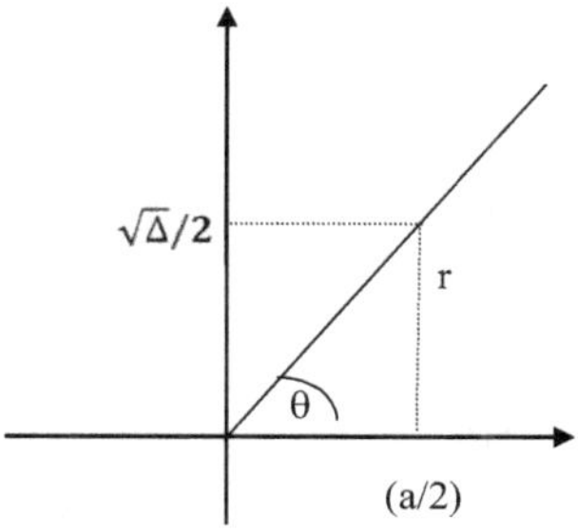

$$A_2 = B_1(\cos B_2 - i\ \sin B_2) \tag{2.478}$$

From which it follows

$$\begin{aligned} A_1\lambda_1^t &= B_1(\cos B_2 + i\ \sin B_2)\ r^t[\cos(\mathrm{t}\theta) + \mathrm{i}\ \sin(\mathrm{t}\theta)] \\ A_2\lambda_2^t &= B_1(\cos B_2 - i\ \sin B_2)\ r^t[\cos(\mathrm{t}\theta) - \mathrm{i}\ \sin(\mathrm{t}\theta)] \end{aligned} \tag{2.479}$$

Rearrange the expression relative to the root λ_1^t

$$\begin{aligned} & B_1(\cos B_2 + i\ \sin B_2)\ \ r^t(\cos(\mathrm{t}\theta) + \mathrm{i}\ \sin(\mathrm{t}\theta)) \\ &= B_1 r^t[(\cos B_2 \cos(\mathrm{t}\theta) + \mathrm{i}\ \cos B_2 \sin(\mathrm{t}\theta) + i \sin B_2 \cos(\mathrm{t}\theta) - \ \sin B_2 \sin(\mathrm{t}\theta)] \\ &= B_1 r^t\{[\cos B_2 \cos(\mathrm{t}\theta) - \ \sin B_2 \sin(\mathrm{t}\theta)] + \mathrm{i}[\cos B_2 \sin(\mathrm{t}\theta) + \ \sin B_2 \cos(\mathrm{t}\theta)]\} \end{aligned} \tag{2.480}$$

Looking at the first of the trigonometric formulas mentioned above in (2.473), the real component can be set as $\cos(\mathrm{t}\theta + B_2)$, while the imaginary component is set as $\sin(\mathrm{t}\theta + B_2)$, and therefore,

$$A_1\lambda_1^t = B_1 r^t[\cos(\mathrm{t}\theta + B_2) + \mathrm{i}\ \sin(\mathrm{t}\theta + B_2)] \tag{2.481}$$

And similarly

$$A_2\lambda_2^t = B_1 r^t[\cos(\mathrm{t}\theta + B_2) - \mathrm{i}\ \sin(\mathrm{t}\theta + B_2)] \tag{2.482}$$

It follows that the solution of the homogeneous associated with the finite-difference equation of the second order becomes

$$y_t = A_1\lambda_1^t + A_2\lambda_2^t = B_1 r^t\ [\cos(\mathrm{t}\theta + B_2) + [\cos(\mathrm{t}\theta + B_2)]$$

$$= 2B_1 r^t [\cos(t\theta + B_2)] \tag{2.483}$$

The term 2B1, since B1 is an arbitrary constant, can be absorbed into the arbitrary constant B, in such a way we can set

$$y_t = Br^t \left[\cos(t\theta + B_2)\right) \tag{2.484}$$

We can now also determine the length of the radius r from the characteristic equation $\lambda^2 - a\lambda - b = 0$.

Since the discriminant is $\Delta < 0$, and the roots are complex, we have $\lambda_{1,2} = \left(\frac{a}{2}\right) \pm i\sqrt{-\frac{\Delta}{4}}$. From $\cos\theta^2 + \sin\theta^2 = 1$ it follows

$$\begin{aligned} &\left(a^2/4r^2\right) - \Delta/4r^2 = 1 \\ &r^2 = \left(a^2 - \Delta\right)/4 = \\ &\left(a^2 - a^2 - 4b\right)/4 = b \end{aligned} \tag{2.485}$$

whence

$$r = (b)^{1/2} \tag{2.486}$$

Therefore, r coincides with the square root of the known term of the characteristic equation.

The term r^t in the solution of a homogeneous second-order difference equation acts as a damping or amplifying factor of oscillations determined by the factor cos $(t\theta + B_2)$.

Depending on whether $r > 1$ or $r < 1$, the oscillations are explosive or damped, unless the initial conditions are $y_0 = 0 = 0$ and $y_1 = 0$. But $r < 1$ means $(b)^{1/2} < 1$ which holds if and only if $b < 1$. Number θ is the frequency or periodicity of oscillations, i.e., it indicates the number of periods in which oscillation proceeds from peak to peak. Known r, it follows $\cos\theta = a_1/2r = a_1/2\,(-a_2)^{1/2}$ and from this

$$\theta = \cos^{-1}\left[a_1/2\,(-a_2)^{1/2}\right] \tag{2.487}$$

while B_1 indicates the length of the period after which a given oscillation occurs (e.g., if the period is measured in years, the number B_1 will be 1½ years, 5 years, and so on).

They are determined by setting two initial conditions, e.g., y_0 and y_1 for t = 0 and t = 1, and forming the following system in unknowns B_1 and B_2[19]

$$\begin{aligned} y_0 &= B\ \cos(B_2) \\ y_1 &= B\ r\ \cos(\theta + B_2) \end{aligned} \tag{2.488}$$

For further general mathematical references on finite difference equations and systems of finite difference equations see Baumol (1970), Bellman and Cooke (1963), Boole (1960), Chiang (1974), Chirichiello (2000), Chow (1997), Elaydi (1996), Galor (2007), Gandolfo (2009), George and Oxley (1994), Ghizzetti and Rosati (1993), Goldberg (1986), Luenberger (1979), Miller (1968), Radin (2019), Simon and Blume (1994), Takajama (1974).

References

Baumol, W. (1970) *Economic Dynamics*, Macmillan, New York.

Bellman, R. and Cooke, K. (1963) *Differential-Difference Equations,* Academic Press, New York.

Blanchard, O. and Kahn, C. (1980) 'The Solution of Linear Difference Models under Rational Expectations', *Econometrica*, 48(5), pp. 1305-1312.

Boole, G. (1960) *A Treatise on the Calculus of finite Differences,* Dover, New York.

Chiang, A. (1974) *Fundamental Methods of Mathematical Economics,* McGraw-Hill, New York.

Chirichiello, G. (2000) *Intertemporal Macroeconomic Models, Money and Rational Choices,* MacMillan Press, London, St's Martin Press, New York.

Chow, G.C. (1997) *Dynamic Economics. Optimization by the Lagrange Method.* New York, Oxford: Oxford University Press.

Collard, F. (2005) *Quantitative Macroeconomics*, web edition (update in October 2015 at http://fabcol.free.fr/notes.htm) (Accessed: 2, July 2016).

Elaydi, S. (1996) *An Introduction to Difference Equations,* Springer Science, New York.

[19]The constants are obtained with the following computations. It is

$$\cos(\theta + B_2) = \cos(\theta)\cos(B_2) - \sin(\theta)\ \sin(B_2)$$

$y_1 = B\ r\cos(\theta)\cos(B_2) - \sin(\theta)\ \sin(B_2) = y_0\ r\cos(\theta) - \sin(\theta)\ \sin(B_2)$

And being $\sin(B_2)^2 = 1 - \cos(B_2)^2 = 1 - \left(\frac{y_0}{B}\right)^2$, it is true that

$y_1 = y_0\ r\cos(\theta) - \left[1 - \left(\frac{y_0}{B}\right)^2\right]\sin(\theta)$

$\frac{y_1}{\sin(\theta)} = y_0\ r\frac{1}{\text{tang}(\theta)} - \left[1 - \left(\frac{y_0}{B}\right)^2\right]$

$$\sqrt{1 + \frac{y_1}{\sin(\theta)} - y_0\ r\frac{1}{\text{tang}(\theta)}} = \left(\frac{y_0}{B}\right)$$

Therefore, $B = \frac{\sqrt{1+\frac{y_1}{\sin(\theta)} - y_0\ r\frac{1}{\text{tang}(\theta)}}}{y_0}$; $y_0 = \frac{\sqrt{1+\frac{y_1}{\sin(\theta)} - y_0\ r\frac{1}{\text{tang}(\theta)}}}{y_0}$ $\cos(B_2)$, from which $\cos(B_2) = \frac{y_0^2}{\sqrt{1+\frac{y_1}{\sin(\theta)} - y_0\ r\frac{1}{\text{tang}(\theta)}}}$ and $B_2 = \cos^{-1}\left[\frac{y_0^2}{\sqrt{1+\frac{y_1}{\sin(\theta)} - y_0\ r\frac{1}{\text{tang}(\theta)}}}\right]$.

Farmer, R. (1993) *The Macroeconomics of Self-Fulfilling Prophecies,* Cambridge: MIT Press.
Galor, O. (2007), *Discrete Dynamical Systems,* Springer, Berlin Heidelberg
Gandolfo, G. (2009) *Economic Dynamics*, 4th ed., Springer-Verlag, Berlin.
George, D. and Oxley L. (1994) 'Linear Saddlepoint Dynamics on Their Head', *European Journal of Political Economy*, vol 10, pp. 389-400.
Ghizzetti, A. and Rosati F. (1993) *Analisi Matematica (Mathematical Analysis, Italian),* Vol. II, Masson, Milan.
Goldberg, S. (1986) *Introduction to Difference Equations,* Dover, New York.
Hadley, G. (1961), *Linear Algebra*, Addison-Wesley, Reading (Mass.).
Klein, P., (2000) 'Using the Generalized Schur Form to Solve a Multivariate Linear Rational Expectations Model', Journal of Economic Dynamics and Control, Vol. 24, pp. 1405-1423.
Luenberger, D. (1979) *Introduction to Dynamic Systems,* Wiley, New York.
Miller, R. (1968) *Linear Difference Equations,*Benjamin, Reading MA.
Radin, M.A. (2019) *Difference equations for scientists and engineering: interdisciplinary difference equations*, World Scientific, New Jersey.
Sargent, T. (1987), *Macroeconomic Theory,* 2nd ed., Academic Press, Orlando.
Simon, C. and Blume, L. (1994) *Mathematics for economists* Vol.7, Norton, New York.
Takajama, A. (1974) *Mathematical Economics*, Dryden Press, Hinsdale.

Chapter 3
Models of Representative Agents and Real Business Cycle Models

In this chapter, after reviewing the use of the Lagrangian methodology in intertemporal maximization, and studying an application, we introduce a distinction between dynamic general equilibrium (DGE) models and dynamic stochastic general equilibrium models to highlight the importance of methodological innovation due to real business cycle (RBC) models of including stochastic shocks in dynamic models. The chapter continues with the examination of a basic RBC model, the methods of solution of log-linearized system, and the applications of Blanchard-Kahn procedures. In the Appendix, the chapter also reviews Bellman's principle and dynamic programming. The determination of aggregate savings in an intertemporal context under conditions of uncertainty further illustrates the use of Bellman's principle in economics.

3.1 Use of the Lagrangian in Intertemporal Maximization

We begin the study of basic models of Real Business Cycle with some methodological notes on the use of Lagrangian in intertemporal maximization.

The case considered here is the one of the choices of a consumer, whose preferences, expressed by a utility function in parametric form, are represented by a Constant Relative Risk Aversion (CRRA), which depends on two arguments, consumption C_t, and labor L_t.

The intertemporal maximum problem is

$$max\ E_0 \sum_{t=0}^{\infty} \beta^t \left[\frac{C_t^{1-\sigma}}{1-\sigma} - \varphi \frac{L_t^{1+\gamma}}{1+\gamma}\right] \tag{3.1}$$

G. Chirichiello, *DSGE Models for Real Business Cycle and New Keynesian Macroeconomics*, Springer Texts in Business and Economics,
https://doi.org/10.1007/978-3-031-56034-7_3

Sub

$$C_t + K_{t+1} = w_t L_t + r_{t+1} K_t + (1-\delta) K_t \qquad \forall t > 0$$

The instantaneous Lagrangian at time t is

$$La_t = \left[\frac{C_t^{1-\sigma}}{1-\sigma} - \varphi \frac{L_t^{1+\gamma}}{1+\gamma}\right] + \lambda_t [w_t L_t + r_{t+1} K_t + (1-\delta) K_t - C_t - K_{t+1}]$$

Intertemporal consumer's maximum problem is solved by maximizing a discounted Lagrangian. The corresponding maximum problem has the following formulation:

$$max \;\; E_0 \sum_{t=0}^{\infty} \beta^t La_t \qquad \forall t > 0 \tag{3.2}$$

where $0 < \beta < 1$ is a discount factor that restores the value of Lagrangian for each future instant to the current value.

Discounted Lagrangian of the example (3.1) is

$$max \; \{E_0 \sum_{t=0}^{\infty} \beta^t \left[\frac{C_t^{1-\sigma}}{1-\sigma} - \varphi \frac{L_t^{1+\gamma}}{1+\gamma}\right]$$
$$+ \lambda_t [w_t L_t + r_{t+1} K_t + (1-\delta) K_t - C_t - K_{t+1}]\} \tag{3.3}$$

Choice's variables in an intertemporal context are (C_t, L_t, K_{t+1}), and in the language of intertemporal optimization, they are *control variables*.

Compared to static maximization, the novelty aspect of intertemporal maximization (3.3) lies in the fact that at each instant t, among the control variables, there is also K_{t+1}, which refers to a future period. Such a variable appears in Lagrangian not only at the instant t but also in the instant t+1, due to updating of the variable K_t.

Therefore, to maximize for K_{t+1} at the instant t, one must consider also those terms of Lagrangian containing K_t updated at time t+1.

Even in the intertemporal context, however, necessary conditions for optimal choice remain first-order conditions.

In the example we are considering they are, respectively,

$$\begin{aligned}
C_t : \;\; & \beta^t C_t^{-\sigma} - \beta^t \lambda_t = 0 \quad \Rightarrow \quad C_t^{-\sigma} = \lambda_t \\
L_t : \;\; & -\beta^t \varphi L_t^{\gamma} + \beta^t \lambda_t w_t = 0 \quad \Rightarrow \quad \varphi L_t^{\gamma} = \lambda_t w_t \\
K_{t+1} : \;\; & -\beta^t \lambda_t + \beta^{t+1} E_t \lambda_{t+1} (r_{t+1} + (1-\delta)) = 0 \\
& \Rightarrow \quad \beta E_t \lambda_{t+1} [r_{t+1} + (1-\delta)] = \lambda_t
\end{aligned} \tag{3.4}$$

Which, by eliminating λ_t and λ_{t+1}, reduce to

$$C_t^{\sigma}\varphi L_t^{\gamma}=w_t$$
$$C_t^{-\sigma}=\beta E_t C_{t+1}^{-\sigma}[\, r_{t+1}+(1-\delta)]$$

Bearing in mind that the constraint must necessarily be satisfied, the solution of intertemporal optimum (3.1) can be reduced to the following three equations relating to period t:

$$\begin{aligned} C_t^{\sigma}\varphi L_t^{\gamma}&=w_t \\ C_t^{-\sigma} &= \beta E_t C_{t+1}^{-\sigma}[\, r_{t+1}+(1-\delta)] \\ C_t+K_{t+1}&=w_tL_t+r_tK_t+(1-\delta)K_t \end{aligned} \tag{3.5}$$

Since these equations must be valid at every instant t, and in them appear variables C_t, C_{t+1}, L_t, K_t, K_{t+1}, we are dealing with a system made up of a static equation, the one referred to the variable L_t, and two dynamic equations, which implicitly define first-order finite-difference equations, i.e., those containing the variables C_t, C_{t+1} and K_t, K_{t+1}.

3.2 A Discussion of the Transversality Condition

To solve for dynamic finite-difference equations, in general, as many initial conditions are required as the number of equations.

But for the system (3.5), we only have one initial condition on capital, K_0. One could, therefore, in principle, assign any initial condition for consumption. A priori, however, there is an infinity of values that an initial consumption can assume, and this causes indeterminacy.

In models of intertemporal choices, indeterminacy is overcome by imposing a further condition called the *transversality condition.*

Following intuition, a further condition could be imposed by considering an economic significance condition on consumption, i.e., $C_t \geq 0$. However, a subtle observation suggests that imposing a condition on consumption would implicitly be the same as indirectly imposing a condition on capital, as well. Indeed, in future periods, given the budget constraint, physical capital is a function of current consumption since it is verified:

$$K_{t+1}=w_tL_t+r_tK_t+(1-\delta)K_t-C_t \tag{3.6}$$

Since K_t is given, for given L_t, imposing a significance condition $C_t \geq 0$ means also imposing another condition on capital, in an indirect way.

For this reason, it is preferable to impose directly on capital a further condition.

From the point of view of the theory of differential equations, this can be justified by the following considerations:

Solving the budget constraint for C_t

$$C_t = w_t L_t + r_t K_t + (1 - \delta) K_t - K_{t+1} \tag{3.7}$$

and

$$C_{t+1} = w_{t+1} L_{t+1} + r_{t+1} K_{t+1} + (1 - \delta) K_{t+1} - K_{t+2} \tag{3.8}$$

Substituting these in the first-order conditions (3.4), the finite-difference system is reduced to a single equation in the variables K_t, K_{t+1}, K_{t+2}. This gives rise to an implicit finite-difference equation of the second order in the variable K_t. But a second-order finite-difference equation in K_t requires two initial conditions. For this reason, in the maximum problem, it makes sense, together with the initial condition K_0, to place the condition of economic significance on the capital

$$K_t \geq 0 \tag{3.9}$$

From the Kuhn-Tucker conditions,[1] referred to (3.9) for the maximum problem (3.3), it results

$$\lambda_t \geq 0; K_t \geq 0; \lim_{t \to \infty} \lambda_t K_t = 0 \tag{3.10}$$

Being $\lambda_t = \beta^t E_t U_c(C_t, L_t)$, that is, for the separable utility function $\lambda_t = \beta^t E_t U_c(C_t)$, surely positive, a transversality condition is obtained:

$$\lim_{t \to \infty} \beta^t E_t U_c(C_t) K_t = 0 \tag{3.11}$$

Condition (3.11) provides the missing condition on K_t. This allows us to obtain a unique solution of the implicit finite-difference equation of the second order on K_t, given the initial condition K_0 and the transversality condition (3.11).

3.3 An Application of the Intertemporal Maximization: The Case of Adjustment Costs of Capital and the Relationship with "Tobin's q" Theory

By anticipating here a maximum problem that will be considered after, in the context of a real business cycle model, we will study the use of Lagrangian when it is assumed that a modification of physical capital is expensive.

[1] See, e.g. Intriligator, M. (1971), pp. 49–60.

The unit cost of capital is supposed to be a quadratic function of kind $\frac{\Psi}{2}\left(\frac{I_t}{K_t}-\delta\right)^2$. The quantity $\frac{I_t}{K_t}$ that appears in the costs definition is equivalent to $\frac{K_{t+1}-K_t}{K_t}$, that is the gross rate of accumulation of capital, so that expression $\left(\frac{K_{t+1}-K_t}{K_t}-\delta\right)^2$ coincides with the square of net rate of capital accumulation.

It is assumed that the unit cost of growth rate of capital is an increasing function of the capital accumulation rate.[2] More exactly, it assumed that unit cost is proportional to the squared net rate of capital accumulation, i.e., the more intensely capital accumulates, the faster the cost of accumulation increases. The total cost of the use of the quantity of capital K_t is $\frac{\Psi}{2}\left(\frac{I_t}{K_t}-\delta\right)^2 K_t$, so that when it is supposed that capital accumulation is carried out directly by the consumer, in the budget constraint, alongside the expenditure for consumption, expenditure for accumulating *new* capital, and expenditure to compensate for the wear and tear of the capital, the consumer must also bear the expenditure connected with the cost of capital accumulation.

Therefore, the budget constraint (3.8) now becomes

$$C_t + \left[K_{t+1} + \delta K_t + \frac{\Psi}{2}\left(\frac{I_t}{K_t}-\delta\right)^2 K_t\right] = w_t L_t + (1+r_t)K_t \tag{3.12}$$

That is to say

$$C_t + I_t = w_t L_t + r_t K_t + (1-\delta)K_t - \frac{\Psi}{2}\left(\frac{I_t}{K_t}-\delta\right)^2 K_t \tag{3.13}$$

which must be valid together with the other constraint:

$$I_t = K_{t+1} - (1-\delta)K_t \tag{3.14}$$

With the parametric utility function considered in problem (3.1), the Lagrangian for the current period, by indicating λ_t and ξ_t the respective Lagrange multipliers relative to constraints (3.13) and (3.14), becomes

$$\begin{aligned} La_t = {} & \left[\frac{C_t^{1-\sigma}}{1-\sigma} - \varphi\frac{L_t^{1-\gamma}}{1-\gamma}\right] \\ & + \lambda_t\left[w_t L_t + r_t K_t + (1-\delta)K_t - C_t - I_t - \frac{\Psi}{2}\left(\frac{I_t}{K_t}-\delta\right)^2 K_t\right] \\ & + \xi_t\left[I_t + (1-\delta)K_t - K_{t+1}\right] \end{aligned} \tag{3.15}$$

The intertemporal problem of choices is stated as

[2] Taubman, P. and Wilkinson, M. (1970).

$$max \quad E_0 \sum_{t=0}^{\infty} \beta^t \{La_t\} = \tag{3.16}$$

$$\max E_0 \sum_{t=0}^{\infty} \beta^t \Bigg\{ \left[\left[\frac{C_t^{1-\sigma}}{1-\sigma} - \varphi \frac{L_t^{1-\gamma}}{1-\gamma} \right] + \lambda_t \left[w_t L_t + r_t K_t + (1-\delta) K_t - C_t - I_t - \frac{\psi}{2} \left(\frac{I_t}{K_t} - \delta \right)^2 K_t \right] \right.$$

$$\left. + \xi_t [I_t + (1-\delta) K_t - K_{t+1}] \right\}$$

First-order conditions of (3.16) are

$$C_t : \qquad C_t^{-\sigma} = \lambda_t \tag{3.17}$$

$$L_t : \qquad \varphi L_t^{-\gamma} \quad = \quad \lambda_t w_t$$

$$I_t : \quad -\beta^t \lambda_t \quad \left[1 + \psi \left(\frac{I_t}{K_t} - \delta \right) \right] = -\beta^t \, \xi_t \qquad \Rightarrow$$

$$\lambda_t \left[1 + \psi \left(\frac{I_t}{K_t} - \delta \right) \right] = \xi_t$$

$$K_{t+1} : \beta^{t+1} E_t \lambda_{t+1} r_{t+1} + \beta^{t+1} E_t \lambda_{t+1} (1-\delta) -$$

$$\beta^{t+1} E_t \lambda_{t+1} \frac{\psi}{2} \left(\frac{I_{t+1}}{K_{t+1}} - \delta \right)^2 + \beta^{t+1} E_t \lambda_{t+1} \psi \left(\frac{I_{t+1}}{K_{t+1}} - \delta \right) \left(\frac{I_{t+1}}{K_{t+1}} \right) +$$

$$\beta^{t+1} E_t \xi_{t+1} (1-\delta) - \beta^t \xi_t = 0$$

From the condition concerning I_t, by dividing both sides by λ_t it follows

$$\left[1 + \psi \left(\frac{I_t}{K_t} - \delta \right) \right] = \frac{\xi_t}{\lambda_t} \tag{3.18}$$

This equality imposes that the ratio between the two Lagrange multipliers relative to constraints for the accumulation of capital and budget constraint must be equal to the cost of increasing one unit of capital, or one unit of investment.

It, therefore, measures the incentive on the part of households to increase or decrease investment in physical capital.

When the ratio between the multipliers is greater than the cost of an investment unit, it is convenient for households to increase investments, by allocating more resources to capital accumulation.

Conversely, when the ratio between Lagrange multipliers is lower than the cost of an investment unit, households find it convenient to reduce resources to be allocated to accumulate capital and, therefore, reduce investments.

This link, between the expenditure for purchasing capital goods and their cost, reproduces the well-known mechanism of *Tobin's q*,[3] which claims that a greater or lesser accumulation of physical capital is guided by the ratio between value attributed to capital and cost of accumulating that capital.

In the case of the representative household, the relationship between value ξ_t attributed to a unit of accumulated capital and cost λ_t of capital accumulation is $\frac{\xi_t}{\lambda_t}$, so that according to Tobin's theory it is $q_t = \frac{\xi_t}{\lambda_t}$.

Following this theory, the condition for optimal capital accumulation, in a microeconomic model cost-per-capital-accumulation-based, becomes

$$\left[1 + \psi\left(\frac{I_t}{K_t} - \delta\right)\right] = q_t \tag{3.19}$$

To further clarify this notion, let us refer to the condition relating to K_{t+1}. That condition can be re-written as

$$\beta E_t\lambda_{t+1}r_{t+1} + \beta E_t\lambda_{t+1}(1-\delta)$$
$$-\beta E_t\lambda_{t+1}\frac{\psi}{2}\left(\frac{I_{t+1}}{K_{t+1}} - \delta\right)^2 + \beta E_t\lambda_{t+1}\psi\left(\frac{I_{t+1}}{K_{t+1}} - \delta\right)\left(\frac{I_{t+1}}{K_{t+1}}\right) + \beta E_t\xi_{t+1}(1-\delta)\Big] = \xi_t \tag{3.20}$$

That is,

$$\beta E_t\lambda_{t+1}r_{t+1} + \beta E_t\xi_{t+1}(1-\delta) + \beta E_t\lambda_{t+1}(1-\delta)$$
$$-\beta\left[E_t\lambda_{t+1}\frac{\psi}{2}\left(\frac{I_{t+1}}{K_{t+1}} - \delta\right)^2 + E_t\lambda_{t+1}\psi\left(\frac{I_{t+1}}{K_{t+1}} - \delta\right)\right] = \xi_t \tag{3.21}$$

And again,

$$\beta E_t\lambda_{t+1}r_{t+1} + \beta(1-\delta)E_t\left(q_{t+1}\lambda_{t+1}\right) + \beta E_t\lambda_{t+1}(1-\delta)$$
$$-\beta E_t\lambda_{t+1}\frac{\psi}{2}\left(\frac{I_{t+1}}{K_{t+1}} - \delta\right)^2 + \beta E_t\lambda_{t+1}\psi\left(\frac{I_{t+1}}{K_{t+1}} - \delta\right)\left(\frac{I_{t+1}}{K_{t+1}}\right) = \xi_t \tag{3.22}$$

The magnitude $\left[E_t\lambda_{t+1}(1-\delta) - E_t\lambda_{t+1}\frac{\psi}{2}\left(\frac{I_{t+1}}{K_{t+1}} - \delta\right)^2\right] K_{t+1})$ can be identified with the *net expected shadow value* of a given future capital stock, so that the expected increase in value of an accumulated capital increase is

[3] See Tobin, J. (1969).

$$\frac{\partial VK_{t+1}}{\partial K_{t+1}} = Net\ marginal\ value\ of\ capital =$$

$$= \frac{\partial\left(E_t\lambda_{t+1}\,(1-\delta)K_{t+1} - E_t\lambda_{t+1}\frac{\Psi}{2}\left(\frac{I_{t+1}}{K_{t+1}}-\delta\right)^2 K_{t+1}\right)}{\partial K_{t+1}} = [E_t\lambda_{t+1}(1-\delta)$$

$$-E_t\lambda_{t+1}\frac{\Psi}{2}\left(\frac{I_{t+1}}{K_{t+1}}-\delta\right)^2 + E_t\lambda_{t+1}\Psi\left(\frac{I_{t+1}}{K_{t+1}}-\delta\right)\left(\frac{I_{t+1}}{K_{t+1}}\right)] \tag{3.23}$$

From the above definition of q_t, we can write

$$\beta\left[E_t\lambda_{t+1}r_{t+1} + (1-\delta)E_t\left(q_{t+1}\lambda_{t+1}\right) + \frac{\partial VK_{t+1}}{\partial K_{t+1}}\right] = q_t\,\lambda_t \tag{3.24}$$

This equality expresses that the expected margin of increase in value of an accumulated capital unit (the term on the left of equality) must be, in present value, equal to the cost $q_t\,\lambda_t$ of sacrificing one unit value of capital.

Acknowledging that capital accumulation requires costs for modifying capital, therefore, provides microeconomic foundations for Tobin's theory of q, originally elaborated in a macroeconomic context.[4]

3.4 From Micro to Macro: A Simple Dynamic General Equilibrium Model (DGE) of Representative Agents (Ramsey) for a Decentralized Economy

Let us reconsider the intertemporal expected utility function

$$E_0\sum_{t=0}^{\infty}\beta^t\left[\frac{C_t^{1-\sigma}}{1-\sigma} - \varphi\frac{L_t^{1-\gamma}}{1-\gamma}\right] \tag{3.25}$$

and set $L_t = 1$ (case of inelastic labor supply).

Ignoring the resulting constant $-\varphi/(1-\gamma)$ (which disappears in derivation computation), a single household optimum problem reduces to

$$max\ E_0\sum_{t=0}^{\infty}\beta^t\left[\frac{C_t^{1-\sigma}}{1-\sigma}\right]$$

[4]For exhaustive discussion on the topic, see Hayashi, F. (1982).

$$C_t + K_{t+1} = w_t + r_t K_t + (1-\delta)K_t \quad \forall t > 0 \tag{3.26}$$

In this intertemporal context, the household's choice is between whether to consume resources, currently earned, or to allocate them to capital accumulation.

The Lagrangian of the constrained maximum problem is

$$\max_{\{C_t, K_{t+1}\}} E_0 \sum_{t=0}^{\infty} \beta^t \{\frac{C_t^{1-\sigma}}{1-\sigma} + \lambda_t [w_t + r_t K_t + (1-\delta)K_t - C_t - K_{t+1}]\} \tag{3.27}$$

and first-order conditions of (3.27) for C_t, K_{t+1} are, respectively,

$$1/C_t^\sigma = \lambda_t$$
$$\beta E_t[\lambda_{t+1}(r_{t+1} + (1-\delta)] = \lambda_t \tag{3.28}$$

Both reduce to a single Euler equation:[5]

$$\beta E_t\left[\left(C_t^\sigma / C_{t+1}^\sigma\right)(r_{t+1} + (1-\delta)\right] = 1 \tag{3.29}$$

Now consider a single representative firm, which confronts with given factor prices, and a production technology (Cobb-Douglas) of kind

$$Y_t = A\left(K_t^d\right)^\alpha \left(L_t^d\right)^{1-\alpha} \tag{3.30}$$

The problem of the firm at any moment is

$$\max_{(L_t, K_t)} \Pi_t = \max A\left(K_t^d\right)^\alpha \left(L_t^d\right)^{1-\alpha} - w_t L_t^d - r_t K_t^d, \forall t > 0 \tag{3.31}$$

First-order conditions for (3.31) are

$$L^d{}_t: \qquad w_t = (1-\alpha)A\left(K_t^d / L_t^d\right)^\alpha \tag{3.32}$$
$$K_t^d: \qquad r_t = \alpha A\left(L_t^d / K_t^d\right)^{1-\alpha}$$

Conditions (3.29) and (3.32), for both a single generic consumer and a single generic firm, are now considered to refer to a *representative consumer* and a *representative firm.*

Setting conditions of equality between magnitudes for individuals and aggregate ones is the same as imposing on the economic system the following conditions of macroeconomic equilibrium:

[5]Tacitly from now on, we will always assume that the necessary condition of transversality is satisfied.

$$L_t = L_t^d = 1$$
$$K_t = K_t^d \tag{3.33}$$

Therefore, by incorporating conditions of equilibrium (3.33) in conditions at the margin of representative firm (3.32), we obtain that, in equilibrium for the economy, must be

$$r_t K_t = \alpha\, A \left(\frac{1}{K_t}\right)^{1-\alpha} K_t = \alpha A\, (K_t)^{\alpha} \tag{3.34}$$

And since it must be valid that

$$w_t + r_t K_t = Y = A\, (K_t)^{\alpha} \tag{3.35}$$

it is also valid that

$$w_t + r_t K_t + (1-\delta)K_t = A\, (K_t)^{\alpha} \; + (1-\delta)K_t \tag{3.36}$$

Thus, a single agent's budget constraint, in the aggregate becomes the following resources constraint for the economy:

$$C_t + K_{t+1} = A\, (K_t)^{\alpha} + (1-\delta)K_t \tag{3.37}$$

Equation (3.37) is the old fundamental equation of ad hoc macroeconomics. In a model without money, it is the aggregate equilibrium condition. In a model with money, it is the aggregate equilibrium condition of the goods market.

Identity between budget constraint and equilibrium conditions (on labor and capital services markets), on the one hand, and equality between aggregate demand and production, on the other, justifies the terminology sometimes used in the DSGE literature. The old Keynesian equilibrium condition in the goods market, as already said, is now called the *resource constraint*. However, in a DGE model, resource constraint must be compatible with an aggregate intertemporal optimality, and this requires compliance with the Euler condition.

Therefore, the simple (optimal) macroeconomic model consists of the three equations:

$$C_t + K_{t+1} = A\, (K_t)^{\alpha} + (1-\delta)K_t \tag{3.38}$$
$$\beta E_t\left[\left(\frac{C_t^{\sigma\sigma}}{C_{t+1}}\right)(\, r_{t+1} + (1-\delta)\right] = 1 \tag{3.39}$$
$$r_t = \alpha A\, (K_t)^{\alpha-1} \tag{3.40}$$

3.5 Discussion of Solution of Simple DGE Macroeconomic Model

How to analytically manage system (3.38)–(3.40)? It is a system of three equations in three unknowns, C_t, K_{t+1}, r_t.

If we were able to solve, e.g., (3.39) for C_t in function of r_{t+1}, given (3.40), we could reduce (3.38) to a finite-difference equation of first order in the variable K_t for each given C^{σ}_{t+1}.

Two considerations on this possibility.

Even after the improbable substitution, Eq. (3.38) would remain nonlinear, since it contains terms like $(K_t)^{\alpha}$.

However, (3.38) is not an ordinary finite-difference equation. It (a) contains the expectations operator, and (b) even if we could ignore the expectation operator, Eq. (3.38) is even nonlinear because in (3.39) the ratio C_t/C_{t+1} appears raised to the power σ.

Finally, (3.40) is also nonlinear, because it contains a term raised to (α−1).

To overcome these difficulties, the strategy is to transform the system (3.38)–(3.40) into one that approximates it but is linear and therefore solvable with methods of linear algebra.

A linear approximation can be obtained using first-order Taylor approximation. This requires knowledge of a solution of the system, in a neighborhood of which to approximate, and therefore, it is necessary to identify for (3.38)–(3.40) a point that constitutes a solution around which to make the approximation.

The natural solution in a dynamic model is a steady state. In the model we are considering, a steady state can be obtained as follows.

From (3.39), at steady state, it is

$$r = \frac{1}{\beta} - (1-\delta) = \frac{1-\beta(1-\delta)}{\beta} \tag{3.41}$$

From (3.40), we obtain[6]

$$(K)^{(1-\alpha)} = \frac{\alpha A\beta}{1-\beta(1-\delta)} \tag{3.42}$$

Equation (3.38) in steady state becomes

$$C + K = A\,(K)^{\alpha} + (1-\delta)K \tag{3.43}$$

And then,

[6]From (2) and (3), it follows $\alpha A\ (K)^{\alpha-1} = \frac{1-\beta(1-\delta)}{\beta}$ that is $(K)^{-(1-\alpha)} = \frac{1-\beta(1-\delta)}{\alpha A\beta}$, and then, $(K)^{(1-\alpha)} = \frac{\alpha A\beta}{1-\beta(1-\delta)}$ from which the Eq. (3.46) is obtained.

$$C = A\ (K)^{\alpha} - \delta K = Y - \delta K \tag{3.44}$$

Complete steady-state solution for variables (C, K, r, Y), therefore, is

$$C = Y - \delta K \tag{3.45}$$

$$K = \left(\frac{\alpha A \beta}{1 - \beta(1 - \delta)}\right)^{\frac{1}{1-\alpha}} \tag{3.46}$$

$$\mathrm{r} = \frac{1}{\beta} - (1 - \delta) \tag{3.47}$$

$$Y = A\ K^{\alpha} \tag{3.48}$$

3.6 Log-Linear Approximation of DGE Macroeconomic Model

To obtain a log-linear approximation of system (3.38)–(3.40), a practical method is to apply to a generic variable X_t the transformation $X_t = X(1+\widehat{x}_t)$,[7] where $\widehat{x}_t$ is the deviation of the log of X_t from steady-state log of X, i.e.,

$$\log X_t - \log X = \widehat{x}_t = x_t - \overline{x}.$$

Operating the proposed transformation on each (and all) variables of system (3.38)–(3.40), it becomes

[7]The logic of the proposed transformation lies in the fact that for each X_t is valid, the identity $X_t = X(\frac{X_t}{X})$, and then, $\log X_t - \log X = \log(\frac{X_t}{X})$. But $\log(\frac{X_t}{X}) = \log(\frac{X_t}{X})\log e = \log e^{\log(\frac{X_t}{X})}$ from which taking anti-logarithm $\frac{X_t}{X} = e^{\log(\frac{X_t}{X})}$ so that $X_t = Xe^{\log(\frac{X_t}{X})} = Xe^{\widehat{x}_t}$. For this function, it is possible to take Taylor approximation of first order around the steady state $\widehat{x}_t$=0 from which we get $X_t = Xe^{\widehat{x_t}}$ $= Xe^0 + e^0X(\widehat{x}_t - 0) \cong X(1+\widehat{x}_t)$. The latter is precisely the proposed variables' transformation.

Note that as a consequence of this result, we get $X_tY_t = X(1 + x_t)Y(1 + \widehat{y}_t) = XY(1 + \widehat{x}_t + \widehat{y}_t + \widehat{x}_t\widehat{y}_t)$. But $\widehat{x}_t\widehat{y}_t$, as $\widehat{x}_t$ and $\widehat{y}_t$ are numbers both close to zero, can be considered null, so that it results, $X_tY_t = X(1 + x_t)Y(1 + \widehat{y}_t) = XY(1 + \widehat{x}_t + \widehat{y}_t)$.

The considerations above carried out highlight that log-linearization of an equation, and therefore of a system, in the neighborhood of the stationary state, can be achieved: (a) by carrying out transformation $X_t = Xe^{\widehat{x_t}}$; or (b) directly by setting $X_t = X(1+\widehat{x}_t)$; or (c) transforming each expression into its logarithm and for each logarithm calculating f'(x)x$\widehat{\boldsymbol{x}}$, where f'(x) is the derivative at the steady state point of each logarithm in each equation. We will normally use the simple transformation $X_t = X(1+\widehat{x}_t)$, but often, depending on the context, we will also use one or the other method indifferently.

On the log-linear approximation, see King et al. (1988a, 1988b); Campbell, J. (1994); and especially Uhlig, H. (1999) in R. Marion, and A. Scott (eds).

$$C(1+\widehat{c}_t)+\mathrm{K}\left(1+\widehat{k}_{t+1}\right)=AK^{\alpha}\left(1+\alpha\widehat{k}_t\right)+(1-\delta)K\left(1+\widehat{k}_t\right) \tag{3.49}$$

$$\beta E_t\{C^{\sigma}\ (1+\sigma\widehat{c}_t)\ C^{-\sigma}\ (1-\sigma\widehat{c}_{t+1})\ [\mathrm{r}(1+\widehat{r}_{t+1})+(1-\delta)]\}=1 \tag{3.50}$$

$$\mathrm{r}(1+E_t\widehat{r}_{t+1})=\alpha AK^{-(1-\alpha)}\left[1+(\alpha-1)\widehat{k}_t\right] \tag{3.51}$$

Expanding (3.49), we get[8]

$$\widehat{k}_{t+1}=\frac{1}{\beta}\widehat{k}_t-\frac{C}{K}\widehat{c}_t \tag{3.52}$$

By referring to (3.50), we obtain[9]

$$E_t\widehat{c}_{t+1}=\frac{\beta}{\sigma}\mathrm{r}E_t\widehat{r}_{t+1}+\widehat{c}_t \tag{3.53}$$

Equation (3.53) can be further transformed by substituting the term $E_t r\widehat{r}_{t+1}$[10] with the equivalent expression

$$E_t r\widehat{r}_{t+1}=\alpha A\ (K)^{\alpha-1}(\alpha-1)\widehat{k}_{t+1}$$

After such substitution, we obtain[11]

---

[8]Equation (3.49) gives

$\mathrm{C}+K+C\widehat{c}_t+K\,\widehat{k}_{t+1}=AK^{\alpha}+(1-\delta)+\alpha AK^{\alpha}\widehat{k}_t+(1-\delta)K\widehat{k}_t.$

Simplifying terms $\mathrm{C}+K=AK^{\alpha}+(1-\delta)K$ and putting $K\widehat{k}_t$ in evidence to the right of equality's sign, it follows:

$$C\widehat{c}_t+K\,\widehat{k}_{t+1}=\left[\alpha AK^{(\alpha-1)}+(1-\delta)\right]K\widehat{k}_t$$

By remembering that $\alpha AK^{(\alpha-1)}+(1-\delta)=r+(1-\delta)=\frac{1}{\beta}$, divide both sides by K and solve for $\widehat{k}_{t+1}$. It follows Eq. (3.52) of the text.

[9]Mathematic steps are $\beta E_t\{(1+\sigma\widehat{c}_t)(1\text{-}\sigma c_{t+1})\ [\mathrm{r}(1+r_{t+1})\text{-}(1\text{-}\delta)]\}=$

$\beta E_t\{(1\text{-}\sigma\widehat{c}_{t+1}+\sigma\widehat{c}_t-\sigma^2\widehat{c}_t\widehat{c}_{t+1})\ [\mathrm{r}+\mathrm{r}\,\widehat{r}_{t+1}+(1\text{-}\delta)]\}=1$, that is

$\beta E_t\{(1\text{-}\sigma\widehat{c}_{t+1}+\sigma\widehat{c}_t)\ [\mathrm{r}\widehat{r}_{t+1}+\frac{1}{\beta}]\}=1.$

Rearranging

$\beta E_t\{(\mathrm{r}\widehat{r}_{t+1}\text{-}\sigma\mathrm{r}r_{t+1}c_{t+1}+\sigma\mathrm{r}r_{t+1}c_t)+(1-\sigma c_{t+1}+\sigma c_t)\frac{1}{\beta}]\}$

$=\beta E_t\{(\mathrm{r}\widehat{r}_{t+1}+[1-\sigma c_{t+1}+\sigma c_t]\ \frac{1}{\beta}]\}=1.$

Simplifying $E_t\{\beta\mathrm{r}\widehat{r}_{t+1}+1-\sigma\widehat{c}_{t+1}+\sigma\widehat{c}_t\}=1$, that is

$E_t\{(\beta\mathrm{r}\widehat{r}_{t+1}\ -\sigma c_{t+1}+\sigma c_t)\}=0$and solving for $E_t\widehat{c}_{t+1}$, it follows Eq. (3.53) of the text.

[10]From (3.51) it results $\mathrm{r}+rr_{t+1}=[\ \alpha AK^{-(1-\alpha)}+\alpha AK^{-(1-\alpha)}\ (\alpha-1)k_t]$ and being $\mathrm{r}=\alpha AK^{-(1-\alpha)}$ by simplifying results

$E_t r\widehat{r}_{t+1}=\alpha A\ (K)^{\alpha-1}(\alpha-1)\widehat{k}_{t+1}$

[11]Instead of referring to (3.50), being $r_{t+1}=\alpha A\ (K_{t+1})^{\alpha-1}$, you can directly refer to Euler's condition in the form:

$$E_t\widehat{c}_{t+1} = \widehat{c}_t + \frac{\beta A\alpha(\alpha-1)(K)^{\alpha-1}}{\sigma}\widehat{k}_{t+1} \tag{3.54}$$

The log-linearized system, therefore, becomes

$$\widehat{k}_{t+1} = \frac{1}{\beta}\widehat{k}_t - \frac{C}{K}\widehat{c}_t \tag{3.55}$$

$$E_t\hat{c}_{t+1} = \hat{c}_t + \frac{\beta\big(\alpha A\ (K)^{\alpha-1}(\alpha-1)}{\sigma}\hat{k}_{t+1} \tag{3.56}$$

$$E_t\widehat{r}_{t+1} = (\alpha-1)\widehat{k}_{t+1} \tag{3.57}$$

However, (3.57) is a multiple of (3.55), and its solution is given as soon as it is known $\widehat{k}_{t+1}$, so that considering only independent log-linearized equations, the system can be reduced to only two equations:

$$\widehat{k}_{t+1} = \frac{1}{\beta}\widehat{k}_t - \frac{C}{K}\widehat{c}_t \tag{3.58}$$

$$E_t\hat{c}_{t+1} = \hat{c}_t + \frac{\beta\big(\alpha A\ (K)^{\alpha-1}(\alpha-1)}{\sigma}\hat{k}_{t+1} \tag{3.59}$$

Equation (3.59) can be rewritten taking into account that from

$$\mathrm{r} = \frac{1}{\beta} - (1-\delta) \tag{3.60}$$

$$\mathrm{r} = \alpha A K^{(\alpha-1)} \tag{3.61}$$

and

$$\beta\left(\alpha A\ (K)^{(\alpha-1)}\right) = 1 - \beta(1-\delta) \tag{3.62}$$

By substituting (3.62) into (3.59), the log-linearized system finally becomes

---

$\beta E_t\{\left(C_t^{\sigma}/C_{t+1}^{\sigma}\right)\ [(\alpha A\ (K_{t+1})^{\alpha-1} + (1-\delta)]\} = 1$

and operate on this the transformation of variable for log-linearization. With transformed variables, it is

$\beta E_t\{C^{\sigma}\ (1+\sigma\widehat{c}_t)\ C^{-\sigma}\ (1-\sigma\widehat{c}_{t+1})\ [\alpha A\ (K)^{\alpha-1}\ (1+(\alpha-1)\widehat{k}_{t+1}) + (1-\delta)]\} = 1$

$\beta E_t\{(1-\sigma\widehat{c}_{t+1} + \sigma\widehat{c}_t - \sigma^2\widehat{c}_t\widehat{c}_{t+1})[\ \alpha A\ (K)^{\alpha-1} + (1-\delta) + (\alpha A\ (K)^{\alpha-1}(\alpha-1)\widehat{k}_{t+1})] = 1$

$\beta E_t\{(1-\sigma\widehat{c}_{t+1} + \sigma\widehat{c}_t - \sigma^2\widehat{c}_t\widehat{c}_{t+1})[\frac{1}{\beta} + (\alpha A\ (K)^{\alpha-1}(\alpha-1)\widehat{k}_{t+1}] = 1.$

Being $\widehat{c}_t\widehat{c}_{t+1} = 0$, and similarly for all the other products of terms with time indices, it follows Eq. (3.54) indicated in the text.

$$\widehat{k}_{t+1} = \frac{1}{\beta}\,\widehat{k}_t - \frac{c}{k}\widehat{c}_t \tag{3.63}$$

$$E_t\widehat{c}_{t+1} = \widehat{c}_t - \frac{(1-\alpha)[1-\beta(1-\delta)]}{\sigma}\widehat{k}_{t+1} \tag{3.64}$$

3.7 Methods of Solution of a Log-Linearized System: Indeterminate Coefficients

The previous model is a simplified one,[12] but it is useful for showing the solution method of indeterminate coefficients. This method exploits the initial intuition that every intertemporal maximum problem can be equivalently formulated as a dynamic programming problem.

A solution to a dynamic programming problem consists of looking for policy functions (the behavioral functions of control variables), invariant over time, which define control variables as functions of state variables, i.e., of variables that in the current instant are considered known and describe the state of the system.

In the problem we have studied so far, there are two control variables (i.e., two variables of choice, c_t, and k_{t+1}) and a state variable k_t, which is given at time t.

As we will soon see, in the stochastic version of the model we are considering, state variables are at least two k_t, a_t.

In that more general model, the policy functions (whose variables are independent of the time index) are those of consumption $c = c(k, a)$ and of capital desired for the next period $k' = f(k, a)$.

However, since the present model version ignores the stochastic variable, we will continue to ignore it for now. The policy functions to which we will refer in applying the method of indeterminate coefficients, therefore, are of the sort

$$c = c(k) \tag{3.65}$$

$$k' = f(k) \tag{3.66}$$

A linear expression of the above policy functions is

$$c = \eta_{ck}k \tag{3.67}$$

$$k' = \eta_{kk}k \tag{3.68}$$

where η_{ck} and η_{kk} are indeterminate coefficients.

[12] In particular, it ignores the stochastic evolution of technology which, as we will see, is the very cause of the economic cycle in the RBC model, according to the original intuition F. Kydland and Prescott; see Kydland, F. and Prescott, E. (1982), and especially Prescott, E. (1986).

Using this information, one can conjecture a simultaneous linear solution for the variables $\widehat{c}_t$ (and for it of the variable $E_t\widehat{c}_{t+1}$) and $\widehat{k}_{t+1}$ dependent on $\widehat{k}_t$, i.e.,

$$\widehat{c}_t = \eta_{ck}\widehat{k}_t \tag{3.69}$$

$$\widehat{k}_{t+1} = \eta_{kk}\widehat{k}_t \tag{3.70}$$

where η_{ck} and η_{kk} are unknown coefficients.

Substituting both (3.69) and (3.70) into (3.62) the assumed dynamics of desired (optimal) capital stock becomes

$$\eta_{kk}\widehat{k}_t = \frac{1}{\beta}\widehat{k}_t - \eta_{ck}\frac{C}{K}\widehat{k}_t \tag{3.71}$$

Identifying coefficients in (3.71), we have the following solution for the capital coefficient:

$$\eta_{kk} = \frac{1}{\beta} - \eta_{ck}\frac{C}{K} \tag{3.72}$$

Let us now consider (3.64). By replacing in it the hypothesized policy functions, it becomes

$$\eta_{ck}E_t\,\widehat{k}_{t+1} = \eta_{ck}\widehat{k}_t - \frac{(1-\alpha)[1-\beta(1-\delta)]}{\sigma}\eta_{kk}\widehat{k}_t$$

That is

$$\eta_{ck}\eta_{kk}\widehat{k}_t = \left[\eta_{ck} - \frac{(1-\alpha)[1-\beta(1-\delta)]}{\sigma}\eta_{kk}\right]\widehat{k}_t \tag{3.73}$$

By identifying coefficients of $\widehat{k}_t$ in (3.73), it follows

$$\eta_{ck}\eta_{kk} = \eta_{ck} - \frac{(1-\alpha)[1-\beta(1-\delta)]}{\sigma}\eta_{kk} \tag{3.74}$$

Substituting (3.72) in (3.74), we will have

$$\eta_{ck}\frac{1}{\beta} - \eta_{ck}^2\frac{C}{K} = \eta_{ck} - \frac{(1-\alpha)[1-\beta(1-\delta)]}{\sigma\beta} + \frac{(1-\alpha)[1-\beta(1-\delta)]}{\sigma}\eta_{ck}\frac{C}{K}$$

i.e.:

$$\eta_{ck}^2 \frac{C}{K} + \left[\frac{(1-\alpha)[1-\beta(1-\delta)]}{\sigma}\frac{C}{K} - \frac{1}{\beta}\right]\eta_{ck} - \frac{(1-\alpha)[1-\beta(1-\delta)]}{\sigma\beta} = 0 \quad (3.75)$$

Equation (3.75) is a quadratic equation in η_{ck}^2 which rewritten compactly appears as

$$a\,\eta_{ck}{}^2 + b\,\eta_{ck} - c = 0 \quad (3.76)$$

where

$$a = \frac{C}{K};\, \mathrm{b} = \left[\frac{(1-\alpha)[1-\beta(1-\delta)]}{\sigma}\frac{C}{K} - \frac{1}{\beta}\right];\ \mathrm{c} = \frac{(1-\alpha)[1-\beta(1-\delta)]}{\sigma\beta}$$

In (3.76), terms a and c are opposite in sign, and the equation has only one variation. The two real roots are therefore opposite, being (by the fact that $-c/a < 0$) their product negative.[13]

Furthermore, their sum (since $-b/a < 0$) is negative. It follows from this, that the minor root, the negative one, must be greater in absolute value.

Let μ_1 the minor root. By considering the product f(1)a, it will be $1 \epsilon\, [\mu_1, \mu_2]$ if f(1) a < 0 or 1 is esternal to interval $[\mu_1, \mu_2]$ if f(1)a > 0.

It turns out

$$\mathrm{f}(1) = \frac{C}{K} + \frac{(1-\alpha)[1-\beta(1-\delta)]}{\sigma}\frac{C}{K} - \frac{1}{\beta} - \frac{(1-\alpha)[1-\beta(1-\delta)]}{\sigma\beta} \quad (3.77)$$

If f(1) > 0 it must also be

$$\frac{C}{K} + \frac{(1-\alpha)[1-\beta(1-\delta)]}{\sigma}\frac{C}{K} > \frac{1}{\beta} + \frac{(1-\alpha)[1-\beta(1-\delta)]}{\sigma\beta} \quad (3.78)$$

or else

$$\frac{C}{K}\left(1 + \frac{(1-\alpha)[1-\beta(1-\delta)]}{\sigma}\right) > \frac{1}{\beta}\left(1 + \frac{(1-\alpha)[1-\beta(1-\delta)]}{\sigma}\right) \quad (3.79)$$

But this would require $C/K > 1/\beta$ which being $1/\beta > 1$ would imply $C > K$, which is impossible to occur, and therefore it holds f(1) < 0. It follows from that $1 \notin [\mu_1, \mu_2]$.

Since the value 1 falls outside the interval that has as lower extreme the absolute value of smallest root, for stability and uniqueness of solution, we take the solution that is minor in absolute value, i.e.,

[13] See Review of quadratic equations, Appendix in Chap. 2.

$$\eta_{ck} = -\frac{1}{2a}\left(b + \sqrt{b^2 - 4ac}\right) \tag{3.80}$$

Finally, substituting (3.80) in the Eq. (3.72) we obtain

$$\eta_{kk} = \frac{1}{\beta} - \frac{1}{2a}\left(b + \sqrt{b^2 - 4ac}\right)\frac{C}{K} \tag{3.81}$$

With (3.80) and (3.81) both coefficients remain determined, and therefore, as the reader can verify, both policy functions are defined.

3.8 A Model of a Decentralized Economy, with Inelastic Labor Supply, as a Basic Model of Real Business Cycle

We will now study the aggregate model of representative agent (3.55)–(3.57) as a basic model of Real Business Cycle.[14]

DGE Model (3.55)–(3.57) becomes a model of a real cycle when among relevant variables is included a variable subject to stochastic shocks over time.

For studying the solution of this stochastic model, rather than replicating the method of indeterminate coefficients, we will consider a theoretical method, due to Blanchard and Kahn.[15]

Preliminarily, let's proceed with the study of the model.

Households

For households, behavioral hypotheses remain the same as before, including the assumption $L_t = 1$, that labor supply is inelastic. Households maximize expected inter-temporal utility, which requires that for the choices' variables C_t, K_{t+1}, are verified first order-conditions, i.e., the same previously seen

$$1/C_t^{\sigma} = \lambda_t \tag{3.82}$$

$$\beta E_t[\lambda_{t+1}(\ r_{t+1} + (1-\delta)] = \lambda_t \tag{3.83}$$

which can be reduced to a unique Euler equation

$$\beta E_t\left[\left(C_t^{\sigma}/C_{t+1}^{\sigma}\right)\ (\ r_{t+1} + (1-\delta)\right] = 1 \tag{3.84}$$

[14]The denomination real business cycle models for this kind of model is due to Long, J. and Plosser, C. (1983).

[15]See Blanchard, O.J. and C.M. Kahn (1980), op cit. On the solution of systems of rational expectations see also Sims, C. A. (2001).

Firms

The representative firm produces only one good Y aiming at maximizing its profit.[16] It has access to a production technology represented by a Cobb-Douglas function, which includes a global productivity factor A_t, that is,

$$Y_t = A_t \left(K_t^d\right)^{\alpha} \left(L_t^d\right)^{1-\alpha}$$

The first-order conditions for maximum profit are

$$L^d{}_t: \quad w_t = (1-\alpha)A_t \left(K_t^d / L_t^d\right)^{\alpha} \tag{3.85}$$

$$K_t^d: \quad r_t = \alpha\, A_t \left(K_t^d / L_t^d\right)^{\alpha - 1} \tag{3.86}$$

It is assumed that global productivity over time is subject to stochastic shock, following a recursive process AR(1) in logarithm, according to equation:[17]

$$\log A_t = \rho \, \log A_{t-1} + \varepsilon_t \qquad\qquad 0 < \rho < 1 \tag{3.87}$$

Equations of Macroeconomic Equilibrium

Equilibrium equations of the model considered become

$$C_t + K_{t+1} = A_t \left(K_t\right)^{\alpha} + (1-\delta)K_t \tag{3.88}$$

$$\beta E_t\left[\left(C_t^{\sigma} / C_{t+1}^{\sigma}\right) \left(r_{t+1} + (1-\delta)\right] = 1 \tag{3.89}$$

$$r_t = \alpha\, A_t \left(\frac{1}{K_t}\right)^{1-\alpha} = \alpha\, A_t (K_t)^{\alpha-1} \tag{3.90}$$

$$\log A_t = \rho \, \log A_{t-1} + \varepsilon_t \tag{3.91}$$

Steady-State Equilibrium

Steady-state of the model is defined by the following conditions:

$$C + K = A\,(K)^{\alpha} + (1-\delta)K \tag{3.92}$$

$$\beta(r + (1-\delta)] = 1 \tag{3.93}$$

---

[16] The goal of a representative firm now becomes

Max Π_t = max $A_t \left(K_t^d\right)^{\alpha} \left(L_t^d\right)^{1-\alpha} - w_t L^d{}_t \text{-} \ r_t K_t^d$.

[17] Technology shocks are supposed to follow an exponential autoregressive process over time of the kind $A_t = A_{t-1}^{\rho} e^{\varepsilon_t}$. The natural logarithm of this process matches Eq. (3.87) above. A more general expression of the stochastic process admits the following trend: $A_t = A^{1-\rho} A_{t-1}^{\rho} e^{\varepsilon_t}$ where A > 0 is a constant and $-1 < \rho < 1$ is the persistence parameter of the first-order autoregressive process. The variable ε_t is the stochastic error term.

$$r = \alpha A(K)^{\alpha-1} \tag{3.94}$$

$$\log A = \rho \log A = 0 \tag{3.95}$$

Log-Linearization Around a Stationary Point
Being log A $= 0$[18], so that logarithmic deviation becomes $\widehat{a}_t = \log A_t$, the log-linear approximation of stochastic process (3.56) gives

$$\widehat{a}_t = \rho\widehat{a}_{t-1} + \varepsilon_t \tag{3.96}$$

By operating the transformation $X_t = X(1+\widehat{x}_t)$, $\widehat{x}_t = \log X_t - \log X$ on each of the remaining variables of the model, the corresponding equations result

$$\frac{c}{k}\widehat{c}_t + \widehat{k}_{t+1} = \frac{1}{\beta}\widehat{k}_t + \frac{1}{\alpha}\left[\frac{1}{\beta} - 1 + \delta\right]\widehat{a}_t \tag{3.97}$$

$$\sigma\widehat{c}_t = -\sigma E_t\widehat{c}_{t+1} + [1-\beta(1-\delta)]\rho\widehat{a}_t + (\alpha-1)\,[1-\beta(1-\delta)]\widehat{k}_{t+1} \tag{3.98}$$

$$\widehat{a}_t = \rho\widehat{a}_{t-1} + \varepsilon_t \tag{3.99}$$

For subsequent considerations, however, it is convenient to rewrite models (3.97)–(3.99) by reporting on the same side as the expected terms for t+1, i.e.,

$$(\alpha-1)[1-\beta(1-\delta)]\widehat{k}_{t+1} - \sigma E_t\widehat{c}_{t+1} = -\sigma\widehat{c}_t - [1-\beta(1-\delta)]\,\rho\widehat{a}_t \tag{3.100}$$

$$\widehat{k}_{t+1} = \frac{1}{\beta}\widehat{k}_t - \frac{c}{k}\widehat{c}_t + \frac{1}{\alpha}\left[\frac{1}{\beta} - 1 + \delta\right]\widehat{a}_t \tag{3.101}$$

$$\widehat{a}_{t+1} = \rho\widehat{a}_t + \varepsilon_{t+1} \tag{3.102}$$

3.9 The Blanchard-Kahn Method for Solving Systems with Rational Expectations

We now review the Blanchard-Kahn method (already seen in general and with an application of economic theory in Sect. 2.8 of Chap. 2) by redefining concepts and symbology appropriate to the models we are considering, even at cost of some redundancy.

A model with rational expectations generally takes a typical form:[19]

[18] The Eq. (3.95) verifies $\log A = 0$ since $\rho \neq 1$ and that implies $A = 1$.

[19] This section goes along the lines of Kolasa M. (Accessed: 10 March 2023).

$$A_1 \begin{bmatrix} X_{t+1} \\ E_t P_{t+1} \end{bmatrix} = A_0 \begin{bmatrix} X_t \\ P_t \end{bmatrix} + \gamma Z_{t+1} \tag{3.103}$$

Variables in (3.103) have the following meaning:

- A_1 and A_0 are matrices of the type (n+m) × (n+m), being n the dimension of vectors $X_t$and X_{t+1}, while m is the dimension of vectors $E_t P_{t+1}$and P_t.
- X_t and X_{t+1} are vectors of predetermined variables at time t and t+1, including the stochastic process, usually of the type AR(1); predetermined variables are state variables.
- P_t and $E_t P_{t+1}$are also vectors of variables that enter the model in the form of expectations variables. They are forward-looking variables, or non-predetermined, or even, jump variables.
- Z_t is a vector of dimension k inclusive of the stochastic shocks, and therefore, the matrix γ is of the type (n+m) × k.

Let A_1 be nonsingular, so that it admits the inverse A_1^{-1}. Pre-multiplying by A_1^{-1}, the system (3.103) becomes

$$\begin{bmatrix} X_{t+1} \\ E_t P_{t+1} \end{bmatrix} = A_1^{-1} A_0 \begin{bmatrix} X_t \\ P_t \end{bmatrix} + A_1^{-1} \gamma Z_{t+1} \tag{3.104}$$

And letting $A = A_1^{-1} A_0$, $R = A_1^{-1} \gamma$, it is

$$\begin{bmatrix} X_{t+1} \\ E_t P_{t+1} \end{bmatrix} = A \begin{bmatrix} X_t \\ P_t \end{bmatrix} + R Z_{t+1} \tag{3.105}$$

By performing already known *Jordan decomposition*, matrix A of system (3.105), can be decomposed in the form:

$$\mathrm{A} = \mathrm{C} \Lambda \mathrm{C}^{-1}$$

Here, Λ is a diagonal matrix, with eigenvalues λ_i on the main diagonal arranged in order of increasing absolute value. It is assumed that A has n+m distinct eigenvalues, and C is the matrix of eigenvector solutions of systems of the type $Ax_i = \lambda_i$ with λ_i given, and coinciding with the i-th eigenvalue, i = 1,. . ., n+m.

Given A = CΛC^{-1}, premultiplying system (3.105) by C^{-1}, we obtain

$$C^{-1} \begin{bmatrix} X_{t+1} \\ E_t P_{t+1} \end{bmatrix} = C^{-1} A \begin{bmatrix} X_t \\ P_t \end{bmatrix} + C^{-1} R Z_{t+1} \tag{3.106}$$

According to Jordan decomposition, being $C^{-1}A = \Lambda C^{-1}$, it follows

$$C^{-1}\begin{bmatrix} X_{t+1} \\ E_t P_{t+1} \end{bmatrix} = \Lambda C^{-1}\begin{bmatrix} X_t \\ P_t \end{bmatrix} + C^{-1} R\, Z_{t+1} \qquad (3.107)$$

System (3.107) can be conveniently decomposed by blocks, by applying the same decomposition of the eigenvalue matrix of the form:

$$\Lambda = \begin{bmatrix} \Lambda_1 & 0 \\ 0 & \Lambda_2 \end{bmatrix} \qquad (3.108)$$

In this decomposition, $\Lambda_1$is a square matrix of order n* × n*, which collects in decreasing order the eigenvalues in modulus smaller than unity (within the circle with unit radius), and Λ_2 of order m* × m*, which collects in decreasing order the eigenvalues outside the circle of unit radius (with modulus greater than unity).

Also, the matrices A, C^{-1}, and R are decomposed by blocks as follows:

$$A = \begin{bmatrix} A_{11[n\ x\ n]} & A_{12\left[n\ x\ m\right.} \\ A_{21[m\ x\ n]} & A_{22\ [m\ x\ m]} \end{bmatrix}; \qquad (3.109)$$

$$C^{-1} = \begin{bmatrix} C_{11[n*x\ n]} & C_{12\left[n*x\ m\right.} \\ C_{21\ [m*x\ n]} & C_{22[m*x\ m]} \end{bmatrix}; \quad R = \begin{bmatrix} R_{1\left[n\ x\ k\right.} \\ R_{2[m\ x\ k]} \end{bmatrix}$$

Let us define vectors $Y_{t[n^* \times 1]}$ and $Q_{t[m^* \times 1]}$ corresponding, respectively, to

$$\begin{bmatrix} Y_t \\ Q_t \end{bmatrix} = C^{-1}\begin{bmatrix} X_t \\ P_t \end{bmatrix} \qquad (3.110)$$

This allows us to rewrite the system (3.110) in the form:

$$\widetilde{E}_t \begin{bmatrix} Y_{t+1} \\ Q_{t+1} \end{bmatrix} = \Lambda \begin{bmatrix} Y_t \\ Q_t \end{bmatrix} + C^{-1} R\, Z_{t+1} \qquad (3.111)$$

where $\widetilde{E}_t$ is the expectation operator modified so that

$$\widetilde{E}_t X_{t+1} = X_{t+1}; \qquad \widetilde{E}_t P_{t+1} = P_{t+1}$$

With this transformation, we consider the bottom block of (3.111) and iterate that block forward into expectations for $j > 0$. Being $E_t\, Z_{t+j} = 0$, you get the solution:

$$E_t Q_{t+1+j} = \Lambda_2^j Q_t \qquad (3.112)$$

But eigenvalues collected in the diagonal matrix Λ_2 are all in modulus greater than unity, so the only nonexplosive solution for this system is the one for $Q_t = 0\ \forall t$.

Using the transformation (3.110), and taking into account the block structure of C^{-1}, condition $Q_t = 0$ becomes

$$\begin{bmatrix} C_{21\,[m*x\,n]} & C_{22[m*x\,m]} \end{bmatrix} \begin{bmatrix} X_t \\ P_t \end{bmatrix} = 0 \tag{3.113}$$

That is,

$$C_{21}X_t + C_{22}\,P_t = 0 \tag{3.114}$$

The latter solved for the vector of non-predetermined variables P_t gives

$$P_t = -C_{22}^{-1}C_{21}X_t \tag{3.115}$$

Solution (3.115), therefore, provides non-predetermined variables as a function of state variables.

Substituting this solution in (3.67), we obtain predetermined variables as a function of state variables

$$X_{t+1} = A_{11} - \left(A_{12}C_{22}^{-1}C_{21}\right)X_t + R_1 Z_{t+1} \tag{3.116}$$

So, we have obtained a complete and unique solution of the system (3.103), written in recurrence form and as a function of state variables.

3.10 Solution of the Basic Real Business Cycle Model with Blanchard-Kahn Method

To apply the Blanchard-Kahn method just described to system (3.100)–(3.102), we must first of all rewrite it in matrix form. The first two equations of (3.100)–(3.102) give

$$E_t\left\{\begin{bmatrix} (\alpha-1)[1-\beta(1-\delta)] & -\sigma \\ 1 & o \end{bmatrix}\begin{bmatrix} \widehat{k}_{t+1} \\ \widehat{c}_{t+1} \end{bmatrix}\right\} = \begin{bmatrix} 0 & -\sigma \\ \frac{1}{\beta} & -\frac{C}{k} \end{bmatrix}\begin{bmatrix} \widehat{k}_t \\ \widehat{c}_t \end{bmatrix}$$
$$+ \begin{bmatrix} -[1-\beta(1-\delta)]\rho \\ \frac{1}{\alpha}\left(\frac{1}{\beta} - 1 + \delta\right) \end{bmatrix}\widehat{a}_t \tag{3.117}$$

Or, naming

$$A = \begin{bmatrix} (\alpha - 1)[1 - \beta(1 - \delta)] & -\sigma \\ 1 & o \end{bmatrix}; B = \begin{bmatrix} 0 & -\sigma \\ \frac{1}{\beta} & \frac{c}{k} \end{bmatrix}$$

$$\text{And } x_t = \begin{bmatrix} \widehat{k}_t \\ \widehat{c}_t \end{bmatrix}; G = \begin{bmatrix} -[1 - \beta(1 - \delta)]\rho \\ \frac{1}{\alpha}\left(\frac{1}{\beta} - 1 + \delta\right) \end{bmatrix},$$

in vector form system (3.117) becomes

$$E_t A x_{t+1} = B x_t + G\widehat{a}_t \tag{3.118}$$

System (3.118), admitting A is invertible, can be set in the canonical form of rational expectations:

$$E_t x_{t+1} = A^{-1} B x_t - A^{-1} G\widehat{a}_t = C x_t + F\widehat{a}_t \tag{3.119}$$

3.11 Jordan Transformation Applied to System in Expectations in the Basic Real Business Cycle Model

We know that matrix C of the system in expectations can be transformed into Jordan decomposition $C = P^{-1}\Lambda\, P$ where P matrix of eigenvectors of Λ, and $P^{-1}$is the inverse matrix of P.

By substituting for C in (3.119), we have

$$E_t x_{t+1} = P^{-1}\Lambda\, P x_t + F\widehat{a}_t \tag{3.120}$$

Pre-multiplying by P, it follows

$$E_t P x_{t+1} = \Lambda\, P x_t + PF\widehat{a}_t \tag{3.121}$$

By defining vectors $y_t = Px_t$, and $Q = PF$, system (3.121) written in recurrence form becomes

$$E_t y_{t+1} = \Lambda y_t + Q\widehat{a}_t \tag{3.122}$$

By carrying the following decomposition out on system (3.123),

$$E_t\begin{bmatrix} y_{1,t+1} \\ y_{2,t+1} \end{bmatrix} = \begin{bmatrix} \lambda_1 & 0 \\ 0 & \lambda_2 \end{bmatrix}\begin{bmatrix} y_{1,t} \\ y_{2,t} \end{bmatrix} + \begin{bmatrix} Q_1 \\ Q_2 \end{bmatrix}\widehat{a}_t \tag{3.123}$$

the following scalar equations to solve are obtained:

$$\begin{aligned} E_t y_{1,t+1} &= \lambda_1\, y_{1t} + Q_1\widehat{a}_t \\ E_t y_{2,t+1} &= \lambda_2\, y_{2t} + Q_2\widehat{a}_t \end{aligned} \tag{3.124}$$

Since eigenvalues in matrix Λ are ordered by increasing absolute value, it will be $|\lambda_1| < 1,\ |\lambda_2| > 1$.

For the second equation of (3.124), where it is $|\lambda_2| > 1$, the stable solution is obtained from the equation:

$$y_{2t} = \left(\frac{1}{\lambda_2}\right)E_t y_{2,t+1} - \frac{Q_2}{\lambda_2}\,\widehat{a}_t \tag{3.125}$$

Indeed, by iterating expectations j periods forward and taking on account $E_t\widehat{a}_{t+j} = \rho^j\widehat{a}_t$, it follows

$$y_{2t+j} = \left(\frac{1}{\lambda_2}\right)^j E_t y_{2,t+1+j} - \frac{Q_2}{\lambda_2}\sum_{i=0}^{j}\left(\frac{\rho}{\lambda_2}\right)^i\widehat{a}_t \tag{3.126}$$

From (3.127) for $j\rightarrow\infty$, you have $E_t y_{2,\,t+1+j} = 0$, and therefore,

$$y_{2t} = -\frac{Q_2}{\lambda_2}\,\widehat{a}_t\sum_{i=0}^{\infty}\left(\frac{\rho}{\lambda_2}\right)^i = -\frac{Q_2}{\lambda_2}\,\frac{1}{1-\frac{\rho}{\lambda_2}}\widehat{a}_t = \frac{Q_2}{\rho-\lambda_2}\,\widehat{a}_t \tag{3.127}$$

The solution (3.127) is in terms of the variables $y_{2,\,t+1}, y_{2t}$.

To rewrite it in terms of original variables, we proceed as follows. We observe that by definition of y_t, it is

$$\begin{bmatrix} y_{1,t} \\ y_{2,t} \end{bmatrix} = Px_t = \begin{bmatrix} u_1 & v_1 \\ u_2 & v_2 \end{bmatrix}\begin{bmatrix} \widehat{k}_t \\ \widehat{c}_t \end{bmatrix} \tag{3.128}$$

where u and v are eigenvectors associated, respectively, to λ_1 and λ_3. So, we can write

$$y_{2,t} = u_2\widehat{k}_t + v_2\widehat{c}_t \tag{3.129}$$

And therefore, from (3.127), it is

$$u_2\widehat{k}_t + v_2\widehat{c}_t = \frac{Q_2}{\rho - \lambda_2}\,\widehat{a}_t \tag{3.130}$$

Solving (3.130) for the control variable $\widehat{c}_t$, you obtain

$$\widehat{c}_t = \frac{Q_2}{v_2(\rho - \lambda_2)}\,\widehat{a}_t - \frac{u_2}{v_2}\widehat{k}_t \tag{3.131}$$

Equation (3.131) gives the control variable $\widehat{c}_t$ as a function of both state variables, i.e., it defines the policy function of $\widehat{c}_t$.

We now write the first equation of the system (3.129) as a policy function. From

$$y_{1,t} = u_1\widehat{k}_t + v_1\widehat{c}_t \tag{3.132}$$

substituting the value of $\widehat{c}_t$ (3.131) in (3.132), it follows that

$$y_{1,t} = u_1\widehat{k}_t + \frac{v_1 Q_2}{v_2(\rho - \lambda_2)}\,\widehat{a}_t - \frac{v_1 u_2}{v_2}\widehat{k}_t \tag{3.133}$$

That is,

$$y_{1,t} = \frac{u_1 v_2 - v_1 u_2}{v_2}\,\widehat{k}_t + \frac{v_1 Q_2}{v_2(\rho - \lambda_2)}\,\widehat{a}_t \tag{3.134}$$

Since we are searching for the solution of $E_t\, y_{1,\ t\ +\ 1}$ in terms of the original variables, the first equation of the system (3.128) is

$$E_t y_{1,t+1} = \lambda_1 y_{1,t} \ + Q_1\widehat{a}_t \tag{3.135}$$

And by substituting in (3.135) the value of $y_{1,\ t}$ in (3.134), it is

$$E_t\left[\frac{u_1 v_2 - v_1 u_2}{v_2}\,\widehat{k}_{t+1} + \frac{v_1 Q_2}{v_2(\rho - \lambda_2)}\,\widehat{a}_{t+1}\right] =$$

$$\lambda_1\frac{u_1 v_2 - v_1 u_2}{v_2}\,\widehat{k}_t + \lambda_1\frac{v_1 Q_2}{v_2(\rho - \lambda_2)}\,\widehat{a}_t + Q_1\widehat{a}_t \tag{3.136}$$

Taking expectations on both sides, it follows that

$$\frac{u_1 v_2 - v_1 u_2}{v_2}\,\widehat{k}_{t+1} + \frac{v_1 Q_2}{v_2(\rho - \lambda_2)}\,\rho\widehat{a}_t$$

$$= \lambda_1 \frac{u_1 v_2 - v_1 u_2}{v_2} \widehat{k}_t + \lambda_1 \frac{v_1 Q_2}{v_2(\rho - \lambda_2)} \widehat{a}_t$$

And more

$$\frac{u_1 v_2 - v_1 u_2}{v_2} \widehat{k}_{t+1}$$

$$= \lambda_1 \frac{u_1 v_2 - v_1 u_2}{v_2} \widehat{k}_t + \lambda_1 \frac{v_1 Q_2}{v_2(\rho - \lambda_2)} \widehat{a}_t - \frac{v_1 Q_2}{v_2(\rho - \lambda_2)} \rho \widehat{a}_t + Q_1 \widehat{a}_t$$

$$= \lambda_1 \frac{u_1 v_2 - v_1 u_2}{v_2} \widehat{k}_t + \frac{v_1 Q_2(\lambda_1 - \rho) + Q_1 v_2(\lambda_2 - \rho)}{v_2(\rho - \lambda_2)} \widehat{a}_t \tag{3.137}$$

Solving (3.137) for $\widehat{k}_{t+1}$

$$\widehat{k}_{t+1} = \frac{v_2}{u_1 v_2 - v_1 u_2} \lambda_1 \frac{u_1 v_2 - v_1 u_2}{v_2} \widehat{k}_t + \frac{v_1 Q_2(\lambda_1 - \rho) + Q_1 v_2(\lambda_2 - \rho)}{v_2(\rho - \lambda_2)} \frac{v_2}{u_1 v_2 - v_1 u_2} \widehat{a}_t \tag{3.138}$$

That is,

$$\widehat{k}_{t+1} = \lambda_1 \widehat{k}_t + \frac{v_1 Q_2(\lambda_1 - \rho) + Q_1 v_2(\lambda_2 - \rho)}{v_2(\rho - \lambda_2)} \frac{1}{u_1 - \frac{v_1}{v_2} u_2} \widehat{a}_t \tag{3.139}$$

And ultimately,

$$\widehat{k}_{t+1} = \lambda_1 \widehat{k}_t + \frac{\frac{v_1 Q_2}{v_2} \frac{(\lambda_1 - \rho)}{(\rho - \lambda_2)} + Q_1}{u_1 - \frac{v_1}{v_2} u_2} \widehat{a}_t \tag{3.140}$$

Equation (3.140) is a policy function of the control variable $\widehat{k}_{t+1}$.

The complete system, solved as a function of the predetermined variables, is

$$\widehat{k}_{t+1} = \lambda_1 \widehat{k}_t + \frac{\frac{v_1 Q_2}{v_2} \frac{(\lambda_1 - \rho)}{(\rho - \lambda_2)} + Q_1}{u_1 - \frac{v_1}{v_2} u_2} \widehat{a}_t = \lambda_1 \widehat{k}_t + g\, \widehat{a}_t \tag{3.141}$$

$$\widehat{a}_{t+1} = \rho \widehat{a}_t + \varepsilon_{t+1} \tag{3.142}$$

$$\widehat{c}_t = \frac{Q_2}{v_2(\rho - \lambda_2)} \widehat{a}_t - \frac{u_2}{v_2} \widehat{k}_t \tag{3.143}$$

The Eqs. (3.141)–(3.143) are the so-called state-space formulation.

They describe recursively, in the first subsystem, the evolution of both state variables, according to the values of the same variables of the previous period.

Further, by distinguishing the state variables into predetermined and non-predetermined, it can be stated that the systems (3.141)–(3.143) show the evolution of the non-predetermined variables as the function of predetermined and exogenous variables, i.e.,

$$\begin{bmatrix} \widehat{k}_{t+1} \\ \widehat{a}_{t+1} \end{bmatrix} = \begin{bmatrix} \lambda_1 & g \\ 0 & \rho \end{bmatrix} \begin{bmatrix} \widehat{k}_t \\ \widehat{a}_t \end{bmatrix} + \begin{bmatrix} 0 \\ 1 \end{bmatrix} \varepsilon_t \tag{3.144}$$

$$\widehat{c}_t = \frac{Q_2}{v_2(\rho - \lambda_2)} \widehat{a}_t - \frac{u_2}{v_2} \widehat{k}_t \tag{3.145}$$

Formulations (3.144)–(3.145) are the ones used in simulations since, given the initial values $\widehat{k}_0, \widehat{a}_0$ and generating random numbers for ε_t, it is possible to construct artificial time series for t = 0 ……T, of all system's variables, whose statistical properties can be compared with the statistical series of the effective economy.

3.12 Basic RBC Model of Centralized Economy with (a) Flexible Labor Supply and (b) Stochastic Shocks to Technology and Aggregate Demand

Generally speaking, by ignoring factors' price equations in RBC model, an equivalent central planner model is obtained, which is more convenient for simulation purposes.

For the models (3.92)–(3.95), a similar procedure leads to the following model for a centralized economy:

$$C_t^{\sigma} \varphi L_t^{1+\gamma} = (1-\alpha) \mathrm{Y_t} \tag{3.146}$$

$$\beta E_t \left[\left(\frac{C_t^{\sigma}}{C_{t+1}^{\sigma}} \right) \left(\alpha \frac{\mathrm{Y_{t+1}}}{K_t} + (1-\delta) \right) \right] = 1 \tag{3.147}$$

$$\mathrm{Y_t} = A_t K_t^{\alpha} L_t^{(1-\alpha)} \tag{3.148}$$

$$K_{t+1} = \mathrm{Y_t} - C_t - G_t + (1-\delta) K_t \tag{3.149}$$

$$\log G_t - \log \overline{G} = \rho_g \left(\log G_{t-1} - \log \overline{G} \right) + \varepsilon_{g,t} \tag{3.150}$$

$$\log A_t = \rho_a \log A_{t-1} + \varepsilon_{a,t} \tag{3.151}$$

Compared to models (3.146)–(3.151), that of Eqs. (3.146)–(3.151) includes further Eq. (3.150) which considers exogenous public expenditure as a stochastic variable, assumed to follow AR(1) process in logarithm distance from the log of steady state.

Steady state of models (3.146)–(3.151) is obtained by solving the following equations:

$$C^{\sigma}\varphi L^{1+\gamma} = (1-\alpha)\mathrm{Y} \tag{3.152}$$

$$K = \beta(\alpha\mathrm{Y} + K(1-\delta)) \tag{3.153}$$

$$\mathrm{Y} = A\, K^{\alpha}L^{(1-\alpha)} \tag{3.154}$$

$$K = \mathrm{Y} - C - G + (1-\delta)K \tag{3.155}$$

$$\mathrm{A} = 1; \quad G = \mathrm{gg}\; Y \tag{3.156}$$

$$\varepsilon_a = \varepsilon_g = 0 \tag{3.157}$$

3.12.1 *Steady-State Variables as Functions of Parameters*

As will be better seen, for a numerical solution, the steady-state variables must expressed as a function of the *fundamental* parameters of the model.

For the systems (3.152)–(3.157), one goes on in the following way. From (3.153), it follows that[20]

$$\frac{K}{\mathrm{Y}} = \frac{\alpha\beta}{1-\beta(1-\delta)} \tag{3.158}$$

From (3.156)

$$\frac{\mathrm{G}}{\mathrm{Y}} = \mathrm{gg} \tag{3.159}$$

From (3.154)[21]

$$\mathrm{Y} = \left(\frac{K}{Y}\right)^{\frac{\alpha}{1-\alpha}} L \tag{3.160}$$

From (3.155)

[20] Here are algebraic steps: $K = (\alpha\beta\mathrm{Y} + \beta K(1-\delta)) \rightarrow K - \beta K(1-\delta) = \alpha\beta\mathrm{Y} \rightarrow K(1-\beta(1-\delta)) = \alpha\beta\mathrm{Y}$, whence (3.158).

[21] Passages are $\mathrm{Y}^{\alpha} = K^{\alpha}\left(\frac{L}{Y}\right)^{(1-\alpha)} \rightarrow \mathrm{Y}^{\frac{\alpha}{1-\alpha}} = K^{\frac{\alpha}{1-\alpha}}\left(\frac{L}{Y}\right) \rightarrow \mathrm{Y}\ \mathrm{Y}^{\frac{\alpha}{1-\alpha}} = K^{\frac{\alpha}{1-\alpha}} L$ from which (3.160).

$$\frac{\mathrm{C}}{\mathrm{Y}} = \left(1 - \frac{\mathrm{G}}{\mathrm{Y}} - \delta\frac{\mathrm{K}}{\mathrm{Y}}\right) \tag{3.161}$$

From (3.152)

$$\varphi L^{1+\gamma} = (1-\alpha)C^{-\sigma}Y \tag{3.162}$$

That is to say

$$\varphi = (1-\alpha)C^{-\sigma}\frac{Y}{L^{1+\gamma}} \tag{3.163}$$

Working time L is taken as a parameter, expressed as a fraction of time endowment. In the applications, the steady-state value L = 1/3 is assumed.

Using notation K = kss, C = css, etc., and for steady-state ratios to Y, notation K/Y = ksy, etc., we will put

$$\mathrm{ksy} = \frac{\mathrm{K}}{\mathrm{Y}} = \frac{\alpha\beta}{1-\beta(1-\delta)} \tag{3.164}$$

$$\mathrm{hss} = \mathrm{L} \tag{3.165}$$

$$\mathrm{gs} = \frac{\mathrm{G}}{\mathrm{y}} = \ \mathrm{ggy} \tag{3.166}$$

$$\mathrm{csy} = \frac{\mathrm{C}}{\mathrm{y}} = 1 - \mathrm{gsy} - \delta\mathrm{ksy} \tag{3.167}$$

so that

$$\mathrm{Kss} = \mathrm{ksy\ Yss} \tag{3.168}$$

$$\mathrm{Gss} = \mathrm{gsy\ Yss} \tag{3.169}$$

$$\mathrm{Css} = \mathrm{csy\ Yss} \tag{3.170}$$

$$Yss = ksy^{\frac{\alpha}{1-\alpha}}\,hss \tag{3.171}$$

$$\varphi = (1-\alpha)Css^{-\sigma}\left(\frac{Yss}{hss^{1+\gamma}}\right) \tag{3.172}$$

Log-linearized equations, corresponding to each of (3.152)–(3.157), are as follows:

$$\sigma\, c_t + \varphi(1+\gamma)l_t = (1-\alpha)y_t \tag{3.173}$$

$$\frac{\sigma}{\beta}\left(c_{t+1}-c_t\right)=\alpha\left(y_{t+1}-k_t\right)+1-\delta \tag{3.174}$$

$$\mathrm{y_t}=a_t+\alpha k_t+(1-\alpha)l_t \tag{3.175}$$

$$k_{t+1}=(1-\mathrm{gg})\,\mathrm{y_t}-c_t+(1-\delta)k_t \tag{3.176}$$

$$g_t=\rho_g g_{t-1}+\left(1-\rho_g\right)\overline{g}+\varepsilon_{g,t} \tag{3.177}$$

$$a_t=\rho_a\,a_{t-1}+\varepsilon_{a,t} \tag{3.178}$$

As it is known, solving the model (3.174)–(3.178) means obtaining analytical expressions of current endogenous variables as policy functions.

In general, obtaining this algebraic solution is difficult, if not impossible, especially for models that become gradually more complex. We will discuss this aspect in detail later in the chapter This, perhaps, is the most important reason for resorting to a numerical solution, obtained in the first instance using calibration, i.e., by assigning appropriate values to parameters and on this basis simulate model so that numerical results are as similar as possible to those shown by the actual data.

Calibrating, in fact, means, given observations of effective economy, finding those parameter values for which time series of theoretical economy matches statistical data observed for effective economy. We will address this issue in the next chapter. For the moment, we continue with the analysis of the Blanchard-Kahn method.

3.13 An Application of the Blanchard-Kahn Method to Hansen's DSGE Model

Hansen's model[22] is an important point of reference in DSGE literature. It is useful to review that model entirely to proceed with an explicit application of the Blanchard-Kahn method. The exercise also aims to show, as anticipated, the complexity of the solution method, despite the essential simplicity of the model.

We will repeat this type of exercise in successive paragraph for a slightly more complex model, and we will show that Blanchard-Kahn conditions give rise to a substantially unmanageable number of calculations for obtaining handmade solutions.

Hansen's model, as for as behavior of representative household, considers the following intertemporal function, logarithmic in consumption and linear in hours worked:

[22] Hansen, G. (1985).

$$E_0 \sum_{t=0}^{\infty} \beta^t (\log C_t - \psi h_t) \tag{3.179}$$

Taking into account budget constraint,

$$C_t + K_{t+1} = \mathrm{W_t h_t} + \mathrm{R_t K_t} + (1-\delta)K_t \tag{3.180}$$

the corresponding intertemporal Lagrangian to maximize is

$$E_0 \sum_{t=0}^{\infty} \beta^t [\log C_t - \psi h_t + \lambda_t(\mathrm{W_t h_t} + \mathrm{R_t K_t} + (1-\delta)K_t - C_t - K_{t+1}] \tag{3.181}$$

As far as production choices are concerned, a decentralized economy is made by firms.

With a Cobb-Douglas production technology $Q_t = \mathrm{A_t} K_t^{\alpha} h_t^{1-\alpha}$, the intertemporal constrained profit maximization of the representative firm is

$$\max_{L_t, K_t} \mathrm{E_0} \sum_{t=0}^{\infty} \beta^t \pi_t \tag{3.182}$$

$$\text{Sub} \quad Q_t = \mathrm{A_t} K_t^{\alpha} h_t^{1-\alpha}$$

In the expression (3.182), the discount factor β^t coincides with the discount factor of the households since by assumption the representative firm is owned by households, for which we have seen the expected present value of a unit of profit at time t +1 is the marginal utility at time t+1, of the marginal utility of current consumption, i.e., $\frac{U'_{c,t+1}}{U'_{c,t}}$. Furthermore, looking at the intertemporal firm problem (3.182), we note that at time t=0, profit does not contain terms at time t=1, so the problem is, in fact, a simple static maximization problem of kind

$$\max_{h_t, K_t} \pi_t = \mathrm{A_t} K_t^{\alpha} h_t^{1-\alpha} - W_t h_t - R_t K_t \tag{3.183}$$

Conversely, in a centralized economy, the productive sector is simply represented by production technology since there are no choices decentralized to firms. In this case in maximizing household utility, the budget constraint is replaced by the resource constraint and the intertemporal Lagrangian is

$$E_0 \sum_{t=0}^{\infty} \beta^t \left[\log C_t - \psi h_t + \lambda_t \left(A_t K_t^{\alpha} h_t^{1-\alpha} - C_t + (1-\delta)K_t - K_{t+1} \right) \right] \tag{3.184}$$

In the remainder of the section, we consider exclusively the centralized economy whose central planner maximizes the intertemporal Lagrangian (3.184).

First-order conditions for control variables C_t, h_t, k_{t+1} for this economy are

$$\frac{1}{C_t} = \lambda_t \tag{3.185}$$

$$-\psi + \lambda_t(1-\alpha)\, A_t K_t^{\alpha}\, h_1^{-\alpha} = -\psi + \lambda_t(1-\alpha)\frac{Y_t}{h_t} = 0; \tag{3.186}$$

$$-\lambda_t + \beta\lambda_{t+1}\alpha\, A_{t+1}\frac{K_{t+1}}{K_t+1} K_{t+1}^{\alpha-1} h_{t+1}^{1-\alpha} + \beta\lambda_{t+1}(1-\delta)$$

$$= -\lambda_t + \beta\left[\lambda_{t+1}\left(\alpha\frac{Y_{t+1}}{K_{t+1}} + 1 - \delta\right)\right] = 0 \tag{3.187}$$

By eliminating λ_t from all Eqs. (3.185)–(3.187), they become

$$C_t = \frac{(1-\alpha)}{\psi}\frac{Y_t}{h_t} \tag{3.188}$$

$$\frac{1}{C_t} = \beta E_t\left[\frac{1}{C_{t+1}}\left(\alpha\frac{Y_{t+1}}{K_{t+1}} + 1 - \delta\right)\right] \tag{3.189}$$

Complete model is

$$Y_t = A_t K_t^{\alpha} h_t^{1-\alpha} \tag{3.190}$$

$$\log(A_t) = (1-\varrho_a)\log\left(\overline{A}\right) + \varrho_a \log(A_{t-1}) + e \tag{3.191}$$

$$Y_t = C_t + I_t \tag{3.192}$$

$$I_t = K_{t+1} - (1-\delta)K_t \tag{3.193}$$

$$C_t = \frac{(1-\alpha)}{\psi}\frac{Y_t}{h_t} \tag{3.194}$$

$$\frac{1}{C_t} = \beta E_t\left[\frac{1}{C_{t+1}}\left(\alpha\frac{Y_{t+1}}{K_{t+1}} + 1 - \delta\right)\right] \tag{3.195}$$

Steady state of the model is

$$Y = AK^{\alpha}h^{(1-\alpha)} \tag{3.196}$$

$$A = 1 \tag{3.197}$$

$$1 = \beta\left(\alpha\frac{Y}{K} + 1 - \delta\right) \tag{3.198}$$

$$\psi C = (1-\alpha)\frac{Y}{h} \tag{3.199}$$

$$\mathrm{Y} = \mathrm{C} + \mathrm{I} \tag{3.200}$$

$$\mathrm{I} = \delta\mathrm{K} \tag{3.201}$$

Log-linearized equations of the model (3.190)–(3.195) are

$$\widehat{y}_t = \widehat{a}_t + \alpha\widehat{k}_t + (1-\alpha)\widehat{h}_t \tag{3.202}$$

$$\widehat{a}_t = \rho\widehat{a}_t + \varepsilon_t \tag{3.203}$$

$$\widehat{y}_t = c_y\widehat{c}_t + i_y\,\widehat{i}_t \tag{3.204}$$

$$\widehat{k}_{t+1} = (1-\delta)\widehat{k}_t + i_k\widehat{i}_t \tag{3.205}$$

$$\frac{\mathrm{c_y}\ \psi}{(1-\alpha)}\ \widehat{c}_t + \frac{\mathrm{c_y}\ \psi}{(1-\alpha)}h_y\ \widehat{h}_t = \widehat{y}_t \tag{3.206}$$

$$-\frac{1}{\beta}\widehat{c}_t = -\beta E_t\widehat{c}_{t+1} + \alpha\widehat{k}_{t+1} + \alpha E_t\widehat{y}_{t+1} \tag{3.207}$$

We distinguish Eqs. (3.202)–(3.207) into two groups, the one relating to expected control variables $(\widehat{k}_{t+1}, E_t\widehat{c}_{t+1})$, and the other relating to expected measurement variables $\left(E_t\widehat{y}_{t+1}, E_t\widehat{i}_{t+1}, E_t\widehat{h}_{t+1}\right)$.

By writing explicitly even variables with zero coefficients, the system of equations becomes

$$\begin{aligned}
&\widehat{k}_{t+1} + 0\,E_t\widehat{c}_{t+1} + 0E_t\widehat{y}_{t+1} + 0E_t\widehat{i}_{t+1} + 0E_t\widehat{h}_{t+1} \\
&\quad = (1-\delta)\widehat{k}_t + 0\widehat{c}_t + 0\,\widehat{y}_t + i_k\widehat{i}_t + 0\,\widehat{h}_t
\end{aligned} \tag{3.208}$$

$$\begin{aligned}
&-\alpha\widehat{k}_{t+1} - \beta E_t\widehat{c}_{t+1} + \alpha E_t\widehat{y}_{t+1} + 0E_t\widehat{i}_{t+1} + 0E_t\widehat{h}_{t+1} \\
&\quad = 0\widehat{k}_t - \frac{1}{\beta}\widehat{c}_t \quad + 0\widehat{y}_t + 0\,\widehat{i}_t + 0\widehat{h}_{t+1}
\end{aligned} \tag{3.209}$$

Written (3.208)–(3.209) in matrix form, it is

$$\begin{pmatrix} 1 & 0 \\ -\alpha & \beta \end{pmatrix}\begin{pmatrix} \widehat{k}_{t+1} \\ E_t\widehat{c}_{t+1} \end{pmatrix} + \begin{pmatrix} 0 & 0 & 0 \\ \alpha & 0 & 0 \end{pmatrix}\begin{pmatrix} E_t\widehat{y}_{t+1} \\ E_t\widehat{i}_{t+1} \\ E_t\widehat{h}_{t+1} \end{pmatrix} = \begin{pmatrix} 1-\delta & 0 \\ 0 & -\frac{1}{\beta} \end{pmatrix}$$

$$\begin{pmatrix} \widehat{k} \\ \widehat{c}_t \end{pmatrix} + \begin{pmatrix} 0 & i_k & 0 \\ 0 & 0 & 0 \end{pmatrix}\begin{pmatrix} \widehat{y}_t \\ \widehat{i}_t \\ \widehat{h}_t \end{pmatrix} \tag{3.210}$$

That is, by putting

$$E_t s_{t+1} = \begin{pmatrix} \widehat{k}_{t+1} \\ E_t \widehat{c}_{t+1} \end{pmatrix}; E_t f_{t+1} = \begin{pmatrix} E_t \widehat{y}_{t+1} \\ E_t \widehat{i}_{t+1} \\ E_t \widehat{h}_{t+1} \end{pmatrix}; \quad s_t = \begin{pmatrix} \widehat{k} \\ \widehat{c}_t \end{pmatrix}; f_t = \begin{pmatrix} \widehat{y}_t \\ \widehat{i}_t \\ \widehat{h}_t \end{pmatrix};$$

And

$$D = \begin{pmatrix} 1 & 0 \\ -\alpha & \beta \end{pmatrix}; \mathrm{F} = \begin{pmatrix} 0 & 0 & 0 \\ \alpha & 0 & 0 \end{pmatrix}; H = \begin{pmatrix} 0 & i_k & 0 \\ 0 & 0 & 0 \end{pmatrix};$$

$$\mathrm{G} = \begin{pmatrix} 1-\delta & 0 \\ 0 & -\dfrac{1}{\beta} \end{pmatrix}$$

in vector notation, we will have

$$DE_t s_{t+1} + FE_t f_{t+1} = Gs_t + Hf_t \tag{3.211}$$

Consider now static equations of (3.190)–(3.195) (which contain only variables referred to time t). They can rewrite

$$\widehat{y}_t + 0\,\widehat{i}_t - (1-\alpha)\widehat{h}_t = \alpha\widehat{k}_t + 0\,\widehat{c}_t + \widehat{a}_t \tag{3.212}$$

$$\widehat{y}_t - i_y\,\widehat{i}_t \;\; + 0\,\widehat{h}_t = \;\; 0\widehat{k}_t + c_y\widehat{c}_t + 0\,\widehat{a}_t \tag{3.213}$$

$$\widehat{y}\;_t - \frac{c_y\,\psi}{1-\alpha} h_y\,\widehat{h}_t = 0\widehat{k}_t + \frac{c_y\,\psi}{1-\alpha}\,\widehat{c}_t + 0\,\widehat{a}_t \tag{3.214}$$

Setting $\frac{c_y\,\psi}{1-\alpha} = \gamma$, system (3.212)–(3.214) has the following matrix form

$$\begin{pmatrix} 1 & 0 & 1-\alpha \\ 1 & -i_y & 0 \\ 1 & 0 & \gamma h_y \end{pmatrix} \begin{pmatrix} \widehat{y}_t \\ \widehat{i}_t \\ \widehat{h}_t \end{pmatrix} = \begin{pmatrix} \alpha & 0 \\ 0 & c_y \\ 0 & \lambda \end{pmatrix} \begin{pmatrix} \widehat{k}_t \\ \widehat{c}_t \end{pmatrix} + \begin{pmatrix} 1 \\ 0 \\ 0 \end{pmatrix} \widehat{a}_t \tag{3.215}$$

That is, by writing

$$A = \begin{pmatrix} 1 & 0 & 1-\alpha \\ 1 & -i_y & 0 \\ 1 & 0 & \lambda h_y \end{pmatrix}; \mathrm{B} = \begin{pmatrix} \alpha & 0 \\ 0 & c_y \\ 0 & \lambda \end{pmatrix}; \mathrm{C} = \begin{pmatrix} 1 \\ 0 \\ 0 \end{pmatrix}$$

in vector notation, we have

$$Af_t = Bs_t + C\widehat{a}_t \tag{3.216}$$

Finally, the equation of technical progress (3.203) can explicitly be solved for expectations $E_{t+j}\widehat{a}_t = \rho^j \widehat{a}_t$ so that dynamic equilibrium system in vector form ultimately is

$$DE_t s_{t+1} + FE_t f_{t+1} = Gs_t + Hf_t \tag{3.217}$$

$$Af_t = Bs_t + C\widehat{a}_t \tag{3.218}$$

$$E_t \widehat{a}_{t+j} = \rho^j \widehat{a}_t \tag{3.219}$$

System (3.217)–(3.219) must be rewritten in the form of expectations vector $E_t\, s_{t+1}$ required by Blanchard-Kahn theorem.

For this purpose, assuming that A is invertible, from (3.216), we will have

$$f_t = A^{-1}Bs_t + A^{-1}C\widehat{a}_t$$

Substituting in (3.216), it follows

$$\begin{aligned} &DE_t s_{t+1} + FE_t\left(A^{-1}Bs_{t+1} + A^{-1}C\widehat{a}_{t+1}\right) \\ &= Gs_t + H\left(A^{-1}Bs_t + A^{-1}C\widehat{a}_t\right) \end{aligned} \tag{3.220}$$

Grouping similar terms

$$\begin{aligned} &\left(D + FA^{-1}B\right)E_t s_{t+1} + \left(FA^{-1}C\right)\rho\widehat{a}_t \\ &= \left(G + HA^{-1}B\right)s_t + \left(HA^{-1}C\right)\widehat{a}_t \end{aligned} \tag{3.221}$$

That is,

$$\begin{aligned} \left(D + FA^{-1}B\right)E_t s_{t+1} &= \left(G + HA^{-1}B\right)s_t + HA^{-1}C\widehat{a}_t - FA^{-1}C\rho\widehat{a}_t \\ &= \left(G + HA^{-1}B\right)s_t + \left(HA^{-1}C - FA^{-1}C\rho\right)\widehat{a}_t \end{aligned} \tag{3.222}$$

And, admitted $((D + FA^{-1}B)$ invertible, it follows

$$\begin{aligned} E_t s_{t+1} = &\left[\left(D + FA^{-1}B\right)^{-1}\left(G + HA^{-1}B\right)\right] s_t \\ &+ \left[\left(D + FA^{-1}B\right)^{-1}\left(HA^{-1}C - FA^{-1}C\rho\right)\right]\widehat{a}_t \end{aligned} \tag{3.223}$$

More compactly, by setting

$$K=\left[\left(D+FA^{-1}B\right)^{-1}\left(G+HA^{-1}B\right)\right]$$

$$\mathrm{L}=\left(D+FA^{-1}B\right)^{-1}\left(HA^{-1}C-FA^{-1}C\rho\right)$$

We will have

$$E_t s_{t+1}=Ks_t+L\widehat{a}_t \tag{3.224}$$

That is, in matrix form

$$\begin{pmatrix} \widehat{k}_{t+1} \\ E_t\widehat{c}_{t+1} \end{pmatrix}=K\begin{pmatrix} \widehat{k} \\ \widehat{c}_t \end{pmatrix}+\mathrm{L}\widehat{a}_t \tag{3.225}$$

The matrix of coefficients K in the system (3.225) is an (n+m)×(n+m) matrix where n refers to the number of predetermined dynamic variables and m is the number of non-predetermined dynamic variables.

By the transformation $K=M^{-1}\Lambda M$, matrix K is transformed into the canonical Jordan matrix, with Λ the diagonal matrix

$$\Lambda=\begin{pmatrix} \Lambda_1 & 0 \\ 0 & \Lambda_2 \end{pmatrix}$$

Submatrices Λ_1 and Λ_2 are, respectively, nXn and mXm and collect the roots in absolute value less than unity N_1 and greater than unity N_2.

Columns of M^{-1} contain the eigenvectors of K, and M can be decomposed as

$$M=\begin{pmatrix} M_{11} & M_{12} \\ M_{21} & M_{22} \end{pmatrix}$$

Matrix M_{11} has dimensions $n\times n$ and then dimensions of M_{21} are $m\times n$, that of M_{12} are $n\times m$, and dimensions of M_{22} are $m\times m$.

In addition, it is $\mathrm{L}=\begin{pmatrix} L_1 \\ L_2 \end{pmatrix}$ where L_1 is $(n\times k)$ and L_2 is $m\times k$, where k refers to exogenous variables.

To solve system (3.224), multiply on the left by matrix M of eigenvectors. It follows

$$ME_t s_{t+1}=MM^{-1}\Lambda Ms_t+ML\widehat{a}_t \tag{3.226}$$

System (3.225), rewritten in matrix form becomes

$$\begin{pmatrix} M_{11} & M_{12} \\ M_{21} & M_{22} \end{pmatrix} E_t \begin{pmatrix} \widehat{k}_{t+1} \\ \widehat{c}_{t+1} \end{pmatrix}$$

$$= \begin{pmatrix} \Lambda_1 & 0 \\ 0 & \Lambda_2 \end{pmatrix} \begin{pmatrix} M_{11} & M_{12} \\ M_{21} & M_{22} \end{pmatrix} \begin{pmatrix} \widehat{k}_t \\ \widehat{c}_t \end{pmatrix} + \begin{pmatrix} M_{11} & M_{12} \\ M_{21} & M_{22} \end{pmatrix} \begin{pmatrix} L_1 \\ L_2 \end{pmatrix} \widehat{a}_t \tag{3.227}$$

And by performing vector products, you will get

$$\begin{pmatrix} M_{11}\,\widehat{k}_{t+1} + M_{12}E_t\widehat{c}_{t+1} \\ M_{21}\widehat{k}_{t+1} + M_{22}E_t\widehat{c}_{t+1} \end{pmatrix}$$

$$= \begin{pmatrix} \Lambda_1 & 0 \\ 0 & \Lambda_2 \end{pmatrix} \begin{pmatrix} M_{11}\widehat{k}_t + M_{12}\widehat{c}_t \\ M_{21}\widehat{k}_t + M_{22}\widehat{c}_t \end{pmatrix} + \begin{pmatrix} M_{11}L_1 + M_{12}L_2 \\ M_{21}L_1 + M_{22}L_2 \end{pmatrix} \widehat{a}_t \tag{3.228}$$

Or calling

$$s_{1t}^1 = M_{11}\widehat{k}_t + M_{12}$$

$$s_{1t}^1 = M_{21}\widehat{k}_t + M_{22}\widehat{c}_t \tag{3.229}$$

You have

$$\begin{pmatrix} E_t s_{1t+1}^1 \\ E_t s_{2t+1}^1 \end{pmatrix} = \begin{pmatrix} \Lambda_1 & 0 \\ 0 & \Lambda_2 \end{pmatrix} \begin{pmatrix} s_{1t}^1 \\ s_{2t}^1 \end{pmatrix} + \begin{pmatrix} M_{11}L_1 + M_{12}L_2 \\ M_{21}L_1 + M_{22}L_2 \end{pmatrix} \widehat{a}_t$$

And again

$$\begin{pmatrix} E_t s_{1t+1}^1 \\ E_t s_{2t+1}^1 \end{pmatrix} = \begin{pmatrix} \Lambda_1 s_{1t}^1 \\ \Lambda_2 s_{2t}^1 \end{pmatrix} + \begin{pmatrix} M_{11}L_1 + M_{12}L_2 \\ M_{21}L_1 + M_{22}L_2 \end{pmatrix} \tag{3.230}$$

By defining,

$$Q_1 = M_{11}L_1 + M_{12}L_2 \text{ and } Q_2 = M_{21}L_1 + M_{22}L_2$$

It follows

$$\begin{pmatrix} E_t s^1_{1t+1} \\ E_t s^1_{2t+1} \end{pmatrix} = \begin{pmatrix} \Lambda_1 s^1_{1t} \\ \Lambda_2 s^1_{2t} \end{pmatrix} + \begin{pmatrix} Q_1 \\ Q_2 \end{pmatrix} \widehat{a}_t \tag{3.231}$$

By equating component by component

$$\begin{aligned} E_t s^1_{1t+1} &= \Lambda_1 s^1_{1t} + Q_1 \widehat{a}_t \\ E_t s^1_{2t+1} &= \Lambda_2 s^1_{2t} + Q_2 \widehat{a}_t \end{aligned} \tag{3.232}$$

Repeating here an already known reasoning, we observe that the equation containing the eigenvalue $|\Lambda_2| > 1$, can be rewritten as

$$s^1_{2t} = \frac{1}{\Lambda_2} E_t s^1_{2t+1} - \frac{Q_2}{\Lambda_2} \widehat{a}_t \tag{3.233}$$

Equation (3.233) is a rational expectations, equation that can be resolved forward. Indeed, moving forward by one period and taking the expectation at time t, you obtain

$$E_t s^1_{2t+1} = = \frac{1}{\Lambda_2} E_t s^1_{2t+2} - \frac{Q_2}{\Lambda_2} E_t \widehat{a}_{t+1} \tag{3.234}$$

Substituting (3.234) in (3.233), it results

$$s^1_{2t} = \left(\frac{1}{\Lambda_2}\right)^2 E_t s^1_{2t+2} - \left(\frac{1}{\Lambda_2}\right)^2 Q_2 E_t \widehat{a}_{t+1} - \frac{1}{\Lambda_2} Q_2 \widehat{a}_t \tag{3.235}$$

And, after T substitutions, (3.235) becomes

$$s^1_{2t} = \left(\frac{1}{\Lambda_2}\right)^T E_t s^1_{2t+T} - \frac{Q_2}{\Lambda_2} \sum_{j=1}^{T} \left(\frac{1}{\Lambda_2}\right)^{j-1} E_t \widehat{a}_{t+j} \tag{3.236}$$

It is $E_{t+j} \widehat{a}_{t+j} = \rho^j \widehat{a}_t$, and $\lim_{T \to \infty} \left(\frac{1}{\Lambda_2}\right)^T E_t s^1_{2t+T} = 0$ so that

$$\lim_{T \to \infty} s^1_{2t} = -\frac{Q_2}{\Lambda_2} \lim_{T \to \infty} \sum_{j=0}^{T} \left(\frac{\rho}{\Lambda_2}\right)^j \widehat{a}_t \tag{3.237}$$

That is,

$$s_{2t}^{1} = -\frac{Q_2}{\Lambda_2}\left(\frac{1}{1-\left(\frac{\rho}{\Lambda_2}\right)}\right)\widehat{a}_t = -\frac{Q_2}{\Lambda_2}\frac{\Lambda_2}{\Lambda_2-\rho}\widehat{a}_t = \frac{Q_2}{\rho-\Lambda_2}\widehat{a}_t \tag{3.238}$$

Taking into account (3.229), we will have

$$M_{21}\widehat{k}_t + M_{22}\widehat{c}_t = \frac{Q_2}{\rho-\Lambda_2}\widehat{a}_t \tag{3.239}$$

Solving (3.239) for $\widehat{c}_t$

$$\widehat{c}_t = -\frac{M_{21}}{M_{22}}\widehat{k}_t + \frac{1}{M_{22}}\frac{Q_2}{\rho-\Lambda_2}\widehat{a}_t = S_1\widehat{k}_t + S_2\widehat{a}_t \tag{3.240}$$

The solution for $\widehat{c}_t$just obtained in (3.240) can be replaced in (3.228) which gives

$$\begin{aligned} s_{1t}^{1} &= M_{11}\widehat{k}_t + M_{12}S_1\widehat{k}_t + M_{12}S_2\widehat{a}_t \\ &= (M_{11} + M_{12}S_1)\widehat{k}_t + M_{12}S_2\widehat{a}_t \end{aligned} \tag{3.241}$$

The latter (3.241), replaced in turn in the first of (3.232), provides

$$\begin{aligned} &(M_{11} + M_{12}S_1)\widehat{k}_{t+1} + M_{12}S_2E_t\widehat{a}_{t+1} \\ &= \Lambda_1\left[(M_{11} + M_{12}S_1)\widehat{k}_t + M_{12}S_2\widehat{a}_t\right] + Q_1\widehat{a}_t \end{aligned} \tag{3.242}$$

i.e.,

$$\begin{aligned} &(M_{11} + M_{12}S_1)\widehat{k}_{t+1} + M_{12}S_2\rho\widehat{a}_t \\ &= \Lambda_1(M_{11} + M_{12}S_1)\widehat{k}_t + (Q_1 + \Lambda_1 M_{12}S_2)\widehat{a}_t \end{aligned} \tag{3.243}$$

And again

$$\begin{aligned} (M_{11} + M_{12}S_1)\widehat{k}_{t+1} = &\Lambda_1(M_{11} + M_{12}S_1)\widehat{k}_t + (Q_1 + \Lambda_1 M_{12}S_2)\widehat{a}_t \\ &- M_{12}S_2\rho\widehat{a}_t \end{aligned} \tag{3.244}$$

Solving (3.244) for $\widehat{k}_{t+1}$, you will obtain

$$\widehat{k}_{t+1} = \Lambda_1\widehat{k}_t + \frac{Q_1 + \Lambda_1 M_{12} - M_{12}S_2\rho S_2}{M_{11} + M_{12}S_1}\widehat{a}_t = S_3\widehat{k}_t + S_4\widehat{a}_t \tag{3.245}$$

Recalling that

$$f_t = A^{-1}Bs_t + A^{-1}C\widehat{a}_t = A^{-1}B\begin{pmatrix}\widehat{k}_t \\ \widehat{c}_t\end{pmatrix} + A^{-1}C\widehat{a}_t \tag{3.246}$$

And replacing the solution of $\widehat{c}_t$ (3.240) into (3.246), we have

$$f_t = A^{-1}B\begin{pmatrix}\widehat{k}_t \\ S_1\widehat{k}_t + S_2\widehat{a}_t\end{pmatrix} + A^{-1}C\widehat{a}_t =$$

$$A^{-1}B\begin{pmatrix}\widehat{k}_t \\ S_1\widehat{k}_t\end{pmatrix} + A^{-1}B\begin{pmatrix}0 \\ S_2\widehat{a}_t\end{pmatrix} + A^{-1}C\widehat{a}_t = A^{-1}B\begin{pmatrix}1 \\ S_1\end{pmatrix}\widehat{k}_t$$

$$+\left[A^{-1}C + A^{-1}B\begin{pmatrix}0 \\ S_2\end{pmatrix}\right]\widehat{a}_t \tag{3.247}$$

That is, writing $S_5 = A^{-1}B\begin{pmatrix}1 \\ S_1\end{pmatrix}; S_6 = \left[A^{-1}C + A^{-1}B\begin{pmatrix}0 \\ S_2\end{pmatrix}\right]$

in compact form, we will have

$$f_t = S_5\ \widehat{k}_t + S_6\ \widehat{a}_t \tag{3.248}$$

Ultimately, the solution of the model is represented by the equations shown below

$$\widehat{k}_{t+1} = S_3\widehat{k}_t + S_4\widehat{a}_t \tag{3.249}$$

$$\widehat{a}_t = \rho\widehat{a}_{t-1} + \varepsilon_t \tag{3.250}$$

$$f_t = S_5\ \widehat{k}_t + S_6\ \widehat{a}_t \tag{3.251}$$

$$\widehat{c}_t = S_1\widehat{k}_t + S_2\widehat{a}_t \tag{3.252}$$

This solution in explicit matrix form is

$$\begin{pmatrix}\widehat{k}_{t+1} \\ \widehat{a}_{t+1}\end{pmatrix} = \begin{pmatrix}S_3 & S_4 \\ 0 & \rho\end{pmatrix}\begin{pmatrix}\widehat{k}_t \\ \widehat{a}_t\end{pmatrix} + \begin{pmatrix}0 \\ \rho\end{pmatrix}\varepsilon_{t+1} \tag{3.253}$$

$$\begin{pmatrix}\widehat{y}_t \\ \widehat{i}_t \\ \widehat{h}_t \\ \widehat{c}_t\end{pmatrix} = \begin{pmatrix}[S_{5(3\times 1)}] & [S_{6(3\times 1)}] \\ S_1 & S_2\end{pmatrix}\begin{pmatrix}\widehat{k}_t \\ \widehat{a}_t\end{pmatrix} \tag{3.254}$$

That is, in vector notation

$$s_{t+1} = \Pi s_t + W\varepsilon_{t+1} \tag{3.255}$$
$$\mathrm{f_t} = Us_t$$

3.14 The Model of a Decentralized Economy, with Flexible Labor Supply and Exogenous Public Spending

The basic RBC model (3.100)–(3.102) is based on a series of hypotheses that today seem natural but which, in reality, represent a substantial inversion with respect to Keynesian macroeconomics, even the hybrid one (neoclassical-Keynesian) of AD/AS model.

It is appropriate to review these hypotheses explicitly. They are as follows:

- Firms are identical and price-takers.
- Households are also identical and price-takers with an infinite time horizon.
- There is perfect competition in all markets.
- There are no frictions, imperfections, and information asymmetries: expectations are rational and all prices adjust instantly.

The dynamic equilibrium that is determined in such a context has the typical characteristics of (static) models of general competitive economic equilibrium, i.e.,

- There is full employment.
- The dynamic competitive equilibrium is Pareto optimal.[23]

Yet, as we saw earlier, even such a model can generate cycles in the equilibrium time paths of consumption and capital. This is an innovative idea. If we admit that global productivity evolves according to a stochastic process, the effects of shocks spread either over time or into the economic space of quantities, generating typical cyclical paths.

In this context, it has been previously seen, also the public administration can be considered a source of cyclical impulses, by equating fiscal policy to a stochastic process, subject to unpredictable shocks, just like technology. In a more complete approach, two further hypotheses allow us to motivate this assimilation. The first is the assumption that fiscal policy follows a simple liberal rule of balanced budgets. According to this rule, public spending is entirely financed by taxation. The second assumption is that taxation is of a kind that does not alter for the worse (does not distort) Pareto-optimal allocation.

This requires that the taxation be lump-sum, i.e.,

[23]This property is established by the well-known first theorem of the welfare theory in Samuelson, P. (1947). See also Intrilligator, M. (1971), pp.269–78.

$$G_t = T_{x_t} \tag{3.256}$$

With the hypotheses just stated, assuming that taxation falls entirely on households alone, their budget constraint becomes

$$C_t + K_{t+1} + T_{x_t} = w_t L_t + r_t K_t + (1-\delta)K_t \tag{3.257}$$

The model, therefore, assumes that public administration interferes, on the one hand, by taxing household disposable income

$$w_t L_t + r_t K_t - T_{x_t} \tag{3.258}$$

and, on the other hand, also interferes with the use of aggregate resources of the economy, with the addition of public demand to that of private demand, so that this interference determines an overall aggregate demand:

$$C_t + I_t + G_t \tag{3.259}$$

A macroeconomic model with public expenditure described above is constructed as follows.

For households, a utility function of CRRA kind in both consumption C_t and labor L_t is admitted. The constrained maximum problem of households, by forming the Lagrangian, equals solving the following maximum problem:

$$max\ E_0 \sum_{t=0}^{\infty} \beta^t \left\{ \left[\frac{C_t^{1-\sigma}}{1-\sigma} - \varphi \frac{L_t^{1+\gamma}}{1+\gamma} \right] + \lambda_t [w_t L_t + r_t K_t + (1-\delta)K_t - C_t - K_{t+1} - T_{x_t}] \right\} \tag{3.260}$$

Control variables in (3.260) are (C_t, L_t, K_{t+1}). Compared to the previous RBC model, the number of hours worked L_t is now among the choices of households, while K_t is, at any instant, a state variable.

First-order conditions for control variables are, respectively,

$$\begin{aligned}
C_t:\ \beta^t C_t^{-\sigma} - \beta^t \lambda_t = 0 \quad \text{that is}\ \ C_t^{-\sigma} &= \lambda_t \\
L_t:\ -\beta^t \varphi L_t^{\gamma} + \beta^t \lambda_t w_t = 0, \text{that is}\ \ \varphi L_t^{\gamma} &= \lambda_t w_t \\
K_{t+1}:\ -\beta^t \lambda_t + \beta^{t+1} E_t[\lambda_{t+1}(r_{t+1} + (1-\delta))] = 0 \quad &\text{that is} \\
\beta E_t \lambda_{t+1}(r_{t+1} + (1-\delta)) &= \lambda_t
\end{aligned}$$

By eliminating λ_t and λ_{t+1}, first-order conditions are reduced to

$$\frac{\varphi L_t^{\gamma}}{C_t^{-\sigma}} = w_t \tag{3.261}$$

$$C_t^{-\sigma} = \beta E_t\left[C_{t+1}^{-\sigma}\left[r_{t+1} + (1-\delta)\right]\right] \tag{3.262}$$

The aggregation procedure now entails

$$w_t L_t + r_t K_t + (1-\delta)K_t = A_t\, K_t^{\alpha} L_t^{(1-\alpha)} + (1-\delta)K_t = \mathrm{Y_t} + (1-\delta)K_t$$

and therefore, from household budget constraint, by symmetry, it follows that

$$C_t + K_{t+1} + T_{x_t} = \mathrm{Y_t} + (1-\delta)K_t \tag{3.263}$$

and from the public budget constraint $T_{x_t} = G_t$, it follows

$$C_t + K_{t+1} + G_t = \mathrm{Y_t} + (1-\delta)K_t \tag{3.264}$$

That is,

$$C_t + K_{t+1} - (1-\delta)K_t + G_t = \mathrm{Y_t} \tag{3.265}$$

Observing that $I_t = K_{t+1} - (1-\delta)K_t$, it follows the usual equality

$$C_t + I_t + G_t = \mathrm{Y_t} \tag{3.266}$$

As far as the firms' sector is concerned, the production technology is, as before, represented by a Cobb-Douglas function with constant returns to scale, i.e.,

$$\mathrm{Y_t} = A_t\, K_t^{\alpha} L_t^{(1-\alpha)} \tag{3.267}$$

Given production technology, the representative firm maximizes instantaneous profit:

$$\max_{L_t, K_t} \pi_t = A_t\, K_t^{\alpha} L_t^{(1-\alpha)} - w_t L_t - r_t K_t \tag{3.268}$$

First-order conditions are

$$L_t : (1-\alpha)A_t\, K_t^{\alpha} L_t^{-\alpha} - w_t = 0$$

That is,

$$w_t = (1-\alpha)A_t\, K_t^{\alpha}\frac{L_t L_t^{-\alpha}}{L_t} = (1-\alpha)\frac{Y_t}{L_t} \tag{3.269}$$

and

$$K_t : \alpha A_t\, K_t^{\alpha-1} L_t^{1-\alpha} - r_t = 0$$

That is,

$$r_t = \alpha A_t\, \frac{K_t^{\alpha}}{K_t} L_t^{1-\alpha} = \alpha\frac{Y_t}{K_t} \tag{3.270}$$

Equations (3.269) and (3.270) define, respectively, inverse demand for labor and for capital services, given current output.

Finally, for technology, we will assume as before that global productivity A_t follows a stochastic process in logarithm

$$\log A_t = \rho_a\ \log A_{t-1} + \varepsilon_{a,t} \tag{3.271}$$

with $\varepsilon_{a,\,t} \sim iid.\ N(0, \sigma^2)$ and $0 < \rho_a < 1$.

Also, for public expenditure G_t, as before, it will be assumed that it follows in logarithm a stochastic process AR(1) of the type

$$\log G_t = \left(1-\rho_g\right)\overline{G} + \rho_g \log G_{t-1} + \varepsilon_{g,t} \tag{3.272}$$

where $\overline{G}$ is the steady-state mean value, and $\varepsilon_{g,\,t} \sim iid.\ N(0, \sigma^2)$; $0 < \rho_g < 1$.

3.15 A Complete Analysis of the RBC Model of the Centralized Economy, with Log-CRRA Utility Function in Consumption and Labor

In a centralized economy, intertemporal choices of economic system are brought out by a central planner whose aim is to maximize the utility of representative family, with the constraint of available resources

$$y_t = c_t + i_t$$

and existing production technology (Cobb-Douglas)

$$y_t = a_t k_t^{\alpha} h_t^{1-\alpha}$$

Technology is subject to a shock of type[24]

$$log\, a_t = (1 - \rho_a)\, log\, \overline{a} + \rho_a\, log\, a_{t-1} + \varepsilon_{at} \tag{3.273}$$

The central planner cares about the well-being not only of the current generation but also of all future generations.

He has the goal to maximize the discounted sum of the utilities of all generations (from here to infinity) by valuing at the present the utility of future generations at the discount rate $\beta^{\tau-t}$.

So, at time t, the central planner solves the problem:

$$\max_{c_{t+\tau}, k_{t+1+\tau}} E_t \sum_{\tau=0}^{\infty} \beta^{\tau-t} \left(log\, c_t - \Psi \frac{h_t^{1+\psi}}{1+\psi} \right) \tag{3.274}$$

$$\text{Sub}: \quad k_{t+1} = a_t k_t^{\alpha} h_t^{1-\alpha} - c_t + (1-\delta) k_t$$

where c_t, h_t, and k_t are, respectively, the consumption at time t, hours worked at time t, and physical capital available at time t. Parameters α and δ are, respectively, the elasticity of production with respect to the physical capital, k_t, and the obsolescence rate of physical capital, assumed constant. Taking into account that $i_t = k_{t+1} - (1 - \delta)$ and given the production technology, the resource constraint is rewritten adequately for the constrained maximization as

$$\begin{aligned} y_t - c_t - i_t &= \\ a_t k_t^{\alpha} h_t^{1-\alpha} - c_t - k_{t+1} + (1-\delta) k_t &= 0 \end{aligned} \tag{3.275}$$

and the dynamic law of capital accumulation becomes

$$k_{t+1} = a_t k_t^{\alpha} h_t^{1-\alpha} + (1-\delta) k_t \tag{3.276}$$

Since conditions repeat identically over time, it is sufficient for the central planner to worry first about the well-being of the current generation by choosing c_t, h_t, and then, through the choice of capital accumulation, of the generation immediately subsequent, solving a maximum problem, considering the constraints concerning instant τ=0 and τ=1. Therefore, the Lagrangian to be considered is as follows:

[24] Here in (3.273) $\overline{a}$ is the unconditional mean of the technology a_t ; ρ_a is the persistence factor, in absolute value less than unity, i.e., $|\rho_a|<1$, and ε_{at} is a Gaussian stochastic variable, with zero mean and finite standard deviation σ_a.

$$\beta^{-t}\left(\log c_t - \Psi \frac{h_t^{1+\psi}}{1+\psi}\right) + \beta^{-t}\lambda_t\left[a_t k_t^{\alpha} h_t^{1-\alpha} - c_t\right.$$
$$\left. + \ (1-\delta)k_t - k_{t+1}\right] + \beta^{1-t}\lambda_{t+1}\left[a_{t+1}k_{t+1}^{\alpha}h_{t+1}^{1-\alpha} + (1-\delta)k_{t+1}\ \right]$$

First-order conditions for control variables are as follows:

$$c_t: \quad \beta^{-t}\frac{1}{c_t} - \beta^{-t}\lambda_t = 0 \tag{3.277}$$

$$h_t: -\beta^{-t}\Psi\, h_t^{\psi} + (1-\alpha)\beta^{-t}\lambda_t a_t k_t^{\alpha}\, h_t^{-\alpha} = 0 \tag{3.278}$$

$$k_{t+1}: -\beta^{-t}\lambda_t + \beta^{1-t}\lambda_{t+1}\left[\alpha\, a_t k_{t+1}^{\alpha-1} h_{t+1}^{1-\alpha} + (1-\delta)\right] = 0 \tag{3.279}$$

Equation (3.279) is equivalent to

$$\beta^{1-t}\lambda_{t+1}\left[\alpha\ \frac{a_t k_{t+1}^{\alpha} h_{t+1}^{1-\alpha}}{k_{t+1}} + (1-\delta)\right] = \beta^{-t}\lambda_t \tag{3.280}$$

Again, dividing both sides by $\beta^{-t}\lambda_t$, and taking into account that $y_{t+1} = a_t\, k_{t+1}^{\alpha} h_{t+1}^{1-\alpha}$, it follows that

$$\beta\frac{\lambda_{t+1}}{\lambda_t}\left[\alpha\ \frac{y_{t+1}}{k_{t+1}} + (1-\delta)\right] = 1 \tag{3.281}$$

The expression in square brackets contains terms at time t+1. These, not being currently known, can only be expected. So, taking these expectations, you get

$$\beta\, E_t\left[\frac{\lambda_{t+1}}{\lambda_t}\left(\alpha\ \frac{y_{t+1}}{k_{t+1}} + (1-\delta)\right)\right] = 1 \tag{3.282}$$

Moreover, (3.282) gives ($\frac{1}{c_t} = \lambda_t$ so that $\frac{1}{c_{t+1}} = \lambda_{t+1}$ and from $\frac{\lambda_{t+1}}{\lambda_t} = \frac{c_t}{c_{t+1}}$ follows the Euler equation:

$$\beta\, E_t\left[\frac{c_t}{c_{t+1}}\left(\alpha\ \frac{y_{t+1}}{k_{t+1}} + (1-\delta)\right)\right] = 1 \tag{3.283}$$

Condition (3.278) becomes

$$\lambda_t\,(1-\alpha)\frac{y_t}{h_t} = \Psi\, h_t^{\psi}$$

And therefore,

$$(1-\alpha)\frac{y_t}{h_t}=\Psi\, c_t\, h_t^{\psi} \tag{3.284}$$

Ultimately, the system of the economy managed by the central planner follows a path over time described by the following equilibrium equations:

$$(1-\alpha)\frac{y_t}{h_t}=\Psi\, c_t\, h_t^{\psi} \tag{3.285}$$

$$y_t=c_t+i_t \tag{3.286}$$

$$y_t=a_t k_t^{\alpha} h_t^{1-\alpha} \tag{3.287}$$

$$k_{t+1}=i_t+(1-\delta)k_t \tag{3.288}$$

$$\beta\, E_t\left[\frac{c_t}{c_{t+1}}\left(\alpha\,\frac{y_{t+1}}{k_{t+1}}+(1-\delta)\right)\right]=1 \tag{3.289}$$

$$log\, a_t=(1-\rho_a)\,log\,\overline{a}+\rho_a\,log\,a_{t-1}+\varepsilon_{at} \tag{3.290}$$

And the transversality condition

$$\lim_{\tau\to\infty}\beta^{t+\tau}\lambda_{t+\tau}\,k_{t+1+\tau}=\beta^{t+\tau}\,\frac{k_{t+1+\tau}}{c_{t+\tau}}=0 \tag{3.291}$$

This system, nonlinear in the unknowns c_t, h_t, y_t,i_t, k_{t+1}, a_t, can be reduced to a linear system by considering a log-linear approximation around the deterministic steady-state solution.

For this purpose, it is necessary to preliminarily determine the steady-state solution.

3.15.1 Steady-State Solution

Steady-state solution of model (3.285)–(3.290) is characterized by the following equations:

$$(1-\alpha)\frac{y}{h}=\Psi\, c\, h^{\psi} \tag{3.292}$$

$$y=c+i \tag{3.293}$$

$$y=ak^{\alpha}h^{1-\alpha} \tag{3.294}$$

$$k=i+(1-\delta)k \tag{3.295}$$

$$\beta\left(\alpha\,\frac{y}{k}+(1-\delta)\right)=1 \tag{3.296}$$

For each of Eqs. (3.292)–(3.296), it is possible to obtain a solution as a function of the fundamental parameters of the model,[25] i.e.:

$$h=\left[\frac{(1-\alpha)}{\Psi}\right]^{\frac{1}{1+\psi}} \tag{3.297}$$

$$y=a^{\frac{1}{1-\alpha}}\left(\frac{\alpha\beta}{1-\beta(1-\delta)}\right)^{\frac{\alpha}{1-\alpha}}h=a^{\frac{1}{1-\alpha}}\left(\frac{\alpha\beta}{1-\beta(1-\delta)}\right)^{\frac{\alpha}{1-\alpha}}\left[\frac{(1-\alpha)}{\Psi}\right]^{\frac{1}{1+\psi}} \tag{3.298}$$

$$c=s_c y=s_c\,a^{\frac{1}{1-\alpha}}\left(\frac{\alpha\beta}{1-\beta(1-\delta)}\right)^{\frac{\alpha}{1-\alpha}}\left[\frac{(1-\alpha)}{\Psi}\right]^{\frac{1}{1+\psi}} \tag{3.299}$$

$$i=s_i y=s_i\,a^{\frac{1}{1-\alpha}}\left(\frac{\alpha\beta}{1-\beta(1-\delta)}\right)^{\frac{\alpha}{1-\alpha}}\left[\frac{(1-\alpha)}{\Psi}\right]^{\frac{1}{1+\psi}} \tag{3.300}$$

$$k=i+(1-\delta)k \tag{3.301}$$

$$\log\overline{a}=0 \tag{3.302}$$

3.15.2 Log-Linearization of the Model

Having steady-state solution (3.292)–(3.296), we can now log-linearize the model around the steady state. To this end, we will use the method of first transforming equations into their logarithms, i.e.,

[25] We proceed in this way. From (3.295), we obtain $i=\delta k$ i.e., $\frac{i}{y}=\delta\frac{k}{y}$.

From (3.293), it is $\frac{c}{y}=1-\frac{i}{y}=1-\delta\frac{k}{y}$. We will set $\frac{i}{y}=s_i$ and $\frac{c}{y}=1-s_i=s_c$.

From (3.296), $\alpha\,\frac{y}{k}+(1-\delta)=\frac{1}{\beta}\rightarrow\frac{y}{k}=\frac{1-\beta(1-\delta)}{\alpha\beta}$; therefore, $\frac{i}{y}=\frac{\alpha\beta\delta}{1-\beta(1-\delta)}$.

From (3.292), $(1-\alpha)\frac{y}{c}=\Psi\,h^{1+\psi}$ and $\frac{(1-\alpha)\frac{y}{c}}{\Psi}=h^{1+\psi}$ from which, being $\frac{y}{c}=\frac{1}{s_c}$, it follows that $h=\left[\frac{(1-\alpha)}{\Psi s_c}\right]^{\frac{1}{1+\psi}}$.

From ((3.294), by dividing both sides for y^{α}

$\frac{y}{y^{\alpha}}=a\frac{k^{\alpha}}{y^{\alpha}}h^{1-\alpha}\rightarrow y^{1-\alpha}=a\left(\frac{k}{y}\right)^{\alpha}h^{1-\alpha}$. Elevating both sides to $\frac{1}{1-\alpha}\rightarrow y^{\frac{1-\alpha}{1-\alpha}}=a^{\frac{1}{1-\alpha}}\left(\frac{k}{y}\right)^{\frac{\alpha}{1-\alpha}}h^{\frac{1-\alpha}{1-\alpha}}$ and considering that $\frac{y}{k}=\frac{1-\beta(1-\delta)}{\alpha\beta}$, it follows that

$$y=a^{\frac{1}{1-\alpha}}\left(\frac{\alpha\beta}{1-\beta(1-\delta)}\right)^{\frac{\alpha}{1-\alpha}}h.$$

$$\log\left[(1-\alpha)y_t\right] = \log\ \left[\Psi\, c_t\, h_t^{1+\psi}\right] \tag{3.303}$$

$$\log\,(y_t) = \log\ (c_t + i_t) \tag{3.304}$$

$$\log\,(y_t) = \log\ \left(a_t k_t^{\alpha} h_t^{1-\alpha}\right) \tag{3.305}$$

$$\log\ k_{t+1} = \log\left[(i_t + (1-\delta)k_t\right] \tag{3.306}$$

$$\log\ \left\{\beta\, E_t\left[\frac{c_t}{c_{t+1}}\left(\alpha\ \frac{y_{t+1}}{k_{t+1}} + (1-\delta)\right)\right]\right\} = \log 1 \tag{3.307}$$

$$\log a_t = (1-\rho_a)\log\overline{a}_t + \rho_a \log a_{t-1} + \varepsilon_{at} \tag{3.308}$$

The corresponding logarithm of each expression is

$$\log\,(1-\alpha) + \log y_t = \log\Psi + \log c_t + (1+\psi)\log h_t \tag{3.309}$$

$$\log\,(y_t) = \log\ (c_t + i_t) \tag{3.310}$$

$$\log\,(y_t) = \log a_t + \alpha\ \log\ k_t + (1-\alpha)\ \log h_t \tag{3.311}$$

$$\log\ k_{t+1} = \log\left[(i_t + (1-\delta)k_t\right] \tag{3.312}$$

$$\log\beta + \log c_t - \log E_t c_{t+1} + \log E_t\left(\alpha\frac{y_{t+1}}{k_{t+1}} + (1-\delta)\right) = 0 \tag{3.313}$$

$$\log a_t = (1-\rho_a)\log\overline{a} + \rho_a \log a_{t-1} + \varepsilon_{at} \tag{3.314}$$

For each logarithm is now obtained f'(x)x$\widehat{x}$, where f'(x) indicates the derivative of each variable at steady state (obviously the rule of derivation of compound function is used in computation).

The log-linearized system finally becomes[26]

---

[26] Computation proceeds as follows. For (3.309), (3.310), and (3.311), it is

$$\frac{1}{y}\ y\widehat{y}_t = \frac{1}{c}c\widehat{c}_t + (1+\psi)\frac{1}{h}\ h\widehat{h}_t$$

$$\tfrac{1}{y}\ y\widehat{y}_t = \tfrac{1}{c+i}\left(c\widehat{c}_t + i\widehat{i}_t\right) = \tfrac{c}{c+i}\ \widehat{c}_t + \tfrac{i}{c+i}\widehat{i}_t = \tfrac{c}{y}\widehat{c}_t + \tfrac{i}{y}\ \widehat{i}_t = s_c\ \widehat{c}_t + s_i\ \widehat{i}_t$$

$$\frac{1}{y}\ y\widehat{y}_t = \frac{1}{a}\ a\,\widehat{a}_t + \alpha\frac{1}{k}\ k\,\widehat{k}_t + (1-\alpha)\frac{1}{h}\ h\,\widehat{h}_t$$

For (3.312), it is $\frac{1}{k}k\widehat{k}_{t+1} = \frac{1}{i+(1-\delta)k}\left(i\widehat{i}_t + (1-\delta)k\widehat{k}_t\right) = \frac{i}{i+(1-\delta)k}\widehat{i}_t + (1-\delta)\ \frac{k}{i+(1-\delta)k}\ \widehat{k}_t$ $= \frac{i}{k}\ \widehat{i}_t + (1-\delta)\frac{k}{k}\widehat{k}_t = \frac{\delta k}{k}\widehat{i}_t + (1-\delta)\widehat{k}_t = \delta\,\widehat{i}_t + (1-\delta)\widehat{k}_t$.

For (3.313), it is $\frac{1}{c}\ c\widehat{c}_t - \frac{1}{c}c\ E_t\widehat{c}_{t+1} + \frac{1}{\alpha\frac{y}{k}+(1-\delta)}\ \alpha\left(\frac{1}{k}\ y\ E_t\widehat{y}_{t+1} - \frac{y}{k^2}\ k\ E_t\widehat{k}_{t+1}\right)$.

Due to $\frac{1}{\alpha\frac{y}{k}+(1-\delta)} = \frac{1}{\frac{1}{\beta}} = \beta$ so that it is

$\frac{1}{\alpha\frac{y}{k}+(1-\delta)}\ \alpha\left(\frac{1}{k}\ y\ E_t\widehat{y}_{t+1} - \frac{y}{k^2}\ k\ E_t\widehat{k}_{t+1}\right)$ from which

$$\widehat{y}_t = \widehat{c}_t + (1+\psi)\widehat{h}_t \tag{3.315}$$

$$\widehat{y}_t = \widehat{a}_t + \alpha\widehat{k}_t + (1-\alpha)\widehat{h}_t \tag{3.316}$$

$$\widehat{y}_t = s_c\widehat{c}_t + s_i\,\widehat{i}_t \tag{3.317}$$

$$\widehat{k}_{t+1} = \delta\widehat{i}_t + (1-\delta)\widehat{k}_t \tag{3.318}$$

$$\widehat{c}_t - E_t\widehat{c}_{t+1} + (1-\beta(1-\delta))\,E_t\left(\widehat{y}_{t+1} - \widehat{k}_{t+1}\right) = 0 \tag{3.319}$$

$$\widehat{a}_t = \rho_a\widehat{a}_{t-1} + \widehat{\boldsymbol{\varepsilon}}_t \tag{3.320}$$

3.15.3 *The State-Space Representation of the Log-Linear System*

To obtain a state-space representation of a log-linearized system, it is now necessary to distinguish static equations, which depend on variables referring only to the current date, and equations containing also variables referred to time t+1 and/or t−1.

The equations are ordered so that the first three contain only variables at time t, and the remaining three contain also variables at time t+1 and t−1.

In the first three equations, variables are $\left\{\widehat{h}_t, \widehat{y}_t, \widehat{i}_t\right\}$, while among variables at time t+1 and t−1, we have $\left\{\widehat{k}_t, \widehat{a}_t, \widehat{c}_t\right\}$. Despite that both $\widehat{c}_t$ and $\widehat{y}_t$ also appear at time t+1, only $\widehat{c}_t$ is a control variable, and $\widehat{y}_t$, in the equation that defines it, is dependent on $\widehat{c}_t$.

Rewriting static equations by considering state and control variables as known terms, we have

$$(1+\psi)\widehat{h}_t - \widehat{y}_t = -\widehat{c}_t \tag{3.321}$$

$$(\alpha-1)\widehat{h}_t + \widehat{y}_t = \widehat{a}_t + \alpha\widehat{k}_t \tag{3.322}$$

$\beta\alpha\frac{y}{k}E_t\left(\widehat{y}_{t+1} - \widehat{k}_{t+1}\right) = \alpha\beta\frac{1-\beta(1-\delta)}{\alpha\beta}E_t\left(\widehat{y}_{t+1} - \widehat{k}_{t+1}\right) =$
$(1-\beta(1-\delta))\,E_t\left(\widehat{y}_{t+1} - \widehat{k}_{t+1}\right)$.
For (3.314), it is

$$\frac{1}{a}\,a\widehat{a}_t = \rho_a\frac{1}{a}\,a\widehat{a}_{t-1} + \frac{1}{\varepsilon_a}\,\varepsilon_a\widehat{\varepsilon}_t$$

Carrying out the necessary simplifications, we obtain the system (3.315)–(3.320) reported in the text.

$$\widehat{y}_t - s_i\,\widehat{i}_t = s_c\widehat{c}_t \tag{3.323}$$

Concerning the vector $(\widehat{h}_t, \widehat{y}_t, \widehat{i}_t)$' the matrix of respective coefficients in equations (3.321)–(3.323) is

$$M_{cc} = \begin{pmatrix} 1+\psi & -1 & 0 \\ (\alpha-1) & 1 & 0 \\ 0 & 1 & -s_i \end{pmatrix}$$

Conversely, the matrix of coefficients of variables related to the vector $\left(\widehat{k}_t, \widehat{a}_t, \widehat{c}_t\right)'$ is

$$M_{cs} = \begin{pmatrix} 0 & 0 & -1 \\ \alpha & 1 & 0 \\ 0 & 0 & s_c \end{pmatrix}$$

Therefore, the Eqs. (3.321)–(3.323) rewritten in matrix form become

$$\begin{pmatrix} 1+\psi & -1 & 0 \\ (\alpha-1) & 1 & 0 \\ 0 & 1 & -s_i \end{pmatrix}\begin{pmatrix} \widehat{h}_t \\ \widehat{y}_t \\ \widehat{i}_t \end{pmatrix} = \begin{pmatrix} 0 & 0 & -1 \\ \alpha & 1 & 0 \\ 0 & 0 & s_c \end{pmatrix}\begin{pmatrix} \widehat{k}_t \\ \widehat{a}_t \\ \widehat{c}_t \end{pmatrix} \tag{3.324}$$

This system, in vector notation, corresponds to the general system:

$$M_{cc}\mathrm{Y_t} = M_{cs}\,\mathrm{S_t} \tag{3.325}$$

Consider now the equations of motion of state variables. Collecting to the left of equality the terms of both state and control variables, related equations are

$$\widehat{k}_{t+1} + (\delta-1)\widehat{k}_t = \delta\widehat{i}_t \tag{3.326}$$

$$\widehat{a}_{t+1} - \rho_a\widehat{a}_t = \widehat{\varepsilon}_{t+1} \tag{3.327}$$

$$(1-\beta(1-\delta))\,\widehat{k}_{t+1} + E_t\widehat{c}_{t+1} - \widehat{c}_t = (1-\beta(1-\delta))E_t\widehat{y}_{t+1} \tag{3.328}$$

Matrix of coefficients related to the vector of expected state and control variables $(\left(\widehat{k}_{t+1}, \widehat{a}_{t+1}, E_t\widehat{c}_{t+1}\right)$' in the Eqs. (3.326)–(3.328) is

$$M_{ss0} = \begin{pmatrix} 1 & 0 & 0 \\ 0 & 1 & 0 \\ 1-\beta(1-\delta) & 0 & 1 \end{pmatrix}$$

In the same Eqs. (3.326)–(3.328), the matrix of coefficients related to $(\widehat{k}_t, \widehat{a}_t, \widehat{c}_t)$' (the vector of variables at time t) is

$$M_{ss1} = \begin{pmatrix} \delta-1 & 0 & 0 \\ 0 & -\rho_a & 0 \\ 0 & 0 & -1 \end{pmatrix}$$

Finally, the matrix of coefficients related to the vector of the variables $(E_t\widehat{h}_{t+1}, E_{t+1}\widehat{y}_{t+1}, E_t\widehat{i}_{t+1})$' in the equations of the state variables is

$$M_{sc0} = \begin{pmatrix} 0 & 0 & 0 \\ 0 & 0 & 0 \\ 0 & -(1-\beta(1-\delta)) & 0 \end{pmatrix}$$

while that relating to the vector of the same variables at time t $(h_t,\ y_t, i_t)$ is

$$M_{sc1} = \begin{pmatrix} 0 & 0 & 0 \\ 0 & 0 & 0 \\ 0 & 0 & \delta \end{pmatrix}$$

Lastly, the coefficient matrix related to stochastic shocks ε_{t+1} is

$$M_{sc} = \begin{pmatrix} 0 \\ 1 \\ 0 \end{pmatrix}$$

Then, the state variable equations in matrix form become

$$\begin{pmatrix} 1 & 0 & 0 \\ 0 & 1 & 0 \\ 1-\beta(1-\delta) & 0 & 1 \end{pmatrix} \begin{pmatrix} \widehat{k}_{t+1} \\ E_t\widehat{a}_{t+1} \\ E_t\widehat{c}_{t+1} \end{pmatrix} + \begin{pmatrix} \delta-1 & 0 & 0 \\ 0 & -\rho_a & 0 \\ 0 & 0 & -1 \end{pmatrix} \begin{pmatrix} \widehat{k}_t \\ \widehat{a}_t \\ \widehat{c}_t \end{pmatrix}$$

$$= \begin{pmatrix} 0 & 0 & 0 \\ 0 & 0 & 0 \\ 0 & -(1-\beta(1-\delta)) & 0 \end{pmatrix} \begin{pmatrix} E_t\widehat{h}_{t+1} \\ E_{t+1}\widehat{y}_{t+1} \\ E_t\widehat{i}_{t+1} \end{pmatrix}$$

$$+ \begin{pmatrix} 0 & 0 & 0 \\ 0 & 0 & 0 \\ 0 & 0 & \delta \end{pmatrix} \begin{pmatrix} \widehat{h}_t \\ \widehat{y}_t \\ \widehat{i}_t \end{pmatrix} + \begin{pmatrix} 0 \\ 1 \\ 0 \end{pmatrix} \varepsilon_{t+1} \tag{3.329}$$

And in vectorial form

$$M_{ss0}\, E_t s_{t+1} + M_{ss1} s_t = M_{sc0} E_t Y_{t+1} + M_{sc1}\, y_t + M_{sc}\varepsilon_{t+1} \tag{3.330}$$

Therefore, considering (3.324) and (3.329) together, the whole model in matrix terms becomes

$$\begin{pmatrix} 1+\psi & -1 & 0 \\ (\alpha-1) & 1 & 0 \\ 0 & 1 & -s_i \end{pmatrix} \begin{pmatrix} \widehat{h}_t \\ \widehat{y}_t \\ \widehat{i}_t \end{pmatrix}$$

$$= \begin{pmatrix} 0 & 0 & -1 \\ \alpha & 1 & 0 \\ 0 & 0 & s_c \end{pmatrix} \begin{pmatrix} \widehat{k}_t \\ \widehat{a}_t \\ \widehat{c}_t \end{pmatrix} \begin{pmatrix} 1 & 0 & 0 \\ 0 & 1 & 0 \\ 1-\beta(1-\delta) & 0 & 1 \end{pmatrix} \begin{pmatrix} \widehat{k}_{t+1} \\ E_t\widehat{a}_{t+1} \\ E_t\widehat{c}_{t+1} \end{pmatrix}$$

$$+ \begin{pmatrix} \delta-1 & 0 & 0 \\ 0 & -\rho_a & 0 \\ 0 & 0 & -1 \end{pmatrix} \begin{pmatrix} \widehat{k}_t \\ \widehat{a}_t \\ \widehat{c}_t \end{pmatrix}$$

$$= \begin{pmatrix} 0 & 0 & 0 \\ 0 & 0 & 0 \\ 0 & (1-\beta(1-\delta)) & 0 \end{pmatrix} \begin{pmatrix} E_t\widehat{h}_{t+1} \\ E_{t+1}\widehat{y}_{t+1} \\ E_t\widehat{i}_{t+1} \end{pmatrix} + \begin{pmatrix} 0 & 0 & 0 \\ 0 & 0 & 0 \\ 0 & 0 & \delta \end{pmatrix}$$

$$\times \begin{pmatrix} \widehat{h}_t \\ \widehat{y}_t \\ \widehat{i}_t \end{pmatrix} + \begin{pmatrix} 0 \\ 1 \\ 0 \end{pmatrix} \varepsilon_{t+1} \tag{3.331}$$

In vectorial form,

$$M_{cc}\mathrm{Y_t} = M_{cs}\,\mathrm{S_t}$$

$$M_{ss0} E_t S_{t+1} + M_{ss1} S_t = M_{sc0} E_t Y_{t+1} + M_{sc1} Y_t + M_{sc}\varepsilon_{t+1} \tag{3.332}$$

These equations coincide with those of starting point (3.321)–(3.323) and (3.326)–(3.341).[27] Having verified this, we can proceed in the next section to the transformation necessary for the application of Blanchard-Kahn conditions.

3.15.4 Transformation of the Real Cycle Model into a System of Rational Expectations

We now transform the model equation into the one in expectations.

The first step involves eliminating measurement variables. This requires obtaining from (3.324) the solution

$$\begin{pmatrix} \widehat{h}_t \\ \widehat{y}_t \\ \widehat{i}_t \end{pmatrix} = \begin{pmatrix} 1+\psi & -1 & 0 \\ (\alpha-1) & 1 & 0 \\ 0 & 1 & -s_i \end{pmatrix}^{-1} \begin{pmatrix} 0 & 0 & -1 \\ \alpha & 1 & 0 \\ 0 & 0 & s_c \end{pmatrix} \begin{pmatrix} \widehat{k}_t \\ \widehat{a}_t \\ \widehat{c}_t \end{pmatrix} \tag{3.333}$$

For purposes of significance of (3.333), it is necessary to verify that the inverse

---

[27] This can be verified as follows. The first system, composed by Eqs. (3.324), is equivalent to

$$\begin{pmatrix} (1+\psi)\widehat{h}_t - \widehat{y}_t \\ (\alpha-1)\widehat{h}_t + \widehat{y}_t \\ \widehat{y}_t - s_i\widehat{i}_t \end{pmatrix} = \begin{pmatrix} -\widehat{c}_t \\ \alpha\widehat{k}_t + \widehat{a}_t \\ s_c\widehat{c}_t \end{pmatrix}$$

By expanding vector products, are obtained initial equations

$$(1+\psi)\widehat{h}_t - \widehat{y}_t = -\widehat{c}_t$$
$$(\alpha-1)\widehat{h}_t + \widehat{y}_t = \alpha\widehat{k}_t + \widehat{a}_t$$
$$\widehat{y}_t - s_i\widehat{i}_t = s_c\widehat{c}_t$$

The second system referring to state variables (3.329), corresponds to equations

$$\begin{pmatrix} \widehat{k}_{t+1} \\ E_t\widehat{a}_{t+1} \\ 1-\beta(1-\delta)\widehat{k}_{t+1} + E_t\widehat{c}_{t+1} \end{pmatrix} + \begin{pmatrix} (\delta-1)\widehat{k}_t \\ -\rho_a\widehat{a}_t \\ -\widehat{c}_t \end{pmatrix} = \begin{pmatrix} 0 \\ 0 \\ (1-\beta(1-\delta))E_{t+1}\widehat{y}_{t+1} \end{pmatrix} + \begin{pmatrix} \delta\widehat{i}_t \\ 0 \\ 0 \end{pmatrix} + \begin{pmatrix} 0 \\ \varepsilon_{t+1} \\ 0 \end{pmatrix}$$

which provides initial equations

$\widehat{k}_{t+1} + (\delta-1)\widehat{k}_t = \delta\widehat{i}_t$

$$\widehat{a}_{t+1} - \rho_a\widehat{a}_t = \varepsilon_{t+1}$$

$(1-\beta(1-\delta))k_{t+1} + E_t c_{t+1} - c_t = (1-\beta(1-\delta))\ E_t(y_{t+1})$.

$$\begin{pmatrix} 1+\psi & -1 & 0 \\ (\alpha-1) & 1 & 0 \\ 0 & 1 & -s_i \end{pmatrix}^{-1} \text{ exists.}$$

The determinant of this matrix is

$$\begin{vmatrix} 1+\psi & -1 & 0 \\ (\alpha-1) & 1 & 0 \\ 0 & 1 & -s_i \end{vmatrix}$$

$$= (1+\psi)\begin{vmatrix} 1 & 0 \\ 1 & -s_i \end{vmatrix} + (1)\begin{vmatrix} (\alpha-1) & 0 \\ 0 & -s_i \end{vmatrix} + (0)\begin{vmatrix} (\alpha-1) & 1 \\ 0 & 1 \end{vmatrix}$$

$$= -s_i(1+\psi) - s_i(\alpha-1) = -s_i(1+\psi+\alpha-1) = -s_i(\psi+\alpha) \neq 0. \quad (3.334)$$

So, an inverse matrix exists.

Once adjunct matrix is obtained,[28] by dividing each term of the adjunct matrix by the determinant $-s_i(\psi+\alpha)$, the inverse matrix is[29]

[28] Computations of the adjunct matrix are as follows:

The minors of the matrix $\begin{pmatrix} 1+\psi & -1 & 0 \\ (\alpha-1) & 1 & 0 \\ 0 & 1 & -s_i \end{pmatrix}$ are as follows:

$$m_{11} = \begin{vmatrix} 1 & 0 \\ 1 & -s_i \end{vmatrix}; m_{12} = -\begin{vmatrix} (\alpha-1) & 0 \\ 0 & -s_i \end{vmatrix}; m_{13} = \begin{vmatrix} (\alpha-1) & 1 \\ 0 & 1 \end{vmatrix};$$

$$m_{21} = -\begin{vmatrix} -1 & 0 \\ 1 & -s_i \end{vmatrix}; m_{22} = \begin{vmatrix} 1+\psi & 0 \\ 0 & -s_i \end{vmatrix}; m_{23} = -\begin{vmatrix} 1+\psi & -1 \\ 0 & 1 \end{vmatrix};$$

$$m_{31} = \begin{vmatrix} -1 & 0 \\ 1 & 0 \end{vmatrix}; m_{32} = -\begin{vmatrix} 1+\psi & 0 \\ (\alpha-1) & 0 \end{vmatrix}; m_{33} = \begin{vmatrix} 1+\psi & -1 \\ (\alpha-1) & 1 \end{vmatrix};$$

By explicitly computation of minors, we get

$m_{11} = -s_i$; $m_{12} = s_i(\alpha-1)$; $m_{13} = (\alpha-1)$;

$m_{21} = -s_i$; $m_{22} = -s_i(1+\psi)$; $m_{23} = -(1+\psi)$;

$m_{31} = 0$; $m_{32} = 0$; $m_{33} = \psi+\alpha$.

Therefore, the adjunct matrix is

$$\begin{pmatrix} m_{11} & m_{21} & m_{31} \\ m_{12} & m_{22} & m_{32} \\ m_{13} & m_{23} & m_{33} \end{pmatrix} = \begin{pmatrix} -s_i & -s_i & 0 \\ s_i(\alpha-1) & s_i(1+\psi) & 0 \\ \alpha-1 & -(1+\psi) & \psi+\alpha \end{pmatrix}$$

[29] i.e., $\begin{pmatrix} \frac{-s_i}{-s_i(\psi+\alpha)} & \frac{-s_i}{-s_i(\psi+\alpha)} & 0 \\ \frac{s_i(\alpha-1)}{-s_i(\psi+\alpha)} & \frac{s_i(1+\psi)}{-s_i(\psi+\alpha)} & 0 \\ \frac{\alpha-1}{-s_i(\psi+\alpha)} & \frac{-(1+\psi)}{-s_i(\psi+\alpha)} & \frac{\psi+\alpha}{-s_i(\psi+\alpha)} \end{pmatrix}$

$$\begin{pmatrix} \frac{1}{\psi+\alpha} & \frac{1}{\psi+\alpha} & 0 \\ \frac{(1-\alpha)}{(\psi+\alpha)} & -\frac{(1+\psi)}{(\psi+\alpha)} & 0 \\ \frac{(1-\alpha)}{s_i(\psi+\alpha)} & \frac{(1+\psi)}{s_i(\psi+\alpha)} & -\frac{1}{s_i} \end{pmatrix} \tag{3.335}$$

The explicit solution (3.333), therefore, is

$$\begin{pmatrix} \widehat{h}_t \\ \widehat{y}_t \\ \widehat{i}_t \end{pmatrix} = \begin{pmatrix} \frac{1}{\psi+\alpha} & \frac{1}{\psi+\alpha} & 0 \\ \frac{(1-\alpha)}{(\psi+\alpha)} & -\frac{(1+\psi)}{(\psi+\alpha)} & 0 \\ \frac{(1-\alpha)}{s_i(\psi+\alpha)} & \frac{1+\psi}{s_i(\psi+\alpha)} & -\frac{1}{s_i} \end{pmatrix} \begin{pmatrix} 0 & 0 & -1 \\ \alpha & 1 & 0 \\ 0 & 0 & s_c \end{pmatrix} \begin{pmatrix} \widehat{k}_t \\ \widehat{a}_t \\ \widehat{c}_t \end{pmatrix}$$

$$= \begin{pmatrix} \frac{\alpha}{\psi+\alpha} & \frac{1}{\psi+\alpha} & -\frac{1}{\psi+\alpha} \\ -\alpha\frac{(1+\psi)}{(\psi+\alpha)} & -\frac{(1+\psi)}{(\psi+\alpha)} & -\frac{(1-\alpha)}{(\psi+\alpha)} \\ -\alpha\frac{1+\psi}{s_i(\psi+\alpha)} & \frac{1+\psi}{s_i(\psi+\alpha)} & -\left(\frac{(1-\alpha)}{s_i(\psi+\alpha)}+\frac{s_c}{s_i}\right) \end{pmatrix} \begin{pmatrix} \widehat{k}_t \\ \widehat{a}_t \\ \widehat{c}_t \end{pmatrix} \tag{3.336}$$

Substituting this solution into the system (3.329), it results

$$\begin{pmatrix} 1 & 0 & 0 \\ 0 & 1 & 0 \\ 1-\beta(1-\delta) & 0 & 1 \end{pmatrix} \begin{pmatrix} \widehat{k}_{t+1} \\ \widehat{a}_{t+1} \\ E_t\widehat{c}_{t+1} \end{pmatrix} + \begin{pmatrix} \delta-1 & 0 & 0 \\ 0 & -\rho_a & 0 \\ 0 & 0 & -1 \end{pmatrix} \begin{pmatrix} \widehat{k}_t \\ \widehat{a}_t \\ \widehat{c}_t \end{pmatrix}$$

$$= \begin{pmatrix} 0 & 0 & 0 \\ 0 & 0 & 0 \\ 0 & (1-\beta(1-\delta)) & 0 \end{pmatrix} \begin{pmatrix} E_t\widehat{h}_{t+1} \\ E_{t+1}\widehat{y}_{t+1} \\ E_t\widehat{i}_{t+1} \end{pmatrix}$$

$$
+\begin{pmatrix} 0 & 0 & 0 \\ 0 & 0 & 0 \\ -\delta\alpha\frac{1+\psi}{s_i(\psi+\alpha)} & \delta\frac{1+\psi}{s_i(\psi+\alpha)} & -\delta\frac{(1-\alpha)}{s_i(\psi+\alpha)}-\delta\frac{s_c}{s_i} \end{pmatrix}\begin{pmatrix} \widehat{k}_t \\ \widehat{a}_t \\ \widehat{c}_t \end{pmatrix}
+\begin{pmatrix} 0 \\ 1 \\ 0 \end{pmatrix}\varepsilon_{t+1} \tag{3.337}
$$

With some further algebraic steps,[30] it results

$$
\begin{pmatrix} 1 & 0 & 0 \\ 0 & 1 & 0 \\ 1-\beta(1-\delta) & 0 & 1 \end{pmatrix}\begin{pmatrix} \widehat{k}_{t+1} \\ E_t\widehat{a}_{t+1} \\ E_t\widehat{c}_{t+1} \end{pmatrix}=\begin{pmatrix} 0 & 0 & 0 \\ 0 & 0 & 0 \\ 0 & (1-\beta(1-\delta)) & 0 \end{pmatrix}\begin{pmatrix} E_t\widehat{h}_{t+1} \\ E_{t+1}\widehat{y}_{t+1} \\ E_t\widehat{i}_{t+1} \end{pmatrix}
$$
$$
+\begin{pmatrix} 1-\delta & 0 & 0 \\ 0 & \rho_a & 0 \\ -\delta\alpha\frac{1+\psi}{s_i(\psi+\alpha)} & \delta\frac{1+\psi}{s_i(\psi+\alpha)} & 1-\delta\frac{(1-\alpha)}{s_i(\psi+\alpha)}-\delta\frac{s_c}{s_i} \end{pmatrix}\begin{pmatrix} \widehat{k}_t \\ \widehat{a}_t \\ \widehat{c}_t \end{pmatrix}
+\begin{pmatrix} 0 \\ 1 \\ 0 \end{pmatrix}\varepsilon_{t+1} \tag{3.338}
$$

Solving (3.338) for the expectation vector of the state and control variables is

[30] Moving to the right-hand side and changing the sign of the system (3.337), we will have

$$
\begin{pmatrix} 1 & 0 & 0 \\ 0 & 1 & 0 \\ 1-\beta(1-\delta) & 0 & 1 \end{pmatrix}\begin{pmatrix} \widehat{k}_{t+1} \\ \widehat{a}_{t+1} \\ E_t\widehat{c}_{t+1} \end{pmatrix}=\begin{pmatrix} 0 & 0 & 0 \\ 0 & 0 & 0 \\ 0 & (1-\beta(1-\delta)) & 0 \end{pmatrix}\begin{pmatrix} E_t\widehat{h}_{t+1} \\ E_{t+1}\widehat{y}_{t+1} \\ E_t\widehat{i}_{t+1} \end{pmatrix}
$$
$$
+\begin{pmatrix} 0 & 0 & 0 \\ 0 & 0 & 0 \\ -\delta\alpha\frac{1+\psi}{s_i(\psi+\alpha)} & \delta\frac{1+\psi}{s_i(\psi+\alpha)} & -\delta\frac{(1-\alpha)}{s_i(\psi+\alpha)}-\delta\frac{s_c}{s_i} \end{pmatrix}\begin{pmatrix} \widehat{k}_t \\ \widehat{a}_t \\ \widehat{c}_t \end{pmatrix}
$$
$$
-\begin{pmatrix} \delta-1 & 0 & 0 \\ 0 & -\rho_a & 0 \\ 0 & 0 & -1 \end{pmatrix}\begin{pmatrix} \widehat{k}_t \\ \widehat{a}_t \\ \widehat{c}_t \end{pmatrix}+\begin{pmatrix} 0 \\ 1 \\ 0 \end{pmatrix}\varepsilon_{t+1}
$$

$$\begin{pmatrix} \widehat{k}_{t+1} \\ E_t\widehat{a}_{t+1} \\ E_t\widehat{c}_{t+1} \end{pmatrix} = \begin{pmatrix} 1 & 0 & 0 \\ 0 & 1 & 0 \\ 1-\beta(1-\delta) & 0 & 1 \end{pmatrix}^{-1} \begin{pmatrix} 0 & 0 & 0 \\ 0 & 0 & 0 \\ 0 & (1-\beta(1-\delta)) & 0 \end{pmatrix} \begin{pmatrix} E_t\widehat{h}_{t+1} \\ E_{t+1}\widehat{y}_{t+1} \\ E_t\widehat{i}_{t+1} \end{pmatrix}$$

$$+ \begin{pmatrix} 1 & 0 & 0 \\ 0 & 1 & 0 \\ 1-\beta(1-\delta) & 0 & 1 \end{pmatrix}^{-1} \begin{pmatrix} 1-\delta & 0 & 0 \\ 0 & \rho_a & 0 \\ -\delta\alpha\dfrac{1+\psi}{s_i(\psi+\alpha)} & \delta\dfrac{1+\psi}{s_i(\psi+\alpha)} & 1-\delta\dfrac{(1-\alpha)}{s_i(\psi+\alpha)}-\delta\dfrac{s_c}{s_i} \end{pmatrix}$$

$$\times \begin{pmatrix} \widehat{k}_t \\ \widehat{a}_t \\ \widehat{c}_t \end{pmatrix}$$

$$+ \begin{pmatrix} 1 & 0 & 0 \\ 0 & 1 & 0 \\ 1-\beta(1-\delta) & 0 & 1 \end{pmatrix}^{-1} \begin{pmatrix} 0 \\ 1 \\ 0 \end{pmatrix} \varepsilon_{t+1} \tag{3.339}$$

It results in $\det \begin{pmatrix} 1 & 0 & 0 \\ 0 & 1 & 0 \\ 1-\beta(1-\delta) & 0 & 1 \end{pmatrix} = 1$,[31] and therefore, the matrix is nonsingular.

To get the explicit expression, we need to compute the inverse matrix $\begin{pmatrix} 1 & 0 & 0 \\ 0 & 1 & 0 \\ 1-\beta(1-\delta) & 0 & 1 \end{pmatrix}^{-1}$.

Since we have seen that det(.) = 1, the inverse matrix coincides with the adjunct matrix, i.e.,

[31] Expanding the determinant for the elements of the first row, the corresponding algebraic minors are $m_{11} = \begin{vmatrix} 1 & 0 \\ 0 & 1 \end{vmatrix} = 1$; $m_{12} = -\begin{vmatrix} 0 & 0 \\ 1-\beta(1-\delta) & 1 \end{vmatrix} = 0$; $m_{13} = \begin{vmatrix} 0 & 1 \\ 1-\beta(1-\delta) & 0 \end{vmatrix} = \beta(1-\delta)-1$; $m_{21} = -\begin{vmatrix} 0 & 0 \\ 0 & 1 \end{vmatrix} = 0$; $m_{22} = \begin{vmatrix} 1 & 0 \\ 1-\beta(1-\delta) & 1 \end{vmatrix} = 1$; $m_{23} = \begin{vmatrix} 1 & 0 \\ 1-\beta(1-\delta) & 0 \end{vmatrix} = 0$; $m_{31} = \begin{vmatrix} 0 & 0 \\ 1 & 0 \end{vmatrix} = 0$; $m_{32} = -\begin{vmatrix} 1 & 0 \\ 0 & 0 \end{vmatrix} = 0$; $m_{33} = \begin{vmatrix} 1 & 0 \\ 0 & 1 \end{vmatrix} = 1$

And so, the determinant is $\begin{vmatrix} 1 & 0 & \beta(1-\delta)-1 \\ 0 & 1 & 0 \\ 0 & 0 & 1 \end{vmatrix} = 1$

$$\begin{pmatrix} 1 & 0 & 0 \\ 0 & 1 & 0 \\ 1-\beta(1-\delta) & 0 & 1 \end{pmatrix}^{-1} = \begin{pmatrix} 1 & 0 & 0 \\ 0 & 1 & 0 \\ \beta(1-\delta)-1 & 0 & 1 \end{pmatrix}$$

System (3.338) becomes[32]

$$\begin{pmatrix} \widehat{k}_{t+1} \\ E_t\widehat{a}_{t+1} \\ E_t\widehat{c}_{t+1} \end{pmatrix} = \begin{pmatrix} 0 & 1-\beta(1-\delta) & 0 \\ 0 & 0 & 0 \\ 0 & (1-\beta(1-\delta)) & 0 \end{pmatrix} \begin{pmatrix} E_t\widehat{h}_{t+1} \\ E_{t+1}\widehat{y}_{t+1} \\ E_t\widehat{i}_{t+1} \end{pmatrix}$$
$$+ \begin{pmatrix} 1-\delta & 0 & 0 \\ 0 & \rho_a & 0 \\ (1-\delta)[\beta(1-\delta)-1] & -\delta\dfrac{1+\psi}{s_i(\psi+\alpha)} & 1-\delta\dfrac{(1-\alpha)}{s_i(\psi+\alpha)}-\delta\dfrac{s_c}{s_i} \end{pmatrix}$$
$$\times \begin{pmatrix} \widehat{k}_t \\ \widehat{a}_t \\ \widehat{c}_t \end{pmatrix} + \begin{pmatrix} 0 \\ 1 \\ 0 \end{pmatrix} \varepsilon_{t+1} \tag{3.340}$$

Being

[32]Product matrices are

$$\begin{pmatrix} 1 & 0 & 0 \\ 0 & 1 & 0 \\ \beta(1-\delta)-1 & 0 & 1 \end{pmatrix} \times \begin{pmatrix} 0 & 0 & 0 \\ 0 & 0 & 0 \\ 0 & (1-\beta(1-\delta)) & 0 \end{pmatrix} = \begin{pmatrix} 0 & 0 & 0 \\ 0 & 0 & 0 \\ 0 & (1-\beta(1-\delta)) & 0 \end{pmatrix}$$

$$\begin{pmatrix} 1 & 0 & 0 \\ 0 & 1 & 0 \\ \beta(1-\delta)-1 & 0 & 1 \end{pmatrix} \times \begin{pmatrix} 1-\delta & 0 & 0 \\ 0 & \rho_a & 0 \\ -\delta\alpha\dfrac{1+\psi}{s_i(\psi+\alpha)} & \delta\dfrac{1+\psi}{s_i(\psi+\alpha)} & 1-\delta\dfrac{(1-\alpha)}{s_i(\psi+\alpha)}-\delta\dfrac{s_c}{s_i} \end{pmatrix}$$

$$\begin{pmatrix} 1 & 0 & 0 \\ 0 & 1 & 0 \\ \beta(1-\delta)-1 & 0 & 1 \end{pmatrix} \times \begin{pmatrix} 1-\delta & 0 & 0 \\ 0 & \rho_a & 0 \\ -\delta\alpha\dfrac{1+\psi}{s_i(\psi+\alpha)} & \delta\dfrac{1+\psi}{s_i(\psi+\alpha)} & 1-\delta\dfrac{(1-\alpha)}{s_i(\psi+\alpha)}-\delta\dfrac{s_c}{s_i} \end{pmatrix}$$
$$= \begin{pmatrix} 1-\delta & 0 & 0 \\ 0 & \rho_a & 0 \\ (1-\delta)[\beta(1-\delta)-1]-\delta\alpha\dfrac{1+\psi}{s_i(\psi+\alpha)} & \delta\dfrac{1+\psi}{s_i(\psi+\alpha)} & 1-\delta\dfrac{(1-\alpha)}{s_i(\psi+\alpha)}-\delta\dfrac{s_c}{s_i} \end{pmatrix}$$

$$\begin{pmatrix} 1 & 0 & 0 \\ 0 & 1 & 0 \\ \beta(1-\delta)-1 & 0 & 1 \end{pmatrix} \times \begin{pmatrix} 0 \\ 1 \\ 0 \end{pmatrix} = \begin{pmatrix} 0 \\ 1 \\ 0 \end{pmatrix}$$

$$\begin{pmatrix} E_t\widehat{h}_{t+1} \\ E_{t+1}\widehat{y}_{t+1} \\ E_t\widehat{i}_{t+1} \end{pmatrix} = \begin{pmatrix} \frac{\alpha}{\psi+\alpha} & \frac{1}{\psi+\alpha} & -\frac{1}{\psi+\alpha} \\ -\alpha\frac{(1+\psi)}{(\psi+\alpha)} & -\frac{(1+\psi)}{(\psi+\alpha)} & 0 \\ -\alpha\frac{1+\psi}{s_i(\psi+\alpha)} & -\frac{1+\psi}{s_i(\psi+\alpha)} & \frac{(1-\alpha)}{s_i(\psi+\alpha)}-\frac{s_c}{s_i} \end{pmatrix} \begin{pmatrix} \widehat{k}_{t+1} \\ E_t\widehat{a}_{t+1} \\ E_t\widehat{c}_{t+1} \end{pmatrix} \tag{3.341}$$

By substituting (3.341) in (3.340), we get

$$\begin{pmatrix} \widehat{k}_{t+1} \\ E_t\widehat{a}_{t+1} \\ E_t\widehat{c}_{t+1} \end{pmatrix} = \begin{pmatrix} \frac{\alpha}{\psi+\alpha} & \frac{1}{\psi+\alpha} & -\frac{1}{\psi+\alpha} \\ -\alpha\frac{(1+\psi)}{(\psi+\alpha)} & -\frac{(1+\psi)}{(\psi+\alpha)} & 0 \\ -\alpha\frac{1+\psi}{s_i(\psi+\alpha)} & -\frac{1+\psi}{s_i(\psi+\alpha)} & \frac{(1-\alpha)}{s_i(\psi+\alpha)}-\frac{s_c}{s_i} \end{pmatrix} \begin{pmatrix} \widehat{k}_{t+1} \\ E_t\widehat{a}_{t+1} \\ E_t\widehat{c}_{t+1} \end{pmatrix}$$
$$+ \begin{pmatrix} 1-\delta & 0 & 0 \\ 0 & \rho_a & 0 \\ (1-\delta)[\beta(1-\delta)-1] & -\delta\frac{1+\psi}{s_i(\psi+\alpha)} & 1-\delta\frac{(1-\alpha)}{s_i(\psi+\alpha)}-\delta\frac{s_c}{s_i} \end{pmatrix}$$
$$\times \begin{pmatrix} \widehat{k}_t \\ \widehat{a}_t \\ \widehat{c}_t \end{pmatrix} + \begin{pmatrix} 0 \\ 1 \\ 0 \end{pmatrix} \varepsilon_{t+1} \tag{3.342}$$

System (3.342) is rewritten as

$$\left[\begin{pmatrix} 1 & 0 & 0 \\ 0 & 1 & 0 \\ 0 & 0 & 1 \end{pmatrix} - \begin{pmatrix} \frac{\alpha}{\psi+\alpha} & \frac{1}{\psi+\alpha} & -\frac{1}{\psi+\alpha} \\ -\alpha\frac{(1+\psi)}{(\psi+\alpha)} & -\frac{(1+\psi)}{(\psi+\alpha)} & 0 \\ -\alpha\frac{1+\psi}{s_i(\psi+\alpha)} & -\frac{1+\psi}{s_i(\psi+\alpha)} & \frac{(1-\alpha)}{s_i(\psi+\alpha)}-\frac{s_c}{s_i} \end{pmatrix} \right] \begin{pmatrix} \widehat{k}_{t+1} \\ E_t\widehat{a}_{t+1} \\ E_t\widehat{c}_{t+1} \end{pmatrix}$$
$$= \begin{pmatrix} 1-\delta & 0 & 0 \\ 0 & \rho_a & 0 \\ (1-\delta)[\beta(1-\delta)-1] & -\delta\frac{1+\psi}{s_i(\psi+\alpha)} & 1-\delta\frac{(1-\alpha)}{s_i(\psi+\alpha)}-\delta\frac{s_c}{s_i} \end{pmatrix} \begin{pmatrix} \widehat{k}_t \\ \widehat{a}_t \\ \widehat{c}_t \end{pmatrix} + \begin{pmatrix} 0 \\ 1 \\ 0 \end{pmatrix} \varepsilon_{t+1} \tag{3.343}$$

That is,

$$\begin{pmatrix} 1-\frac{\alpha}{\psi+\alpha} & -\frac{1}{\psi+\alpha} & \frac{1}{\psi+\alpha} \\ \alpha\frac{(1+\psi)}{(\psi+\alpha)} & 1+\frac{(1+\psi)}{(\psi+\alpha)} & 0 \\ \alpha\frac{1+\psi}{s_i(\psi+\alpha)} & \frac{1+\psi}{s_i(\psi+\alpha)} & 1+\frac{s_c}{s_i}-\frac{(1-\alpha)}{s_i(\psi+\alpha)} \end{pmatrix}\begin{pmatrix} \widehat{k}_{t+1} \\ E_t\widehat{a}_{t+1} \\ E_t\widehat{c}_{t+1} \end{pmatrix}$$

$$= \begin{pmatrix} 1-\delta & 0 & 0 \\ 0 & \rho_a & 0 \\ (1-\delta)[\beta(1-\delta)-1] & -\delta\frac{1+\psi}{s_i(\psi+\alpha)} & 1-\delta\frac{(1-\alpha)}{s_i(\psi+\alpha)}-\delta\frac{s_c}{s_i} \end{pmatrix}\begin{pmatrix} \widehat{k}_t \\ \widehat{a}_t \\ \widehat{c}_t \end{pmatrix}+\begin{pmatrix} 0 \\ 1 \\ 0 \end{pmatrix}\varepsilon_{t+1} \tag{3.344}$$

And the solution for the expectations is

$$\begin{pmatrix} \widehat{k}_{t+1} \\ E_t\widehat{a}_{t+1} \\ E_t\widehat{c}_{t+1} \end{pmatrix}$$

$$= \begin{pmatrix} 1-\frac{\alpha}{\psi+\alpha} & -\frac{1}{\psi+\alpha} & \frac{1}{\psi+\alpha} \\ \alpha\frac{(1+\psi)}{(\psi+\alpha)} & 1+\frac{(1+\psi)}{(\psi+\alpha)} & 0 \\ \alpha\frac{1+\psi}{s_i(\psi+\alpha)} & \frac{1+\psi}{s_i(\psi+\alpha)} & 1+\frac{s_c}{s_i}-\frac{(1-\alpha)}{s_i(\psi+\alpha)} \end{pmatrix}^{-1}$$

$$\begin{pmatrix} 1-\delta & 0 & 0 \\ 0 & \rho_a & 0 \\ (1-\delta)[\beta(1-\delta)-1] & -\delta\frac{1+\psi}{s_i(\psi+\alpha)} & 1-\delta\frac{(1-\alpha)}{s_i(\psi+\alpha)}-\delta\frac{s_c}{s_i} \end{pmatrix}\begin{pmatrix} \widehat{k}_t \\ \widehat{a}_t \\ \widehat{c}_t \end{pmatrix}$$

$$+\begin{pmatrix} 1-\frac{\alpha}{\psi+\alpha} & -\frac{1}{\psi+\alpha} & \frac{1}{\psi+\alpha} \\ \alpha\frac{(1+\psi)}{(\psi+\alpha)} & 1+\frac{(1+\psi)}{(\psi+\alpha)} & 0 \\ \alpha\frac{1+\psi}{s_i(\psi+\alpha)} & \frac{1+\psi}{s_i(\psi+\alpha)} & 1+\frac{s_c}{s_i}-\frac{(1-\alpha)}{s_i(\psi+\alpha)} \end{pmatrix}^{-1}\begin{pmatrix} 0 \\ 1 \\ 0 \end{pmatrix} \tag{3.345}$$

3.15.5 The Blanchard-Kahn Transformation of the RBC Model of the Centralized Economy

With the appropriate change of notation

$$\mathrm{E_t s_{t+1}} = \begin{pmatrix} \widehat{k}_{t+1} \\ E_t\widehat{a}_{t+1} \\ E_t\widehat{c}_{t+1} \end{pmatrix}; \mathrm{s_t} = \begin{pmatrix} \widehat{k}_t \\ \widehat{a}_t \\ \widehat{c}_t \end{pmatrix} \quad \text{and}$$

$$\mathrm{W_s} = \begin{pmatrix} 1-\dfrac{\alpha}{\psi+\alpha} & -\dfrac{1}{\psi+\alpha} & \dfrac{1}{\psi+\alpha} \\ \alpha\dfrac{(1+\psi)}{(\psi+\alpha)} & 1+\dfrac{(1+\psi)}{(\psi+\alpha)} & 0 \\ \alpha\dfrac{1+\psi}{s_i(\psi+\alpha)} & \dfrac{1+\psi}{s_i(\psi+\alpha)} & 1+\dfrac{s_c}{s_i}-\dfrac{(1-\alpha)}{s_i(\psi+\alpha)} \end{pmatrix}^{-1}$$

$$\begin{pmatrix} 1-\delta & 0 & 0 \\ 0 & \rho_a & 0 \\ (1-\delta)[\beta(1-\delta)-1] & -\delta\dfrac{1+\psi}{s_i(\psi+\alpha)} & 1-\delta\dfrac{(1-\alpha)}{s_i(\psi+\alpha)}-\delta\dfrac{s_c}{s_i} \end{pmatrix};$$

$$\mathrm{W_e} = \begin{pmatrix} 1-\dfrac{\alpha}{\psi+\alpha} & -\dfrac{1}{\psi+\alpha} & \dfrac{1}{\psi+\alpha} \\ \alpha\dfrac{(1+\psi)}{(\psi+\alpha)} & 1+\dfrac{(1+\psi)}{(\psi+\alpha)} & 0 \\ \alpha\dfrac{1+\psi}{s_i(\psi+\alpha)} & \dfrac{1+\psi}{s_i(\psi+\alpha)} & 1+\dfrac{s_c}{s_i}-\dfrac{(1-\alpha)}{s_i(\psi+\alpha)} \end{pmatrix}^{-1} \begin{pmatrix} 0 \\ 1 \\ 0 \end{pmatrix}$$

System (3.345) is equivalent to the following system of expectations, in vectorial form:

$$\mathrm{E_t s_{t+1}} = \mathrm{W_s s_t} + \mathrm{W_e}\boldsymbol{\varepsilon}_{t+1} \tag{3.346}$$

For the Blanchard-Kahn procedure, setting

$$\mathrm{E_t s_{t+1}} = \mathrm{s_{t+1}} - \mathrm{z_{t+1}}$$

where $\mathrm{E_t\, z_{t+1}} = 0$, it is

$$\mathrm{s_{t+1}} - \mathrm{z_{t+1}} = \mathrm{W_s s_t} + \mathrm{W_e}\boldsymbol{\varepsilon}_{t+1}$$

So that the system (3.346) in state variables becomes

$$s_{t+1} = W_s s_t + W_e \boldsymbol{\varepsilon}_{t+1} + z_{t+1} \tag{3.347}$$

The long and detailed calculation carried out up to now was performed by hand to expressly show the laboriousness of calculations necessary to obtain a specific expression of matrices in terms of model parameters.

Yet, the model here is just a little more complicated than the basic one and still remains simple. A minimally realistic model of the economy would in practice become unsolvable with the Blanchard-Kahn procedure, and this is sufficient for suggesting the search for other methods that can count on the aid of the computer.

But that's not enough. It should be noted that to continue from the expectation system just obtained in the application of the Blanchard-Kahn procedure, we will need further calculations since it will be recalled that it is necessary to apply Jordan's diagonalization $W_s = PDP^{-1}$ to the expectation system and then also to consider the partition of the matrices P, D, and P^{-1} into the submatrices of dimensions corresponding, respectively, to the number of eigenvalues inside and outside the unit circle, which in turn should be explicitly calculated.

Partition, as it has been previously seen, is

$$P = \begin{pmatrix} P_{BB} & P_{BF} \\ P_{FB} & P_{FF} \end{pmatrix}; D = \begin{pmatrix} D_B & 0 \\ 0 & D_F \end{pmatrix}; P^{-1} = \begin{pmatrix} P^*_{BB} & P^*_{BF} \\ P^*_{FB} & P^*_{FF} \end{pmatrix}$$

By defining the new vector of state variables $\bar{s}_t = P^1 s_t$, diagonalized subsystems corresponding to the partition become

$$\begin{pmatrix} \bar{s}_{Bt} \\ \bar{s}_{Ft} \end{pmatrix} = \begin{pmatrix} D_B & 0 \\ 0 & D_f \end{pmatrix} \begin{pmatrix} \bar{s}_{Bt} \\ \bar{s}_{Ft} \end{pmatrix} + \begin{pmatrix} R_B \\ R_F \end{pmatrix} \boldsymbol{\varepsilon}_{t+1} + \begin{pmatrix} P^*_B \\ P^*_F \end{pmatrix} z_{t+1} \tag{3.348}$$

where $\begin{pmatrix} R_B \\ R_F \end{pmatrix}$ is the partition of the matrix $R = P^{-1}W_{e\_}$ and $\begin{pmatrix} P^*_B \\ P^*_F \end{pmatrix}$ is that of P^{-1}.

From this point on, we proceed as from (2.302), and following, of Sect. 2.20 of Chap. 2.[33]

[33] For the convenience of the reader, albeit at the cost of some repetition, we here give a hint of the continuation of the procedure.

Given (3.348), the system relating to forward variables is

$$\bar{s}_{Ft} = D_f \bar{s}_{Ft} + R_F \boldsymbol{\varepsilon}_{t+1} + P^*_F z_{t+1} \tag{3.349}$$

The forward solution in expectations of (3.349) yields $\bar{s}_{Ft} = 0$, which, being by construction, $\bar{s}_{Ft} = \begin{pmatrix} P^*_{FB} & P^*_{FF} \end{pmatrix} \begin{pmatrix} s_{Bt} \\ s_{Ft} \end{pmatrix}$, holds

$$P^*_{FB} s_{Bt} + P^*_{FF} s_{Ft} = 0 \tag{3.350}$$

And therefore,

If we also wanted to express the matrices and variables considered up to now in their explicit values of the parameters' model, we would have to repeat the calculations just carried out on the parameter matrices, and this would still require a substantially unmanageable number of calculations.

We can conclude by observing that the attempt made in this section illuminates the reasons why, from a practical point of view, it is preferable and convenient to refer not to the theoretical solution but to a solution obtained with numerical methods.[34]

We will deal with the topic of numerical methods in the next chapter.

$$s_{Ft} = \left(P^*_{FF}\right)^{-1} P^*_{FB} s_{Bt} = \Gamma s_{Bt} \tag{3.351}$$

Given the law of motion of backward variables obtained from partition

$$\begin{pmatrix} s_{Bt+1} \\ s_{Ft+1} \end{pmatrix} = \begin{pmatrix} W_{s,BB} & W_{s,BF} \\ W_{s,FB} & W_{s,FF} \end{pmatrix} \begin{pmatrix} s_{Bt} \\ s_{Ft} \end{pmatrix} + \begin{pmatrix} W_{e,B} \\ W_{e,F} \end{pmatrix} \varepsilon_{t+1} + \begin{pmatrix} z_{B.t+1} \\ z_{F,t+1} \end{pmatrix}$$

It holds

$$s_{Bt+1} = W_{s,BB} s_{Bt} + W_{s,BF} s_{Bt} + W_{e,B} \varepsilon_{t+1} + z_{B.t+1} \tag{3.352}$$

Since it is $z_{B.\ t\ +\ 1} = 0$, as there are no forecast errors in the predetermined variables, by substituting for s_{Bt} and setting $M_{ss} = (W_{s,\ BB} + W_{s,\ BF}\Gamma)$, the solution for predetermined variables is

$$s_{Bt+1} = M_{ss}\ s_{Bt} + M_{se} \varepsilon_{t+1}$$

Where for uniformity of notation it has been written $M_{se} = W_{e,\ B}$.
The system's solution for backward and forward variables can, therefore, be written

$$\begin{aligned} s_{Bt+1} &= M_{ss}\ s_{Bt} + M_{se} \varepsilon_{t+1} \\ s_{Ft} &= \Gamma s_{Bt} \end{aligned} \tag{3.353}$$

Finally, recall that for the measurement variables (see Chap. 2, Sect. 2.18), we have $y_t = M_{cc}^{-1} M_{cs} s_t$, and by setting $\phi = M_{cc}^{-1} M_{cs}$, it follows

$$y_t = \phi s_t$$

By partitioning matrix ϕ according to the same criterion as the other partitions $\phi = \begin{pmatrix} \phi_B & 0 \\ 0 & \phi_F \end{pmatrix}$, the solution can be completed by adding to the system (3.353) the vector equation

$$y_t = \begin{pmatrix} \phi_B & 0 \\ 0 & \phi_F \end{pmatrix}) \begin{pmatrix} s_{Bt} \\ s_{F,t} \end{pmatrix} = \phi_B s_{Bt} + \phi_F\ s_{F,t} = (\phi_B + \phi_F \Gamma) s_{Bt} \tag{3.354}$$

where it has been used the fact that $s_{Ft} = \Gamma s_{Bt}$.

[34] A solution resulting from the application of MATLAB software is in F. Collard (2015). There the code of the model we have considered, written in the MATLAB language, is reported in a zip folder called Matlab_codes.

Appendix

A.1 Bellman and Dynamic Programming

In this Appendix, Bellman's principle will be illustrated[35] by resorting to the representative agent problem.[36]

Agent's objective is to find a sequence $\{u_t\}_{t=0}^{\infty}$ of control, i.e., a decision u_t, at each instant t of a time horizon. Control u_t is exercised on a system, which over time follows a given trajectory $x_{t+1} = F(x_t, u_t, z_t)$. This control, u_t, is optimally selected, in the sense that it maximizes some merit criterion, expressed in general by an objective function, and in the economic example, we will consider by function $E_0 \sum_{t=0}^{\infty} \beta^t U(x_t, \ u_t)$.

This optimal control problem is reducible to a familiar intertemporal maximization problem of kind:

$$\max_{\{u_t\}_{t=0}^{\infty}} E_0 \left[\sum\nolimits_{t=0}^{\infty} \beta^t U(x_t, u_t) \right] \tag{3.355}$$

$$\text{Sub} \quad x_{t+1} = F(\, x_t, u_t, z_t)$$

$$(x_0, z_0) = \text{given} \tag{3.356}$$

In the notation here introduced, x_t is a vector of m state variables in period t; u_t is a vector of n control variables at instant t; z_t is a vector of s exogenous variables whose dynamics at every t does not depend on x_t and u_t; E_t is the mathematical expectation, conditional on the information available at time t, and $\beta \in (0, 1)$ denotes the discount factor.

A further hypothesis, which we have seen largely widespread in DSGE models, refers to the dynamics of z_t since it is assumed that z_t follows an AR(1) process:

$$z_{t+1} = Pz_t + p + \varepsilon_{t+1} \tag{3.357}$$

The solution to the problem (3.355)–(3.356) is a function G, invariant over time, called *policy function*, or even *control equation*. The policy function maps (x, z) in the optimal control u. Given the control function, the resulting dynamic system describes temporal sequences which, for a given sequence of the exogenous process $\{z_t\}_{t=0}^{\infty}$, are composed of values of state variable $\{x_t\}_{t=1}^{\infty}$ and control variable $\{u_t\}_{t=0}^{\infty}$, generated by iteration by the system:

[35] Bellman, R. (1957); Bertsekas, D. (1976), in particular chapters 2 and 6.

[36] An elegant and comprehensive treatment of dynamic programming is in Stokey et al. (1989). See also Sargent, T. (1987).

$$\begin{aligned} u_t &= G(x_t, z_t) \\ x_{t+1} &= F(x_t, u_t, z_t) \\ z_{t+1} &= Pz_t + p + \epsilon_{t+1} \end{aligned} \tag{3.358}$$

given an initial condition (x_0, z_0).

The control function G(.) is determined by iteration based on the *Bellman equation*, whose construction precisely reveals the iterated nature of the problem (3.355)–(3.356).

To this end, consider the maximum function of problem (3.355)–(3.356)

$$V(x_0, z_0) = \max_{u_t} E_0 \left[\sum_{t=0}^{\infty} \beta^t U(x_t, u_t) \right] \tag{3.359}$$

Function V(.) is the *value function*. This function expresses values of the objective function resulting from the effective implementation of optimal control (the value assumed by objective function corresponding to choices made, at instant t, in an optimal way).

If it is considered value function V (3.359) at time 1, by taking expectation at time 0, it results

$$E_0 V(x_1, z_1) = \max_{u_t} E_0 \left[\sum_{t=0}^{\infty} \beta^t U(x_t, u_t) \right] \tag{3.360}$$

With obvious considerations, function (3.359) can be set

$$V(x_0, z_0) = \max_{u_t} \left\{ U(x_0, u_0) + E_0 \left[\sum_{t=1}^{\infty} \beta^t U(x_t, u_t) \right] \right\} =$$

$$\max_{u_t} \left\{ U(x_0, u_0) + \beta\, E_0 \left[\sum_{t=1}^{\infty} \beta^t U(x_{t+1}, u_{t+1}) \right] \right\} \tag{3.361}$$

By replacing (3.360) in (3.361), it follows

$$V(x_0, z_0) = \max_{u_t} \left\{ U(x_0, u_0) + \beta\, E_0[V(x_1, z_1)] \right\} \tag{3.362}$$

Formulation (3.362) constitutes a *dynamic programming problem* that highlights the sequential structure of the operator's decision problem. Indeed, in period 0, an operator is confronted with the problem $V(x_0, z_0)$. In period 1, the operator is confronted with problem $V(x_1, z_1)$. In period 3.... and so on.

In each period t, therefore, the operator is confronted with the same type of problem, namely, choosing the control variable u_t that maximizes the current *gain* (utility) plus the discounted value of the optimal plan from the period t+1.

Since this problem repeats identically in each period, we can ignore the time suffix in (3.362), and rewrite the value function[37] as

$$V(x.z) = \max_{u_t} \{U(x, u) + \beta\, E_0[V(\tilde{x}, \tilde{z})]\} \quad (3.363)$$

In (3.363), the tilde sign (~) on x and z denotes respective values in the following period. Both values $(\tilde{x}, \tilde{z})$ in (3.363) are also subject to (3.356) and (3.357), i.e., they must be

$$\tilde{x} = F(x, u, z) \quad (3.364)$$
$$\tilde{z} = Pz + p + \tilde{\varepsilon}$$

Given (3.363) if we knew function V(.), we could solve the conditions for a maximum for u, and the solution to the problem, given (3.358), would be completely determined from since we also obtain $(\tilde{x}, \tilde{z})$. The problem, however, is that V(.) is unknown, and this qualifies Eq. (3.362) as a *functional equation*, in which, in fact, unknown is a function.

A typical method for solving this functional equation is to construct a sequence of value functions, through the iteration of the following value function:

$$V_{j+1}(x.z) = \max_{u_t} \left\{U(x, u) + \beta\, E_0\left[V_j(\tilde{x}, \tilde{z})\right]\right\} \quad (3.365)$$

This method, in terms of algorithm, consists of the following steps:

- Step 1. A concave and differentiable function (e.g., one of known utility functions) is proved as a possible value function, V_j.
- Step 2. Bellman's equation is applied to find the optimal value of u, and together in (3.356), we obtain V_{j+1} according to (3.365).
- Step 3. Step 1 is repeated with V_{j+1} as the initial value, repeating the procedure until $V_{j'+1} = V_j$ occurs for some index js.

The difficulty of this method is that each step 2 requires solving a maximum problem for finding the optimum, from the maximization of the right side of (3.363).

In principle, if the functions U(.) and F(.) appearing in problem (3.355)–(3.356) satisfy certain conditions of regularity, by virtue of a theorem called *contractions' theorem*,[38] we are sure that a solution exists and is unique.

---

[37] A setup similar to the one adopted here for obtaining the value function is also in Gong, G. and Semmler, W. (2006), pp. 25–27.

[38] An accessible exposition of the theorem of contractions (In Italian) is in Stampacchia, G. (1973), Chapter 1, Section 3.

However, in practical terms, the difficulty remains in obtaining, except in rare cases, an explicit form for Bellman's equation. This difficulty also explains the use of approximation and numerical calculation procedures, and therefore of various methods applied in the literature.

It should be noted, however, that using first-order conditions allows one to characterize and, in some cases, obtain the sequence of decisions of the representative operator.

Maximizing (3.363) for u requires that the following first-order condition must be satisfied:

$$\frac{\partial U(x,u)}{\partial u} + \beta E\left[\frac{\partial F}{\partial u}(x,u,z)\frac{\partial V}{\partial \widetilde{x}}(\widetilde{x},\widetilde{z})\ \right] = 0 \qquad (3.366)$$

Term in square brackets in (3.366) derives from the fact that $\widetilde{x} = F(x,u,z)$, and therefore, $\frac{dV}{du} = \frac{\delta V}{\delta \widetilde{x}}\frac{\delta F}{\delta u}$.

In (3.366) appears the derivative $\frac{\partial V}{\partial \widetilde{x}}$ of the unknown function we want to determine.

Given the solution for u, which is represented by the policy function $u_t = G(x_t, z_t)$, by substituting, function (3.363) will write as follows:

$$V(x,z) = U(x, G(x,z)) + \beta E[V(F(x, G(x,z), z, \widetilde{z}\ )] \qquad (3.363\text{-a})$$

By differentiating (3.363-a) for x, we obtain

$$\frac{\partial V(x,z)}{\partial x} = \partial U\left(\frac{x, G(x,z)}{\partial x + \beta E\left[\frac{\partial V}{\partial F}(\widetilde{x},\widetilde{z})\frac{\partial F}{\partial x}\ (x, G(x,z), z)\right]}\right. \qquad (3.367)$$

Condition (3.367) is known in economic literature as the *Benveniste-Scheinkman equation.*[39]

By the envelope theorem (see below), you have $\partial F/\partial x = 0$, and (3.367) becomes

$$\frac{\partial V(x,z)}{\partial x} = \partial U\left(\frac{x, G(x,z)}{\partial x}\right. \qquad (3.368)$$

Considering (3.368) for future variables, it becomes

See also Sargent, T. (1987) op. cit., Stokey et al. (1989), op. cit.

[39] Benveniste, L.M. and. Scheinkman, J.A (1979), pp.727–33. On the Benveniste- Scheinkman equation, see also Sargent, T. (1987) pp.21–22.

$$\frac{\partial V(\widetilde{x},\widetilde{z})}{\partial \widetilde{x}} = \frac{\partial U(\widetilde{x},\widetilde{u})}{\partial \widetilde{u}} \tag{3.369}$$

Replacing (3.369) in (3.366) gives the Euler equation

$$\frac{\partial U(x,u)}{\partial u} + \beta E\left[\frac{\partial F}{\partial u}(x,u,z)\ \frac{\partial U}{\partial \widetilde{x}}(\widetilde{x},\widetilde{u})\right] = 0 \tag{3.370}$$

It is important to stress the role of condition $\partial F / \partial x = 0$ in obtaining the Euler equation.

This condition was imposed by invoking the envelope theorem. For a full understanding of dynamic programming, it is useful to review it here.

To introduce the topic, let us consider a simple static optimization problem that we know appears to us in the form:

$$\max_x F(x) \tag{A}$$

$$\text{Sub } c \geq G(x)$$

In applications, it is possible that (A) is presented in a generalized form

$$\max_x F(x,\theta) \tag{B}$$

$$\text{Sub } c \geq G(x,\theta)$$

In optimal problem (B), functions F(.) and G(.) (objective and constraint functions), concerning version (A), depend both on parameter $\theta \in R$.

Concerning (B), we now define the maximum value function V: $R \to R$ given by

$$V(\theta) = \max_X F(x,\theta) \tag{3.371}$$

$$\text{Sub } c \geq G(x,\theta)$$

Evaluation of V requires a two-stage procedure:

- In the first stage, for a given value of θ, we solve for value x^* that satisfies the constrained optimum problem.
- In the second stage, substituting x^*, together with the given value of θ, we obtain

$$V\ (\theta) = F\ (x^*,\theta) \tag{3.372}$$

We now want to obtain an expression for the derivative of V for θ, based on the data we know.

We know that the solution x^* satisfies the Lagrangian

$$L(x^*, \lambda^*, \theta) = F(x^*, \theta) + \lambda^*[c - G(x^*, \theta)] \quad (3.373)$$

together with the *slackness-conditions* imposed by the Kuhn-Tucker theorem

$$\lambda^*[c - G(x^*, \theta)] = 0 \quad (3.374)$$

Given the latter, the following identity is true:

$$V(\theta) = L(x^*, \lambda^*, \theta) = F(x*, \theta) \quad (3.375)$$

and from this, it follows that

$$V'(\theta) = \frac{\partial L}{\partial \theta} = \frac{\partial F}{\partial \theta} \quad (3.376)$$

In principle, in computing the first derivative $V'(\theta)$ in (3.376), we should take into account the dependence of both x^*, λ^* on the parameter θ and therefore also differentiating quantities x^*, λ^* for θ. But the envelope theorem consists precisely in the property that in differentiation operation we can ignore this dependence. That is, given the value $x^*(\theta)$ which solves the maximum problem for the assigned value of θ, substituting value in objective function is obtained:

$$V(\theta) = F[x^*(\theta), \theta] \quad (3.377)$$

Differentiating with respect to θ, by the rule of derivation of the compound function:

$$V'(\theta) = F_1[x^*(\theta), \theta]\, x^{*'}(\theta) + F_2[x^*(\theta), \theta] \quad (3.378)$$

But $x^*(\theta)$ is the value of x that maximizes F given θ, and therefore, it must be true:

$$F_1[x^*(\theta), \theta] = 0 \quad (3.379)$$

Therefore, the envelope theorem implies a free maximum problem:

$$V'(\theta) = F_2[x^*(\theta), \theta] \quad (3.380)$$

In the derivation of the function of maximum (3.377) for θ, we can ignore the dependence of x^* on this parameter.

It is important to note that this result is obtained not because it is assumed that x^* does not depend on θ, but because, being x^* chosen optimally, it is a critical point of F, given θ.

In the case of a constrained maximum, $x^*(\theta)$ is a critical point not only of the objective function but also of the entire Lagrangian. Indeed, the definition of the maximum value function shows that it coincides not only with the objective function but also with the Lagrangian evaluated at the optimum point, and the Kuhn-Tucker theorem tells us that for a problem with a constrained maximum, the solution x $*(\theta)$ is a critical point of the Lagrangian.

We are now able to formulate the following:[40]

Envelope Theorem

Let F(.) and G(.) be continuous functions with continuous derivatives for x and θ. For any given θ, let $x^*(\theta)$ be the value that maximizes $F(x, \theta)$ subject to $c \geq G(x, \theta)$, and let $\lambda^*(\theta)$ be the value of the associated Lagrange multiplier for given θ. Assuming that $x^*(\theta)$ and $\lambda^*(\theta)$ are also continuous and differentiable functions and that the qualification $G_1[x^*(\theta), \theta] \neq 0$ of the constraint by the Kuhn-Tucker theorem is valid for all values of θ, the function of maximum value

$$V(\theta) = max\ F(x, \theta)\ sub \quad c \geq G(x, \theta)$$

Verifies

$$V'(\theta) = F_2[x^*(\theta), \theta] - \lambda^*(\theta) G_2[x^*(\theta), \theta]$$

And therefore,

$$F_1\ (x * (\theta), \theta)\ x' * (\theta) = 0$$

Proof:

The proof follows the intuitive reasoning set out above.

The Kuhn-Tucker theorem tells us that for any given value of θ, the quantities $x^*(\theta)$ and $\lambda^*(\theta)$ verify

$$V(\theta) = F[x^*(\theta), \theta] = F[x^*(\theta), \theta] + \lambda^*(\theta)\{c - G[x^*(\theta), \theta]\} \tag{3.381}$$

Differentiating with respect to θ, we have

$$V'(\theta) = F_1[x^*(\theta), \theta]x^{*\prime}(\theta) + F_2[x^*(\theta), \theta] + \lambda^{*\prime}(\theta)\{c - G[x^*(\theta), \theta]\}$$
$$-\lambda^*(\theta)G_1[x^*(\theta), \theta]x^{*\prime}(\theta) - \lambda^*(\theta)G_2[x^*(\theta), \theta] \tag{3.382}$$

Equation (3.382) shows that, CORRECTLY, in the derivation to obtain $V'(\theta)$, the dependence of x^* and λ^* on θ must be taken into account. However, rewriting:

[40] An exposition of the envelope theorem is in Takayama, A. (1985) *Mathematical Economics*, (second ed.), Cambridge University Press, New York, pp. 137–38.

$$V'(\theta) = \{F_1[x^*(\theta), \theta] - \lambda^*(\theta)G_1[x^*(\theta), \theta]\}x^{*\prime}(\theta) + F_2[x^*(\theta), \theta]$$
$$+\lambda^{*\prime}(\theta)\{c - G[x^*(\theta), \theta]\} - \lambda^*(\theta)G_2[x^*(\theta), \theta] \quad (3.383)$$

it is noted that as a result of the condition

$$F_1\ [x^*(\theta), \theta] - \lambda^*(\theta)G_1[x^*(\theta), \theta]\}x^{*\prime}(\theta) = 0 \quad (3.384)$$

$V'(\theta)$ reduces to

$$V'(\theta) = F_2[x^*(\theta), \theta] + \lambda^{*\prime}(\theta)\{c - G[x^*(\theta), \theta]\} - \lambda^*(\theta)G_2[x^*(\theta), \theta]$$

It remains to ascertain that x*(θ) and λ*(θ) also satisfy the Kuhn-Tucker condition

$$\lambda^{*\prime}(\theta)\{c - G[x^*(\theta), \theta]\} = 0 \quad (3.385)$$

Equation (3.384) is valid for any θ, if the constraint is satisfied as equality (the constraint is binding).

For θ for which the constraint is not binding, i.e., it is satisfied as an inequality, (3.385), λ*(θ) is zero. But if the constraint is non-binding for θ, for the continuity of G and x*(), there will exist an $\varepsilon^* > 0$ such that for all values θ+ε with $\varepsilon^* > |\varepsilon|$ the constraint still remains unbinding. Therefore $\lambda^*(\theta+\varepsilon) = 0$ for all $\varepsilon^* > |\varepsilon|$.

Appealing to the definition of derivative as the limit of the incremental ratio follows

$$\lambda^{*\prime}(\theta) = \lim_{\varepsilon \to \infty} \frac{\lambda * (\theta + \varepsilon) - \lambda * (\theta)}{\varepsilon} = -\lim_{\varepsilon \to \infty} \frac{\lambda^*(\theta)}{\varepsilon} = 0$$

And (3.385) must hold also when the constraint is nonbinding. Therefore:

$$V'(\theta) = F_2[x^*(\theta), \theta] - \lambda^*(\theta)G_2[x^*(\theta), \theta] \quad (3.386)$$

and this proves the envelope theorem.

In the light of these considerations, it only remains to observe that the problem

$$\max_u \{U(x, u) + \beta E[V(\widetilde{x}, \widetilde{z})]\} \quad (3.387)$$
$$\text{Sub } \widetilde{x} = F(x, u, z)$$

It can be reduced to the (free) maximum problem

$$\max_u \{U(x,u) + \beta E[V(F(x,u,z),\tilde{z})]\} \tag{3.388}$$

in which the objective function to be maximized for u depends on the parameter x, and therefore the envelope theorem is applies to it.

This conclusion justifies the use that hs been made of the envelope theorem in the determination of the Euler equation.

A.2 An Economic Example of the Application of Bellman's Principle: Aggregate Savings in an Intertemporal Context Under Conditions of Uncertainty

As an example of the application of Bellman's principle, consider the problem of a representative *consumer-saver* who must optimally allocate the available resources between consumption and savings over an infinite time horizon.

Available resources derive from a production activity subject to uncertainty $Q_t = A_t k_t^{\alpha}$ and savings take place through the acquisition of physical capital.

The constrained maximum problem is

$$\max \sum_{i=0}^{\infty} (1+\theta)^{-i} E[\ln\ c_{t+i} |\ t]$$
$$\text{sub } k_{t+1+i} + c_{t+i} = A_t k_t^{\alpha} \tag{3.389}$$

Corresponding to (3.389), a dynamic programming problem is defined by the Bellman equation:

$$V_t\ (k_t) = \max_{(c_t,k_t)} \ln c_t + (1+\theta)^{-1}\ E[V_{t+1}(k_{t+1})] \tag{3.390}$$

Maximizing the value function for c_t requires that the corresponding first-order condition be satisfied:

$$\frac{1}{c_t} + E\left[(1+\theta)^{-1} V'_{t+1} \frac{\partial k_{t+1}}{\partial c_t} \middle|\ t\right] = 0 \tag{3.391}$$

On the other hand, for the value function, differentiating for k_t must be verified:

$$V'_t(k_t) = (1+\theta)^{-1}\ E\left[V'_{t+1}(k_{t+1}) \frac{\partial k_{t+1}}{\partial k_t} \middle|\ t\right] \tag{3.392}$$

From the resources' constrain, it is obtained

$$k_{t+1} = A_t k_t^{\alpha} - c_t \tag{3.393}$$

from which $\frac{\partial k_{t+1}}{\partial c_t} = -1$, so that the necessary condition concerning consumption becomes

$$\frac{1}{c_t} - (1+\theta)^{-1} E\left[V'_{t+1}(k_{t+1}) \middle| t\right] = 0 \tag{3.394}$$

Still, from the resources' constraint follows

$$\frac{\partial k_{t+1}}{\partial k_t} = \alpha A_t k_t^{\alpha - 1} \tag{3.395}$$

and so

$$V'_t(k_t) = (1+\theta)^{-1} E\left[V'_{t+1}(k_{t+1}) \alpha A_t k_t^{\alpha-1} \middle| t\right] \tag{3.396}$$

A necessary condition for maximum consumption is

$$\frac{1}{c_t} = (1+\theta)^{-1} E\left[V'_{t+1}(k_{t+1}) \middle| t\right] \tag{3.397}$$

and substituting (3.397) in (3.396), it follows

$$V'_t(k_t) = \frac{\alpha A_t k_t^{\alpha-1}}{c_t} \tag{3.398}$$

By taking the expectation of (3.398) at time t+1, it follows

$$E\, V'_t(k_{t+1}) = E\left(\frac{\alpha A_{t+1} k_{t+1}^{\alpha-1}}{c_{t+1}}\right) \tag{3.399}$$

Substituting (3.399) in (3.397), we obtain

$$\frac{1}{c_t} = (1+\theta)^{-1} E[A_{t+1} \alpha k_{t+1}^{\alpha-1} \frac{1}{c_{t+1}} \mid t] \tag{3.400}$$

This (Euler's) condition expresses that the optimality of saving requires that the cost of giving up current consumption, as measured by the marginal utility of current consumption, must be equal to the marginal utility of future consumption, capitalized at the stochastic rate of return of savings in real activity (i.e., return of physical capital) $\alpha A_{t+1} k_{t+1}^{\alpha-1}$ discounted at the intertemporal preference rate.

The rule for optimal savings in conditions of uncertainty is the same as the one obtained if we consider the case of the individual consumer, or a representative consumer, who holds a portfolio of assets and is faced with the choice between investing a portion of the portfolio on certain security and the remaining portion of assets in risky assets.

Consider a consumer who at time 0 solves the problem

$$\max \sum_{t=0}^{\infty} (1+\theta)^{-i} U(\, c_t |\, 0) \tag{3.401}$$

$$sub \;\; A_{t+1} = (A_t + y_t - c_t)[(1+r_t)w_t + (1+z_t)(1-w_t)]$$

Here, w_t is the portion of portfolio A_t increased by current savings $y_t - c_t$ invested in the asset with a certain return r_t, while $(1 - w_t)$ is the portion of the portfolio invested in risky assets whose yield z_t is uncertain (and therefore it is a stochastic variable).

In terms of dynamic programming, the Bellman equation defines the following function of maximum value:

$$V_t(A_t) = \max_{(c_t,\, w_t)} \; [U(c_t) + (1+\theta)^{-1} E\, [V_{t+1}\, (A_{t+1})|t] \tag{3.402}$$

The value function verifies the condition

$$\frac{dV_t(A_t)}{dA_t} = (1+\theta)^{-1} E\left[\frac{dV_{t+1}(A_{t+1})}{dA_{t+1}} \frac{\partial A_{t+1}}{\partial A_t}\right] \tag{3.403}$$

From the budget constraint, it is

$$\frac{\partial A_{t+1}}{\partial A_t} = (1+r_t)w_t + (1+z_t)(1-w_t)] \tag{3.404}$$

and therefore, the (3.403) becomes

$$\frac{dV_t(A_t)}{dA_t} = (1+\theta)^{-1}[(1+r_t)w_t + (1+z_t)(1-w_t)]E\left[\frac{dV_{t+1}(A_{t+1})}{dA_{t+1}}\right] \tag{3.405}$$

Now consider the derivative of the value function for w_t. It is

$$\frac{dV_t(A_t)}{dw_t} = (1+\theta)^{-1} E\left[\frac{dV_{t+1}(A_{t+1})}{dw_t}\right] \tag{3.406}$$

But

$$\frac{dV_{t+1}(A_{t+1})}{dw_t} = \frac{dV_{t+1}(A_{t+1})}{dA_{t+1}} \frac{\partial A_{t+1}}{\partial w_t} \tag{3.407}$$

and from the budget constraint, we get

$$\frac{\partial A_{t+1}}{\partial w_t} = (1 + r_t) - (1 + z_t) \tag{3.408}$$

Therefore, (3.404) becomes

$$\frac{dV_t(A_t)}{dw_t} = (1+\theta)^{-1}[\,(1+r_t) - (1+z_t)]E\left[\frac{dV_{t+1}(A_{t+1})}{dA_{t+1}}\right] \tag{3.409}$$

In both conditions, (3.403) and (3.409) appear derivative $\frac{dV_{t+1}(A_{t+1})}{dA_{t+1}}$, which is unknown since the function $V_{t\,+\,1}(A_{t\,+\,1})$ is unknown. Observing that from the envelope theorem, it follows

$$\frac{dV_t(A_t)}{dA_t} = U'(c_t) \tag{3.410}$$

and moving forward the index t by one period to t+1, we have

$$\frac{dV_{t+1}(A_{t+1})}{dA_{t+1}} = EU'(c_{t+1}) \tag{3.411}$$

It turns out that the Benveniste-Scheinkman condition of the value function concerning A_t requires

$$U'(c_t) = (1+\theta)^{-1}\ \{[(1+r_t)w_t + (1+z_t)(1-w_t)]EU'(c_{t+1})||\ t\} \tag{3.412}$$

On the other hand, maximizing the value function for c_t and w_t also requires that there are satisfied conditions for vanishing respective first derivatives.[41]

---

[41] The condition of vanishing first-derivative for c_t is

$\frac{dV_t(A_t)}{dc_t} = U'(c_t) + (1+\theta)^{-1}E\left[\frac{dV_{t+1}(A_{t+1})}{dc_t}\Big|t\right] = 0.$

But $\frac{dV_{t+1}(A_{t+1})}{dc_t} = \frac{dV_{t+1}(A_{t+1})}{dA_{t+1}}\frac{\partial A_{t+1}}{\partial c_t}$ and from the budget constraint, we get $\frac{\partial A_{t+1}}{\partial c_t} = -[(1+r_t)w_t + (1+z_t)(1-w_t)]$, so that the first expression becomes

$\frac{dV_t(A_t)}{dc_t} = U'(c_t) - (1+\theta)^{-1}E\left[\frac{dV_{t+1}(A_{t+1})}{dA_{t+1}}[(1+r_t)w_t + (1+z_t)(1-w_t)]\Big|t\right] = 0.$

This is equivalent to

$$U'(c_t) = (1+\theta)^{-1}\ [(1+r_t)w_t + (1+z_t)(1-w_t)]E[\ U'(c_{t+1})]$$

Maximum for w_t requires $\frac{dV_t(A_t)}{dw_t}=0$, and therefore, it must hold

$$E\left[U'(c_{t+1})(1+r_t))\right]-E\left[U'(c_{t+1})(1+z_t)\right]=0 \tag{3.413}$$

that is to say

$$E\left[U'(c_{t+1})(1+r_t))\right]=E\left[U'(c_{t+1})(1+z_t)\right] \tag{3.414}$$

Substituting (3.414) in (3.412), we obtain

$$\begin{aligned} U'(c_t) &= (1+\theta)^{-1}E[(1+z_t)U'(c_{t+1})w_t+(1+z_t)U'(c_{t+1})(1-w_t)] \\ &= (1+\theta)^{-1}\mathrm{E}[(1+z_t)U'(c_{t+1})] \end{aligned} \tag{3.415}$$

Equation (3.415) is a generalization to a context of uncertainty of the Keynes-Ramsey rule for optimal saving.

It requires that to have optimal savings, the cost of the current giving up of a unit of consumption must be equal to the currently expected value of the marginal utility of future consumption, valued at the current stochastic rate (1+z_t) of capitalization, and further discounted at the rate of intertemporal preference.

As can now be easily verified, in the two problems of savings considered in this section, the optimal saving rule is, in both cases, conceptually identical.

References

Bellman, R. (1957) *Dynamic Programming*, Princeton University Press.

Benveniste, L.M. and Scheinkman, J.A. (1979) "On the differentiability of the value function in dynamic models of economics", *Econometrica,* 47(3), pp. 727-33.

Bertsekas, D. (1976) *Dynamic Programming and Stochastic Control*, Academic Press, New York.

Blanchard, O.J. and Kahn, C.M. (1980) "The solution of linear difference models under rational expectations." Econometrica, 48(1), 305-311.

Campbell, J. (1994) "Inspecting the Mechanism: An Analytical Approach to the Stochastic Growth Model." *Journal of Monetary Economics,* 33(3), pp. 463–506.

Collard, F. (2015), Lectures, Available at: http://fabcol.free.fr/notes.html (Accessed: October 2020).

Gong, G. and Semmler, W. (2006) "*Stochastic dynamic macroeconomics: theory and empirical evidence*", Oxford University Press. Oxford, New York, pp. 25-27.

Hansen, G. (1985) "Indivisible labor and the business cycle", *Journal of Monetary Economics,* 16(3), pp. 309-27.

Hayashi, F. (1982) "Tobin's Marginal q and Average q: A Neoclassical Interpretation", Econometrica, 50(1), pp. 213-224.

The necessary condition for a maximum for consumption c_t appears redundant, since it coincides with the expression already obtained from the Benveniste-Scheinkman condition, and therefore, it can be ignored.

Intriligator, M. (1971) *Mathematical Optimization and Economic Theory*, Prentice-Hall, inc., Englewood Cliffs, N.J, pp. 269-78

King, R. and Plosser, I., Rebelo S. (1988b). "Production, Growth and Business Cycles II: New Directions." *Journal of Monetary Economics,* 21(2/3), pp. 309–341.

King, R. and Plosser, I., Rebelo S., (1988a). "Production, Growth and Business Cycles I: The Basic Neo-classical Model." *Journal of Monetary Economics*, 21(2/3), pp. 195–232.

Kydland, F. and Prescott, E. (1982) "Time to build and aggregate fluctuations", *Econometrica*, 50(6), 1345-1371.

Long, J. and Plosser, C. (1983), "Real Business cycles", *Journal of Political Economy,* 9(1), pp. 1345-370.

Prescott, E. (1986) "Theory ahead of business-cycle measurement", *Federal Reserve Bank of Minneapolis Quarterly Report*, 10(Fall), pp. 9-23.

Samuelson, P. A. (1947) *Foundations of Economic Analysis,* Harvard University Press, Cambridge Mass.

Sargent, T. (1987) *Dynamic Macroeconomic Theory,* Harvard University Press, Cambridge, MA.

Sims, C. A. (2001) "Solving Linear Rational Expectations Models", *Computational Economics,* 20(1), pp. 1-20.

Stampacchia, G. (1973), *Lezioni di Analisi Matematica (Lectures on Mathematical Analysis)*, Vol. II, Liguori publisher, Neaples.

Stokey, N.L. and Lucas R.E., with Prescott E. (1989) *Recursive Methods in Economic Dynamic*, Harvard University Press, Cambridge Mass.

Takayama, A. (1985), *Mathematical Economics*, (second ed.), Cambridge University Press, New York, pp. 137–38

Taubman, P. Wilkinson, M. (1970) "User cost, capital utilization and investment theory", *International Economic Review*, 11(2), pp. 209-215

Tobin, J. (1969) "A general equilibrium approach to monetary theory", *Journal of Money, Credit and Banking*, 1(1), pp. 15-29.

Uhlig, H. (1999) "A Toolkit for Analyzing Nonlinear Dynamic Stochastic Models Easily" in R. Marion, and A. Scott (eds) *Computational Methods for the Study of Dynamic Economies*, Oxford University Press, New York, pp. 30-61.

Chapter 4
A Simplified Illustration of Numerical Solution Methods of DSGE Models with DYNARE Software

Blanchard-Kahn's procedure for the solution of real business cycle (RBC) models is powerful and elegant, but it has evident limits: it requires a lot of calculations, which for more complex models make it substantially inapplicable. For these reasons, economic theory has moved toward numerical calculus. This chapter considers the numerical solution method contained in the DYNARE software by exposing the writing of the DSGE model code in a simplified way. In Sect. 4.4, there is a detailed comment on DYNARE's numerical simulation of the model of the centralized economy in level form, with a flexible labor supply. This chapter continues by examining the model of the centralized economy in (log) linear form and alternative ways of encoding the model. A complete DYNARE code of the log-linearized model with public expenditure is also considered. After a note on CALIBRATION, a detailed discussion of different ways for calculating the steady state in DYNARE concludes the chapter.

4.1 DYNARE Coding as a Method for Numerical Solving DSGE Models

Compared to initial applications, concerning above all *MATLAB* software, the *DYNARE* software has subsequently established itself among the tools available to economists for numerical calculus of DSGE models. In DYNARE, in fact, the writing of a *code* allows one to carry out numerical simulations of each of DSGE models.

The fundamental reference equations for writing the DYNARE code of DSGE models are those of first-order conditions and steady-state solutions. These allow both variables and parameters of a model to be identified and defined in the DYNARE language. Steady-state conditions are useful for identifying the initial values of each of the variables to be determined.

G. Chirichiello, *DSGE Models for Real Business Cycle and New Keynesian Macroeconomics*, Springer Texts in Business and Economics,
https://doi.org/10.1007/978-3-031-56034-7_4

Shocks present in a model, since they are supposed stochastic, are not known; either in the "if" nor in the *quantum* they could occur (they are obviously uncertain), for each of the future instants considered. However, it is admitted that the distribution of probability and therefore mean and variance are known.

Knowledge of the mean is built into the steady state, because shocks are assumed to have zero mean.

The variance is assumed to be finite, and therefore its knowledge is included among the parameters of the model, generally in the form of the value assigned to mean squared deviation.

However, it is necessary to distinguish whether a single shock or multiple shocks are being admitted. This second possibility introduces a problem of possible correlation between various shocks.

A DYNARE code consists of blocks, each of which is labeled at the beginning of the block itself.

Such blocks consist of the following:

1. **Labeling block**: the labeling block specifies symbols with which variables and parameters are indicated.
   - The variables in "var"
   - The exogenous shocks in "varexo"
   - The parameters in "parameters"
2. **Block of parameter values**
   In this block, values to parameters are assigned.
3. **Program blocks**
   Blocks of the DYNARE program are divided into

3.a) **Model block**: this block starts with the instruction **model** and ends with the instruction **end**.

Between the two instructions, the n equations for the n variables of the model are written.

Each equation ends with a semicolon instruction, i.e., **;** at the end of the line.

Equations have conditional expectations. Placing (+1) next to a variable makes DYNARE understand that in the equation, there is a conditional expectation of that variable.

3.b) **Initialization block**: DYNARE needs to resolve the steady state. This may be the hardest part (when dealing with a nonlinear problem). So, it is important to assign good initial conditions.

4. **Random shock block**: indicates the standard deviation for exogenous innovation.
5. **Solution block:** this block contains instructions to DYNARE to solve the program. These instructions are

5.1 **command for first order approximation:** *stoch_simul(order=1, nocorr, nomoments, IRF=0);*

5.2 **command for second order approximation**: *stoch_simul(order=2, nocorr, nomoments, IRF=0).*

To instruct DYNARE to calculate IRF and business cycle statistics of the model's theoretical values, modify the stoch_simul command as follows *stoch_simul (order=1, IRF=30).*

4.2 Three Different Ways of Writing Model Block Equations

When writing the model, the following specifications must be taken into account:

1. Model equations can be written in three different forms:

1.1 *Equations in the levels*
First-order conditions are resumed as they have been formulated in the nonlinear model

1.2 *Equations in the form exp-log*
Each variable is interpreted as if it were a log and its level is referred to with the transformation **exp(.)**.

1.3 *Equations in linear form*
In this case, first-order conditions considered are those of the model previously log-linearized "by hand."

2. DYNARE uses both first-order approximation and second-order approximation.
When using second-order approximation, it must be considered that second-order moments (variances and covariances) are in general different, in different forms of writing the model.
3. DYNARE can distinguish endogenous state variables from exogenous state variables as long as the latter (exogenous) is followed by the index (−1).

4.3 The Code of the Centralized Economy Model, with Flexible Labor Supply, in the Form of Levels

We will now apply the various forms previously indicated for writing DYNARE code to a real business cycle model.

Let us consider an economy run by the central planner, whose performance we know to be represented by the following equations:[1]

---

[1]Lagrangian that central planner maximizes for control variables c_t, k_{t+1}, is:

$$E_0 \sum_{t=0}^{\infty} \beta^t \left[\log c_t - \theta \frac{h^{1+\psi}}{1+\psi} + \lambda_t \left(a_t k_t^{\alpha} h_t^{1-\alpha} - c_t - k_{t+1} + (1\text{-}\delta) k_t \right) \right].$$

$$(1-\alpha)y_t = c_t\theta\, h_t^{1+\psi} \tag{4.1}$$

$$y_t = c_t + i_t \tag{4.2}$$

$$y_t = a_t k_t^{\alpha} h_t^{1-\alpha} \tag{4.3}$$

$$k_{t+1} = i_t + (1-\delta)k_t \tag{4.4}$$

$$\beta\, E_t\left[\frac{c_t}{c_{t+1}}\left(\alpha\,\frac{y_{t+1}}{k_{t+1}} + (1-\delta)\right)\right] = 1 \tag{4.5}$$

$$log\, a_t = (1-\rho_a)\, log\, \overline{a} + \rho_a\, log\, a_{t-1} + \varepsilon_{at} \tag{4.6}$$

The *model* block of Eqs. (4.1)–(4.6), with the parameters rewritten, not already with their correct Greek name, but with some mangling words to avoid conflicts with prenamed functions of MATLAB, and therefore malfunctions of the code, is

```
model;

(1-alph)*y= thet*c*h^(1+psi);
y = c+i;
y = a*k(-1)^alph*h^(1-alph);
k = i + (1-delt)*k(-1);
k= betta*(c/c(+1)*(alph*(y(+1) + (1-delt)*k)));
log(a) = (1-rhoa)*log(abar) +(rhoa)*log(a(-1))+ea;
end;
```

The complete code with all the four blocks is

```
var y, c, k, I, h, a;
varexo ea;
parameters abar, rhoa, betta, delt, alph, psi, thet;
abar =1;
rhca = 0.025;
betta =0.99;
delt = 0.025;
psi = 0;
thet = 2.95;
alph = 0.36;
model;
(1-alph)*y= thet*c*h^(1+psi);
y = c+i;
y = a*k(-1)^alph*h^(1-alph);
```

Compared to the basic model, the one considered here includes also the central planner's choice of worked hours, h, to be distributed to households. The parametric utility function considered is logarithmic in consumption, and CRRA, for worked hours.

```
k = i + (1-delt)*k(-1);
k= betta*(c/c(+1)*(alph*(y(+1) + (1-delt)*k)));
log(a) = (1-rhoa)*log(abar) +(rhoa)*log(a(-1))+ea;
end;
initval;
y = 1.08;
c = 0.80;
h = 0.33;
k = 11.08;
a=1;
ea = 0;
end;
shocks;
var ea; stderr 0.009;
end;
stoch_simul;
```

In my PC, this code was saved in the folder (C:\dynare\4.6.4\examples) with the extension *m_RBC1.mod*, and it was tested with DYNARE version 4.6.4. It works properly.

4.4 A Comment on DYNARE's Numerical Simulation of the Model of the Centralized Economy in Level Form, with a Flexible Labor Supply

At the end of processing the code, DYNARE provides, each code, with the following results:

- *Summary of the model*
- *Variance-covariance matrix of exogenous shocks*
- *Policy and transition functions*
- *Statistical moments of endogenous variables (mean, variance, standard deviation, skewness, kurtosis)*
- *Matrix of contemporaneous correlations*
- *Table of autocorrelation coefficients*
- *Graphic representation of impulse responses*

The following is a representation of the results DYNARE provided for the above code:

```
MODEL SUMMARY
Number of variables: 6
Number of stochastic shocks: 1
```

Table 4.1 Policy and transition functions

	y	c	k	i	h	a
Constant	0.156527	0.154389	0.085495	0.002137	0.219953	1.000000
k(−1)	0.323987	0.836028	0.462959	−0.512041	0.735787	0
a(−1)	0.005032	0.003239	0.001794	0.001794	0.002457	0.025000
ea	0.201293	0.129552	0.071741	0.071741	0.098290	1.000000
k(−1),k(−1)	−2.913014	−1.874816	−1.038198	−1.038198	2.561922	0
a(−1),k(−1)	0.019457	0.012522	0.006934	0.006934	0.011630	0
a(−1),a(−1)	−0.002450	−0.001577	−0.000873	−0.000873	−0.001248	−0.012188
ea,ea	0.105277	0.067756	0.037521	0.037521	−0.031072	0.500000
k(−1),ea	0.778273	0.500896	0.277376	0.277376	0.465197	0
a(−1),ea	0.005264	0.003388	0.001876	0.001876	0.001554	0.025000

```
Number of state variables: 2
Number of jumpers: 2
Number of static variables: 2
```

```
MATRIX OF COVARIANCE OF EXOGENOUS SHOCKS
Variables ea
ea C.000081
```

The following table, starting from the second row, describes policy and transition functions of the model.

Reading the matrix of Table 4.1 provides the following information:

- By rows: period t values of variables
- By columns: values of state variables + shock (e) in period t−1

The constant is the steady state. It enters as an intercept in all functions defined therein.

Thus, for example, considering variable y, reading by column provides the following information on the corresponding policy function in period t−1:

$$y = 0.156527 + 0.323987\ k(-1) + 0.005032\ a(-1) + 0.201293\ ea \tag{4.7}$$

Equation (4.7) shows values of measurement variable y as a function of state variables and stochastic shock.

The measurement nature of variable y qualifies this function as a *transition function*, since, being the system stable, it indicates the values assumed over time by variable y in its path of returning to the initial steady-state value 0.156527.

Conversely, concerning, e.g., consumption and capital stock, which are control variables, the functions

Table 4.2 Approximated theoretical moments

Variable	Mean	Std. Dev.	Variance
y	0.1565	0.0018	0.0000
c	0.1544	0.0013	0.0000
k	0.0855	0.0007	0.0000
i	0.0021	0.0007	0.0000
h	0.2199	0.0010	0.0000
a	1.0000	0.0090	0.0001

Table 4.3 Approximated matrix of correlations

Variables	y	c	k	i	h	a
y	1.0000	0.9392	0.9392	0.7869	0.7735	0.9915
c	0.9392	1.0000	1.0000	0.5271	0.5087	0.8864
k	0.9392	1.0000	1.0000	0.5271	0.5087	0.8864
i	0.7869	0.5271	0.5271	1.0000	0.9998	0.8605
h	0.7735	0.5087	0.5087	0.9998	1.0000	0.8494
a	0.9915	0.8864	0.8864	0.8605	0.8494	1.0000

$$\mathrm{c} = 0.154389 + 0.836028\ \mathrm{k}(-1) + 0.003239\ \mathrm{a}(-1) + 0.129552\ \mathrm{ea} \tag{4.8}$$

$$\mathrm{k} = 0.085495 + 0.462959\ \mathrm{k}(-1) + 0.001794\ \mathrm{a}(-1) + 0.071741\ \mathrm{ea} \tag{4.9}$$

constitute *policy functions*.

Equations (4.8)–(4.9) indicate how the system, following an exogenous impulse due to changes in state variables, modifies control variables.

Subsequent lines consider second-degree level effects in the exogenous variables and can be ignored in a linear, first-degree approximation.

The next Table 4.2 on theoretical moments shows the values of the statistics for each model variable.

These values are those resulting from theoretical data obtained from the simulation carried out by DYNARE.

The next matrix of correlations Table 4.3 specifies the nature of the respective *co-movements* of the model's variables simulated by DYNARE.

So, e.g., the first column indicates how system variables move according to GDP trend over time.

Literature on the business cycle has crystallized the characteristics of co-movements by indicating that the variable moves with the business cycle (e.g., it increases when GDP increases and vice versa) if it exhibits a positive correlation greater than 0.25.

Conversely, the variable moves countercyclically if it moves in the opposite direction of the business cycle (i.e., it increases when GDP decreases and vice versa), with a negative correlation of less than −0.25.

Table 4.4 Approximated coefficients of autocorrelation

Order	1	2	3	4	5
y	0.1469	0.0601	0.0276	0.0128	0.0059
c	0.4824	0.2238	0.1036	0.0480	0.0222
k	0.4824	0.2238	0.1036	0.0480	0.0222
i	−0.2498	−0.1335	−0.0622	−0.0288	−0.0133
h	−0.2502	−0.1337	−0.0623	−0.0289	−0.0134
a	0.0250	0.0006	0.0000	0.0000	0.0000

Finally, a variable exhibits an acyclical movement if it does not move with the business cycle and exhibits a correlation included in the interval [−0.25, 0.25].

In general, the closer correlation to +1, the greater the degree of pro-cyclicality, and conversely, the closer correlation to (−1), the greater the degree of countercyclicality.

Reading the first column of Table 4.3 shows that the model forecasts a strong cyclicality between total factor productivity and GDP, as well as between GDP and capital, and consumption, less cyclicality for investments and hours worked.

The following Table 4.4 of autocorrelation coefficients shows the effects of changes of each variable on itself at any instant. So, e.g., the effect of innovation on total productivity, after the first reaction, disappears at the end of the second period and is zero in the third period.

GDP shows greater persistence. In period 5, the autocorrelation coefficient shows that, to a lesser extent, GDP is positively affected by the positive effect previously recorded, i.e., to the end of period 1. Conversely, in the same period 5, greater autocorrelation coefficient of consumption shows a greater persistence to positive changes occurring, e.g., in period 1.

Finally, for each variable, DYNARE provides a graphical description of the response, for the period specified in the code, to the initial exogenous impulse, e.g., a positive shock on production technology initially increases GDP, consumption, capital stock, investment, and hours worked, but the latter approximate steady state in a different way concerning the other variables, since both investment and hours worked, after initially reaching steady state, decrease for some time before returning to steady state again.

Impulse response functions describe the equilibrium time trend of variables after that shock initially hits the economy.

A fundamental difference emerges here relative to static models. In static models, a conventional adjustment mechanism toward equilibrium is considered.

In dynamic models, of which here graphs of Fig. 4.1 represent an example, co-movements describe mechanisms of *diffusion* of initial impulses *over time, and in the economy* between the different variables, generated by changes in exogenous variables.

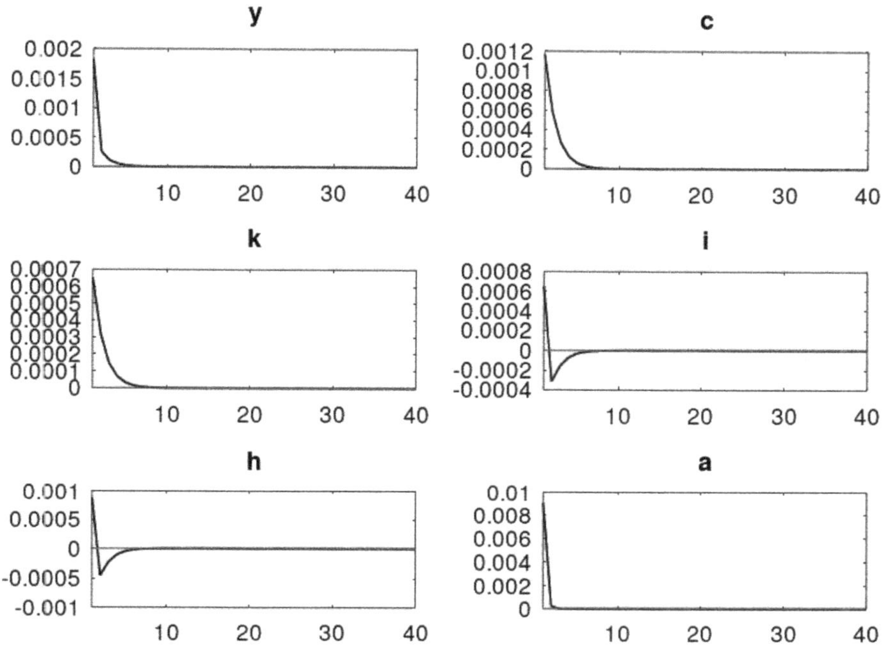

Fig. 4.1 Transition functions

4.5 The Code of Model of the Centralized Economy with Flexible Labor Supply, in Exp-Log Form

Regarding the previous model of a centralized economy, the version of DYNARE's model block in exp-log form is

```
model;
theta * exp (c) * exp (h) ^ (1 + psi) = (1 − alpha) * exp (y);
exp(y) = exp (a) * exp (k(−1)) ^ alpha * exp (h) ^ (1 − alpha);
exp(k) = exp (y − c) + (1 − delta) exp (k(−1));
exp(k) = beta * (exp(c)/exp(c(+1)) * (alpha * exp(y(+1)) + (1−delta) * exp (k));
end;
```

As can be verified, this code considers transformation exp(x) of each variable x, interpreting a variable x as if it were its logarithm.

The complete code is

```
var y,c,k,h,a;
varexo ea;
parameters abar,betta, rhoa, alph, delt, psi, thet;
```

```
abar=1;
alph = 0.36;
rhoa = 0.95;
betta =0.99;
delt = 0.025;
psi = 0;
thet = 2.95;
model;
thet*exp(c)*exp(h)^(1+psi)=(1-alph)*exp(y);
exp(y)=exp(a)*exp(k(-1))^alph*exp(h)^(1-alph);
exp(k)=exp(y-c)+(1-delt)*exp(k(-1));
exp(k)=betta*(exp(c)/exp(c(+1))*(alph*exp(y(+1))+(1delt)*exp(k));
a=(1-rhoa)*abar+rhoa*a(-1)+ea;
end;
initval;
y = 0.1;
c = -0.2;
h = -1.2;
k = 2.4;
a = abar;
ea = 0;
end;
steady;
shocks;
var ea = 0.009^2;
end;
stoch_simul;
```

The code, saved in my PC at folder *C:\dynare\4.6.4\examples* with the extension *m_RBC2.mod*, has been tested in DYNARE version 4.6.4 and it works properly .

Please note: Griffoli, in his well-known DYNARE's guide, on page 21[2] uses the notation exp(repeated variable), e.g., for consumption exp(cc), to make it clear that the repeated variable cc means the logarithm of c, and the same for the other variables.

[2] See Griffoli (2011).

4.6 The Code of the Model of the Centralized Economy in (Log) Linear Form, i.e., in the Form of Percentage Deviations from the Steady State

Log-linearization of the previous model of centralized economy, which includes choice of worked hours, gives the equations

$$\widehat{y}_t = \widehat{c}_t + (1 + \psi)\widehat{h}_t \tag{4.10}$$

$$\widehat{\mathrm{y}}_{\mathrm{t}} = \mathrm{s_c}\ \widehat{\mathrm{c}}_{\mathrm{t}} + \mathrm{s_i}\widehat{\mathrm{i}}_{\mathrm{t}} \tag{4.11}$$

$$\widehat{y}_t = \widehat{a}_t + \alpha\widehat{k}_t + (1-\alpha)\widehat{\mathrm{h}}_t \tag{4.12}$$

$$\widehat{k}_{t+1} = \delta\widehat{i}_t + (1-\delta)\widehat{k}_t \tag{4.13}$$

$$\widehat{c}_t - E_t\widehat{c}_{t+1} + \left(1 - \beta(1-\delta)E_t\left(\widehat{y}_{t+1} - \widehat{k}_{t+1}\right) = 0\right. \tag{4.14}$$

$$\widehat{a}_t = \rho_a\widehat{a}_{t-1} + \varepsilon_t \tag{4.15}$$

In Eqs. (4.10)–(4.15), the symbol hat on variables indicates the distance in the log from the steady-state log or more simply percentage deviation of each variable from the steady state. In writing the model block of this system in DYNARE, the "hat" symbol is ignored, but, in any case, variables are to be interpreted as percentage deviations from steady state. Therefore, e.g., y will be the percentage deviation from the steady state of production and so on for the other symbols.

The model block for the log-linearized model therefore becomes

```
model (linear);
y = c + (1 + pssi)*h;
y=s_c*c + s_i*i;
y= a+ aplh*k(-1)+ (1-alph)*h;
k= delt*i+ (1-delt)*k(-1);
c= c(+1)-(1-betta*(1-delt))*(y(+1)-k);
a= rho_a*a(-1)+e:
end;
```

Two remarks

1. Equations of the model considered in the block are those previously linearized in the log, and therefore next to the command "model" in the code, it is also necessary to write the word "(linear)."
2. The parameters are rewritten not with the correct Greek name to avoid DYNARE or MATLAB being misled.

The full model code is

```
var y, c, k, i, a, h;
varexo e;
parameters betta, rhoa, alph, delt, phi, pssi, s_c, s_i;
alph = 0.36;
rhoa = 0.025;
betta =0.99;
delt = 0.25;
phi = 0;
pssi = 2.95;
s_c = 0.85 ;
s_i = 0.13 ;
sigma = 0.63;

model (linear);
y = c + (1 + pssi)*h;
y=s_c*c + s_i*i;
y= a+ alph*k(-1)+ (1-alph)*h;
k= delt*i+ (1-delt)*k(-1);
c= c(+1)-(1-betta*(1-delt))*(y(+1)-k);
a= rhoa*a(-1)+e;
end;
shocks;
var e = sigma^2;
end;
stoch_simul(periods=2000, drop=200);
```

The code shown here (saved in my PC in folder *C:\dynare\4.6.4\examples* with the *m_RB3_loglin.mod* extension) has been tested, like the previous ones, with DYNARE 4.6.4 and works correctly.

4.7 An Alternative Way of Encoding Model Block

It is also possible to write the linearized model not in terms of the log-linear transformation but in terms of the original variables, adding, however, to variables in the model block a log transformation of kind ly, lh, lc, li, lk for each variable.

In the code of the model of the centralized economy, therefore, in the model block, in addition to equations of the model in levels, the following equations of logarithmic transformation of variables are also written as

```
ly=log(Y);
lh=log(L);
lc=log(C);
li=log(I);
```

```
lk=log(K);
end;
```

and among the initial values of steady state, their logarithms must also be included, i.e.,

```
Initval

C=Css;
K=Kss;
Y=Yss;
A=Ass;
lyss=log(yss);
lhss=log(hss);
lcss=log(css);
liss=log(iss);
lkss=log(kss);
```

Moreover, in the list of parameter values, values of variables in the steady state must be declared.

As an example, consider Hansen's model.

The complete model is

$$\mathrm{Y_t} = A_t K_t^{\alpha} h_t^{1-\alpha} \tag{4.16}$$

$$log(A_t) = (1-\varrho_a)\log(\bar{A}) + \varrho_a \log(\mathrm{A_{t-1}}) + \mathrm{e} \tag{4.17}$$

$$\mathrm{C_t} = \frac{(1-\alpha)}{\psi}\frac{\mathrm{Y_t}}{\mathrm{h_t}} \tag{4.18}$$

$$\frac{1}{C_t} = \beta \mathrm{E_t}\left[\frac{1}{\mathrm{C_{t+1}}}\left(\alpha\frac{\mathrm{Y_{t+1}}}{\mathrm{K_{t+1}}} + 1 - \delta\right)\right] \tag{4.19}$$

$$\mathrm{Y_t} = \mathrm{C_t} + K_{t+1} - (1-\delta)K_t \tag{4.20}$$

Steady state is

$$\mathrm{Y} = \mathrm{AK^{\alpha}h^{(1-\alpha)}} = \mathrm{A} * (\mathrm{K/h})^{\alpha} \tag{4.21}$$

$$\overline{\mathrm{A}} = 1 \tag{4.22}$$

$$1 = \beta\left(\alpha\frac{\mathrm{Y}}{\mathrm{K}} + 1 - \delta\right) \tag{4.23}$$

$$\psi C = (1 - \alpha)\frac{Y}{h} \quad (4.24)$$

$$Y = C + I \quad (4.25)$$

$$I = \delta K \quad (4.26)$$

From steady-state solution (4.20)–(4.26),[3] the following values of ratios of variables to the GDP as a function of the parameters are obtained:

$$\text{ksy} = \frac{K}{Y} = \frac{\beta\alpha}{(1-\beta)+\beta\delta} \quad (4.27)$$

$$\text{isy} = \frac{I}{Y} = \frac{\delta\alpha}{(1-\beta)+\beta\delta} \quad (4.28)$$

$$\text{csy} = \frac{C}{Y} = \frac{(1-\beta)+\beta\delta(1-\alpha)}{(1-\beta)+\beta\delta} \quad (4.29)$$

$$\psi = (1-\alpha)\frac{1}{\text{csy}}\frac{1}{h} \quad (4.30)$$

where h is treated as a parameter. Hence,

$$\text{Kss} = \text{ksy Yss} \quad (4.31)$$

$$\text{Iss} = \text{isy Yss} \quad (4.32)$$

$$\text{Css} = \text{csy Yss} \quad (4.33)$$

$$\text{Yss} = \text{ksy}^{\frac{\alpha}{1-\alpha}}\,h \quad (4.34)$$

The complete code of Hansen's model is

```
var Y, C, K, A, ly,lc,lk;
varexo e;
```

[3] Since for the scope of writing DYNARE code it is necessary to obtain the solution of steady-state variables as a function of parameters, we proceed in this way.

Assuming known Y, considering (4.23), by multiplying both sides by K, it follows K=β(-αY + $K(1-\delta)$)] that is K= ($\alpha\beta$Y + $K\beta(1-\delta)$). Rearranging K-$K\beta(1-\delta)$ =$\alpha\beta$Y, i.e., K(1-β(1 − δ))= $\alpha\beta$Y; hence, K/Y = $\beta\alpha$/(1-β) + β δ.

From (4.26) substituting for K, we get $I = \delta K = \frac{\delta\beta\alpha}{(1-\beta)+\beta\delta}$ Y, from which is y $= \frac{\delta\beta\alpha}{(1-\beta)+\beta\delta}$.

From (4.24), it follows $\frac{C}{Y} = \frac{(1-\alpha)}{\psi}\frac{1}{h}$.

Finally from (4.21) being A=1 and noting that $Y = Y^{\alpha-\alpha+1} = Y^{\alpha}Y^{1-\alpha}$, dividing both sides of this equality for $Y^{1-\alpha}$, it follows $Y^{\alpha} = K^{\alpha}\left(\frac{h}{Y}\right)^{(1-\alpha)}$; $Y^{\frac{\alpha}{1-\alpha}} = K^{\frac{\alpha}{1-\alpha}}\left(\frac{h}{Y}\right)$; that is, Y $Y^{\frac{\alpha}{1-\alpha}} = K^{\frac{\alpha}{1-\alpha}}h$ and therefore $Y = \frac{K^{\frac{\alpha}{1-\alpha}}}{Y^{\frac{\alpha}{1-\alpha}}}h = \left(\frac{K}{Y}\right)^{\frac{\alpha}{1-\alpha}}h = ksy^{\frac{\alpha}{1-\alpha}}h$.

```
parameters beta, rho_a, Abar, alpha, delta, psi, h;
alpha = 0.33;
rho_a = 0.74;
beta = 0.99;
delta = 0.24;
h=1/3;
Abar=1;
psi = 0.02;

// Steady-state values expressed in terms of parameters

ksy = (beta *alpha)/((1-beta)+beta*delta)
csy = ((1-alpha)/psi*h);
Ass=1;
Yss=Ass*(ksy/h)^(alpha*(1-alpha)*h;
Kss =ksy*Yss;
Css =csy*Yss;

// The model directly translated into levels

model;
(1/beta)*C(+1)/C= alpha*Y(+1)/K(+1)+1-delta;//Euler equation
 C = ((1-alpha)/psi*h)*Y; //Capital market equilibrium
C +K(+1)-(1-delta)*K(-1) = A*(K(-1)^alpha)*h^(1-alpha); //Production
function

A = (1-rho_a)*Abar+(rho_a)*A(-1)+e; // schock

// Log transformations of endogenous variables

ly=log(Y);
lc=log(C);
lk=log(K);
end;

// Initial steady-state values and their transformation into log

initval;
C=Css;
K=Kss;
Y=Yss;
A=Ass;
lc=log(Css);
lk=log(Kss);
ly=log(Yss);
```

```
e=0;
end;
steady;
shocks;
var e;
stderr 0.007;
end;
stoch_simul(order=1, irf=100) Y C K ly lc lk A;
```

The code shown here (saved in *C:\dynare\4.6.4\examples* with the extension *m_hansen1.mod*) has been verified (like the previous ones) with DYNARE 4.6.4 and works correctly.

4.8 Code of the Basic RBC Model with a CRRA Utility Function and Government Spending as a Shock

Let us now consider a more complete model of the economy run by a central planner, with flexible labor supply and public spending as a shock.

It considers the instantaneous utility function of the kind

$$U_t = \frac{C_t^{1+\sigma}}{1+\sigma} - \varphi \frac{h_t^{1+\psi}}{1+\psi}$$

The budget constraint of a representative household is

$$\mathrm{C_t} + \mathrm{K_{t+1}} - (1-\delta)K_t = W_t h_t + R_t K_t - T_x$$

Taking into account also public budget constraint $T_x = G_t$, the model consists of the following equations:

$$C_t^{\sigma} \varphi h_t^{1+\psi} = (1-\alpha)\mathrm{Y_t} \tag{4.35}$$

$$\beta E_t \left[\left(\frac{C_t^{\sigma}}{C_{t+1}^{\sigma}} \right) \left(\alpha \frac{\mathrm{Y_{t+1}}}{K_{t+1}} + (1-\delta) \right) \right] = 1 \tag{4.36}$$

$$\mathrm{Y_t} = A_t K_t^{\alpha} h_t^{(1-\alpha)} \tag{4.37}$$

$$K_{t+1} = \mathrm{Y_t} - C_t - G_t + (1-\delta)K_t \tag{4.38}$$

$$\log G_t - \log \overline{G} = \rho_g \left(\log G_{t-1} - \log \overline{G} \right) + \varepsilon_{g,t} \tag{4.39}$$

$$\log A_t = \rho_a \log A_{t-1} + \varepsilon_{a,t} \tag{4.40}$$

4.8.1 Steady-State Variables as Functions of Parameters of the Model

Steady-state corresponds to the solutions of the following equations:

$$C^{\sigma}\varphi h^{1+\psi} = (1-\alpha)\mathrm{Y} \tag{4.41}$$

$$K = \beta(\alpha \mathrm{Y} + K(1-\delta)) \tag{4.42}$$

$$\mathrm{Y} = A\ K^{\alpha} h^{(1-\alpha)} \tag{4.43}$$

$$K = Y - C - G + (1-\delta)K \tag{4.44}$$

$$\mathrm{A} = 1; \tag{4.45}$$

$$\overline{G} = gg\,\overline{Y} \tag{4.46}$$

$$\varepsilon_a = \varepsilon_g = 0 \tag{4.47}$$

As a function of parameters, a steady state is obtained as follows:
From (4.42),[4]

$$\frac{K}{Y} = \frac{\beta\alpha}{(1-\beta(1-\delta))}\quad \frac{\mathrm{G}}{\mathrm{Y}} = \mathrm{gg}$$

From (4.43),[5]

$$Y = \left(\frac{K}{Y}\right)^{\frac{\alpha}{1-\alpha}} h$$

From (4.44),

[4]The steps required are those already seen in the Hansen model and are

$$K = (\alpha\beta\mathrm{Y} + \beta K(1-\delta)) \rightarrow K - \beta K(1-\delta) = \alpha\beta\mathrm{Y}$$
$$K(1-\beta(1-\delta) = \alpha\beta\mathrm{Y}$$
$$\frac{K}{Y} = \frac{\beta\alpha}{(1-\beta(1-\delta))}$$

[5]Setting A=1 and observing that $\mathrm{Y} = \mathrm{Y}^{\alpha - \alpha + 1} = \mathrm{Y}^{\alpha}\mathrm{Y}^{1-\alpha}$, dividing both sides by $\mathrm{Y}^{1-\alpha}$, it follows $\mathrm{Y}^{\alpha} = K^{\alpha}\left(\frac{h}{Y}\right)^{(1-\alpha)}$, that is, $\mathrm{Y}^{\frac{\alpha}{1-\alpha}} = K^{\frac{\alpha}{1-\alpha}}\left(\frac{h}{Y}\right)$, and multiplying both sides by Y Y $\mathrm{Y}^{\frac{\alpha}{1-\alpha}} = K^{\frac{\alpha}{1-\alpha}}\,h$ so that $\mathrm{Y} = \frac{K^{\frac{\alpha}{1-\alpha}}}{\mathrm{Y}^{\frac{\alpha}{1-\alpha}}}\,h = \mathrm{Y} = \left(\frac{K}{Y}\right)^{\frac{\alpha}{1-\alpha}} h = (ksy)^{\frac{\alpha}{1-\alpha}}\,h.$

$$\frac{\mathrm{C}}{\mathrm{Y}} = \left(1 - \frac{\mathrm{G}}{\mathrm{Y}} - \delta\frac{\mathrm{K}}{\mathrm{Y}}\right)$$

From (4.41),

$$\varphi h^{1+\psi} = (1-\alpha)C^{-\sigma}Y, \text{ That is to say}$$

$$\varphi = (1-\alpha)C^{-\sigma}\frac{Y}{h^{1+\psi}}$$

The number of worked hours h is taken as a parameter and expressed as a fraction of the time. In the applications, steady-state trend value h = 1/3 is assumed. Using, for steady-state ratios to Y, the notation K/Y = ksy, etc., and for steady-state values $K = Kss$, C = Css, etc., we set

$$\frac{\mathrm{K}}{\mathrm{Y}} = \mathrm{ksy} = \frac{\alpha\beta}{1-\beta(1-\delta)} \tag{4.48}$$

$$\frac{\mathrm{G}}{\mathrm{y}} = \mathrm{gg} = \mathrm{gsy} \tag{4.49}$$

$$\frac{\mathrm{C}}{\mathrm{y}} = \mathrm{csy} = 1 - \mathrm{gsy} - \delta\mathrm{ksy} \tag{4.50}$$

Therefore,

$$\mathrm{Kss} = \mathrm{ksy\ Yss} \tag{4.51}$$

$$\mathrm{Gss} = \mathrm{gsy\ Yss} \tag{4.52}$$

$$\mathrm{Css} = \mathrm{csy\ Yss} \tag{4.53}$$

$$Yss = ksy^{\frac{\alpha}{1-\alpha}}\, hss \tag{4.54}$$

$$\varphi = (1-\alpha)Css^{-\sigma}\left(\frac{Yss}{hss^{1+\psi}}\right) \tag{4.55}$$

The DYNARE code of the model is

```
var Y, C, K, A, G;
varexo ea, eg;
parameters beta, sigma, phi, psi, alpha, delta, Abar, Gbar, h, sea,
rhoa, rhog, seg, gsy;
beta = 0.990;
sigma = 2.00;
phi = 0.100;
alpha = 0.400;
```

```
delta = 0.025;
gsy = 0.20;
h= 1/3;
rhoa = 0.95;
rhog = 0.95;
sea = 0.009;
seg = 0.009;
ksy = alpha*beta/(1-beta*(1-delta));
csy = 1- gsy- delta*ksy;
Ass=1;
Abar=Ass;
Yss= Ass*(ksy)^(alpha/(1-alpha))*h;
Gbar=gsy*Yss;
Gss = gsy*Yss;
Kss = ksy*Yss;
Css = csy*Yss;
psi = (1-alpha)*Css^(-sigma)*Yss/(h^(1+phi));
model ;
C^sigma*psi*h^(1+psi)= (1-alpha)*Y;
(1/beta)*(C(+1)/C)^sigma= alpha*Y(+1)/K(+1)+1-delta;
K(+1)= A*K^alpha*h^(1-alpha)-C-G+(1-delta)*K;
G=(1- rhog)*Gbar+ (rhog)* G(-1)+eg;
A= (1-rhoa)*Abar+(rhoa)*A(-1)+ea;
end;
shocks;
var ea; stderr sea;
var eg; stderr seg;
var ea, eg=0;
end;
stoch_simul(order=1,irf=20, relative_irf) Y C K A G;
```

The code (saved in *C:\dynare\4.6.4\examples* with the extension *m_rbc_public_spending.mod)* has been tested with DYNARE 4.6.4 and works correctly.

4.9 The Complete DYNARE Code of the Log-Linearized Model with Public Expenditure

Now let's look at coding the previous model, log-linearized, which includes government spending.

Log-linearized equations are

$$\sigma\, c_t + \varphi(1+\psi)h_t = (1-\alpha)[a_t + \alpha k_t + (1-\alpha)]h_t \tag{4.56}$$

$$\frac{\sigma}{\beta}(c_{t+1} - c_t) = \alpha\big(y_{t+1} - k_t\big) + 1 - \delta \tag{4.57}$$

$$k_{t+1} = (1-\mathrm{gg})\, y_t - c_t + (1-\delta)k_t \tag{4.58}$$

$$g_t = \rho_g g_{t-1} + \big(1-\rho_g\big)\overline{g} + \varepsilon_{g,t} \tag{4.59}$$

$$a_t = \rho_a\, a_{t-1} + \varepsilon_{a,t} \tag{4.60}$$

The model code is

```
var y, c, k, a, g;
varexo ea, eg;
parameters alpha, beta, delta, h, gg, phi, psi, rhoa, rhog, sea, seg,
sigma;
alpha = 0.400;
beta = 0.990;
delta = 0.025;
sigma = 2.00;
psi = 0.100;
h = 1/3;
phi =0.1;
rhoa = 0.95;
rhog = 0.95;
sea = 0.009;
seg = 0.009;
gg=0.20
gbar= gg
model (linear) ;
// The model in log
sigma*c+ psi*(1+phi)*h =(1-alpha)*y;
(sigma/beta)*(c(+1) - c)= alpha*(y(+1) - k)+ 1-delta;
k = (1-gg)*y- c + (1-delta)*k(-1);
y = a+alpha*k(-1)+(1-alpha)*h;
a = rhoa*a(-1)+ ea;
g =(1-rhog)*(gbar)+ rhog*g(-1)+ + eg;
end;
shocks;
var ea; stderr sea;
var eg; stderr seg;
end;
stoch_simul(order=1,irf=20, relative_irf) y c k;
```

The code (saved in *C:\dynare\4.6.4\examples* with the extension *m_rbc_publicspending_loglinear.mod*) has been tested with DYNARE 4.6.4 and works correctly.

4.10 A Note on CALIBRATION, i.e., Assigning Numerical Values to Parameters

Calibration is the process of choosing values for the parameters by a researcher. Such choice is not arbitrary but is based on the correspondence of chosen parameters to the moments of a sample of observed data. The reason why parameters are not estimated using the least squares method is due to the simultaneity of macroeconomic variables. Furthermore, the fact that generally there is only one source or few sources of stochastic disturbances, i.e., that covariances between shocks are assumed to be zero, indicates that the considered model is stochastically singular.

As a general method, looking at steady-state equations, the values of parameters can be obtained individually, by reversing the usual optics. The values of parameters in the steady-state equations are regarded as the unknowns to be solved. Thus, e.g., from the steady-state equation $\mathrm{w} = (1-\alpha)\frac{\mathrm{Y}}{\mathrm{h}}$, the labor share of income, solved as unknown, is $\alpha = 1 - \frac{hw}{Y}$. It is admitted, based on observed US data, that labor share is generally two-thirds of the GDP. Therefore, we set $\alpha = 1-2/3 = 1/3$.

In the same vein, the parameter δ is obtained from $\delta K = I$ which results in $\delta = I/K$. Considering the annual US data, the indication $\delta \cong 10\%$ is obtained using the quarterly data:

$$(1-0.1)^{\frac{1}{4}} \cong \frac{1}{4} * 1 \cong 2.5\%.$$

The net return on investments is $\mathrm{r} = \alpha\frac{Y}{K} - \delta = \frac{1}{3} * \frac{1}{3} \cong 0.10$, and the quarterly return is $(0.10)/4 = 0.025$.

The quarterly discount rate is $\beta = \left(\frac{1}{1+\mathrm{R}}\right)^{\frac{1}{4}}$ which, given a real bond interest rate of around 4%, results in $\beta = \left(\frac{1}{1.04}\right)^{\frac{1}{4}} \cong 0.9902 \cong 0.99$.

As can be seen, in general, the parameters depend on steady-state values of relevant variables, the values of which are obtained from the statistical data.

4.11 Different Ways for Calculating the Steady State in DYNARE

In log-linearized models, it is not necessary to calculate the steady state, being, for each variable, the logarithm of the steady state equal to zero.[6] Therefore, for such models, it is not necessary to declare the initial value.

For non-log-linearized models, it is necessary to calculate the steady state.

DYNARE identifies four different ways to calculate the steady state in non-log-linearized models.

They are as follows:

1. *steady_state_model* block if the steady state is available in closed form
2. Same *steady_state_model* block with a *helper* function if some variables are not available in closed form
3. Writing a steady-state MATLAB function
4. Writing the already seen *initval* block

As an example, we use a variant of the RBC model which considers leisure time and assumes, respectively, an instantaneous utility function log in all arguments or an instantaneous utility function CRRA for both arguments, i.e.,

$$U_t = \log C_t + \psi \log (1 - L_t) \tag{4.61}$$

$$U_t = \frac{C_t^{1-\eta_C}}{1-\eta_c} + \psi \frac{(1-L_t)^{1-\eta L}}{1-\eta_L} \tag{4.62}$$

When considering the utility function logarithmic in consumption C_t and leisure time $(1 - L_t)$, the steady state is analytically solvable.

Conversely, in the case of a CRRA utility function, we cannot solve labor in closed form, as we will now verify.

4.11.1 Method 1: steady_state_model *Block*[7]

Consider the case of log utility for a decentralized economy. The model is

$$\frac{1}{C_t} = \beta E_0 \left(\frac{1}{C_{t+1}} (\mathrm{R_{t+1}} + 1 - \delta \right) \tag{4.63}$$

[6]Indeed, it is $\log\overline{x}\text{-}\log\overline{x} = \log(\frac{\overline{x}}{\overline{x}}) = \log(1) = 0$.

[7]This and the following sections are adapted from W. Mutschler, "Best practices in Dynare," (2023).

$$\psi \frac{C_t}{(1-L_t)} = W_t \tag{4.64}$$

$$Y_t = C_t + K_{t+1} - (1-\delta)K_t \tag{4.65}$$

$$Y_t = A_t K_t^{\alpha} L_t^{1-\alpha} \tag{4.66}$$

$$I_t = Y_t - C_t \tag{4.67}$$

$$W_t = (1-\alpha)\frac{Y_t}{L_t} \tag{4.68}$$

$$R_{t+1} = \alpha A_t\, K_{t+1}^{\alpha-1} L_{t+1}^{1-\alpha} \tag{4.69}$$

$$\log\ A_t = (1-\varphi_a)\log\ A + \varphi\ \log\ A_{t-1} + \varepsilon_t \tag{4.70}$$

The stationary solution of model (4.63)–(4.70) considers steady-state equations rewritten so that they can be solved in terms of the parameters, as soon as L is known. This solution is the following:

For the variable A, we set A = 1, and from Eq. (4.63), we obtain R= $(1/\beta) + \delta - 1$.

From (4.69), you get[8]

$$K\_L = \left(\frac{\alpha A}{R}\right)^{\frac{1}{1-\alpha}} \tag{4.71}$$

Equation (4.68) corresponds to

$$W = (1-\alpha)A(K\_L)^{\alpha} \tag{4.72}$$

From (4.67) and (4.68), it follows[9]

$$I\_L = \delta\ K\_L \tag{4.73}$$

Equation (4.66)[10] can be written

$$Y\_L = A(K\_L)^{\alpha} \tag{4.74}$$

Finally, from definition of consumption,[11]

---

[8] Steady-state equation becomes $R=\alpha A(\frac{K}{L})^{\alpha-1}$; that is, $\left(\frac{K}{L}\right)^{\alpha-1} = \frac{R}{\alpha A}$ also $\left(\frac{K}{L}\right)^{1-\alpha} = \frac{\alpha A}{R}$, and setting $K\_L = \frac{K}{L}$, it follows $K\_L^{1-\alpha} = \frac{\alpha A}{R}$ from which (4.71).

[9] From definition I= K-(1-δ)K= δK, by dividing both sides by L setting $\frac{I}{L} = I\_L$ and $\frac{K}{L} = K\_L$, it follows (4.73).

[10] It is $\frac{Y}{L} = A\left(\frac{K}{L}\right)^{\alpha}$.

[11] That is, C=Y-I, and by dividing both sides by L and rearranging, we get (4.75).

$$C\_L = Y\_L - I\_L = A(K\_L)^{\alpha} - \delta\, K\_L$$

We obtain A $\left(\frac{\alpha A}{R}\right)^{\frac{\alpha}{1-\alpha}}$- $\delta\left(\frac{\alpha A}{R}\right)^{\frac{1}{1-\alpha}}$

$$C\_L = = A\left(\frac{\alpha A}{R}\right)^{\frac{\alpha}{1-\alpha}} - \delta\left(\frac{\alpha A}{R}\right)^{\frac{1}{1-\alpha}} \tag{4.75}$$

Solution of L[12] is

$$L = \frac{\frac{W}{\psi C\_L}}{1 + \frac{W}{\psi C\_L}} = \frac{(1-\alpha)A(K\_L)^{\alpha}}{\psi C\_L + (1-\alpha)A(K\_L)^{\alpha}} \tag{4.76}$$

Steady state is rewritten in a *steady_state_model* block by setting

$$C = C\_L\,L \tag{4.77}$$

$$I = I\_L\,L \tag{4.78}$$

$$K = K\_L\,L \tag{4.79}$$

$$Y = Y\_L\,L \tag{4.80}$$

The full DYNARE's code is

```
var Y C K L A R W I;
varexo eps_A;
parameters alph, betta, delt, pssi, rhoA;
alph = 0.35;
betta = 0.99;
delt = 0.025;
pssi = 1.6;
rhoA = 0.9;
sigma = 0.01;
Ass=1;
Rss = (1/betta)+delt-1;
K_L = ((alph*Ass)/Rss)^(1/(1-alph));
I_L = delt*K_L;
```

[12] Solution (4.76) is obtained in the following way. From (4.66), it results $\psi\frac{C}{1-L}$= W, that is, $1 - L = \psi\frac{C}{W}$. By multiplying both sides by $\frac{1}{L}$, we get $\frac{1-L}{L} = \psi\frac{C\_L}{W}$ from which L = (1-L)$\frac{W}{\psi C\_L}$. This expression is not yet the solution for L since to the right of the equality appears the term (1-L) which contains the unknown L. By considering that 1-L=1-(1-L)$\frac{W}{\psi C_L}$and by dividing both sides by (1-L), it follows 1=$\frac{1}{1-L}$- $\frac{W}{\psi C_L}$and therefore 1 +$\frac{W}{\psi C_L}$=$\frac{1}{1-L}$from which 1-L = $\frac{1}{1+\frac{W}{\psi C\_L}}$, and by substituting in L, we obtain L = $\frac{1}{1+\frac{W}{\psi C\_L}}\,\frac{W}{\psi C\_L}$, i.e., (4.76).

```
Y_L = Ass*(K_L)^alph;
C_L = Y_L-I_L;
Wss=(1-alph)*Ass*(K_L)^alph;
Lss= (Wss/pssi*C_L)*(1/(1+(Wss/pssi*C_L)));
Yss = Y_L*Lss;
Css = C_L*Lss;
Iss = I_L*Lss;
Kss = K_L*Lss;
model;
1/C = betta*(1/C(+1)*(1-delt+R));
W = (pssi*(1-L)^(-1))/C^(-1);
K= (1-delt)*K(-1)+I;
Y = I+C;
Y = A*K(-1)^alph*L^(1-alph);
W= (1-alph)*Y/L;
R = alph*Y/K(-1);
log(A) = rhoA*log(A(-1))+ eps_A;
end;
initval;
Y=Yss;
C=Css;
K=Kss;
L=Lss;
A=Ass;
W=Wss;
I=Iss;
end;
steady;
shocks;
var eps_A = sigma^2;
end;
stoch_simul(order = 1,irf=40) Y C I K L W R A;
```

This code was saved in *C:\dynare\4.6.4\examples* with the extension *m_rbc_logutil.mod* and was verified with DYNARE 4.6.4. It works properly.

It is important to point out that the method just seen for specifying stationary state in the mod file requires having previously obtained solutions in closed form, and, despite the laboriousness of calculations, in general, it is the one to be preferred.[13]

[13]Note that standard deviation σ appears among parameter values even though it is not declared in parameters block. However, σ is contained in shock block. In general, this is a convenient procedure for declaring σ explicitly.

4.11.2 *Method 2: steady_state with the* steady state_helper *Function*

In the RBC model with CRRA utility, it is not possible to solve analytically for labor L, but once a value has been preassigned to L, all other variables can be calculated in closed form. Such cases can be addressed by using a helper function in the *steady_state_model* block.

By taking the CRRA utility function, in the model of a market economy, the intertemporal consumer problem is to maximize the Lagrangian function:

$$E_0 \sum_{t=0}^{\infty} \beta^t \left(\frac{C_t^{1-\eta_C}}{1-\eta_c} - \psi \frac{(1-L_t)^{1-\eta L}}{1-\eta_L} \right)$$

$$+\lambda_t [W_t L_t + R_t K_t + (1-\delta) K_t - C_t - K_{t+1}] \tag{4.81}$$

Except for first-order conditions relative to consumption and labor, the other equations of the model remain identical to previous ones.

The full model is

$$\frac{1}{C_t^{\eta_C}} = \beta E_0 \left(\frac{1}{C_{t+1}^{\eta_C}} (R_{t+1} + 1 - \delta) \right. \tag{4.82}$$

$$\psi \frac{C_t^{\eta_c}}{(1-L_t)^{\eta L}} = (1-\alpha) A_t\, K_t^{\alpha}\, L_t^{-\alpha} \tag{4.83}$$

$$Y_t = C_t + K_{t+1} - (1-\delta) K_t \tag{4.84}$$

$$Y_t = A_t K_t^{\alpha} L_t^{1-\alpha} \tag{4.85}$$

$$I_t = Y_t - C_t \tag{4.86}$$

$$W_t = (1-\alpha) \frac{Y_t}{L_t} \tag{4.87}$$

$$R_{t+1} = \alpha A_t\, K_{t+1}^{\alpha-1} L_{t+1}^{1-\alpha} \tag{4.88}$$

$$\log\, A_t = (1-\varphi_a) \log\, A + \varphi\, \log\, A_{t-1} + \varepsilon_t \tag{4.89}$$

ε_t is i.i.d., with zero conditioned mean.

In this model, a steady state for labor has no explicit solution.

In fact, the first-order condition for L now becomes

$$\psi \frac{1}{(1-L)^{\eta L}} = \frac{W}{C^{\eta_c}} \tag{4.90}$$

That is, multiplying both sides by L^{η_c},

$$L^{\eta_c}\frac{1}{(1-L)^{\eta L}}=\frac{W}{(C\_L)^{\eta_c}} \tag{4.91}$$

This is a nonlinear expression for L that cannot be solved analytically. The corresponding DYNARE code, in addition to the model block, also contains a *steady_state_model* block. In this block, steady-state solutions are reported, on the one hand, as functions of parameters of ratios for L and prices of factors on the other.

Given ratios, steady-state quantities are obtained for each of the variables from identities, e.g., X_L*L.

Alongside these equations, now appears the helper function named *m_rbc_crra_steadystate_helper.m.*

The *helper* function uses MATLAB to calculate L, given an initial value of L_0 and parameters, and quantities that appear in the expression that solves L.

It is necessary to create this file in the same folder as the mod file but with the *.m* extension (it is indicated here with the same name as the mod file, followed by *steadystate_helper.m*, but it can also be called differently). In the case considered here, the file has the following extension:

m_rbc_crra_steadystate_helper.m; the commands of the file are:
function L=m_rbc_crra_steady_state_helper(L0,pssi,etaL,etaC,C_L,W)
options = optimset('Display', 'Final', 'TolX',1e-10, 'TolFun',1e-10);
L = fsolve(@(L) C_L^(-etaC)*W-pssi*(1-L)^(-etaL)*L^etaC , L0,options);

In the *.m file*, the command *fsolve* is used to calculate steady-state labor value, and some options are set using *optimset.*

Other optimizers that possibly work better are possible.

Furthermore, with an "if" statement, the special case of log utility is also taken, since, as we have seen, there is a closed-form solution.

The *steady_state_model* block concludes with the definition of the values in steady-state levels with the obvious definition of each of the variables as a product of the steady-state ratio to L.

Ultimately, the complete code is

```
var Y C K L A R W I;
varexo eps_A;
parameters alph betta delt pssi rhoA etaC etaL;
alph=0.35; betta=0.99; delt=0.25; pssi=1.6; rhoA=0.99; etaC=2;
etaL=1.5; sigma=0.01;
model;
C^(-etaC) = betta*C(+1)^(-etaC)*(1-delt+R);
W = pssi*(1-L)^(-etaL)/C^(-etaC);
K = (1-delt)*K(-1)+I;
Y = I+C;
Y = A*K(-1)^alph*L^(1-alph);
W = (1-alph)*Y/L;
```

```
R = alph*Y/K(-1);
log(A) = rhoA*log(A(-1))+eps_A;
end;
steady_state_model;
A = 1;
R = (1/betta)+delt-1;
K_L = ((alph*A)/R)^(1/(1-alph));
W = (1-alph)*A*K_L^alph;
I_L = delt*K_L;
Y_L = A*K_L^alph;
C_L = Y_L-I_L;

% Since an analytical expression cannot be obtained
for %labor, a helper function is used

L0 = 1/3;
L=m_rbc_crra_steady_state_helper(L0,C_L,W,pssi,etaL, etaC);
C = C_L*L;
I = I_L*L;
K = K_L*L;
Y = Y_L*L;
end;
steady;
shocks;
var eps_A= sigma^2;
end;
stoch_simul;
```

The code was saved in *C:\dynare\4.6.4\examples* with the extension *m_rbc_crra.mod* and has been verified with DYNARE 4.6.4. It works properly.

4.11.3 *Method 3: Assigning Initial Values in the* initval *Block*

We have already seen that, if we do not want to calculate the steady state of the model, we can resort to numerical methods, specifying an *initval* block with initial values for the endogenous variables whose equations are

$$\frac{1}{C_t^{\eta_C}} = \beta E_0 \left(\frac{1}{C_{t+1}^{\eta_C}} (R_{t+1} + 1 - \delta) \right. \tag{4.92}$$

$$\psi \frac{C_t^{\eta_c}}{(1-L_t)^{\eta L}} = (1-\alpha)\mathrm{A_t}\, K_t^{\alpha}\, L_t^{-\alpha} \tag{4.93}$$

$$Y_t = \mathrm{C_t} + \mathrm{K_{t+1}} - (1-\delta)K_t \tag{4.94}$$

$$Y_t = \mathrm{A_t} K_t^{\alpha} L_t^{1-\alpha} \tag{4.95}$$

$$I_t = Y_t - \mathrm{C_t} \tag{4.96}$$

$$\mathrm{W_t} = (1-\alpha)\frac{Y_t}{L_t} \tag{4.97}$$

$$R_{t+1} = \alpha \mathrm{A_t}\, \mathrm{K_{t+1}^{\alpha-1} L_{t+1}^{1-\alpha}} \tag{4.98}$$

$$\log\ \mathrm{A_t} = (1-\varphi_a)\log\ \mathrm{A} + \varphi\ \log\ \mathrm{A_{t-1}} + \varepsilon_t \tag{4.99}$$

with ε_t i.i.d.

This is the DYNARE code:

```
var Y C K L A R W I;
varexo eps_A;
parameters alph betta delt pssi rhoA etaC etaL;
alph = 0.35; betta = 0.99; delt = 0.025; pssi = 1.6; rhoA = 0.9;
etaC = 2; etaL = 1.5;sigma=0.01;
model;
C^(-etaC) = betta*C(+1)^(-etaC)*(R+1-delt);
W = pssi*C^(etaC) /(1-L)^(etaL);
K = (1-delt)*K(-1)+I;
Y = I+C;
Y = A*K(-1)^alph*L^(1-alph);
W = (1-alph)*Y/L;
R = alph*Y/K(-1);
log(A) = rhoA*log(A(-1))+eps_A;
end;
initval;
Y = 1.2;
C = 0.9;
K = 12;
L = 0.35;
A = 1;
R = 0.03;
W = 2.24;
I = 0.3;
end;
steady;
resid;
shocks;
```

```
var eps_A= sigma^2;
end;
stoch_simul;
```

For the intuition behind initial values, see the previous section on calibration.

Note that if you don't specify a variable explicitly, DYNARE uses 0 as the initial value.

The code was saved with the extension *m_rbc_logutil_num.mod* in *C:\dynare \4.6.4\examples* and has been verified with DYNARE 4.6.4.

It works properly.

There are various authors which have contributed to how to write Dynare's code. Here there is a little but significant sampling of contributions: Adjemian et al. (2011), Barillas et al. (2010), Collard and Juillard (2003), DYNARE (n.d.), Ireland (2004), Judd (1998), Juillard (2001), Pfeifer (2013), Pfeifer (2023), User Guide (n.d.), Wiki (n.d.).

4.11.4 A Focus on External Steady-State File

This section is optional and can be disregarded at first reading.

To have full control of steady-state calculations, a file YOURMODFILENAME_steadystate.m. must be created.

So, let us consider another filemod # rbc_crra2.mod:

```
var Y C K L A R W I;
varexo eps_A;
parameters alph betta delt pssi rhoA etaC etaL;
alph = 0.35; betta = 0.99; delt = 0.025; pssi = 1.6; rhoA = 0.9;
etaC = 2; etaL = 1.5;
model;
C^(-etaC) = betta*C(+1)^(-etaC)*(1-delt+R);
W = -pssi*(1-L)^(-etaL)/C^(-etaC);
K = (1-delt)*K(-1)+I;
Y = I+C;
Y = A*K(-1)^alph*L^(1-alph);
W = (1-alph)*Y/L;
R = alph*Y/K(-1);
log(A) = rhoA*log(A(-1))+eps_A;
end;
steady;
resid;
```

Note that there is no steady_state_model or initval block in this code. The only command written is *steady* which tells DYNARE to calculate steady state.

Now let's create another MATLAB file, called *rbc_ces2_steadystate.m*, which calculates the steady state:

function [ys,params,check] = rbc_ces2_steadystate(ys,exo,M_,options_)

Inputs of previous instruction are the following:

ys [vector] steady-state initial value vector of endogenous variables
exo [vector] exogenous variable vector values
M_ [[structure] DYNARE model structure
options [structure] DYNARE options structure

As for the output,

- ys [vector] vector of steady-state values of endogenous variables
params [vector] vector of parameter values
check [scalar] 0 if steady-state computation worked and 1 if not (allows to impose restrictions on parameters)

Instructions for completing the MATLAB file are as follows:

Step 0, initialize indicator and set options for numerical solver:

```
check = 0;
options = optimset('Display','Final','TolX',1e-10,'TolFun',1e-10);
```

Step 1, read out parameters to access them with their name:

```
for ii = 1:M_.param_nbr
eval([M_.param_names{ii} ' = M_.params(' int2str(ii) ');']);
end
```

Step 2, Check parameter restrictions:

```
if etaC*etaL<1 (% parameter violates restriction (here it
is artificial)
check=1; %set failure indicator
return; %return without updating steady states
end
```

Step 3, enter model equations here:

```
A = 1;
R = 1/betta+delt-1;
```

```
K_L = ((alph*A)/R)^(1/(1-alph));
if K_L <= 0
check = 1; % set failure indicator
return; % return without updating steady states
end
W = (1-alph)*A*K_L^alph;
I_L = delt*K_L;
Y_L = A*K_L^alph;
C_L = Y_L-I_L;
if C_L <= 0
check = 1; % set failure indicator
return; % return without updating steady states
end
if etaC == 1 && etaL == 1 % The labor level
% Closed-form solution for labor
L = 1/pssi*C_L^(-1)*W/(1+1/pssi*C_L^(-1)*W);
else
% No closed-form solution uses a fixed-point algorithm
L0 = 1/3;
[L,~,exitflag] = fsolve(@(L) pssi*(1-L)^(-etaL)*L^etaC -
C_L^(-etaC)*W, L0,options);
if exitflag <= 0
check = 1; % set failure indicator
return % return without updating steady
states
end
end
C = C_L*L; % consumption level
I = I_L*L; % investment level
K = K_L*L; % capital level
Y = Y_L*L; % output level
```

Step 4, update parameters and variables:

```
params=NaN(M_.param_nbr,1);
for iter = 1:M_.param_nbr %update parameters set in the file
eval([ 'params(' num2str(iter) ') = ' M_.param_names{iter} ';' ])
end
for ii = 1:M_.orig_endo_nbr %auxiliary variables are set
automatically
eval(['ys(' int2str(ii) ') = ' M_.endo_names{ii} ';']);
end
```

Some remarks

1. It is usually not recommended to write your own file to calculate steady state as it is error-prone. But it has the undoubted advantage of allowing full control of calculations.
2. *_steady_state.m* file must have the same first part of the name as the mod file.
3. Steps 1 and step 4 are still the same and are very important to include in your steady-state file.
4. Before actually calling the numeric optimizer, examples of how to check parameters and variable constraints are included. If they are not satisfied, the function returns a flag that the steady state could not be calculated. This is a good practice as the numerical solver may take a long time or lead to unfeasible results.
5. Finally, you need to specify values for all declared variables and return both parameters and variables. DYNARE then internally updates the auxiliary variables.

4.12 Another DYNARE Focus: Model with Different Parameter Values

This section, like the previous one, can be disregarded in the first reading.

Once the mod file has been set up, a loop to experiment with different parameter settings can be created.

You set up a Matlab.m script that loops through an array containing different values of a given parameter. Suppose we want to vary σ:

clear all ;
sigma s = [1, 2, 4] ;
% specifies a vector of values for sigma
results = struct
% creates an empty result containment structure
for i = 1 : length (sigma s)
sigma = sigma s (i) ;
% open cycle

% saves the current value(s) of sigma with the name of parameters used in the. mod file

save sigma ;
% start DYNARE
dynare your_mod _ file _ here no clear all ;
% saves results in a subtree
results. (sprint f (' sigma%d ' , i)) = oo_ ;
end;

In the mod file, after declaring parameters, we insert two lines

% loads previously saved parameter values
load sigma;
% overrides previously specified parameter values;
set _ param_value (' sigma ' , sigma) ;

You can access the results structure to inspect them and graphically project the results. When creating a loop, it is useful to use the nograph option to suppress printing of IRFs.

References

Adjemian, S. and Bastani, H. and Juillard, M. and Karamé, F. and Maih, Jr and Mihoubi, F. and Mutschler, W. and Perendia, G. and Pfeifer, J. and Ratto, M. and Villemot, S. (2011) 'Dynare: Reference Manual Version 4,' Dynare Working Papers 1, CEPREMAP, revised Mar 2021.

Barillas, F. and Bhandari, A. and Colacito, R. and Kitao, S. and Matthes, C., Sargent, T. and Shin,Y. (2010) 'Practicing Dynare' web address https://forum.dynare.org/t/practicing-dynare-2019-updated-version/13389 (Accessed june 2023)

Collard, F. and Juillard, M. (2003) 'Stochastic Simulations with DYNARE. A Practical Guide'. CEPREMAP

DYNARE in the Web: -Examples:(Accessed May 2023); `https://github.com/DynareTeam/dynare/tree/master/examples`-Forum: (Accessed May 2023); `https://forum.dynare.org/`

Griffoli, T. (2011) 'Dynare 4: User Guide', web address: https://archives.dynare.org/documentation-and-support/user-guide.1.html (Accessed May 2023).

Ireland, P. (2004) 'A Method for Taking Models to the Data', *Journal of Economic Dynamics and Control*, 28(6), pp. 1205–26

Judd, K. L. (1998) *Numerical methods in economics*, MIT press.

Juillard, M. (2001). 'DYNARE: A program for the resolution and simulation of dynamic models with forward variables through the use of a relaxation algorithm'. CEPREMAP working papers.

Mutschler, W. 'Best practices in Dynare' tutorial at https://mutschler.eu/dynare (Accessed: 10 Feb 2023).

Pfeifer, J. (2013). *A guide to DYNARE for the use of students.* Humboldt University Berlin, School of Business and Economics.

Pfeifer, J. DSGE_mod: 'A collection of Dynare models', on Web, https://github.com/JohannesPfeifer/DSGE_mod (Accessed: April 2023)

User Guide. (n.d.). (Accessed May 2023), web address: `https://www.dynare.org/documentation-and-support/user-guide/`

Wiki. (n.d.). (Accessed May 2023), web address: `https://github.com/DynareTeam/dynare/wiki`

Chapter 5
A Basic Version of the Micro-founded Neo-Keynesian Model

This chapter considers a basic Neo-Keynesian micro-founded model. In particular, for the choices of firms, it distinguishes various forms of production technology: linear, Cobb-Douglas, and CES technologies.

After introducing Calvo stickiness and Rotemberg stickiness in price formation, this chapter considers the general equilibrium of the new Keynesian economics (NKE) model with linear production technology and sets out Blanchard-Kahn conditions for stability and uniqueness of solutions and a DYNARE code for the definitive basic model of the NKE.

5.1 A Decentralized Economy: Choices of Representative Household

In DSGE models of new Keynesian macroeconomics, aggregate consumption C_t, meant as consumption of representative household, is defined as a composite good, represented by an index of CES kind,[1] which is assumed as a unit of measurement of all different individual goods c_{jt}.

If we suppose that the number of individual goods n is sufficiently large but finite and attribute to each j-th good a uniform weight equal to (1/n) within a typical basket, we can define a C_t index CES as

[1] See Dixit, A. K., and Stiglitz, J. E. (1977).

G. Chirichiello, *DSGE Models for Real Business Cycle and New Keynesian Macroeconomics*, Springer Texts in Business and Economics,
https://doi.org/10.1007/978-3-031-56034-7_5

$$C_t = \left[\sum_{j=1}^{n} \left(\frac{1}{n} c_{it} \right)^{\frac{\theta-1}{\theta}} \right]^{\frac{\theta}{\theta-1}} \qquad \theta > 1 \tag{5.1}$$

However, it is convenient from the analytical point of view to assume an infinity of goods, each corresponding to infinite points of the interval [0, 1] of real numbers, each with negligible relative weight, to be able to represent aggregate consumption C_t with a continuous measurement as follows:

$$C_t = \left[\int_0^1 c_{jt}^{\frac{\theta-1}{\theta}} dj \right]^{\frac{\theta}{\theta-1}} \qquad \theta > 1 \tag{5.2}$$

This way of understanding consumption has two implications that will be soon demonstrated:

a) The price general level is an index of individual prices of goods p_{jt} of the type

$$P_t = \left[\int_0^1 p_{jt}^{(1-\theta)} dj \right]^{\frac{1}{1-\theta}} \tag{5.3}$$

b) Consumption demand for each goods c_{jt} has a constant elasticity and depends on the level of aggregate consumption, according to the following relationship:

$$c_{jt} = \left(p_{jt}/P_t \right)^{-\theta} C_t \tag{5.4}$$

The general price-level index coincides with the shadow price of consumption by a consumer who chooses individual goods to minimize overall expenditure, for a given aggregate consumption.

This minimum spending problem for the consumer has the following formulation:

$$\min_{c_{jt}} \int_0^1 p_{jt} c_{Jt} dj \tag{5.5}$$

$$\text{Sub} \quad \left[\int_0^1 c_{jt}^{\frac{\theta-1}{\theta}} dj \right]^{\frac{\theta}{\theta-1}} = C_t \tag{5.6}$$

Calling λ_t the Lagrange multiplier, first-order conditions with respect to c_{jt} provide[2]

---

[2]First-order condition for c_{jt} is

$p_{jt} - \lambda_t \frac{\theta}{\theta-1} [\int_0^1 c_{jt}^{\frac{\theta-1}{\theta}} dj]^{\frac{1}{\theta-1}} \frac{\theta-1}{\theta} c_{jt}^{-\frac{1}{\theta}} = 0.$

$$\left[\int_0^1 p_{jt}^{1-\theta} dj\right]^{\frac{1}{1-\theta}} = \lambda_t \tag{5.7}$$

That this effectively is an aggregate price index can be deduced from the following considerations:

The price p_{jt} of jth good is

$$p_{jt} = \lambda_t C_t^{\frac{1}{\theta}} c_{jt}^{-\frac{1}{\theta}} = \left[\int_0^1 p_{jt}^{1-\theta} dj\right]^{\frac{1}{1-\theta}} C_t^{\frac{1}{\theta}} c_{jt}^{-\frac{1}{\theta}} \tag{5.8}$$

Multiplying both sides of (5.8) by c_{jt},

$$p_{jt} c_{jt} = \left[\int_0^1 p_{jt}^{1-\theta} dj\right]^{\frac{1}{1-\theta}} C_t^{\frac{1}{\theta}} c_{jt}^{1-\frac{1}{\theta}} \tag{5.9}$$

By integrating (5.9), total expenditure is

$$\int_0^1 p_{jt} c_{jt} dj = \left[\int_0^1 p_{jt}^{1-\theta} dj\right]^{\frac{1}{1-\theta}} C_t^{\frac{1}{\theta}} \int_0^1 c_{jt}^{\frac{\theta-1}{\theta}} dj \tag{5.10}$$

From the definition of the consumption index, it follows

$$\int_0^1 c_{jt}^{\frac{\theta-1}{\theta}} dj = C_t^{-\frac{1-\theta}{\theta}} \tag{5.11}$$

And from (5.11), it follows

It follows
$p_{jt} = \lambda_t [\int_0^1 c_{jt}^{\frac{\theta-1}{\theta}} dj]^{\frac{1}{\theta-1}} c_{jt}^{-\frac{1}{\theta}} = \lambda_t \int_0^1 c_{jt}^{\frac{\theta-1}{\theta}} dj]^{\frac{\theta}{(\theta-1)\theta}} c_{jt}^{-\frac{1}{\theta}} = \lambda_t C_t^{\frac{1}{\theta}} c_{jt}^{-\frac{1}{\theta}}$
From which

$$p_{jt}^{1-\theta} = \lambda_t^{1-\theta} C_t^{\frac{1-\theta}{\theta}} c_{jt}^{-\frac{1-\theta}{\theta}}$$

By integrating over the interval [0, 1] and raising to the power $\frac{1}{1-\theta}$

$$\left[\int_0^1 p_{jt}^{1-\theta} dj\right]^{\frac{1}{1-\theta}} = \lambda_t C_t^{\frac{1}{\theta}} \left[\int_0^1 c_{jt}^{\frac{\theta-1}{\theta}} dj\right]^{\frac{1}{1-\theta}}$$

But $\left[\int_0^1 c_{jt}^{\frac{\theta-1}{\theta}} dj\right]^{\frac{1}{1-\theta}} = C_t^{-\frac{1}{\theta}}$ so that $\left[\int_0^1 p_{jt}^{1-\theta} dj\right]^{\frac{1}{1-\theta}} = \lambda_t$.

$$\int_0^1 p_{jt}c_{jt}dj = \left[\int_0^1 p_{jt}^{1-\theta}dj\right]^{\frac{1}{1-\theta}} C_t^{\frac{1}{\theta}} C_t^{-\frac{1-\theta}{\theta}} = \left[\int_0^1 p_{jt}^{1-\theta}dj\right]^{\frac{1}{1-\theta}} C_t \tag{5.12}$$

But the term to the left of the equality sign is monetary expenditure on all consumer goods, so that

$$\int_0^1 p_{jt}c_{jt}dj = P_t C_t$$

and therefore

$$P_t = \left[\int_0^1 p_{jt}^{1-\theta}dj\right]^{\frac{1}{1-\theta}} \tag{5.13}$$

Consumption demand for each good c_{jt} is the solution of a problem, dual to the previous one, of choosing consumption's mix of individual goods which, for a given expenditure, maximizes the total consumption, i.e.,

$$\max_{c_{jt}} \int_0^1 c_{jt}^{\frac{\theta-1}{\theta}} dj]^{\frac{\theta}{\theta-1}} \tag{5.14}$$

$$\text{sub} \quad \int_0^1 p_{jt}c_{jt}dj = P_t C_t \tag{5.15}$$

For generic i-th good, the demand function[3] is

$$c_{it} = \left(\frac{p_{it}}{P_t}\right)^{-\theta} C_t \tag{5.16}$$

[3]Calling λ_t the Lagrange multiplier, the first-order condition is

$\frac{\theta}{\theta-1}\int_0^1 c_{jt}^{\frac{\theta-1}{\theta}} dj]^{\frac{1}{\theta-1}} \frac{\theta-1}{\theta} c_{jt}^{-\frac{1}{\theta}} - \lambda_t p_{jt} = 0$. That is, taking into account that $\int_0^1 c_{jt}^{\frac{\theta-1}{\theta}} dj]^{\frac{1}{\theta-1}} = C_t^{\frac{1}{\theta}}$, the first-order condition is $C_t^{\frac{1}{\theta}} c_{jt}^{-\frac{1}{\theta}} = \lambda_t p_{jt}$. For an index i≠j, it holds $C_t^{\frac{1}{\theta}} c_{it}^{-\frac{1}{\theta}} = \lambda_t p_{it}$, and eliminating λ_t follows

$\frac{c_{jt}^{-\frac{1}{\theta}}}{c_{it}^{-\frac{1}{\theta}}} = \frac{p_{jt}}{p_{it}} \rightarrow \left(\frac{c_{it}}{c_{jt}}\right)^{-\frac{1}{\theta}} = \frac{p_{jt}}{p_{it}} \rightarrow \frac{c_{jt}}{c_{it}} = \left(\frac{p_{jt}}{p_{it}}\right)^{-\theta}$, that is, $c_{jt} = \left(\frac{p_{jt}}{p_{it}}\right)^{-\theta} c_{it}$. Substituting into the definition of expenditure follows

$\int_0^1 p_{jt}\left[\frac{p_{jt}}{p_{it}}\right]^{-\theta} c_{it}\, dj = P_t C_t \Rightarrow p_{it}{}^{\theta} c_{it} \int_0^1 p_{jt}{}^{1-\theta}\, dj = P_t C_t$

From the definition of aggregate price index, it follows

$\int_0^1 p_{jt}{}^{1-\theta}\, dj = P_t^{1-\theta}$ and therefore $p_{it}^{\theta} c_{it} = P_t^{\theta} C_t \Rightarrow P_t^{-\theta} c_{it} = p_{it}^{-\theta} C_t$ whence $c_{it} = \left(\frac{p_{it}}{P_t}\right)^{-\theta} C_t$.

Aggregate consumption C_t is the result of rational choices of the typical consumer-worker, with an infinite time horizon and whose utility function on that horizon is the expected flow of instantaneous utilities

$$E_0 \sum_{1=0}^{\infty} \beta^t U\left(C_t, \frac{M_t}{P_t}, L_t\right) \tag{5.17}$$

Choices of typical consumer-worker are constrained by instantaneous budget constraint:

$$C_t + \left(\frac{M_t}{P_t}\right) + \left(\frac{B_t}{P_t}\right) = \left(\frac{W_t}{P_t}\right)L_t + \left(\frac{M_{t-1}}{P_{t-1}}\right) + (1 + i_{t-1})\left(\frac{B_{t-1}}{P_{t-1}}\right) + \frac{\Pi_t}{P_t} \tag{5.18}$$

Writing (5.18) assumes that households are actual owners of firms, and therefore, they are entitled to obtain profits Π_t earned by firms in each period, in the form of distributed profits.

We indicate $\{\Omega_t\}$ the sequence of baskets entering the utility function, being $\Omega_t \equiv (C_t, M_t/P_t, L_t)$.

In addition to basket Ω_t, households also purchase securities (B_t/P_t), which have unitary periods of duration and gross yield $(1+i_{t-1})$. Therefore, when B_{t-1} matures at the beginning of the current period, the representative household receives an additional quantity of money equal to $(1+i_{t-1})(B_{t-1}/P_{t-1})$ which is added to the initial stock already owned (M_{t-1}/P_{t-1}).[4]

The term $(W_t/P_t)L_t$ in budget constraint is labor income available to households during period t.

Given the current budget constraint, bonds holding (B_t/P_t) are a residual choice, and the conditions at margin for $\Omega_t \equiv (C_t, M_t/P_t, L_t)$ give the following (necessary) conditions for optimal choices:[5]

[4] Alternatively, as often occurs in economic literature, it can be assumed that the interest on securities is not paid at maturity, but securities are at a discount, i.e., that they are sold at the current price, different from the face value so that interest is implicitly defined by the difference between nominal value repaid at maturity and value paid at the time of subscription.

Being so, if we say B_t is the nominal amount of securities currently purchased, and D_t is subscription price incorporating a given discount (D_t is the current value of a security with a nominal unit value), it must be $D_t = \frac{1}{1+i_t}$).

In this case, the household budget constraint takes the form

$$C_t + \left(\frac{M_t}{P_t}\right) + \left(\frac{D_t B_t}{P_t}\right) = \left(\frac{W_t}{P_t}\right)N_t + \left(\frac{M_{t-1}}{P_{t-1}}\right) + \left(\frac{B_{t-1}}{P_{t-1}}\right) + \Pi$$

The analytical substance of first-order conditions does not change.

[5] See Galí, J. (2008) and also Chirichiello, G. (2010).

$$\mathrm{U_C}(\Omega_t/\mathrm{U_{M/P}}(\Omega_t) = [\mathrm{i_t}/(1+\mathrm{i_t})] \tag{5.19}$$

$$-\mathrm{U_L}(\Omega_t/\mathrm{U_C}(\Omega_t) = \mathrm{W_t}/\mathrm{P_t} \tag{5.20}$$

$$\mathrm{U_C}(\Omega_t) = \beta(1+\mathrm{i_t})\,\mathrm{E_t}\,[\mathrm{U_C}(\Omega_t)(\mathrm{P_t}/\mathrm{P_{t+1}})] \tag{5.21}$$

The last condition (Euler) can be put as

$$\frac{1}{(1+\mathrm{i_t})} = \beta\,\mathrm{E_t}\left[\frac{U_C(\Omega_{t+1})}{U_C(\Omega_t)}\left(\frac{P_t}{\mathrm{P_{t+1}}}\right)\right] \tag{5.22}$$

In this form, Euler's condition highlights that to discount future values, a consumer uses the term in square brackets (to the right of equation) as a discount rate, i.e., the expected intertemporal rate of substitution between future and current consumption, weighted with the rate of inflation.[6]

He will modify his present and future choices $\mathrm{V_t}$ and Ω_{t+1}, until his expected individual discount rate coincides with the discount market's rate $\frac{1}{(1+\mathrm{i_t})}$.

With a parametric expression of the household's utility function of type already known,

$$U\left(C_t, \frac{M_t}{P_t}, L_t\right) = \frac{C_t^{1-\sigma}}{1-\sigma} + \frac{(M_t/P_t)^{1-\eta}}{1-\eta} - \frac{L_t^{1+\nu}}{1+\nu} \tag{5.23}$$

First-order conditions for maximum expected utility are equal to

$$\frac{\left(\frac{M_t}{P_t}\right)^{-\eta}}{C_t^{-\sigma}} = \frac{\mathrm{i_t}}{1+\mathrm{i_t}} \tag{5.24}$$

$$\frac{L_t^{\nu}}{C_t^{-\sigma}} = \frac{W_t}{P_t} \tag{5.25}$$

$$1 = \beta(1+\mathrm{i_t})\,\mathrm{E_t}\left[\frac{C_{t+1}^{-\sigma}}{C_t^{-\sigma}}\frac{P_t}{P_{t+1}}\right] \tag{5.26}$$

From these, we deduce, respectively, a function of real money demand, a function of labor supply, and a function of current consumption demand, given by

[6] On the other hand, this is confirmed by Euler's condition obtained in the case of securities at a "discounted" price, of the previous note. In that case, the Euler condition becomes $D_t = \beta\,\mathrm{E_t}\,[\frac{U_C(\Phi_{t+1})}{U_C(\Phi_t)}(\frac{P_t}{\mathrm{P_{t+1}}})]$, and the equivalence to (5.23) immediately derives from the fact that $D_t = \frac{1}{1+\mathrm{i_t}}$.

$$\frac{M_t^d}{P_t} = \left(\frac{\mathrm{i_t}}{1+\mathrm{i_t}}\, C_t^{-\sigma}\right)^{-\frac{1}{\eta}} \tag{5.27}$$

$$L_t^s = \left(\frac{W_t}{P_t} C_t^{-\sigma}\right)^{\frac{1}{\nu}} \tag{5.28}$$

$$C_t = [\beta(1+\mathrm{i_t})]^{-\frac{1}{\sigma}} \left\{ \mathrm{E_t}\left[C_{t+1}^{-\sigma} \frac{P_t}{P_{t+1}} \right] \right\}^{-\frac{1}{\sigma}} \tag{5.29}$$

5.2 Firms' Choices in the Case of Linear Production Technology and Flexible Prices

Concerning firms, also it is assumed they are a continuum, and the generic firm is denoted by index $\mathrm{j} \in [0,1]$.

Each firm produces a single good, distinct from the others, under competitive monopolistic conditions, so that a single firm acts as a small monopolist in its market.

It is assumed that the production technology is linear and the same for all firms, i.e.,

$$\mathrm{Q_t(j)} = \mathrm{A_t\, L_t(j)} \qquad \forall \mathrm{j} \in [0, 1] \tag{5.30}$$

Following the RBC approach, the time evolution of $\mathrm{A_t}$ is assumed to follow some exogenously given stochastic process. Since each firm faces the entire demand for its good, we can set $\mathrm{Q_t(j)} = \mathrm{c_{jt}}$ so that the instantaneous real profit of the firm producing good j-th is

$$\frac{\Pi_\mathrm{t}(\mathrm{j})}{\mathrm{P_t}} = \frac{\mathrm{p_{jt}}}{\mathrm{P_t}} \mathrm{c_{jt}} \left(\frac{\mathrm{W_t}}{\mathrm{P_t}} \frac{1}{\mathrm{A_t}}\right) \mathrm{c_{jt}} \tag{5.31}$$

The firm maximizes (5.31) subject to the constraint

$$\mathrm{c_{jt}} = \left(\frac{p_{it}}{P_t}\right)^{-\theta} C_t \tag{5.32}$$

If each firm was free to fix the price of its good, conditions for maximum profit would lead the individual firm to fix the price of its j-th good according to the rule[7]

$$p_{jt} = \frac{\theta}{\theta - 1}\frac{W_t}{A_t} = \mu\frac{W_t}{A_t} \tag{5.33}$$

Giving (W_t/A_t), whose appropriate interpretation is the real marginal cost of product, the optimal pricing rule has a markup interpretation, being μ the markup coefficient.

For this purpose, consider the optimal quantity of labor demanded by firms solution of a standard minimum constrained cost problem:

$$\min_{L_t(j)} \frac{W_t}{P_t} L_t(j) \tag{5.34}$$

$$\text{sub} \quad Q_t(j) = A_t L_t(j)$$

Forming the Lagrangian,

$$\frac{W_t}{P_t} L_t(j) + \gamma_t[Q_t(j) - A_t L_t(j)] \tag{5.35}$$

Efficiency condition is

$$\frac{W_t}{P_t} = \gamma_t A_t \tag{5.36}$$

And minimum total cost becomes

$$\gamma_t A_t L_t(j) = \gamma_t Q_t(j) \tag{5.37}$$

Therefore, when a firm efficiently organizes its production, its nominal (optimal) total cost function is

---

[7] With the assumed technology of production, the real profit function for firm j-th is

$\Pi_t(j)/P_t = (p_{jt}/P_t)\, c_{jt} - (W_t/P_t)(1/A_t)\, c_{jt} = (p_{jt}/P_t) \left(\frac{p_{jt}}{P_t}\right)^{-\theta} C_t \text{ -}(W_t/P_t)(1/A_t)\left(\frac{p_{jt}}{P_t}\right)^{-\theta} C_t.$

Differentiating for $\left(\frac{p_{jt}}{P_t}\right)$, first-order condition is

$\left(\left(\frac{p_{jt}}{P_t}\right)^{-\theta} - \theta\frac{p_{jt}}{P_t}\left(\frac{p_{jt}}{P_t}\right)^{-\theta-1}\right) C_t + \theta\,(W_t/P_t)(1/A_t)\left(\frac{p_{jt}}{P_t}\right)^{-\theta-1} C_t =$

$\left[(1-\theta) + \theta\,(W_t/P_t)(1/A_t)\left(\frac{p_{jt}}{P_t}\right)^{-1}\right]\left(\frac{p_{jt}}{P_t}\right)^{-\theta} C_t = 0$

that is to say,

$\frac{(1-\theta)}{\theta}\left(\frac{p_{jt}}{P_t}\right) = -\left(\frac{W_t}{P_t}\right)\left(\frac{1}{A_t}\right)$

from which, solving, it is $\left(\frac{p_{jt}}{P_t}\right) = \frac{\theta}{(\theta-1)}(W_t/P_t)(1/A_t).$

$$C(Q_t(j)) = \gamma_t P_t Q_t(j) \tag{5.38}$$

Real total cost of production is

$$C(Q_t(j))/P_t = \gamma_t Q_t(j) \tag{5.39}$$

So that real marginal cost becomes

$$\gamma_t = \frac{d[C(Q_t(j))/P_t]}{dQ_t(j)} = (W_t/P_t 1/A_t) \tag{5.40}$$

Given the previous position, taking into account the constraint $Q_t(j)=c_{jt}$, real total profit becomes

$$\Pi_t\, j/P_t = \left(p_{jt}/P_t\right) c_{jt} - (W_t/P_t 1/A_t)c_{jt} = \left(p_{jt}/P_t\right) c_{jt} - \gamma_t c_{jt} \tag{5.41}$$

That is,

$$\Pi_t\, j/P_t = \left(p_{jt}/P_t\right) \left(\frac{p_{it}}{P_t}\right)^{-\theta} C_t - \gamma_t \left(p_{jt}/P_t\right) \left(\frac{p_{it}}{P_t}\right)^{-\theta} C_t \tag{5.42}$$

and condition for maximum profit becomes

$$\left(p_{jt}/P_t\right) = \quad (\theta/\theta - 1)\ (W_t/P_t 1/A_t) = (\theta/\theta - 1)\ \gamma_t \tag{5.43}$$

This equality shows, therefore, that $(W_t/P_t)(1/A_t)$ coincides with the real marginal cost of labor, γ_t, and the setting rule for real price becomes

$$\left(p_{jt}/P_t\right) = (\theta/\theta - 1)\ Mc_t \tag{5.44}$$

Note that, by the assumption that the labor market is competitive, the real cost of labor per unit of product, given uniform productive technology, is the same for all firms and therefore

$$Mc_{jt} = \quad Mc_t \quad \forall j \tag{5.45}$$

and if the elasticity of demand θ is the same for all firms, which is certainly verified since the demand function is of the same type for all firms, all they will fix the same real price, despite the conditions of imperfect competition, i.e.,

$$\left(p_{jt}/P_t\right) = (p_t/P_t) \tag{5.46}$$

5.3 Firm Choices in the Case of Cobb-Douglas Production Technology

Assume now that production technology is Cobb-Douglas, the same for all firms, i.e.,[8]

$$Q_{jt} = A_t K_{jt}{}^{\alpha} L_{Jt}{}^{1-\alpha} \qquad \forall j \in [0, 1] \tag{5.47}$$

Firm j-th produces the good it monopolizes in a way that minimizes the total cost of production, which, since inputs markets are both competitive, is defined by

$$CT_{jt} = P_t\ W_t L_{jt} + P_t\ r_t^k K_{jt} \tag{5.48}$$

Given Cobb-Douglas production technology, firm j-th demands for the inputs are obtained by solving the following constrained minimum problem:

$$\min_{L_{jt},\, K_{jt}} P_t\ W_t L_{jt} + P_t\ r_t^k k_{Jt} \tag{5.49}$$

$$\text{sub}\ \ Q_{jt} = A_t K_{jt}{}^{\alpha} L_{jt}{}^{1-\alpha}$$

Calling λ_t Lagrange multiplier, the first-order conditions for $L_{jt}$and K_{jt} are, respectively,

$$W_t = \frac{\lambda_t}{P_t}\ (1-\alpha) A_t K_{jt}{}^{\alpha} L_{jt}{}^{-\alpha} \tag{5.50}$$

$$r_t^k = \frac{\lambda_t}{P_t}\ \alpha A_t K_{jt}{}^{\alpha-1} L_{Jt}{}^{1-\alpha} \tag{5.51}$$

Dividing member by member (5.51) by (5.50),

[8] As it is known, a general neoclassical production function F(.) is assumed to satisfy the following properties: (a) F(.) is strictly increasing ($F_K > 0$ and $F_L > 0$), twice differentiable, and strictly concave ($F_{KK} < 0$ and $F_{LL} < 0$); (b) constant returns to scale are admitted, i.e., for $z > 0$, it verifies $zQ_t = F(zK_t,\ zL_t)$; and (c) Inada's conditions are satisfied: $\lim_{K \to 0} F_K = \infty$; $\lim_{K \to \infty} F_K = 0$; $\lim_{L \to 0} F_L = \infty$; and $\lim_{L \to \infty} F_L = 0$. Conditions (a), (b), and (c) are in particular satisfied by the Cobb-Douglas function.

$$\frac{r_t^k}{W_t} = \frac{\alpha A_t K_{jt}{}^{\alpha-1} L_{jt}{}^{1-\alpha}}{(1-\alpha) A_t K_{jt}{}^{\alpha} L_{jt}{}^{-\alpha}} = \frac{\alpha}{(1-\alpha)} \frac{L_{jt}}{K_{jt}} \tag{5.52}$$

From which

$$\frac{K_{jt}}{L_{jt}} = \frac{\alpha}{(1-\alpha)} \frac{W_t}{r_t^k} \tag{5.53}$$

As was to be expected, as a consequence of the first-degree homogeneity of production function, firm i-th, in minimizing production costs, determines the optimal ratio of production inputs, but not their levels.

Furthermore, the term on the right of (5.53) is independent of the firm's indices, so the relationship between factors is the same for all firms and is equal to the aggregate capital-labor ratio $\frac{K}{L}$.

The total cost of a firm, already expressed as expenditure for purchasing production factors, can also be expressed as a function of the total product as follows. Given the optimal ratio between factors, it is possible to define total cost concerning only one of the factors, e.g., labor, since capital remains determined according to the optimal ratio between labor and capital.

The marginal product of labor is

$$\frac{\partial Q_{jt}}{\partial Lj_t} = (1-\alpha)\, a_t K_{jt}{}^{\alpha} L_{jt}{}^{-\alpha} \tag{5.54}$$

Its reverse is

$$\begin{aligned} \frac{\partial L_{jt}}{\partial Q_{jt}} &= \frac{1}{\frac{\partial y_{jt}}{\partial Lj_t}} = \frac{1}{(1-\alpha)\, A_t K_{jt}{}^{\alpha} L_{jt}{}^{-\alpha}} = \frac{1}{(1-\alpha)\, A_t \frac{K_{jt}{}^{\alpha}}{L_{jt}{}^{\alpha}}} \\ &= \frac{1}{(1-\alpha) A_t} \left(\frac{K_{jt}}{L_{jt}} \right)^{-\alpha} \end{aligned} \tag{5.55}$$

This expression measures marginal labor factor *requirement*, i.e., the amount of labor required by j-th firm to increase output by one unit. This requirement depends on the ratio $\frac{K_{jt}}{L_{jt}}$. But optimal $\frac{K_{jt}}{L_{jt}}$ equals $\frac{\alpha}{(1-\alpha)} \frac{W_t}{r_t^k}$ and by substituting

$$\begin{aligned} \frac{\partial L_{jt}}{\partial Q_{jt}} &= \frac{1}{(1-\alpha) A_t} \left(\frac{w_t}{r_t^k} \frac{\alpha}{(1-\alpha)} \right)^{-\alpha} = \left(\frac{1}{(1-\alpha)} \right)^{1-\alpha} \left(\frac{1}{\alpha} \right)^{\alpha} \frac{r_t^{k\alpha}}{A_t} w_t{}^{-\alpha} \\ &= \frac{1}{A_t} \frac{1}{(1-\alpha)} \left(\frac{\alpha}{(1-\alpha)} \right)^{-\alpha} \left(\frac{r_t^k}{w_t} \right)^{\alpha} \end{aligned} \tag{5.56}$$

Real marginal cost is measured by the marginal requirement for labor multiplied by the real unit wage, i.e.,

$$mc_t = w_t \frac{\partial L_{jt}}{\partial Q_{jt}} = \left(\frac{1}{(1-\alpha)}\right)^{1-\alpha} \left(\frac{1}{\alpha}\right)^{\alpha} \frac{1}{A_t} \, w_t{}^{1-\alpha} r_t^{k\alpha} = \frac{1}{A_t}\left(\frac{r_t^k}{\alpha}\right)^{\alpha}\left(\frac{W_t}{(1-\alpha)}\right)^{1-\alpha} \tag{5.57}$$

We note that being W_t and r_t^k given at every instant t, and also other parameters of (5.57) given at every instant t, (5.57) is constant. Therefore, real marginal cost of labor is constant and equal for all firms. Moreover, a marginal cost constant is equal to the average cost at all times. So, given

$$\mathrm{mc_t} = \textit{real marginal cost} = \textit{real average cost} \tag{5.58}$$

the real total cost of production of firm j-th, $C_t(y_{jt})/P_t$, is

$$\frac{C_t(Q_{jt})}{P_t} = mc_t Q_{jt} \tag{5.59}$$

This definition allows us to define the nominal profit of firm j-th as

$$\Pi_{jt} = p_{jt} Q_{jt} - P_t mc_t Q_{jt} \tag{5.60}$$

Fixing price by firm producer of good j-th under monopolistic competition, in a context of full price flexibility, now requires solving the problem

$$\max_{p_{jt}} p_{jt} Q_{jt} - P_t \, mc_t \, Q_{jt} \tag{5.61}$$

$$\text{sub} \quad Q_{jt} = \left(\frac{P_{jt}}{P_t}\right)^{-\theta} Q_t$$

This is equivalent to

$$\max_{P_{jt}} \; P_t^{\theta} P_{jt}^{1-\theta} \, Q_t - P_t{}^{1+\theta} mc_t \, P_{jt}{}^{-\theta} \, Q_t \tag{5.62}$$

The first-order condition for P_{jt} is

$$(1-\theta)\left(\frac{P_{jt}}{P_t}\right)^{-\theta} + \theta \; mc_t \left(\frac{P_{jt}}{P_t}\right)^{-(1+\theta)} = 0 \tag{5.63}$$

That is,

$$\left(\frac{P_{jt}}{\mathrm{P_t}}\right)^{-\theta}\left[(1-\theta)+\theta\frac{\mathrm{P_t}}{P_{jt}}\,mc_t\right]=0 \tag{5.64}$$

And the optimal real price for firm j-th results

$$\frac{P_{jt}}{\mathrm{P_t}}=\frac{\theta}{(\theta-1)}\,mc_t \tag{5.65}$$

This is the usual rule according to which a firm in a monopolistic competitive market sets its price by applying a markup on marginal cost. Note: for the firm i-th, for i≠ j, it holds $\frac{P_{it}}{\mathrm{P_t}}=\frac{\theta}{(\theta-1)}\,mc_t$, and therefore the term to the right of equality is independent of the firm index, since for any pair of indices (j, i), it holds

$$\frac{P_{jt}}{\mathrm{P_t}}=\frac{P_{it}}{\mathrm{P_t}} \tag{5.66}$$

5.4 Firm Choices in the Case of Production Technology CES for Final Goods, Cobb-Douglas Technology for Intermediate Goods, and Full Flexible Prices

In a basic NK model, the productive sector, compared to the previous description, is characterized by a further hypothesis: there are two productive sectors, one sector of the final good and the other of intermediate goods.

The final goods sector is competitive. Firms produce a single identical good by combining an assortment of intermediate goods.

Intermediate goods are aggregated in a way that the final good is a CES basket of all intermediate goods. The intermediate productive sector, by assumption, uses all labor. Therefore, the supply of labor by households is directed only to firms producing intermediate goods.

The intermediate goods sector is further characterized by

c.1) Monopolistic competition market structure
c.2) Cobb-Douglas production technology

5.4.1 Choices of Firm Producing Final Good

Representative firm in the sector of final good produces final good $\mathrm{Q_t}$ using intermediate goods $\mathrm{y_{it}}$, each produced by the corresponding i-th firm.

Having assumed a competitive context, in which for a single firm prices P_t and P_{it} are given, the representative firm solves the profit maximization problem:

$$\max \quad P_t\, Q_t - \left[\int_0^1 P_{it}\, y_{it}\, di\right] \tag{5.67}$$

$$\text{Sub} \quad Q_t = \left[\int_0^1 y_{it}^{\frac{\theta-1}{\theta}} di\right]^{\frac{\theta}{\theta-1}}$$

Constraint in (5.67) comes down from the assumption that the production technology of the final good is CES in intermediate goods.

Maximizing profit by the representative firm, for given P_t and P_{it}, means solving for optimal quantities of intermediate goods y_{it} used in the production of the final good. Indeed, by substituting technological constraint into the definition of total profit of the final goods sector, it follows

$$\max_{y_{i,t}} \quad P_t \left[\int_0^1 y_{it}^{\frac{\theta-1}{\theta}} di\right]^{\frac{\theta}{\theta-1}} - \left[\int_0^1 P_{it}\, y_{it}\, di\right] \tag{5.68}$$

The first-order condition for the demand for $y_{i,\,t}$ intermediate good is

$$P_t \frac{\theta}{\theta-1} \left[\int_0^1 y_{it}^{\frac{\theta-1}{\theta}} di\right]^{\frac{1}{\theta-1}} \frac{\theta-1}{\theta}\, y_{it}^{-\frac{1}{\theta}} - P_{it} = 0 \tag{5.69}$$

By rewriting

$$\left[\int_0^1 y_{it}^{\frac{\theta-1}{\theta}} di\right]^{\frac{1}{\theta-1}} = Q_t^{\frac{1}{\theta}} \tag{5.70}$$

It follows

$$P_t\, Q_t^{\frac{1}{\theta}}\, y_{it}^{-\frac{1}{\theta}} - P_{it} = 0 \tag{5.71}$$

It again follows

$$y_{it}^{-\frac{1}{\theta}} = \frac{P_{it}}{P_t} Q_t^{-\frac{1}{\theta}}$$

From which, the demand for i-th input by a representative firm is

$$y_{it} = \left(\frac{P_{it}}{\mathrm{P_t}}\right)^{-\theta} \mathrm{Q_t} \tag{5.72}$$

The final good is sold at a price[9]

$$\mathrm{P_t} = \left[\int_0^1 P_{it}^{1-\theta} di\right]^{\frac{1}{\theta-1}} \tag{5.73}$$

5.4.2 Choices of Firm Producing Intermediate Goods

Each of i-th intermediate goods producer, belonging to the set of indices $i \in (0, 1)$, produces its intermediate good y_{it} to minimize the total cost of production:

$$CT_{it} = P_t\, W_t L_{it} + P_t\, r_t^k K_{it} \tag{5.74}$$

Minimizing total cost is equivalent for the firm to solving the following constrained minimum problem:

$$\min \quad P_t\, W_t L_{it} + P_t\, r_t^k k_{it} \tag{5.75}$$
$$\text{sub } y_{it} = A_t K_{it}{}^{\alpha} L_{it}{}^{1-\alpha}$$

from whose first-order conditions, it follows

$$\frac{K_{it}}{L_{it}} = \frac{\alpha}{(1-\alpha)} \frac{W_t}{r_t^k} \tag{5.76}$$

The optimal ratio of productive inputs is the same for all firms and is equal to the aggregate capital-labor ratio $\frac{K}{L}$. The total cost of a firm as a function of total product, as we have already seen, is obtained starting from the notion of marginal requirement for labor input, i.e.,

[9] This follows from the condition of null profit for a competitive firm

$\mathrm{P_tQ_t} = \int_0^1 P_{it}\, y_{it}\, di = \int_0^1 P_{it} \left(\frac{P_{it}}{\mathrm{P_t}}\right)^{-\theta} \mathrm{Q_t}\, di = \mathrm{Q_t} \int_0^1 P_{it} \left(\frac{P_{it}}{\mathrm{P_t}}\right)^{-\theta} di = 0$

i.e., $\mathrm{P_t} = \frac{1}{\mathrm{P_t}^{-\theta}} \int_0^1 P_{it} P_{it}{}^{-\theta}\, di$, from which $\mathrm{P_t}^{1-\theta} = \int_0^1 P_{it}{}^{1-\theta}\, di$, so that, by solving for $\mathrm{P_t}$, Eq. (5.73) obtains.

$$\frac{\partial L_{it}}{\partial y_{it}} = \frac{1}{(1-\alpha)A_t}\left(\frac{K_{it}}{L_{it}}\right)^{-\alpha} \tag{5.77}$$

Since the optimal ratio of inputs is

$$\frac{K_{it}}{L_{it}} = \frac{\alpha}{(1-\alpha)}\frac{W_t}{r_t^k} \tag{5.78}$$

By substituting, it follows

$$\frac{\partial L_{it}}{\partial y_{it}} = \frac{1}{A_t}\frac{1}{(1-\alpha)}\left(\frac{\alpha}{(1-\alpha)}\right)^{-\alpha}\left(\frac{r_t^k}{w_t}\right)^{\alpha} \tag{5.79}$$

Real marginal cost is the marginal requirement for labor multiplied by real wage, i.e.,

$$mc_t = \frac{1}{A_t}\left(\frac{r_t^k}{\alpha}\right)^{\alpha}\left(\frac{W_t}{(1-\alpha)}\right)^{1-\alpha} \tag{5.80}$$

which is the same for all firms.

The nominal profit of a firm producing intermediate a i-th good is

$$\Pi_{\mathrm{it}} = \mathrm{p}_{\mathrm{it}} y_{it} - \mathrm{P}_{\mathrm{t}}\, mc_t y_{it} \tag{5.81}$$

Firm i-th under monopolistic competition, and fully flexible prices, chooses the price P_{it} of good y_{it} that solves the problem

$$\max_{\mathrm{p}_{\mathrm{it}}} \mathrm{P}_{\mathrm{it}} y_{it} - \mathrm{P}_{\mathrm{t}} mc_t\, y_{it} \tag{5.82}$$

$$\text{Sub} \quad y_{it} = \left(\frac{P_{it}}{\mathrm{P}_{\mathrm{t}}}\right)^{-\theta} \mathrm{Q}_{\mathrm{t}}$$

And from the first-order condition, it turns out

$$\frac{P_{it}}{\mathrm{P}_{\mathrm{t}}} = \frac{\theta}{(\theta-1)} mc_t \tag{5.83}$$

For any pair of indices (j, i), it holds

$$\frac{P_{jt}}{\mathrm{P}_{\mathrm{t}}} = \frac{P_{it}}{\mathrm{P}_{\mathrm{t}}} \tag{5.84}$$

All firms producing intermediate goods will set the same selling price for the goods they produce.

5.5 Firms' Pricing in the Presence of Price Stickiness: (a) The Case of Costs of Price Adjustment

Frictions, which prevent firms in monopolistic competition from freely changing the price of goods they produce, introduce stickiness into the price-fixing process. We have already seen that, in literature, there are two approaches for representing such stickiness in the economic system:

1. The price adjustment costs approach of Rotemberg (1982)
2. A random process (proposed by Calvo 1983) according to which an individual firm is randomly called to change the price of the good it produces

This latter approach is the most widely followed in the literature, due to its elegance and greater analytical simplicity. In this section, however, we will consider Rotenberg's approach, and we will show its implications for the firm conduct, by assuming a quadratic function of real costs changing the price of the type

$$\frac{\varphi_p}{2}\left(\frac{P_{it}}{P_{it-1}}-1\right)^2 \mathrm{Q_t} \tag{5.85}$$

The dependence on the level of aggregate output Q_t expresses the idea that real costs are measured in terms of resources of the economy as a whole, absorbed in the activity of price formation.

Taking into account costs of price changes incurred by the firm, i-th firm's current profit in period t from producing the intermediate good y_i now becomes

$$\mathrm{P_t}^{\theta}\mathrm{P_{it}^{1-\theta}Q_t} - \mathrm{P_t}^{1+\theta} mc_t P_{it}{}^{-\theta}\mathrm{Q_t} - \mathrm{P_t}\frac{\varphi_p}{2}\left(\frac{P_{it}}{P_{it-1}}-1\right)^2 \mathrm{Q_t} \tag{5.86}$$

The presence of the term $\frac{P_{it}}{P_{it-1}} - 1$ now makes the firm profit maximization problem an intertemporal one.

Just like the past price P_{it-1} affects the optimal current price P_{it}, also the current price P_{it}will affect the future price through the future cost component of price changes, and the firm must account for this influence. Let's move forward by one period the expression of costs $\mathrm{P_t}\frac{\varphi_p}{2}\left(\frac{P_{it}}{P_{it-1}}-1\right)^2 \mathrm{Q_t}$, considered in expectation as they refer to the future, and let a discount factor be $\frac{\Lambda_{t+1}}{\Lambda_t}$ (compatible with consumer preferences).

The problem of choosing the optimal price by a single firm over an infinite horizon becomes

$$E_t \sum_{n=0}^{\infty} \left(\beta \frac{\Lambda_{t+n+1}}{\Lambda_{t+n}} \right)^n \left[\mathrm{P_{t+n}}^{\theta} \ \mathrm{P_{it+n}^{1-\theta}} - \mathrm{P_{t+n}}^{1+\theta} P_{it+n}{}^{-\theta} \ mc_{t+n} \right] \mathrm{Q_{t+n}}$$
$$- P_{t+n+1} \frac{\varphi_p}{2} \left(\frac{P_{it+n+1}}{P_{it+n}} - 1 \right)^2 \mathrm{Q_{t+n+1}}] \tag{5.87}$$

At instant t, the expression to which i-th firm must refer to maximize profit becomes

$$\max_{\mathrm{P_{it}}} \ \mathrm{P_t}^{\theta} \mathrm{P_{it}^{1-\theta}} \ \mathrm{Q_t} - \mathrm{P_t}^{1+\theta} \ mc_t \ P_{it}{}^{-\theta} \ \mathrm{Q_t} - \mathrm{P_t} \frac{\varphi_p}{2} \left(\frac{P_{it}}{P_{it-1}} - 1 \right)^2 \mathrm{Q_t}$$
$$- \beta E_t \left[\frac{\Lambda_{t+1}}{\Lambda_t} \ \mathrm{P_{t+1}} \ \frac{\varphi_p}{2} \ \left(\frac{P_{it+1}}{P_{it}} - 1 \right)^2 \mathrm{Q_{t+1}} \right] \tag{5.88}$$

And the optimal price $\frac{P_{it}}{P_t}$ is derived from the first-order condition:

$$(1-\theta)\mathrm{P_t}^{\theta}\mathrm{P_{it}^{-\theta}}\mathrm{Q_t} + \theta \ mc_t \frac{\mathrm{P_t}}{P_{it}} \mathrm{P_t}^{\theta} P_{it}{}^{-\theta}\mathrm{Q_t} - \frac{P_t}{P_{it-1}} \varphi_p \left(\frac{P_{it}}{P_{it-1}} - 1 \right) \mathrm{Q_t}$$
$$+ \beta E_t \left[\frac{\Lambda_{t+1}}{\Lambda_t} \ \left(\frac{\mathrm{P_{t+1}}}{P_{it}} \right)^2 \varphi_p \left(\frac{P_{it+1}}{P_{it}} - 1 \right) \mathrm{Q_{t+1}} \right] = 0 \tag{5.89}$$

That is to say,[10]

$$\theta \ mc_t \frac{\mathrm{P_t}}{P_{it}} \left(\frac{P_{it}}{\mathrm{P_t}} \right)^{-\theta} - \varphi_p \frac{P_t}{P_{it-1}} \left(\frac{P_{it}}{P_{it-1}} - 1 \right)$$
$$+ \beta \varphi_p E_t \left[\frac{\Lambda_{t+1}}{\Lambda_t} \ \left(\frac{P_{t+1}}{P_{it}} \right)^2 \left(\frac{P_{it+1}}{P_{it}} - 1 \right) \frac{\mathrm{Q_{t+1}}}{\mathrm{Q_t}} \right] = (\theta - 1) \ \left(\frac{\mathrm{P_{it}}}{\mathrm{P_t}} \right)^{-\theta} \tag{5.90}$$

With regard to productive factors pricing, the model has the following implications. Being the marginal product of labor also[11]

[10] For $\varphi_p = 0$, (5.90) becomes $(\theta - 1) \left(\frac{\mathrm{P_{it}}}{\mathrm{P_t}} \right)^{-\theta} = \theta \ mc_t \frac{\mathrm{P_t}}{P_{it}} \left(\frac{P_{it}}{\mathrm{P}} \right)^{-\theta}$ from which it follows that the optimal real price for $\varphi_p = 0$ is the one already known in the absence of friction in price setting $\frac{P_{it}}{\mathrm{Pt}} = \frac{\theta}{(\theta-1)} mc_t$. We find here that in the absence of price-changing costs, the i-th firm producing the corresponding intermediate good fixes the price by applying a markup equal to $\frac{\theta}{(\theta-1)}$ on its own marginal cost, being θ the elasticity of demand for the good it produces.

[11] As a reminder, $(1-\alpha) \ a_t k_{it}{}^{\alpha} N_{it}{}^{-\alpha} = (1-\alpha) \ a_t k_{it}{}^{\alpha} \frac{N_{it}{}^{1-\alpha}}{N_{it}} = (1-\alpha) \frac{y_{it}}{N_{it}}$.

$$\frac{\partial y_{it}}{\partial L_{it}} = (1 - \alpha) \frac{y_{it}}{L_{it}} \tag{5.91}$$

It follows that in terms of labor, the real marginal cost is

$$w_t \frac{\partial L_{it}}{\partial y_{it}} = w_t \frac{1}{(1 - \alpha) \frac{y_{it}}{L_{it}}} \tag{5.92}$$

But the real marginal cost is also mc_t so that

$$w_t \frac{1}{(1 - \alpha) \frac{y_{it}}{L_{it}}} = mc_t \tag{5.93}$$

from which

$$w_t = (1 - \alpha) mc_t \frac{y_{it}}{L_{it}} \tag{5.94}$$

Similarly, being real marginal cost of capital given by

$$r_t^k \frac{1}{\alpha \frac{y_{it}}{K_{it}}} = mc_t \tag{5.95}$$

also follows

$$r_t^k = mc_t \alpha \frac{y_{it}}{K_{it}} \tag{5.96}$$

5.6 Firm's Pricing in the Presence of Price Stickiness: (b) Price Stickiness a-la-Calvo in a Model of Linear Production Technology

Calvo's approach to price stickiness also makes it possible to represent individual firms, at the time of fixing price, as a forward-looking operator, but now this implication is a consequence of admitting uncertainty about the moment in which it will be able to change its price.

As a result of this uncertainty, the individual monopolistic competitive firm will have to take into account the entire profit stream, from the current instant when setting the price up to the point in time when it will eventually be able to change the price again.

The value of this flow coincides with the present value of future profits, including the current period, discounted at an appropriate discount rate applied by firms. Since, by assumption, households own firms, and information is symmetrical, there are no divergences or conflicts of interest between firms and households.

The instantaneous discount rate applied by firms coincides with the discount rate applied by households which, has been seen, in general, is

$$\left[\beta^i \frac{U(\Omega_{t+i})_{C_{t+I}}}{U(\Omega_t)_{C_t}} \frac{P_t}{P_{t+i})}\right] \tag{5.97}$$

Regarding the parametric representation considered above, this discount rate becomes $\beta^i C_{t+i}/C_t)^{-\sigma} P_t/P_{t+i}$.

In each period, it is assumed that firms called upon to change the price are a constant proportion of the total, equal to $(1-\psi)$, so that ψ is the probability that the representative firm cannot change the price in the current period. For a generic instant t, the probability that in the following period $t+\tau$ the price remains unchanged is ψ^τ.

Assume for simplicity a linear production:

$$y_{jt} = A_t L_{jt} \tag{5.98}$$

The j-th firm faces a demand $c_{j,t+i}$ bearing a total cost $\frac{W_{t+i}}{P_{t+i}} \frac{1}{A_{t+i}} c_{j,t+i}$ for its output. Value of instantaneous profit at any time t+i, with $i \geq 0$, is

$$\left[\frac{p_{jt}}{P_{t+i}} c_{j,t+i} - \frac{W_{t+i}}{P_{t+i}} \frac{1}{A_{t+i}} c_{j,t+i}\right] \tag{5.99}$$

Over an infinite time horizon, with uncertainty about future possibilities of changing currently fixed price, the expected discounted flow of profits is

$$E_t \sum_{i=0}^{\infty} (\beta\psi)^i \left(\frac{C_{t+i}}{C_t}\right)^{-\sigma} \frac{P_t}{P_{t+i}} \left[\left(\frac{p_{jt}}{P_{t+i}}\right) c_{j,t+i} - \left(\left(\frac{W_{t+i}}{P_{t+i}}\right)\left(\frac{1}{A_{t+i}}\right)\right) c_{j,t+i}\right] \tag{5.100}$$

Taking into account the demand constraint,

$$c_{j,t+i} = \left(\frac{p_{j,t+i}}{P_{t+i}}\right)^{-\theta} C_{t+i} \tag{5.101}$$

and being, for throughout the time horizon, $p_{j,\,t+i} = p_{jt}$, the firm will choose optimal real price p_{jt}/P_t that solves the maximum problem:

$$\max_{p_{jt}/P_t} E_t \sum_{i=0}^{\infty} (\beta\psi)^i \left(\frac{C_{t+i}}{C_t}\right)^{-\sigma} C_{t+i} \frac{P_t}{P_{t+i}} \left(\frac{p_{jt}}{P_{t+i}}\right) \left(\frac{p_{jt}}{P_{t+i}}\right)^{-\theta} - \left(\frac{W_{t+i}}{P_{t+i}}\right)\left(\frac{1}{A_{t+i}}\right)\Big) \left(\frac{p_{jt}}{P_{t+i}}\right)^{-\theta} \tag{5.102}$$

A necessary condition for a maximum for $\left(\frac{p_{jt}}{P_{t+i}}\right)$ is

$$E_t \sum_{i=0}^{\infty} (\beta\psi)^i \left(\frac{C_{t+i}}{C_t}\right)^{-\sigma} C_{t+i} \frac{P_t}{P_{t+i}} \times \left[\left(\frac{p_{jt}}{P_{t+i}}\right)^{-\theta} - \theta \left(\frac{p_{jt}}{P_{t+i}}\right) \left(\frac{p_{jt}}{P_{t+i}}\right)^{-1-\theta} \right] + \theta \left(\frac{W_{t+i}}{P_{t+i}}\right)\left(\frac{1}{A_{t+i}}\right)\Big) \left(\frac{p_{jt}}{P_{t+i}}\right)^{-1-\theta}]=0 \Big] \tag{5.103}$$

which, solved for $\left(\frac{p_{jt}}{P_t}\right)$, and after some algebraic transformations,[12] becomes

---

[12]Putting $\left(\frac{p_{jt}}{P_{t+i}}\right)^{-\theta}$ outside of parentheses

$\sum_{i=0}^{\infty} (\beta\psi)^i \left(\frac{C_{t+i}}{C_t}\right)^{-\sigma} C_{t+i} \frac{P_t}{P_{t+i}} \left(\frac{p_{jt}}{P_{t+i}}\right)^{-\theta} [(1-\theta) + \theta \left(\frac{W_{t+i}}{P_{t+i}}\right)\left(\frac{1}{A_{t+i}}\right)\Big) \left(\frac{p_{jt}}{P_{t+i}}\right)^{-1}]=0$

or even

$\frac{1}{C_t^{-\sigma}} \sum_{i=0}^{\infty} (\beta\psi)^i (C_{t+i})^{1-\sigma} \frac{P_t}{P_{t+i}} \left(\frac{p_{jt}}{P_{t+i}}\right)^{-\theta} \left[(1-\theta) + \theta \left(\frac{W_{t+i}}{P_{t+i}}\right)\left(\frac{1}{A_{t+i}}\right)\Big) \left(\frac{p_{jt}}{P_{t+i}}\right)^{-1} = 0.\right.$

Being $\frac{1}{C_t^{-\sigma}} > 0$, this requires

$$\sum_{i=0}^{\infty} (\beta\psi)^i (C_{t+i})^{1-\sigma} \frac{P_t}{P_{t+i}} \left(\frac{p_{jt}}{P_{t+i}}\right)^{-\theta} \left[(1-\theta) + \theta \left(\frac{W_{t+i}}{P_{t+i}}\right)\left(\frac{1}{A_{t+i}}\right)\Big) \left(\frac{p_{jt}}{P_{t+i}}\right)^{-1}]=0 \right]$$

Or

$$\sum_{i=0}^{\infty} (\beta\psi)^i (C_{t+i})^{1-\sigma} \frac{P_t}{P_{t+i}} \left(\frac{p_{jt}}{P_t}\right)^{-\theta} \left(\frac{P_t}{P_{t+i}}\right)^{-\theta} \left[(1-\theta) + \theta \left(\frac{W_{t+i}}{P_{t+i}}\right)\left(\frac{1}{A_{t+i}}\right)\Big) \left(\frac{p_{jt}}{P_t}\right)^{-1} \left(\frac{P_t}{P_{t+i}}\right)^{-1}]=0 \right]$$

That is,

$$\left(\frac{p_{jt}}{P_t}\right)^{-\theta} \sum_{i=0}^{\infty} (\beta\psi)^i (C_{t+i})^{1-\sigma} \frac{P_t}{P_{t+i}} \left(\frac{P_t}{P_{t+i}}\right)^{-\theta} \left[(1-\theta) + \theta \left(\frac{W_{t+i}}{P_{t+i}}\right)\left(\frac{1}{A_{t+i}}\right)\Big) \left(\frac{p_{jt}}{P_t}\right)^{-1} \left(\frac{P_t}{P_{t+i}}\right)^{-1}]=0 \right]$$

So that necessary condition becomes

$$\sum_{i=0}^{\infty} (\beta\psi)^i (C_{t+i})^{1-\sigma} \left(\frac{P_t}{P_{t+i}}\right)^{1-\theta} \left[(1-\theta) + \theta \left(\frac{W_{t+i}}{P_{t+i}}\right)\left(\frac{1}{A_{t+i}}\right)\Big) \left(\frac{p_{jt}}{P_t}\right)^{-1} \left(\frac{P_t}{P_{t+i}}\right)^{-1}]=0 \right]$$

This is rewritten

$(\theta-1)\sum_{i=0}^{\infty} (\beta\psi)^i (C_{t+i})^{1-\sigma} \left(\frac{P_t}{P_{t+i}}\right)^{1-\theta} = \theta \sum_{i=0}^{\infty} (\beta\psi)^i (C_{t+i})^{1-\sigma} \left(\frac{P_t}{P_{t+i}}\right)^{-\theta} \left(\frac{W_{t+i}}{P_{t+i}}\right)\left(\frac{1}{A_{t+i}}\right)\Big) \left(\frac{p_{jt}}{P_t}\right)^{-1}$

That is,

$$\frac{p_{jt}}{P_t} = \frac{\theta}{(\theta - 1)} \frac{\sum_{i=0}^{\infty}(\beta\psi)^i (C_{t+i})^{1-\sigma}\left(\frac{W_{t+i}}{P_{t+i}}\left(\frac{1}{A_{t+i}}\right)\right)\left(\frac{P_{t+i}}{P_t}\right)^{\theta}}{\sum_{i=0}^{\infty}(\beta\psi)^i (C_{t+i})^{1-\sigma}\left(\frac{P_{t+i}}{P_t}\right)^{\theta-1}} \tag{5.104}$$

Two annotations about this expression

Optimal price p^*_{jt} fixed by the j-th firm is $\frac{p^*_{jt}}{P_t} = \frac{p*_t}{P_t}$, that is, the firm j-th fixes optimal price p^*_t which is common to other firms. If we also consider the firm with index k, it results $\frac{p_{jt}}{P_t} = \frac{p_{kt}}{P_t}$. This is true $\forall$(k, j).

This property is a consequence of the fact that all firms have the same technology, and therefore same marginal costs; also they face the same type of demand functions and therefore have the same elasticity.

Note that both numerator and denominator summations can be written, respectively,

$$(C_t)^{1-\sigma}\left(\frac{W_t}{P_t}\left(\frac{1}{A_t}\right)\right)\left(\frac{P_t}{P_t}\right)^{\theta} + \sum_{i=1}^{\infty}(\beta\psi)^i (C_{t+i})^{1-\sigma}\left(\frac{W_{t+i}}{P_{t+i}}\left(\frac{1}{A_{t+i}}\right)\right) \tag{5.105}$$

and

$$(C_t)^{1-\sigma}\left(\frac{P_t}{P_t}\right)^{\theta-1} + \sum_{i=1}^{\infty}(\beta\psi)^i (C_{t+i})^{1-\sigma}\left(\frac{P_{t+i}}{P_t}\right)^{\theta-1} \tag{5.106}$$

From which, it follows that, if $\psi = 0$, i.e., if there is perfect price flexibility, the optimal price becomes

$$\frac{p_{jt}}{P_t} = \frac{\theta}{(\theta - 1)} \frac{(C_t)^{1-\sigma}\left(\frac{W_t}{P_t}\left(\frac{1}{A_t}\right)\right)}{(C_t)^{1-\sigma}} \tag{5.107}$$

This is the already referred $\frac{p_{jt}}{P_t} = \frac{\theta}{(\theta-1)} \frac{W_t}{P_t}\left(\frac{1}{A_t}\right)$, where $\frac{\theta}{(\theta-1)}$ is markup *desired* by firms.

In the expression of the common optimal real price $\frac{p_{1t}}{P_t} = \ldots \frac{p_{jt}}{P_t} \ldots = p^*_t/P_t$, it is convenient to consider also $(W_{t+i}/P_{t+i})(1/A_{t+i})$ as a single quantity, and since it corresponds to the real marginal cost of labor at time t+i, it can be denoted by mc_t

---

$$\left(\frac{p_{jt}}{P_t}\right)(\theta - 1)\sum_{i=0}^{\infty}(\beta\psi)^i (C_{t+i})^{1-\sigma}\left(\frac{P_{t+i}}{P_t}\right)^{\theta-1}$$
$$= \theta\sum_{i=0}^{\infty}(\beta\psi)^i (C_{t+i})^{1-\sigma}\left(\frac{P_{t+i}}{P_t}\right)^{\theta}\left(\frac{W_{t+i}}{P_{t+i}}\right)\left(\frac{1}{A_{t+i}}\right)$$

From this, solving for $\left(\frac{p_{jt}}{P_t}\right)$, Eq. (5.104) follows.

$_{+i}$, placing essentially $mc_{t+i} = (W_{t+i}/P_{t+i})(1/A_{t+i})$, and the optimal pricing rule becomes

$$\frac{p_t^*}{P_t} = \frac{\theta}{(\theta-1)} \frac{\sum_{i=0}^{\infty}(\beta\psi)^i (C_{t+i})^{1-\sigma} mc_{t+i}\left(\frac{P_{t+i}}{P_t}\right)^{\theta}}{\sum_{i=0}^{\infty}(\beta\psi)^i (C_{t+i})^{1-\sigma}\left(\frac{P_{t+i}}{P_t}\right)^{\theta-1}} \tag{5.108}$$

5.7 Firm's Pricing in the Presence of Price Stickiness: (c) Price Stickiness a-la-Calvo and Nonlinear Production Technology

The last expression of the pricing rule (5.108) refers to the i-th firm's real marginal cost mc_{t+i}. This makes the formula for fixing optimal real price, in a context of price stickiness, compatible with a more general technology, with flexible coefficients of production, not just linear. For example, with the Cobb-Douglas technology, we saw that real marginal cost is the marginal requirement for labor multiplied by the real unit wage, i.e., $mc_t = \frac{1}{A_t}\left(\frac{r_t^k}{\alpha}\right)^{\alpha}\left(\frac{W_t}{(1-\alpha)}\right)^{1-\alpha}$. Even assuming that mc_t differs for each firm, and the nominal profit of the firm producer of the i-th intermediate good differs for each firm, the nominal profit of the firm producing i-th intermediate good is

$$\Pi_{it} = p_{it} y_{it} - P_t\, mc_{t+i} y_{it}$$

and price of i-th firm in a regime of monopolistic competition, and full price flexibility, is the solution to the constrained maximum problem.

$$\max_{p_{it}} p_{jt} y_{it} - P_t mc_{t+i}\, y_{it} \tag{5.109}$$

$$\text{Sub} \quad y_{it} = \left(\frac{P_{it}}{P_t}\right)^{-\theta} C_{t+i}$$

In the presence of Calvo price stickiness, the discounted flow of profits of the i-th firm over an infinite time horizon becomes

$$\max_{p_{j^*}/P_t} E_t \sum_{i=0}^{\infty}(\beta\psi)^i \left(\frac{C_{t+i}}{C_t}\right)^{-\sigma} C_{t+i} \frac{P_t}{P_{t+i}}\left[\left(\frac{p_{jt}}{P_{t+i}}\right)\left(\frac{p_{jt}}{P_{t+i}}\right)^{-\theta} - (mc_t)\left(\frac{p_{jt}}{P_{t+i}}\right)^{-\theta}\right] \tag{5.110}$$

From conditions of maximum profit, it derives the already anticipated optimal real price expression, i.e.,

$$\frac{p_t^*}{P_t} = \frac{\theta}{(\theta - 1)} \frac{\sum_{i=0}^{\infty}(\beta\psi)^i (C_{t+i})^{1-\sigma} mc_{t+i}\left(\frac{P_{t+i}}{P_t}\right)^{\theta}}{\sum_{i=0}^{\infty}(\beta\psi)^i (C_{t+i})^{1-\sigma}\left(\frac{P_{t+i}}{P_t}\right)^{\theta-1}} \tag{5.111}$$

5.8 Differences Between Rotemberg and Calvo Price Stickiness

In the Rotemberg approach, unlike Calvo's approach, there is no dispersion in price changes. In each period t, firm j-th can freely change the price P_{tj} for its intermediate good, by incurring the corresponding cost. All firms face the same problem. They will choose the same price and produce the same amount of each differentiated good (symmetry of choices).

In Calvo's approach, firms do not set the same price (there is dispersion), unless symmetry (same price) is explicitly assumed.

In Rotemberg, the assumed rigidities create a wedge between aggregate demand ($C_t + I_t + G_t$) and aggregate output Q_t, since a fraction of output is used to support price adjustment costs.

Vice versa, in Calvo, nominal rigidities lead the economy to an aggregate production lower than the efficient one.

Despite the conceptual differences concerning price stickiness, in a first-order approximation and a neighbor of zero inflation, the two models, as we will see, reproduce the same reduced form of the New Keynesian Phillips curve.

Conversely, the Rotemberg model seems to provide much more robust results in the presence of nonlinearities.[13]

5.9 Implications for the Inflation Rate of Firm's Way of Setting Prices

Firms' price choices have implications for aggregate inflation. Indeed, having admitted that the fraction of firms who do not change their price is ψ, while the remaining $1-\psi$ re-optimizes price, implies that the CES general price-level index is the weighted average of price choices of the two groups of firms, i.e.,

[13] Born, B. and Pfeifer, J. (2020). On the implications of the presence of trends in inflation; Ascari, G. and Ropele, T. (2007); Ascari, G. and Merkl, C. (2009); Ascari, G. and Rossi, L. (2011).

$$P_t = \left[\int_{S(t)}^{1} P_{i,t-1}^{(1-\theta)} di + (1-\psi) P_t^{*(1-\theta)} \right]^{\frac{1}{1-\theta}} \tag{5.112}$$

In (5.112), S(t) indicates the subset of firms' indices that do not change prices. Since $\int_{S(t)}^{1} P_{i,t-1}^{(1-\theta)} di = \psi\, P_{t-1}^{(1-\theta)}$, the general price-level index can also be written

$$P_t = \left[\psi\, P_{t-1}^{(1-\theta)} + (1-\psi) P_t^{*(1-\theta)} \right]^{\frac{1}{1-\theta}} \tag{5.113}$$

A simple algebraic transformation allows us to describe the consequent trend of aggregate inflation. Indeed, it is

$$P_t^{1-\theta} = \psi\, P_{t-1}^{(1-\theta)} + (1-\psi) P_t^{*(1-\theta)} \tag{5.114}$$

And also

$$\left(\frac{P_t}{P_{t-1}} \right)^{1-\theta} = \psi + (1-\psi) \left(\frac{P_t^*}{P_{t-1}} \right)^{1-\theta} \tag{5.115}$$

From which

$$\Pi_t = \left[\psi + (1-\psi) \left(\frac{P_t^*}{P_{t-1}} \right)^{1-\theta} \right]^{\frac{1}{1-\theta}} \tag{5.116}$$

Equation (5.123) highlights that two forces tend to change current economy's rate of inflation.

The first is the inertial component of the group of firms that does not change current prices and therefore does not currently exert any pressure on inflation other than the one in the past, and the second is instead the pressure exerted by the group of firms that wishes to adjust their prices to the amount deemed optimal.

We will see below the implications of the presence of these forces on the equilibrium trend of the inflation rate.

5.10 The Aggregate Economic System with Price Stickiness a-la-Calvo and Linear Production Technology: The Demand Side

Concerning the aggregate system, we will now consider the general equilibrium of each market composing the economy.

We will look separately at conditions of supply and demand, limiting ourselves for the moment to the model with linear production technology.

On the demand side, the system is characterized by the following properties:

a) *Aggregate demand for goods*

Since there is no accumulation of capital and no public expenditure, the entire product of each period is consumed. It follows that aggregate demand in the goods market coincides with consumption.

On the market, the equilibrium for every single good is

$$Q^d_{jt} = c_{jt} \tag{5.117}$$

From which

$$\left(Q^d_{jt}\right)^{\frac{\theta-1}{\theta}} = \left(c_{jt}\right)^{\frac{\theta-1}{\theta}} \tag{5.118}$$

Integrating and after raising to power $\frac{\theta}{\theta-1}$

$$Q^d_t = \left[\int_0^1 Q^{d\,\frac{\theta-1}{\theta}}_{jt}\, dj\right]^{\frac{\theta}{\theta-1}} = \left[\int_0^1 \left(c_{jt}\right)^{\frac{\theta-1}{\theta}} dj\right]^{\frac{\theta}{\theta-1}} \tag{5.119}$$

Since $c_{jt} = (p_{jt}/P_t)^{-\theta}\, C_t$, it follows

$$Q^d_t = \left[C_t^{\frac{\theta-1}{\theta}} \int_0^1 \left(\frac{p_{jt}}{P_t}\right)^{1-\theta} dj\right]^{\frac{\theta}{\theta-1}} = \left[C_t^{\frac{\theta-1}{\theta}}\, P_t^{\theta-1} \int_0^1 \left(p_{jt}\right)^{1-\theta} dj\right]^{\frac{\theta}{\theta-1}}$$

$$= C_t^{\frac{\theta-1}{\theta}\frac{\theta}{\theta-1}} P_t^{(\theta-1)\frac{\theta}{\theta-1}} \left[\int_0^1 \left(p_{jt}\right)^{1-\theta} dj\right]^{-\frac{1}{1-\theta}\theta} \tag{5.120}$$

From which, at the aggregate level is

$$Q^d_t = C_t\, P_t^{\theta} P_t^{-\theta} = C_t \tag{5.121}$$

Given the Euler equation relating to consumption C_t, it follows that aggregate demand for goods can be characterized by the following expression:

$$Q^d_t = [\beta(1+i_t)]^{-\frac{1}{\sigma}} \left\{E_t\left[\left(Q^d\right)^{-\sigma}_{t+1} \frac{P_t}{P_{t+1}}\right]\right\}^{-\frac{1}{\sigma}} \tag{5.122}$$

b) *Aggregate demand for labor*

Demand for labor results from the aggregation of optimal labor requirements of individual firms, i.e., starting from

$$L_{it}^{d} = \frac{Q_{jt}}{A_t} \tag{5.123}$$

By integrating

$$\mathrm{L}_{\mathrm{t}}^{\mathrm{d}} = \int_0^1 \left(\frac{Q_{jt}}{A_t}\right) dj = \left(\frac{Q_t}{A_t}\right) \int_0^1 \frac{Q_{jt}}{Q_t}\, dj \tag{5.124}$$

From

$$\mathrm{Q_{jt} = c_{jt} = \left(p_{jt}/P_t\right)^{-\theta} C_t = \left(p_{jt}/P_t\right)^{-\theta} Q_t} \tag{5.125}$$

It follows

$$\mathrm{L}_{\mathrm{t}}^{\mathrm{d}} = \left(\frac{Q_t}{A_t}\right) \int_0^1 \frac{Q_{jt}}{Q_t}\, dj = \left(\frac{Q_t}{A_t}\right) \int_0^1 \left(\frac{p_{jt}}{P_t}\right)^{-\theta} dj \tag{5.126}$$

The term $\int_0^1 \left(\frac{p_{jt}}{P_t}\right)^{-\theta} dj$ measures the price dispersion reflecting the fact that price formation is precisely dispersed among many potentially different firms.

A linear log approximation of $\int_0^1 \left(\frac{p_{jt}}{P_t}\right)^{-\theta} dj$ gives

$$\int_0^1 \left(\frac{p_{jt}}{P_t}\right)^{-\theta} dj \cong 1. \tag{5.127}$$

Hence the aggregate demand for labor[14] can be approximated by

[14]Let us consider a second-order linear log approximation around the steady state of the term $\int_0^1 \left(\frac{p_{jt}}{P_t}\right)^{-\theta} dj$. This approximation, by operating the transformation $x e^{\widehat{x}}$, gives

$\int_0^1 \left(\frac{p_{jt}}{P_t}\right)^{-\theta} dj = e^{\int_0^1 -\theta\left(\widehat{p}_{jt} - \widehat{p}_t\right) dj + \frac{\theta^2}{2}\int_0^1 \left(\widehat{p}_{jt} - \widehat{p}_t\right)^2 dj} = 1 - \theta \int_0^1 \left(\widehat{p}_{jt} - \widehat{p}_t\right) dj + \frac{\theta^2}{2} \int_0^1 \left(\widehat{p}_{jt} - \widehat{p}_t\right)^2 dj.$

With a further step, the second-degree term can be written with an explicit expression. From definition $P_t = \left[\int_0^1 p_{jt}^{1-\theta} dj\right]^{\frac{1}{1-\theta}}$ so that $P_t^{1-\theta} = \left[\int_0^1 p_{jt}^{1-\theta} dj\right]$, it is

$$\int_0^1 \left(\frac{p_{jt}}{P_t}\right)^{1-\theta} dj = 1$$

And therefore,

$1 = e^{\int_0^1 (1-\theta)\left(\widehat{p}_{jt} - \widehat{p}_t\right) dj + \frac{(1-\theta)^2}{2}\int_0^1 \left(\widehat{p}_{jt} - \widehat{p}_t\right)^2 dj} \cong 1 + (1-\theta) \int_0^1 \left(\widehat{p}_{jt} - \widehat{p}_t\right) dj + \frac{(1-\theta)^2}{2} \int_0^1 \left(\widehat{p}_{jt} - \widehat{p}_t\right)^2 dj.$

$$L_t^d = \left(\frac{Q_t}{A_t}\right) \tag{5.128}$$

c) *Aggregate demand for money*

Demand for money function is the one already seen for the representative household, i.e.,

$$\frac{M_t}{P_t} = \left(\frac{\mathrm{i_t}}{1+\mathrm{i_t}}\, C_t^{-\sigma}\right)^{-\frac{1}{\eta}} \tag{5.129}$$

5.11 The Aggregate Economic System with Price Stickiness a-la-Calvo and Linear Production Technology: The Supply Side

On the supply side, the system is characterized by the following properties:

a) *Aggregate supply of goods*

In each market, the supply of goods is determined by the firms' optimal output:

$$Q_{jt}^s = A_t L^d{}_{it} \tag{5.130}$$

which, given previous considerations, at the aggregate level becomes

$$Q_t^s = A_t L_t^d = A_t \left(\frac{Q_t}{A_t}\right) = Q_t \tag{5.131}$$

Therefore, the aggregate supply of goods simply coincides with the aggregate production.

From this, it follows
$-(1-\theta)\int_0^1 \left(\widehat{\mathrm{p}}_{\mathrm{jt}}-\widehat{\mathrm{p}}_{\mathrm{t}}\right)\mathrm{dj}=\frac{(1-\theta)^2}{2}\int_0^1 \left(\widehat{\mathrm{p}}_{\mathrm{jt}}-\widehat{\mathrm{p}}_{\mathrm{t}}\right)^2 - \int_0^1 \left(\widehat{\mathrm{p}}_{\mathrm{jt}}-\widehat{\mathrm{p}}_{\mathrm{t}}\right)\mathrm{dj} =$
$\frac{(1-\theta)^2}{2(1-\theta)}\int_0^1 \left(\widehat{\mathrm{p}}_{\mathrm{jt}}-\widehat{\mathrm{p}}_{\mathrm{t}}\right)^2 - \theta\int_0^1 \left(\widehat{\mathrm{p}}_{\mathrm{jt}}-\widehat{\mathrm{p}}_{\mathrm{t}}\right)\mathrm{dj} = \frac{\theta(1-\theta)}{2}\int_0^1 \left(\widehat{\mathrm{p}}_{\mathrm{jt}}-\widehat{\mathrm{p}}_{\mathrm{t}}\right)^2.$
So, it is definitely

$$\int_0^1 \left(\frac{P_{jt}}{P}\right)^{-\theta} dj = 1 + \frac{\theta(1-\theta)}{2}\int_0^1 \left(\widehat{\mathrm{p}}_{\mathrm{jt}}-\widehat{\mathrm{p}}_{\mathrm{t}}\right)^2 + \frac{\theta^2}{2}\int_0^1 \left(\widehat{\mathrm{p}}_{\mathrm{jt}}-\widehat{\mathrm{p}}_{\mathrm{t}}\right)^2 dj = 1 + \frac{\theta}{2}\int_0^1 \left(\widehat{\mathrm{p}}_{\mathrm{jt}}-\widehat{\mathrm{p}}_{\mathrm{t}}\right)^2 dj$$

In a first-order approximation, the second-order term appearing in this expression can be neglected and, therefore, can be approximately $\int_0^1 \left(\frac{P_{jt}}{P_t}\right)^{-\theta} dj \cong 1$.

b) *Aggregate supply of labor*

Supply of labor is the one that results from first-order conditions of households that we have seen is equal to equation

$$L_t^s = \left(\frac{W_t}{P_t} C_t^{-\sigma} \right)^{\frac{1}{\nu}} \tag{5.132}$$

c) *Supply of money*

In DSGE models of new Keynesian macroeconomics, money supply plays no role, as it is assumed that the central bank controls interest rates. In NK general equilibrium models, the money market counts only for purposes of determining money stock that households at any moment wish to hold. Therefore, the money supply is totally endogenous and coincides identically with the demand for money.

5.12 General Equilibrium of NKE Model with Linear Technology

We can now proceed to the representation of general equilibrium by considering all markets, including the securities market. The equilibrium conditions on the respective markets are

Goods Market
From

$$Q_t^s = Q_t^d \tag{5.133}$$

It follows

$$Q_t = [\beta(1 + \mathrm{i}_t)]^{-\frac{1}{\sigma}} \left\{ \mathrm{E}_t \left[Q_{t+1}^{-\sigma} \frac{P_t}{P_{t+1}} \right] \right\}^{-\frac{1}{\sigma}} \tag{5.134}$$

Labor Market
Labor market equilibrium is

$$L_t^d = L_t^s \tag{5.135}$$

Therefore,

$$\left(\frac{Q_t}{A_t}\right) = \left(\frac{W_t}{P_t} C_t^{-\sigma}\right)^{\frac{1}{\nu}} \tag{5.136}$$

Money Market

For any given stock of money M_t/P_t, the money market aggregate equilibrium is $M_t/P_t = M^d{}_t/P_t$.

Bond Market

By aggregation of budget constraints, bond market equilibrium is $\frac{B_t}{P_t} = 0$.

By Walras' law, this condition is automatically satisfied as soon as goods and money markets are in equilibrium and therefore can be ignored.

5.12.1 The Log-Linear Version of Model

By approximating log-linearly in the neighborhood of stationary equilibrium each of the equilibrium equations, and indicating a logarithm of variables with lowercase, we have

Goods Market

In a steady state, condition (5.141)becomes

$$Q = [\beta(1 + i)]\{[Q^{-\sigma}]\}^{-\frac{1}{\sigma}} \tag{5.137}$$

Log-linear approximation is

$$Q(1 + \widehat{q}_t) = Q\{\left[1 - \frac{1}{\sigma}[\log\beta + \log(1 + i_t)] + E_t\,\widehat{q}_{t+1} + \frac{1}{\sigma} E_t\,\widehat{\pi}_{t+1}\right\} \tag{5.138}$$

That is,

$$\widehat{q}_t = -\frac{1}{\sigma}[\log\beta + \log(1 + i_t)] + E_t\,\widehat{q}_{t+1} + \frac{1}{\sigma} E_t\,\widehat{\pi}_{t+1} \tag{5.139}$$

Putting $-\log\beta = \rho$; $\log(1 + i_t) = r_t$, it follows

$$\widehat{q}_t = \left(\frac{\rho}{\sigma}\right) + E_t\widehat{q}_{t+1} - \frac{1}{\sigma}(r_t - E_t\,\widehat{\pi}_{t+1}) \tag{5.140}$$

Equation (5.140) defines, for given expectations, the set of pairs (r_t, q_t) that realize equilibrium in the goods market. This is the usual definition of the IS curve of conventional macroeconomic models. However, Eq. (5.140) includes both future production and inflation expectations, and for this reason, (5.140) is a dynamic IS equation. In fact, to distinguish it from the traditional one, it is often denominated in the literature new dynamic IS curve.

Labor Market

Being $C_t = Q_t$, the log-linear approximation of (5.143) gives

$$\left(\frac{Q}{A}\right)(1+\widehat{q}_t-\widehat{a}_t)=\left(\frac{W}{P}Q^{-\sigma}\right)^{\frac{1}{\nu}}\left[1+\frac{1}{\nu}(\widehat{w}_t-\widehat{p}_t)-\frac{\sigma}{\nu}\widehat{q}_t\right]$$

Simplifying, it follows

$$\widehat{q}_t-\widehat{a}_t=\left(\frac{1}{\nu}\right)(\widehat{w}_t-\widehat{p}_t)-\left(\frac{\sigma}{\nu}\right)\widehat{q}_t \tag{5.141}$$

from which we obtain the following log-deviation of equilibrium real wage:

$$(\widehat{w}_t-\widehat{p}_t)=(\sigma+\nu)\,\widehat{q}_t-\nu\,\widehat{a}_t$$

By recalling that real marginal cost in the model with linear production technology is $mc_t = (W_t/P_t)(1/A_t)$, so that from transformation $mc_t e^{\widehat{mc}_t}=\frac{W}{P}\frac{1}{A}e^{\widehat{w}_t-\widehat{p}_t-\widehat{a}_t}$, it follows

$$mc(1+\widehat{mc}_t)=\frac{W}{P}\frac{1}{A}(1+\widehat{w}_t-\widehat{p}_t-\widehat{a}_t) \tag{5.142}$$

Logarithmic approximation of real marginal cost is

$$\widehat{mc}_t=(\widehat{w}_t-\widehat{p}_t)-\widehat{a}_t$$

Therefore,

$$\widehat{mc}_t=(\sigma+\nu)\widehat{q}_t-\nu\,\widehat{a}_t-\widehat{a}_t=(\sigma+\nu)\widehat{q}_t-(1+\nu)\widehat{a}_t \tag{5.143}$$

Money Market

As already mentioned, on the money market, for any exogenously given stock of money, the equilibrium condition is always verified and can be ignored.[15]

[15]For the sake of completeness, the equilibrium condition of the money market is $\frac{M_t}{P_t}=\left(\frac{i_t}{1+i_t}C_t^{-\sigma}\right)^{-\frac{1}{\eta}}$, and the distance in the log from the steady state is
(logM_t- logM) - (log P_t- logP)

5.13 Dynamics of the Equilibrium Inflation

We are now able to examine the dynamics of equilibrium inflation, in a given context in which only some firms are required to change the price of the goods they produce.

The general price level P_t, we have seen, at any instant is the aggregate of an average between the proportion $(1-\psi)$ of adjusted prices and that ψ of unchanged prices, i.e.,[16]

$$P_t^{1-\theta} = (1-\psi)p_t^{*1-\theta} + \psi P_{t-1}^{1-\theta} \tag{5.144}$$

Equivalently,

$$1 = (1-\psi)\left(\frac{p_t^*}{P_t}\right)^{1-\theta} + \psi\left(\frac{P_{t-1}}{P_t}\right)^{1-\theta} \tag{5.145}$$

$= -\frac{1}{\eta}$[log i_t - log i - (log(1+i_t) - log (1+i)]+ $\frac{\sigma}{\eta}$ ($log\ C_t - logC$).

The first-order Taylor approximation for the first two terms to the right of the equality sign is log i_t - log i = (1/i) (i_t-i) and log(1+i_t) - log (1+i) = (1/1+i) (i_t – i)

from which

(log i_t - log i) - log(1+ i_t) + log (1+i) = (1/i) (i_t-i) - (1/1+i) (i_t – i)

= (i_t – i)[(1/i) - (1/1+i)].

The latter is equal to (i_t -i)/i(1+i) = $\widehat{i_t}$/i. Setting the semielasticity of the demand for money with respect to i equal to (1/ηi) = χ and setting $\widehat{i_t} = r_t$, it follows

$$\widehat{m}_t - \widehat{p}_t = -\chi r_t + \frac{\sigma}{\eta}\widehat{q}_t.$$

As already stated, in the DSGE models of new Keynesian macroeconomics, the money market plays no role, as the central bank controls the interest rate, and the corresponding equilibrium being automatically verified can be ignored.

A detailed discussion of the real business cycle model with linear technology is in Galì, J. (2008), op. cit.

[16]The same result can be obtained formally by observing that from the condition of uniformity of the price of intermediate goods $\frac{p_{1t}^*}{P_t} = \ldots \frac{p_{jt}^*}{P_t} = \frac{p_t^*}{P_t}$, ∀ j∈[0, 1] and from the definition of general price level follows

$$(1-\psi)P_t^{(1-\theta)} = (1-\psi)\int_0^1 p_{jt}^{*(1-\theta)}dj = (1-\psi)p_t^{*(1-\theta)}\int_0^1 dj = (1-\psi)p_t^{*(1-\theta)}$$

and

$$\psi P_t^{(1-\theta)} = \psi P_{t-1}^{1-\theta}.$$

Adding the two terms, Eq. (5.152) follows.

As usual, the log-linear approximation of this expression is obtained from the transformation

$$1 = (1-\psi)\, e^{(1-\theta)\left(\widehat{p}_t^* - \widehat{p}_t\right)} + \psi\, e^{(1-\theta)\left(\widehat{p}_{t-1} - \widehat{p}_t\right)} \tag{5.146}$$

Or

$$1 = (1-\psi)\left[1 + (1-\theta)\left(\widehat{p}_t^* - \widehat{p}_t\right)\right] + \psi\left[1 + (1-\theta)\left(\widehat{p}_{t-1} - \widehat{p}_t\right)\right]$$

That is,

$$0 = (1-\psi)\,\left(\widehat{p}_t^* - \widehat{p}_t\right) + \psi\left(\widehat{p}_{t-1} - \widehat{p}_t\right)] \tag{5.147}$$

From (5.147) follows

$$\left(\widehat{p}_t^* - \widehat{p}_t\right) = \frac{\psi}{(1-\psi)\,\pi_t} \tag{5.148}$$

Dynamics of inflation expressed by Eq. (5.156) must be compatible with that resulting from the practice of fixing the common optimal real price of goods $\frac{p_t^*}{P_t}$ by firms based on the equation

$$\frac{p_t^*}{P_t} = \frac{\theta}{(\theta-1)} \frac{\sum_{i=0}^{\infty}(\beta\psi)^i (C_{t+i})^{1-\sigma} mc_{t+i}\left(\frac{P_{t+i}}{P_t}\right)^{\theta}}{\sum_{i=0}^{\infty}(\beta\psi)^i (C_{t+i})^{1-\sigma}\left(\frac{P_{t+i}}{P_t}\right)^{\theta-1}} \tag{5.149}$$

The log-linear approximation of optimal real price deviations around the steady state ($C°$, $P_{t+i}/P_t = 1$, mc) gives the following rule for fixing (log of deviation) price of goods:[17]

[17] To obtain the log-linear approximation, some algebraic steps are necessary, explicitly reported here. Rewrite the expression of real price in the form

$$\left(E_t \sum_{i=0}^{\infty}(\beta\psi)^i C_{t+i}^{1-\sigma}\left(\frac{P_{t+i}}{P_t}\right)^{\theta-1}\right)\frac{p_t^*}{P_t} = \left(\frac{\theta}{(\theta-1)} E_t \sum_{i=0}^{\infty}(\beta\psi)^i C_{t+i}^{1-\sigma}\left[\left(mc_{t+i}\left(\frac{P_{t+i}}{P_t}\right)^{\theta}\right]\right)$$

First, consider the term to the left of the equality, and perform the aforementioned transformation of the type $X\widehat{e^x}$. Linear approximation is obtained by replacing $\widehat{e^x}$ with $1+\widehat{x}$, and therefore the term on the left of the equality is

$$E_t \sum_{i=0}^{\infty}(\beta\psi)^i C^{1-\sigma}\frac{p^*}{P}\left[1 + (1-\sigma)\widehat{c}_{t+i} + (\theta-1)\left(\widehat{p}_{t+i} - \widehat{p}_t\right) + \widehat{p}_t^* - \widehat{p}_t\right]$$

Similarly, the expression to the right of equality sign is

$$\widehat{p}_t^* - \widehat{p}_t = \mu + (1 - \beta\psi)\left[E_t \sum_{i=0}^{\infty} (\beta\psi)^i \left(\widehat{mc}_{t+i} + \widehat{p}_{t+i} - \widehat{p}_t\right)\right. \tag{5.150}$$

Equation (5.150), with some transformations, may be set:[18]

$$\frac{\theta}{(\theta-1)} E_t \sum_{i=0}^{\infty} (\beta\psi)^i C^{1-\sigma} mc\left[1 + \log\frac{\theta}{(\theta-1)} + (1-\sigma)\widehat{c}_{t+i} + \widehat{mc}_{t+i} + \theta\left(\widehat{p}_{t+i} - \widehat{p}_t\right)\right]$$

The transformed equation therefore is

$E_t \sum_{i=0}^{\infty} (\beta\psi)^i C^{1-\sigma} \frac{p^*}{P} \left[(1-\sigma)\widehat{c}_{t+i} + (\theta-1)\left(\widehat{p}_{t+i} - \widehat{p}_t\right) + \widehat{p}_t^* - \widehat{p}_t\right]$

$= E_t \sum_{i=0}^{\infty} (\beta\psi)^i C^{1-\sigma} \frac{\theta}{(\theta-1)} MC + \left((\beta\psi)^i C^{1-\sigma} \frac{\theta}{(\theta-1)} MC\left[\log\frac{\theta}{(\theta-1)} + (1-\sigma)\widehat{c}_{t+i}\right.\right.$

$+ \widehat{mc}_{t+i} + \theta\left(\widehat{p}_{t+i} - \widehat{p}_t\right)]$

Simplifying

$E_t \sum_{i=0}^{\infty} (\beta\psi)^i (1-\sigma)\widehat{c}_{t+i} + E_t \sum_{i=0}^{\infty} (\beta\psi)^i (\theta-1)\left(\widehat{p}_{t+i} - \widehat{p}_t\right) + E_t \sum_{i=0}^{\infty} (\beta\psi)^i \left(\widehat{p}_t^* - \widehat{p}_t\right)$

$$= \sum_{i=0}^{\infty} (\beta\psi)^i \log\frac{\theta}{(\theta-1)} + E_t \sum_{i=0}^{\infty} (\beta\psi)^i (1-\sigma)\widehat{c}_{t+i} + E_t \sum_{i=0}^{\infty} (\beta\psi)^i \left[\widehat{mc}_{t+i} + \theta\left(\widehat{p}_{t+i} - \widehat{p}_t\right)\right]$$

And again

$-E_t \sum_{i=0}^{\infty} (\beta\psi)^i \left(\widehat{p}_{t+i} - \widehat{p}_t\right) + E_t \sum_{i=0}^{\infty} (\beta\psi)^i \left(\widehat{p}_t^* - \widehat{p}_t\right) = \sum_{i=0}^{\infty} (\beta\psi)^i \log\frac{\theta}{(\theta-1)} + E_t \sum_{i=0}^{\infty} (\beta\psi)^i \widehat{mc}_{t+i}$

from which

$$\left(\widehat{p}_t^* - \widehat{p}_t\right) \sum_{i=0}^{\infty} (\beta\psi)^i = \log\frac{\theta}{(\theta-1)} \sum_{i=0}^{\infty} (\beta\psi)^i + E_t \sum_{i=0}^{\infty} (\beta\psi)^i \widehat{mc}_{t+i} + E_t \sum_{i=0}^{\infty} (\beta\psi)^i \left(\widehat{p}_{t+i} - \widehat{p}_t\right)]$$

and being $\sum_{i=0}^{\infty} (\beta\psi)^i = \frac{1}{1-\beta\psi}$, solving for $\left(\widehat{p}_t^* - \widehat{p}_t\right)$ we get

$$\left(\widehat{p}_t^* - \widehat{p}_t\right) = \log\frac{\theta}{(\theta-1)} + (1-\beta\psi) E_t \sum_{i=0}^{\infty} (\beta\psi)^i \left[\widehat{mc}_{t+i} + \left(\widehat{p}_{t+i} - \widehat{p}_t\right)\right]$$

Setting $\log\frac{\theta}{(\theta-1)} = \mu$ follows Eq. (5.150).

[18] Here, there are required transformations. By setting $\mu = \frac{(1-\beta\psi)\mu}{(1-\beta\psi)}$ $= (1-\beta\psi) \sum_{i=0}^{\infty} (\beta\psi)^i \mu$, Eq. (5.158) rewrites

$$\widehat{p}_t^* - \widehat{p}_t = (1-\beta\psi)\left[E_t \sum_{i=0}^{\infty} (\beta\psi)^i (\widehat{mc}_{t+i} + \mu) + \widehat{p}_{t+i} - \widehat{p}_t\right)$$

which is

$\widehat{p}_t^* - \widehat{p}_t = (1-\beta\psi)(\widehat{mc}_t + \mu) + (1-\beta\psi) E_t \sum_{i=1}^{\infty} (\beta\psi)^i \left(\widehat{mc}_{t+i} + \mu + \widehat{p}_{t+i} - \widehat{p}_t\right).$

Consider the Eq. $\widehat{p}_t^* - \widehat{p}_t = (1-\beta\psi)\left[E_t \sum_{i=0}^{\infty} (\beta\psi)^i (\widehat{mc}_{t+i} + \mu) + \widehat{p}_{t+i} - \widehat{p}_t\right.$; moving the index t forward one period, taking the expected values, and then multiplying both sides by $\beta\psi$, we get

$$\beta\psi E_t\widehat{p}_{t+1}^* - \beta\psi E_t\widehat{p}_{t+1} = (1-\beta\psi)E_t \sum_{i=0}^{\infty} (\beta\psi)^{i+1} \left(\widehat{mc}_{t+i+1} + \mu + \widehat{p}_{t+i+1} - E_t\widehat{p}_{t+1}\right)$$

Set the term to the right-hand as

$$(1-\beta\psi)E_t \sum_{i=0}^{\infty} (\beta\psi)^{i+1} \left(\widehat{mc}_{t+i+1} + \mu + \widehat{p}_{t+i+1} - \widehat{p}_t + \widehat{p}_t - E_t\widehat{p}_{t+1}\right)$$

it follows

$$\beta\psi E_t\widehat{p}_{t+1}^* - \beta\psi E_t\widehat{p}_{t+1} = (1-\beta\psi)E_t \sum_{i=0}^{\infty} (\beta\psi)^{i+1} \left(\widehat{mc}_{t+i+1} + \mu + \widehat{p}_{t+i+1} - \widehat{p}_t\right)$$

$$+\beta\psi(1-\beta\psi)E_t \sum_{i=0}^{\infty} (\beta\psi)^{i+1} \left(\widehat{p}_t - E_t\widehat{p}_{t+1}\right)$$

Bearing in mind that the term on the right is the expression

$$\beta\psi(1-\beta\psi)E_t \sum_{i=0}^{\infty} (\beta\psi)^i (\widehat{p}_t - E_t\widehat{p}_{t+1}$$

$$= -\beta\psi(1-\beta\psi)E_t\pi_{t+1} \sum_{i=0}^{\infty} (\beta\psi)^i = -\beta\psi E_t\pi_{t+1}$$

it follows

$$\beta\psi E_t\widehat{p}_{t+1}^* - \beta\psi E_t\widehat{p}_{t+1} + \beta\psi E_t\pi_{t+1}$$

$$= (1-\beta\psi)\, E_t \sum_{i=0}^{\infty} (\beta\psi)^{i+1} \left(\widehat{mc}_{t+i+1} + \mu)\, \widehat{p}_{t+i+1} - \widehat{p}_t\right)$$

From $\widehat{p}_t^* - \widehat{p}_t = (\psi/1-\psi)\,\pi_t$ by moving the index t forward and taking the expectation, the term on the left of the equality of the previous equation becomes
$\beta\psi\left(E_t\widehat{p}_{t+1}^* - E_t\widehat{p}_{t+1}\right) + \beta\psi E_t\pi_{t+1} = \beta\psi\, \frac{\psi}{1-\psi} E_t\pi_{t+1} + \beta\psi E_t\pi_{t+1} = \frac{\beta\psi}{1-\psi}\, E_t\pi_{t+1}$
so

$$\frac{\beta\psi}{1-\psi}\, E_t\pi_{t+1} = (1-\beta\psi)E_t \sum_{i=0}^{\infty} (\beta\psi)^{i+1} \left(\widehat{mc}_{t+i+1} + \mu) + \widehat{p}_{t+i+1} - \widehat{p}_t\right)$$

$$= (1-\beta\psi)E_t \sum_{i=1}^{\infty} (\beta\psi)^i \left(\widehat{mc}_{t+i} + \mu) + \widehat{p}_{t+i} - \widehat{p}_t\right)$$

and therefore

$(1-\beta\psi)(\widehat{mc}_t + \mu) + \frac{\beta\psi}{1-\psi}\, E_t\pi_{t+1} = (1-\beta\psi)(\widehat{mc}_t + \mu) + (1-\beta\psi)E_t \sum_{i=1}^{\infty} (\beta\psi)^i$
$\left(\widehat{mc}_{t+i} + \mu + \widehat{p}_{t+i} - \widehat{p}_t\right)$.

$$\widehat{p}_t^* - \widehat{p}_t = \frac{\beta\psi}{1-\psi} E_t\pi_{t+1} + (1-\beta\psi)(\widehat{mc}_t + \mu) \tag{5.151}$$

But it is also

$$\widehat{p}_t^* - \widehat{p}_t = (\psi/1-\psi)\,\pi_t \tag{5.152}$$

and comparing (5.151) and (5.152), we get

$$\left(\frac{\psi}{1-\psi}\right)\pi_t = \frac{\beta\psi}{1-\psi} E_t\pi_{t+1} + (1-\beta\psi)(\widehat{mc}_t + \mu) \tag{5.153}$$

Solving for π_t, it follows

$$\pi_t = +\beta\, E_t\pi_{t+1} \frac{(1-\psi)(1-\beta\psi)}{\psi} (\widehat{mc}_t + \mu) \tag{5.154}$$

From which by setting $k = \frac{(1-\psi)(1-\beta\psi)}{\psi}$, we can rewrite

$$\pi_t = \beta\, E_t\pi_{t+1} + k\,(\widehat{mc}_t + \mu) \tag{5.155}$$

Equation (5.155), just proposed, relates current inflation to expected future inflation and captures the idea that, even with zero future expected inflation $E_t\, \pi_{t+1} = 0$ or even if inflation expectations were static $E_t\, \pi_{t+1} = \pi_t$, the driving force behind current inflation is cost-push, including markup, which is captured by the term $\widehat{mc}_t + \mu$.

Furthermore, the equation explains both the intensity of the inflationary process through the parameter k and the weight that the structural components ψ and β assume in this parameter k.

As it will be readily seen, the term $\widehat{mc}_t + \mu$ measures the divergence, in percentage terms, of the (log of) the current real marginal cost with respect to the corresponding value assumed in case of full price flexibility.

Ultimately, then, simultaneous equilibrium in goods and labor markets, in log-linear terms in the neighborhood of the steady state, is described by the following equations:

$$\widehat{q}_t = \frac{\rho}{\sigma} + E_t\widehat{q}_{t+1} - \frac{1}{\sigma}(r_t - E_t\,\pi_{t+1}) \tag{5.156}$$

Given that the term on the right of equality sign is the expression of $\widehat{p}_t^* - \widehat{p}_t$, it is $(1-\beta\psi)(\widehat{mc}_t + \mu) + \frac{\beta\psi}{1-\psi} E_t\pi_{t+1} = \widehat{p}_t^* - \widehat{p}_t$, i.e., Eq. (5.151).

$$\pi_t = \beta E_t \pi_{t+1} + k\,(\widehat{mc}_t + \mu) \tag{5.157}$$

$$\widehat{mc}_t = (\sigma + \nu)\widehat{q}_t - (1 + \nu)\,\widehat{a}_t \tag{5.158}$$

The dynamics of the system expressly depend on the fundamental parameters, which are in turn precisely defined when behavioral functions of economic operators in the parametric form are assumed, and this allows the overcoming of the famous "Lucas's critique".[19]

5.14 The Notion of GDP Gap and the New Keynesian Phillips' Curve

The interpretation of the first two equations as equivalent to IS and Phillips' curve explicitly suggests a parallelism between this model and the conventional ad hoc AS/AD model. But the conventional AD/AS model is formulated in terms of GDP gap, so to complete such parallelism requires revisiting Eqs. (5.156)–(5.157), for reformulating even the New Keynesian Phillips curve and dynamic IS curve in terms of GDP gap.

The notion of GDP gap in DSGE models requires the definition of potential GDP, or rather of natural GDP, about which the GDP gap can be defined.

Since the natural GDP is identified with full employment production reached when prices and wages are fully flexible, in a general equilibrium model, it is really natural to assume that natural GDP is the aggregate production resulting from equilibrium in the case of *perfectly flexible prices*. Such an expression can be obtained in the following way. We have seen that the price formation rule when prices are flexible is

$$\left(p * _{jt}/P_t\right) = \mu_{jt} mc_t \tag{5.159}$$

Log-linearizing (5.159) around the steady state as usual requires the transformation

$$\frac{p^*}{P} e^{\widehat{p^*}_{jt} - \widehat{p}_t} = \mu_j mc\, e^{\left(\widehat{\mu}_{jt} + \widehat{mc}_t\right)} \tag{5.160}$$

That is,

$$\widehat{p}^*_{jt} - \widehat{p}_t = \widehat{\mu}_{jt} + \widehat{mc}_t \tag{5.161}$$

By integrating (5.161), it follows

[19] Lucas, R. (1976).

$$\int_0^1 \widehat{\mathrm{p}}_{\mathrm{jt}}\, dj - \widehat{\mathrm{p}}_{\mathrm{t}} = 0 = \int_0^1 \widehat{\mu}_{\mathrm{jt}}\, dj + \widehat{\mathrm{mc}}_{\mathrm{t}} \tag{5.162}$$

The term $\int_0^1 \widehat{\mu}_{\mathrm{jt}}\, dj = \mu$ is the aggregate deviation of markup from its steady state (a kind of average of the log of individual producers' markups), while $\int_0^1 \widehat{\mathrm{p}}_{\mathrm{jt}}\, dj$ is (approximately, ignoring a second-order term) the log of the general price level p_{t} *when prices are flexible*, that is,

$$\int_0^1 \widehat{\mathrm{p}}_{\mathrm{jt}}\, dj = \widehat{\mathrm{p}}_{\mathrm{t}} \tag{5.163}$$

It follows that with flexible prices,

$$\widehat{\mathrm{mc}}_{\mathrm{t}} = -\mu \tag{5.164}$$

Note that this means that deviation $\widehat{mc}_t$ of log of marginal cost with full price flexibility is a constant, i.e.,

$$\widehat{\mathrm{mc}}_{\mathrm{t}} = \widehat{\mathrm{mc}} = -\mu \tag{5.165}$$

The relation (5.165) makes now possible to define the deviation in the log of the production which (in a context of monopolistic competition) prevails in the event of full price flexibility. That is, (5.165) allows us to define the percentage deviation of potential or natural production from its steady state.

We denote this quantity with $\widehat{q}_{\mathrm{pt}}$ and proceed as follows.

From (5.158), given (5.165), when $\widehat{q}_{\mathrm{t}} = \widehat{q}_{\mathrm{pt}}$, it follows

$$\widehat{mc} = (\sigma + \nu)\, \widehat{q}_{\mathrm{pt}} - (1 + \nu)\, \widehat{a}_{\mathrm{t}} \tag{5.166}$$

with $\widehat{q}_{\mathrm{pt}}$ unknown. Solving for $\widehat{q}_{\mathrm{pt}}$ gives

$$\widehat{q}_{pt} = \frac{\widehat{mc}}{\sigma + \nu} + \frac{1 + \nu}{\sigma + \nu} \widehat{\mathrm{a}}_{\mathrm{t}} \tag{5.167}$$

Equation (5.167) shows that, concerning the conventional definition (in AD/AS models of ad hoc macroeconomics), in DSGE models, potential output $\widehat{q}_{pt}$ is not constant over time. In fact, it depends on the technology that changes over time (unless it is $\widehat{a}_{\mathrm{t}} = 0\ \forall t$).

Having the result (5.167), it is possible giving to the equilibrium real marginal cost a suggestive interpretation.

Since $\widehat{\mathrm{mc}}_{\mathrm{t}} = -\mu$, it is also true that

$$\widehat{mc}_t + \mu = \widehat{mc}_t - \widehat{mc} = (\sigma + \nu)\,\widehat{q}_t - (1+\nu)\,\widehat{a}_t \;-(\sigma+\nu)\,\widehat{q}_{pt} + (1+\nu)\widehat{a}_t$$

That is,

$$\widehat{mc}_t + \mu = (\sigma + \nu)\left(\widehat{q}_t - \widehat{q}_{pt}\right) \tag{5.168}$$

Equation (5.168) shows that divergence $\widehat{mc}_t + \mu$ turns out to be proportional [according to the proportionality factor $(\sigma + \nu)$] to GDP gap in terms of natural production $(\widehat{q}_t - \widehat{q}_{pt})$.

Substituting in (5.157) the expression (5.168), the dynamics of inflation expressed in terms of deviations of the GDP gap from the steady state becomes the definitive New Keynesian Phillips curve:

$$\pi_t = \beta E_t \pi_{t+1} + \lambda\left(\widehat{q}_t - \widehat{q}_{pt}\right) \tag{5.169}$$

where it has been set $\lambda = k\,(\sigma + \nu)$.

Also, the IS can be reformulated in terms of the GDP gap. Indeed, since[20]

$$\widehat{q}_t = -(1/\sigma)[(r_t - E_t\,\pi_{t+1}) - \rho] + E_t\widehat{q}_{t+1} \tag{5.170}$$

By subtracting natural GDP from both sides, it follows

$$\widehat{q}_t - \widehat{q}_{pt} = \left(E_t\widehat{q}_{t+1} - \widehat{q}_{pt}\right) - (1/\sigma)(r_t - E_t\,\pi_{t+1} - \rho) \tag{5.171}$$

5.15 The Definitive Basic Model of the New Keynesian Economics (NKE)

The basic NKE model includes a dynamic "IS curve," which represents equilibrium in the goods market, and a "Phillips curve" which represents equilibrium in output, labor market, and prices. Setting

$$x_t = \widehat{q}_t - \widehat{q}_{pt} \tag{5.172}$$

$$E_t x_{t+1} = E_t\widehat{q}_t - \widehat{q}_{pt} \tag{5.173}$$

The initial aggregate New Keynesian aggregate model, in terms of GDP gap, becomes

[20] It is obtained from
$\widehat{q}_t = (\rho/\sigma) + E_t\widehat{q}_{t+1} - (1/\sigma)(r_t - E_t\pi_{t+1}) = (-\rho)(-1/\sigma) - (1/\sigma)(r_t - E_t\,\pi_{t+1}) + E_t\widehat{q}_{t+1}$.

$$x_t = E_t x_{t+1} - (1/_{\sigma})(r_t - E_t \pi_{t+1} - \rho) \tag{5.174}$$

$$\pi_t = \beta E_t \pi_{t+1} + \lambda\, x_t \tag{5.175}$$

From a mathematical point of view, the NKE equilibrium is a system of two finite linear difference equations in expectations, which, however, also includes the variable r_t.

The system (5.174)–(5.175) is indeterminate.

It admits infinity sequences (x_t, π_t), as many as infinite sequences of values that r_t can assume.

The analogy to the indeterminacy of systems of linear equations is immediately highlighted if the stationary solution is considered.

In this case, the system appears as a system of two equations in the three unknowns (x, π, r), which admits an infinity of solutions.

However, model (5.174)–(5.175) can be closed by assuming monetary policy follows a simple Taylor monetary rule of the kind

$$r_t = \varphi_\pi \pi_t + \varphi_x x_t \tag{5.176}$$

Adding (5.176) to (5.174)–(5.175) defines a system of three difference equations with expectations in three variables. This permits checking conditions for uniqueness of solutions, by verifying whether or not the system satisfies Blanchard-Kahn conditions.

5.16 Blanchard-Kahn Conditions for Stability and Uniqueness of Solutions of the Basic NKE Model

In verifying Blanchard-Khan conditions, it is better to refer to a reduced system of equations, in which the monetary policy rule is substituted into the IS equation.

Going ahead with the substitution, we get

$$\begin{aligned} x_t &= E_t x_{t+1} - \frac{1}{\sigma}(r_t - E_t \pi_{t+1} - \rho) = \\ & E_t x_{t+1} - \frac{1}{\sigma}(\varphi_\pi \pi_t + \varphi_x x_t - E_t \pi_{t+1} - \rho) \end{aligned} \tag{5.177}$$

Rewriting system (5.174) and (5.175) in the canonical form of finite difference equations with expectations, it follows

$$(\sigma + \varphi_x) x_t + \varphi_\pi \pi_t = \sigma E_t x_{t+1} + E_t \pi_{t+1} + \rho \tag{5.178}$$

$$\pi_t - \lambda x_t = \beta E_t \pi_{t+1} \tag{5.179}$$

System in expectations (5.178)–(5.179) needs to be transformed to bring it back to the other canonical form required by the Blanchard-Kahn conditions.

First, in matrix terms, system (5.178)–(5.179) becomes

$$\begin{pmatrix} \sigma + \varphi_x & \varphi_\pi \\ -\lambda & 1 \end{pmatrix} \begin{pmatrix} x_t \\ \pi_t \end{pmatrix} = \begin{pmatrix} \sigma & 1 \\ 0 & \beta \end{pmatrix} \begin{pmatrix} E_t x_{t+1} \\ E_t \pi_{t+1} \end{pmatrix} + \begin{pmatrix} 1 \\ 0 \end{pmatrix} (\rho) \tag{5.180}$$

Setting

$$A = \begin{pmatrix} \sigma + \varphi_x & \varphi_\pi \\ -\lambda & 1 \end{pmatrix}; B = \begin{pmatrix} \sigma & 1 \\ 0 & \beta \end{pmatrix}; c = \begin{pmatrix} 1 \\ 0 \end{pmatrix};$$

$$y_t = \begin{pmatrix} x_t \\ \pi_t \end{pmatrix} \tag{5.181}$$

System (5.180) in vectorial form rewrites

$$Ay_t = BE_t y_{t+1} + c \tag{5.182}$$

Let us calculate inverse matrix A using the rule

$$A^{-1} = \frac{1}{detA} \, adj \, A \tag{5.183}$$

Since

$$detA = \sigma + \varphi_x + \lambda \varphi_\pi \neq 0 \tag{5.184}$$

Matrix inverse A^{-1} exists. *AdjA* matrix is

$$adj \, A = \begin{pmatrix} 1 & -\varphi_\pi \\ \lambda & \sigma + \varphi_x \end{pmatrix} \tag{5.185}$$

So that

$$A^{-1} = \frac{1}{\sigma + \varphi_x + \lambda \varphi_\pi} \begin{pmatrix} 1 & -\varphi_\pi \\ \lambda & \sigma + \varphi_x \end{pmatrix} \tag{5.186}$$

The system (5.182) in the canonical form required by Blanchard-Kahn conditions is

$$\begin{pmatrix} x_t \\ \pi_t \end{pmatrix} = A^{-1}B\begin{pmatrix} E_t x_{t+1} \\ E_t \pi_{t+1} \end{pmatrix} + A^{-1}c\rho \tag{5.187}$$

That is, by setting $\frac{1}{\sigma+\varphi_x+\lambda\,\varphi_\pi} = \Omega$

$$\begin{pmatrix} x_t \\ \pi_t \end{pmatrix} = \Omega\begin{pmatrix} 1 & -\varphi_\pi \\ \lambda & \sigma+\varphi_x \end{pmatrix}\begin{pmatrix} \sigma & 1 \\ 0 & \beta \end{pmatrix}\begin{pmatrix} E_t x_{t+1} \\ E_t \pi_{t+1} \end{pmatrix} + \Omega\begin{pmatrix} 1 & -\varphi_\pi \\ \lambda & \sigma+\varphi_x \end{pmatrix}\begin{pmatrix} 1 \\ 0 \end{pmatrix} \tag{5.188}$$

And setting

$$\Omega\begin{pmatrix} 1 & -\varphi_\pi \\ \lambda & \sigma+\varphi_x \end{pmatrix}\begin{pmatrix} \sigma & 1 \\ 0 & \beta \end{pmatrix} = \Omega\begin{pmatrix} \sigma & 1-\beta\varphi_\pi \\ \lambda\sigma & \lambda+\beta(\sigma+\varphi_x) \end{pmatrix} = \mathrm{F} \tag{5.189}$$

and

$$G = \Omega\begin{pmatrix} 1 & -\varphi_\pi \\ \lambda & \sigma+\varphi_x \end{pmatrix}\begin{pmatrix} 1 \\ 0 \end{pmatrix} \tag{5.190}$$

System (5.194) becomes

$$\begin{pmatrix} x_t \\ \pi_t \end{pmatrix} = F\begin{pmatrix} E_t x_{t+1} \\ E_t \pi_{t+1} \end{pmatrix} + G\rho \tag{5.191}$$

Autovalues α of matrix F are obtained by solving the characteristic equation:

$$|\,F-\alpha I\,| = 0 \tag{5.192}$$

That is,

$$\begin{vmatrix} (\sigma\Omega)-\alpha & (1-\beta\varphi_\pi)\Omega \\ \lambda\sigma\Omega & [\lambda+\beta(\sigma+\varphi_x)]\Omega-\alpha \end{vmatrix} = 0 \tag{5.193}$$

Expanding the null condition (5.193), the associated characteristic equation results

$$\alpha^2 - Tr(F)\alpha + \det F = 0 \tag{5.194}$$

The equivalent algebraic expression of (5.194)[21] is

[21] It is

TR(F)= $\Omega[\sigma + \lambda + \beta(\sigma + \varphi_x)]$ and det(F)= $\Omega^2\{\sigma(\lambda + \beta(+\sigma\varphi_x) - \lambda\sigma(1 - \beta\varphi_\pi)]$.

Conversely, the characteristic equation results from the development of characteristic determinant. We have

$$\alpha^2 - \Omega([\sigma + \lambda + \beta(\sigma + \varphi_x)]\alpha - \Omega^2\{\sigma[\lambda + \beta(\sigma + \varphi_x) - \lambda\sigma(1 - \beta\varphi_\pi)] = 0 \quad (5.195)$$

and expanding the term in brackets of (5.195) follows

$$\alpha^2 - \Omega[\sigma + \lambda + \beta(\sigma + \varphi_x)]\alpha + \sigma\beta\Omega^2[\sigma + \varphi_x + \varphi_\pi)] = 0 \quad (5.196)$$

The quadratic characteristic equation in α admits distinct real roots if

$$1 - \beta\varphi_\pi > 0 \quad (5.197)$$

which is certainly verified.[22] Moreover, being

$$TrF > 0 \quad and\ \det F > 0 \quad (5.198)$$

Equation (5.196) has two variations. Due to Descartes' rule, it admits two positive roots.

A necessary and sufficient condition for both (positive) roots to be less than unity is that both the following inequalities are verified:[23]

$(\sigma\Omega - \alpha)[\lambda\Omega + \beta\Omega(\sigma + \varphi_x) - \alpha]$-$\sigma\lambda\Omega^2(1 - \varphi_\pi\beta)$=$[(\sigma\Omega - \alpha)\lambda\Omega + (\sigma\Omega - \alpha)\beta\Omega(\sigma + \varphi_x) - (\sigma\Omega - \alpha)\alpha]$-$\sigma\lambda\Omega^2(1 - \beta\varphi_\pi)$= 0

and again

$\sigma\Omega\lambda - \lambda\Omega\alpha + \sigma\beta\Omega^2(\sigma + \varphi_x) - \beta\Omega(\sigma + \varphi_x)\alpha + \alpha^2 - \sigma\alpha -]$-$\sigma\lambda\Omega^2(1 - \beta\varphi_\pi) = 0$,

That is,

$[(-\lambda\Omega\alpha) - \sigma\Omega\alpha - \beta\Omega(\sigma + \varphi_x)\alpha + \alpha^2] + \lambda\sigma\Omega^2 + \sigma\beta\Omega^2(\sigma + \varphi_x)$- $\sigma\lambda\Omega^2(1 - \beta\varphi_\pi)$= 0.

And therefore, the characteristic equation is (5.195):

$\alpha^2 - \Omega[\sigma + \lambda + \beta(\sigma + \varphi_x)]\alpha + \lambda\sigma\Omega^2 - \sigma\lambda\Omega^2 + \sigma^2\beta\Omega^2 + \sigma\beta\Omega^2\varphi_x + \sigma\lambda\Omega^2\beta\varphi_\pi = 0$.

By simplifying, Eq. (5.196) follows.

[22] The roots of characteristic equation are real and distinct if $\Delta > 0$, which requires $\lambda\sigma(1 - \beta\varphi_\pi) > 0$. This condition is obtained by observing that the explicit expression of the discriminant Δ is

$\{\Omega[\sigma + \lambda + \beta(\sigma + \varphi_x)]\}^2$-$4\sigma\beta\Omega^2[\sigma + \varphi_x + \lambda\varphi_\pi)$=

$\{\Omega[\sigma + \lambda + \beta(\sigma + \varphi_x)]\}^2 - 4\sigma\Omega^2(\beta\sigma + \beta\varphi_x + \beta\lambda\varphi_\pi)$.

Rewriting $4\sigma\Omega^2(\beta\sigma + \beta\varphi_x + \beta\lambda\varphi_\pi)$= $4\sigma\Omega^2(\lambda - \lambda + \beta\sigma + \beta\varphi_x + \beta\lambda\varphi_\pi)$= $4\sigma\Omega^2(\lambda$+$\beta(\sigma + \varphi_x)$-$\lambda(1$-$\beta\varphi_\pi)$, it is

$\Delta = \{\Omega[\sigma + \lambda + \beta(\sigma + \varphi_x)]\}^2 - 4\Omega^2\sigma[\lambda + \beta(\sigma + \varphi_x)$ - $\lambda(1 - \beta\varphi_\pi)]$.

Since $[\lambda + \beta(\sigma + \varphi_x) + \sigma]^2 = [\lambda + \beta(\sigma + \varphi_x)]^2 + \sigma^2 + 2\sigma(\lambda + \beta(\sigma + \varphi_x)$;

the condition $\Delta > 0$ requires

$\Omega^2\{[\lambda + \beta(\sigma + \varphi_x)]^2 + \sigma^2 + 2\sigma(\lambda + \beta(\sigma + \varphi_x)\} > \Omega^2\{4\sigma[\lambda + \beta(\sigma + \varphi_x)$- $\lambda(1 - \varphi_\pi\beta)]\}$, that is,

$$[\lambda + \beta(\sigma + \varphi_x)]^2 + \sigma^2 - 2\sigma(\lambda + \beta(\sigma + \varphi_x) > -4\lambda\sigma(1 - \varphi_\pi\beta)$$

which rewrites

$$[\lambda + \beta(\sigma + \varphi_x) - \sigma]^2 > -4\lambda\sigma(1 - \varphi_\pi\beta).$$

This, being $\lambda > 0$, $\sigma > 0$, is certainly verified when $(1 - \varphi_\pi\beta) > 0$.

[23] See Chirichiello, G. (2000) work cit., p.252.

$$| \ TrF \ | \ < 2 \tag{5.199}$$

$$| \ \det F \ | \ < 1 \ | \tag{5.200}$$

Conditions (5.199) and (5.200) are equivalent to

$$| \ \det F < 1 \ | \tag{5.201}$$

$$| \ TrF \ | \ - \ | \ \det F \ | \ < 1 \tag{5.202}$$

Both (5.201) and (5.202) are traceable to those indicated in the literature:[24]

$$| \ \sigma\beta\Omega^2[\sigma + \varphi_x + \varphi_\pi)] \ | \ < 1 \tag{5.203}$$

$$| \ \Omega([\sigma + \lambda + \beta(\sigma + \varphi_x)] \ | \ < 1 + \sigma\beta\Omega^2[\sigma + \varphi_x + \varphi_\pi)] \tag{5.204}$$

Considering (5.203) and (5.204), and by taking into account the nature of monetary rule, the conditions of stability can be searched in the set $\varphi_x \geq 0$, $\varphi_\pi \geq 0$. Moreover, the sign of absolute value of both TrF and detF can be ignored since they are both positive.

Condition (5.203), taking into account that $\Omega = \frac{1}{\sigma + \varphi_x + \lambda\ \varphi_\pi}$ is equivalent to requiring that

$$\sigma\beta\Big([\sigma + \varphi_x + \varphi_\pi)] < (\sigma + \varphi_x + \lambda\ \varphi_\pi)^2 \tag{5.205}$$

That is,

$$[\sigma + \varphi_x + \varphi_\pi)] < \frac{\{[\sigma + \varphi_x + \varphi_\pi] + \varphi_\pi(\lambda - 1)\}^2}{\sigma\beta} \tag{5.206}$$

which is immediately true since the term on the left-hand of (5.206) is included in the square of term on the right-hand of (5.206).

Equation (5.204) requires

$$\frac{\sigma + \lambda + \beta(\sigma + \varphi_x)}{\sigma + \varphi_x + \lambda\ \varphi_\pi} < \frac{\sigma + \varphi_x + \lambda\ \varphi_\pi + \sigma\beta}{\sigma + \varphi_x + \lambda\ \varphi_\pi} \tag{5.207}$$

That is,

$$\sigma + \beta\sigma + \lambda + \beta\varphi_x < \sigma + \sigma\beta + \varphi_x + \lambda\ \varphi_\pi \tag{5.208}$$

which is equivalent to

[24] See Bullard, J. and Mitra, K. (2002), App. A.

$$\lambda + \beta\varphi_x < \varphi_x + \lambda\, \varphi_\pi \tag{5.209}$$

which still requires[25]

$$\lambda\, (\varphi_\pi - 1) + \varphi_x(1 - \beta) > 0 \tag{5.210}$$

In (5.210), taking φ_x=0 and being $\lambda > 0$, we obtain

$$\varphi_\pi > 1 \tag{5.211}$$

Condition (5.211) expresses the *Taylor's principle*[26] according to which, to guarantee the stability of the system, monetary policy authorities must change the interest rate by more than proportionally to the rate of inflation.[27]

[25]The same condition can be found with some passages of elementary algebra. The trinomial $f(\alpha) = \alpha_2 - TrA_T\alpha + DetA_T$ assumes a sign in agreement with that of the term α^2 for $\alpha > max\,(\alpha_1, \alpha_2)$, being both roots (α_1, α_2) of equation $f(\alpha) = 0$ positive.

Since the coefficient of α^2 is 1, obviously positive, it will be $1 > \max\,(\alpha_1, \alpha_2)$ if $f(1) > 0$, that is, if $f(1) = 1 - \frac{\sigma+\lambda+\beta(\sigma+\varphi_x)}{\sigma+\varphi_x+\lambda\,\varphi_\pi} + \frac{\sigma\beta}{\sigma+\varphi_x+\lambda\,\varphi_\pi} > 0.$

It turns out that the condition

$f(1) = 1 - \frac{\sigma-\lambda-\beta\varphi_x}{\sigma+\varphi_x+\lambda\,\varphi_\pi} = \frac{\lambda\,(\varphi_\pi-1)+\varphi_x(1-\beta)}{\sigma+\varphi_x+\lambda\,\varphi_\pi} > 0$, since the denominator is positive, is verified if and only if

$$\lambda\, (\varphi_\pi - 1) + \varphi_x(1 - \beta) > 0$$

which is the same as (5.210).

It is also interesting to observe that necessary and sufficient conditions for the roots to be stable derive from the relationship between the roots and the coefficients of characteristic equation. As a consequence of this relation, it must be $-(-TrA_T) = \alpha_1 + \alpha_2$; $DetA_T = \alpha_1\alpha_2$. The roots are positive since $TrA_T > 0$, $Det\,A_T > 0$, so that even their sum and their product are positive.

If both must be $\alpha_1 < 1$, $\alpha_2 < 1$, then it must be true $\alpha_1 + \alpha_2 < 1 + 1$, *i. e.*, $TrA_T < 2$, and for the same reason

$$\alpha_1\alpha_2 < \alpha_2 < 1, \text{that is } DetA_T < 1.$$

[25]Taylor, J. (1993).

[27]Actually, as seen in the Footnote 21, Taylor's rule should be amended in $\varphi_\pi \in \left(1, \frac{1}{\beta}\right)$. This observation is of some theoretical interest, as it imposes an upper bound on the aggressiveness in the central bank's inflation reaction function.

5.17 Numerical Solution of the Basic NKE Model and the DYNARE Code

To elaborate on a DYNARE code, it is necessary to specify the nature of the shocks that unpredictably affect the economy. For simplicity, we will assume that in the basic model, the technology does not undergo unpredictable changes. Instead, it is admitted that both the dynamics of inflation and the rule of monetary policy suffer unpredictable shocks.

The inflation equation inclusive of cost-push shocks becomes

$$\pi_t = \beta E_t \pi_{t+1} + \lambda\, x_t + u_t \tag{5.212}$$

With u_t stochastic process AR(1) of the kind $u_t = \rho_\pi u_{t-1} + e_{tu}$, $e_{tu} \sim N(0, \sigma_u)$. Likewise, the monetary policy rule is

$$r_t = \varphi_\pi \pi_t + \varphi_x x_t + z_t$$

with z_t stochastic process AR(1) of the kind

$$z_t = \rho_z z_{t-1} + e_{tz}, e_{tz} \tilde{N}(0, \sigma_\omega)$$

The complete DYNARE code of the model is as follows:[28]

```
// New Keynesian model with Taylor's rule
//m_NKM.mod
var
x pi r rho_r z u;
varexo e_z, e_u;
parameters
beta nu sigma phi lambda phi_pi phi_x rho rho_z rho_u;
//parameters values
beta = 0.99;
nu = 1.0;
sigma =1.0;
phi = 0.8;
phi_pi = 1.5;
phi_x = 0; //.5/4;
rho_z = 0.5;
rho_u = 0.9;
sde_z = 0.01;
```

[28] The code is in C. Walsh (2017). Compared to Walsh's version, some changes here have been made.

```
sde_u = 0.002;
// Implicit parameters
lambda = (sigma + nu)*(1-phi)*(1-phi*beta)/phi;
rho = -log(beta);
model(linear);
x = x(+1) - (1/sigma)*(r-rho-pi(+1));
pi = beta*pi(+1) + lambda*x + u;
r = phi_pi *pi + phi_x *x + z;
rho_r = r-rho-pi(+1);
z = rho_z*z(-1) + e_z;
u = rho_u* u(-1) + e_u;
end;
steady;
check;
shocks;
var e_z = 1;
var e_u = 1;
end;
stoch_simul(order=1,ar=1,irf=20, graph,print);
```

The code was saved with the extension *m_NKM.mod* (in my desktop directory *C:\dynare\5.6.4\examples*) and has been verified with DYNARE 5.6.5. It works properly.

References

Ascari, G. and Ropele, T. (2007) 'Trend Inflation, Taylor Principle, and Indeterminacy', *Journal of Money, Credit and Banking*, 41(8), pp. 1557-1585.

Ascari, G. and Merkl, C. (2009) 'Real Wage Rigidities and the Cost of Disinflations', *Journal of Money, Credit and Banking,* 41 (2/3), pp. 417-43.

Ascari G. and L. Rossi (2011) 'Real wage rigidities and disinflation dynamics: Calvo vs. Rotemberg pricing', *Economics Letters*, 110(2) pp. 126-131.

Born, B. and Pfeifer, J. (2020) 'The new Keynesian wage Phillips Curve: Calvo vs. Rotemberg', *Macroeconomic Dynamics,* 24(5), pp.1017-1041.

Bullard, J. and Mitra, K. (2002) 'Learning about monetary policy rules', *Journal of Monetary Economics*, 49(6), pp. 1105-1129.

Calvo, G. (1983) 'Staggered prices in a utility-maximizing framework'. Journal of Monetary Economics, 12:383-98.

Chirichiello, G. (2000) *Intertemporal Macroeconomic Models, Money and Rational Choices*, MacMillan Press, London, St's Martin Press, New York.

Chirichiello, G. (2010) 'Vecchie e nuove controversie sulla Curva di Phillips' (italian), in AA.VV. *Scritti in onore di Manlio Resta,* Cedam, Padova ("Phillips Curve: Old and New Disputes"(Italian).

Dixit, A. K., and Stiglitz, J. E. (1977) 'Monopolistic Competition and Optimum Product Diversity', American Economic Review, American Economic Association, vol. 67(3), pages 297-308, June.

Galí, J. (2008) *Monetary Policy, Inflation, and the Business Cycle: An Introduction to the New Keynesian Framework,* Princeton University Press, N.J.

Lucas, R. (1976) 'Econometric Policy Evaluation: A Critique'. In Brunner, K. and Meltzer, A. *The Phillips Curve and Labor Markets,*Carnegie-Rochester Conference Series on Public Policy 1, New York: American Elsevier, pp. 1946.

Taylor, J. B. (1993) 'Discretion versus policy rules in practice'. In Carnegie-Rochester conference series on public policy, Vol. 39, pp. 195-214.

Walsh, C. (2017) *Monetary theory*, 4th ed. The MIT Press, Cambridge, MA.

Rotemberg, J.J. (1982) 'Sticky prices in the United States', Journal of Political Economy, 90, pp.1187-211.

Chapter 6
More Complex NKE Models: Stickiness in Money Wages, Real Stickiness, and Extensions to a Medium-Size Model

This chapter addresses aspects of the NKE that are progressively more complex than the basic model previously considered. First, a nonlinear technology of production, the accumulation of capital, and the setting of wages by families in conditions of monopolistic competition or by a representative union are considered. Then, a complete log-linearized version of the NKE model with physical capital and adjustment costs is discussed, and the DYNARE code of this model is also examined. In the following sections, some extensions of this NKE model relating to Calvo stickiness in wage modifications, habit persistence and adjustment costs of capital and labor, "rules of thumb," and non-Ricardian households are briefly mentioned. The main characteristics of these phenomena are given, but a specific model is not considered for each one. The reason is that many of the stated stickinesses are jointly considered in a final medium-sized model which includes many of the nominal stickinesses (prices and wages, backward indexing of out-of-date prices and wages) and the real stickinesses, relating to consumption and the production sector (such as habit formation in consumption, variable use of physical capital, adjustment costs, etc.) together with shocks in monetary and fiscal policies. The final two sections include the DYNARE code for the numerical solution of the medium-sized NK model and the presentation of the results of the DYNARE code for the medium-sized NK model.

G. Chirichiello, *DSGE Models for Real Business Cycle and New Keynesian Macroeconomics*, Springer Texts in Business and Economics,
https://doi.org/10.1007/978-3-031-56034-7_6

6.1 Complex Model of the NKE with (a) Nonlinear Production Technology and Capital Accumulation; (b) Money Wages Setting by Households Acting as Monopolists in Specific Labor Market Services

The basic NKE model assumes only labor as a factor of production, thus excluding physical capital and its accumulation. Furthermore, under the assumption of perfect competition and perfectly flexible money wages, the labor market is treated asymmetrically to the goods market. It is possible to extend the basic model both by including physical capital as a factor of production and by assuming that money wages, just like prices of goods, are fixed also under monopolistic competition. The hypotheses that allow us to consider the phenomena just indicated are as follows:

- There is a continuum of households that consume, own capital, and supply differentiated work services.
- Each household, being the only supplier of specific labor service, acts as a monopolist, setting the corresponding monetary wage.
- There is a continuum of producers of intermediate goods, each of which employs differentiated labor, rents physical capital from households, and produces its differentiated intermediate goods in a monopolistic competitive market.
- There is a continuum of producers of a single final good, each of which operates in a perfectly competitive market, using intermediate goods for the production of a single final good consumed by households.

Two public operators will also be considered:

- Government, which autonomously determines public spending and taxation
- Central bank, which implements and controls monetary policy

Furthermore, assumptions of the basic model relating to stickiness in price changes, economic cycles generated by nominal and real shocks, absence of information asymmetries, and rational expectations on the part of operators will be maintained.

6.1.1 *The Representative Firm Producing Final Good*

As before, the final good Q_t is obtained in a competitive sector whose firm uses only intermediate goods $Q_t(j)$, $j \in [0,1]$, purchased at the current price $P_t(j)$ taken as given. The production technology is CES, with constant returns to scale:

$$Q_t = \left[\int_0^1 Q_t(j)^{\frac{\theta-1}{\theta}} dj \right]^{\frac{\theta}{\theta-1}} \tag{6.1}$$

where $\theta > 1$ is the elasticity of substitution between intermediate goods.

The representative firm aims at maximizing profits, given the production technology.

From these assumptions, it follows that

(a) The demand for the j-th intermediate good by the firm producing the final good Q_t has the form:[1]

$$Q_t(j) = \left(\frac{P_t(j)}{P_t}\right)^{-\theta} Q_t \qquad \forall j \in [0, 1] \tag{6.2}$$

(b) The price of the final good P_t is an aggregate of the prices of intermediate goods of kind:

$$P_t = \left(\int_0^1 P_t(j)^{1-\theta} dj\right)^{\frac{1}{1-\theta}} \tag{6.3}$$

which is also the expression of the general price level.[2]

---

[1] The underlying reasoning is the one already seen above. The firm producing the final good solves the problem:

$$\max P_t Q_t - \int_0^1 P_t(j) Q_t(j) dj \;\; sub \;\; Q_t = \left(\int_0^1 Q_t(j)^{\frac{\theta-1}{\theta}} dj\right)^{\frac{\theta}{\theta-1}}$$

Substituting the constraint in the definition of profit, the function to be maximized with respect to $Q_t(j)$ becomes

$$P_t\left(\int_0^1 Q_t(j)^{\frac{\theta-1}{\theta}} dj\right)^{\frac{\theta}{\theta-1}} - \int_0^1 P_t(j) Q_t(j) dj$$

The first-order condition for $Q_t(j)$ is

$$P_t \frac{\theta}{\theta-1}\left(\int_0^1 Q_t(j)^{\frac{\theta-1}{\theta}} dj\right)^{\frac{1}{\theta-1}} \frac{\theta-1}{\theta} Q_t(j)^{-\frac{1}{\theta}} - P_t(j) = 0$$

Being $\left(\int_0^1 Q_t(j)^{\frac{\theta-1}{\theta}} dj\right)^{\frac{\theta}{(\theta-1)\theta}} = Q_t^{\frac{1}{\theta}}$, it follows $P_t(j) = P_t Q_t^{\frac{1}{\theta}} Q_t(j)^{-\frac{1}{\theta}}$ and also $\frac{P_t(j)}{P_t} Q_t^{-\frac{1}{\theta}} = Q_t(j)^{-\frac{1}{\theta}}$ from which $Q_t(j) = \left(\frac{P_t(j)}{P_t}\right)^{-\theta} Q_t, \quad \forall j \in [0, 1]$.

[2] As we have seen, the derivation of the price index of final goods makes use of the property that, in perfect competition, in the production sector of the final good the zero profit condition is verified in the long run, i.e., $P_t Q_t - \int_0^1 P_t(j) Q_t(j) dj = Q_t\left[P_t - \int_0^1 P_t(j)\left(\frac{P_t(j)}{P_t}\right)^{-\theta} dj\right] = 0$; therefore, the price of the final good verifies $P_t = P_t^{\theta} \int_0^1 P_t(j)^{1-\theta} dj$. From this, it follows Eq. (6.3).

6.1.2 Firms Producing Intermediate Goods

Each intermediate good j is obtained by a specialized firm using a Cobb-Douglas production function:

$$Q_t(j) = A_t\, K_t(j)^{\alpha}\, N_t(j)^{1-\alpha}, \quad 0<\alpha<1 \tag{6.4}$$

Total productivity, as before, evolves stochastically over time according to an exponential process of type

$$A_t = e^{\varepsilon_{A,t}} \tag{6.5}$$

where $\varepsilon_{A,\,t} = \rho_{A,\,t}\,\varepsilon_{A,\,t-1} + \xi_{A,\,t}$ and $\xi_{A,t}\quad iid.N\left(0, \sigma^2_{A,t}\right)$.

It is assumed, following Rotemberg (1982), that prices of intermediate goods are sticky, because each monopoly firm producing intermediate goods must incur costs to make adjustments in nominal prices.

As already known, these costs are measured in real terms, i.e., they constitute resources in terms of the quantity of the final good that is necessary to make price adjustments. As previously known, it is admitted that costs of price adjustment, per unit of product, follow a quadratic function:

$$\frac{C\_P_t(j)}{Q_t} = \frac{\gamma_p}{2}\left(\frac{P_t(j)}{P_{t-1}(j)} - 1\right)^2 \tag{6.6}$$

where γ_p indicates the degree of stickiness of intermediate goods' nominal prices. In the absence of price adjustment costs, monopolistic firm producer of the intermediate good j-th sets the optimal price:[3]

[3]Remember that the function to be maximized for firm j-th is $\left[P^*_t(j)\left(\frac{P^*_t(j)}{P_t}\right)^{-\theta} - mc_t(j)\left(\frac{P^*_t(j)}{P_t}\right)^{-\theta}\right]Q_t$. Since the term in brackets has the first derivative for $P^*_t(j)$ equal to

$$-\theta P^*_t(j)\left(\frac{1}{P_t}\right)^{-\theta} P^*_t(j)^{-(1+\theta)} + \left(\frac{P^*_t(j)}{P_t}\right)^{-\theta} = -\theta\left(\frac{P^*_t(j)}{P_t}\right)^{-\theta} + \left(\frac{P^*_t(j)}{P_t}\right)^{-\theta} = (1-\theta)\left(\frac{P^*_t(j)}{P_t}\right)^{-\theta}$$

The first-order condition for optimal $P^*_t(j)$ becomes

$$(1-\theta)\left(\frac{P^*_t(j)}{P_t}\right)^{-\theta} + \theta\, mc_t(j)\left(\frac{P^*_t(j)}{P_t}\right)^{-\theta-1} = \left(\frac{P^*_t(j)}{P_t}\right)^{-\theta}\left((1-\theta) + \theta\, mc_t(j)\frac{P_t}{P^*_t(j)}\right) = 0$$

Solving for $\frac{P^*_t(j)}{P_t}$, Eq. (6.7) is obtained.

$$P_t^*(j) = \frac{\theta}{(\theta - 1)} \text{ mc (j)} \tag{6.7}$$

Facing a convex cost function, the firm producing the intermediate good will set a price different from the level (6.7) of full flexibility.

Assumed given sequences of wage index W_t and price of use of capital $r^k{}_t$, the objective of firm producing j-th intermediate goods, in the presence of price adjustment costs, becomes one of choosing the infinite sequence $\{L_t(j), K_t(j), P_t(j)\}_{j=0}^{\infty}$ that maximizes discounted expected future real profits:

$$E_0 \sum\nolimits_{t=0}^{\infty} \Phi_{0,t} \left[\frac{P_t(j)}{P_t} Q_t(j) - \frac{W_t}{P_t} L_t(j) - r_t^k K_t(j) - CJ\_P_t(j) \right] \tag{6.8}$$

$$\text{Sub } Q_t(j) = A_t \; K_t(j)^{\alpha} L_t(j)^{1-\alpha}$$

In (6.8), the symbol $\Phi_{0,\,t}$ indicates the instantaneous discount rate.[4]

First-order conditions are as follows:[5]

[4]Since households own firms, the discount rate, as before, is

$$\Phi_{0,t+i} = \left[\beta^i \frac{U(\Omega_{t+i})_{C_{t+i}}}{U(\Omega_t)_{C_t}} \frac{P_t}{P_{t+i})} \right].$$

[5]Taking that into account $Q_t(j) = \left(\frac{P_t(j)}{P_t}\right)^{-\theta} Q_t$, the Lagrangian is

$$E_0 \sum\nolimits_{t=0}^{\infty} \Phi_{0,t} \left\{ \frac{P_t(j)}{P_t} \left(\frac{P_t(j)}{P_t}\right)^{-\theta} Q_t - \frac{W_t}{P_t} L_t(j) - r_t^k K_t(j) - CJ\_P_t(j) + \lambda_t(j) \left[A_t K_t(j)^{\alpha} L_t(j)^{1-\alpha} - \left(\frac{P_t(j)}{P_t}\right)^{-\theta} Q_t \right] \right\}$$

Concerning partial first derivative for $P_t(j)$, it is

$$\frac{1}{P_t} \left(\frac{P_t(j)}{P_t}\right)^{-\theta} Q_t - \theta \frac{P_t(j)}{P_t} \left(\frac{P_t(j)}{P_t}\right)^{-\theta-1} \frac{1}{P_t} Q_t - \frac{\partial CJ_{P_t}(j)}{\partial P_t(j)} - E_t \left[\Phi_{0,t+1} \frac{\partial CJ_{P_{t+1}}(j)}{\partial P_t(j)} \right]$$
$$+ \lambda_t(j) \theta \left(\frac{P_t(j)}{P_t}\right)^{-\theta-1} \frac{1}{P_t} Q_t \} = 0$$

And being $\left(\frac{P_t(j)}{P_t}\right)^{-\theta} Q_t = Q_t(j)$, it can be written

$$\frac{1}{P_t} Q_t(j) - \theta \frac{1}{P_t} Q_t(j) + \theta \frac{\lambda_t(j)}{P_t(j)} Q_t(j) = \frac{\partial CJ_{P_t}(j)}{\partial P_t(j)} + E_t \left[\Phi_{0,t+1} \frac{\partial CJ_{P_{t+1}}(j)}{\partial P_t(j)} \right]$$

From which $\left[(1-\theta)\frac{1}{P_t} + \theta \frac{\lambda_t(j)}{P_t(j)}\right] Q_t(j) = \frac{\partial CJ_{P_t}(j)}{\partial P_t(j)} + E_t \left[\Phi_{0,t+1} \frac{\partial CJ_{P_{t+1}}(j)}{\partial P_t(j)} \right].$

$$\mathrm{L_t(j)}: \qquad \frac{W_t}{P_t} = \lambda_t(j)\,(1-\alpha)\mathrm{A_t K_t(j)^{\alpha}\, L_t(j)^{-\alpha}} \tag{6.9}$$

$$\mathrm{K_t\,(j)}: \qquad r_t^k = \lambda_t(j)\,\alpha \mathrm{A_t\, K_t(j)^{\alpha-1} L_t(j)^{1-\alpha}} \tag{6.10}$$

$$\mathrm{P_t(j)}: \qquad \left[(1-\theta)\frac{1}{P_t} + \lambda_t(j)\frac{1}{P_t(j)}\right] Q_t(j) =$$

$$\frac{\partial \mathrm{CJ\_P_t\,(j)}}{\partial \mathrm{P_t\,(j)}} + \mathrm{E_t}\left[\Phi_{0,t+1}\frac{\partial \mathrm{CJ\_P_{t+1}\,(j)}}{\partial \mathrm{P_t\,(j)}}\right] \tag{6.11}$$

Condition (6.11) is written in compact form. In explicit form, since $\frac{\partial \mathrm{CJ\_P_t\,(j)}}{\partial \mathrm{P_t\,(j)}} = \gamma_p\left(\frac{P_t(j)}{P_{t-1}(j)} - 1\right)\frac{1}{P_{t-1}(j)}$ moving forward by one time index, the adjustment cost term is $\mathrm{CJ_{P_{t+1}(j)}} = \frac{\gamma_p}{2}\left(\frac{P_{t+1}(j)}{P_t(j)} - 1\right)^2$, so that an expected term appears in the Lagrangian at time t+1, $E_t\,[\Phi_{0,\,t+1}\mathrm{CJ_P_{t+1}\,(j)}]$whose partial derivative with respect to $P_t(j)$ is

$$\mathrm{E_t}\left[\Phi_{0,t+1}\frac{\partial \mathrm{CJ\_P_{t+1}\,(j)}}{\partial \mathrm{P_t\,(j)}}\right] = -\gamma_p \mathrm{E_t}\left[\Phi_{0,t+1}\left(\frac{P_{t+1}(j)}{P_t(j)} - 1\right)\frac{P_{t+1}(j)}{P_t(j)^2}\right]$$

The extended expression of the first-order condition for $P_t(j)$ which we will refer to below is

$$\left[(1-\theta) + \theta\frac{\lambda_t(j)}{P_t(j)}\right]\left(\frac{P_t(j)}{P_t}\right)^{-\theta}\mathrm{Q_t} = \gamma_p\left(\frac{P_t(j)}{P_{t-1}(j)} 1\right)\frac{1}{P_{t-1}(j)}$$

$$-\gamma_p \mathrm{E_t}\left[\Phi_{0,t+1}\left(\frac{P_{t+1}(j)}{P_t(j)} - 1\right)\frac{P_{t+1}(j)}{P_t(j)^2}\right] \tag{6.12}$$

Concerning the other above first-order conditions, multiplying (6.9) by $\mathrm{L_t(j)}$ both sides of the equality, and (6.10) by $\mathrm{K_t(j)}$, by taking into account

$\mathrm{Q_t\,(j) = A_t\,K_t(j)^{\alpha} L_t(j)^{1-\alpha}}$, it follows[6]

[6]The proof is done by considering the explicit expression of real marginal cost obtained by solving the minimum cost problem:

$$\min_{N_t(j),K_t(j)} \quad \frac{W_t}{P_t}L_t(j) + r_t^k\,K_t(j)$$

$$\text{Sub}\quad \mathrm{Q_t\,(j) = A_t\,K_t(j)^{\alpha}\,L_t(j)^{1-\alpha}}$$

Considering the Lagrangian,

$(\mathrm{La}) = \frac{W_t}{P_t}\,L_t(j) + r_t^k\,K_t(j) + \lambda_t(j)\left[\mathrm{Q_t\,(j) - A_t\,L_t(j)^{\alpha}\,K_t(j)^{1-\alpha}}\right]$, the necessary conditions for a minimum are $L_t(j)$: $\frac{W_t}{P_t}$-λ_t(j) $(1-\alpha\,)\mathrm{A_t\,K_t(j)^{\alpha}L_t(j)^{-\alpha}} = 0$; $K_t(j)$: r_t^k-λ_t (j) $\alpha\mathrm{A_t\,\,K_t(j)^{\alpha-1}L_t(j)^{1-\alpha}} = 0$,

$$\lambda_t(j)\,(1-\alpha)\mathrm{Q_t}\,(\mathrm{j}) = \frac{W_t}{P_t}\mathrm{L_t(j)} \tag{6.13}$$

$$\lambda_t(j)\,\alpha\mathrm{Q_t}\,(\mathrm{j}) = r_t^k\mathrm{K_t(j)} \tag{6.14}$$

Thus, the instantaneous profit for firm j-th can also be set:

$$\left[\frac{P_t(j)}{P_t} - \lambda_t(j)\right]\mathrm{Q_t}\,(\mathrm{j}) - \mathrm{CJ\_P_t}\,(\mathrm{j}) \tag{6.15}$$

Real profit-maximizing production requires equality between real marginal revenue and real marginal cost, i.e.,

$$\frac{P_t(j)}{P_t} = \lambda_t(j) \tag{6.16}$$

Therefore, the real marginal cost (of production) coincides with the Lagrange multiplier $\lambda_t(j)$ of profit maximization, and by calling $mc_t(j)$ the real marginal cost of j-th intermediate good, it can also be set:[7]

$$\frac{P_t(j)}{P_t} = mc_t(j) \tag{6.17}$$

6.1.3 Households

Households are a continuum, indexed in the set i ∈[0, 1].

Household i-th is entitled to dividend share $\mathrm{D_t(i)}$ and maximizes the following constrained utility function:[8]

---

that is, $\frac{W_t}{P_t} = \lambda_t(\mathrm{j})(1-\alpha)\frac{\mathrm{Q_t\,(j)}}{\mathrm{L_t(j)}}$ and $r_t^k = \lambda_t(\mathrm{j})\alpha\,\frac{\mathrm{Q_t\,(j)}}{\mathrm{K_t(j)}}$. By substituting into the cost function to be minimized, the real minimum cost function is

$$C_{Rt}[Q_t(j)] = \lambda_t(\mathrm{j})(1-\alpha)\frac{\mathrm{Q_t\,(j)}}{\mathrm{L_t(j)}}\,L_t(j) + \lambda_t(\mathrm{j})\alpha\,\frac{\mathrm{Q_t\,(j)}}{\mathrm{K_t(j)}}\mathrm{K_t(j)} = \lambda_t(j)\mathrm{Q_t}(j)$$

Hence, we find the already-known result $\frac{\mathrm{d}C_{Rt}[Q_t(j)]}{\mathrm{d}Q_t(j)} = \lambda_t(\mathrm{j}) = \mathrm{mc}_t(\mathrm{j})$.

[7] Summing marginal conditions,

$\lambda_t(j)\;(1-\alpha)\mathrm{Q_t}\;(\mathrm{j}) + \lambda_t(j)\alpha\mathrm{Q_t}\;(\mathrm{j}) = \frac{W_t}{P_t}\mathrm{L_t(j)} + r_t^k\mathrm{K_t(j)}$ and therefore $\lambda_t(j)\mathrm{Q_t}\;(\mathrm{j}) = \frac{W_t}{P_t}\mathrm{L_t(j)} + r_t^k\mathrm{K_t(j)}$, from which substituting into the definition of total profit and taking into account that $Q_t(j) = \left(\frac{P_t(j)}{P_t}\right)^{-\theta} Q_t$, it follows (6.17).

[8] It's the same problem as before when $\nu = 1$.

$$\text{Max} \quad E_0 \sum_{t=0}^{\infty} \beta^t \left[\log C_t(i) - \varphi \frac{L_t(i)^{1-\upsilon}}{1-\nu} \right]$$

$$\text{Sub}:$$

$$P_t C_t(i) + B_t(i) + P_t I_t(i) + P_t TX_t(i)$$

$$= W_t L_t(i) + R_{t-1} B_{t-1}(i) + P_t r_t^k K_t(i) + D_t(i) \tag{6.18}$$

where

$$R_{t-1} = (1 + r_{t-1}); \tag{6.19}$$

$$I_t(i) = K_{t+1}(i) - (1-\delta) K_t(i) \tag{6.20}$$

and $L_t(i)$ is the amount of working hours.

Here, compared to previous positions, the nominal interest rate is indicated with the symbol r to avoid confusion with the symbol i used to index families.

Formed the Lagrangian

$$E_0 \sum_{t=0}^{\infty} \beta^t \left\{ \log C_t(i) - \varphi \frac{L_t(i)^{1-\upsilon}}{1-\nu} \right\} + \lambda_t(i) \frac{W_t(i)}{P_t} L_t(i) + R_{t-1} \frac{P_{t-1}}{P_t} \frac{B_{t-1}(i)}{P_{t-1}}$$

$$+ r_t^k K_t(i) + \frac{D_t(i)}{P_t} - C_t(i) - \frac{B_t(i)}{P_t} - I_t(i) - TX_t(i) \tag{6.21}$$

Setting $\frac{P_t}{P_{t-1}} = \pi_t$, first-order conditions are:

$$C_t(i): \quad \frac{1}{C_t(i)} - \lambda_t(i) = 0 \tag{6.22}$$

$$\frac{B_t(i)}{P_t}: \quad -\lambda_t(i) + \beta E_t \left[\frac{R_t}{\pi_{t+1}} \lambda_{t+1}(i) \right] = 0 \tag{6.23}$$

$$L_t(i): \quad -\varphi L_t(i)^{-\upsilon} + \lambda_t(i) \frac{W_t(i)}{P_t} = 0 \tag{6.24}$$

$$K_{t+1}: \quad \beta E_t \left[\lambda_{t+1}(i) \left(r_{t+1}^k + 1 - \delta \right) \right] - \lambda_t(i) = 0 \tag{6.25}$$

From (6.23) and (6.25), it follows

$$\beta E_t \left[\lambda_{t+1}(i) \frac{R_t}{\pi_{t+1}} \right] = E_t \beta E \left[\lambda_{t+1}(i) \left(r_{t+1}^k + 1 - \delta \right) \right] \tag{6.26}$$

The (6.26) is the condition of the absence of arbitrage opportunities between physical capital and bonds. It implicitly defines the real interest rate

$$\frac{R_t}{\pi_{t+1}} = \left(r_{t+1}^k + 1 - \delta\right) \tag{6.27}$$

Furthermore, from (6.22) and (6.27), it follows Euler's condition:

$$\beta E_t\left[\frac{1}{C_{t+1}(i)}\frac{R_t}{\pi_{t+1}}\right] = \frac{1}{C_t(i)} \tag{6.28}$$

It is assumed that for the economy as a whole aggregate labor input results from aggregation through a CES function, of specific quantities of labor offered by an infinite number of households.

The aggregator is

$$L_t = \left[\int_0^1 L_t(i)^{\frac{\theta_L - 1}{\theta_L}} di\right]^{\frac{\theta_L}{\theta_L - 1}} \qquad \theta_L \quad > 1 \tag{6.29}$$

Just as in the case of demand for consumption from households, this way of meaning aggregate labor supply has two implications:

(a) The demand for labor by firms for the i-th labor service, for any given overall level of labor demand, has constant elasticity θ_L and is

$$\mathrm{L_t(i)} = \left(\frac{\mathrm{W_t(i)}}{\mathrm{W_t}}\right)^{-\theta_L} L_t \tag{6.30}$$

(b) The average level of money wages of the economy is an aggregate index of individual wages $W_t(i)$ fixed by individual families:

$$\mathrm{W_t} = \left[\int_0^1 \mathrm{W_t(i)}^{(1-\theta_N)}\mathrm{di}\right]^{\frac{1}{1-\theta_L}} \tag{6.31}$$

The proof of (a) and (b) occurs along the lines of that for consumption index. In fact, (6.30) is obtained from a condition of efficiency in production, i.e., a solution to the problem

$$\min_{L_{t(i)}} \left[\int_0^1 L_t(i)^{\frac{\theta_L - 1}{\theta_L}} di\right]^{\frac{\theta_L}{\theta_L - 1}} \tag{6.32}$$

$$\text{Sub} \qquad \int_0^1 \mathrm{W_t(i)L_t(i)}di = W_t L_t$$

The demand for i-th labor can be expressed as a function of the relative wage and demand for other types of work,[9] i.e.,

$$L_t(i)=\left[\frac{\mathrm{W_t(i)}}{\mathrm{W_t(j)}}\right]^{-\theta_L}L_t(j) \tag{6.33}$$

6.1.4 General Wage Index

The general wage index W_t is the result of minimizing labor costs

$$\min_{L_{t(i)}} \int_0^1 W_t(i)L_t(i)di \tag{6.34}$$

$$\text{Sub}\ \left(\int_0^1 \mathrm{L_t(i)}^{\frac{\theta_L-1}{\theta_L}}di\right)^{\frac{\theta}{\theta_L-1}}=\mathrm{L_t}$$

From the first-order necessary condition, it follows

$$\mu_{Lt}=W_t=\left[\int_0^1 W_t(i)^{1-\theta_L}di\right]^{\frac{1}{1-\theta_L}} \tag{6.35}$$

where μ_{Lt} is the Lagrange multiplier.

The Lagrangian of the problem (6.34) to be minimized is

[9] Called λ_{Lt} the Lagrange multiplier, the first-order condition is $\frac{\theta_L}{\theta_L-1}\left[\int_0^1 L_t(i)^{\frac{\theta_L-1}{\theta_L}}di\right]^{\frac{1}{\theta_L-1}}\frac{\theta_L-1}{\theta_L}L_t(i)^{-\frac{1}{\theta_L}}-\lambda_{Lt}\mathrm{W_t(i)}=0$. That is, taking into account that $\left[\int_0^1 L_t(i)^{\frac{\theta_L-1}{\theta_L}}di\right]^{\frac{1}{(\theta_L-1)}}=L_t^{\frac{1}{\theta_L}}$, it follows $L_t^{\frac{1}{\theta_L}}L_t(i)^{-\frac{1}{\theta_L}}=\lambda_{Lt}\mathrm{W_t(i)}$ from which $L_t(i)=[\lambda_{Lt}\mathrm{W_t(i)}]^{-\theta_L}L_t$. By taking two different indices i, j, we have

$$L_t^{\frac{1}{\theta_L}}L_t(i)^{-\frac{1}{\theta_L}}=\lambda_{Lt}\mathrm{W_t(i)}$$
$$L_t^{\frac{1}{\theta_L}}L_t(j)^{-\frac{1}{\theta_L}}=\lambda_{Lt}\mathrm{W_t(j)}$$

Eliminating λ_{Lt},

$$\frac{L_t(i)^{-\frac{1}{\theta_L}}}{L_t(j)^{-\frac{1}{\theta_L}}}=\frac{\mathrm{W_t(i)}}{\mathrm{W_t(j)}}\Rightarrow\left[\frac{L_t(i)}{L_t(j)}\right]^{-\frac{1}{\theta_L}}=\frac{\mathrm{W_t(i)}}{\mathrm{W_t(j)}}\Rightarrow\left[\frac{L_t(i)}{L_t(j)}\right]=\left[\frac{\mathrm{W_t(i)}}{\mathrm{W_t(j)}}\right]^{-\theta_L}$$

$$\int_0^1 W_t(i)L_t(i)di + \mu_{Lt}\left[\mathrm{L_t(j)} - \left(\int_0^1 \mathrm{L_t(i)}^{\frac{\theta_L - 1}{\theta_L}} di\right)^{\frac{\theta_L}{\theta_L - 1}}\right] \tag{6.36}$$

The first order condition of nulling derivative for $L_t(i)$ requires

$$W_t(i) - \mu_{Lt}\ \frac{\theta_L}{\theta_L - 1}\left(\int_0^1 \mathrm{L_t(i)}^{\frac{\theta_L - 1}{\theta_L}} di\right)^{\frac{1}{\theta_L - 1}} \frac{\theta_L - 1}{\theta_L} \mathrm{L_t(i)}^{-\frac{1}{\theta_L}} = 0 \tag{6.37}$$

And so,

$$W_t(i) = \mu_{Lt}\left(\int_0^1 L_t(i)^{\frac{\theta_L - 1}{\theta_L}} di\right)^{\frac{1}{\theta_L - 1}} L_t(i)^{-\frac{1}{\theta_N}}$$

$$= \mu_{Lt}\left(\int_0^1 L(i)^{\frac{\theta_L - 1}{\theta_L}} di\right)^{\frac{\theta_L}{(\theta_L - 1)\theta_L}} L_t(i)^{-\frac{1}{\theta_L}} = \mu_{Lt}\, L_t^{\frac{1}{\theta_L}}\, L_t(i)^{-\frac{1}{\theta_L}} \tag{6.38}$$

That is to say

$$W_t(i)^{1-\theta_N} = \mu_{Lt}{}^{1-\theta_L}\, L_t^{\frac{1-\theta_L}{\theta_L}}\ L_t(i)^{-\frac{1-\theta_L}{L}} \tag{6.39}$$

Integrating and elevating to $\frac{1}{1-\theta_L}$,

$$\left[\int_0^1 W_t(i)^{1-\theta_L} di\right]^{\frac{1}{1-\theta_L}} = \mu_{Lt} L_t^{\frac{1}{\theta_L}}\left[\int_0^1 L_t(i)^{\frac{\theta_L - 1}{\theta_L}} di\right]^{\frac{1}{1-\theta_L}} \tag{6.40}$$

$$\text{But}\quad \left[\int_0^1 L_t(i)^{\frac{\theta_L - 1}{\theta_L}} di\right]^{\frac{1}{1-\theta_L}} = L_t{}^{-\frac{1}{\theta_L}}$$

And so,

$$\left[\int_0^1 W_t(i)^{1-\theta_L} di\right]^{\frac{1}{1-\theta_L}} = \mu_{Lt} \tag{6.41}$$

That μ_{Lt} is an aggregate index of wages in the economy can be deduced by the following considerations:

Given the expression of μ_{Nt},

$$W_t(i) = \mu_{Lt} L_t^{\frac{1}{\theta_L}} \ L_t(\mathrm{i})^{-\frac{1}{\theta_L}} = \left[\int_0^1 W_t(i)^{1-\theta_L} di\right]^{\frac{1}{1-\theta_L}} L_t^{\frac{1}{\theta_L}} \ L_t(i)^{-\frac{1}{\theta_L}} \tag{6.42}$$

Multiplying both sides of equality (6.41) by $L_t(i)$,

$$W_t(i) L_t(i) = \left[\int_0^1 W_t(i)^{1-\theta_L} di\right]^{\frac{1}{1-\theta_L}} L_t^{\frac{1}{\theta_L}} \ L_t(i)^{1-\frac{1}{\theta_L}} \tag{6.43}$$

Integrating for the index i,

$$\int_0^1 W_t(i) L_t(i) \mathrm{di}$$
$$= \left[\int_0^1 W_t(i)^{1-\theta_L} di\right]^{\frac{1}{1-\theta_L}} L_t^{\frac{1}{\theta_L}} \int_0^1 L_t(i)^{\frac{\theta_L - 1}{\theta_L}} di \tag{6.44}$$

From the definition of aggregate labor demand index, it follows

$$\int_0^1 L_t(i)^{\frac{\theta_L - 1}{\theta_L}} di = L_t^{-\frac{1-\theta_L}{\theta_L}} \tag{6.45}$$

From which

$$\int_0^1 W_t(i) L_t(i) \mathrm{di} = \left[\int_0^1 W_t(i)^{1-\theta_L} di\right]^{\frac{1}{1-\theta_L}} L_t^{\frac{1}{\theta_L}} L_t^{-\frac{1-\theta_L}{\theta_L}}$$
$$= \left[\int_0^1 W_t(i)^{1-\theta_L} di\right]^{\frac{1}{1-\theta_L}} L_t \tag{6.46}$$

But the term to the left of (6.45) is the cost for firms purchasing labor from households, i.e.,

$$\int_0^1 W_t(i) L_t(i) \mathrm{di} = W_t L_t \tag{6.47}$$

So that

$$W_t = \left[\int_0^1 W_t(i)^{1-\theta_L} di\right]^{\frac{1}{1-\theta_L}} \tag{6.48}$$

Note that in the previous problem (6.34) of minimizing the labor input at a given cost, from the first-order condition, we have $L_t^{\frac{1}{\theta_L}} L_t(i)^{-\frac{1}{\theta_L}} = \lambda_{Lt} \mathrm{W_t(i)}$, while in the present problem, from the first-order condition of minimization of the cost of labor for a given quantity of aggregate labor, it is $W_t(i) = \mu_{Lt}\, L_t^{\frac{1}{\theta_L}}\, L_t(i)^{-\frac{1}{\theta_L}}$.

Substituting this in the previous one,

$$L_t^{\frac{1}{\theta_L}} L_t(i)^{-\frac{1}{\theta_L}} = \lambda_{Lt}\, \mu_{Lt}\, L_t^{\frac{1}{\theta_L}}\, L_t(i)^{-\frac{1}{\theta_L}} \tag{6.49}$$

i.e.,

$$\lambda_{Lt} = \frac{1}{\mu_{Lt}} = \frac{1}{W_t} \tag{6.50}$$

Therefore, taking into account the condition on demand for the i-th labor,

$$L_t(i) = [\lambda_{Lt} \mathrm{W_t(i)}]^{-\theta_N} L_t \tag{6.51}$$

It follows

$$L_t(i) = \left[\frac{\mathrm{W_t(i)}}{\mathrm{W_t}}\right]^{-\theta_N} L_t \tag{6.52}$$

6.2 Nominal Wage's Setting for Labor Service by the Representative Household

The setting of nominal i-th wage by each i-th household occurs under monopoly conditions.

The maximization problem by households, therefore, involves the maximization of utility for consumption and labor for each period and also, given the demand by firms for the specific labor service supplied, involves the maximization of income from labor through the optimal choice of monetary wage to be quoted.

The component of the instantaneous Lagrangian of i-th household relating to choices wages is

$$\max_{\mathrm{W_t(i)}} -\varphi \frac{L_t(i)^{1-\upsilon}}{1-\nu} + \lambda_t(i)\, \frac{W_t(i)}{P_t}\, L_t(i) \tag{6.53}$$

subject to the constraint of the given demand for labor for the i-th type of labor by firms

$$L_t(i) = \left(\frac{\mathrm{W_t(i)}}{W_t}\right)^{-\theta_L} L_t \tag{6.54}$$

Therefore, the choice of monetary wage by the i-th household can be regarded as a solution to the free maximum problem:

$$\max_{\mathrm{W_t(i)}} -\varphi \frac{\left[\left(\frac{\mathrm{W_t(i)}}{W_t}\right)^{-\theta_L} L_t\right]^{1-\upsilon}}{1-\nu} + \lambda_t(i)\frac{W_t(i)}{P_t}\left(\frac{\mathrm{W_t(i)}}{W_t}\right)^{-\theta_L} L_t \tag{6.55}$$

The first-order condition[10] for $W_t(i)$ provides the following i-th real-wage-setting rule:

$$\frac{\mathrm{W_t(i)}}{P_t} = \frac{\theta_L}{(\theta_L - 1)} \frac{\varphi L_t(i)^{-\nu}}{\lambda_t(i)} \tag{6.56}$$

With a utility function like the one admitted, it turns out $\lambda_t(i) = \frac{1}{C_t(i)}$, and therefore,

$$\frac{\mathrm{W_t(i)}}{P_t} = \frac{\theta_L}{(\theta_L - 1)} C_t(i)\varphi L_t(i)^{-\nu} \tag{6.57}$$

More generally, the rule of formation of the real wage is

$$\frac{\mathrm{W_t(i)}}{P_t} = \frac{\theta_L}{(\theta_L - 1)} \frac{U_L}{U_c} = \frac{\theta_L}{(\theta_L - 1)} \mathrm{MRS_t(i)} \tag{6.58}$$

Equation (6.58) highlights that households determine real wage by applying a kind of markup on the marginal rate of substitution between consumption and labor:

---

[10]The first-order condition is

$$\theta_L\varphi\left[\left(\frac{\mathrm{W_t(i)}}{W_t}\right)^{-\theta_N} L_t\right]^{-\nu} \frac{1}{\mathrm{W_t(i)}}\left(\frac{\mathrm{W_t(i)}}{W_t}\right)^{-\theta_L} L_t + (1-\theta_L)\lambda_t(i)\frac{1}{P_t}\left(\frac{\mathrm{W_t(i)}}{W_t}\right)^{-\theta_L} L_t = 0$$

Hence

$$\theta_L\varphi\left[\left(\frac{\mathrm{W_t(i)}}{W_t}\right)^{-\theta_L} L_t\right]^{-\nu} \frac{1}{\mathrm{W_t(i)}}\left(\frac{\mathrm{W_t(i)}}{W_t}\right)^{-\theta_L} L_t = (\theta_L - 1)\lambda_t(i)\frac{1}{P_t}\left(\frac{\mathrm{W_t(i)}}{W_t}\right)^{-\theta_L} L_t$$

Simplifying, $\theta_L\varphi[L_t(i)]^{-\nu}\frac{1}{\mathrm{W_t(i)}} = (\theta_L - 1)\lambda_t(i)\frac{1}{P_t}$
and from this, $\frac{\mathrm{W_t(i)}}{P_t} = \frac{\theta_L}{(\theta_L - 1)}\frac{\varphi L_t(i)^{-\nu}}{\lambda_t(i)}$.

$$\mu_w = \frac{\theta_L}{(\theta_L - 1)} \tag{6.59}$$

In symmetric equilibrium, from the aggregate point of view, it will be

$$C_t(i) = C_t; \;\; L_t(i) = L_t; \;\; W_t(i) = W_t \tag{6.60}$$

and therefore,

$$\frac{W_t}{P_t} = \frac{\theta_L}{(\theta_L - 1)} \; C_t \varphi L_t^{\;-\nu} \tag{6.61}$$

6.3 The Aggregate Labor Supply and Representative Trade Union

An equivalent way to aggregate the labor market is to look at specific labors in the same way as intermediate products for the production of the final good. From this perspective, it is possible to imagine that there is a final representative trade union whose task, exactly like the representative firm producing the final good, is to aggregate intermediate jobs into a single final job to be sold on the market, at a single aggregate salary.

The objective of this representative union is to maximize overall aggregate net income from work, the latter defined as the difference between what is obtained from the sale of aggregate labor to the firms' sector and the value resulting from aggregation of income from specific labors, in a context of zero profit, comparable to markets of perfect competition.

In symbols, the representative trade union solves the following problem:

$$\begin{aligned} &\max_{L_t(i)} W_t L_t - \int_0^1 W_t(i) L_t(i) di \\ &sub \; L_t = \left[\int_0^1 L_t(i)^{\frac{\theta_L - 1}{\theta_L}} di \right]^{\frac{\theta_L}{\theta_L - 1}} \end{aligned} \tag{6.62}$$

By substituting the constraint into the objective function, the function to maximize becomes

$$W_t\left[\int_0^1 L_t(i)^{\frac{\theta_L-1}{\theta_L}}di\right]^{\frac{\theta_L}{\theta_L-1}} - \int_0^1 W_t(i)L_t(i)di \tag{6.63}$$

And from the first-order condition for $L_t(i)$[11] of (6.63), it follows

$$L_t(i)=\left(\frac{W_t(i)}{W_t}\right)^{-\theta_L}L_t \tag{6.64}$$

which coincides with (6.54).

Note also that from the first-order condition follows

$$W_tL_t^{\frac{1}{\theta_L}}\ L_t(i)^{-\frac{1}{\theta_L}}=W_t(i) \tag{6.65}$$

and dividing member by member the same condition for a different index j≠i, it follows

$$\frac{L_t(i)^{-\frac{1}{\theta_L}}}{L_t(j)^{-\frac{1}{\theta_L}}}=\frac{W_t(i)}{W_t(i)};\ \text{ from which }\ L_t(i)^{-\frac{1}{\theta_L}}=\frac{W_t(i)}{W_t(i)}L_t(j)^{-\frac{1}{\theta_L}}$$

and elevating both sides to $-\theta_L$, it follows

$$L_t(i)=\left(\frac{W_t(i)}{W_t(j)}\right)^{-\theta_L}L_t(j) \tag{6.66}$$

Finally, operating the representative union by hypothesis in conditions similar to perfect competition, from condition of zero profit, it follows

$$W_tL_t=\int_0^1 W_t(i)L_t(i)di=\int_0^1 W_t(i)\left(\frac{W_t(i)}{W_t}\right)^{-\theta_L}L_tdi \tag{6.67}$$

That is,

[11] Such a condition is

$$W_t\frac{\theta_L}{\theta_L-1}\left[\int_0^1 L_t(i)^{\frac{\theta_L-1}{\theta_L}}di\right]^{\frac{1}{\theta_L-1}}\frac{\theta_L-1}{\theta_L}L_t(i)^{-\frac{1}{\theta_L}}-W_t(i)=0$$

and since $\left[\int_0^1 L_t(i)^{\frac{\theta_L-1}{\theta_L}}di\right]^{\frac{1}{\theta_L-1}}=L_t^{\frac{1}{\theta_L}}$, Eq. (6.64) is obtained.

$$W_t = \int_0^1 W_t(i) \left(\frac{W_t(i)}{W_t} \right)^{-\theta_L} di \tag{6.68}$$

which is equivalent to

$$W_t^{1-\theta_L} = \int_0^1 W_t(i)^{1-\theta_L} di \tag{6.69}$$

From which

$$W_t = \left[\int_0^1 W_t(i)^{1-\theta_L} di \right]^{\frac{1}{1-\theta_L}} \tag{6.70}$$

which is the same as (6.48).

6.4 The Public Administration and the Central Bank

As far as public administration is concerned, the hypothesis is that the public sector conducts a balanced budget policy and, therefore, that is valid:

$$R_t\, B_{t-1} + P_t G_t = B_t + P_t TX_t \tag{6.71}$$

Public spending is assumed to grow exponentially, i.e.,

$$G_t = G\, e^{\varepsilon_{g,t}} \tag{6.72}$$

where the growth rate $\varepsilon_{g,\,t}$ follows a stochastic process:

$$\varepsilon_{g,t} = \rho_g \varepsilon_{g,t-1} + \xi_{g,t} \quad \text{with } \xi_{g,t} \sim iid\, N\left(0, \sigma_g^2\right) \tag{6.73}$$

To guarantee a nonexplosive growth of public debt, it is assumed that taxation follows a fiscal rule according to which taxation is commensurate with the current amount of public debt.

This tax rule (known from Leeper (1991), as *passive* tax rule[12]) is defined in the following way:

$$P_t TX_t = TX + \tau B_t \tag{6.74}$$

By defining

$$\mathrm{T_t} = TX_t - \frac{TX}{\mathrm{P_t}} = \tau b_t \tag{6.75}$$

We will refer to (6.75).

As for the Central Bank, it is assumed that it sets the short-term nominal interest rate following monetary rule:

$$\frac{R_t}{\overline{R}} = \left[\left(\frac{R_{t-1}}{\overline{R}}\right)^{l_r}\left(\frac{\pi_t}{\overline{\pi}}\right)^{l_\pi}\left(\frac{Q_t}{\overline{Q}}\right)^{l_q}\right]^{\frac{1}{1-l_r}} u_t^R \tag{6.76}$$

where

$$\overline{R} = \text{steady} - \text{state (gross) interest rate}$$

and

$$u_t^R = e^{\varepsilon_{u,t}} \tag{6.77}$$

with

$$\varepsilon_{u,t} = \rho_u \varepsilon_{u,t-1} + \xi_{u,t}, \quad \xi_{u,t} \sim iid\, N\left(0, \sigma_u^2\right) \tag{6.78}$$

6.5 Equilibrium of Model with Rotemberg Price Stickiness and Flexible Wages

Assuming that macroeconomic equilibrium is identical to individual equilibrium, the macro equilibrium is described by the following equations:

$$\frac{1}{C_t} = \beta E_t\left[\frac{1}{C_{t+1}} \frac{R_t}{\pi_{t+1})}\right] \tag{6.79}$$

(*Euler's equation*)

---

[12]E. Leeper (1991), 'Equilibria under 'active' and 'passive' monetary and fiscal policies', *Journal of Monetary Economics*, vol. 27, issue 1, 129–147.

$$\beta E_t\left[\frac{R_t}{\pi_{t+1}}\frac{1}{C_{t+1}}\right]=\beta E_t\left[\frac{1}{C_{t+1}}\left(r_{t+1}^k+1-\delta\right)\right] \tag{6.80}$$

(*Absence of arbitrage opportunities between securities and physical capital*)

$$\frac{\mathrm{W_t}}{P_t}=\frac{\theta_\mathrm{L}}{(\theta_\mathrm{L}-1)}\varphi \mathrm{L_t}^{-\nu}C_t \tag{6.81}$$

(*real wage equation*)

$$Q_t=\mathrm{A_t}\,\mathrm{K_t^\alpha}\,\mathrm{L_t^{1-\alpha}} \tag{6.82}$$

(*Aggregate production equation*)[13]

$$A_t=e^{\varepsilon_{A,t}} \tag{6.83}$$

(*total productivity growth trend*)

[13]This is obtained by aggregating the production function of intermediate goods as follows:

$$\int_0^1 \mathrm{Q_t}\,(\mathrm{j})\mathrm{dj}=\mathrm{A_t}\int_0^1 \mathrm{K_t(j)}^\alpha \mathrm{L_t(j)}^{1-\alpha}\,\mathrm{dj}$$

Substituting production level with the demand for intermediate goods $\int_0^1 \mathrm{Q_t}\,(\mathrm{j})\mathrm{dj}=\int_0^1\left(\frac{P_t(j)}{P_t}\right)\mathrm{dj}^{-\theta}Q_t$ follows

$$Q_t\int_0^1\left(\frac{P_t(j)}{P_t}\right)^{-\theta}\mathrm{dj}=\mathrm{A_t}\int_0^1 \mathrm{K_t(j)}^\alpha\,\mathrm{L_t(j)}^{1-\alpha}\mathrm{dj}$$

To the left of the equality sign, we have already seen that the price dispersion index can be set, with the first-order approximation:

$\int_0^1\left(\frac{P_t(j)}{P_t}\right)^{-\theta}dj\cong 1$ to the right, it is $\int_0^1\frac{\mathrm{K_t(j)}^\alpha}{\mathrm{L(j)}^\alpha}\mathrm{L_t(j)dj}$. In the productive factors' market, capital and labor are employed according to a common proportion, identical to the aggregate one. This implies

$\left(\frac{\mathrm{K_t(j)}}{\mathrm{L_t(j)}}\right)^\alpha=\left(\frac{\mathrm{K_t}}{\mathrm{L_t}}\right)^\alpha$ and being $\int_0^1\mathrm{L_t(j)dj}=\mathrm{L_t}$, it follows

$\int_0^1\left(\frac{\mathrm{K_t(j)}}{\mathrm{L_t(j)}}\right)^\alpha\mathrm{L_t(j)dj}=\mathrm{K_t^\alpha}\,\mathrm{L_t^{1-\alpha}}$.

$$mc_t(1-\alpha)\mathrm{A_t\,K_t^{\alpha}L_t^{-\alpha}} = (1-\alpha)mc_t\frac{Q_t}{L_t} = \frac{\mathrm{W_t}}{P_t} \tag{6.84}$$

(*labor demand*)

$$mc_t\alpha\mathrm{A_t\,K_t^{\alpha-1}L_t^{1-\alpha}} = \alpha\, mc_t\frac{Q_t}{K_t} = r_t^k \tag{6.85}$$

(*capital services demand*)

$$\theta(1-mc_t) = 1-\gamma_{\mathrm{p}}(\pi_{\mathrm{t}}-1)\pi_{\mathrm{t}} + \beta\gamma_p E_t\left[\left(\frac{C_t}{C_{t+1}}\right)(\pi_{t+1}-1)\pi_{t+1}\frac{Q_{t+1}}{Q_t}\right] \tag{6.86}$$

(*dynamics of the inflation rate*[14])

$$Q_t = C_t + I_t + G_t + \frac{\gamma_p}{2}\,(\pi_t-1)^2 Q_t \tag{6.87}$$

(the resource constraint)

---

[14] Inflation dynamics results from the optimality condition of the j-th price

$(1-\theta)\frac{1}{P_t}\left(\frac{P_t(j)}{P_t}\right)^{-\theta}Q_t + \lambda_t(j)\theta\,\frac{1}{P_t}\left(\frac{P_t(j)}{P_t}\right)^{-\theta-1}Q_t$

$= \gamma_p\left(\frac{P_t(j)}{P_{t-1}(j)}-1\right)\frac{1}{P_{t-1}(j)}Q_t - \gamma_p \mathrm{E_t}\left[\Phi_{0,t+1}\frac{P_{t+1}(j)}{P_t(j)^2}\left(\frac{P_{t+1}(j)}{P_t(j)}-1\right)Q_{t+1}\right]$

Imposing the symmetry condition follows

$(1-\theta)\frac{1}{P_t} + \lambda_t\,\theta\,\frac{1}{P_t} = \gamma_p(\pi_t-1)\frac{1}{P_{t-1}} \quad -\gamma_p\mathrm{E_t}\left[\Phi_{0,t+1}\frac{P_{t+1}}{P_t^2}(\pi_{t+1}-1)\frac{Q_{t+1}}{Q_t}\right]$

Multiplying both sides by $\mathrm{P_t}$ follows

$(1-\theta)+\lambda_t\theta = \gamma_p(\pi_t-1)\pi_t - \gamma_p\mathrm{E_t}\left[\Phi_{0,t+1}(\pi_{t+1}-1)\pi_{t+1}\frac{Q_{t+1}}{Q_t}\right]$

and changing its sign

$\theta-1-\lambda_t\,\theta = -\gamma_p(\pi_t-1)\pi_t + \gamma_p\mathrm{E_t}\left[\Phi_{0,t+1}(\pi_{t+1}-1)\pi_{t+1}\frac{Q_{t+1}}{Q_t}\right]$, from which

$\theta\,(1-\lambda_t) = 1-\gamma_p(\pi_t-1)\pi_t+\gamma_p\mathrm{E_t}\left[\Phi_{0,t+1}(\pi_{t+1}-1)\pi_{t+1}\frac{Q_{t+1}}{Q_t}\right]$. Remembering that in the firm problem $mc_t(j) = \lambda_t(j)$, and that at aggregate level $mc_t = \lambda_t$, so that it follows

$\theta\,(1-mc_t) = 1-\gamma_p(\pi_t-1)\pi_t+\gamma_p\mathrm{E_t}\left[\Phi_{0,t+1}(\pi_{t+1}-1)\pi_{t+1}\frac{Q_{t+1}}{Q_t}\right]$. The stochastic discount factor $\Phi_{0,t+1}$ is calculated taking into account that the firms belong to families and that in aggregate they apply the discount factor obtained from the Euler condition $\beta E_t\left[\frac{1}{C_{t+1}}\frac{R_t}{\pi_{t+1}}\right] = \frac{1}{C_t}$. Being $E_t\left[\beta\frac{C_t}{C_{t+1}}\frac{R_t}{\pi_{t+1}}\right] = 1 = E_t\left(\Phi_{t,t+1}\frac{R_t}{\pi_{t+1}}\right)$ from $E_t\left(\Phi_{t,t+1}\frac{R_t}{\pi_{t+1}}\right) = 1$ is obtained $\beta\frac{C_t}{C_{t+i}} = \Phi_{t,t+1}$. More generally, the value of $\Phi_{t,t+i}$ between the date 0 and the date t+i is the one obtained according to the recursive formula:

$\Phi_{t,t+i} = \Phi_{t,t}\Phi_{t,t+1}\cdots\Phi_{t,t+i}$, and therefore,

$\Phi_{t,t+i} = \beta\frac{C_t}{C_{t+1}}\beta\frac{C_{t+1}}{C_{t+2}}\ldots\beta\frac{C_t}{C_{t+i}} = \beta^i\frac{C_t}{C_{t+i}}$.

From $\Phi_{0,t+1} = \beta\frac{C_t}{C_{t+1}}$, it follows

$\theta\,(1-mc_t) = 1-\gamma_p(\pi_t-1)\pi_t + \beta\gamma_p\mathrm{E_t}\left[\frac{C_t}{C_{t+1}}(\pi_{t+1}-1)\pi_{t+1}\frac{Q_{t+1}}{Q_t}\right]$.

$$K_{t+1} - (1-\delta)K_t = I_t \tag{6.88}$$

(capital accumulation equation)

$$B_t = R_t\, B_{t-1} + P_t G_t - P_t T_t \tag{6.89}$$

(budget constraint of public administration)

$$G_t = G\, e^{\varepsilon_{g,t}} \tag{6.90}$$

(public spending growth equation)

$$P_t T_t = \tau\, B_t \tag{6.91}$$

(Fiscal rule)

$$\frac{R_t}{\overline{R}} = \left(\frac{R_{t-1}}{\overline{R}}\right)^{l_r} \left[\left(\frac{\pi_t}{\overline{\pi}}\right)^{l_\pi} \left(\frac{Q_t}{\overline{Q}}\right)^{l_q}\right]^{1-l_r} u_t^R \tag{6.92}$$

(monetary rule)

$$u_t^R = e^{\varepsilon_{u,t}} \tag{6.93}$$

(shock to monetary policy)

$$\varepsilon_{A,t} = \rho_A \varepsilon_{A,t-1} + \xi_{A,t}, \quad \text{with} \quad \xi_{A,t}\ iid.N\left(0, \sigma_{A,t}^2\right) \tag{6.94}$$

(shock to total productivity)

$$\varepsilon_{g,t} = (1-\rho_g) g\_q + \rho_g\ \varepsilon_{g,t-1} + \xi_{g,t}$$
$$\text{with}\ \ \xi_{g,t} \sim iid\ N\left(0, \sigma_g^2\right) \tag{6.95}$$

(shock to public spending)

$$\varepsilon_{u,t} = \rho_u \varepsilon_{u,t-1} + \xi_{u,t}, \text{with} \quad \xi_{u,t} \sim iid\ N\left(0, \sigma_u^2\right) \tag{6.96}$$

(shock to monetary policy)

6.6 The Phillips Curve with Rotemberg Price Adjustment Costs

With the Rotenberg price setting, the log-linear expression of inflation dynamics can be obtained by referring to the following rewriting of the optimal price equation:

$$\frac{\theta}{\theta-1}\,mc_t-\frac{\varphi_p}{\theta-1}\pi_t(\pi_t-1)+\beta\frac{\varphi_p}{\theta-1}E_t\left[\left(\frac{\mathrm{C_t}}{\mathrm{C}_{t+1}}\right)\pi_{t+1}(\pi_{t+1}-1)\frac{\mathrm{Q_{t+1}}}{\mathrm{Q_t}}\right]=1 \tag{6.97}$$

By applying exponential transformation,

$$\frac{\theta}{(\theta-1)}mc\;e^{\widehat{mc}_t}-\frac{\varphi_p}{(\theta-1)}\;e^{2\widehat{\pi}_t-\widehat{\pi}_t}+\beta\frac{\varphi_p}{(\theta-1)}e^{-E_t\Delta\widehat{\mathrm{c}}_\mathrm{t}+E_t\left(2\widehat{\pi}_{t+1}-\widehat{\pi}_{t+1}\right)+E_t\Delta\widehat{\mathrm{q}}_\mathrm{t}}=1 \tag{6.98}$$

The log-linearization around the steady state provides

$$\frac{\theta}{(\theta-1)}mc\,(1+\widehat{mc}_t)-\frac{\varphi_p}{(\theta-1)}\,(1+\widehat{\pi}_t)+\beta\frac{\varphi_p}{(\theta-1)}\,(1-E_t\Delta\widehat{\mathrm{c}}_\mathrm{t}+E_t\widehat{\pi}_{t+1}+E_t\Delta\widehat{\mathrm{q}}_\mathrm{t})=1 \tag{6.99}$$

Expanding

$$\left[\frac{\theta}{(\theta-1)}mc-\frac{\varphi_p}{(\theta-1)}+\beta\frac{\varphi_p}{(\theta-1)}\right]+\frac{\theta}{(\theta-1)}mc\,\widehat{mc}_t-\frac{\varphi_p}{(\theta-1)}\widehat{\pi}_t+\beta\frac{\varphi_p}{(\theta-1)}(E_t\Delta\widehat{\mathrm{q}}_\mathrm{t}-E_t\Delta\widehat{\mathrm{c}}_\mathrm{t})+\beta\frac{\varphi_p}{(\theta-1)}E_t\widehat{\pi}_{t+1}=1 \tag{6.100}$$

But $\left[\frac{\theta}{(\theta-1)}mc-\frac{\varphi_p}{(\theta-1)}+\beta\frac{\varphi_p}{(\theta-1)}\right]=1$ and $mc=\frac{(\theta-1)}{\theta}$, so that[15]

[15]The latter derives from the fact that by definition of a steady state, firms do not re-optimize prices, and therefore, they do not bear the costs for their modification. Since the prices setting rule in the absence of costs is $\frac{P_{jt}}{\mathrm{P_t}}=\frac{\theta}{(\theta-1)}mc_t$, in steady state, it is $1=\frac{\theta}{(\theta-1)}mc$. On the other hand, in the price equation, since in steady state still results $\pi=1$; again it is $\frac{\theta}{\theta-1}\;mc=1$.

$$\widehat{mc}_t - \frac{\varphi_p}{(\theta-1)}\widehat{\pi}_t + \beta\frac{\varphi_p}{(\theta-1)}(E_t\Delta\widehat{\mathrm{q}}_t - E_t\Delta\widehat{\mathrm{c}}_t) + \beta\frac{\varphi_p}{(\theta-1)}E_t\widehat{\pi}_{t+1} = 0 \quad (6.101)$$

Rewriting

$$\frac{\varphi_p}{(\theta-1)}\widehat{\pi}_t = \beta\frac{\varphi_p}{(\theta-1)}E_t\widehat{\pi}_{t+1} + \beta\frac{\varphi_p}{(\theta-1)}(E_t\Delta\widehat{\mathrm{q}}_t - E_t\Delta\widehat{\mathrm{c}}_t) + \widehat{mc}_t \quad (6.102)$$

Solving (6.102) for $\widehat{\pi}_t$, still follows

$$\widehat{\pi}_t = \beta E_t\widehat{\pi}_{t+1} + \beta(E_t\Delta\widehat{\mathrm{q}}_t - E_t\Delta\widehat{\mathrm{c}}_t) + \frac{(\theta-1)}{\varphi_p}\widehat{mc}_t \quad (6.103)$$

The term $E_t\Delta\widehat{\mathrm{q}}_t - E_t\Delta\widehat{\mathrm{c}}_t$ in (6.103) is obtained by considering the constraint of the aggregate resources. The Phillips curve in Rotemberg, therefore, differs from the one a-la Calvo.

However, in the basic NKE model, there is no capital accumulation and public administration. If we ignore public spending, taxation, and capital accumulation, here too, the resource constraint in this case becomes

$$\mathrm{Q}_t = \mathrm{C}_t + \frac{\varphi_p}{2}(\pi_t - 1)^2\,\mathrm{Q}_t \quad (6.104)$$

That is,

$$\mathrm{C}_t = \left(1 - \frac{\varphi_p}{2}(\pi_t - 1)^2\right)\mathrm{Q}_t = \left(1 - \frac{\varphi_p}{2} - \frac{\varphi_p}{2}\pi_t^2 + \varphi_p\ \pi_t\right)\mathrm{Q}_t \quad (6.105)$$

From this is obtained[16] $E_t\Delta\widehat{\mathrm{q}}_t = E_t\Delta\widehat{\mathrm{c}}_t$ so that the Phillips curve is like that of the basic model having dynamics of prices a-la Calvo:

[16] Here is the proof. Log-linearizing around the steady state

$$Ce^{\widehat{c}_t} = Qe^{\widehat{q}_t} - \frac{\varphi_p}{2}\,Qe^{\widehat{q}_t} - \frac{\varphi_p}{2}\pi^2 Qe^{2\widehat{\pi}_t + \widehat{q}_t} + \varphi_p Q\pi e^{\widehat{\pi}_t + \widehat{q}_t}$$

$$\mathrm{C}(1+\widehat{c}_t) = Q(1+\widehat{q}_t) - \frac{\varphi_p}{2}\,Q(1+\widehat{q}_t) - \frac{\varphi_p}{2}\pi^2 Q(1 + 2\widehat{\pi}_t + \widehat{q}_t) + \varphi_p Q\pi(1 + \widehat{\pi}_t + \widehat{q}_t)$$

$$\mathrm{C} + \mathrm{C}\widehat{c}_t = Q + Q\widehat{q}_t - \frac{\varphi_p}{2}\,Q - \frac{\varphi_p}{2}Q\widehat{q}_t - \frac{\varphi_p}{2}\pi^2 Q - \varphi_p\pi^2 Q\widehat{\pi}_t - \frac{\varphi_p}{2}\pi^2 Q\widehat{q}_t + \varphi_p Q\pi + \varphi_p Q\pi\,\widehat{\pi}_t + \varphi_p Q\pi\widehat{q}_t$$

$$\mathrm{C} + \mathrm{C}\widehat{c}_t = \left(Q - \frac{\varphi_p}{2}\,Q - \frac{\varphi_p}{2}\pi^2 Q + \varphi_p Q\pi\right) + Q\widehat{q}_t - \frac{\varphi_p}{2}\,Q\widehat{q}_t$$

$$\widehat{\pi}_t = \beta E_t \widehat{\pi}_{t+1} + \frac{(\theta - 1)}{\varphi_p} \widehat{mc}_t \quad (6.106)$$

6.7 Steady State and Details of Log-Linearization Algebra

Steady-state conditions are as follows:

$$\frac{1}{C} = \beta \frac{1}{C} \frac{R}{\pi}$$

That is for $\pi = 1$

$$1 = \beta R = r^k + 1 - \delta \quad (6.107)$$

$$r^k = mc\ \alpha\ \frac{\mathrm{Q}}{\mathrm{K}} \quad (6.108)$$

$$\frac{W}{P} = mc(1 - \alpha)\frac{Q}{N} \quad (6.109)$$

$$\frac{\mathrm{W}}{P} = \frac{\theta_{\mathrm{L}}}{(\theta_{\mathrm{L}} - 1)} \varphi \mathrm{L}^{-\nu} C \quad (6.110)$$

θ (1 − mc)= 1, that is to say

$$\mathrm{mc} = \frac{\theta - 1}{\theta} \quad (6.111)$$

$b = \frac{R}{\pi} b + G - \tau\, b$ i.e., $b = b + G - \tau\, b$ and therefore

---

$$- \frac{\varphi_p}{2}\pi^2 Q\widehat{q}_t + \varphi_p Q\pi\widehat{q}_t - \varphi_p \pi^2 Q\widehat{\pi}_t + \varphi_p Q\pi\, \widehat{\pi}_t$$

$$C\widehat{c}_t = Q\widehat{q}_t - \frac{\varphi_p}{2} Q\widehat{q}_t - \frac{\varphi_p}{2}\pi^2 Q\widehat{q}_t + \varphi_p Q\pi\widehat{q}_t - \varphi_p \pi^2 Q\widehat{\pi}_t + \varphi_p Q\, \pi\widehat{\pi}_t$$

$$C\widehat{c}_t = \left(1 - \frac{\varphi_p}{2}\pi^2 + \varphi_p \pi\right) Q\widehat{q}_t \quad - \frac{\varphi_p}{2} Q\widehat{q}_t - \varphi_p \pi^2 Q\widehat{\pi}_t + \varphi_p Q\pi\widehat{\pi}_t$$

$$= \left(1 - \frac{\varphi_p}{2} - \frac{\varphi_p}{2}\pi^2 + \varphi_p \pi\right) Q\widehat{q}_t + (1 - \pi)\varphi_p Q\pi\, \widehat{\pi}_t$$

$$\widehat{c}_t = \widehat{q}_t + \ (1 - \pi)\varphi_p \pi \frac{Q}{C} \widehat{\pi}_t = \widehat{q}_t + \left[\frac{(1 - \pi)\varphi_p}{\left(1 - \frac{\varphi_p}{2}(\pi - 1)^2\right)} \pi \right] \widehat{\pi}_t$$

Since log-linearization occurs at the point $\pi = 1$, it follows $\widehat{c}_t = \widehat{q}_t$; therefore, $\Delta\widehat{c}_t = \Delta\widehat{q}_t$.

$$G = \tau\, b = T \tag{6.112}$$

$$I = \delta K \tag{6.113}$$

$$Q = C + I + G \tag{6.114}$$

$$Q = \mathrm{A}\, \mathrm{K}^{\alpha}\, \mathrm{L}^{1-\alpha} \tag{6.115}$$

We log-linearize around the steady-state values. We will use the symbol $\widehat{\mathrm{n}}_{\mathrm{t}}$ for the log deviation of the work from steady state, to avoid confusion with similar symbols.

We have

– *Euler's equation (6.79) when transformed becomes*

$$\frac{1}{C + C\widehat{c}_{t+1}} = \frac{1}{C + C\widehat{c}_{t+1}} \frac{\beta R + \beta R\widehat{r}_t}{1 + \widehat{\pi}_{t+1}}$$

and being $\beta\mathrm{R} = 1$, it follows

$$\frac{1}{(1 + \widehat{c}_t)(1 + \widehat{r}_t)} = E_t \left(\frac{1}{(1 + \widehat{c}_{t+1})(1 + \widehat{\pi}_{t+1})} \right).$$

Rearranging and taking into account that

$$\widehat{c}_t \widehat{r}_t = \widehat{c}_{t+1} \widehat{\pi}_{t+1} = 0$$

it follows $\frac{1}{1+\hat{c}_t+\hat{r}_t} = E_t\left(\frac{1}{1+\hat{c}_{t+1}+\hat{\pi}_{t+1}}\right)$ i.e.,
$1 + \widehat{c}_t + \widehat{r}_t = 1 + E_t\widehat{c}_{t+1} + E_t\, \widehat{\pi}_{t+1}$, and therefore,

$$(\widehat{r}_t - E_t \pi_{t+1}) = E_t \widehat{c}_{t+1} - \widehat{c}_t \tag{6.116}$$

– *Absence of arbitrage opportunities (6.80) when transformed becomes*

$$\beta \mathrm{E}_{\mathrm{t}} \left[\frac{\mathrm{R}}{\pi} (1 + \widehat{\mathrm{r}}_{\mathrm{t}} - \widehat{\pi}_{\mathrm{t}+1}) - \mathrm{C}\, (1 + \widehat{\mathrm{c}}_{\mathrm{t}+1}) \right] = \beta \mathrm{E}_{\mathrm{t}} [-\mathrm{C}(1 + \widehat{\mathrm{c}}_{\mathrm{t}+1})$$
$$+ \left(\mathrm{r}^{\mathrm{k}} + 1 - \delta\right) \left(1 + \widehat{\mathrm{r}}^{\mathrm{k}}_{\mathrm{t}+1} + 1 - \delta\right)]$$

that is,

$$\frac{\mathrm{R}}{\pi} (1 + \widehat{\mathrm{r}}_{\mathrm{t}} - \mathrm{E}_{\mathrm{t}} \widehat{\pi}_{\mathrm{t}+1}) = \left[\, \left(\mathrm{r}^{\mathrm{k}} + 1 - \delta\right) \right] \left[\, 1 + \mathrm{E}_{\mathrm{t}} \widehat{\mathrm{r}}^{\mathrm{k}}_{\mathrm{t}+1} + 1 - \delta \right)$$

From $r^k_{t+1} + 1 - \delta = \frac{R_t}{\pi_{t+1}}$ and $\mathrm{r}^{\mathrm{k}} + 1 - \delta = \frac{\mathrm{R}}{\pi}$, we have

$$1+\widehat{r}_t-E_t\widehat{\pi}_{t+1}=1+E_t\widehat{r}^k_{t+1}+1-\delta$$

From which

$$\widehat{r}_t-E_t\widehat{\pi}_{t+1}=E_t\widehat{r}^k_{t+1}+1-\delta \tag{6.117}$$

– *Real-wage equation (6.81) when transformed becomes*

$$\frac{W}{P}(1+\widehat{w}_t-\widehat{p}_t)=\frac{\theta_L}{(\theta_L-1)}\varphi L^{-\nu}C(1-\nu\widehat{n}_t+\widehat{c}_t)$$

That is

$$1+\widehat{w}_t-\widehat{p}_t=1-\nu\widehat{n}_t+\widehat{c}_t$$

And setting $\widehat{w}_{rt}=\widehat{w}_t-\widehat{p}_t$

One has

$$\widehat{w}_{rt}=-\nu\widehat{n}_t+\widehat{c}_t \tag{6.118}$$

– *Aggregate production function (6.82) when transformed is*

$$Q(1+\widehat{q}_t)=AK^{\alpha}L^{1-\alpha}\Big(1+\widehat{a}_t+\alpha\widehat{k}_t+(1-\alpha)\widehat{n}_t$$

or

$$1+\widehat{q}_t=1+\widehat{a}_t+\alpha\widehat{k}_t+(1-\alpha)\widehat{n}_t$$

From which

$$\widehat{q}_t=\widehat{a}_t+\alpha\widehat{k}_t+(1-\alpha)\widehat{n}_t \tag{6.119}$$

– *Total productivity growth (6.83) when transformed becomes*

$$A\,(1+\widehat{a}_t)=A\,(1+\varepsilon_{A,t})$$

From which

$\widehat{a}_t=\ \xi_{A,t}$ where $\xi_{A,\,t}=\rho_{\xi}\,\xi_{A,\,t-1}+\varepsilon_{gt}$

That is,

$$\widehat{a}_t = \rho_a \widehat{a}_{t-1} + \varepsilon_{gt} \tag{6.120}$$

– *Demand for labor (6.84) when transformed is*

$$(1-\alpha)\mathrm{mc}\,\frac{\mathrm{Q}}{\mathrm{L}}\,(1+\widehat{\mathrm{mc}}_t+\widehat{\mathrm{q}}_t-\widehat{\mathrm{n}}_t)=\frac{\mathrm{w}}{\mathrm{P}}(1+\widehat{\mathrm{w}}_{\mathrm{rt}})$$

That is, $1+\widehat{\mathrm{mc}}_t+\widehat{\mathrm{q}}_t-\widehat{\mathrm{n}}_t= 1+\widehat{\mathrm{w}}_{\mathrm{rt}}$

So that

$$\widehat{\mathrm{w}}_{\mathrm{rt}} = \widehat{\mathrm{mc}}_t+\widehat{\mathrm{q}}_t-\widehat{\mathrm{n}}_t \tag{6.121}$$

– *Demand for capital services (6.85) when transformed becomes*

$$\alpha\, mc\,\frac{Q}{K}\left(1+\widehat{\mathrm{mc}}_t+\widehat{\mathrm{q}}_t-\widehat{\mathrm{k}}_t\right)=\mathrm{r}^{\mathrm{k}}\left(1+\widehat{\mathrm{r}}_t^{\mathrm{k}}\right)$$

And therefore,

$$\widehat{r}_t^{\,k} = \widehat{\mathrm{mc}}_t+\widehat{\mathrm{q}}_t-\widehat{\mathrm{k}}_t \tag{6.122}$$

– *The dynamics of inflation* in log-linear terms is the one already described by Eq. (6.103) obtained in the section on the Rotenberg Phillips curve, i.e.,

$$\widehat{\pi}_t = \beta E_t\widehat{\pi}_{t+1} + \beta(\mathrm{E_t}\Delta\widehat{\mathrm{q}}_t - \mathrm{E_t}\Delta\widehat{\mathrm{c}}_t) + \frac{(\theta-1)}{\varphi_p}\widehat{mc}_t \tag{6.123}$$

– *The resource constraint (6.87) subject to transformation becomes*

$$\mathrm{Q}\left[1-\frac{\gamma_p}{2}(\pi-1)^2\right](1+\widehat{\mathrm{q}}_t)=\mathrm{C}(1+\widehat{\mathrm{c}}_t)+\mathrm{I}\left(1+\widehat{\mathrm{i}}_t\right)+G(1+\widehat{g}_t)$$

That is to say

$$\mathrm{Q}\widehat{\mathrm{q}}_t = \mathrm{C}\widehat{\mathrm{c}}_t + \mathrm{I}\widehat{\mathrm{i}}_t + \mathrm{G}\widehat{\mathrm{g}}_t$$

And therefore,

$$\widehat{q}_t = \frac{C}{Q}\widehat{c}_t + \frac{I}{Q}\widehat{i}_t + \frac{G}{Q}\widehat{g}_t$$

setting $c_q = \frac{C}{Q}; i_q = \frac{I}{Q}; g_q = \frac{G}{Q}$, it is

$$\widehat{q}_t = c\_q\,\widehat{c}_t + i\_q\,\widehat{i}_t + g\_q\,\widehat{g}_t \tag{6.124}$$

– *Equation for the trend of public expenditure (6.90) when transformed becomes*

$$G(1+\widehat{g}_t) = G\left(1+\varepsilon_{g,t}\right)$$

That is,

$$\widehat{g}_t = \varepsilon_{g,t} \quad \text{with} \quad \varepsilon_{g,t} = \left(1-\rho_g\right)g\_q + \rho_g\,\varepsilon_{g,t-1} + \xi_{g,t}$$

$$\widehat{g}_t = \left(1-\rho_g\right)g\_q + \rho_g\widehat{g}_{t-1} + \xi_{g,t} \tag{6.125}$$

– *Capital accumulation equation (6.88) when transformed becomes*

$$K\left(1+\widehat{k}_{t+1}\right) = (1-\delta)\,K\left(1+\widehat{k}_t\right) + I\left(1+\widehat{i}_t\right)$$

i.e.,

$$K\widehat{k}_{t+1} = (\,1-\delta)K\widehat{k}_t + I\widehat{i}_t;$$

from which

$$\widehat{k}_{t+1} = \frac{(1-\delta)K}{K}\widehat{k}_t + \frac{I}{K}\widehat{i}_t$$

And $\frac{I}{K} = \delta$, segue

$$\widehat{k}_{t+1} = (1-\delta)\widehat{k}_t + \delta\,\widehat{i}_t \tag{6.126}$$

– *The budget constraint of public administration rewritten in real terms is*

$$b_t = R_t\,\frac{P_{t-1}}{P_t}\,\frac{B_{t-1}}{P_{t-1}} + G_t - T_t = \frac{R_t}{\pi_t}\,b_{t-1} + G_t - T_t$$

which when transformed becomes

$$b\left(1+\widehat{b}_t\right)=\frac{R}{\pi}b\left(1+\widehat{r}_t-\widehat{\pi}_t+\widehat{b}_{t-1}\right)+G(1+\widehat{g}_t)-T\left(1+\widehat{t}_t\right)$$

After some simplifications, it is[17]

$$\widehat{b}_t=\frac{1}{1+\tau}\left(\widehat{r}_t-\widehat{\pi}_t+\widehat{b}_{t-1}\right)+\frac{\tau}{1+\tau}\widehat{g}_t \tag{6.127}$$

– *Monetary rule equation (6.92) subject to transformation becomes*

$$1+\widehat{r}_t=1+\left[(1-l_r)\left(l_r\widehat{r}_{t-1}+l_\pi\pi_t+l_q\widehat{q}_t\right)\right]+\widehat{u}_t^R)$$

That is,

$$\widehat{r}_t=l_r\widehat{r}_{t-1}+(1-l_r)\left(l_\pi\pi_t+l_q\widehat{q}_t\right)+\widehat{u}_t^R \tag{6.128}$$

– *Equation (6.93) of monetary policy shock when transformed becomes*

$$1+\widehat{u}_t^R=1+\varepsilon_{u,t}$$

That is,

$$\widehat{u}_t^R=\varepsilon_{u,t} \quad \text{with } \varepsilon_{u,t}=\rho_\varepsilon\varepsilon_{u,t-1}+\xi_{\varepsilon,t}$$

And therefore,

$$\widehat{u}_t^R=\rho_u\widehat{u}_{t-1}^R+\xi_{\varepsilon,t} \tag{6.129}$$

[17] Simplifications are as follows

$b+b\widehat{b}_t=\frac{R}{\pi}b+\frac{R}{\pi}b\,\widehat{r}_t-\frac{R}{\pi}b\widehat{\pi}_t+\frac{R}{\pi}b\,\widehat{b}_{t-1}+G\widehat{g}_t-T\,\widehat{t}_t;$

$b\widehat{b}_t=\frac{R}{\pi}b\,\widehat{r}_t-\frac{R}{\pi}b\widehat{\pi}_t+\frac{R}{\pi}b\,\widehat{b}_{t-1}+G\widehat{g}_t-T\widehat{t}_t$

$b\widehat{b}_t=b\left(\widehat{r}_t-\widehat{\pi}_t+\widehat{b}_{t-1}\right)+\tau b(\widehat{g}_t-\widehat{b}_t)$

$\widehat{b}_t+\tau\widehat{b}_t=\widehat{r}_t-\widehat{\pi}_t+\widehat{b}_{t-1}+\tau\,\widehat{g}_t$

and solving for $\widehat{b}_t$, Eq. (6.127) follows.

6.8 The Complete Log-Linearized NKE Model, with Physical Capital and Price Adjustment Costs

By grouping log-linearized equations, the complete system in log-linear deviations from steady state becomes

$$(\widehat{r}_t - E_t\pi_{t+1}) = E_t\widehat{c}_{t+1} - \widehat{c}_t \tag{6.130}$$

$$\widehat{r}_t - E_t\pi_{t+1} = E_t\widehat{r}^k_{t+1} + 1 - \delta \tag{6.131}$$

$$\widehat{\mathrm{q}}_t = \widehat{a}_t + \alpha\widehat{\mathrm{k}}_t + (1-\alpha)\widehat{\mathrm{n}}_t \tag{6.132}$$

$$\widehat{r}_t{}^k = \widehat{\mathrm{mc}}_t + \widehat{\mathrm{q}}_t - \widehat{\mathrm{k}}_t \tag{6.133}$$

$$\widehat{w}_{rt} = \widehat{\mathrm{mc}}_t + \widehat{\mathrm{q}}_t - \widehat{\mathrm{n}}_t \tag{6.134}$$

$$\widehat{w}_{rt} = -\nu\widehat{\mathrm{n}}_t + \widehat{\mathrm{c}}_t \tag{6.135}$$

$$\widehat{\pi}_t = \beta E_t\widehat{\pi}_{t+1} + \beta(\mathrm{E}_t\Delta\widehat{\mathrm{q}}_t - \mathrm{E}_t\Delta\widehat{\mathrm{c}}_t) + \frac{(\theta-1)}{\varphi_p}\widehat{mc}_t \tag{6.136}$$

$$\widehat{k}_{t+1} = (1-\delta)\widehat{k}_t + \delta\widehat{i}_t \tag{6.137}$$

$$\widehat{q}_t = \frac{C}{Q}\widehat{c}_t + \frac{I}{Q}\widehat{i}_t + \frac{G}{Q}\widehat{g}_t \tag{6.138}$$

$$\widehat{\mathrm{b}}_t = \frac{1}{1+\tau}\left(\widehat{\mathrm{r}}_t - \widehat{\pi}_t + \widehat{\mathrm{b}}_{t-1}\right) + \frac{\tau}{1+\tau}\widehat{\mathrm{g}}_t \tag{6.139}$$

$$\widehat{r}_t = l_r\,\widehat{r}_{t-1} + (1-l_r)\left(l_\pi\widehat{\pi}_t + l_q\,\widehat{q}_t\right) + \widehat{u}^R_t \tag{6.140}$$

$$\widehat{a}_t = \rho_A\,\widehat{a}_{t-1} + \xi_{A,t} \tag{6.141}$$

$$\widehat{g}_t = \left(1-\rho_g\right)\mathrm{g}_\mathrm{q} + \rho_g\widehat{g}_{t-1} + \xi_{g,t} \tag{6.142}$$

$$\widehat{\mathrm{u}}^R_t = \rho_u\,\widehat{\mathrm{u}}^R_{t-1} + \quad \xi_{u,t} \tag{6.143}$$

6.9 DYNARE's Code for the Numerical Solution of the NKE Model with Physical Capital and Price Adjustment Costs

The numerical solution of the log-linearized NKE model, with physical capital and price adjustment costs, is obtained with the following DYNARE code:

```
% m_NKE_physicalK_adjcosts.mod
var a b c g i k mc n pi q r r_k u w_r;
```

```
varexo z_a z_g z_u;
parameters alpha beta delta theta phi_p c_q gau gs i_q g_q l_r l_pi l_q mu
nu rho_a rho_g rho_u tau;
alpha = 0.34;
beta  = 0.99;
delta = 0.025;
theta = 0.66;
phi_p = 65.5;
c_q   = 0.66;
i_q   = 0.17;
g_q   = 0.17;
l_r   = 0;
l_pi  = 1.6;
l_q   = 0.12;
nu    = 0.8;
rho_a = 0.95;
rho_g = 0.95;
rho_u = 0.95;
tau   = 0.05;
gau   = 1/1+tau;
gs    = tau*gau;
mu    = (theta-1)*(1/phi_p);

model(linear);
r-pi(+1)= c(+1)-c;
r-pi(+1) = r_k(+1)+ 1-delta;
q =a +alpha*k(-1)+(1-alpha)*n;
r_k=mc+q-k(-1);
w_r= mc+q-n;
w_r=-nu*n+c;
  pi=beta*pi(+1)+beta *(q(+1)-q +c(+1)-c)+mu*mc;
k=(1-delta)*k(-1)+delta*i;
q= c_q*c(-1)+i_q*i+ g_q*g;
r= l_r*r(-1)+(1-l_r)*(l_pi*pi+l_q*q)+u;
b = gau*(r-pi+b(-1))+gs*g;
a= rho_a*a(-1)+z_a;
g= (1-rho_g)*g_q +rho_g*g(-1)+z_g;
u= rho_u*u(-1)+z_u;
end;
steady;
check;
shocks;
var z_a; stderr .01;
var z_g; stderr .01;
var z_u; stderr .01;
```

```
end;
stoch_simul(order=1, irf=30) a b c g i k mc n pi q r r_k u w_r;
```

The code was saved in the folder *(C:\dynare\4.6.4\examples)* with the extension *m_NKE_physicalK_adjcosts.mod* in my PC and was tested with DYNARE version 4.6.4. It works properly.

6.10 Some Specific Extensions of the NKE Model

This section and the following subsections contain some further extensions of the NKE model, by considering in sequence (a) Calvo stickiness in salary changes; (b) persistence in consumption habits ("habit persistence"), and (c) adjustment costs of labor as well as capital.

6.10.1 Calvo Stickiness in Wage Modifications

Extending Calvo's approach to the wages setting by households, in each period only a share of households, equal to $1 - \theta_w$, is called in a completely random way to choose wages optimally.

The remaining share of families θ_w will maintain the current monetary wage $W_t(i)$ at the same level as the previous period $W_{t-1}(i)$.

If a household could choose the optimal wage of its specific labor service, in each period it would solve, over an infinite time horizon, a problem of the kind

$$\max_{W^*_{t+n}(i)} \mathrm{E_t} \sum_{n=0}^{\infty} (\beta\theta_w)^n \left[-\varphi \frac{L_{t+n}(i)^{1-\upsilon}}{1-\nu} + \lambda_{t+n}(i)\, \frac{W^*_{t+n}(i)}{P_{t+n}}\, L_{t+n}(i) \right]$$

$$\text{Sub} \quad L_{t+n}(i) = \left(\frac{W^*_{t+n}(i)}{W_{t+n}} \right)^{-\theta_L} L_{t+n} \tag{6.144}$$

But households know that the wage chosen today will remain fixed for T future periods with probability θ_w^T. Since with known probability the wage determined at time t could not adjust in the future, the real wage at time t will change over time only due to inflation.

This means that the real wage sequence $\frac{W_{t+n}(i)}{P_{t+n}}$ to be considered by households for the maximization problem is given by

$$\frac{W_{t+1}(i)}{P_{t+1}} = \frac{W_t^*(i)}{P_{t+1}} = \frac{W_t^*(i)}{P_t}\frac{P_t}{P_{t+1}} = \frac{W_t^*(i)}{P_t\pi_t}$$

$$\frac{W_{t+2}(i)}{P_{t+2}} = \frac{W_t^*(i)}{P_{t+2}} = \frac{W_t^*(i)}{P_{t+1}}\frac{P_{t+1}}{P_{t+2}} = \frac{W_t^*(i)}{P_t}\frac{P_t}{P_{t+1}}\frac{P_{t+1}}{P_{t+2}}$$

$$= \frac{W_t^*(i)}{P_t\pi_t\pi_{t+1}} = \frac{W_t^*(i)}{P_t\prod_{n=0}^{1}\pi_{t+n}} \tag{6.145}$$

And more generally,

$$\frac{W_{t+n}(i)}{P_{t+n}} = \frac{W_t^*(i)}{P_t\prod_{n=0}^{n-1}\pi_{t+n}} = \frac{W_t^*(i)}{P_t}\frac{P_t}{P_{t+n}} = \frac{W_t^*(i)}{P_{t+n}} \tag{6.146}$$

Therefore, at times t the maximum problem for households becomes the intertemporal one

$$\max_{W_t^*(i)} E_t \sum_{n=0}^{\infty} (\beta\theta_w)^n \left[-\varphi \frac{L_{t+n}(i)^{1-\upsilon}}{1-\nu} + \lambda_{t+n}(i)\frac{W_t^*(i)}{P_{t+n}} L_{t+n}(i) \right]$$

$$\text{Sub} \quad L_{t+n}(i) = \left(\frac{W_t^*(i)}{W_{t+n}}\right)^{-\theta_L} L_{t+n} \tag{6.147}$$

That is, by substituting the constraint into the objective function, the problem is

$$\max_{W_t^*(i)} E_t \sum_{n=0}^{\infty} (\beta\theta_w)^n \left[-\varphi \frac{\left[\left(\frac{W_t^*(i)}{W_{t+n}}\right)^{-\theta_L} L_{t+n}\right]^{1-\upsilon}}{1-\nu} + \lambda_{t+n}(i)\frac{W_t^*(i)}{P_{t+n}}\left(\frac{W_t^*(i)}{W_{t+n}}\right)^{-\theta_L} L_{t+n} \right] \tag{6.148}$$

The optimal wage results[18]

[18]The first-order condition is

$$\theta_L\varphi\, E_t \sum_{n=0}^{\infty} (\beta\theta_w)^n \left[\left[\left(\frac{W_t^*(i)}{W_{t+n}}\right)^{-\theta_L} L_{t+n}\right]^{-\upsilon} \frac{1}{W_{t+n}} \left[\left(\frac{W_t^*(i)}{W_{t+n}}\right)^{-\theta_L-1} L_{t+n}\right]\right] =$$

$$(\theta_L - 1)E_t \sum_{n=0}^{\infty} (\beta\theta_w)^n \left[\lambda_{t+n}(i)\frac{1}{P_{t+n}}\left(\frac{W_t^*(i)}{W_{t+n}}\right)^{-\theta_L} L_{t+n}\right]$$

and taking into account that $\frac{\lambda_{t+n}(i)}{P_{t+n}} = \frac{1}{P_{t+n}C_{t+n}(i)}$, symplifying and solving for $W_t^*(i)$, Eq. (6.149) follows.

$$W_t^*(i) = \frac{\theta_L}{\theta_L - 1} \frac{\varphi E_t \sum_{n=0}^{\infty} (\beta\theta_w)^n L_{t+n}(i)^{1-\upsilon}}{E_t \sum_{n=0}^{\infty} (\beta\theta_w)^n (P_{t+n} C_{t+n}(i))^{-1}(i) L_{t+n}(i)} \tag{6.149}$$

Note that for $\theta_w = 0$, we deduce

$$\frac{W_t(i)}{P_t} = \frac{\theta_L}{(\theta_L - 1)} C_t(i) \varphi L_t(i)^{-\nu} \tag{6.150}$$

which is the rule already known for determining the optimal real wage in the case of full flexibility of money wages.

At the aggregate level, since a fraction $1 - \theta_w$ of households set the wage at the optimal level $W_t^*(i)$ while the remaining fraction of households keep the monetary wage unchanged $W_t = W_{t-1}$, in a symmetric equilibrium $W_t^*(i) = W_t^*$, it must be valid

$$W_t^{1-\theta_N} = \theta_w W_{t-1}^{1-\theta_N} + (1 - \theta_w) W_t^{*1-\theta_L}$$

From which

$$W_t = \left[\theta_w W_{t-1}^{1-\theta_L} + (1 - \theta_w) W_t^{*1-\theta_L}\right]^{\frac{1}{1-\theta_L}} \tag{6.151}$$

6.10.2 Habit Persistence and Adjustment Costs of Capital and Labor

With "external" habit persistence (in which current individual consumption is influenced by past level of aggregate consumption), the household utility function is assumed to be[19]

$$E_0 \sum_{t=0}^{\infty} \beta^t \left[\log(C_{it} - h^e C_{t-1}) - \varphi \frac{N_{it}^{1-\upsilon}}{1-\upsilon}\right] \tag{6.152}$$

Here and in the following symbol, N_{it} indicates labor.

Constraints are

[19] On habit formation, see Pollak, R. (1970), Abel A. (1990), Overland, C. and Weil D. (2000), Lettau, M. and Uhlig, H. (2000), Boldrin, M. et al. (2001), Ravn M. et al. (2006).

1. Instantaneous budget constraint

$$P_tC_{it} + B_{it} + P_tI_{it} + P_tTX_{it} + P_tCJ(I_{it}, K_{it}) = W_tN_{it} + (1 + r_{t-1})B_{i,t-1} + P_t\, r_t^k\, K_{i,t} + D_{it} \quad (6.153)$$

2. Net accumulation of capital

$$I_{it} = \mathrm{K}_{\mathrm{i,t+1}} - (1 - \delta)\mathrm{K}_{\mathrm{it}} \quad (6.154)$$

Also, it is valid

$$CJ(I_{it}, K_{it}) = \frac{\gamma_I}{2}\left(\frac{I_{it}}{K_{it}} - 1\right)^2 K_{it} \quad (6.155)$$

Named ξ_{it} Lagrange multiplier of investments and ignoring the index i, the first-order conditions are

$$C_t: \quad \frac{1}{C_{it} - h^e C_{t-1}} = \lambda_t \quad (6.156)$$

$$N_t: \quad \varphi\,(1 - N_{it})^{-\upsilon} = \lambda_t \frac{W_t}{P_t} \quad (6.157)$$

$$B_t: \quad \frac{\lambda_t}{P_t} = \beta E_t \frac{\lambda_{t+1}}{P_{t+1}}(1 + \mathrm{r_t}) \quad (6.158)$$

$$I_t: \quad \lambda_t\left[1 + \gamma_I\left(\frac{I_t}{K_t} - 1\right)\right] = \xi_t \quad (6.159)$$

$$\mathrm{K}_{t+1}: \xi_t = \beta\, E_t\lambda_{t+1} r_{t+1} + \beta\,(1 - \delta)E_t\xi_{t+1} - \beta\, E_t\, \lambda_{t+1}\frac{\partial CJ}{\partial K_{t+1}} \quad (6.160)$$

Defining marginal "Tobin's $\mathrm{q_t}$" the ratio between the shadow price of investment (the shadow value of increased capital) and the shadow price of adjustment of investment (the cost of reproduction of capital), it follows

$$I_t: \quad \left[1 + \gamma_I\left(\frac{I_t}{K_t} - 1\right)\right] = \frac{\xi_t}{\lambda_t} = q_t \quad (6.161)$$

$$\text{From which } \gamma_I\left(\frac{I_t}{K_t} - 1\right) = q_t - 1 \quad (6.162)$$

By taking into account that $\xi_t = \lambda_t q_t$, (6.160) becomes

$$\lambda_t q_t = \beta\, E_t \lambda_{t+1} r_{t+1} + \beta(1-\delta) E_t \lambda_{t+1} q_{t+1} - \beta E_t \lambda_{t+1} \frac{\partial CJ}{\partial K_{t+1}} \tag{6.163}$$

The implications of the costs of adjusting physical capital were already examined in the first chapter of this book.

We will now extend the same logic to adjustment costs for employment.

For firms producing intermediate goods, we will assume that it is expensive to adjust the level of employment (there are costs for hiring and firing).

The adjustment cost function, similar to capital adjustment costs, is quadratic and is of the kind

$$CJ[N_t(j)] = \frac{\gamma_N}{2} \left(\frac{N_t(J)}{N_{t-1}(j)} - 1 \right)^2 \mathrm{Q_t} \tag{6.164}$$

The presence of adjustment costs transforms the static problem of cost minimization into an intertemporal problem. The cost function is made up of two components, one relating to the present and the other relating to the future.

The instantaneous objective function is

$$\min_{\mathrm{N_t, K_t}} \mathrm{E_t} \left\{ \left(\beta^{\mathrm{i}} \Phi_{\mathrm{t,t+i}}\right) \left[\frac{W_{\mathrm{t}}}{P_t} N_t(j) \right.\right.$$
$$\left.\left. + r_t^k K_t(j) + \frac{\gamma_N}{2} \left(\frac{N_{t+i}(J)}{N_{t-1+i}(j)} - 1 \right)^2 \mathrm{Q_{t+i}(j)} \right] \right\} \tag{6.165}$$

The first-order condition for $K_t(j)$ remains unchanged (there is no intertemporal component), while the one for $N_t(j))$ is obtained by forming the Lagrangian taking into account the constraint[$\mathrm{Q_t}$ (j) = $\mathrm{A_t\ N_t(J)^\alpha\ K_t(j)^{1-\alpha}}$] and for given sequences $\{\mathrm{Q_{t+i}(j)}\}_{\mathrm{i}=0}^{\infty}$, $\left\{\frac{\mathrm{W_{t+i}}}{\mathrm{P_{t+i}}}(\mathrm{j})\right\}_{\mathrm{i}=0}^{\infty}$, $\{r_{t+i}^k(\mathrm{j})\}_{\mathrm{i}=0}^{\infty}$. Limiting only to instants t and t+1, the Lagrangian is

$$\frac{W_{\mathrm{t}}}{P_t} N_t(j) + r_t^k K_t(j) + \frac{\gamma_N}{2} \left(\frac{N_t(J)}{N_{t-1}(j)} - 1 \right)^2 \mathrm{Q_t(j)}$$
$$+ \mathrm{E_t} \beta \Phi_{\mathrm{t,t+1}} \left[\frac{W_{\mathrm{t+1}}}{P_{t+1}} N_{t+1}(j) + r_{t+1}^k K_{t+1}(j) + + \frac{\gamma_N}{2} \left(\frac{N_{t+1}(J)}{N_t(j)} - 1 \right)^2 Q_{t+1}(j) \right]$$
$$+ \lambda_{\mathrm{t}}(\mathrm{j}) \left[\mathrm{Q_t\ (j) - A_t N_t(j)^\alpha K_t(j)^{1-\alpha}} \right] \tag{6.166}$$

And differentiating for $N_t(j)$

$$
\begin{aligned}
N_t(j) : & \frac{W_t}{P_t} + \gamma_N \left(\frac{N_t(J)}{N_{t-1}(j)} - 1 \right) \frac{Q_t(j)}{N_{t-1}(j)} \\
& - E_t \beta \Phi_{t,t+1} \gamma_N \left(\frac{N_{t+1}(J)}{N_t(j)} - 1 \right) \frac{N_{t+1}(J)}{N_t(j)^2} Q_{t+1}(j) \\
& - \lambda_t \, \alpha A_t N_t(j)^{1-\alpha} K_t(j)^{1-\alpha} = 0
\end{aligned} \tag{6.167}
$$

From (6.167), solving with respect to $\frac{W_t}{P_t}$, it is

$$
\begin{aligned}
\frac{W_t}{P_t} = & \lambda_t(j) \alpha A_t N_t(j)^{1-\alpha} K_t(j)^{1-\alpha} + E_t \beta \Phi_{t,t+1} \gamma_N \left(\frac{N_{t+1}(J)}{N_t(j)} - 1 \right) \frac{N_{t+1}(J)}{N_t(j)^2} Q_{t+1}(j) \\
& - \gamma_N \left(\frac{N_t(J)}{N_{t-1}(j)} - 1 \right) \frac{Q_t(j)}{N_{t-1}(j)}
\end{aligned} \tag{6.168}
$$

And remembering that $\lambda_t(j) = MC_t(j)$ it is

$$
\begin{aligned}
\frac{W_t}{P_t} = & \lambda_t(j) \alpha \frac{Q_t}{N_t} + E_t \beta \Phi_{t,t+1} \gamma_N \left(\frac{N_{t+1}(J)}{N_t(j)} - 1 \right) \frac{N_{t+1}(J)}{N_t(j)^2} Q_{t+1}(j) \\
& - \gamma_N \left(\frac{N_t(J)}{N_{t-1}(j)} - 1 \right) \frac{Q_t(j)}{N_{t-1}(j)}
\end{aligned} \tag{6.169}
$$

The resource constraint with adjustment costs of both capital and labor becomes

$$
Q_t = C_t + I_t + G_t + \frac{\gamma_P}{2} \left(\frac{P_t(j)}{P_{t-1}(j)} - 1 \right)^2 Q_t + \frac{\gamma_P}{2} \left(\frac{P_t(j)}{P_{t-1}(j)} - 1 \right)^2 K_t \tag{6.170}
$$

6.10.3 "Rules of Thumb" and Non-Ricardian Households

A significant part of the literature has highlighted an "excessive" dependence of consumption on current income, reporting important deviations from the permanent income hypothesis.[20]

To capture these aspects, some NKE-DSGE models divide households into two types: "non-Ricardian" households who do not save, do not go into debt, and consume all their income from work (households living from hand to mouth) and

[20]The topic has been the subject of study and debate in an extensive literature. See among others Souleles, N. (1999), Mankiw, N. (2000), Wolff, M. (2003), Johnson, D. et al. (2006), Galí, J. et al. (2007), and Arias, A. et al. (2007).

Ricardian households, who act for smoothing consumption over time, save, and go into debt.

It is assumed that s_{NR} is the share of the non-Ricardian population, and $1 - s_{NR}$ is the share of Ricardian households.

The Ricardian representative household solves the problem:

$$Max_{C_{it}}\ E_0 \sum_{t=0}^{\infty} \beta^t \left[\log\left(C_{it} - h^e C_{t-1}\right) - \varphi\ \frac{{N_{it}}^{1-\upsilon}}{1-\upsilon} \right] \tag{6.171}$$

$$\begin{aligned} \text{Sub}:\quad & P_t C_{it} + B_{it} + P_t I_{it} + P_t TX_{it} + P_t CJ(I_{it}, K_{it}) = W_t N_{it} \\ & +(1 + r_{t-1}) B_{i,t-1} + P_t\, r_t^k\, K_{i,t} + D_{it}; \\ & I_{it} = \mathrm{K}_{\mathrm{i,t+1}} - (1 - \delta)\mathrm{K}_{\mathrm{it}} \end{aligned}$$

First-order conditions are similar to the previous ones.

For the non-Ricardian households, the following utility function is assumed:

$$\log C_{it}^{NR} - \varphi\ \frac{\left(1 - L_t^{NR}\right)^{1-v_{NA}}}{1-v} \tag{6.172}$$

But consumption is assumed to be equal to labor income, i.e., given the current budget constraint:

$$P_t C_{it}^{NR} = W_t N_{it}^{NR} - P_t TX_{it}^{NR} \tag{6.173}$$

Consumption of a typical non-Ricardian household is

$$C_{it}^{NR} = \frac{W_t}{P_t} N_{it}^{NR} - TX_{it}^{NR} \tag{6.174}$$

By imposing symmetry property on aggregate equilibrium, the overall aggregate consumption is a weighted average of consumption of the two categories of households, i.e.,

$$C_t = s_{NR}\ C_{it}^{NR} + (1 - s_{NR}) C_{it}^{R} \tag{6.175}$$

While the investments and accumulation of aggregate capital coincide with the investments and accumulation of aforementioned Ricardian households,

$$I_t = I_t^R \tag{6.176}$$

$$K_t = K_t^R \tag{6.177}$$

A different hypothesis assumes that the fraction of non-Ricardian and Ricardian households is uniformly distributed among the different types of workers (and therefore, among representative unions that set wages). In this context, it is assumed that in each period, for the i-th worker, the wage is set to maximize an objective function, a combination of the components of the Lagrangian of interest for each type of household, i.e.,

$$\text{Max } s_{RN}\left[\varphi \frac{(1-N_{it})^{1-\upsilon}}{1-\upsilon}+\lambda_{it}^{NR}\frac{W_{it}}{P_t}N_{it}\right]+(1-s_{RN})$$
$$\times\left[\varphi \frac{(1-N_{it})^{1-\upsilon}}{1-\upsilon}+\lambda_{it}^{R}\frac{W_{it}}{P_t}N_{it}\right]$$
$$\text{Sub} \qquad N_t(i)=\left(\frac{\mathrm{W_t(i)}}{W_t}\right)^{-\theta_N}N_t(i) \tag{6.178}$$

And the wage equation becomes

$$\frac{\theta_n}{\theta_N-1}\varphi(1-N_{it})^{-\upsilon}=\left[\lambda_{it}^{NR}s_{RN}+\lambda_{it}^{R}(1-s_{RN})\right]\frac{W_t}{P_t} \tag{6.179}$$

However, we will not develop separately these models further,[21] by focusing instead on the study of a detailed version of New Keynesian Macroeconomics which brings together, in a single DSGE model, many of economic stickiness considered in the literature.

6.11 The Medium-Sized Micro-founded Keynesian Model (E. Sims 2016)[22]

It has been seen that the basic DSGE model of New Keynesian Macroeconomics admits a series of extensions, which include various stickiness not only nominal of prices and wages but also real, relating to the productive sector.

Furthermore, in models that aim at understanding the causes and effects of financial crises, the basic NKE is extended to include firstly a financial sector and

[21] A full exposition of the model with Ricardian and non-Ricardian families is in Costa, C. J. Jr (2016), pp. 192–227.

[22] The original version of the lecture was modified by E. Sims himself, in the version available at https://sites.nd.edu/esims/courses/ph-d-macro-theory-ii/

However, a complete exposition of the model is in Xu, W. (2019).

then various stickiness in the financial sector also to try to understand financial and real implications of such stickiness.[23]

Here, only the extensions of stickiness to the real sector will be considered, by examining a comprehensive model of physical capital accumulation which, in the context of fixing prices of goods à la Calvo, in addition to sticky wages, contains other stickiness consisting in:

1. *Backward indexing of out-of-date prices and wages*
2. *Habits formation in consumption*
3. *Investment adjustment costs*
4. *Variable use of physical capital*
5. *A fixed cost of production*
6. *Monetary policy conducted according to a Taylor rule*
7. *Fiscal policies*

Furthermore, although not all of them will be considered in the code, the following shocks are supposed:

(a) *Total Productivity*
(b) *Marginal efficiency of investments*
(c) *Public spending*
(d) *Monetary policy*
(e) *Intertemporal preference*
(f) *Intratemporal preference, between work and consumption (labor supply shock)*

The model considers the following operators:

- Labor broker that combines heterogeneous labor inputs into a single, homogeneous labor available as input for the firm production.
- Households that consume, invest in physical capital, provide labor, decide on the degree of utilization of capital, rent capital services to businesses, and set wages of their heterogeneous labor input, based on a downward sloping demand, accumulate bonds.
- One firm producing final good that groups heterogeneous goods produced by intermediate firms into a single final product.
- Intermediate goods firms that use capital and labor services to produce heterogeneous production goods.
- A Central Bank that conducts monetary policy according to Taylor rule.
- Public Authority (i.e., Government) that chooses exogenous public spending, which is financed by a mix of taxes and public debt.

The following sections illustrate decision problems and optimality conditions of various operators just indicated and then discuss aggregation and equilibrium conditions.[24]

---

[23] This is an important topic of analysis, and there is a vast literature on the subject. We limit ourselves to reporting here a small significant sample of contributions: Gerali A. et al. (2010), Gertler, M. and Karadi, P. (2011), Brázdik, F. et al. (2012), Benes, J. et al. (2014), Adrian, T. et al. (2022).

[24] The model abstracts from money, and the economy considered is "cashless." Money could be introduced as done in previous models assuming that households obtain direct utility from a stock of

6.12 Labor's Supply Aggregation and Representative Trade Union Choices

The examination of the model begins with the study of the labor market which is regarded, from the supply side, as an aggregator of various specific types of work.

To this end, it is possible, as already previously done, to imagine that there is a final representative trade union (symmetrically to a representative firm producing the final good) whose task is to amalgamate the heterogeneous intermediate labors $N_t(i)$ in a single final aggregate labor N_t to be sold on the market at the single aggregate wage W_t.

The role of this representative union is to request from households a package of specific labor services to be resold as an aggregate, to maximizing aggregate net income from labor, defined, as previously, by the difference between what is obtained from the sale of aggregated labor to firms' sector, and the value resulting from the aggregation of income from specific labors.

The determination of the labor supply and the monetary wage, along the lines of the previous analysis, is carried out assuming that the representative union has the objective of maximizing net income, with the constraint of labor supply by households:

$$\begin{aligned} &\max_{N_t(i)} W_t N_t - \int_0^1 W_t(i) N_t(i) di \\ &sub\ N_t = \left[\int_0^1 N_t(i)^{\frac{\theta_N - 1}{\theta_N}} di \right]^{\frac{\theta_N}{\theta_N - 1}} \end{aligned} \tag{6.180}$$

By substituting constraint into the objective function, the function to be maximized becomes

$$W_t \left[\int_0^1 N_t(i)^{\frac{\theta_N - 1}{\theta_N}} di \right]^{\frac{\theta_N}{\theta_N - 1}} - \int_0^1 W_t(i) N_t(i) di \tag{6.181}$$

The first-order for $N_t(i)$ is

money that enters the utility function in an additive and separable manner. As seen, this would not affect the balance of the model. No utility for public spending is considered. Even for public spending, one could assume that households obtain direct utility from public spending and consider an additional, separate additive component, and the equilibrium of the economy would not be compromised (see R. Barro (1997) *New-Keynesian Model with government*, MIT Press Cambridge). An extensive discussion of the public sector in the DSGE model is in Torres, J.L. (2014).

$$W_t \frac{\theta_N}{\theta_N - 1}\left[\int_0^1 N_t(i)^{\frac{\theta_N - 1}{\theta_N}} di\right]^{\frac{1}{\theta_N - 1}} \frac{\theta_N - 1}{\theta_N} N_t(i)^{-\frac{1}{\theta_N}} - W_t(i) = 0 \tag{6.182}$$

And taking into account that $\left[\int_0^1 N_t(i)^{\frac{\theta_N - 1}{\theta_N}} di\right]^{\frac{1}{\theta_N - 1}} = N_t^{\frac{1}{\theta_N}}$, it follows

$$N_t(i) = \left(\frac{W_t(i)}{W_t}\right)^{-\theta_N} N_t \tag{6.183}$$

Also note that from the first-order condition is

$$W_t N_t^{\frac{1}{\theta_N}} \; N_t(i)^{-\frac{1}{\theta_N}} \; = W_t(i) \tag{6.184}$$

and dividing member by member (6.183) for the same condition for a different index j, it follows

$$\frac{N_t(i)^{-\frac{1}{\theta_N}}}{N_t(j)^{-\frac{1}{\theta_N}}} = \frac{W_t(i)}{W_t(j)} \tag{6.185}$$

From which

$$N_t(i)^{-\frac{1}{\theta_N}} = \frac{W_t(i)}{W_t(J)} N_t(j)^{-\frac{1}{\theta_N}} \tag{6.186}$$

and raising both sides of (6.186) to $-\theta_N$, it follows

$$N_t(i) = \left(\frac{W_t(i)}{W_t(j)}\right)^{-\theta_N} N_t(j) \tag{6.187}$$

Expression (6.187) gives the demand for i-th labor as a function of relative wage at time t.

The representative trade union is assumed to operate in a context (similar to a perfectly competitive sector) of zero profit. From this condition, it follows

$$W_t N_t = \int_0^1 W_t(i) N_t(i) di = \int_0^1 W_t(i) \left(\frac{W_t(i)}{W_t}\right)^{-\theta_N} N_t di$$

That is to say

$$W_t = \int_0^1 W_t(i)\left(\frac{W_t(i)}{W_t}\right)^{-\theta_N} di \tag{6.188}$$

which is equivalent to

$$W_t^{1-\theta_N} = \int_0^1 W_t(i)^{1-\theta_N} di \tag{6.189}$$

from which the aggregate wage index follows:

$$W_t = \left[\int_0^1 W_t(i)^{1-\theta_N} di\right]^{\frac{1}{1-\theta_N}} \tag{6.190}$$

The overall supply of labor to the economy, as has been said, is an aggregation of a set of specific quantities of labor $N_t(i)$, requested from households by the representative union, and therefore must be valid:

$$N(t) = \int_0^1 N_t(i)di \tag{6.191}$$

Taking into account demands of specific types of work by the representative union follows

$$N(t) = \int_0^1 \left(\frac{W_t(i)}{W_t}\right)^{-\theta_N} N(t)di \tag{6.192}$$

By setting

$$N(t) = N(t)\int_0^1 \left(\frac{W_t(i)}{W_t}\right)^{-\theta_N} di \tag{6.193}$$

Equation (6.193) requires

$$\int_0^1 \left(\frac{W_t(i)}{W_t}\right)^{-\theta_N} di = 1 \tag{6.194}$$

The expression $\int_0^1 \left(\frac{W_t(i)}{W_t}\right)^{-\theta_N} di$ is an index of the dispersion of specific wages regarding the aggregate wage.

Setting (6.194) to unit indicates that there is no dispersion between monetary wages of various types of labor or that on average higher wages are compensated by lower ones compared to the one of the economy.

The absence of inhomogeneity between wages, however, depends on having admitted in the problem of the representative union that the quantity of labor made available for the economy through CES technology coincides with actual employment.

If we admit that the two may differ, i.e., if we assume that labor input available for the economy is the one resulting from the CES aggregation

$$N_d(t) = \left[\int_0^1 N_t(i)^{\frac{\theta_N - 1}{\theta_N}} di\right]^{\frac{\theta_N}{\theta_N - 1}} \tag{6.195}$$

in this case, aggregate supply of labor results from the aggregation

$$N(t) = \int_0^1 \left(\frac{W_t(i)}{W_t}\right)^{-\theta_N} N_d(t) di = N_d(t) \int_0^1 \left(\frac{W_t(i)}{W_t}\right)^{-\theta_N} di \tag{6.196}$$

Setting $v^d(t) = \int_0^1 \left(\frac{W_t(i)}{W_t}\right)^{-\theta_N} di$ follows

$$N(t) = v^d(t) N_d(t) \tag{6.197}$$

In general, it can now also be $N(t) \neq N_d(t)$ unless $v^d(t) = 1$. In particular, the quantity of aggregate labor supplied by households $N(t)$is greater than the quantity $N_d(t)$ (employment) which is made available (demanded) by firms if $v^d(t) > 1$, since in this case, trivially, it results $\frac{N(t)}{N_d(t)} > 1$.

6.12.1 Households

There is a continuum of families indexed by i∈[0, 1]. These households set monetary wages for their specific work in a context of monopolistic competition and in this determination, they are subject to a Calvo-type friction, which means that there will be heterogeneous labor inputs and heterogeneous wages, and therefore differentiated labor income. There are also bonds, conditioned by the state of nature, which insure households against idiosyncratic wage risk.[25] If utility is separable in consumption

[25] State-of-nature bonds operate as a sort of income insurance, upon the occurrence of the state of nature, for which the bond pays the corresponding value. Indeed, it is as if the security "insured" the corresponding value to the owner, upon the occurrence of the expected state of nature, and the purchase price of this security is equivalent to an "insurance premium." If a complete security

and labor (which is assumed here), households will be identical on all margins except labor supply and wages. This allows us to suppress the dependence of choices on index i except for those two margins.

Household owns capital stock. It can choose also the intensity of use u(t) of this capital stock then rent capital services to firms (which correspond to the arithmetic product of physical capital times the degree of capital use).

Household pays taxes, invests, and can even choose how many securities to accumulate.

The problem of choices of i-th household is

$$\max_{C_t, N_t(i), W_t(i), u_t, K_{t+1}, B_{t+1}} E_t \sum_{n=0}^{\infty} \beta^n \nu_{t+n} \Big[\log \left[C_{t+n} - bC_{t+n-1} \right] - \psi_{t+n} \frac{N(i)_{t+n}^{1+\upsilon}}{1+\upsilon} \qquad (6.198)$$

$$sub: P_t C_t + P_t I_t + B_{t+1} \leq W_t(i) N_t(i) + R_t K_t u_t + \Pi_t - P_t T_t + (1 + i_{t-1}) B_t;$$

$$K_{t+1} = Z_t \left[1 - \frac{\kappa}{2} \left(\frac{I_t}{I_{t-1}} - 1 \right)^2 \right] I_t + (1 - \delta(u_t)) K_t;$$

$$N_t(i) = \left(\frac{W_t(i)}{W_t} \right)^{-\theta_N} N_t;$$

$$\delta(u_t) = \delta_0 + \delta_1 (u_t - 1) + \frac{\delta}{2} (u_t - 1)^2;$$

Symbols have the following meaning: β is the discount factor of future preferences, b is a measure of external consumption habits, and υ is the inverse of the Frisch elasticity of labor supply (labor elasticity to the real wage). The magnitudes ν_{t+n} and ψ_{t+n} indicate, respectively, ν_{t+n} an intertemporal shock to preferences, whereas ψ_{t+n} is an intratemporal shock to the relative evaluation of the utility of consumption and disutility of work.

Adjusting investment involves costs, and κ is a measure of these adjustment costs.

The function $\delta(u_t)$ indicates that the rate of deterioration of capital depends on the level of use of capital and captures the idea that the wear and tear of capital increases with its use. Since wear and tear is a quadratic function of the net utilization rate $u_t - 1$, the parameters δ_0, δ_1, and $\frac{\delta}{2}$ are respective coefficients of the second-degree polynomial in $u_t - 1$.

Magnitudes C_t, I_t, $N_t(i)$, and K_t are, respectively, consumption, investments, specific work of the i-th household and physical capital; Z_t is an exogenous shock

market exists, it will be possible to insure for any permissible circumstances, by paying the value of the corresponding portfolio of conditional securities of the Arrow-Debreu type.

to marginal efficiency of investments, R_t is the unit rental price of capital goods services, Π_t is nominal profit distributed by firms to household who own physical capital, and T_t is the real taxation, for the moment assumed lump-sum (flat rate); i_{t-1} indicates the nominal interest rate paid at the beginning of period t, and B_t is the nominal stock of securities owned by household at the beginning of period t.

For convenience, it is advisable, as has already been done previously, to form the Lagrangian relating to the representative family, distinguishing two parts, the part not connected to wage setting, and the part relative to wage setting, specific for each i-th household.

The Lagrangian relating to the part not connected to wage setting of representative household is

$$\max_{C_t, u_t, B_{t+1}, I_t, K_{t+1}} E_t \sum_{n=0}^{\infty} \beta^n \{\nu_{t+n} \ln (C_{t+n} - bC_{t+n-1})$$
$$+\lambda'_{t+n} \left[W(i)_{t+n} N(i)_{t+n} + R'_{t+n} K_{t+n} u_{t+n} + (1 + i_{t+n-1}) B_{t+n} + \Pi_{t+n} \right.$$
$$\left. - P_{t+n} T_{t+n} - P_{t+n} C_{t+n} - P_{t+n} I_{t+n} - B_{t+n+1}\right] + \mu_{t+n}\{Z_{t+n}$$
$$\times \left[1 - \frac{\kappa}{2}\left(\frac{I_{t+n}}{I_{t+n-1}} - 1\right)^2 I_{t+n}\right]$$
$$+[1 - \delta(u_{t+n})]K_{t+n} - K_{t+n+1}\} \tag{6.199}$$

The first-order conditions are

$$C_t: \quad \frac{\nu_t}{C_t - bC_{t-1}} - \beta b E_t \frac{\nu_{t+1}}{C_{t+1} - bC_t} - P_t \lambda'_t = 0 \;\Rightarrow$$
$$P_t \lambda'_t = \frac{\nu_t}{C_t - bC_{t-1}} - \beta b E_t \frac{\nu_{t+1}}{C_{t+1} - bC_t} \tag{6.200}$$
$$u_t: \quad \lambda'_t R'_t K_t - \mu_t \delta'(u_t) K_t = 0 \quad \Rightarrow$$
$$\lambda'_t R'_t K_t = \mu_t \delta'(u_t) K_t \tag{6.201}$$
$$B_{t+1}: \quad \beta E_t \lambda'_{t+1} (1 + i_t) - \lambda'_t = 0 \quad \Rightarrow$$
$$\lambda'_t = \beta E_t \lambda'_{t+1} (1 + i_t) \tag{6.202}$$
$$I_t: \; - P_t \lambda'_t + \mu_t Z_t \left[\left(1 - \frac{\kappa}{2}\left(\frac{I_t}{I_{t-1}} - 1\right)^2 - \kappa\left(\frac{I_t}{I_{t-1}} - 1\right) \frac{I_t}{I_{t-1}}\right]\right.$$
$$+\beta E_t \mu_{t+1} Z_{t+1} \kappa \left(\frac{I_{t+1}}{I_t} - 1\right)\left(\frac{I_{t+1}}{I_t}\right)^2 = 0 \quad \Rightarrow$$

$$P_t\lambda'_t = \mu_t Z_t \left[\left(1 - \frac{\kappa}{2}\left(\frac{I_t}{I_{t-1}} - 1\right)^2 - \kappa\left(\frac{I_t}{I_{t-1}} - 1\right)\frac{I_t}{I_{t-1}}\right]\right.$$
$$+ \beta E_t \mu_{t+1} Z_{t+1} \kappa \left(\frac{I_{t+1}}{I_t} - 1\right)\left(\frac{I_{t+1}}{I_t}\right)^2 \tag{6.203}$$

$$K_{t+1}: \quad \beta E_t\left(\lambda'_{t+1} R'_{t+1} u_{t+1} + \mu_{t+1}[1 - \delta(u_{t+1})] - \mu_t = 0 \Rightarrow\right.$$
$$\mu_t = \beta E_t\left(\lambda'_{t+1} u_{t+1} + \mu_{t+1}[1 - \delta(u_{t+1})]\right) \tag{6.204}$$

To rewrite the first-order conditions in real terms, let

$$\lambda_t = P_t \lambda'_t; R_t = \frac{R'_t}{P_t}; \left(P_t \lambda'_t \frac{R'_{t+1}}{P_t} = \lambda_t R_t\right) \qquad \text{and}$$
$$1 + \pi_{t+1} = \frac{P_{t+1}}{P_t} \tag{6.205}$$

You can rewrite

$$C_t: \qquad \lambda_t = \frac{\nu_t}{C_t - bC_{t-1}} - \beta b E_t \frac{\nu_{t+1}}{C_{t+1} - bC_t} \tag{6.206}$$

$$u_t: \qquad P_t \lambda'_t \frac{R'_t}{P_t} = \lambda_t R_t = \mu_t \delta'(u_t) \tag{6.207}$$

$$B_{t+1}: \qquad \lambda_t = \beta E_t \lambda_{t+1} \frac{1 + i_t}{1 + \pi_{t+1}} \tag{6.208}$$

$$I_t: \quad \lambda_t = \mu_t Z_t \left[\left(1 - \frac{\kappa}{2}\left(\frac{I_t}{I_{t-1}} - 1\right)^2 - \kappa\left(\frac{I_t}{I_{t-1}} - 1\right)\frac{I_t}{I_{t-1}}\right]\right.$$
$$+ \beta E_t \mu_{t+1} Z_{t+1} \kappa \left(\frac{I_{t+1}}{I_t} - 1\right)\left(\frac{I_{t+1}}{I_t}\right)^2 \tag{6.209}$$

$$\mu_t = \beta E_t\left[\lambda_{t+1} R_{t+1} u_{t+1} + \mu_{t+1}(1 - \delta(u_{t+1}))\right] \tag{6.210}$$

Now consider the other part of the Lagrangian related to wage setting.

In each period, a randomly selected fraction of households have probabilities $1 - \theta_w$ to adjust wages, and conversely, a fraction θ_w of households will not be able to adjust their nominal wages. Households that are not called to update their money wages are assumed to have wages indexed to the rate of inflation, lagged at a rate $\zeta_w \in [0, 1]$.

In other words, the wage of period t of a household i-th who cannot freely choose desired money wage is automatically set to $(1 + \pi_{t-1})^{\zeta_w} W_{t-1}(i)$, being $W_{t-1}(i)$ specific wage of the previous period.

Mathematically

$$W_t(i) = \begin{cases} W_t^*(i) & \text{if } W_t(i) \text{ is chosen optimally} \\ (1+\pi_{t-1})^{\zeta_w} W_{t-1}(i) & \text{otherwise} \end{cases} \tag{6.211}$$

The failing-to-adjust wage, applied in each subsequent period, due to indexation, will be

$$\begin{aligned} W_{t+1}(i) &= (1+\pi_t)^{\zeta_w} W_t^*(i); \\ W_{t+2}(i) &= [(1+\pi_{t+1})(1+\pi_t)]^{\zeta_w} W_t^*(i) \\ &\ldots\ldots\ldots\ldots \\ &\ldots\ldots\ldots\ldots \\ W_{t+n}(i) &= \left[\prod_{J=0}^{s-1}(1+\pi_{t+j})\right]^{\zeta_w} W_t^*(i) \end{aligned} \tag{6.212}$$

where:

$$\prod_{j=0}^{n-1}(1+\pi_{t+j}) = (1+\pi_t)(1+\pi_{t+1})(1+\pi_{t+2}) \times \cdots \times (1+\pi_{t+n-1}) \tag{6.213}$$

In terms of price levels, (6.213) can be written:

$$\prod_{j=0}^{n-1}(1+\pi_{t+j}) = \frac{P_t}{P_{t-1}}\frac{P_{t+1}}{P_t}\frac{P_{t+2}}{P_{t+1}} \times \ldots \times \frac{P_{t+n-1}}{P_{t+n-2}} = \frac{P_{t+n-1}}{P_{t-1}} \tag{6.214}$$

In other words, all but the last and first terms of general price level expression cancel each other out. Thus, we can express the not revised wage in period t+n as

$$W_{t+n}(i) = \left(\frac{P_{t+n-1}}{P_{t-1}}\right)^{\zeta_w} W_t^*(i) \tag{6.215}$$

Let us now refer to the part of the Lagrangian of the household connected to the setting of wages.

A household that has the opportunity of adjusting its wage in period t knows that with probability θ_w^n, the wage chosen today will still be valid at t+n. Taking into account the overall demand for labor for the given specific job, the household will actualize the generic period t + n at the rate $(\beta\theta_w)^n$.

In setting the optimal wage, the objective of a representative household is to maximize labor income, solving the following problem:[26]

$$\max_{W_t(i)} L_t = \max E_t \sum_{n=0}^{\infty} (\beta\theta_w)^n \left\{ -\nu_{t+n}\Psi_{t+n}(1+\upsilon)^{-1} \left(\frac{\left(\frac{P_{t+n-1}}{P_{t-1}}\right)^{\zeta_w} W_t^*(i)}{W_{t+n}} \right)^{-\theta_N(1+\upsilon)} N_{t+n}^{1+\upsilon} \right.$$

$$\left. + \lambda'_{t+n} \left[\left(\frac{P_{t+n-1}}{P_{t-1}}\right)^{\zeta_w} W_t^*(i) \right]^{(1-\theta_N)} (W_{t+n})^{\theta_N} N_{t+n} \right\} \tag{6.216}$$

The first-order condition for $W_t^*(i)$ is

$$\theta_N \left(W_t^*(i)^{-\theta_N(1+\upsilon)-1} E_t \sum_{n=0}^{\infty} \left((\beta\theta_w)^n \nu_{t+n}\Psi_{t+n} \left(\frac{P_{t+n-1}}{P_{t-1}}\right)^{-\zeta_w\theta_N(1+\upsilon)} (W_{t+n})^{\theta_N(1+\upsilon)} N_{t+n}^{1+\upsilon} \right.\right.$$

$$+(1-\theta_N) \left(W_t^*(i)^{-\theta_N} E_t \sum_{n=0}^{\infty} \left((\beta\theta_w)^n \lambda'_{t+n} \left(\frac{P_{t+n-1}}{P_{t-1}}\right)^{\zeta_w(1-\theta_N)} (W_{t+n})^{\theta_N} N_{t+n} = 0 \right.\right.$$

$$\tag{6.217}$$

After some mathematical steps,[27] you have

[26]The last term of the Lagrangian, $\lambda'_{t+n}(W_{t+n}(i)N_{t+n}(i)$ referring to wage income that cannot be adjusted at time t+n, is obtained by rewriting

$$\lambda'_{t+n}(W_{t+n}(i))N_{t+n}(i) = \lambda'_{t+n} \left(\frac{P_{t+n-1}}{P_{t-1}}\right)^{\zeta_w} W_t^*(i) N_{t+n}(i)$$

$$= \lambda'_{t+n} \left(\frac{P_{t+n-1}}{P_{t-1}}\right)^{\zeta_w} W_t^*(i) \left(\frac{W_{t+n}(i)}{W_{t+n}}\right)^{-\theta_N} N_{t+n}$$

$$= \lambda'_{t+n} \left(\frac{P_{t+n-1}}{P_{t-1}}\right)^{\zeta_w} \left(\frac{P_{t+n-1}}{P_{t-1}}\right)^{-\zeta_w\theta_N} (W_t^*(i))^{1-\theta_N} (W_{t+n})^{\theta_N} N_{t+n}$$

$$= \lambda'_{t+n} \left(\frac{P_{t+n-1}}{P_{t-1}}\right)^{\zeta_w(1-\theta_N)} (W_t^*(i))^{1-\theta_N} (W_{t+n})^{\theta_N} N_{t+n}$$

$$= \lambda'_{t+n} \left[\left(\frac{P_{t+n-1}}{P_{t-1}}\right)^{\zeta_w} W_t^*(i) \right]^{(1-\theta_N)} (W_{t+n})^{\theta_N} N_{t+n}.$$

[27]By simplifying, it follows

$$\theta_N \left(W_t^*(i)^{-\theta_N(1+\upsilon)-1} E_t \sum_{n=0}^{\infty} (\beta\theta_w)^n \nu_{t+n}\Psi_{t+n} \left(\frac{P_{t+n-1}}{P_{t-1}}\right)^{-\zeta_w\theta_N(1+\upsilon)} (W_{t+n})^{\theta_N(1+\upsilon)} N_{t+n}^{1+\upsilon} \right.$$

$$= (\theta_N - 1) \left(W_t^*(i)^{-\theta_N} E_t \sum_{n=0}^{\infty} \left((\beta\theta_w)^n \lambda'_{t+n} \left(\frac{P_{t+n-1}}{P_{t-1}}\right)^{\zeta_w(1-\theta_N)} (W_{t+n})^{\theta_N} N_{t+n} \right.\right.$$

That is,

$$W_t^*(i)^{(1+\theta_N v)} = \frac{\theta_N}{(\theta_N - 1)} \frac{E_t \sum_{n=0}^{\infty} (\beta\theta_w)^n \nu_{t+n} \Psi_{t+n} \left(\frac{P_{t+n-1}}{P_{t-1}}\right)^{-\zeta_w \theta_N (1+v)} (W_{t+n})^{\theta_N(1+v)} N_{t+n}}{E_t \sum_{n=0}^{\infty} \left((\beta\theta_w)^n \lambda'_{t+n} \left(\frac{P_{t+n-1}}{P_{t-1}}\right)^{\zeta_w (1-\theta_N)} (W_{t+n})^{\theta_N} N_{t+n}\right.} \tag{6.218}$$

Note that the term on the right of the equality sign does not depend on the i-th index and is the same for all households, so the term on the left will also be identical for all households, which, when they readjust the optimal money wage, will all set it at the same level.

Furthermore, in the absence of stickiness, for $\theta_w = 0$, it turns out

$$W_t^* = \frac{\theta_N}{(\theta_N - 1)} \frac{\nu_t \Psi_t \; N_t^v}{\lambda'_t}.$$

It is now useful to obtain an expression of the real wage

$$w_t = \frac{W_t^*}{P_t}.$$

The expression of optimal monetary wages can be rewritten as

$$W_t^{*(1+\theta_N v)} = \frac{\theta_N}{(\theta_N - 1)} \frac{H_{1,t}}{H_{2,t}} = \frac{\theta_N}{(\theta_N - 1)} \frac{\frac{H_{1,t}}{P_t^{\theta_N(1+v)}} P_t^{\theta_N(1+v)}}{\frac{H_{2,t}}{P_t^{\theta_N - 1}} P_t^{\theta_N - 1}} \tag{6.219}$$

where at numerator, it is

$\frac{\theta_N}{(\theta_N - 1)} \left(W_t^*(i)^{-(1+\theta_N v)} E_t \sum_{n=0}^{\infty} (\beta\theta_w)^n \nu_{t+n} \Psi_{t+n} \left(\frac{P_{t+n-1}}{P_{t-1}}\right)^{-\zeta_w \theta_N (1+v)} (W_{t+n})^{\theta_N(1+v)} N_{t+n}\right.$

$= E_t \sum_{n=0}^{\infty} \left((\beta\theta_w)^n \lambda'_{t+n} \left(\frac{P_{t+n-1}}{P_{t-1}}\right)^{\zeta_w (1-\theta_N)} (W_{t+n})^{\theta_N} N_{t+n}\right.$ from which solving for $W_t^*(i)^{(1+\theta_N v)}$, the first-order condition (6.218) is obtained.

$$
\begin{aligned}
\mathrm{H}_{1,\mathrm{t}} &= E_t \sum_{n=0}^{\infty} (\beta\theta_w)^n \upsilon_{t+n} \Psi_{\mathrm{t+n}} \left(\frac{P_{t+n-1}}{P_{t-1}}\right)^{-\zeta_w \theta_N(1+\upsilon)} \left(\frac{W_{t+n}}{P_{t+n}}\right)^{\theta_N(1+\upsilon)} (P_{t+n})^{\theta_N(1+\upsilon)} N_{t+n} \\
&= E_t \sum_{n=0}^{\infty} (\beta\theta_w)^n \upsilon_{t+n} \Psi_{\mathrm{t+n}} \left(\frac{P_{t+n-1}}{P_{t-1}}\right)^{-\zeta_w \theta_N(1+\upsilon)} w_{t+n}{}^{\theta_N(1+\upsilon)} (P_{t+n})^{\theta_N(1+\upsilon)} N_{t+n}^{1+\upsilon}
\end{aligned}
\tag{6.220}
$$

And at denominator is

$$
\begin{aligned}
H_{2,t} &= E_t \sum_{n=0}^{\infty} (\beta\theta_w)^n \lambda'_{t+n} \left(\frac{P_{t+n-1}}{P_{t-1}}\right)^{\zeta_w(1-\theta_N)} W_{t+n}{}^{\theta_N} N_{t+n} \\
&= E_t \sum_{n=0}^{\infty} (\beta\theta_w)^n \lambda_{t+n} \left(\frac{P_{t+n-1}}{P_{t-1}}\right)^{\zeta_w(1-\theta_N)} w_{t+n}{}^{\theta_N} (P_{t+n})^{\theta_N - 1} N_{t+n}
\end{aligned}
\tag{6.221}
$$

By defining $\frac{\mathrm{H}_{1,\mathrm{t}}}{P_t{}^{\theta_N(1+\upsilon)}} = \mathrm{h}_{1,\mathrm{t}}$ and $\frac{H_{2,t}}{P_t{}^{\theta_N - 1}} = \mathrm{h}_{2,\mathrm{t}}$, you have

$$
\begin{aligned}
W_t^{*(1+\theta_N\upsilon)} &= \frac{\theta_N}{(\theta_N - 1)} \frac{\mathrm{h}_{1,\mathrm{t}}}{\mathrm{h}_{2,\mathrm{t}}} \frac{P_t{}^{\theta_N(1+\upsilon)}}{P_t{}^{\theta_N - 1}} \\
&= \frac{\theta_N}{(\theta_N - 1)} \frac{\mathrm{h}_{1,\mathrm{t}}}{\mathrm{h}_{2,\mathrm{t}}} P_t{}^{\theta_N + \theta_N\upsilon} P_t{}^{1-\theta_N} = \frac{\theta_N}{(\theta_N - 1)} \frac{\mathrm{h}_{1,\mathrm{t}}}{\mathrm{h}_{2,\mathrm{t}}} P_t{}^{(1+\theta_N\upsilon)}
\end{aligned}
\tag{6.222}
$$

This in terms of the optimal real wage is written as

$$
\frac{W_t^{*(1+\theta_N\upsilon)}}{P_t{}^{(1+\theta_N\upsilon)}} = w_t^{*(1+\theta_N\upsilon)} = \frac{\theta_N}{(\theta_N - 1)} \frac{\mathrm{h}_{1,\mathrm{t}}}{\mathrm{h}_{2,\mathrm{t}}}
\tag{6.223}
$$

Equations (6.222) and (6.223) both characterize the process of setting the optimal wage, respectively, the money wage and the real wage. By redefining

$$
w_t^{*(1+\theta_N\upsilon)} = \frac{\theta_N}{(\theta_N - 1)} \frac{\frac{\mathrm{h}_{1,\mathrm{t}}}{w_t^{*\theta_N(1+\upsilon)}} w_t^{*\theta_N(1+\upsilon)}}{\frac{\mathrm{h}_{2,\mathrm{t}}}{w_t^{*\theta_N}} w_t^{*\theta_N}}
$$

and setting $\widehat{\mathrm{h}}_{1,\mathrm{t}} = \frac{\mathrm{h}_{1,\mathrm{t}}}{w_t^{*\theta_N(1+\upsilon)}}$ and $\widehat{\mathrm{h}}_{2,\mathrm{t}} = \frac{\mathrm{h}_{2,\mathrm{t}}}{w_t^{*\theta_N}}$, Eq. (6.223) of real wage becomes

$$w_t^{*(1+\theta_N \upsilon)} = \frac{\theta_N}{(\theta_N - 1)} \frac{\widehat{\mathrm{h}}_{1,\mathrm{t}}}{\widehat{\mathrm{h}}_{2,\mathrm{t}}} w_t^{*\theta_N (1+\upsilon)} w_t^{* - \theta_N} = \frac{\theta_N}{(\theta_N - 1)} \frac{\widehat{\mathrm{h}}_{1,\mathrm{t}}}{\widehat{\mathrm{h}}_{2,\mathrm{t}}} w_t^{*\theta_N \upsilon} \tag{6.224}$$

so that the optimal real wage ultimately turns out:

$$w_t^* = \frac{\theta_N}{(\theta_N - 1)} \frac{\widehat{\mathrm{h}}_{1,\mathrm{t}}}{\widehat{\mathrm{h}}_{2,\mathrm{t}}} \tag{6.225}$$

In the same way, defining $\widehat{\mathrm{H}}_{1,\mathrm{t}} = \frac{\mathrm{H}_{1,\mathrm{t}}}{W_t^{*\theta_N (1+\upsilon)}}$ and $\widehat{\mathrm{H}}_{2,\mathrm{t}} = \frac{H_{2,t}}{W_t^{*\theta_N}}$, also the monetary wage can be set as

$$W_t^{*(1+\theta_N \upsilon)} = \frac{\theta_N}{(\theta_N - 1)} \frac{\frac{\mathrm{H}_{1,\mathrm{t}}}{W_t^{*\theta_N (1+\upsilon)}} W_t^{*\theta_N (1+\upsilon)}}{\frac{H_{2,t}}{W_t^* (i)^{\theta_N}} W^{\theta_N}}$$

$$= \frac{\theta_N}{(\theta_N - 1)} \frac{\widehat{\mathrm{H}}_{1,\mathrm{t}}}{\widehat{\mathrm{H}}_{2,\mathrm{t}}} W_t^{*\theta_N \upsilon} \tag{6.226}$$

So that, in a symmetric way to real wage, the level of monetary wage becomes

$$W_t^*(i) = \frac{\theta_N}{(\theta_N - 1)} \frac{\widehat{\mathrm{H}}_{1,\mathrm{t}}}{\widehat{\mathrm{H}}_{2,\mathrm{t}}} \tag{6.227}$$

To calculate the steady state, it is appropriate to transform the expressions of $\mathrm{H}_{1,\ \mathrm{t}}$, $\mathrm{H}_{2,\ \mathrm{t}}$, $\mathrm{h}_{1,\ \mathrm{t}}$, $\mathrm{h}_{2,\ \mathrm{t}}$, and also those of $\widehat{\mathrm{h}}_{1,\mathrm{t}}$, $\widehat{\mathrm{h}}_{2,\mathrm{t}}$. For each of these quantities, a recursive relation will be obtained in which the expression at time t is a function of the same expression at time t+1. Starting with $\mathrm{H}_{1,\ \mathrm{t}}$, the recursive form follows from the following steps:[28]

[28] Here, it is useful to review a bit of mathematics. To obtain the recursive form, from a sum of infinite terms, let x_{t} ; $0 < \beta < 1$ and $y_t = \sum_{k=0}^{\infty} \beta^k x_{t+k}$. By moving the time index of one period forward from t to t+1, it is

$y_{t+1} = \sum_{k=0}^{\infty} \beta^k x_{t+1+k}$. From $y_t = \sum_{k=0}^{\infty} \beta^k x_{t+k}$, it follows

$$y_t = \sum_{k=0}^{\infty} \beta^{k+1} x_{t+1+k} + \beta^0 x_{t+0} = \beta \sum_{k=0}^{\infty} \beta^k x_{t+1+k} + x_t$$

But the summation at the first term is indeed y_{t+1}, and therefore, $\beta \sum_{k=0}^{\infty} \beta^k x_{t+1+k} + x_t = \beta\ y_{t+1} + x_t$, and this provides the recurrence form $y_t = \beta\ y_{t+1} + x_t$.

The opposite passage, from the form by recurrence to the representation as a sum of infinite terms, uses the lag operator L. From $y_t = \beta\ y_{t+1} + x_t$, it follows $y_t - \beta\ \mathrm{L}^{-1}\ y_t = x_t$; that is,

$$\mathrm{H}_{1,t}=\nu_t\Psi_t w_t^{\theta_N(1+\upsilon)}P_t^{\theta_N(1+\upsilon)}N_t^{1+\upsilon}E_t\sum_{n=1}^{\infty}(\beta\theta_w)^n\nu_{t+n}\Psi_{t+n}\left(\frac{P_{t+n-1}}{P_{t-1}}\right)^{-\zeta_w\theta_N(1+\upsilon)}(w_{t+n})^{\theta_N(1+\upsilon)}(P_{t+n})^{\theta_N(1+\upsilon)}N_{t+n}^{1+\upsilon}$$

$$=\nu_t\Psi_t w_t^{\theta_N(1+\upsilon)}P_t^{\theta_N(1+\upsilon)}N_t^{1+\upsilon}$$

$$+E_t\left(\frac{P_t}{P_{t-1}}\right)^{-\zeta_w\theta_N(1+\upsilon)}E_t\sum_{n=0}^{\infty}(\beta\theta_w)^n\nu_{t+1+n}\Psi_{t+1+n}\left(\frac{P_{t+1+n-1}}{P_{t-1}}\right)^{-\zeta_w\theta_N(1+\upsilon)}(w_{t+1+n})^{\theta_N(1+\upsilon)}(P_{t+1+n})^{\theta_N(1+\upsilon)}N_{t+1+n}^{1+\upsilon}$$

$$=\nu_t\Psi_t w_t^{\theta_N(1+\upsilon)}P_t^{\theta_N(1+\upsilon)}N_t^{1+\upsilon}+\beta\theta_w\ E_t\left(\frac{P_t}{P_{t-1}}\right)^{-\zeta_w\theta_N(1+\upsilon)}H_{1,t+1} \tag{6.228}$$

In the same way, for $H_{2,\ t}$is obtained[29]

$(1-\beta\,\mathrm{L}^{-1})\,y_t=x_t$, from which
$y_t=(1-\beta\,\mathrm{L}^{-1})^{-1}x_t=$
$(1+\beta\,\mathrm{L}^{-1}+\beta^2\,\mathrm{L}^{-2}+\ldots+\beta^k\,\mathrm{L}^{-k}+\ldots)x_t=$
$\sum_{k=0}^{\infty}(\beta^k L^{-k})x_t=\sum_{k=0}^{\infty}\beta^k L^{-k}x_t=\sum_{k=0}^{\infty}\beta^k x_{t+k}$

[29] Since $H_{2,t}=E_t\sum_{n=0}^{\infty}(\beta\theta_w)^n\lambda_{t+n}\left(\frac{P_{t+n-1}}{P_{t-1}}\right)^{\zeta_w(1-\theta_N)}(w_{t+n})^{\theta_N}(P_{t+n})^{\theta_N-1}N_{t+n}$ moving the time index t one step forward:

$$H_{2,t+1}=E_t\sum_{n=0}^{\infty}(\beta\theta_w)^n\lambda_{t+1+n}\left(\frac{P_{t+1+n-1}}{P_{t+1-1}}\right)^{\zeta_w(1-\theta_N)}(w_{t+1+n})^{\theta_N}(P_{t+1+n})^{\theta_N-1}N_{t+1+n}$$

Now consider the expression

$$H_{2,t}=\lambda_t w_t^{\theta_N}(P_t)^{\theta_N}N_t$$
$$+E_t\sum_{n=1}^{\infty}(\beta\theta_w)^n\lambda_{t+n}\left(\frac{P_{t+n-1}}{P_{t-1}}\right)^{\zeta_w(1-\theta_N)}w_{t+n}^{\theta_N}(P_{t+n})^{\theta_N-1}N_{t+n}$$

The summation which starts from the index n = 1 in this expression can be started from the index n = 0 by increasing the index itself by one unit, i.e., by setting

$\mathrm{E}_t\sum_{n=1}^{\infty}(\beta\theta_w)^n\lambda_{t+n}\left(\frac{P_{t+n-1}}{P_{t-1}}\right)^{\zeta_w(1-\theta_N)}(w_{t+n})^{\theta_N}(P_{t+n})^{\theta_N-1}N_{t+n}$
$=E_t\sum_{n=0}^{\infty}(\beta\theta_w)^{n+1}\lambda_{t+n+1}\left(\frac{P_{t+n+1-1}}{P_{t-1}}\right)^{\zeta_w(1-\theta_N)}(w_{t+n+1})^{\theta_N}(P_{t+n+1})^{\theta_N-1}N_{t+n+1}.$

But

$$\left(\frac{P_{t+n+1-1}}{P_{t-1}}\right)^{\zeta_w(1-\theta_N)}=\left(\frac{P_{t+n+1-1}}{P_{t+1-1}}\frac{P_{t+1-1}}{P_{t-1}}\right)^{\zeta_w(1-\theta_N)}=\left(\frac{P_{t+n+1-1}}{P_{t+1-1}}\right)^{\zeta_w(1-\theta_N)}\left(\frac{P_{t+1-1}}{P_{t-1}}\right)^{\zeta_w(1-\theta_N)}$$

and therefore,

$$H_{2,t} = \lambda_t w_t^{\theta_N} P_t^{\theta_N - 1} N_t + \beta\theta_w E_t \left(\frac{P_t}{P_{t-1}}\right)^{\zeta_w} H_{2,t+1} \tag{6.229}$$

In terms of the inflation rate, the same expressions (6.228) and (6.229) are

$$\mathrm{H}_{1,t} = \nu_t \Psi_t w_t^{\theta_N(1+\upsilon)} P_t^{\theta_N(1+\upsilon)} N_t^{1+\upsilon} + \beta\theta_w\ E_t(1+\pi_t)^{-\zeta_w\theta_N(1+\upsilon)} H_{1,t+1} \tag{6.230}$$

$$H_{2,t} = \lambda_t w_t^{\theta_N} P_t^{\theta_N - 1} N_t + \beta\theta_w E_t (1+\pi_t)^{\zeta_w(1-\theta_N)} H_{2,t+1} \tag{6.231}$$

To replace the price level, that still appears in the expressions (6.230) and (6.231), with the inflation rate, we can refer to the equivalent expressions of $\mathrm{h}_{1,\ t}$ and $\mathrm{h}_{2,\ t}$.

Being $\mathrm{h}_{1,t} = \frac{\mathrm{H}_{1,t}}{P_t^{\theta_N(1+\upsilon)}}$, by dividing (6.230) at both sides for $P_t^{\theta_N(1+\upsilon)}$, it follows[30]

$$\mathrm{h}_{1,t} = \nu_t \Psi_t w_t^{\theta_N(1+\upsilon)} N_t^{1+\upsilon}$$
$$+\beta\theta_w\ (1+\pi_t)^{-\zeta_w\theta_N(1+\upsilon)} E_t(1+\pi_{t+1})^{\theta_N(1+\upsilon)} \mathrm{h}_{1,t+1} \tag{6.232}$$

Analogously, being $\mathrm{h}_{2,t} = \frac{H_{2,t}}{P_t^{\theta_N - 1}}$, by dividing (6.231) at both sides for $P_t^{\theta_N - 1}$, it follows[31]

$$\mathrm{h}_{2,t} = \lambda_t w_t^{\theta_N} N_t$$
$$+\beta\theta_w (1+\pi_t)^{\zeta_w(1-\theta_N)} E_t (1+\pi_{t+1})^{\theta_N - 1} h_{2,t+1} \tag{6.233}$$

$$\mathrm{E_t} \sum_{n=0}^{\infty} (\beta\theta_w)^{n+1} \lambda_{t+n+1} \left(\frac{P_{t+n+1-1}}{P_{t-1}}\right)^{\zeta_w(1-\theta_N)} (w_{t+n+1})^{\theta_N} (P_{t+n+1})^{\theta_N - 1} N_{t+n+1}$$
$$= E_t(\beta\theta_w) \left(\frac{P_t}{P_{t-1}}\right)^{\zeta_w(1-\theta_N)} \sum_{n=0}^{\infty} (\beta\theta_w)^n \lambda_{t+n+1} \left(\frac{P_{t+n+1-1}}{P_{t+1-1}}\right)^{\zeta_w(1-\theta_N)} (w_{t+n+1})^{\theta_N} (P_{t+n+1})^{\theta_N - 1} N_{t+n+1}$$

$= (\beta\theta_w) E_t \left(\frac{P_t}{P_{t-1}}\right)^{\zeta_w(1-\theta_N)} H_{2,t+1}$. By substituting in $H_{2,\ t}$ follows (6.229).

[30]Last term in (6.232) follows from

$$\frac{P_{t+1}^{\theta_N(1+\upsilon)}}{P_t^{\theta_N(1+\upsilon)}} \frac{H_{1,t+1}}{P_{t+1}^{\theta_N(1+\upsilon)}} = E_t(1+\pi_{t+1})^{\theta_N(1+\upsilon)} \mathrm{h}_{1,t+1}.$$

[31]Also in (6.233), the last term follows from

$$\frac{H_{2,t+1}}{P_{t+1}^{\theta_N - 1}} \frac{P_{t+1}^{\theta_N - 1}}{P_t^{\theta_N - 1}} = E_t(1+\pi_{t+1})^{\theta_N - 1} h_{2,t+1}.$$

And finally, being $\widehat{\mathrm{h}}_{1,t} = \frac{\mathrm{h}_{1,t}}{w_t^{*\theta_N(1+\upsilon)}}$, by dividing (6.232) at both sides for $w_t^{*\theta_N(1+\upsilon)}$, it follows

$$\widehat{\mathrm{h}}_{1,t} = \frac{\mathrm{h}_{1,t}}{w_t^{*\theta_N(1+\upsilon)}} = \nu_t \Psi_t \left(\frac{w_t}{w_t^*}\right)^{\theta_N(1+\upsilon)} N_t^{1+\upsilon}$$

$$+\beta\theta_w(1+\pi_t)^{-\zeta_w\theta_N(1+\upsilon)} \; E_t(1+\pi_{t+1})^{\theta_N(1+\upsilon)} \frac{\mathrm{h}_{1,t+1}}{w_{t+1}^{*\;\theta_N(1+\upsilon)}} \frac{w_{t+1}^{*\;\theta_N(1+\upsilon)}}{w_t^{*\theta_N(1+\upsilon)}} \tag{6.234}$$

And therefore,

$$\widehat{\mathrm{h}}_{1,t} = \nu_t \Psi_t \left(\frac{w_t}{w_t^*}\right)^{\theta_N(1+\upsilon)} N_t^{1+\upsilon}$$

$$+\beta\theta_w(1+\pi_t)^{-\zeta_w\theta_N(1+\upsilon)} E_t(1+\pi_{t+1})^{\theta_N(1+\upsilon)} \left(\frac{w_{t+1}^*}{w_t^*}\right)^{\theta_N(1+\upsilon)} \widehat{\mathrm{h}}_{1,t+1} \tag{6.235}$$

Similarly, being $\widehat{\mathrm{h}}_{2,t} = \frac{\mathrm{h}_{2,t}}{w_t^{*\theta_N}}$, by dividing (6.233) at both sides for $w_t^{*\theta_N}$

$$\widehat{\mathrm{h}}_{2,t} = \lambda_t \left(\frac{w_t}{w_t^*}\right)^{\theta_N} N_t$$

$$+\beta\theta_w(1+\pi_t)^{\zeta_w(1-\theta_N)} E_t(1+\pi_{t+1})^{\theta_N - 1} \left(\frac{w_{t+1}^*}{w_t^*}\right)^{\theta_N} \widehat{h}_{2,t+1} \tag{6.236}$$

6.12.2 Firm Producer of the Final Good

The final good sector, as in the basic model, is made up of a representative firm that produces final good $\mathrm{Q_t}$, using intermediate goods y_{it} as inputs, and using CES technology:

$$\mathrm{Q_t} = \left[\int_0^1 y_t(i)^{\frac{\theta-1}{\theta}} di\right]^{\frac{\theta}{\theta-1}} \tag{6.237}$$

The representative firm, in a competitive context with given $\mathrm{P_t}$ and P_{it}, has the objective of maximizing profit, from whose first-order condition, the demand for the intermediate good i-th from the final sector can be deduced:

$$y_t(i) = \left(\frac{P_{it}}{\mathrm{P_t}}\right)^{-\theta} \mathrm{Q_t} \tag{6.238}$$

Conversely, from the zero-profit condition, the price at which the final good is sold is obtained.

This price represents the general price level, which is

$$\mathrm{P_t} = \left[\int_0^1 P_{it}^{1-\theta} di\right]^{\frac{1}{\theta-1}} \tag{6.239}$$

6.12.3 Firm Producer of Intermediate Goods

There is a continuum of firms $j \in [0, 1]$ each one producing the intermediate good $y_t(j)$ by utilizing the production function

$$y_t(j) = A_t \widehat{K}_t(j)^{\alpha} N_t(j)^{1-\alpha} - F \tag{6.240}$$

Symbol $\mathrm{F} \geq 0$ indicates fixed costs expressed in terms of product, while $\widehat{K}_t(j)$ indicates the amount of capital services rented from households (physical capital multiplied by the degree of use). The production of firm jth is determined by the choice of optimal quantities of inputs to be used that are the solution to a cost minimization problem, subject to a given demand for the good to be produced. From first-order conditions,[32] optimal ratio of production factors is obtained as a function of the factor's prices ratio so that

[32] The problem is

$$\min_{\widehat{K}_t(j), N_t(j)} \quad W_t N_t(j) + R'_t \widehat{K}_t(j)$$

$$\text{sub} \quad A_t \widehat{K}_t(j)^{\alpha} N_t(j)^{1-\alpha} - F = \left(\frac{P_{jt}}{\mathrm{P_t}}\right)^{-\theta} \mathrm{Q_t}$$

Setting $\gamma_t(j)$ Lagrange's multiplier, the Lagrangian is

$$W_t N_t(j) + R'_t \widehat{K}_t(j) + \gamma_t(j) \left[\left(\frac{P_{jt}}{\mathrm{P_t}}\right)^{-\theta} \mathrm{Q_t} - A_t \widehat{K}_t(j)^{\alpha} N_t(j)^{1-\alpha} + F\right]$$

The first-order conditions are

$N_t(j)$: $W_t - \gamma_t(j)(1-\alpha) A_t \widehat{K}_t(j)^{\alpha} N_t(j)^{-\alpha} = 0 \Rightarrow W_t = \gamma_t(j)(1-\alpha) A_t \left(\frac{\widehat{K}_t(j)}{N_t(j)}\right)^{\alpha}$

$\widehat{K}_t(j)$: $R'_t - \gamma_t(j) \alpha A_t \widehat{K}_t(j)^{\alpha-1} N_t(j)^{1-\alpha} = 0 \Rightarrow R'_t = \gamma_t(j) \alpha A_t \left(\frac{\widehat{K}_t(j)}{N_t(j)}\right)^{\alpha-1}$. Dividing member by member follows Eq. (6.241).

$$\frac{W_t}{R'_t} = \frac{\lambda_t(1-\alpha)A_t\left(\frac{\widehat{K_t(j)}}{N_t(j)}\right)^{\alpha}}{\lambda_t\alpha A_t\left(\frac{\widehat{K_t(j)}}{N_t(j)}\right)^{\alpha-1}} = \frac{(1-\alpha)}{\alpha}\frac{\widehat{K}_t(j)}{N_t(j)} \tag{6.241}$$

The term to the left of (6.241) does not depend on the index j so the ratio $\frac{\widehat{K_t(j)}}{N_t(j)}$ is the same for all the firms. Therefore, ignoring the index j, dividing the numerator and denominator by P_t the equivalent price ratio of production factors in real terms is obtained:

$$\frac{w_t}{R_t} = \frac{(1-\alpha)}{\alpha}\frac{\widehat{K}_t}{N_t} \tag{6.242}$$

Since, as it has been seen, firms face the same price ratio and, therefore, use production factors in the same proportion, they also have the same real marginal cost. This marginal cost (considering an implicit function of the total product y(j) (N)) can be expressed regarding the labor and is the inverse of the marginal product of labor multiplied by the real wage, so we can put

$$\frac{1}{\frac{\partial y_t(j)}{\partial N_t(j)}}\mathrm{w_t} = \frac{\mathrm{w_t}}{(1-\alpha)A_t\left(\frac{\widehat{K_t(j)}}{N_t(j)}\right)^{\alpha}} = \frac{\mathrm{w_t}}{(1-\alpha)A_t\left(\frac{\widehat{K_t}}{N_t}\right)^{\alpha}} = mc_t \tag{6.243}$$

Note that from the first-order conditions, it follows

$$\frac{W_t}{P_t} = \frac{\gamma_t(j)}{P_t}(1-\alpha)A_t\left(\frac{\widehat{K}_t(j)}{N_t(j)}\right)^{\alpha} \tag{6.244}$$

From (6.244) is obtained

$$mc_t = \frac{\frac{\gamma_t(j)}{P_t}(1-\alpha)A_t\left(\frac{\widehat{K_t(j)}}{N_t(j)}\right)^{\alpha}}{(1-\alpha)A_t\left(\frac{\widehat{K_t(j)}}{N_t(j)}\right)^{\alpha}} = \frac{\gamma_t(j))}{P_t}$$

This allows the nominal profit of firm j-th to be rewritten as follows:

$$\Pi_t(j) = P_t(j)y_t(j) - \gamma_t(j)y_t(i) = P_t(j)y_t(j) - P_t\, mc_t y_t(i) \tag{6.245}$$

Firms set prices of intermediate goods according to the Calvo procedure. Each period a firm j-th has a probability $1-\theta_p$ to adjust its price. If it is unable to adjust the price optimally, it can partially index the current price to the past period's aggregate inflation at the rate $\zeta_p \in [0,1]$.

Therefore, the price that a firm can set in period t is

$$P_t(j) = \begin{cases} P^*{}_t(j) & \textit{if } P_t(j) \textit{ is chosen optimally} \\ (1+\pi_{t-1})^{\zeta_p}\, P_{t-1}(j) & \text{otherwise} \end{cases} \tag{6.246}$$

If the firm does not have the opportunity to adjust optimally in period t+1, the current price will be

$$P_{t+1}(j) = (1+\pi_t)^{\zeta_p} P^*{}_t(j) \tag{6.247}$$

If the firm does not have the opportunity to adjust optimally in period t+2, the current price will be

$$\begin{aligned} P_{t+2}(j) &= (1+\pi_{t+1})^{\zeta_p} P_{t+1}(j) = (1+\pi_{t+1})^{\zeta_p}(1+\pi_t)^{\zeta_p} P^*{}_t(j) \\ &= [(1+\pi_{t+1})(1+\pi_t)]^{\zeta_p}\, P^*{}_t(j) \end{aligned} \tag{6.248}$$

If firm does not have the opportunity to adjust optimally in period t+n, the current price will be

$$\begin{aligned} P_{t+n}(j) &= (1+\pi_{t+n-1})^{\zeta_p}..(1+\pi_t)^{\zeta_p}(1+\pi_{t-1})^{\zeta_p} P^*{}_t(j) \\ &= \prod_{g=0}^{n-1} (1+\pi_{t+g})^{\zeta_p} P^*{}_t(j) \end{aligned} \tag{6.249}$$

Since

$$\Big[(1+\pi_{t+n-1})..((1+\pi_t)(1+\pi_{t-1})]^{\zeta_p} = \left(\frac{P_{t+n-1}}{P_{t+n-2}}\frac{P_{t+n-2}}{P_{t+n-3}}\cdots\frac{P_t}{P_{t-1}}\right)^{\zeta_p} = \left(\frac{P_{t+n-1}}{P_{t-1}}\right)^{\zeta_p} \tag{6.250}$$

So it is

$$P_{t+n}(j) = \left(\frac{P_{t+n-1}}{P_{t-1}}\right)^{\zeta_p} P^*{}_t(j) \tag{6.251}$$

Consider now the optimal price at time t.

The firm chooses a price that maximizes profit, regarding the period for which the chosen price can be expected to be valid with the respective probability.

The firm discounts the flow of nominal profits at the stochastic discount rate used by households:

$$\frac{1}{(1+i_t)^n} = \frac{\beta^n E_t \lambda'_{t+n}}{\lambda'_t} \tag{6.252}$$

The instantaneous profit function is

$$P_{t+n}(j) y_{t+n}(j) - P_{t+n} mc_{t+n} y_{t+n}(j) \tag{6.253}$$

Taking into account that for the j-th intermediate good, given the demand function, it holds

$$y_{t+n}(j) = \left(\frac{P_{t+n}(j)}{P_{t+n}}\right)^{-\theta} Q_{t+n} = \left[\frac{\left(\frac{P_{t+n-1}}{P_{t-1}}\right)^{\zeta_p} P^*{}_t(j)}{P_{t+n}}\right]^{-\theta} Q_{t+n} \tag{6.254}$$

The total revenue function is

$$P_{t+n}(j) y_{t+n}(j) = \left(\frac{P_{t+n-1}}{P_{t-1}}\right)^{\zeta_p} P^*{}_t(j) \left[\frac{\left(\frac{P_{t+n-1}}{P_{t-1}}\right)^{\zeta_p} P^*{}_t(j)}{P_{t+n}}\right]^{-\theta} Q_{t+n} \tag{6.255}$$

Similarly, the total cost function is

$$\begin{aligned} P_{t+n} mc_{t+n} y_{t+n}(j) &= P_{t+n} mc_{t+n} \left[\frac{\left(\frac{P_{t+n-1}}{P_{t-1}}\right)^{\zeta_p} P^*{}_t(j)}{P_{t+n}}\right]^{-\theta} Q_{t+n} \\ &= mc_{t+n} \left(\frac{P_{t+n-1}}{P_{t-1}}\right)^{-\zeta_p \theta} P_t^*(j)^{-\theta} P_{t+n}^{1+\theta} Q_{t+n} \end{aligned} \tag{6.256}$$

The intertemporal profit function to be maximized is

$$\begin{aligned} \max_{P_t^*(j)} E_t \sum_{n=0}^{\infty} (\beta\theta_p)^n \frac{\lambda'_{t+n}}{\lambda'_t} &\left[\left(\frac{P_{t+n-1}}{P_{t-1}}\right)^{\zeta_p(1-\theta)} P_t^*(j)^{1-\theta} P_{t+n}{}^{\theta} Q_{t+n}\right. \\ &\left. - mc_{t+n} \left(\frac{P_{t+n-1}}{P_{t-1}}\right)^{-\zeta_p \theta} P_t^*(j)^{-\theta} P_{t+n}^{1+\theta} Q_{t+n}\right] \end{aligned} \tag{6.257}$$

The first-order condition for $P_t^*(j)$ is

$$(1-\theta)P_t^*(j)^{-\theta}E_t\sum_{n=0}^{\infty}(\beta\theta_p)^n\frac{\lambda'_{t+n}}{\lambda'_t}\left[\left(\frac{P_{t+n-1}}{P_{t-1}}\right)^{\zeta_p(1-\theta)}P_{t+n}{}^{\theta}Q_{t+n}\right]$$

$$+\theta\, P_t^*(j)^{-\theta-1}E_t\sum_{n=0}^{\infty}(\beta\theta_p)^n\frac{\lambda'_{t+n}}{\lambda'_t}\left[mc_{t+n}\left(\frac{P_{t+n-1}}{P_{t-1}}\right)^{-\zeta_p\theta}P_{t+n}^{1+\theta}Q_{t+n}\right]=0 \quad (6.258)$$

And solving for $P_t^*(j)$, it is obtained

$$P_t^*(j)=\frac{\theta}{(\theta-1)}\frac{E_t\sum_{n=0}^{\infty}(\beta\theta_p)^n\frac{\lambda'_{t+n}}{\lambda'_t}\left[mc_{t+n}\left(\frac{P_{t+n-1}}{P_{t-1}}\right)^{-\zeta_p\theta}P_{t+n}^{1+\theta}Q_{t+n}\right]}{E_t\sum_{n=0}^{\infty}(\beta\theta_p)^n\frac{\lambda'_{t+n}}{\lambda'_t}\left[\left(\frac{P_{t+n-1}}{P_{t-1}}\right)^{\zeta_p(1-\theta)}P_{t+n}{}^{\theta}Q_{t+n}\right]}$$

$$=\frac{\theta}{(\theta-1)}\frac{\frac{1}{\lambda'_t}E_t\sum_{n=0}^{\infty}(\beta\theta_p)^n\lambda'_{t+n}\left[mc_{t+n}\left(\frac{P_{t+n-1}}{P_{t-1}}\right)^{-\zeta_p\theta}P_{t+n}^{1+\theta}Q_{t+n}\right]}{\frac{1}{\lambda'_t}E_t\sum_{n=0}^{\infty}(\beta\theta_p)^n\lambda'_{t+n}\left[\left(\frac{P_{t+n-1}}{P_{t-1}}\right)^{\zeta_p(1-\theta)}P_{t+n}{}^{\theta}Q_{t+n}\right]} \quad (6.259)$$

Note that the term to the right of the equality sign does not depend on the index j, and therefore, it is

$$P_t^*(j)=P_t^* \quad \forall j\in[0,1] \quad (6.260)$$

Setting

$$X_{1,t}=E_t\sum_{n=0}^{\infty}(\beta\theta_p)^n\lambda'_{t+n}\left[mc_{t+n}\left(\frac{P_{t+n-1}}{P_{t-1}}\right)^{-\zeta_p\theta}P_{t+n}^{1+\theta}Q_{t+n}\right] \quad (6.261)$$

and

$$X_{2,t}=E_t\sum_{n=0}^{\infty}(\beta\theta_p)^n\lambda'_{t+n}\left[\left(\frac{P_{t+n-1}}{P_{t-1}}\right)^{\zeta_p(1-\theta)}P_{t+n}{}^{\theta}Q_{t+n}\right] \quad (6.262)$$

the optimum pricing equation (6.259) can be written more compactly:

$$P_t^*=\frac{\theta}{(\theta-1)}\frac{X_{1,t}}{X_{2,t}} \quad (6.263)$$

Also regarding $X_{1,\,t}$, $X_{2,\,t}$, the necessary transformations can be made to write the relevant expressions in recursive form and as expressions with respect to the inflation rate. Starting with $X_{1,\,t}$, the form for recurrence follows from the following steps:

$$X_{1,t} = E_t \sum_{n=0}^{\infty} (\beta\theta_p)^n \lambda'_{t+n} \left[mc_{t+n} \left(\frac{P_{t+n-1}}{P_{t-1}} \right)^{-\zeta_p\theta} P_{t+n}^{1+\theta} Q_{t+n} \right]$$

$$= \lambda'_t mc_t P_t^{1+\theta} Q_t + E_t \sum_{n=1}^{\infty} (\beta\theta_p)^n \lambda'_{t+n} \left[mc_{t+n} \left(\frac{P_{t+n-1}}{P_{t-1}} \right)^{-\zeta_p\theta} P_{t+n}^{1+\theta} Q_{t+n} \right] \quad (6.264)$$

That is,

$$X_{1,t} = \lambda'_t mc_t P_t^{1+\theta} Q_t$$
$$+ \sum_{n=0}^{\infty} (\beta\theta_p)^{n+1} \lambda'_{t+1+n} \left[mc_{t+1+n} \left(\frac{P_{t+1+n-1}}{P_{t-1}} \right)^{-\zeta_p\theta} P_{t+1+n}^{1+\theta} Q_{t+1+n} \right] \quad (6.265)$$

But $\left(\frac{P_{t+1+n-1}}{P_{t-1}}\right)^{-\zeta_p\theta} = \left(\frac{P_t}{P_{t-1}}\right)^{-\zeta_p\theta} \left(\frac{P_{t+1+n-1}}{P_{t+1-1}}\right)^{-\zeta_p\theta}$ so that it can be written as

$$X_{1,t} = \lambda'_t mc_t P_t^{1+\theta} Q_t$$
$$-\beta\theta_p \left(\frac{P_t}{P_{t-1}} \right)^{-\zeta_p\theta} E_t \sum_{n=0}^{\infty} (\beta\theta)^{n+1} \lambda'_{t+1+n} \left[mc_{t+1+n} \left(\frac{P_{(t+1)+n-1}}{P_{(t+1)-1}} \right)^{-\zeta_p\theta} P_{t+1+n}^{1+\theta} Q_{t+1+n} \right] \quad (6.266)$$

That is,

$$X_{1,t} = \lambda'_t mc_t P_t^{1+\theta} Q_t + \beta\theta_p \left(\frac{P_t}{P_{t-1}} \right)^{-\zeta_p\theta} E_t X_{1,t+1} \quad (6.267)$$

Similarly, by rewriting

$$X_{2,t} = \sum_{n=0}^{\infty} (\beta\theta_p)^n \lambda'_{t+n} \left[\left(\frac{P_{t+n-1}}{P_{t-1}} \right)^{\zeta_p(1-\theta)} P_{t+n}{}^{\theta} Q_{t+n} \right] = \lambda'_t P_t{}^{\theta} Q_t$$
$$+ \sum_{n=1}^{\infty} (\beta\theta_p)^n \lambda'_{t+n} \left[\left(\frac{P_{t+n-1}}{P_{t-1}} \right)^{\zeta_p(1-\theta)} P_{t+n}{}^{\theta} Q_{t+n} \right] \quad (6.268)$$

Since

$$\sum_{n=1}^{\infty}(\beta\theta_p)^n\lambda'_{t+n}\left[\left(\frac{P_{t+n-1}}{P_{t-1}}\right)^{\zeta_p(1-\theta)}P_{t+n}{}^{\theta}Q_{t+n}\right]$$
$$=\sum_{n=0}^{\infty}(\beta\theta_p)^{n+1}\lambda'_{t+1+n}\left[\left(\frac{P_{t+n+1-1}}{P_{t-1}}\right)^{\zeta_p(1-\theta)}P_{t+1+n}{}^{\theta}Q_{t+1+n}\right] \tag{6.269}$$

and

$$\left(\frac{P_{t+1+n-1}}{P_{t-1}}\right)^{\zeta_p(1-\theta)}=\left(\frac{P_t}{P_{t-1}}\right)^{\zeta_p(1-\theta)}\left(\frac{P_{t+1+n-1}}{P_{(t+1)-1}}\right)^{\zeta_p(1-\theta)} \tag{6.270}$$

it follows

$$X_{2,t}=\lambda'_tP_t{}^{\theta}Q_tn$$
$$+(\beta\theta_p)\left(\frac{P_t}{P_{t-1}}\right)^{\zeta_p(1-\theta)}E_t\sum_{n=0}^{\infty}(\beta\theta)^n\lambda'_{t+1+n}\left[\left(\frac{P_{(t+1)+n-1}}{P_{(t+1)-1}}\right)^{\zeta_p(1-\theta)}P_{t+1+n}{}^{\theta}Q_{t+1+n}\right] \tag{6.271}$$

whence

$$X_{2,t}=\lambda'_tP_t{}^{\theta}Q_t+(\beta\theta_p)\left(\frac{P_t}{P_{t-1}}\right)^{\zeta_p(1-\theta)}E_tX_{2,t+1} \tag{6.272}$$

In terms of inflation rate, the two Eqs. (6.267) and (6.272) are rewritten:

$$X_{1,t}=\lambda'_tmc_tP_t^{1+\theta}Q_t+\beta\theta_p\,(1+\pi_t)^{-\zeta_p\theta}E_tX_{1,t+1} \tag{6.273}$$
$$X_{2,t}=\lambda'_tP_t{}^{\theta}Q_t+(\beta\theta_p)(1+\pi_t)^{\zeta_p(1-\theta)}E_tX_{2,t+1} \tag{6.274}$$

Dividing both members of (6.273) by P_t^{θ}, setting $x_{1,t}=\frac{X_{1,t}}{P_t^{\theta}}$ and taking into account that $\lambda'_tP_t=\lambda_t$, it follows

$$x_{1,t}=\lambda_tmc_tQ_t+\beta\theta_p(1+\pi_t)^{-\zeta_p\theta}E_t\frac{X_{1,t+1}}{P_{t+1}^{\theta}}\left(\frac{P_{t+1}}{P_t}\right)^{\theta}$$
$$=\lambda_tmc_tQ_t+\beta\theta_p\,(1+\pi_t)^{-\zeta_p\theta}E_t(1+\pi_{t+1})^{\theta}x_{1,t+1} \tag{6.275}$$

Likewise, dividing both sides of (6.274) by $P_t{}^{\theta-1}$ and setting $x_{2,t}=\frac{X_{2,t}}{P_t^{\theta-1}}$, it follows

$$x_{2,t} = \lambda_t Q_t + (\beta\theta_p)(1+\pi_t)^{\zeta_p(1-\theta)} E_t\,(1+\pi_{t+1})^{\theta-1}\,x_{2,t+1} \tag{6.276}$$

Finally, the equation of price formation can be set

$$\frac{P_t^*}{P_{t-1}} = \frac{\theta}{(\theta-1)}\frac{1}{P_{t-1}}\frac{\frac{X_{1,t}}{P_t^\theta}P_t^\theta}{\frac{X_{2,t}}{P_t^{\theta-1}}P_t^{\theta-1}} =$$

$$\frac{\theta}{(\theta-1)}\frac{1}{P_{t-1}}\frac{x_{1,t}P_t^\theta}{x_{2,t}P_t^{\theta-1}} = \frac{\theta}{(\theta-1)}\frac{P_t}{P_{t-1}}\frac{x_{1,t}}{x_{2,t}} \tag{6.277}$$

So that

$$1+\pi_t^* = \frac{\theta}{(\theta-1)}(1+\pi_t)\frac{x_{1,t}}{x_{2,t}} \tag{6.278}$$

6.12.4 Public Administration and Central Bank

Public administration consumes an exogenous quantity of production G_t.Public spending follows an AR (1) process in logarithm:

$$ln\,G_t = (1-\rho_G)\,lnG + \rho_G\,ln\,G_{t-1} + \varepsilon_{G,t} \tag{6.279}$$

It is assumed that $0 \le \rho_G < 1$. Stochastic error $\varepsilon_{G,\,t}$ is assumed to be extracted from a standard normal distribution. The government's budget constraint is

$$P_tG_t + i_{t-1}D_t \le P_tT_t + D_{t+1} - D_t \tag{6.280}$$

where D_t is the starting stock of nominal debt of the government at the current period t and on which the government must pay (end-period) i_{t-1}interest rate. To finance nominal spending including interest on the debt, the government obtains revenue from lump-sum taxes T_t or the issuance of new debt, $D_{t+1} - D_t$.

As regards monetary policy, it assumed following a Taylor rule of partial adjustment:

$$i_t = (1-\rho_i)i + \rho_i i_{t-1} + (1-\rho_i)[\varphi_\pi(\pi_t - \pi) + \varphi_y(lnQ_t - lnQ_{t-1})] + \varepsilon_{i,t} \tag{6.281}$$

It is assumed that $0 \le \rho_i < 1$. Symbols i and π indicate, respectively, steady-state interest rate and target steady-state inflation rate. Coefficients φ_π and φ_y are positive and are assumed to keep the economy in the region of determination of the dynamic system that represents it. The Taylor rule considered here allows Central Bank's response to refer, rather than to the output gap, to output growth (implicitly, relative to steady-state growth, which is zero in the model).

6.13 Equilibrium and Aggregation

In this section, we will consider the aggregation procedure that allows the transition from micro to macro. This procedure demonstrates that

(a) The usual fundamental identity of ad hoc macroeconomic models results from the aggregation of individual family budgets, also understood at the aggregate level as equilibrium on the goods market.
(b) From the condition of equality between the production and demand for intermediate goods for all types of goods and all firms, the aggregate production of intermediate goods, and the equality of this with the overall demand for them, are obtained taking into account an index of dispersion of prices of intermediate goods.
(c) The dynamics of inflation are expressed in terms of an aggregate index of the general price level, taking into account price change a la Calvo, and hypothesized indexation for prices not changed optimally.
(d) The dynamics of aggregate wages are defined both in monetary and real terms.

The results of the aggregation procedure from (a) to (d) will allow us in a subsequent section to formulate the overall set of equilibrium conditions of the entire economic system.

Point (a) is verified as follows.

Starting from the total profit of the intermediate companies in the economy, it results

$$\begin{aligned} \Pi_t &= \int_0^1 \Pi_t(j)dj \\ &= \int_0^1 P_t(j)y_t(j)dj - W_t\int_0^1 N_t(j)dj - R'_t\int_0^1 \widehat{K}_t(j)dj \end{aligned} \tag{6.282}$$

In market equilibrium, in aggregate, the following must be valid:

$$W_t\int_0^1 N_t(j)dj = W_tN_t \text{ e } R'_t\int_0^1 \widehat{K}_t(j)dj = R'_tu_tK_t \tag{6.283}$$

And therefore,

$$\Pi_t = \int_0^1 \Pi_t(j)dj = \int_0^1 P_t(j)y_t(j)dj - W_tN_t - R_t'u_tK_t \tag{6.284}$$

The demand for the j-th intermediate good is $y_t(j) = \left(\frac{P_t(j)}{P_t}\right)^{-\theta}Q_t$ whence

$$\begin{aligned}\Pi_t &= \int_0^1 P_t(j)\left(\frac{P_t(j)}{P_t}\right)^{-\theta}Q_t\,dj - W_tN_t - R_t'u_tK_t \\ &= P_t^{\theta}Q_t\int_0^1 P_t(j)^{1-\theta}dj - W_tN_t - R_t'u_tK_t\end{aligned} \tag{6.285}$$

and being $\int_0^1 P_t(j)^{1-\theta}dj = P_t^{1-\theta}$, it turns out

$$\Pi_t = P_tQ_t - W_tN_t - R_t'u_tK_t$$

Aggregating the budget constraint of families, it is

$$\begin{aligned}P_tC_t + P_tI_t + B_{t+1} = &\int_0^1 W_t(i)N_t(i)di + R_t'u_tK_t + \Pi_t - P_tT_t \\ &+(1+i_{t-1})B_t\end{aligned} \tag{6.286}$$

Demand for the i-th labor service is $N_t(i) = \left(\frac{W_t(i)}{W_t}\right)^{-\theta_N}N_t$, and therefore,

$$\begin{aligned}&\int_0^1 W_t(i)N_t(i)di = \int_0^1 W_t(i)\left(\frac{W_t(i)}{W_t}\right)^{-\theta_N}N_t = W_t^{\theta_N}N_t\int_0^1 W(i)^{1-\theta_N}di \\ &= W_t^{\theta_N}N_t\,W^{1-\theta_N} = W_tN_t\end{aligned} \tag{6.287}$$

Then,

$$\begin{aligned}P_tC_t + P_tI_t + B_{t+1} = &W_tN_t + R_t'u_tK_t + \Pi_t - P_tT_t \\ &+(1+i_{t-1})B_t\end{aligned} \tag{6.288}$$

In equilibrium, the public debt is entirely owned by families, and therefore, it must be $B_t = D_t$ and $B_{t+1} = D_{t+1}$, and from the budget constraint of public administration, it follows

$$B_{t+1} + P_tT_t - (1+i_{t-1})B_t = P_tG_t \tag{6.289}$$

and so

$$P_tC_t + P_tI_t + \mathrm{P_tG_t} = W_tN_t + R_t'u_tK_t + \Pi_t \tag{6.290}$$

Remembering that

$$\Pi_t = \mathrm{P_tQ_t} - \mathrm{W_tN_t} - R_t'u_tK_t$$

it follows

$$P_tC_t + P_tI_t + \mathrm{P_tG_t} = \mathrm{P_tQ_t} \tag{6.291}$$

That is, in real terms

$$C_t + I_t + \mathrm{G_t} = \mathrm{Q_t} \tag{6.292}$$

Let us now prove (b).

The aggregate production of intermediate goods, i.e., the integral of the production of such goods by all firms, must be equal to the aggregate demand for such goods:

$$\int_0^1 \left[A_t\widehat{K}_t(j)^\alpha N_t(j)^{1-\alpha}dj\text{–}F\right] = \int_0^1 Y_t(j)dj$$
$$= Q_t\int_0^1 \left(\frac{P_t(j)}{\mathrm{P_t}}\right)^{-\theta}\mathrm{dj} \tag{6.293}$$

Remembering that firms employ capital and labor in the same ratio $\frac{\widehat{K}_t}{N_t} = \frac{\widehat{K}_t(j)}{N_t(j)}$, it follows

$$A_t\left(\frac{\widehat{K}_t}{N_t}\right)^\alpha \int_0^1 N_t(j)dj - F] = Q_t\int_0^1 \left(\frac{P_t(j)}{\mathrm{P_t}}\right)^{-\theta}\mathrm{dj} \tag{6.294}$$

Demand for labor by firms coincides with employment; $\int_0^1 N_t(j) = N_t$, therefore

$$A_t\widehat{K}_t^{\ \alpha} N_t^{\ 1-\alpha} - F = Q_t v_p(t) \tag{6.295}$$

At the aggregate level, therefore, demand differs from aggregate production due to price dispersion $v_p(t)$ unless $v_p(t) = 1$.[33]

---

[33] Prices' dispersion is due to the stickiness with which firms, in a Calvo context, optimally adjust the price of their goods. This is shown by rewriting $v_p(t)$ as a function of the inflation rate. From this, a reformulation by recurrence makes clear the presence of an inertial phenomenon of price dispersion, which is also present in the inflation rate.

Indeed $v_p(t)$ can be rewritten as

As regards point (c) relating to the general price level index, we can proceed in the same way by writing

$$\mathrm{P_t}^{1-\theta} = \int_0^{1-\theta_p} \mathrm{P_t^*}^{1-\theta} \mathrm{dj} + \int_{1-\theta_p}^{1} (1+\pi_{t-1})^{\zeta_p(1-\theta)}\, \mathrm{P_{t-1}}^{1-\theta} \mathrm{dj} \tag{6.296}$$

Therefore,

$$\mathrm{P_t}^{1-\theta} = (1-\theta_p)\mathrm{P_t^*}^{1-\theta} + (1+\pi_{t-1})^{\zeta_p(1-\theta)}\, \theta_p \int_0^1 \mathrm{P_{t-1}}^{1-\theta} dj \tag{6.297}$$

But the integral in the last term of (6.297) coincides with $\mathrm{P_{t-1}}^{1-\theta}$,so that

$$\mathrm{P_t}^{1-\theta} = (1-\theta_p)\mathrm{P_t^*}^{1-\theta} + (1+\pi_{t-1})^{\zeta_p(1-\theta)}\, \theta_p \mathrm{P_{t-1}}^{1-\theta} \tag{6.298}$$

Dividing both sides of (6.298) by $\mathrm{P_{t-1}}^{1-\theta}$, in terms of inflation rate is

---

$$v_p(t) = \int_0^1 \left(\frac{P_t(j)}{\mathrm{P_t}}\right)^{-\theta} \mathrm{d(j)} = \int_0^{1-\theta_p} \left(\frac{P_t^*(j)}{\mathrm{P_t}}\right)^{-\theta} \mathrm{d(j)} + \int_{1-\theta_p}^{1} \left(\frac{(1+\pi_{t-1})^{\zeta_p} P_{t-1}(j)}{\mathrm{P_t}}\right)^{-\theta} \mathrm{dj}$$

This is equivalent to

$$v_p(t) = (1-\theta_p)\left(\frac{P_t^*}{\mathrm{P_t}}\right)^{-\theta} + \int_{1-\theta_p}^{1} (1+\pi_{t-1})^{-\zeta_p\theta} \left(\frac{P_{t-1}(j)}{\mathrm{P_t}-1}\right)^{-\theta} \left(\frac{P_{t-1}}{\mathrm{P_t}}\right)^{-\theta} \mathrm{dj} =$$
$$(1-\theta_p)\left(\frac{P_t^*}{\mathrm{P_t}}\right)^{-\theta} + (1+\pi_{t-1})^{-\zeta_p\theta}(1+\pi_t)^{\theta} \int_{1-\theta_p}^{1} \left(\frac{P_{t-1}(j)}{\mathrm{P_t}-1}\right)^{-\theta} \mathrm{dj}$$

The last integral equals

$$\int_{1-\theta_p}^{1} \left(\frac{P_{t-1}(j)}{\mathrm{P_t}-1}\right)^{-\theta} \mathrm{dj} =$$
$$\left(\frac{P_{t-1}}{P_{t-1}}\right)^{-\theta} - (1-\theta_p)\left(\frac{P_{t-1}}{P_{t-1}}\right)^{-\theta} = \theta_p \left(\frac{P_{t-1}}{P_{t-1}}\right)^{-\theta} = \theta_p \int_0^1 \left(\frac{P_{t-1}(j)}{\mathrm{P_t}-1}\right)^{-\theta} \mathrm{dj} = \theta_p v_p(t-1)$$

So that $v_p(t) = (1-\theta_p)\left(\frac{P_t^*}{\mathrm{P_t}}\right)^{-\theta} + (1+\pi_{t-1})^{-\zeta_p\theta}(1+\pi_t)^{\theta}\theta_p v_p(t-1)$. Also writing the first term to the right of equality sign in terms of the inflation rate
$(1-\theta_p)\left(\frac{P_t^*/P_{t-1}}{\mathrm{P_t}/\mathrm{P_{t-1}}}\right)^{-\theta} = (1-\theta_p)\frac{(1+\pi_t^*)}{(1+\pi_t)}$, we'll have
$v_p(t) = (1-\theta_p)\left(\frac{1+\pi_t^*}{1+\pi_t}\right)^{-\theta} + (1+\pi_{t-1})^{-\zeta_p\theta}(1+\pi_t)^{\theta}\theta_p v_p(t-1)$.

$$(1+\pi_t)^{(1-\theta)} = (1-\theta_p)\left(1+\pi_t^*\right)^{1-\theta} + \theta_p(1+\pi_{t-1})^{\zeta_p(1-\theta)} \tag{6.299}$$

Lastly, the demonstration of point (d), relating to the dynamics of aggregate wages both in monetary and real terms.

Remembering, for the monetary salary, it is $W_t^{1-\theta_N} = \int_0^1 W_t(i)^{1-\theta_N} di$, so that as in the previous cases, it can be written as

$$W_t^{1-\theta_N} = \int_0^1 W_t(i)^{1-\theta_N} di$$

$$= \int_0^{1-\theta_w} W_t^{*1-\theta_N} + \int_{1-\theta_w}^1 (1+\pi_{t-1})^{\zeta_w(1-\theta_N)} W_{t-1}(i)^{1-\theta_N} di \tag{6.300}$$

That is,

$$W_t^{1-\theta_N} = (1-\theta_w) W_t^{*1-\theta_N} + \theta_w(1+\pi_{t-1})^{\zeta_w(1-\theta_N)} \int_0^1 W_{t-1}(i)^{1-\theta_N} di \tag{6.301}$$

The integral in the last term of (6.300) must be $W_{t-1}^{1-\theta_N}$, and therefore,

$$W_t^{1-\theta_N} = (1-\theta_w) W_t^{*1-\theta_N} + \theta_w(1+\pi_{t-1})^{\zeta_w(1-\theta_N)} W_{t-1}^{1-\theta_N} \tag{6.302}$$

To obtain the dinamics of wage in real terms, dividing both sides of (6.302) by $P_t^{1-\theta_N}$, it follows

$$w_t^{1-\theta_N} = (1-\theta_w) w_t^{*1-\theta_N} + \theta_w(1+\pi_{t-1})^{\zeta_w(1-\theta_N)} w_{t-1}^{1-\theta_N} \frac{P_{t-1}^{1-\theta_N}}{P_t^{1-\theta_N}} \tag{6.303}$$

$$w_t^{1-\theta_N} = (1-\theta_w) w_t^{*1-\theta_N} + \theta_w(1+\pi_{t-1})^{\zeta_w(1-\theta_N)} (1+\pi_t)^{(\theta_N-1)} w_{t-1}^{1-\theta_N} \tag{6.304}$$

6.13.1 Exogenous Stochastic Processes

It is assumed that global productivity, A_t, marginal efficiency of investment Z_t, and intertemporal preference shock ν_t, all follow AR(1) processes in the log, with a non-stochastic mean normalized to unity (therefore, zero in logarithms):

$$ln\, A_t = \rho_A \;\; ln\, A_{t-1} + \varepsilon_{A,t} \tag{6.305}$$

$$ln\, Z_t = \rho_Z \;\; ln\, Z_{t-1} + \varepsilon_{Z,t} \tag{6.306}$$

$$ln\, \nu_t = \rho_\nu \;\; ln\, \nu_{t-1} + \varepsilon_{\nu,t} \tag{6.307}$$

$$\ln(G_t) = (1-\rho_G)\, ln\,(\omega Q) + \rho_G\, ln\,(G_{t-1}) + e_{G,t} \tag{6.308}$$

where ωQ indicates the share of public spending on GDP in the steady state.

All the AR parameters are assumed to be between 0 and 1, and shocks are assumed to be drawn from standard normal distributions.

The intratemporal preference shock follows an AR(1) process in the logarithm with non-stochastic averaging $\ln\psi$:

$$ln\, \psi_t = \left(1-\rho_\psi\right) \;\; ln\, \psi\_\text{bar} + \rho_\psi \;\; ln\, \psi_{t-1} + \varepsilon_{\psi,t} \tag{6.309}$$

6.14 The Complete Set of Equilibrium Equations

Grouping the equilibrium conditions, the medium-sized New Keynesian model is

$$\lambda_t = \frac{\nu_t}{C_t - bC_{t-1}} - \beta b E_t \frac{\nu_{t+1}}{C_{t+1} - bC_t} \tag{6.310}$$

$$P_t \lambda'_t \frac{R'_t}{P_t} = \lambda_t R_t = \mu_t\, [\delta_1 + \delta(u_t - 1)] \tag{6.311}$$

$$\lambda_t = \beta E_t \lambda_{t+1} \; \frac{1 + i_t(+1)}{1 + \pi_{t+1}} \tag{6.312}$$

$$\lambda_t = \mu_t Z_t \left[\left(1 - \frac{\kappa}{2}\left(\frac{I_t}{I_{t-1}} - 1\right)^2 - \kappa\left(\frac{I_t}{I_{t-1}} - 1\right) \frac{I_t}{I_{t-1}}\right]\right.$$

$$+\beta E_t \mu_{t+1} Z_{t+1} \kappa \left(\frac{I_{t+1}}{I_t} - 1\right)\left(\frac{I_{t+1}}{I_t}\right)^2 \tag{6.313}$$

$$\mu_t = \beta E_t \{[\, \lambda_{t+1} R_{t+1} u_{t+1}$$

$$+\mu_{t+1} 1 - \delta_0 + \delta_1 (u_{t+1} - 1) + \frac{\delta}{2} (u_{t+1} - 1)^2]\} \tag{6.314}$$

$$\widehat{h}_{1,t} = \nu_t \psi_t \left(\frac{w_t}{w_t^*}\right)^{\theta_N(1+\upsilon)} N_t^{1+\upsilon}$$

$$+\beta\theta_w (1+\pi_t)^{-\zeta_w \theta_N(1+\upsilon)} E_t (1+\pi_{t+1})^{\theta_N(1+\upsilon)} \left(\frac{w_{t+1}^*}{w_t^*}\right)^{\theta_N(1+\upsilon)} \widehat{h}_{1,t+1} \tag{6.315}$$

$$\widehat{\mathrm{h}}_{2,\mathrm{t}} = \lambda_t \left(\frac{w_t}{w_t^*}\right)^{\theta_N} N_t$$

$$+\beta\theta_w(1+\pi_t)^{\zeta_w(1-\theta_N)} E_t(1+\pi_{t+1})^{\theta_N-1}\left(\frac{w_{t+1}^*}{w_t^*}\right)^{\theta_N}\widehat{h}_{2,t+1} \tag{6.316}$$

$$\frac{w_t}{R_t} = \frac{(1-\alpha)}{\alpha}\frac{\widehat{K}_t}{N_t} \tag{6.317}$$

$$w_t^* = \frac{\theta_N}{(\theta_N-1)}\frac{\widehat{\mathrm{h}}_{1,\mathrm{t}}}{\widehat{\mathrm{h}}_{2,\mathrm{t}}} \tag{6.318}$$

$$mc_t = \frac{\mathrm{w_t}}{(1-\alpha)A_t\left(\frac{\widehat{K}_t}{N_t}\right)^{\alpha}} \tag{6.319}$$

$$x_{1,t} = \lambda_t \mathrm{mc_t} Q_t + \beta\theta_p\,(1+\pi_\mathrm{t})^{-\zeta_\mathrm{p}\theta}\mathrm{E_t}(1+\pi_{\mathrm{t+1}})^{\theta}\,\mathrm{x_{1,t+1}} \tag{6.320}$$

$$x_{2,t} = \lambda_t \mathrm{Q_t} + (\beta\theta_p)(1+\pi_\mathrm{t})^{\zeta_\mathrm{p}(1-\theta)}\mathrm{E_t}\,(1+\pi_{\mathrm{t+1}})^{\theta-1}\,x_{2,t+1} \tag{6.321}$$

$$1+\pi_\mathrm{t}^* = \frac{\theta}{(\theta-1)}\,(1+\pi_\mathrm{t})\frac{x_{1,t}}{x_{2,t}} \tag{6.322}$$

$$\mathrm{Q_t} = C_t + I_t + \mathrm{G_t} \tag{6.323}$$

$$\mathrm{K_{t+1}} = \mathrm{Z_t}\left[1-\frac{\kappa}{2}\left(\frac{\mathrm{I_t}}{\mathrm{I_{t-1}}}-1\right)^2\right]\mathrm{I_t}$$

$$+\left(1-\delta_0+\delta_1(\mathrm{u_t}-1)+\frac{\delta}{2}(\mathrm{u_t}-1)^2\right)\mathrm{K_t} \tag{6.324}$$

$$\widehat{K}_t = u_t K_t \tag{6.325}$$

$$v_p(t) = (1-\theta_p)\left(\frac{1+\pi_t^*}{1+\pi_t}\right)^{-\theta}$$

$$+(1+\pi_{t-1})^{-\zeta_p\theta}(1+\pi_t)^{\theta}\theta_p v_p \tag{6.326}$$

$$Q_t = \left(A_t\widehat{K}_t^{\ \alpha} N_t^{\ 1-\alpha} - F/v_p(t)\right) \tag{6.327}$$

$$(1+\pi_t)^{(1-\theta)} = (1-\theta_p)(1+\pi_t^*)^{1-\theta}$$

$$+(1+\pi_{t-1})^{\zeta_p(1-\theta)}\,\theta_p \tag{6.328}$$

$$w_t^{1-\theta_N} = (1-\theta_w)w_t^{*\,1-\theta_N}$$

$$+(1+\pi_{t-1})^{\zeta_w(1-\theta_N)}\theta_w(1+\pi_t)^{(\theta_N-1)}w_{t-1}^{1-\theta_N} \tag{6.329}$$

$$i_t(+1) = (1-\rho_i)i + \rho_i i_t + (1-\rho_i)\left[\varphi_\pi\left(\pi_t - \pi^T\right)\right.$$
$$\left.+\varphi_y(lnQ_t - lnQ_{t-1})\right] + s_i\varepsilon_{i,t}) \tag{6.330}$$

$$ln\,G_t = (1-\rho_G)\ln(\omega Q) + \rho_G\,ln\,(\omega Q_{t-1}) + \varepsilon_{G,t} \tag{6.331}$$

$$ln\,A_t = \rho_A\;\;ln\,A_{t-1} + \varepsilon_{A,t} \tag{6.332}$$

$$ln\,Z_t = \rho_Z\;\;ln\,Z_{t-1} + \varepsilon_{Z,t} \tag{6.333}$$

$$ln\,\nu_t = \rho_\nu\;\;ln\,\nu_{t-1} + \varepsilon_{\nu,t} \tag{6.334}$$

$$ln\,\psi_t = \left(1-\rho_\psi\right)\,ln\psi + \rho_\psi\;\;ln\,\psi_{t-1} + \varepsilon_{\psi,t} \tag{6.335}$$

This is a model of 26 equations in the following 26 variables:

$\lambda_t, \mu_t, C_t, , \widehat{h}_{1,t}, \widehat{h}_{2,t}, w_t^*, R_t, N_t, mc_t, x_{1,t}, x_{2,t}, I_t, Q_t, u_t, K_t, \widehat{K}_t,\ \pi_t^*,$
$w_t,\ i_t,\ G_t,\ A_t,\ Z_t,\ \nu_t,\ \psi_t.$

Parameters, with F = 0 in number of 25,are

b, β, α, δ_0, δ_1, δ, π_s, κ, θ_N, θ_w, θ_p, θ, υ, ζ_w, ζ_p, ρ_i, φ_π, φ_y, ρ_G, ω, ρ_A, ρ_Z, ρ_ν, ρ_ψ, ψ.

The parameters also include the steady-state inflation rate π_s which, as coincides with the target of monetary authorities, in the steady state does not necessarily coincide with zero inflation.

6.14.1 Calculation of the Steady-State Solution

In this section, calculations of the steady-state equations are considered. It is a bit tedious but a necessary step. We consider the previous model by obtaining the steady state from Eqs. (6.310)–(6.335), one after another, without renumbering each one. In the next section, the complete set of steady-state equations will be reconsidered in a fully correct formal numeration.

From (6.312), at steady state, it is $1 = \beta\,\frac{1+i}{1+\pi}$, and it follows

$$i = \frac{1+\pi}{\beta} - 1.$$

From (6.313) being trivially at steady state I/I=1, it follows $\lambda = \mu Z$, but Z = 1, and therefore, $\lambda = \mu$. So that, in a steady state, Lagrange's multiplicators are equal.

Equivalently $q = \frac{\mu}{\lambda} = 1$, which is the long-run Tobin's equilibrium condition.

As for $u_t = u$, it is set u = 1 since with u = 1, it follows

$$\delta(\mathrm{u}) = \delta_0 + \delta_1(u-1) + \frac{\delta}{2}(u-1)^2 = \delta_0$$

Taking note of these results, from Euler's equation (6.314) is $\mu = \beta[(R\mu + \mu(1 - \delta_0)]$ from which is obtained $\beta[(R + (1 - \delta_0)] = 1$, and therefore,

$$R = \frac{1}{\beta} - (1 - \delta_0)$$

Note that from (6.311), compatibly with the restriction u = 1, it must be $\delta_1 = \mathrm{R} = \frac{1}{\beta} - (1 - \delta_0)$.

As regards the evolution of inflation, it is best to refer to Eq. (6.328) from which in steady state

$$(1+\pi^*) = \left[\frac{(1+\pi)^{(1-\theta)} - (1+\pi)^{\zeta_p(1-\theta)}\,\theta_p}{(1-\theta_p)}\right]^{\frac{1}{1-\theta}}$$

Solving for π^*, it is

$$\pi^* = \left[\frac{(1+\pi)^{(1-\theta)} - (1+\pi)^{\zeta_p(1-\theta)}\,\theta_p}{(1-\theta_p)}\right]^{\frac{1}{1-\theta}} - 1$$

This provides steady-state inflation of prices readjusted optimally, as a function of the parameters, among which also appears the steady-state price inflation.If it were $\pi = 0$, as normally assumed in the literature, to the right of the numerator, we would have $(1 - \theta_p)$, and therefore, also $\pi^* = 0 = \pi$. Similarly for $\zeta_p = 1$, the term in brackets becomes $(1 + \pi)^{(1 - \theta)}$ so that $(1 + \pi^*) = (1 + \pi)$, and therefore $\pi^* = \pi$.

Now the steady-state expression of price dispersion can also be obtained from (6.326). It is

$$v_p\left(1 - (1+\pi)^{-\zeta_p\theta}(1+\pi)^{\theta}\theta_p\right) = (1-\theta_p)\left(\frac{1+\pi^*}{1+\pi}\right)^{-\theta}$$

And solving for v_p

$$\mathrm{v_p} = \frac{(1-\theta_p)\left(\frac{1+\pi^*}{1+\pi}\right)^{-\theta}}{1-(1+\pi)^{-\zeta_p\theta}(1+\pi)^{\theta}\theta_p} = \frac{(1-\theta_p)\left(\frac{1+\pi^*}{1+\pi}\right)^{-\theta}}{1-\theta_p(1+\pi)^{\theta(1-\zeta_p)}}$$

Worth noting: for $\pi = 0 = \pi^*$, it is $v_p = 1$, and for $\zeta_p = 1$ since $\pi = \pi^*$, then $v_p = 1$.

Now consider (6.320) and (6.321). In a steady state, you have

$$x_1 = \lambda \mathrm{mc} Q + \beta\theta_p\, (1+\pi)^{-\zeta_p\theta}\, x_1 (1+\pi)^{\theta}$$

That is,

$$x_1 = \frac{\lambda \mathrm{mc}\, Q}{1 - \beta\theta_p\, (1+\pi)^{\theta(1-\zeta_p)}}$$

and

$$x_2 = \lambda \mathrm{Q} + \left(\beta\theta_p\right)(1+\pi)^{\zeta_p(1-\theta)} \mathrm{E_t}\, (1+\pi)^{\theta-1}\, x_2$$

That is,

$$x_2 = \frac{\lambda \mathrm{Q}}{1 - \beta\theta_p (1+\pi)^{(\theta-1)(1-\zeta_p)}}$$

It follows $\frac{x_1}{x_2} = \frac{1-\beta\theta_p(1+\pi)^{(\theta-1)(1-\zeta_p)}}{1-\beta\theta_p\, (1+\pi)^{\theta(1-\zeta_p)}}\mathrm{mc}$, from which

$$\mathrm{mc} = \frac{1 - \beta\theta_p\, (1+\pi)^{\theta(1-\zeta_p)}}{1 - \beta\theta_p (1+\pi)^{(\theta-1)(1-\zeta_p)}}\, \frac{x_1}{x_2}$$

From (6.322) in steady state follows $1+\pi^* = \frac{\theta}{(\theta-1)}\, (1+\pi)\frac{x_1}{x_2}$ so that $\frac{x_1}{x_2} = \frac{(\theta-1)}{\theta}\frac{1+\pi^*}{1+\pi}$, and by substituting in mc, it is

$$\mathrm{mc} = \frac{(\theta-1)}{\theta}\, \frac{1+\pi^*}{(1+\pi)}\, \frac{1 - \beta\theta_p\, (1+\pi)^{\theta(1-\zeta_p)}}{1 - \beta\theta_p (1+\pi)^{(\theta-1)(1-\zeta_p)}}$$

Once mc is known, you can solve for the real wage, given the relationship between the steady-state production factors, going on as follows:

From (6.319), it is $mc = \frac{\mathrm{w}}{(1-\alpha)A\left(\widehat{\frac{K}{N}}\right)^{\alpha}} = \frac{\mathrm{w}}{(1-\alpha)\left(\frac{K}{N}\right)^{\alpha}}$

The ratio $\widehat{\frac{K}{N}}$ matches with $\frac{K}{N}$ (which is not yet known) since the steady-state utilization rate is u = 1. Moreover, $A = 1$. It is observed, however, that from (6.317) in steady-state, it is $w = R\frac{(1-\alpha)}{\alpha}\,\frac{K}{N}$ and so substituting follows

$$mc = \frac{R\frac{(1-\alpha)}{\alpha}\,\frac{K}{N}}{(1-\alpha)\left(\frac{K}{N}\right)^{\alpha}} = \frac{R}{\alpha\left(\frac{K}{N}\right)^{\alpha-1}}$$

But R is known and mc is known, and therefore, it can be solved for $\frac{K}{N}$ which from $mc\ \alpha\left(\frac{K}{N}\right)^{\alpha-1}=R$ is $\frac{K}{N}=\left(\frac{R}{mc\ \alpha}\right)^{\frac{1}{\alpha-1}}$. Given the ratio between the quantities of production factors, the real wage is obtained from

$$\mathrm{w}= (1-\alpha)\mathrm{mc}\left(\frac{\mathrm{K}}{\mathrm{N}}\right)^{\alpha}=(1-\alpha)\mathrm{mc}\left(\frac{\mathrm{R}}{\mathrm{mc}\ \alpha}\right)^{\frac{\alpha}{\alpha-1}}$$

Let us now refer to the equation of the real wage dynamics (6.329). In a steady state, it is

$$w^{1-\theta_N}=(1-\theta_w)w^{*1-\theta_N}+(1+\pi)^{\zeta_w(1-\theta_N)}(1+\pi)^{(\theta_N-1)}\theta_w w^{1-\theta_N}$$
$$w^{1-\theta_N}=(1-\theta_w)w^{*1-\theta_N}+\theta_w(1+\pi)^{(\theta_N-1)(1-\zeta_w)}w^{1-\theta_N}$$

The last equation can be solved for w^* which is equal to

$$w^*=\left(\frac{w^{1-\theta_N}\left[1-\theta_w(1+\pi)^{(\theta_N-1)(1-\zeta_w)}\right]}{1-\theta_w}\right)^{\frac{1}{1-\theta_N}}$$
$$=w\left(\frac{\left[1-\theta_w(1+\pi)^{(\theta_N-1)(1-\zeta_w)}\right]}{1-\theta_w}\right)^{\frac{1}{1-\theta_N}}$$

Once w* is known, we solve for the steady-state values of $\widehat{\mathrm{h}}_1$ and $\widehat{\mathrm{h}}_2$. From (6.315) and (6.316), by remembering that in steady state the shock ν_t is $\nu=1$, it is obtained

$$\widehat{\mathrm{h}}_1=\psi\left(\frac{w}{w^*}\right)^{\theta_N(1+\upsilon)}N^{1+\upsilon}+\beta\theta_w(1+\pi))^{\theta_N(1+\upsilon)(1-\zeta_w)}\widehat{\mathrm{h}}_1$$

and

$$\widehat{\mathrm{h}}_2=\lambda\left(\frac{w}{w^*}\right)^{\theta_N}N+\beta\theta_w(1+\pi))^{(\theta_N-1)(1-\zeta_w)}\widehat{h}_2$$

From the first equation, it follows

$$\widehat{\mathrm{h}}_1=\frac{\varphi\left(\frac{w}{w^*}\right)^{\theta_N(1+\upsilon)}N^{1+\upsilon}}{1-\beta\theta_w(1+\pi)^{\theta_N(1+\upsilon)(1-\zeta_w)}}$$

And from the second equation, it is

$$\widehat{h}_2 = \frac{\lambda\left(\frac{w}{w^*}\right)^{\theta_N} N}{1 - \beta\theta_w (1+\pi))^{(\theta_N - 1)(1-\zeta_w)}}$$

The ratio between these two values appears in the optimal real-wage equation. This ratio is

$$\frac{\widehat{h}_1}{\widehat{h}_2} = \frac{\psi\left(\frac{w}{w^*}\right)^{\theta_N(1+\upsilon)} N^{1+\upsilon}}{\lambda\left(\frac{w}{w^*}\right)^{\theta_N} N} \frac{1 - \beta\theta_w (1+\pi))^{(\theta_N - 1)(1-\zeta_w)}}{1 - \beta\theta_w (1+\pi))^{\theta_N(1+\upsilon)(1-\zeta_w)}}$$

$$= \psi\lambda^{-1}\left(\frac{w}{w^*}\right)^{\theta_N\upsilon} N^{\upsilon} \frac{1 - \beta\theta_w (1+\pi))^{(\theta_N - 1)(1-\zeta_w)}}{1 - \beta\theta_w (1+\pi))^{\theta_N(1+\upsilon)(1-\zeta_w)}}$$

By substituting into the equation of optimal wage is obtained

$$w^* = \frac{\theta_N}{(\theta_N - 1)} \psi\lambda^{-1}\left(\frac{w}{w^*}\right)^{\theta_N\upsilon} N^{\upsilon} \frac{1 - \beta\theta_w (1+\pi))^{(\theta_N - 1)(1-\zeta_w)}}{1 - \beta\theta_w (1+\pi))^{\theta_N(1+\upsilon)(1-\zeta_w)}}$$

In this expression, the only unknown magnitude is N^{υ}. Solving for it, we obtain

$$N^{\upsilon} = \frac{(\theta_N - 1)}{\theta_N} \frac{1}{\psi} \lambda w^* \left(\frac{w}{w^*}\right)^{-\theta_N\upsilon} \frac{1 - \beta\theta_w (1+\pi))^{\theta_N(1+\upsilon)(1-\zeta_w)}}{1 - \beta\theta_w (1+\pi))^{(\theta_N - 1)(1-\zeta_w)}}$$

The term λ is obtained from (6.310) which at steady state equals $\lambda = \frac{1}{C}\frac{1-\beta b}{1-b}$, so that substituting it follows

$$N^{\upsilon} = \frac{(\theta_N - 1)}{\theta_N} \frac{1}{\psi} \frac{1}{C} \frac{1-\beta b}{1-b} w^* \left(\frac{w}{w^*}\right)^{-\theta_N\upsilon} \frac{1 - \beta\theta_w (1+\pi))^{\theta_N(1+\upsilon)(1-\zeta_w)}}{1 - \beta\theta_w (1+\pi))^{(\theta_N - 1)(1-\zeta_w)}}$$

Multiplying this expression on both sides by N follows

$$N^{1+\upsilon} = \frac{(\theta_N - 1)}{\theta_N} \frac{1}{\psi} \frac{N}{C} \frac{1-\beta b}{1-b} w^* \left(\frac{w}{w^*}\right)^{-\theta_N\upsilon} \frac{1 - \beta\theta_w (1+\pi))^{\theta_N(1+\upsilon)(1-\zeta_w)}}{1 - \beta\theta_w (1+\pi))^{(\theta_N - 1)(1-\zeta_w)}}$$

This equation is useful for solving for N consistent with the writing of resource constraint.

Assume that in the steady state $G = \omega Q$. Aggregate resource constraint becomes $(1 - \omega)Q = C + I$, and from the steady-state capital accumulation equation $I = \delta_0 K$, you can write $(1 - \omega)Q = C + \delta_0 K$, and dividing by N, you get

$$(1-\omega)\frac{Q}{N}=\frac{C}{N}+\frac{\delta_0 K}{N}$$

From which

$$\frac{C}{N}=(1-\omega)\frac{Q}{N}-\frac{\delta_0 K}{N}$$

The ratio $\frac{K}{N}$ is already known, so if we know also $\frac{Q}{N}$, we can use this equation to get $\frac{C}{N}$ and solve for N.

From (6.327) in steady state is

$$A\widehat{K}^{\alpha}N^{1-\alpha}-F=Qv_p$$

i.e.,

$$\frac{\boldsymbol{Q}}{\boldsymbol{N}}=\frac{\left(\frac{K}{N}\right)^{\alpha}-\frac{F}{N}}{v_p}$$

In a model with no fixed costs, and F = 0, this is the solution. With positive fixed costs, the expression for $\frac{F}{N}$ must also be obtained. This is deduced from the nullification condition of the stationary aggregate profit.

From the nominal aggregate profit equation

$\Pi^n_t = P_tQ_t - W_tN_t - R'_t u_t K_t$ in steady state, it is

$\Pi^n = PQ - WN - R'K$. In real terms, it is

$$\Pi=\mathrm{Q}-\mathrm{WN}-RK$$

We can now assume F is compatible with the condition $\Pi = 0$, from which it follows $\frac{Q}{N}=w+\frac{K}{N}R$ so that can be written as

$$\frac{C}{N}=(1-\omega)\frac{Q}{N}-\frac{\delta_0 K}{N}=(1-\omega)\frac{\left(w+\frac{K}{N}R\right)}{v_p}-\delta_0\frac{K}{N}$$

Knowing $\frac{C}{N}$, we can substitute in $N^{1+\upsilon}$ and obtain N, which is

$$N=\left[\frac{(\theta_N-1)}{\theta_N}\frac{1}{\Psi}\frac{1}{(1-\omega)\frac{\left(w+\frac{K}{N}R\right)}{v_p}-\delta_0\frac{K}{N}}\frac{1-\beta b}{1-b}w^*\left(\frac{w}{w^*}\right)^{-\theta_N\upsilon}\frac{1-\beta\theta_w(1+\pi))^{\theta_N(1+\upsilon)(1-\zeta_w)}}{1-\beta\theta_w(1+\pi))^{(\theta_N-1)(1-\zeta_w)}}\right]^{\frac{1}{1+\upsilon}}$$

Once N is obtained, from $\frac{Q}{N}=\left(\frac{K}{N}\right)^{\alpha}-\frac{F}{N}$, we can also obtain F compatible with zero condition of aggregate profits $\frac{F}{N}=\left(\frac{K}{N}\right)^{\alpha}-\frac{Q}{N}=\left(\frac{K}{N}\right)^{\alpha}-\left(w+\frac{R}{N}K\right)$

From which trivially, it is

$$F = N\left[\left(\frac{K}{N}\right)^{\alpha} - \frac{Q}{N}\right] = N\left[\left(\frac{K}{N}\right)^{\alpha} - \left(\mathrm{w} + \frac{\mathrm{R}}{\mathrm{N}}\,\mathrm{K}\right)\right]$$

Finally, from the monetary policy rule, it follows that the inflation target assumed in the Central Bank's reaction function must be consistent with the steady-state inflation rate. In fact, from the Central Bank reaction function (6.330) in the steady state must be

$$0 = (1 - \rho_i)\varphi_{\pi}\left(\pi - \pi_{target}\right)$$

which requires

$$\pi - \pi_{target} = 0$$

6.14.2 The Complete Set of Steady-State Equations

Grouping the steady-state conditions, the complete set of equations is

$$\mathrm{A} = 1 \tag{6.336}$$

$$\mathrm{Z} = 1 \tag{6.337}$$

$$\nu = 1 \tag{6.338}$$

$$\psi_t = \psi\_bar \tag{6.339}$$

$$\pi = \pi_{target} \tag{6.340}$$

$$\left[\frac{F}{N} = \left(\frac{K}{N}\right)^{\alpha} - \left(\mathrm{w} + \frac{\mathrm{R}}{\mathrm{N}}\,\mathrm{K}\right)\right]] \tag{6.341}$$

$$i = \frac{1 + \pi}{\beta} - 1 \tag{6.342}$$

$$\lambda = \mu \tag{6.343}$$

$$\mathrm{u} = 1 \tag{6.344}$$

$$R = \frac{1}{\beta} - (1 - \delta_0) \tag{6.345}$$

$$\delta_1 = \mathrm{R} \tag{6.346}$$

$$(1 + \pi^*) = \left[\frac{(1 + \pi)^{(1-\theta)} - (1 + \pi)^{\zeta_p(1-\theta)}\theta_p}{(1 - \theta_p)}\right]^{\frac{1}{1-\theta}} \tag{6.347}$$

$$v_p = \frac{\left(1-\theta_p\right)\left(\frac{1+\pi^*}{1+\pi}\right)^{-\theta}}{1-(1+\pi)^{-\zeta_p\theta}(1+\pi)^{\theta}\theta_p} = \frac{\left(1-\theta_p\right)\left(\frac{1+\pi^*}{1+\pi}\right)^{-\theta}}{1-\theta_p(1+\pi)^{\theta\left(1-\zeta_p\right)}} \tag{6.348}$$

$$\mathrm{mc} = \frac{(\theta-1)}{\theta}\,\frac{1+\pi^*}{(1+\pi)}\,\frac{1-\beta\theta_p\,(1+\pi)^{\theta\left(1-\zeta_p\right)}}{1-\beta\theta_p(1+\pi)^{(1-\theta)\left(\zeta_p-1\right)}} \tag{6.349}$$

$$w = (1-\alpha)mc\left(\frac{K}{N}\right)^{\alpha} = (1-\alpha)mc\left(\frac{R}{mc\,\alpha}\right)^{\frac{\alpha}{\alpha-1}} \tag{6.350}$$

$$w^* = \left(\frac{w^{1-\theta_N}\left[1-\theta_w(1+\pi)^{(\theta_N-1)(1-\zeta_w)}\right]}{1-\theta_w}\right)^{\frac{1}{1-\theta_N}}$$

$$= w\left(\frac{\left[1-\theta_w(1+\pi)^{(\theta_N-1)(1-\zeta_w)}\right]}{1-\theta_w}\right)^{\frac{1}{1-\theta_N}} \tag{6.351}$$

$$\mathrm{N} = \left[\frac{\frac{(\theta_N-1)}{\theta_N}}{\varphi}\,\frac{1-\beta \mathrm{b}}{1-b}\,\frac{1}{(1-\omega)\frac{\left(\frac{mc\,\alpha}{R}\right)^{\frac{\alpha}{1-\alpha}}}{v_p}-\delta_0\left(\frac{R}{mc\,\alpha}\right)^{\frac{1}{\alpha-1}}}\,w^*\left(\frac{w}{w^*}\right)^{-\theta_N\upsilon}\,\frac{1-\beta\theta_w(1+\pi))^{\theta_N(1+\upsilon)(1-\zeta_w)}}{1-\beta\theta_w(1+\pi))^{(\theta_N-1)(1-\zeta_w)}}\right]^{\frac{1}{1+\upsilon}} \tag{6.352}$$

$$\widehat{K} = \left(\frac{R}{mc\,\alpha}\right)^{\frac{1}{\alpha-1}} N = \left(\frac{mc\,\alpha}{R}\right)^{\frac{1}{1-\alpha}} N \tag{6.353}$$

$$G = \omega\, Q \tag{6.354}$$

$$I = \delta_0 K \tag{6.355}$$

$$Q = C + I + \mathrm{G} \tag{6.356}$$

$$Q = K^{\alpha}\, N^{1-\alpha} \tag{6.357}$$

$$\mathrm{C} = \mathrm{Q} - \mathrm{I} - \mathrm{G} \tag{6.358}$$

$$\widehat{\mathrm{h}}_1 = \frac{\psi\left(\frac{w}{w^*}\right)^{\theta_N(1+\upsilon)} N^{1+\upsilon}}{1-\beta\theta_w(1+\pi))^{\theta_N(1+\upsilon)(1-\zeta_w)}} \tag{6.359}$$

$$\widehat{\mathrm{h}}_2 = \frac{\lambda\left(\frac{w}{w^*}\right)^{\theta_N} N}{1-\beta\theta_w(1+\pi))^{(\theta_N-1)(1-\zeta_w)}} \tag{6.360}$$

$$x_1 = \frac{\lambda \mathrm{mc}\; Q}{1-\beta\theta_p\;(1+\pi)^{\theta\left(1-\zeta_p\right)}} \tag{6.361}$$

$$x_2 = \frac{\lambda \mathrm{Q}}{1-\beta\theta_p(1+\pi)^{(\theta-1)\left(1-\zeta_p\right)}} \tag{6.362}$$

6.15 DYNARE Code for the Numerical Solution of the Medium-Sized NK Model

In this section, at the end of the chapter, the DYNARE code for the numerical solution of the medium-sized NK model is presented.

This code, like the previous codes, has also been verified with DYNARE 4.6.4 with the name m_NK_medium_size.mod and it works perfectly.

To simplify, the code was written by considering only stochastic disturbances to technical progress and public spending, but all the shocks previously considered can be included together in the code, except for some difficulties in the screen of the simulation by DYNARE.

```
//m_ NK_medium_size.mod

var A C G h1 h2 i I K K_ha lamb mc mu N pi pi_star phi Q R t u
nu v_p x1 x2 w_star w Z;
varexo e_i  e_A e_G e_Z e_v e_phi;
parameters alpha b beta delta0 delta1 delta pi_target kappa
theta_N upsilon theta_w zeta_p zeta_w theta theta_p F rho_i
phi_pi phi_y s_i rho_G s_G rho_A s_A rho_Z s_Z rho_v s_v
rho_phi phi_bar s_phi,omega;
  alpha = 0.33;
  b = 0.7;
  beta = 0.995;
  delta0 = 0.025;
  delta = 0.05;
  pi_target= 0.02;
  kappa = 4;
  theta_N = 3;
  upsilon=2;
  theta_w=0.75;
  zeta_p = 0.2;
  zeta_w= 0.2;
  theta = 3;
  theta_p = 0.66;
  F=0;
  rho_i = 0.8;
  phi_pi= 1.5;
  phi_y = 0.2;
  rho_G= 0.72;
  rho_A = 0.92;
  rho_Z= 0.94;
  rho_nu= 0.9;
  rho_psi=0.7;
```

```
psi_bar=6;
omega= 0.2;
delta1=1/beta -(1-delta0);
% F=0
%N*((R/mc**alfa)^(alfa/alfa-1)-w+(R*(R/mc*alfa)^(1/alfa-
1)))%

model;
lamb= v/(C-b*C(-1)) - b*beta*v(+1)/(C(+1)-b*C);
lamb*R=mu*( delta1*u+ delta*(u-1));
lamb= (beta*lamb(+1)*(1+i)/1+pi(+1);
lamb=mu*Z*(1-kappa/2*(I/I(-1)-1)^2-kappa*(I/I(-1)-1)*I/I(-
1))+ beta*mu(+1)*Z(+1)*kappa*(I(+1)/I- 1)*(I(+1)/I)^2;
mu=beta*(lamb(+1)*R(+1)*u(+1)+mu(+1)*(1-
delta0+delta1*(u(+1)-1)+ delta/2 *(u(+1)-1)^2));
w_star= ( theta_N/ (theta_N -1)) * h1/ h2;
h1=nu*phi*(w/w_star)^(theta_N*(1+upsilon))*N^(1+upsilon)
+beta*theta_w*(1+pi)^(-
zeta_w*theta_N*(1+upsilon))*(1+pi(+1))^(theta_N*(1+upsilon))
* (w_star(+1)/w_star)^(theta_N*(1+upsilon))* h1(+1);
h2=lamb*(w/wstar)^theta_N*N+beta*theta_w*(1+pi)^(zeta_
w*(1-theta_N))*(1+pi(+1))^(theta_N-1)* (w_star(+1)/wstar)^
theta_N * h2(+1);
w/R= (1-alpha)/alpha * (K_hat(-1)/N);
mc = w/(1-alpha)*A*(K_hat(-1)/N)^alpha;
1+pi_star = theta/(theta-1) * (1+pi)* x1/x2;
x1=lamb*mc*Q+beta*theta_p*(1+pi)^(-
zeta_p*theta)*(1+pi(+1))^theta *x1(+1);
x2=lamb*Q+beta*theta_p*(1+pi)^zeta_p*(1-
theta)*(1+pi(+1))^(theta-1)*x2(+1);
Q=C+I+G;
K=Z*((1-kappa/2*(I/I(-1)-1))^2)*I*+K(-1)*(1-delta0-
delta1*(u-1))- delta/2*(u-1)^2);
A*K_hat(-1)^alpha*N^(1-alpha) = Q*v_p;
K_hat = u*K(-1) ;
v_p=(1-theta_p)*((1+pi_star)/(1+pi))^(-theta)+(1+pi(-
1))^(zeta_p*theta)*(1+pi)^theta *theta_p*v_p(-1);
(1+pi)^(1-theta)=(1-theta_p)*(1+pi_star)^(1-theta)+(1+pi(-
1))^(zeta_p*(1-theta))*theta_p;
w^(1-theta_N)=(1-theta_w)*w_star^(1-theta_N)+(1+pi(-
1))^zeta_w*(1-theta_N)*theta_w*(1+pi)^ (theta_N-1)*w(-1)^(1-
theta_N);
i=(1-rho_i)*i+rho_i*i(-1)+(1-rho_i)*(phi_pi*(pi-
pi_target)+phi_y*(logQ-logQ(-1)))+ s_i*e_i;
log(G)=(1-rho_G)*log(omega*Q)+rho_G*log(omega*Q(-
```

```
1))+s_G*e_G ;
 log(A)= rho_A*log(A(-1))+s_A*e_A;
 log(Z)= rho_Z*log(Z(-1))+s_Z*e_Z;
 log(v)= rho_v*log(v(-1))+s_v*e_v;
 log(phi)= (1-rho_phi)*log(phi_bar) + rho_phi* log(phi(-1)+
s_psi*e_psi
 %F=0/ (R/mc*alpha)-w+R*(alpha*mc/R)^(1/(1-alpha))* ;
 end;
 initval;
 A=1;
 Z=1;
 v=1;
 phi=phi_bar;
 pi=pi_target;
 i=((1+pi)/beta)-1;
 u=1;
 R=1/beta-(1-delta0);
 pi_star=(((1+pi)^(1-theta)-theta_p*(1+pi)^(zeta_p*(1-
theta)))/(1-theta_p))^(1/(1-theta))-1;
 v_p=(1-theta_p)*((1+pi_star)/(1+pi))^(-theta)/(1-
theta_p*(1+pi)^(theta*(1-zeta_p)));
 mc=(theta-1)/theta*(1+pi_star)/(1+pi)*(1-
beta*theta_p*(1+pi)^(theta*(1-zeta_p)))/(1-
beta*theta_p*(1+pi)^((1-zeta_p)*(theta-1)));
 w=(1-alfa)*mc*(alfa*mc/R)^(alfa/(1-alfa));
 w_star=w*(1-(theta_w*(1+pi)^((theta_N-1)*(1-z_w))/(1-
theta_w))^(1/(1-theta_N));
 N=((theta_N-1)/theta_N*phi)*(1-beta*b)/(1-b)*1/(1-omega)*
(alfa*mc/R)^(alfa/(1-alfa))/v_p-delta0*(mc*alpha/R)^1/(1-
alpha)*w_star*(w/w_star)^(-theta_N*upsilon)*((1-
theta_w*beta*(1+pi)^(theta_N*(1+upsilon)*(1-zeta_w)))/(1-
beta*thetaw*(1+pi)^thet_N-1*(1-zeta_w))))^ (1/(1+upsilon));
 K_hat=(alfa*mc/R)^(1/(1-alpha))*N;
 K=K_hat;
 I=delta0*K;
 Q=A*K_hat^alfa*N^(1-alfa)/v_p;
 G=omega*Q;
 C=Q-G-I;
 lamb=1/C*(1-beta*b)/(1-b);
 mu= lamb;
 x1=lamb*mc*Q/(1-theta_p*beta*(1+pi)^((1-zeta_p)*theta));
 x2=lamb*Q/(1-theta_p*beta*(1+pi)^((theta-1)*(1-zeta_p)));
 h1=phi*(w/w_star)^(theta_N*(1+upsilon))*N^(1+upsilon)/(1
-theta_w*beta*(1+pi)^(theta_N*(1+upsilon)*(1-zeta_w)));
 h2=lamb*((w/w_star)^theta_N*)*N/(1-
theta_w*beta*(1+pi)^((theta_N-1)*(1-zeta_w)));
```

```
end;
resid;
check;
steady;
model_diagnostics;
shocks;
var e_A;
s_A=stderr;
stderr 0.01;
var e_G;
s_A=stderr;
stderr 0.01;
var e_i;
s_i=stderr;
stderr 0.01;
var e_Z;
s_Z=stderr;
stderr 0.01;
var e_v;
s_v=stderr;
stderr 0.01;
var e_phi;
s_phi=stderr;
stderr 0.01;
end;
stoch_simul(order=1, irf=30) A Q C I N R i w pi;
```

6.16 The Results of the DYNARE code for the Medium-Sized NK Model

For the sake of accuracy's confirmation of the DYNARE'S code and convenience of the reader, this section reports in full results from running the DYNARE'S code of the medium-sized NK model. Below is the output of running DYNARE'S code:

Residuals of the static equations:

```
Equation number 1 : 0 : lamb
Equation number 2 : 0 : 2
Equation number 3 : 0 : 3
Equation number 4 : 0 : 4
Equation number 5 : 0 : mu
Equation number 6 : 0 : h1
Equation number 7 : 0 : h2
Equation number 8 : 0 : w_star
```

```
Equation number 9 : 0 : 9
Equation number 10 : 0 : mc
Equation number 11 : 0 : x1
Equation number 12 : 0 : x2
Equation number 13 : 0 : 13
Equation number 14 : 0 : Q
Equation number 15 : 0 : K
Equation number 16 : 0 : 16
Equation number 17 : 0 : K_hat
Equation number 18 : 0 : v_p
Equation number 19 : 0 : 19
Equation number 20 : 0 : 20
Equation number 21 : 0 : i
Equation number 22 : 0 : 22
Equation number 23 : 0 : 23
Equation number 24 : 0 : 24
Equation number 25 : 0 : 25
Equation number 26 : 0 : 26
```

There are 14 eigenvalue(s) larger than 1 in modulus for 14 forward-looking variable(s). The rank condition is verified.

STEADY-STATE RESULTS:

```
lamb        1.49384
mu          1.49384
C           0.677228
i           0.0251256
pi          0.02
R           0.0300251
u           1
Z           1
I           0.201262
v           1
phi         6
w           1.18784
w_star      1.24972
h1          1.92203
h2          2.30696
N           0.413152
K_hat       8.0505
K           8.0505
mc          0.665393
pi_star     0.0534455
x1          3.50589
x2          6.09188
```

Table 6.1 Eigenvalues

Modulus	Real	Imaginary
1.312e-17	−1.312e-17	0
0.2045	0.2045	0
0.6602	0.6586	0.0448
0.6602	0.6586	−0.0448
0.6912	0.6912	0
0.7	0.7	0
0.733	0.733	0
0.7557	0.7557	0
0.8434	0.8434	0
0.8973	−0.8973	0
0.9	0.9	0
0.92	0.92	0
0.94	0.94	0
0.9722	0.9722	0
1.057	1.057	0.02532
1.057	1.057	−0.02532
1.075	1.065	0.1476
1.075	1.065	−0.1476
1.308	1.308	0
1.39	1.388	0.06175
1.39	1.388	−0.06175
1.599	1.599	0
1.044e+15	−1.044e+15	0
4.413e+17	4.413e+17	0
2.744e+18	−2.744e+18	0
1.288e+50	−1.288e+50	0
Inf	Inf	0
Inf	Inf	0

Table 6.2 Matrix of covariance of exogenous shocks

Variables	e_G	e_i	e_A	e_Z	e_v	e_phi
e_G	0.000100	0.000000	0.000000	0.000000	0.000000	0.000000
e_i	0.000000	0.000000	0.000000	0.000000	0.000000	0.000000
e_A	0.000000	0.000000	0.000100	0.000000	0.000000	0.000000
e_Z	0.000000	0.000000	0.000000	0.000000	0.000000	0.000000
e_v	0.000000	0.000000	0.000000	0.000000	0.000000	0.000000
e_phi	0.000000	0.000000	0.000000	0.000000	0.000000	0.000000

```
Q            1.09811
G            0.219622
A            1
v_p           1.00246
```

Table 6.3 Policy and transition functions

	C N	i K_hat	pi K	R Q	I G	w A
Constant	0.677228 0.413152	0.025126 8.050498	0.020000 8.050498	0.030025 1.098112	0.201262 0.219622	1.187841 1.00000
i(-1)	0.319561	0.664879	−0.373981	−0.026122	−0.274601	0.049316
phi(-1)	−0.000339 −0.000371	0.000119 0.004274	0.000482 −0.000477	0.000005 −0.000713	−0.000334 −0.000040	0.001248 0
w(-1)	0.049951 −0.049727	0.035265 2.928945	0.130041 −0.139298	0.013455 −0.102887	−0.047174 −0.005762	0.675251 0
K_hat(-1)	0.000444 −0.025102	−0.001160 −0.881369	−0.003957 0.027553	−0.005445 0.000748	0.000262 0.000042	0.004295 0
K(-1)	0.011661 0.005997	−0.001642 1.138718	−0.006862 0.969040	0.000651 0.011436	−0.000865 0.000640	0.008508 0
Q(-1)	0.014550 0.017147	−0.030274 −0.382378	0.017028 0.024727	0.001189 0.028659	0.012503 0.001605	−0.002246 0
G(-1)	−0.021894 0.411356	0.043223 4.877378	0.055879 −0.163767	0.029123 0.726378	−0.012406 0.760677	−0.030529 0
A(-1)	0.154975 −0.409550	0.068525 −5.133187	0.266090 0.301087	0.021258 0.017375	0.137922 0.310272	0.336485 0.920000
v_p(-1)	−0.015025 0.414302	0.013132 4.761405	0.046875 −0.156759	0.029279 −0.025546	−0.009091 −0.001431	−0.032807 0
C(-1)	0.680524 0.401540	0.041624 4.754976	0.052629 −0.158515	0.028442 0.709255	−0.010987 0.039718	−0.029244 0
pi(-1)	−0.027234 −0.032681	0.047535 0.567753	0.165048 −0.042388	−0.002276 −0.054346	−0.024069 −0.003043	0.003909 0
Z(-1)	−0.035663 0.037931	0.016552 2.942864	0.047610 0.201345	0.003608 0.062299	0.094473 0.003489	0.033672 0
I(-1)	−0.011604 0.510690	0.060854 7.906306	0.093676 0.642254	0.036764 0.899104	0.860358 0.050350	−0.013817 0
v(-1)	0.119665 0.054181	0.015462 0.840892	0.040365 −0.059828	0.004052 0.092035	−0.032783 0.005154	0.004528 0
e_G	−0.006678 0.125476	0.013184 1.487753	0.017045 −0.049954	0.008883 0.221568	−0.003784 0.232030	−0.009312 0
e_i	−0.399451 −0.470740	0.831099 10.497363	−0.467476 −0.678817	−0.032652 −0.786760	−0.343251 −0.044059	0.061645 0
e_A	0.168451 0.445163	−0.074484 −5.579551	−0.289228 0.327269	−0.023107 0.337252	0.149916 0.018886	0.365744 1.000000
e_Z	−0.037939 0.040352	0.017609 3.130707	0.050648 0.214197	0.003838 0.066275	0.100503 0.003711	0.035822 0
e_v	0.132961 0.060201	0.017180 0.934324	0.044850 −0.066475	0.004502 0.102262	−0.036426 0.005727	0.005031 0
e_phi	−0.002908 −0.003178	0.001016 0.036636	0.004130 −0.004087	0.000039 −0.006114	−0.002864 −0.000342	0.010695 0

Table 6.4 Theoretical moments

Variable	Mean	Std. Dev.	Variance
C	0.6772	0.0207	0.0004
i	0.0251	0.0026	0.0000
pi	0.0200	0.0038	0.0000
R	0.0300	0.0008	0.0000
I	0.2013	0.0183	0.0003
w	1.1878	0.0314	0.0010
N	0.4132	0.0080	0.0001
K_hat	8.0505	0.3495	0.1221
K	8.0505	0.3838	0.1473
Q	1.0981	0.0451	0.0020
G	0.2196	0.0094	0.0001
A	1.0000	0.0255	0.0007

Table 6.5 Variance decomposition (in percent)

Variable	e_G	e_i	e_A	e_Z	e_v	e_phi
C	0.05	0.00	99.95	0.00	0.00	0.00
i	0.75	0.00	99.25	0.00	0.00	0.00
pi	0.33	0.00	99.67	0.00	0.00	0.00
R	2.67	0.00	97.33	0.00	0.00	0.00
I	0.02	0.00	99.98	0.00	0.00	0.00
w	0.01	0.00	99.99	0.00	0.00	0.00
N	4.22	0.00	95.78	0.00	0.00	0.00
K_hat	0.44	0.00	99.56	0.00	0.00	0.00
K	0.05	0.00	99.95	0.00	0.00	0.00
Q	0.48	0.00	99.52	0.00	0.00	0.00
G	14.15	0.00	85.85	0.00	0.00	0.00
A	0.00	0.00	100.00	0.00	0.00	0.00

MODEL_DIAGNOSTICS: No obvious problems with this mod-file were detected.

MODEL SUMMARY

```
Number of variables:      26
Number of stochastic shocks: 6
Number of state variables:  14
Number of jumpers:        14
Number of static variables: 3
```

Table 6.6 Matrix of correlations

Variable	C	i	pi	R	I	w	N	K_hat	K	Q	G	A
C	1.0000	−0.7157	−0.2740	−0.0585	0.7512	0.9663	0.5532	0.8992	0.9049	0.9457	0.8691	0.7401
i	−0.7157	1.0000	0.6825	−0.1528	−0.6005	−0.7334	−0.0076	−0.3985	−0.4501	−0.6686	−0.4597	−0.8509
pi	−0.2740	0.6825	1.0000	0.1502	−0.1789	−0.2957	0.5725	0.0356	−0.1292	−0.2150	−0.0786	−0.6025
R	−0.0585	−0.1528	0.1502	1.0000	0.4407	0.1213	0.3381	−0.0928	−0.3704	0.1687	0.0790	0.3309
I	0.7512	−0.6005	−0.1789	0.4407	1.0000	0.8927	0.5739	0.5670	0.4536	0.9159	0.7892	0.8829
w	0.9663	−0.7334	−0.2957	0.1213	0.8927	1.0000	0.5657	0.8173	0.7847	0.9922	0.8904	0.8577
N	0.5532	−0.0076	0.5725	0.3381	0.5739	0.5657	1.0000	0.7445	0.5340	0.6373	0.7199	0.2048
K_hat	0.8992	−0.3985	0.0356	−0.0928	0.5670	0.8173	0.7445	1.0000	0.9482	0.8178	0.8371	0.4371
K	0.9049	−0.4501	−0.1292	−0.3704	0.4536	0.7847	0.5340	0.9482	1.0000	0.7615	0.7752	0.4146
Q	0.9457	−0.6686	−0.2150	0.1687	0.9159	0.9922	0.6373	0.8178	0.7615	1.0000	0.9283	0.8379
G	0.8691	−0.4597	−0.0786	0.0790	0.7892	0.8904	0.7199	0.8371	0.7752	0.9283	1.0000	0.6675
A	0.7401	−0.8509	−0.6025	0.3309	0.8829	0.8577	0.2048	0.4371	0.4146	0.8379	0.6675	1.0000

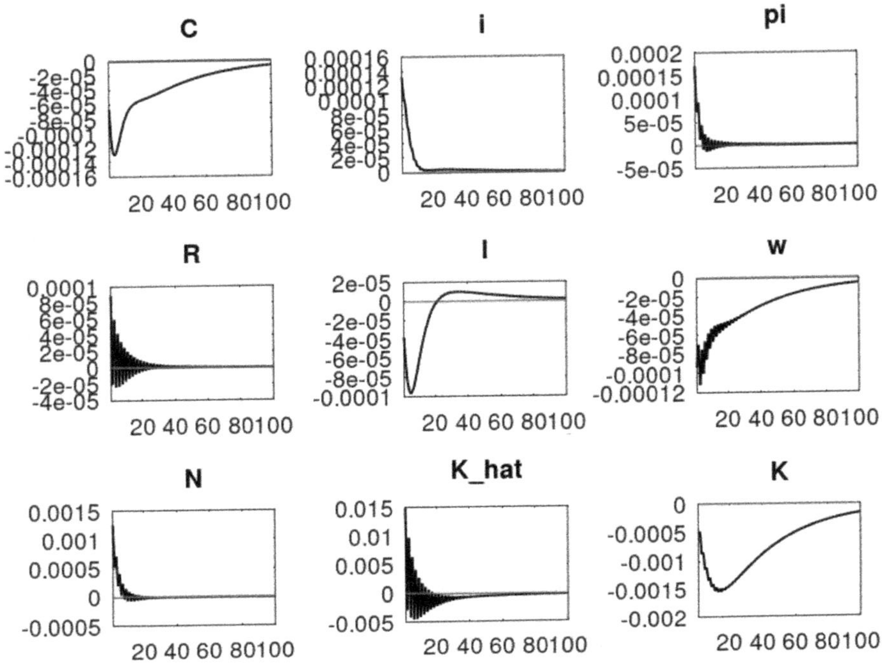

Fig. 6.1 Orthogonalized shock to e_G

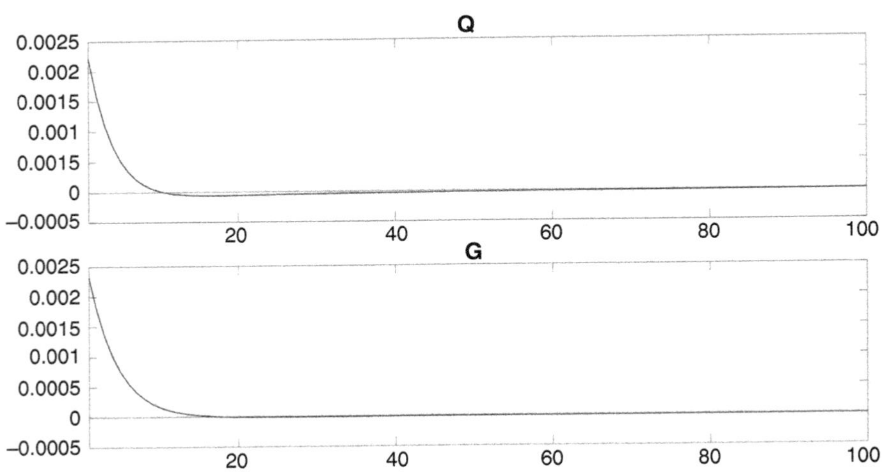

Fig. 6.2 Orthogonalized shock to e_G

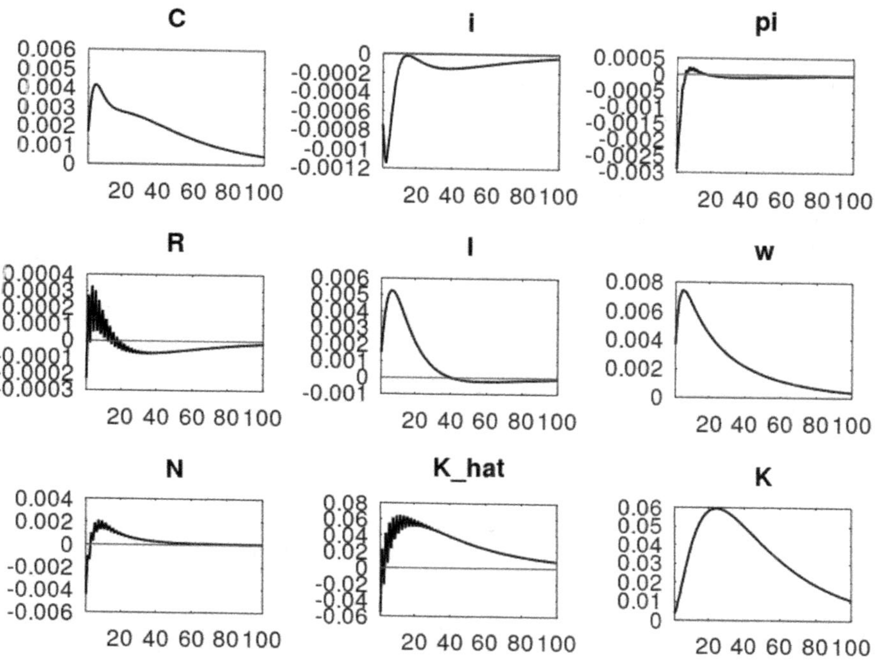

Fig. 6.3 Orthogonalized shock to e_A

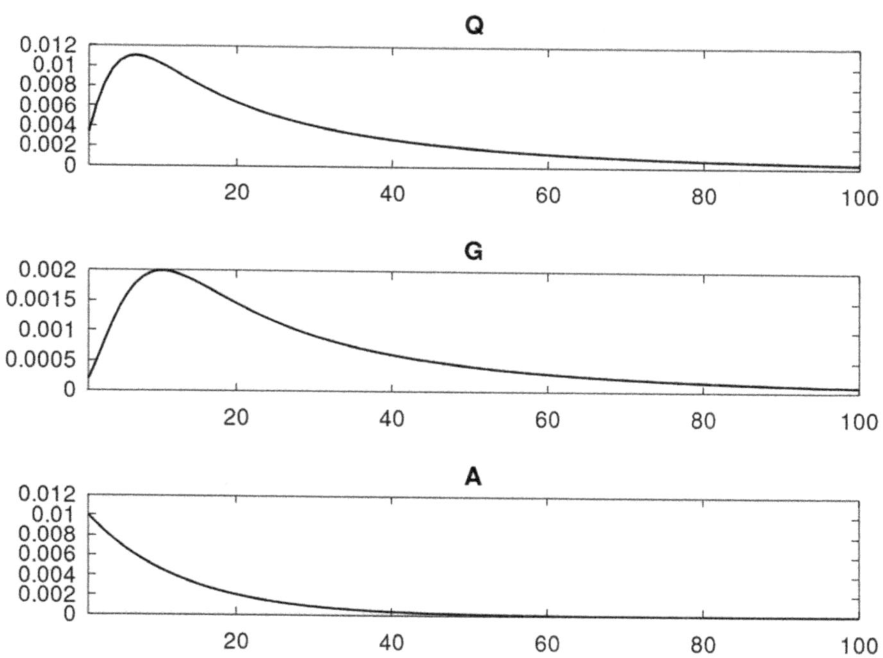

Fig. 6.4 Orthogonalized shock to e_A

References

Abel, A. (1990) 'Asset prices under habit formation and catching up with the Joneses', *American Economic Review*, 80 (May), pp. 38-42.

Adrian, T. Gaspar, V. and Vitek, F. (2022) 'A Medium-Scale DSGE Model for the Integrated Policy Framework', *IMF Working Papers*, 2022/016.

Arias, A. and Hansen, G. and Ohanian, L. (2007) 'Why have business cycle fluctuations become less volatile?', *Economic Theory*, 32(1), 43-58.

Barro R. (1997) *New-Keynesian Model with government*, MIT Press Cambridge.

Benes, J. and Kumhof, M. and Laxton D. (2014) 'Financial Crises in DSGE Models: A Prototype Model', *IMF Working Paper,* April, WP/14/57.

Boldrin, M. and Christiano, J. and Fisher J. (2001) 'Habit persistence, asset returns, and the business cycle', *American Economic Review*, 91(1), 149-166.

Brázdik, F. and Hlaváček, M. and Maršál, A. (2012) 'Survey of Research on Financial Sector Modeling within DSGE Models: What Central Banks Can Learn from It ', *Czech Journal of Economics and Finance*, 62 (3) pp. 252-77.

Costa, C. J. Jr (2016) *Understanding DSGE,* Vernon Press, Delaware.

Galí, J. and López-Salido, J.D. and Vallés J. (2007) 'Understanding the Effects of Government Spending on Consumption', *Journal of the European Economic Association*, 5(1), pp. 227–270.

Gerali, A. and Neri, S. and Sessa, L. and Signoretti F. (2010) 'Credit and Banking in a DSGE Model of the Euro Area', *Journal of Money, Credit and Banking,* 42(Supp. 1), pp. 107-41.

Gertler, M. and Karadi P. (2011), "A model of unconventional monetary policy", *Journal of Monetary Economics*, 58(1), pp. 17-34.

Johnson, D. and Parker J. and Souleles N. (2006) 'Household expenditure and the income tax rebates of 2001', *American Economic Review*, 96(5), 1589-1610.

Leeper, E. (1991), 'Equilibria under 'active' and 'passive' monetary and fiscal policies', *Journal of Monetary Economics*, 27(1), pp. 129-147.

Lettau, M. and Uhlig H. (2000) 'Can habit formation be reconciled with business cycle facts?' *Review of Economic Dynamics,* 3, pp. 79–99.

Mankiw, N. (2000) 'The savers-spenders theory of fiscal policy', *American Economic Review,* 90(2), 120-126.

Overland, C. and Weil D. (2000)'Saving and Growth with Habit Formation', *American Economic Review,* vol. 90, no. 3, pp. 341-355.

Pollak, R. (1970) 'Habit formation and dynamic demand functions', *Journal of Political Economy,* 78, pp. 745–63.

Ravn, M. and Schmitt-Grohé, S., Uribe M. (2006) 'Deep habits', *Review of Economic Studies*, 73, pp. 1–24.

Rotemberg, J.J. (1982) 'Sticky prices in the United States'. *Journal of Political Economy*, 90:1187–211

Sims, E. (2016) *Ph.D. Macro Theory II- Lectures* Avalaible at https://sites.nd.edu/esims/courses/ph-d-macro-theory-ii/ (Accessed: 7 July 2023).

Souleles, N. (1999) 'The response of household consumption to income tax refunds', *American Economic Review*, 89(4), 947-958.

Torres, J.L. (2014) *Introduction to Dynamic Macroeconomic General Equilibrium Models,* Vernon Press, Malaga.

Wolff, M. (2003) 'Recent trends in the size distribution of household wealth", *Journal of Economic Perspectives*, 12, 131-150.

Xu, W. (2019) *A Baseline Medium-Scale NK DSGE Model for Policy Analysis* Avalaible at: https://mpra.ub.uni-muenchen.de/id/eprint/93167 (Accessed: 7 July 2023)

Index

A
Abel, A., 302
Absence of arbitrage opportunities, 276, 287, 293
Adjustment costs
  of Capital, 2, 110–114, 269, 298–300, 302–305
  of employment, 304
Aggregate consumption, 221, 222, 225, 302, 306
  differentiated goods, 246, 332
  single good, 246
Alternative way
  of encoding model block, 198–202
Arias, A., 305
Arrow-Debreu, 313
Ascari, G., 244
Asymptotically stable, 5
Autocorrelation coefficients, 52, 191, 194
Autoregressive process AR(1), 1, 17, 21, 51, 79, 80, 84, 125, 127, 135, 151, 172, 266, 336, 337

B
Backward expansion, 11
Backward factorization, 13
Backward iteration, 7, 22–26
Balanced budget policy, 285
Barro, R., 309
Basic DSGE model
  basic NKE model, 2, 259–267, 270, 291
  basic RBC model, 134, 148, 202–205
  code of NKE model, 266–267
  code of Real Business Cycle, 202–205
Beliefs, 26, 27
  See also Speculative factors
Bellman, R., 172
Bellman equation, 173, 180, 182
Bellman's principle, 172, 180–184
  application of, 180–184
  and dynamic programming, 107, 172–180
Benes, J., 308
Benveniste Scheinkman equation, 175
Blanchard, O.J., 62, 65, 124
Blanchard-Kahn conditions, 65, 137, 161, 221, 260–265
  of basic NKE model, 260–265
Blanchard-Kahn procedure, 62, 67–70, 84–93, 107, 169, 170
Blocks
  of DYNARE code, 188, 213
Boldrin, M., 302
Bonds holding, 225
Born, B., 244
Bounded solution, 8, 12, 13, 24
Brázdik, F., 308
Bubbles, 26–28, 71, 72
Budget constraint, 109–112, 116, 138, 149, 150, 182, 183, 202, 225, 250, 289, 296, 303, 306, 333
Bullard, J., 264
Business cycle, 1, 2, 107, 110, 124–126, 129–134, 189, 193, 194
  basic RBC model, 134
  log-linearized model, 155–157

G. Chirichiello, *DSGE Models for Real Business Cycle and New Keynesian Macroeconomics*, Springer Texts in Business and Economics,
https://doi.org/10.1007/978-3-031-56034-7

C

Calibration, 137, 207, 216
Calvo, G., 221, 239, 243, 244, 269, 291, 300–302, 308, 312, 325, 332, 334
Calvo's approach
  to price setting, 239, 243
  to wages setting, 300–302
Campbell, J., 118
Canonical form, 14, 16, 63, 64, 73, 93, 130, 260, 261
Capital and labor usage, 3
Cashless economy, 308
Central bank, 3, 249, 265, 270, 285–286, 308, 331–332, 345
Central planner model, 134
CES
  basket of intermediate goods, 233
  production function, 2, 221, 233, 234, 270, 277
Characteristic equation
  properties of, 30–34
Chirichiello, G., 225, 263
Classics vs. Keynes, 3
Cobb-Douglas function, 125, 150
Co movements, 193, 194
Constant Relative Risk Aversion (CRRA), 107, 149, 202–205, 208, 212
Constant returns to scale, 150, 230, 270
Constrained minimum problem, 230, 235
  minimum expenditure problem, 239–243
Consumption demand, 222, 224, 226
Contractions' theorem, 174
Control equation, 172
Control variables, 108, 121, 132, 133, 139, 140, 149, 153, 157, 158, 164, 172, 174, 192, 193
Convolution
  of two sequences, 47
Costa, C.J. Jr., 307
Costs for hiring and firing, 304
Costs for using labor, 74
Costs of price adjustment, 235–239, 272

D

Decentralized economy, 114–116, 124–126, 138, 148–151, 208, 221–227
Demand for intermediate good, 287, 332
Demand for labor, 74, 151, 246, 247, 277, 281, 295, 316, 334
  in an inter-temporal context, 74
Demand side of basic NKE, 245–248
Descartes' rule, 97
Diagonalization, 56, 66, 71, 170
Difference equations, 2, 5–105, 260
  general solution, 6, 13, 35
  linear homogeneous, 5, 6
  n-th order, 44
  second order, 28–35, 44–59
  stochastic, 14, 17, 19, 26, 27, 51, 63, 69
  system of, 5–105
  with expectations, 14–15
Diffusion mechanisms
  in the economy, 194
  of initial impulses, 194
  over time, 194
Discounted Lagrangian, 108
Discriminant, 29, 30, 77, 96, 97, 101, 104, 263
Dispersion
  of prices of intermediate goods, 332
  of specific wages, 311
Dispersion of specific wages, 311
Divergence
  in expectations, 23
Dixit, A., 2, 221
Dominant root, 31
Dynamic General Equilibrium (DGE) model
  from DGE to DSGE model, 1
Dynamic maximization problem
  of central planner, 152
  of firm, 138, 234, 237, 281
  of household, 114, 115, 124, 138, 149, 275, 281, 301
Dynamic programming problem, 121, 173, 180
Dynamics
  of equilibrium inflation, 252–257
  of expectations, 15, 22
DYNARE codes
  m_hansen1.mod, 202
  m_NK_medium_size.mod, 347
  m_NKM.mod, 267
  m_RB3_loglin.mod, 198
  m_rbc_crra.mod, 214
  m_rbc_crra_steadystate_helper.mod, 213
  m_rbc_logutil.mod, 211
  m_rbc_logutil_num.mod, 216
  m_RBC1.mod, 191
  m_RBC2.mod, 196
  m_rbc_publicspending_loglinear.mod, 205
  m_rbc_public_spending.mod, 205
DYNARE codes blocks
  initialization block, 188
  labeling block, 188
  model block, 188
  parameter values' block, 188

random shock block, 188
solution block, 188
DYNARE equation format
equations in linear form, 189
equations in the form exp-log, 189
equations in the levels, 189
DYNARE results
graphic representation of impulse responses, 191
matrix of contemporaneous correlations, 191
model diagnostic, 354
policy and transition functions, 191
statistical moments of endogenous variables, 191
summary of the model, 191
table of autocorrelation coefficients, 191
variance-covariance matrix of exogenous shocks, 191

E
Economic policy, 2, 3
Efficiency condition, 228
Eigenvalue-eigenvector problem, 60
Elasticity
of demand for consumption good, 277
of demand for labor, 277
of production, 75, 152
of substitution between intermediate goods, 270
Endogenous variables, 65, 137, 191, 214, 217
statistical moments of, 191
Envelope theorem, 175–180, 183
Estimation methods, 3
Euler equation, 115, 124, 153, 176, 180, 246
Exogenous variables, 65, 134, 143, 172, 193, 194, 217
Exponential process, 272
"External" habits, 302
permanent income hypothesis, 305
External steady state file, 216–219

F
Factorization method, 10–14, 19, 20, 30, 83
Final good sector, 323
Finite difference equations
first-order (linear), 5–9
second-order, 48–54
with rational expectations, 28–30
systems of
example of economic theory, 74–93
with rational expectations, 63, 64
First order
conditions, 76, 108, 110, 112, 115, 124, 125, 139, 149, 150, 153, 175, 180, 187, 189, 212, 222, 224–226, 228, 230, 232, 234–236, 238, 249, 271, 272, 274, 278, 280, 282, 284, 301, 303, 304, 306, 310, 314, 315, 317, 318, 324, 325, 327
difference equation (*see* Finite difference equations)
Fiscal policy, 3, 148, 269, 308
Fixed costs, 308, 324, 344
Forward
expansion, 12, 14
factorization, 10, 12
operator, 10, 19, 52
polynomial in the lag operator, 10
solution, 14–22, 26, 93, 170
Functional equation, 174
See also Bellman equation
Fundamental
parameters, 135, 155, 257
solutions, 20, 26

G
Galí, J., 225, 252, 305
Gaussian stochastic variable, 152
GDP gap, 257–259
General Equilibrium model
of DGE, 1, 107, 110–114, 117–120, 124
of NKE, 221–267
of RBC, 107–171
General price level index, 222, 244, 245, 335
General solution
difference equation, 6, 13
of linear homogeneous first difference equation, 6, 13
General wage index, 278–281
Gerali, A., 308
Gertler, M., 308
Global productivity, *see* Total factor productivity (TFP)
Government's budget constraint, 331
Government spending, 202–205
as a shock, 202–205
Griffoli, T., 196

H
Habits formation, 308
Hansen, G., 137
Hansen's DSGE model, 137–147
DYNARE code of, 199, 200

Hayashi, F., 114
Helper function, 208, 212, 213

I
Identity
  between micro and macro variables, 116, 332
Impulse response function
  definition, 194
  graphical representation of, 191
Indeterminacy, 51, 57, 70–73, 109, 260
Indeterminate coefficients (method of), 16, 20–22, 29, 49–52, 54, 55, 60, 80–83, 121–124
Indexation
  of wages, 316
Induction, *see* Solutions of difference equations
Inelastic labor supply, 114, 124–126
Inertial component of inflation, 245
Initialization block, *see* DYNARE codes blocks
Initial value, 6, 8, 15, 22, 58, 61, 134, 174, 187, 199, 208, 213–217
Initval block, *see* DYNARE codes blocks
Instantaneous
  and intertemporal Lagrangian, 108
  and intertemporal Profit function, 75, 150, 327
  and intertemporal utility function, 107, 114
Intensity of the inflationary process, 256
Intermediate goods, 233–237, 243, 244, 270–275, 304, 308, 323–334
Intra-temporal preference shock, 308, 313, 337
Intriligator, M., 110
Inverse forward operator, 10
Investment costs, 3
Iterated substitution
  of expectations, 16–19
  of initial value, 6

J
Johnson, D., 305
Jordan transformation, 62, 67, 89, 90, 130–134
Jump variables, 65, 69, 70, 127

K
Kahn, C.M., 62, 65, 124
Karadi, P., 308
Keynes Ramsey rule, 184
King, R., 3
Kolasa M., 126
Kuhn-Tucker conditions, 110, 179
  and transversality condition, 109, 110
Kydland, F., 121

L
Labeling block, *see* DYNARE codes blocks
Lag operator, 10, 35, 40, 320
Lagrangian methodology
  and consumption in NKE, 222
  and discounted expected profits, 108
  and external habit persistence
    in medium-size NKE, 304
  and Hansen's model, 137–147
  in a central planner problem, 152, 154
  in a complex NKE model, 274, 278, 281, 307, 314, 315
  in the intertemporal maximization, 107–114
  and minimum cost problem, 110–114
  and Tobin's q theory, 110–114
Law of iterated expectations, 16
Leeper, E., 286
Lettau, M., 302
Limited solutions
  with methods of indeterminate coefficients, 20–22, 49–52, 80–83, 121–124
  methods of solution, 26
  non-homogeneous linear equation, 6, 7, 12, 60, 61
Linear approximation, *see* Taylor first-order approximation
Linear factors, 40, 53, 78, 98
Log-linear approximation, 118–120, 126, 154, 250, 251, 253
Log-linearization, 126, 155–157, 197, 290, 292–297
Log-linearized systems, solution to
  by Blanchard-Kahn method, 107, 140
  by indetermined coefficient method, 121–124
Log-utility function, 208, 213
Long, J., 124
Loop
  for different parameters, 219, 220
Lucas's critique, 257

M
Mankiw, N., 305
Marginal cost, 228, 229, 232, 233, 236, 239, 242, 243, 251, 256, 258, 275, 325
Marginal requirement
  for labor, 232, 235, 236, 243

Marginal "Tobin's q, 303
Marion, R., 118
Mark-up coefficient, 228
MATLAB software, 64, 187
Matrix
  for solving ordinary difference equations, 14
  of contemporaneous correlations, 191
  of covariance of exogenous shocks, 352
  and systems of finite difference equations, 54–59
  and systems with rational expectations, 161–169
Medium-sized NKE model
  DYNARE code of, 269, 347–351
Method
  of factorization, 49, 77–80
  of indeterminate coefficient, 16, 20–22, 29, 49–52, 54, 55, 60, 80–83, 121, 124
  of partial fractions, 42, 44
Minimum
  cost problem for firms, 228
  spending problem for consumers, 222
Mitra, K., 264
Model block, *see* DYNARE codes blocks
Monetary policy rule, 260, 266, 345
Monetary wage, 270, 281, 282, 300, 302, 309, 312, 318, 320
Monopolistic competition, 2, 232, 233, 236, 237, 243, 258, 269, 270, 312
Mutschle, W., 208

N
Neo-Keynesian micro-founded model
  with CES production technology for final goods, 233, 234
  with linear production technology, 221, 227–229, 245–249
  with non-linear Cobb-Douglas production technology, 243
Net income from work, 283
Net marginal value of capital, 114
New Keynesian
  basic DSGE model, 307
  extensions of, 269, 300–307
  medium size model, 269, 337, 347–351
Non-homogeneous linear equation, 6
Non-Ricardian households, 269, 305–307
Numerical solution
  method, 2, 187
  of the basic NKE model, 266–267
  of the log-linearized NKE model, 298
  of the medium-size NKE model, 347

O
Optimal
  price, 228, 237, 238, 242, 243, 272, 290, 326
  quantity of labor demanded, 228
  ratio between labor and capital, 231
  savings in conditions of uncertainty, 181
  wages, 300, 301, 316, 319, 343
Optimal control problem, 172
  See also Bellman's principle
Overland, C., 302

P
Parametric utility function, 111
Pareto optimality, 1
Particular solution, 7, 12, 25, 35, 37, 39, 41
Passive tax rule, 286
Path towards steady state
  increasing/decreasing mode, 6
  oscillatory mode, 6
Persistence factor, 17
Persistence in consumption habits, 300
Pfeifer, J., 244
Phase diagram, 15, 57
Phillips curve
  with Calvo price-stickiness, 244
  with Rotemberg price-stickiness, 244, 290–291
Policy and transition functions, 192
Policy functions, 121, 122, 124, 132, 133, 137, 172, 175, 192, 193
Pollak, R., 302
Polynomial
  characteristic, 85, 86
  in the lag operator, 10
Portfolio of assets, 182
Predetermined variables, 65–67, 69, 70, 72, 127, 129, 133, 171
Prescott, E., 1, 121
Price
  dispersion of, 332
  general level, 222
  of the final good, 271 (*see also* Optimal price)
Production function
  CES, 2, 221, 233, 234, 270, 277
  Cobb-Douglas, 2, 115, 125, 150, 221, 230
  linear, 2, 221, 227–229, 239–243, 245–249, 251
  linear quadratic, 74
Program blocks, *see* DYNARE codes blocks
Public administration, 148, 149, 285–286, 289, 291, 296, 331–333

Q

Quadratic function
 of adjustment costs, 304
 of production technology, 74
Quantum mechanics, 1

R

Ramsey, F., 1, 114–116
Random Shock Block, *see* DYNARE codes blocks
Rate of accumulation of capital, 111
Rational expectations
 Blanchard-Kahn method of solution of systems of, 126–129
 example of economic theory, 74–93
 first-order difference equation in
  backward iteration method, 22–26
  bubbles, 26–28
  forward solution, 15–22
  methods of solution, 10–14
 second-order finite difference equations in
  solution methods, by factorization, 35–37
  solution methods, by indeterminate coefficients, 49–52
  solution methods, by matrix approach, 54–59
 systems of finite difference equations with, 59–64
 See also Finite Difference Equations
Rational polynomial, 10, 39, 42–44
Ravn, M., 302
RBC vs. NKE, 3
Real Business Cycle model (RBC)
 basic model
  decentralized economy, 124–126
  with flexible labor supply, 134–137
  with inelastic labor supply and stochastic shocks to technology, 124–126, 134–137
 DYNARE code of
  centralized economy, 187, 189
  with CRRA utility function and government spending as a shock, 202–205
Real marginal cost
 of labor, 229, 232, 242
 of production, 275
Real rigidities, 3
Real total profit, 229
Rebelo, S., 3
Reduction to partial fractions, 39
Representative
 agents, 1, 107–184
 consumer-saver, 180
 trade union, 283–285, 309–332
Resources constraint, 116
Ricardian households, 305, 306
Roots of quadratic equation
 and comparison to two given real numbers, 99–101
 complex conjugate, 30, 96, 98, 101, 102
 real, 30, 94, 123, 263
 real and coincident, 30
 and relations with coefficients, 96–99
Ropele, T., 244
Rossi, L., 244
Rotemberg, J., 244, 272
Rules-of thumb, 269, 305–307

S

Saddle point property, 50, 65, 66, 78, 82
Samuelson, P., 148
Sargent, T., 38–41, 74, 172, 175
Sargent's decomposition, 38
Scott, A., 118
Second-degree trinomial, 97
Self-fulfilling increasing expectations, 15
Significance condition, 109
Sims, C.A., 124
Sims, E., 3, 307–308
Simulations of DSGE models, *see* DYNARE codes
Singular problems, 73–74
Slackness-conditions, 177
 See also Kuhn-Tucker conditions
Solution Block, *see* DYNARE codes blocks
Souleles, N., 305
Source, 57, 65, 148, 207
Speculative
 bubble, 15, 27
 factors, 26 (*see also* Beliefs)
Stability conditions, 34–35
State-space representation, 70, 157–161
Statistical moments
 of endogenous variables, 191
 steady state_helper function, 212–214
 steady_state_model block, 208–211
Steady-state solution, 118, 154–155, 187, 200, 213, 339–345
Stickiness, 2, 3, 221, 237–249, 269–357
 See also Optimal, price; Optimal, wages

Stickiness to the real sector, 308
Stiglitz, J.E., 221
Stochastic
  linear equation, 27
  Neo Keynesian DSGE models, 221, 249, 252, 307
  RBC Dynamic Models, 1
  See also Autoregressive process
Sunspot variables, 70, 71
System
  of equations in rational expectation, 2, 5–105
  of finite difference equations, 12
  with rational expectation, 63, 64, 126–129

T
Taubman, P., 111
Taylor first-order approximation, 117, 118 252
  See also Log-linear approximation; Log-linearization
Taylor rule, 308, 331, 332
Taylor's principle, 265
Terminal condition, 15
Tobin, J., 2, 110–114, 303, 339
Tobin's q, 2, 113
Total factor productivity (TFP), 194
Transition function, 191, 192
Transversality condition, 13, 17, 20, 109, 110, 154
Trigonometric
  component, 47
  identities, 5, 101–105
  representation of complex numbers, 101–105
Trinomial of lags, 38

U
Uhlig, H., 118, 302
Unit circle, 50, 51, 65, 67, 70, 170
Utility function
  CRRA, 149, 202–205, 208, 212
  general, 114, 225, 282, 306
  parametric, 107, 111, 190, 226

V
Value function, 173, 174, 176, 178, 180, 182, 183
Variable capital utilization, 3
Vortex property, 65, 66

W
Walsh, C., 266
Weil, D., 302
Wilkinson, M., 111
Wolff, M., 305

X
Xu, W., 307

Z
Zero profit condition, 324

www.ingramcontent.com/pod-product-compliance
Lightning Source LLC
Chambersburg PA
CBHW071700221225
37172CB00003B/71
9783031560330

Springer Texts in Business and Economics

Springer Texts in Business and Economics (STBE) delivers high-quality instructional content for undergraduates and graduates in all areas of Business/Management Science and Economics. The series is comprised of self-contained books with a broad and comprehensive coverage that are suitable for class as well as for individual self-study. All texts are authored by established experts in their fields and offer a solid methodological background, often accompanied by problems and exercises.